Curtis H. Kobrio

DIAGNOSTIC PSYCHOLOGICAL TESTING

DIAGNOSTIC PSYCHOLOGICAL TESTING

by

DAVID RAPAPORT
Merton M. Gill and Roy Schafer

Revised Edition

Edited by
Robert R. Holt

INTERNATIONAL UNIVERSITIES PRESS, INC.

NEW YORK, NEW YORK

Contents

DIAGNOSTIC
PSYCHOLOGICAL
TESTING

Editor's Foreword

When the first edition of *Diagnostic Psychological Testing* appeared just 20 years ago, it met a highly polarized reception. Reviews by clinicians hailed it as the most important and valuable book of its kind; evaluations by statisticians were scathing because of deficiencies in the design of the research reported in it and in the statistical analysis. In the perspective of the ensuing two decades, both evaluations seem to have been correct: as a compilation of clinical wisdom, it has been equaled only by some of the work of Rapaport's own students, but its shortcomings as a piece of controlled quantitative research are glaringly apparent. It sold steadily, however, and went through numerous printings; finally, the plates and stock were exhausted before 1960.

During that year, the accumulated demand seemed great enough to warrant republication, and publishers were ready to republish the two volumes in their original form. But David Rapaport had been hurt by the criticisms of the book and had taken them to heart; he realized that many were justified, and he did not feel that he could allow so many undeniable errors to stand in a reissued book; yet he did not have time or inclination to undertake a revision. His own interests and practice had turned toward theory, experimental research, and therapy, and those of Roy Schafer had similarly grown away from testing into psychoanalysis. As for the third member of the original team, though he remained interested in and informed about testing beyond most of his psychiatric and psychoanalytic colleagues, Merton Gill was clearly not the man for the job. It happened that Rapaport was spending a sabbatical year at New York University as a guest of the Research Center for Mental Health during 1959–1960, so that he and I had many opportunities for conversations about matters of mutual interest. It was early in 1960 that he told me about this situation

1

and asked my opinion. I agreed that the book ought to be kept in print, but in condensed form, and I outlined my thoughts about how a condensation might be done. Some time later Rapaport wrote to me that, after thinking it over and discussing it with others, he had decided that he agreed with my ideas; would I undertake the job? Shortly before his death, I agreed to do so, somewhat hesitantly because I had many other prior commitments which I knew would stand in the way of a quick job. It has taken even longer than I feared; even so, it would have been impossible for me to have taken the time to work on the book if it had not been for the Public Health Service research career program award (No. MH-K6-12,455) that I received from the National Institute of Mental Health in 1962.

PLAN OF THIS REVISION

In its original form, the two-volume work comprised 1089 pages, a high proportion of which were set in small type. The reader's task was made difficult by the masses of statistical tables and graphs, and by the fact that there was considerable redundancy in the exhaustive quantitative analyses and discussions of the data. It struck me that there was a happy correlation between the lasting value of the various parts of the totality and their readability, and that the two volumes could be reduced to one by making it into a clinical manual, deleting the research aspects. Therefore, I have taken out the description of procedure, the statistical analyses and tables, and the presentation of quantitative results, leaving only those diagnostic guidelines that are supported by other clinical experience. Some of the detailed description of tests and of elementary aspects of administration have been compressed, particularly when they are readily available elsewhere.

Two other major decisions helped cut out many pages. First, I decided to omit discussion of the Hanfmann-Kasanin test and of all parts of the Babcock except the one subtest that has remained in active use (Story Recall). By the time the second volume was on sale, the battery of tests routinely given at the Menninger Clinic had been reduced to the Wechsler-Bellevue, Story Recall, Sorting, Word Association, Rorschach, and Thematic Apperception Tests; that is the battery of Schafer's *The Clinical Application of Psychological Tests* (1948), and it is the one presented and discussed in detail here. Second, the numerous appendices have been omitted: the presentation of all the raw scores used in the research, the condensed clinical descriptions of the cases, and the reviews of literature (contributed by Martin Mayman). The point of the first kinds of appendices has vanished with the decision to omit the research report, and the bibliographic studies are of course completely out of date. To replace the latter would be an enormous task; in addition, extensive bibliographies of the tests covered here are available in Buros's series of *Mental Measurements Yearbooks*. A complete listing of David Rapaport's writings on psychological testing has been added, and the list of works referred to in the text includes many of the more important contributions to this field by his students. There was one more appendix, which has also been left out: a compilation of all the deviant verbalizations in the Rorschachs of all the research subjects. That has been replaced by a more liberal use of examples (drawn from this source) in the text of Chapter 9.

What remains, only slightly condensed and edited, is a focused and theoretically oriented handbook of diagnostic psychological testing. It expounds a way of working with a selected battery of tests to further the description and understanding of adults suffering from a restricted range of neurotic and psychotic conditions. Except for occasional incidental remarks (a good many of which are my interpolations), there is no substantial consideration of organic states, character disorders, mania and hypomania, or psychosomatic disorders, nor the special problems associated with the early or the late years of life (e.g., adolescent identity crises, senile psychoses). When he had made original contributions, Rapaport's brief advices about administration and scoring have been retained. The emphasis, however, is upon rationale and upon diagnostic suggestions from specific test findings, arranged test by test. Schafer's book (1948), originally presented in lieu of a third volume, integrates the diagnostic indications by presenting sample cases, organizing the material by diagnosis rather than by test. The two books still serve to complement and supplement each other: Rapaport's supplies the theoretical basis of Schafer's, and guides the diagnostic tester through the initial stages of his professional task—the process of gathering and scoring his test data, reflecting on them, and forming his primary inferences about psychopathological trends that may be present. He will then want to refer to the relevant sections of Schafer for aid in deciding on the major diagnostic grouping and then in synthesizing a picture of an individual human being in difficulty.

I have resisted the temptation to alter the rationales (except for very occasional points involving what I knew to be errors of fact; doubtless I have not succeeded in getting completely rid of all errors) or to present my own views when they varied somewhat from Rapaport's. It is his book, and only confusion would result from any attempt of mine to try to "update" his ideas or to argue with them. The first edition was occasionally criticized on the grounds that it did not present all points of view, but that was a deliberate decision, which has been retained: let it be understood that this book aims for some depth in the application of a single point of view (the psychoanalytic) to tests, not for eclectic comprehensiveness. It should be enough for one book to present the mature wisdom of one man who was virtually the dean of modern psychodiagnostic testing, and surely the founder of one of its most influential and respected traditions or schools of thought.

Some progress has been made in the field during a score of years, of course, and several kinds of changes have been necessary. The Wechsler-Bellevue (or W-B) has been substantially replaced in general use by Wechsler's Adult Intelligence Scale (WAIS); many items of the Word Association Test and TAT originally presented have been replaced by other words and pictures. It was easier to accommodate to the latter changes than to the former; after considerable consultation, I decided to keep the chapter on the W-B essentially as it was, but adding to it an appendix discussing the relevant similarities and differences between the two Wechsler tests. In the chapters on Word Association and TAT, however, I eliminated certain examples and other references to the items that have been changed with the revisions of the tests and introduced some new normative data to replace those on the old Word Association list which were deleted. Even psychoanalytic theory has changed, in no mean part because of the efforts of David Rapaport. Where recent developments seemed relevant, I have inserted references to them. Such editorial interpolations are easily distinguished from the original authors' footnotes because they are designated as the editor's and are placed within square brackets.

Incidentally, some readers may recall the fact that Rapaport, Schafer, and Gill also issued a *Manual of Diagnostic Psychological Testing* (1944–1946) in two slim paperback volumes under the imprint of the Josiah Macy Jr. Foundation, and may wonder how the present condensation differs from that one, prepared by the original authors. Indeed, one possibility Rapaport and I considered when the issue of republication first came up was to publish these manuals again instead of the larger monograph. When we reviewed them, however, we found them not to be suitable for the contemporary psychologist. Those manuals were written and distributed during the war for immediate use by people who were doing clinical psychological work in the armed services, many of them without adequate training and even without access to other books. They carry the stamp of their time even more than the big books do, and condense the presentation of rationale more than that of administration and scoring, while still containing a good deal about the research project. In the end, I did not use them at all in preparing this revision.

THE DIAGNOSTIC RESEARCH PROJECT

Though the full account of the research is not being republished, for the reasons given above, it was a significant piece of work which must be at least briefly described. It was harshly—and justly—criticized; yet it was a milestone in the development of research in clinical psychology, and a good deal can be learned from its failures as well as from its achievements.

The situation of clinical psychology just before and during World War II is difficult to recall or reconstruct, since it was in a real sense a prehistoric era. Our science and profession might fairly be said to have had its true beginning after the war; surely the numbers of clinical psychologists were very small and their influence slight before the heroic efforts to expand training that began in the 1940's. The psychologist was just earning a place on the clinical team in hospitals and clinics, by his special skill of testing. Private practice was virtually unheard of, and the psychologist who practiced adult psychotherapy to any extent and in any setting was exceptional. The traditional function of the clinical psychologist was to work with children. His testing centered on furnishing a measure of intelligence (the IQ), and his remedial work was largely what is today called counseling and guidance. But in the 1930's a small band of pioneers, beginning with Samuel Beck and John Benjamin and followed by an immigration of Europeans (including Klopfer, Oberholzer, Piotrowski, Rickers-Ovsiankina, and Schachtel in addition to Rapaport), introduced the Rorschach test to this country and spread its use. During the same decade, the researches of Murray and his collaborators (1938) stimulated interest in a wider range of projective techniques, most notably of course the Thematic Apperception Test (TAT; Morgan & Murray, 1935). As clinical psychologists started applying these instruments along with a slowly growing group of nonprojective individual tests to adult psychiatric patients, there began to develop a body of psychodiagnostic lore. It was loose, difficult to lay one's hands on, unsystematized, and mostly empirical—not much of a foundation for the development of a profession with a sound basis for self-assurance.

When he began work at the Menninger Clinic in 1940, two years after his arrival in this country, David Rapaport knew the literature on psychological tests and had studied with some of those who had been involved in attempts to apply tests to diagnosis; he had also had a couple of years' intensive experience in a state hospital. It was no surprise to him that his own efforts to contribute to the appraisal of patients were initially met with skepticism and even suspicion; no basis existed for faith in his ability to do much more than measure intelligence. By the time he left Topeka eight years later, he had succeeded so well that his psychiatric colleagues regarded testing (but particularly his application of it) with almost superstitious awe. Aside from the impact of his own personal presence and talents, he achieved this result by three principal means: first, by several years of immersing himself in clinical data through testing "blind" every patient who was evaluated at the Clinic and then participating in the staff discussions, afterwards studying the clinical and historical data in relation to the test responses, and following each patient as long as possible; second, by an unremitting attempt to understand and conceptualize these data in terms of psychoanalytic theory, particularly the theory of thought organization; and third, by planning and carrying out a systematic re-evaluation of the test scores of carefully diagnosed patients. The first procedure provided a maximal opportunity for learning, since his first evaluation of the subject had to be concentrated on extracting everything possible from the tests themselves, while the subsequent study of the nontest clinical data provided validation for hypotheses and surprises that would send him back to restudy the tests, finding new ways to interpret them. The second strategy resulted in the rationale section of this book, and, more generally, contributed to the development of a later way of working with theory which never lost touch with clinical reality. The third means by which Rapaport established testing locally was the research project; it was an attempt to learn as well as to test what was by then known clinically.

Rapaport acknowledged the role of his colleagues in the research as follows: "Merton Gill, M.D., had a major share in planning the project upon which these volumes are based; the nosological classification of all our cases, the psychiatric examination and evaluation of the control-group, and the chapter on nosology have been contributed by him. Roy Schafer, B. S., planned and contributed the statistical analyses of our material, as well as the entire section on the Babcock Test; he has in addition influenced the formulation of our material in almost all of its parts. In the second volume not only the statistical work, but many of the formulations are also his."

The basic data of the research were the batteries of tests given to 217 patients, selected from among the patients seen at the Menninger Clinic and Hospital over a period of three and one-half years. The only patients excluded from the sample were children, organic, character-disordered, and addictive cases, "and those atypical cases which in terms of clinical findings did not lend themselves easily to nosological classification" (Rapaport et al., 1945-1946, Vol. 1, pp. 12-13). The objective was to make the samples as uniform and internally consistent as possible; an additional reason for excluding the available character disorders and organic conditions was that they were considered "not sufficiently representative." The tests, which had been given in routine practice, were rescored by Rapaport, usually in conferences with two or three junior colleagues.

The diagnostic groupings of these cases were carried out by Gill, who studied and discussed the psychiatric data on each patient in a series of conferences with Rapaport, but without reference to the tests. The material used was mainly the case abstract,[1] "a condensation into ten or twelve typewritten pages of all the material and examinational information concerning the patient" (Rapaport et al., 1945-1946, Vol. 1, p. 15), plus the record of the staff conference at which the case had been discussed and follow-up notes after discharge. "In more dubious cases we had recourse to the detailed records of the examinations, observations, and consultations with relatives and informants, upon which the case abstract was based: [and] . . . often . . . the 'progress notes' reflecting the patient's course in the Sanitarium"; in addition, when necessary the therapist in question was consulted about particular cases. Thus, the study did not depend upon the limited information available at the time of the initial diagnosis but was able to use the fruits of a longer period of observation.

This intensive scrutiny of the cases led to one controversial decision: to introduce some novel diagnostic categories. "Although we decided to keep as much as possible within the framework of accepted nosological categories, our chief concern was to make a classification which would express the coherence of our cases—that is to say, the clustering shown by our psychiatric material." Though pains were taken not to let the test results influence the categorization, "special efforts were made to reach an understanding of what kind of nosological classification would not cloud, but rather help to bring clearly to relief, the diagnostic features of the tests for different psychiatric, nosological categories" (Rapaport et al., 1945-1946, Vol. 1, p. 17). The resulting diagnostic groupings are described in Chapter 1, below.

From a clinical standpoint, it is hard to find fault with this procedure. Considering the generally high level of routine clinical work at the Menninger Clinic, and the outstanding ability of the people who did the rediagnosis of the cases by a systematic and uniform procedure, the resulting categorization of the clinical material is probably as good as has ever been achieved in a study of this size. The very fact that schizophrenics, who are usually thrown together into one virtually meaningless ragbag in much psychopathological research, are here subdivided into nine homogeneous and clinically meaningful subgroups, is a major point of this study's superiority which was rarely enough appreciated by its critics.

---

[1] Usually written by a psychiatric resident or junior member of the psychiatric staff.

Yet viewed from the standpoint of research design, the study has obvious deficiencies. The unbiased procedure of taking cases as they came along in routine clinical practice did result in their having too little comparability in many relevant respects. The underlying difficulty, with which this research never grappled, is that the test findings investigated are importantly determined not just by personality and its disorders but also by age, sex, education, socioeconomic status, and ethnic or cultural identity; and the diagnostic groups were quite variously constituted in these latter respects. The result was so much confounding of the independent variables under consideration with others, which should have been held constant, that it is impossible to know what the resulting test differences are attributable to. It would of course never be possible to select involutional depressives and overideational preschizophrenics so that they would be matched for age (the groups used ranged from 55 to 67 and from 16 to 40 years, respectively); but it would have been possible to correct at least the W-B results for the effect of age before comparing groups, since the requisite data were available. For other tests and other variables, no such normative data were at hand, and it would still be difficult to come by them without a major, independent piece of research.

A further defect of the design became apparent only with the development of the general rationale of diagnostic testing (see next section). As our understanding has grown about just what it is that can be gotten from tests, and how that is used in the process of creating a diagnostic picture, it has become clear that a comparison of diagnostic groups can throw only indirect light on the validity of test interpretation. Schafer put it thus (1948, p. 22 fn.):

> Unfortunately most research into the clinical usefulness of tests has attempted to correlate test "signs" with diagnoses, and not with characteristics of thinking or behavior. These studies, when they have obtained positive results, have then tried, by reasoning rather than by experiment, to establish which personality characteristics assumed to be widespread among the members of any diagnostic group were responsible for the significantly frequent occurrence of the established "sign" or "signs." This is a fault of the statistical investigations in *Diagnostic Psychological Testing*. It is a roundabout method and can never yield conclusive results.

The study made use of a control group of "54 randomly-chosen members of the Kansas Highway Patrol" (Rapaport et al., 1945-1946, Vol. 1, p. 28). This group is of course subject to the same kind of criticism, for its members differed notably (in occupation, intelligence, cultural background, and socioeconomic status) from the great run of patients at this expensive private clinic and sanitorium. This obvious vulnerability blinded some critics to an important research value of the group: it was internally homogeneous in all of these respects; the tests were administered and scored uniformly and consistently; and good clinical data were available from an hour's psychiatric interview with each man by Dr. Gill and a social and developmental history taken by a highly competent social worker, Mrs. Marjorie Lozoff, in another hour's interview. On the basis of these data, plus the record of a discussion of each man with the Chief of the Patrol, and quite without any possible contamination from knowledge of the tests, the psychiatrist assigned three-point ratings to each policeman on the following variables: adjustment, anxiety, depressive mood, schizoid trends, inhibition, and impulsiveness. He also noted the presence or absence of cultural interests, and of idealistic conceptions of their work. These ratings on the normal subjects were subsequently used wherever possible for an independent check on comparable trends in the clinical cases. The impressive fact was that these checks did usually substantiate the much more methodologically suspect group differences, without danger of contamination or of confounding. In this sense, the Patrolmen did serve the true function of a control group, despite the fact that their means or distributions on test scores could not be meaningfully compared with those of the clinical groups. Moreover, this aspect of the research is not subject to the criticism quoted above from Schafer.

The statistical treatment of the data was simple enough: each group was compared with every other on just about every score or combination of scores that was used clinically, plus a good many others. Differences between pairs of means were tested by Student's t, and differences between distributions were tested by chi square. Several major errors were committed aside from the failure to control the confounding effect of unwanted variables. No effort was made to take into account the great numbers of comparisons actually and implicitly made, when the p-values of the findings were evaluated. Moreover, the distributions of scores were scrutinized in a deliberate effort to find cutting points that would maximize the differences among groups—a procedure that is justified in exploratory research, but one that completely equivocates the alleged significance of the findings. Add to this certain technical errors in the application of chi square (such as its occasional use with frequencies of scores rather than of subjects), and not much remains that can be relied on at face value, in what superficially appeared to be a huge mass of highly significant differences.

It is not difficult to discredit this research, therefore, and some of the reviews by statisticians were scathing. By concentrating on its weaknesses, they quite overlooked the presence of such compensating strengths as the intracontrol-group comparisons just mentioned, the careful selection of cases, the high quality of test data, and the fact that trends emerging in the data were constantly subjected to an informal but real check against the accumulated clinical experience of the authors and their theoretical understanding. With all of its vulnerabilities, this research remains a landmark. The blueprint that must be used to surpass it has been available for decades, partly in the early pages of Chapter 9, below, and partly in the reviews of the first edition: one need only build on this study, retaining its strengths and avoiding its shortcomings. To my knowledge, no one has done so.

It would have been possible to redo some of the statistics, applying some relevant corrections and avoiding some fallacies, but that would have left untouched the most important ambiguities in the design, and it would still have been virtually impossible to evaluate the significance of the differences. It seemed best, therefore, simply to omit the whole thing, the good along with the bad.

THE DEVELOPMENT OF RAPAPORT'S APPROACH TO DIAGNOSTIC TESTING

Unfortunately, the exigencies of the research project distorted the presentation of Rapaport's style of working with tests, in ways I have not been able to modify significantly in this condensation. It seems best, therefore, to call specific attention to them, and to outline in some detail the guiding principles that Rapaport actually taught and practiced, and some of the resulting tradition of diagnostic testing.

Because the design of the research necessarily called for the separation of subjects into as homogeneous and sharply differentiated groups as possible, so that associated patterns of test scores might emerge, the book has an ineradicable overemphasis on the categorizing function of diagnosis. It can hardly be stressed too strongly that as Rapaport and the Menningers conceived of diagnosis, it had only begun when the decision was made about the major diagnostic grouping (e.g., chronic paranoid schizophrenia) to which a patient could be referred. Conversely, the requirements of statistical quantification put a heavy emphasis in most of the chapters on *scores,* to the neglect of qualitative features of the test performance and the subject's behavior during testing.

The former distortion plays right into the hands of the advocates of an actuarial approach to clinical problems, for whom diagnosis must be pigeonholing—again, because of the exigencies of their method. A better example of the artifactual effect of an investigative technique would be hard to find: first, reality is distorted to fit a convenient mathematical model; then the failure of the resulting investigations is laid to the clinical method, not the research method. Clinical psychologists and psychiatrists alike have become increasingly dissatisfied in recent years with the whole enterprise of diagnosis, whether carried out by means of tests or otherwise, partly for the reason that real people rarely fit the classical diagnostic entities very well, partly because it tells relatively little about a person to know only that he is a hysteric. All too many clinicians, therefore, have mistakenly rejected diagnosis altogether as "static," or "nondynamic," and have advocated instead a kind of boneless, literary description laced with "deep" speculations about genetic sequences, traumas, fixations, and unconscious fantasies. Such a Charybdis of swirling, murky prose is as much a disservice to the diagnostic art and has brought it as much discredit as the Scylla of sterile categorizing.

The course that Rapaport steered was not so much between these two dangers as in a somewhat different direction. The new conception of diagnostic work may be glimpsed only fitfully and imperfectly in the first edition, partly because of the fact that it was matured considerably by the process of preparing this book. And others whom Rapaport had trained, most notably Schafer, had important parts in shaping it. It became not only a Rapaport tradition, but also one of the Menninger Foundation and the Riggs Center; and the enlightened, sophisticated psychiatric approaches of the Menningers and of R. P. Knight were also important contributing forces.

As far as *diagnosis* is concerned, this tradition conceives the job to be done as the analysis and description of individual personalities (who are usually having some kind of difficulty in adaptation) to assist in planning what can be done to help them, not the attaching of a label to facilitate "disposition": storage or shipping. Rapaport stated it in a highly condensed manner, as follows: "To describe a personality structure verbally, one must first state the next of kind, which implies an interpersonal comparison; and second, designate the features specifically differentiating each, which implies intrapersonal comparisons as well" (see below, p. 227). There are several points in this passage that call for a little elaboration.

First, the diagnostic task is to describe a personality, and to do it verbally (not by a set of quantitative ratings, or by a Q sort). The description is, moreover, to emphasize the *structure* of personality, its enduring principles of organization such as defenses, abilities, and styles of adaptation, with only secondary concern for so-called dynamics, by which is usually meant hypothetical reconstructions of genetic sequences such as the fate of the oedipus complex, and statements about the relative strength of various motives. When Rapaport refers to stating "the next of kind," he means specifying the types of personality structure that are most closely related. An interpersonal comparison is implied, because to locate a person means to specify his position in relation to others. Thus, when we say that a subject has hysterical naïveté and lability of affect but is obsessional in having distressingly recurrent ego-alien ideas, we are locating him between two adjacent types of neurotics. Moreover, we have already begun to designate specific differentiating features. And by singling out the presence of clinical obsessions, we have implicitly stated that the other aspects of the obsessive-compulsive syndrome, such as isolating and intellectualizing defenses, are less prominent. This is intrapersonal comparison, the logical equivalent of the Q sort.

But, one may ask, is "to describe a personality structure verbally" a *diagnostic* procedure? Diagnosis is after all a medical term, meaning "the art or act of identifying a disease from its signs and symptoms" (Webster's Seventh *New Collegiate Dictionary*). True, diagnostic psychological testing developed in a medical setting and out of a medical tradition, in which the ideal conception of disease was one of a clearly identifiable, unique pattern of symptoms arising from the deleterious effect of an external agent upon a healthy organism. But even in the practice of nonpsychiatric medicine, this conception has proved oversimple and is grossly applicable to only a fraction of the conditions which the physician must treat. The struggles of the classical descriptive psychiatrists to classify their charges according to this model are instructive (see the excellent history of diagnosis in Menninger et al , 1963): it took enormous integrative efforts and concept attainment of the highest order for such a man as Kraepelin to come up with his diagnostic system, and one can only have great respect for his achievement by comparison with less inspired efforts of others to find useful categories.

Yet the difference is probably quantitative, not qualitative. All classification, whether in psychiatry, medicine, or descriptive biology, makes the simplifying assumption that nature is particulate yet typical—that individuals for all their uniqueness do fall into definable and discriminable types. When viewed closely, however, the subject matters of all these taxonomic endeavors seem continuous; all contours lose their sharpness on a close approach and turn into gradients. Lamarck was so impressed with this fact that he denied the existence of species altogether, arguing for a continuum of animal forms, and though he lost decisively to Linnaeus, controversy still rages in descriptive biology. Even the advent of the computer has by no means provided a satisfactory cookbook solution to the classification of species. The resulting so-called "phenetic numerical taxonomy" has enabled A. J. Royce to discover that female gorillas have closer "affinities" with the male *Homo sapiens* than with the male *Gorilla gorilla gorilla,* so Simpson (1965) tells us. It is no wonder that Polanyi (1962, p. 603) comments: "The identification of the species to which an animal or plant belongs, resembles the task of diagnosing a disease; it too can be learnt only by practicing it under a teacher's guidance. A medical practitioner's diagnostic ability continues to develop by further practical experience; and a taxonomist can become an expert . . . only after many years of professional practice. Thus, both the medical diagnostician and the taxonomist acquire much diagnostic knowledge that they could not learn from books." How much more true these words are for the psychological diagnostician!

The medical model against which many clinical psychologists are revolting today, under the leadership of Szasz (1961), may be an anachronism within medicine itself, therefore. Traces of the old conception of diseases, as discrete diagnostic entities, can be found in the first edition of this book, for the Topeka orientation in the 1940's used the concept of disease as one of its starting points. Yet it is interesting to note that the term disease hardly ever appears in the two volumes. There was no conscious focusing on the issue, no polemical attacks on the medical model; but the terminology was rather consistently avoided. Even before Rapaport left the Menninger Foundation, there were other signs of change, staff discussions about the nature of diagnosis and illness, culminating in books by Karl A. Menninger, Martin Mayman, and collaborators (1962, 1963) outlining a new approach to diagnosis, close to the new spirit of diagnosis in medicine under the impact of Selye's ideas.

Rapaport himself began to grow less concerned with the problem of diagnosis at about this time, and after he left Topeka became increasingly preoccupied with theory, research, and to some extent with therapy. Nevertheless, what he taught us was never compatible with a cookbook approach. It contained within it the seeds of a very different theory of psychopathology than the taxonomic one, which at the same time preserved what was lastingly valuable in the approach typified by Kraepelin.

Many psychologists and psychiatrists alike, when confronted by the unpleasant discovery that nosology is procrustean, while reality is protean, have either rejected diagnosis altogether (see Rogers, 1951) or have decided that the old approach was too "static" and what was needed was something "dynamic" instead. A great deal of time has been wasted in the effort to set up dynamic diagnostic categories, which would be characterized by common etiological sequences, or "impulse-defense configurations." Such an approach lends itself to discrete rubrics even less well than the nomenclature of descriptive psychiatry. Nevertheless, it is to this day common for clinical psychologists to deal with the problem by a kind of resigned, cynical shrug, conveying a disillusionment with "pigeonholing" but admitting an inability to find anything to take its place. Indeed, this state of affairs undoubtedly is a powerful contributor to the present low esteem for diagnosis as a focus of professional activity for clinical psychologists.

Rapaport taught, and by his example demonstrated, that diagnostic testing could be and was: first, clinically most useful; second, personally challenging and exciting; third, intellectually respectable and meaningful. For most of his life it was his only clinical practice, and his students are unusual in that so many of them have been able to find it a professionally satisfying activity despite the lures of psychotherapy. But neither he nor we could have found it so if it were a matter of nothing more than intuitively "instantiating modules" (Sarbin, Taft, & Bailey, 1960) or constructing cookbooks.

What, then, is the role of diagnosis (in the sense of using a nosology) in clinical practice? *A diagnosis is not a sufficient classification but a necessary constituent of a personality description.* In order to explain how it is used, it will be necessary to state a conception of how typological concepts such as diagnoses are useful in a world of continuous variation.

Let me suggest a spatial metaphor, in which diagnoses are not addresses of buildings into which people may be put, but landmarks with respect to which people may be located. Imagine an unbroken surface, representing the people who get defined as patients (not because they are "ill" but because they show up at psychological or psychiatric clinics or hospitals). Any one region on this surface shades imperceptibly into the next; yet if we have a system of reference points, we can locate it more or less precisely. In geography, it seems probable that points on the earth's surface were first located by reference to prominent landmarks—a mountain, a river, a ravine. Nosology is still in this state of development, naming outstanding features of the psychopathological landscape in terms of what is perceptually striking about them, so that the diagnostic terms do not stand in any very easily determined relation to one another. Perhaps, however, we may be able to move on to the next step, corresponding in geography to the isolation of the basic directions in three-dimensional space. These form a coordinate system in a simple, logical relation to one another, making it possible to locate something on the earth about as precisely as desired. In psychopathology, workers like Wittenborn and Holzberg (1951) and Lorr, O'Connor, and Stafford (1957) hope to discover such an abstract set of orthogonal dimensions by means of factor analysis. Their results to date are relatively encouraging: such a structure does seem to be inherent in our descriptive psychiatric terminology, and though it is early to say just how many dimensions will be necessary, the principal impediment to further progress along these lines is the lack of precise and objective measuring instruments, analogues of the compass and sextant.

Until this dimensional approach is developed and perfected, then, the diagnostician will have to stick to the landmark approach, using the classical diagnostic categories as orienting points. Occasionally, a person may be close enough to the center of the hypothetical region defining a diagnostic entity so that he can be located almost entirely by reference to it, without discussing the "next of kind"; in this limiting case only, diagnosis can approach pigeonholing. Usually, however, the diagnostician will have to triangulate by reference to several such landmarks.

So far, the diagnostic process has been described in reverse. An important principle in the tradition that Rapaport started is that diagnosis is a semiquantitative assessment of many separate *variables* of intellect, defense, affect, motivation, and other aspects of personality. One can read in Schafer (1949) and in Sargent (1953), but oddly enough *not* in the original edition of *Diagnostic Psychological Testing,* the fundamental tenet of psychodiagnosis: from clinical data such as tests provide, one can proceed by means of what I call primary inference only to variables, not to diagnoses. Yet both writers learned this conception of diagnosis directly from Rapaport.

The basis of primary inference from test data is either actuarial or theoretical. That is, an interpretive rule may be an empirical rule of thumb, based on clinical experience or on a statistical study; or else it may be deductive instead of inductive, an implication derived from some theoretical rationale. Ideally, we know that a certain test indicator is associated with an aspect of personality at a specific level of probability, and also are able to understand the relationship by reference to a theory of personality. Without rationale, the diagnostician has only isolated bits of information with which it is difficult to do anything clinically valuable. By its very nature, of course, the actuarial method is restricted to unintegrated, fragmentary inferences.

A diagnostic entity is a syndrome, a pattern of several simpler, constituent elements; it is a good example of what Max Weber (1904-1917) called an ideal type. It may not exist at all in nature in pure form, but it expresses recurrent tendencies for certain variables to cluster. Careful diagnostic work therefore demands a knowledge of the range of expectable syndromes, what their constituent variables are, and some means of measuring (if only by subjective estimation) the strength of each variable. By drawing on this knowledge and on his knowledge of theory, the diagnostician puts together his primary inferences and in an act of secondary inference locates the subject with reference to diagnostic syndromes.

Without at least an effort at ordinal quantification through the use of intensifying and qualifying language in describing the subject, the multidimensional approach degenerates into an easily caricatured mishmash: every patient becomes a little paranoid, a little hysterical, somewhat schizophrenic but with depression and obsession also present. Some order (the intraindividual comparison of which Rapaport spoke) must be sought by decisions about which types describe the patient best, and which variables are noticeably operative at what estimated levels of strength or prominence. By failing to commit themselves in this way, some diagnostic testers arouse negative feelings in their psychiatric colleagues, beginning with impatience and ranging through rejection to contempt.

In the diagnostic tradition associated with the Menningers, Knight, and Rapaport, every patient was given a *characterological* as well as a *symptomatic* diagnosis. The former characterized the style of a person's adaptation before the development of symptoms; for it has long been noticed that there are normal equivalents or approximations to many of the so-called psychiatric diseases. Kretschmer (1921), for example, describes "schizothymic" and "cyclothymic" personalities in the normal range, noting that their characteristic ways of coping with their own drives and with the demands of reality may grow more extreme until one has to call them first schizoid or cycloid, and finally schizophrenic or manic-depressive. It has often been noted, also, that many schizophrenics have premorbid personalities marked not so much by schizoid as by hysterical or obsessional features (e.g., Fairbairn, 1952). A symptomatic condition (like schizophrenia) will have quite a different appearance and clinical course depending on the premorbid make-up, so that characterological diagnosis not only adds to the differentiation and descriptive adequacy of the diagnostic picture but to its clinical utility as well.

In reflecting on these matters and trying as always to put the lore of the clinic together with theoretical concepts, Rapaport came to see that part of the perennial vitality of Kraepelin's concepts, despite the many attacks on them, was that they represent pathological extremes of ideal types of ego structure, conceived of as organized systems of defensive and adaptive apparatuses. There do seem to be natural lines of cleavage, certain gestalts that are "better" than others, so that a typology is not wholly indefensible (see Murphy, 1947, Chapter 31; and Stein, 1963). Yet just as in the realm of symptomatic diagnosis, the ego-structural point of view did not lead to classification so much as to measurement, via diagnostic tests: the ideal types remained as orienting reference points, in terms of which to organize the discussion of the simpler and more abstract variables that were assessed by primary inference.

A further extension of the thinking that led to the distinction between characterological and symptomatic diagnosis was the insight that any given ego structure could exist in adaptive or maladaptive variants. The characterological diagnosis of compulsive character, for instance, was not necessarily a prediction that compulsions and related symptoms would perforce develop, nor a statement that the person was "a little sick." It was a recognition that the same pattern of abilities and defenses that could decompensate into a hand washer paralyzed with doubt and indecision could also subserve the most useful kind of well-organized, orderly, hard-working, conscientious behavior. The logical extension of the diagnostic process that is involved is to assess the degree to which the defenses are decompensated, which means not only taking note of anxiety, depression, or other forms of incapacitating distress, or breakdowns of contact with reality, but knowing and describing the variant forms of any particular defense. To put it crudely, there is intellectualizing and also overintellectualizing; the more tediously pedantic, inappropriately precise, or pretentiously technical a person's style of talking and dealing with problems, the more decompensated we recognize his defense of intellectualization to be. When, however, a person can use the resources of a large vocabulary to express precise shadings of meaning instead of merely clogging the channels of communication with big words, when he can draw on a wide range of information without having to use it for self-indulgent display, when he uses orderly methods of working without being seriously disturbed if they have to be interrupted or cannot be employed on a task, then we make a serious error to conclude that he must be suffering from an obsessive-compulsive *neurosis*.

The final step of the diagnostic process, once empathy and primary inferences have led to the evaluation of clinically relevant variables of personality and their adaptive or maladaptive (compensated or decompensated) status, is the construction by secondary inference of an organized picture of a personality. Typological concepts such as ego structures and pathological syndromes are standard forms of organization, simplified paradigms of ways people tend to be put together; but good diagnostic work uses them in a differentiated way as starting points for the construction of *individualized models of personality*. These must be so organized and oriented that they are capable of being used to generate predictions about how the person would behave in specifiable circumstances—for example, when exposed to the psychoanalytic situation, would he be able to make good use of this therapeutic technique, or would he decompensate further, or simply be unable to produce the kind of material needed for the method to have any effects? Depending on the kind of predictions likely to be needed, which will be a function of the kind of persons being tested and the context (e.g., outpatient or inpatient clinical setting, personnel selection, etc.), the verbal description of a personality structure will need to emphasize different types of variables. Usually, however, such a model will include statements about intellectual functioning, defenses and other structural features, motives and affects, object relations (attitudes and feelings about principal types of figures—parents, peers, sexual partners, et al.), identity and related issues such as self-esteem, genetic hypotheses and reconstructions, pathological trends, and often general values and attitudes.

The diagnostic tradition of which this book is a part may be summarized in the following eight propositions:

(1) Diagnosis is not classification but construction of a verbal model of a personality in adaptive difficulty, or suffering from some malformation or dilapidation.

(2) Such a verbal model must be hierarchically organized, by means of intrapersonal comparisons or quantification of the variables used.

(3) Typological concepts, like diagnoses, are useful as reference points to aid the description of personalities by means of interpersonal comparison.

(4) The central emphasis of diagnosis is structural, using a typology of ego structures based mainly on defenses; dynamic and genetic considerations are important, but secondary.

(5) The diagnostic process begins with the identification and measurement of variables by empathic observation and primary inference directly from clinical data (including tests); the clinician then examines the patterning of these variables, and by reference to empirical knowledge about what goes with what and to relevant theory, he makes secondary inferences of a more constructional kind.

(6) The clinical usefulness of a personality description is enhanced if it includes both characterological and symptomatic diagnosis.

(7) The diagnostician should strive to assess the degree to which aspects of personality play an adaptive role and are well compensated, as against being maladaptive (decompensated).

(8) The ultimate purpose of diagnosis is to facilitate understanding and individualized predictions about the behavior of uniquely organized persons. Since a broad range of possible predictions may be clinically called for, the diagnostic description must cover most of the important aspects of personality.

The above principles are applicable to diagnostic work whether carried out by psychiatrist or psychologist, with the aid of social-historical or of test data. Certain further aspects of the tradition are more specific to testing.

The role of theory in testing has already been implied, above, but needs to be explicated further. Perhaps it is as well epitomized by an ideal as any other way: the neophyte should aspire to become the kind of tester who *understands* the relations between all of his test data and personality in terms of a systematic theory. The contrasting ideal that defines another prominent tradition in psychodiagnosis is the intuitive wizard who performs astonishing predictive prodigies, introduced by the disarming remark, "Don't ask me how I know this, but . . ." Rapaport saw how little lasting value there was to such personal virtuosity (though he was himself quite capable of it) if it could not be analyzed and thus taught to others. He had less respect for or interest in the pragmatic value of an observation that some feature of tests was regularly associated with something diagnostically relevant than in the theoretical challenge posed by such a correlation. Until some inner necessity could be elucidated for a relationship of this kind, he distrusted it because the limits of its applicability were unknown.

Out of this orientation came Rapaport's stress on what he called the *rationale* of tests: a systematic linkage of the test-responding process (and its products) to a theory of personality, thought organization, and psychopathology. The theory he found most useful was Freudian psychoanalysis, expanded and enriched by any contributions from other psychologies and behavioral sciences he could make consistent with it. One might characterize his stance as a rooted eclecticism, always willing to borrow but not easily being convinced to change a fundamental proposition.

The relation between testing and theory was a two-way street in this tradition, also. Much of Rapaport's later important contribution to psychoanalytic ego psychology and metapsychology grew directly out of his years of diagnostic testing: observing patients, trying empathically and analytically to understand the processes by which the various kinds of test responses came about, and relating all of this to psychoanalysis. In the process, he found operational definitions for many psychoanalytic concepts, made microanalyses of processes and structural relations which Freud had been able to describe only in the macrocosm of life events, and generated many theoretical hypotheses. All of his students learned theory as well as diagnosis, and were shown how diagnostic work can be exciting and productive, as dignified a source of ideas for theory construction as psychotherapy. An excellent recent example from the Menninger-Riggs testing tradition is Shapiro (1965).

The second most distinctive contribution to diagnostic testing from the Rapaport tradition is the insistence on using a battery of tests to evaluate a patient. *Diagnostic Psychological Testing* was the first major advocacy and exposition of clinical work with a balanced group of instruments, called a battery. Even when psychologists began to see the need to supplement the Rorschach with other tests (despite the chauvinism, or perhaps merely overoptimism, that led some of its early partisans to declare the Rorschach a measure of the total personality), what they added was all too often merely other projective techniques. In this book, and in his paper on nonprojective tests (1946), Rapaport made it clear that it is indispensable to include tests that pose a definite adaptive challenge, in which there *are* "right and wrong answers"—at the least, one of Wechsler's intelligence tests. The similarity or difference in the patient's performance on the more and less structured or permissive tests is often most instructive (see the last chapter, below).

The principle of the battery meant in practice that every subject would be given the same three or four tests, but to this core would be added an equal number of others from a fairly restricted armamentarium. It was good not to be limited to just the tests described in this book, Rapaport taught, and unwise to hold rigidly to precisely the same battery for all comers. Yet it takes time to build up skill with each extra test you add to your working stock, and few psychologists indeed can hope to maintain a high level of competence with each of a score of tests. For the beginner, it was always considered his first order of business to learn the basic battery as thoroughly as possible, and to build up his experience with it on as wide a range of subjects as he could, before adding others.

A closely related principle of testing buttresses the case for using several tests: the inferential process of interpretation is probabilistic, not certain. This principle is opposed to the notion of the "pathognomic sign," a chimerical dream that always vanishes in practice, no matter how dogmatic the books may be about the exclusive association of a certain type of response with schizophrenia or the like. Every diagnostic conclusion is a hypothesis, therefore, and it behooves the tester to test all hypotheses that occur to him as he goes over his data, buttressing his final conclusions as well as possible by a multiplicity of converging probabilities. If the content of one TAT story suggests a hypothesis, only weak confirmation is supplied by the emergence of similar content in another story, because there is little independence of approach to the construct in question. If the subject's test behavior, or formal aspects of his stories, lead to the same hypothesis, the probability that it is correct is more usefully enhanced; while convergence of interpretations arising from different tests and different types of interpretive principles is the soundest basis of all for the tester's having enough confidence in his point to include it in his report. Since most notable aspects of a test performance lend themselves to more than one interpretive hypothesis, ideally all should be held in mind and tested against as much other and as independent data as possible; in practice, a good deal of this goes on automatically in the well-trained and experienced tester without the necessity of conscious attention, thanks to a process that Hartmann (1939) called automatization. Note that this approach makes it not only possible but desirable to use a multiplicity of indicators each of which has only a low empirical validity. The substantial redundancy or overlap within a good battery of tests thus makes possible an excellent level of validity for a tester's interpretations, even though the probability that any one of his hypotheses is true may actually be poor. (See the discussion of scatter analysis of the Wechsler tests, in the Appendix to Chapter 3.)

When hypotheses agree, the tester's course is plain; but what about the more common cases of only partial overlap, or outright disagreement? The point of view Rapaport taught emphasized the need to make sense out of all the data; therefore, an apparent contradiction was treated as a challenge to seek a new synthesis, a hypothesis on another level that would embrace and make intelligible both of the apparently clashing facts. To be sure, there is some danger of overinterpretation in this approach. It is not always possible to discern the true determinants of all aspects of a group of test results; the tester should never lose sight of the possibility that he is interpreting error variance. Yet there are greater fallacies and pitfalls in the principal alternative, which is to assume that, when one test—let us say, the Wechsler Information subtest—implies hysterical flightiness and another (perhaps Rorschach verbalizations) schizoid looseness, one of them is right, the other wrong. On closer re-examination, one or the other may prove to have been misinterpreted, or it may lend itself equally well to the rival interpretation; or both may be right. In any event, the good clinician calls on his stock of knowledge about syndromes in which these hysterical and schizoid trends usually occur, and sets up new arrays of possibilities to check against other data in his battery. In this instance, he would probably check his notes on the patient's test behavior—observations of affects actually displayed—and also formal indications of the ways affects are handled, as in the color scores in the Rorschach. Warm, openly displayed feelings plus several *CF* responses would be consistent with the former interpretation and argue against the latter. Yet all of these bits in the context of a performance level in the WAIS well above the verbal, especially Picture Arrangement, and accompanied by a poverty of introspection when the patient was confronted by the inquiries in the Rorschach and Word Association tests, might suggest a character disorder in which underlying schizoid trends are covered by a hysteriform display of agreeable affect which proves on closer examination to be shallow and ingratiating. I will not pursue this hypothetical example through the further internal checks the last hypothesis would generate, but only indicate that even these steps have been much simplified and abbreviated for ease of exposition. It takes many words to describe a process that can occur quite quickly, despite many steps of forming and verifying hypotheses.

Granted this much of an outlook on test interpretation, it should follow naturally enough that clinical data need to be integrated with those of the tests in exactly the same way. Again, disagreement between the diagnostic conclusions of tester and social worker or psychiatrist need not mean that one of them is simply incompetent and wrong (though that can indeed be the case!). Neither testing nor interviewing is any better or more valid than the interpretive intelligence through which the resulting data are filtered. Usually everyone on a clinical team has hold of at least some fragment or transformation of the truth, and a synthesis that takes into account a *maximum* of information can theoretically achieve a maximum of validity. Human integrative capacities being what they are, however, it should not be surprising that some research has shown many clinicians to reach an optimal level of informational input quite soon, after which they may even do more poorly with an increase in load.

The reasons for Rapaport's strong advocacy of blind testing were partly local and historically temporary; but there remains a good deal to be said for keeping alive its spirit. If the tester will gather his own type of data with only a minimum of necessary history and presenting complaint, and make as many purely internal checks of his hypotheses as possible, he will be in a strong position to look intelligently at the clinical story, with an increased likelihood of being able to see in it something that his clinical colleagues have not already picked up. Even if he is working alone, and interprofessional rivalries or the like do not operate to narrow the scope of his interviewing, he may find it economical of his time and effort to hold to a minimum his gathering of nontest data.

Despite his advocacy of blind testing, Rapaport always valued what could be learned from nontechnical information of the type on a usual face-sheet or application form: the implications for personality development of the educational and occupational history, of belonging to various sub-cultures, ethnic or religious groups, or of having lived in a cultivated or a poor family in an urban or rural setting. Each bit of even such apparently bland information, he taught and demonstrated, serves to narrow the range of possible interpretive significance for the test findings themselves, as well as more positively suggesting a range of inferences.

Similarly, while he was highly skeptical about the claims of enthusiasts, Rapaport taught us not to despise what could be learned from noticing a person's physiognomy, his bodily build, posture, expressive movements, clothing, tone of voice, etc. Anything the sharpened wits of the psychologist could seize upon to notice might be used to suggest hypotheses, so long as they were entertained only tentatively and were viewed with skepticism until subjected to independent test by as many other sources of data as possible. It was therefore of first importance that the diagnostic tester be as curious as possible about all aspects of human behavior, that he observe sharply, and that he record in writing any potentially useful results of this process. Recent research (summarized by Masling, 1966) shows that clinicians are influenced by the kinds of information discussed in this and the preceding paragraph whether they think so or not; it is far better to have conscious control of this as well as other aspects of the inferential process.

A related principle which Rapaport never tired of impressing on his students was the absolutely primary importance of verbatim recording in all testing. The chapters on the Rorschach and TAT, below, will give most eloquent testimony to the creative use he made of psycholinguistic analyses which obviously require accurate verbal protocols, but he brought the same principles to the analysis of the Wechsler-Bellevue. It is unfortunate that the almost exclusive emphasis on the quantitative data in Chapter 3 has given some readers the wholly mistaken impression that the Topeka-Stock-bridge tradition pays no attention to qualitative analysis of verbalization in tests of intellectual function. (Some leads to qualitative analysis will be found in Schafer, 1948, and Mayman, Schafer, & Rapaport, 1951). Again, the exigencies of a research orientation distorted the presentation, though it must be admitted also that the analysis of verbalization in tests of intelligence and concept formation is not easy to expound with any degree of brevity.

A final principle of testing has been adumbrated in the above several times; Schafer (1954) has expounded it most explicitly: by "test data" we mean a great deal more than the scores. We do not underestimate the scores and what can be suggested by their quantitative patterns; but they are only a set of abstracted dimensions from a much richer reality. In addition to what is explicitly *scored,* test data include *content* (in the sense of ideational content, as discussed in Chapter 10), *formal aspects* (only some of which are typically scored), *verbalizations,* and observations of *test behavior* (e.g., affect expressive style). The relative independence of these types of data makes them a valuable resource for testing interpretive hypotheses, and no battery has been thoroughly analyzed until all five of these types of test data have been scrutinized and understood.

From the tone of the preceding sections, one might get the impression that they were written with the assumption that the world of clinical psychology into which this revision is being sent is much the same as the world that received the first edition, except perhaps for some additional sophistication. That is obviously not the case; the situation has changed so radically that some might even question the need for any more books on testing. It will be worth our while, therefore, to examine in some detail what has been happening to psychodiagnosis as a preoccupation of the clinical psychologist, and where it may be headed.

The Present Situation and Future Prospects of Diagnostic Testing[2]

In the score of years after the appearance of the first edition of this book, diagnostic testing reached an early zenith and then went into a de-

---

[2] A somewhat longer and more fully documented version of this section has been published elsewhere (Holt, 1967d).

cline, both in the amount of time psychologists devote to it and in their estimation of it. Several surveys (including some made by Division 12 and other arms of the American Psychological Association, and by the National Institute of Mental Health) support the impression that among clinical psychologists there has been a significant drop-off of involvement in diagnosis. The disillusionment has been particularly marked in the academic sector of the profession, so that recent trainees in clinical psychology characteristically bring to their internships more skepticism about the whole psychodiagnostic enterprise than skill in giving and interpreting tests.

POSSIBLE REASONS FOR THE DECLINE OF DIAGNOSTIC TESTING

A number of hypotheses have been advanced to account for the hard times that diagnostic testing has fallen upon. First, there is the obvious fact that such a decline was inevitable since testing and psychodiagnosis began as virtually the only function of the clinical psychologist, to whom many more patterns of professional activity have been progressively opened: psychotherapy, ward administration, consultation, and other forms of community mental-health activity, as well as research and teaching of various sorts. The story is by no means just one of freedom gained from institutional hierarchies; the same development has taken place within psychiatry. Not many years ago, the psychiatrist's clinical work too was almost entirely diagnostic, because there was little else (besides administration) for him to do. As mental-health workers have expanded their fields of operation from closed hospitals to include clinics, private office practice, schools and other community agencies, the amount of time they devote to any one function—even psychotherapy—is bound to decline.

A second possible reason is an outgrowth of the extraordinarily rapid expansion of clinical psychology, much of it at a time when the principal form of professional training given was in testing. With great amounts of federal money force-feeding its growth and more jobs constantly available than could be filled, clinical psychology multiplied its own numbers many times during the immediate postwar period. On the whole, this was a remarkable achievement and one to be proud of, but such a great expansion in the quantitative production of anything is bound to be achieved at the cost of quality. There were not enough testers of sufficient skill, experience, and ability to communicate what they knew to teach all the new students, so that much of the training had to be done by poorly qualified persons. There was not enough time for slow learning by apprenticeship, or for individually supervised practice with a wide variety of cases—as much as possible had to be taught in large lecture courses supplemented by a few "clinical demonstrations" of cases and the whole thing polished off by a one-year's internship, which as often as not was not even a full year of immersion in clinical work. Then the products of this accelerated training were picked while still green for full clinical jobs or, what was worse, for university positions in which they themselves soon began training the next crop even more superficially.

The result was not only that the intellectual content of diagnostic training suffered, but its emotional aspects as well. The older generation of clinicians had learned diagnostic testing from men like Rapaport, Klopfer, Beck, and others who respected themselves and their own work, who could transmit a sense of intellectual excitement about it, and who offered role models of considerable prestige and substance for their students to emulate. But the vast majority of today's psychodiagnosticians were given no such opportunity to study with a master tester; their teachers were all too often insecure in their own competence, doubtful about the validity of what they had to offer, and bored with the very function they were trying to teach.

Meanwhile, another consequence of the burgeoning of clinical psychology came into play: Nonclinical psychologists who saw their own hegemony in the science and profession threatened by the far greater growth rate of their applied colleagues often reacted with suspicion, hostility, and rejection. Being in positions of power in university departments, they put the young clinical faculty members on the defensive, to which many reacted by identification with the aggressor. Their own status as scientists impugned, they became devotees of rigor at all costs, racing to be the first to attack any clinician's pronouncement that was not backed up by extensive research.

Meanwhile, the never-satisfied demand for the Ph.D.'s to fill empty positions in the growing numbers of hospitals and clinics also tended to debase the quality of diagnostic work. While psychologists were struggling to establish themselves and to win a place on the mental health team, they had to deliver useful service or face dismissal. Once they had proved their value and the role of the clinical psychologist had been institutionalized, so that a clinic had to have one on its staff in some states by law in order to qualify for financial aid, the most routine and perfunctory diagnostic performance became acceptable, at least in many settings.

A third reason for the diminishing luster of psychodiagnosis is that it was initially oversold. Just where the mystique of diagnostic testing came from is uncertain; partly, however, it undoubtedly stems from the fact that much of what the expert achieves is a matter of art, the exercise of intuition and craft in a way that is difficult to verbalize, simultaneously with the manipulation of an impressive physical apparatus of test equipment. It was contributed to, also, by the unfortunate penchant of some elder statesmen of psychodiagnosis for an opaque and idiosyncratic jargon, which made some of their inferences irrefutable even though they *seemed* to be asserting something. To many a psychiatrist, when the judgments of the tester were borne out by clinical experience, it seemed as if objective measurement was being performed and by means he could not follow, which awed him all the more. By a similar process of displacement, the equally impressed student of a diagnostic "wizard" wishfully located the latter's skill in what he himself could inherit with minimal pain, the tests themselves. Elated by the success and acceptance that came to them in the 1940's, clinical psychologists became overconfident and began claiming far too much. They thus set themselves up for a hard fall; the evidence pretty quickly began coming in that they had no magical wands in their grasp. If the pendulum of professional opinion has swung past realism toward pessimistic disillusionment, that is part of an inevitable process of adjustment.

Fourth, and for many the major factor, there is the controversy over clinical versus statistical prediction, as it was epitomized in Meehl's (1954) highly influential book. What began as a question in the logic of prediction and the analysis of the inferential processes of a person who works with complex meaningful data ended up as a rout for the diagnosticians. I have stated in some detail elsewhere (Holt, 1958a) why I believe that the issues were misleadingly drawn and the available research data wrongly interpreted; whether my reading of the situation was right or wrong, the harm was done. Meehl did not intend his survey as a propaganda attack, but it functioned superbly as such. Did the clinician really contribute something to the analysis of data that could not be achieved by objective means? Formulas could obviously not function alongside the psychologist as part of an interdisciplinary group evaluating and working with patients; therefore, the only way to answer the question was to force the diagnostic tester to operate in an artificial manner, on unfamiliar materials and making predictions concerning matters he knew little of, like success in flight training. In research project after project, it was shown conclusively that diagnostic skill did not enable a man to predict, for example, who would make a good clinical psychologist (Kelly & Fiske, 1951). That last was a damaging failure: there was no *rational* reason why being a clinician oneself should enable someone to predict whether a first-year graduate student was going to succeed in terms of the available criteria, yet the failure of even recognized and respected masters of diagnostic testing to perform this feat of prophecy made it look as if they were hardly better than poseurs.

Not only did clinical psychologists fail to beat the machines in most of the races they entered on foreign ground, they also did not produce much evidence that they could do their own job well. As we have seen, it is extremely difficult to plan and carry out a valid test of the psychodiagnostic function; in one of the rare instances where it has been done, a tester of many years of experience (Harrower, 1965) had to give up her practice and devote herself to research in order to follow up her tested cases and demonstrate that her test-based judgments had had a high degree of validity. (For a small-scale example, see Lindzey, 1965). It is safe to say that a graduate student doing research for his dissertation virtually never has the resources available to him to carry out a meaningful study of the validity of diagnostic testing, even if he were to understand the nature of the function well enough to plan such a project (see, however, Silverman, 1959). What *is* within his grasp is a test of the validity of some isolated diagnostic indicator; and so a lot of this kind of work was done. Perhaps it has not all been useless: we have had many demonstrations by now that there are no quick, easy, and simple diagnostic shortcuts. The search for "pathognomic signs" has been fruitless, and the validities of isolated scores, indicators, or lists thereof have proved low, fluctuating, and of no practical usefulness. A similar fate has met the naïve conception of projective techniques as psychological X rays that could penetrate the superfices of personality, undisturbed by momentary situational influences or by the subject's conscious conceptions (Masling, 1960, 1966).

We are left, then, with the alternative of giving up diagnostic testing altogether and leaving the field to statistical cookbook approaches, or doing a professional, responsible job in the slow, thoughtful, informed way that was developed in the Menninger-Riggs tradition. I shall come back to this alternative later; here I want only to note that the wrong conclusion has been difficult to resist. In a situation where valid demonstrations of competence are difficult to produce, and irrelevant demonstrations that what should not work does not are abundant, the sheer weight of numbers will impress those outside the field that research has proved psychodiagnosis worthless.

The next set of hypotheses that has been adduced for the present discontents of psychodiagnosis has to do with the nature of the work itself. As currently practiced in many settings, it is undeniably frustrating in a number of ways. The inner strains in the testing role were brilliantly analyzed by Schafer (1954). Briefly, here are a few of his major points: the role of the clinical psychologist is not crystallized and thus not protected by traditions and standardization; practice lacks a firm foundation of theory and research findings; testing is a service often performed for a psychiatrist, a member of a profession with which psychology competes and struggles for professional status, autonomy, and power. Then, the tester's livelihood depends on the value of his reports to those for whom he provides service, not to the patient; they are often psychiatric residents, whose needs and demands necessarily reflect their professional immaturity;

when only difficult cases are referred for testing, the psychologist has to carry heavy responsibility when it is hardest to do a good job, especially if he is unrealistically looked on as a final authority. Schafer describes the tester's flight into pseudo omniscience, hedging, propitiation, rebellion, or withdrawal in the face of overvaluation, and his similar reactions to being "a second-class citizen in a psychiatric setting," viewed as ancillary even though his training may exceed that of the residents he serves. If the psychologist longs for the superior status and privileges of the M.D., he may use testing as a back door to therapy, giving up the means when the end has been attained. In many hospitals, the tester's role is particularly frustrating in that he never finds out the fate of his report, much less that of the patient; for all he knows, the product of his labors may simply be filed unread, which effectively undermines morale. There are strains in the nature of the relationship to the patient, too, Schafer tells us: the kind of data he needs (rich, revealing, scorable responses but not too many of them) only an exceptional patient can easily provide, and as a consequence the tester may be seduced into various kinds of more or less pathological behavior. The role itself has aspects that are voyeuristic, autocratic, oracular, and saintly, which in turn usually stir up anxiety, guilt, and other personal problems as the tester is successively tempted to become Peeping Tom, authoritarian dictator, omniscient and infallible seer, or kind mother.

Such a cursory summary cannot hope to do more than hint at the clinical richness of Schafer's presentation. It has been usefully supplemented by two recent papers: a brief one by Appelbaum and Siegal (1965) bringing out, for example, the stresses in certain unusual kinds of tasks that testers occasionally face, and a longer and particularly valuable one by Rosenwald (1963). The scientific training of the psychologist, Rosenwald points out, makes him uncomfortable with the artistic nature of psychodiagnosis, which nevertheless demands the integration of objective and technological elements along with the intuitive. Further, it makes the tester want to generate data to show the intrinsic validity of his inferences, yet the nature of the professional role is to provide a service, the usefulness of which depends to a great extent on the person being served: "The consumer's personal equation is not usually kept in mind in conventional studies of test validity. Generally speaking, significant research into the *clinical* usefulness of tests cannot be performed until clearer formulations are made of what is expected of and by therapists" (p. 229).

Rosenwald instructively emphasizes the passivity of the psychodiagnostic role: "The tester does little. He speaks to the patient mostly instrumentally—to induce him to talk more. He depends on his test material, while the interviewer uses his own person, his own ingenuity. The tester is ideally seen but not heard. The therapist, in contrast, is seen as a powerful and miraculous figure who says little but wields a potent influence. The tester merely sits in his office and quietly studies the test responses." Moreover, in addition to the greater activity and potency attributed to the therapist is his greater validity: "The question of validity is usually posed competitively as: 'Can the tester do and discern what the therapist does and discerns?'—never vice versa. . . . If the therapist cannot utilize test findings, it is easy for them to be discarded as meaningless" (p. 228). But as Rosenwald proceeds to demonstrate, the therapist's judgment is not a good criterion against which to check much that can be learned from tests; they are valuable partly owing to the very fact that they contribute information not otherwise obtainable so quickly.

To these excellent discussions I should like to add only one point, which is related to Schafer's concept of the saintly aspect of testing. The psychodiagnostic role is a peculiar one in that it never allows the psychologist a simple, direct, and human responsiveness to the patient, no matter how much he would like to be helpful. Behind his poker face he must be passing judgments which it would be destructive, at times, to reveal to his subject; he has to consider a suffering human being as if he were a specimen to be analyzed and described. Moreover, the tester must demand without ever giving. At best, diagnostic testing is only indirectly helpful to the patient; thus, the usually nurturant motivation of the good clinician is somewhat irrelevant to the testing role if not an actual interference with it. The fact that the psychologist typically has only a brief and impersonal contact with the subject, often never finding out what became of him, tends to make him hold back from any empathic engagement; this makes his task more difficult and pushes him toward the waiting stereotype of the schizoid intellectual who is interested in people only as objects of his dispassionate scrutiny and scientific dissection.

Testing does, typically, appeal to and satisfy intellectual curiosity, as research does. But the latter allows the investigator to be his own boss, or, if he is part of an interdisciplinary team, to be the intellectual center of a group enterprise. All in all, diagnostic testing is not an emotionally and motivationally satisfying activity for the full-time endeavors of the kind of person who is likely to be best at it.

The culture of clinical psychology is strongly antiauthoritarian, perhaps even more so than psychology at large because of the nurturant motivation just mentioned. These values are, however, incompatible with the traditionalism and with the respect for authority that are required for the transmission of a skill or art, like psychodiagnosis. As the eminent scientist-philosopher Polanyi has written:

> . . . the aim of a skilful performance is achieved by the observance of a set of rules which are not known as such to the person following them. . . .

An art which cannot be specified in detail cannot be transmitted by pre-scription, since no prescription for it exists. It can be passed on only by example from master to apprentice. . . . To learn by example is to submit to authority. You follow your master because you trust his manner of do-ing things even when you cannot analyse and account in detail for its effectiveness. By watching the master and emulating his efforts in the pres-ence of his example, the apprentice unconsciously picks up the rules of the art, including those which are not explicitly known to the master himself. These hidden rules can be assimilated only by a person who surrenders himself to that extent uncritically to the imitation of another [1958, pp. 49, 53].

Rapaport knew this and insisted on the kind of apprenticeship Polanyi describes. I can well remember how we, his students, chafed under this alien requirement and resented the demand for submission to a tradition, when all our rationalist training had told us that the only valid knowledge was that of explicit science. Yet there was, and still is, no substitute for apprenticeship, something that is recognized in the persistence of clerk-ships, practica, and the formal year of internship that remain part of most clinical training programs.

The implication is not that we should turn the clock back to the era of the guilds and unquestioningly imitate all that a supposed expert does. We need to steer, as usual, a middle course, retaining our skepticism and in-sisting on an ultimate objective test while suspending the demand that every procedure be documented by controlled research. This is easier to do in a science where valid pragmatic tests are readily available, and a true master can easily be distinguished from a poseur. In psychodiagnosis, the real villain of the piece is the lack of satisfactory criteria about the validity of which everyone agrees. The student who wishes to learn experimental research by apprenticeship does not have much trouble in finding men to work with who are generally conceded to be productive contributors. A truly expert diagnostic tester can make himself known only gradually, through the gratification of clinical colleagues who find that they are not led astray by relying on his statements about patients.

The situation is further confused by the fact, which Polanyi has so clearly demonstrated, that "practical wisdom is more truly embodied in action than expressed in rules of action" (1958, p. 54). Thus, in the tradi-tionalistic field of common law, a judge's decision is rightly given a great deal more weight than his verbal explanation. Even a true expert does not know to any great extent how he achieves what he does. Indeed, a major reason for this introduction was the feeling I and other students of Rapa-port had on rereading the book that "that wasn't really the way he did it." I hope that I have succeeded in setting out in words a little more of the process, but I am not self-deceived enough to believe that any book of this kind can have more than a limited value in the present state of the art.

The sad thing about the great bulk of psychodiagnostic research is that it seems uninformed about the artistic nature of the skill. We would have done well to emulate the approach adopted by industrial researchers in the cotton-spinning mills: "most of the initial decade's work on the part of the scientist will have to be spent merely in defining what the spinner knows" (W. L. Balls, quoted by Polanyi, 1958, p. 52). It actually took that long to explicate the skilled process of spinning enough so that the scientists could begin to improve and finally to automate it. What happened in our own field?—the verbal statements of the experts were taken at face value, as if they knew exactly how they worked; each cue relationship was treated as if it must have a validity that could be demonstrated in isolation from a complex judgmental process, by people who themselves were neophytes in testing. In retrospect, it is hard to see how the results could have been positive except in occasional samples. They were not, as we well know; and a nihilistic conclusion was drawn by all too many psychologists, particularly those who did not know enough about the skill to see that something was wrong with the research.

It has not been easy to say just how the research was at fault. The initial reaction of many experts, when their verbal rules failed to work, was to invoke the configurational nature of the data. This principle has undoubted validity, but it should lend itself to explication and to testing; so far, very little research has demonstrated that configurational rules work where linear ones do not. The real trouble, I believe, is that the experts do not know enough about how they themselves work, and that the problem of the criterion has never been satisfactorily solved.

A few masters of testing (for example, Schafer, 1949) have had the insight to see that the only validational research that made much sense used clinical judgments, not objective scores or signs in the tests, as the predictors. Most of the positive results have been obtained in studies of this kind (Rotter, 1940; Harrison, 1940; Symonds, 1955; Sohler et al., 1957; Silverman, 1959). My impression, from a casual scanning of the literature, is that less of this kind of work is being published today than a decade or two ago. No wonder; such research is only demonstrational, and needs not so much to be repeated as to be followed up by the patient application of job-analytic techniques—the study of the good diagnostic tester at work.

Another blow to testing has been struck from entirely outside the profession. Beginning about a decade ago with *The Organization Man* (Whyte, 1956), a series of books aimed at the general public has attacked psychological tests of all kinds and on many grounds (Packard, 1957, 1964;

Gross, 1962; Hoffman, 1962; Black, 1962; Brenton, 1964): although their instruments are unscientific and invalid, psychologists are reading our minds, invading our privacy, imposing a yoke of conformity on employees and stifling originality in school children, driven by morbid sexual curiosity and the cynical pursuit of money. Some of these authors were invited to testify at Congressional and Senatorial investigations of personality testing in June, 1965 (see *American Psychologist,* November, 1965, Vol. 20, No. 11). The main brunt of the attack has been borne by such self-administering tests as the MMPI when used by industrial psychologists for the selection of personnel, and the investigations have served the useful purpose of focusing the attention of psychology on the neglected ethical and civil-libertarian aspects of personality tests when they are taken semivoluntarily as a condition of employment. Nevertheless, psychologists who are professionally identified with testing of any kind have been put on the defensive, and a great deal of confusion and misinformation has been broadcast to a large segment of the public. Furthermore, clinical diagnostic testing was exempt from Congressional criticism only because it was considered part of a medical inquiry. There still remains some danger that *all* psychological testing may be subjected to clumsy and overrestrictive legal regulation.

Subject to all of these stresses and strains, both external and internal, it is no wonder that psychodiagnosticians are in a state of poor morale today. Two questions remain to be answered, however: What is the value of psychodiagnostic testing and thus the place of training in this function in the doctoral curriculum for clinical psychologists? And what is the future likely to be for diagnostic psychological testing?

THE USES OF DIAGNOSTIC TESTING

Let us recall, first, that the shrunken part played by diagnosis in the work of the clinical psychologist is a relative matter, caused by competition for his time; the demand for diagnostic service has surely not dropped off despite all of the attacks on testing (justified and unjustified) but has if anything increased. And to some extent the glamor that testing has lost was false, so that the reappraisal has been in part healthy. The old "medical model" of clinical psychological work created a natural place for diagnosis; now it is passing, and it will be a good thing for psychologists to take a close look at psychodiagnosis, asking just what value it has.

With the emergence of a vocal minority of clinical psychologists in private practice, who are a conspicuous group in the great cities, it is easy to lose sight of the fact that clinical psychologists predominantly work in medical institutions. *Action for Mental Health* (Joint Commission, 1961) helped remind us that huge numbers of hospital beds continue to be occupied by psychotic persons, and that schizophrenia remains the major mental-health problem of our day. Despite all the hopeful promise of preventive psychiatry, there is little realistic prospect that the number of psychotics is going to decline. The pattern of institutional practice will eventually change in unpredictable ways; but for the next few decades, it seems safe to predict that medically dominated institutions will continue to have primary responsibility for identifying and taking care of psychotic people, and that diagnosis will continue to be a necessity for the administration of such institutions. The contribution of the diagnostic tester may be unrealistically evaluated in many institutions at various times, but there is a core of solid acceptance for it that will not easily be worn away, which generates a steady demand.

Is this faith justified, despite the failure of most research to produce impressive evidence of the validity of diagnostic tests? We have already seen that most of this research is off the point. One persistently overlooked but major source of variance in diagnostic testing is the talent and skill of the psychologist who does it. It is all too easy to exaggerate the degree of objectivity that is introduced by the standardization of test materials, instructions, etc., as compared to the interview; it is still possible for one practitioner to do a consistently brilliant job, and another to be hopelessly incompetent to get anything of value out of his tests. In these circumstances, it is as meaningful to ask what is "the validity of the Rorschach" or of a battery of tests, as it is to ask about the validity of oil painting as a means of representing faces. In the hands of a master, oils can produce portraits that not only easily match photographs for excellence of likeness, but convey a good deal more about the personality; which says exactly nothing about the probability that a picture painted by an unknown person can be matched to the face of the person portrayed better than chance.

Viewed from this perspective, the problem of validity becomes first one of establishing the upper limits of what can be done by the most gifted diagnosticians, and then of finding out how they do it. Little research of these kinds has been done. It is of relatively little lasting importance what the level of competence of the average practitioner may be. If one were to evaluate the problem-solving skill of a group of people, many of whom had little talent for mathematics or interest in it for its own sake, and who had been poorly trained in the solution of differential equations by teachers who were not skilled at it themselves, the prevailing poor level of proficiency would not tell us a thing about the utility of the calculus itself.

Yet there remains a vast difference between a branch of mathematics and the scientific art of psychodiagnosis, apart from the fact that one is a formal, the other an empirical science. In the physical sciences, two experts often reach the same solution to a problem requiring the application of a set of laws to a body of facts; but when experts in diagnostic testing are given the same battery of test data, they never reach exactly the same conclusions. The comparison suggests a reason for the difference: psychology lacks a substantial body of laws that are relevant to the diagnostic task, as outlined above. We are forced to improvise, to create hypotheses where someday it may be possible simply to invoke established laws. Each new subject for testing might be compared to an unsolved problem in theory for another science: different experts will approach it differently, drawing on their intuition, hunches, purely heuristic rules of thumb, anything to make possible some start; and they may end up with different solutions, sometimes partly overlapping, sometimes equally plausible but unrelated to one another. At this point, the two situations diverge, for the hard sciences by definition are those that have precise and rigorous methods of testing theories. A diagnostic test report is a theory of a particular person, which is in principle testable; in practice, however, it would be extremely slow, laborious, and even so not very rigorous, if we brought to bear all the resources of psychology to confirm or refute it.

In the end, we are left without hard research evidence that there exist many practitioners of diagnostic testing who can do the job well enough to deserve the name of expert. In the lack of an easily obtained criterion, skeptics like Eysenck are ready to assume that psychodiagnosticians who claim that they know something about diagnostic testing are at best self-deceived, at worst charlatans. But it is possible to maintain such a cynical view of "clinical validation"—the ability of diagnostic testers to create a respected place for themselves on clinical teams over a period of years—only if one maintains that all psychiatrists, social workers, nurses, and others who work with patients in clinics and mental hospitals are a pack of rogues and fools, who either are in collusion to bilk the public, or can be consistently gulled into accepting empty formulations in obscure jargon instead of the evidence of their senses. For a while, a charlatan can get by undetected even in as concrete a discipline as surgery, as certain notorious imposters have demonstrated in recent years, on the strength of an impressive, assured manner, a superficial command of shop talk, and a bit of native shrewdness in practical situations. In isolated private practice, practitioners of less definitive healing arts like psychotherapy can doubtless survive for years despite the lack of any valid knowledge or skill, simply because their work is not observed and checked by colleagues, and because people tend on the average to get better anyway.

But to anyone who has participated in the daily work of a mental-health team, particularly in a hospital, it is perfectly evident that there is such an entity as clinical competence and that the lack of it cannot long be concealed. This evidence of validity is admittedly fallible, and it would be dangerous to rely on it too much, but it is real and important evidence.

The rather undifferentiated clinical usefulness of diagnostic testing in a hospital or clinic may be further analyzed.[3] The psychodiagnostician first of all contributes to the understanding of etiology, the causes of the suffering person's present predicament. He weighs the relative contribution of organic and functional factors, and reconstructs a plausible history of the way the personality developed to its contemporary status. Of special value is the picture of the person's ego structure that tests allow the diagnostician to draw. Tests are also unexcelled in enabling a precise and differentiated account to be given of the person's abilities, and the degree of their functional and organic impairment. The good psychodiagnostician then contributes to prognosis, predicting the probable course of the patient's condition if untreated and if subjected to various types of therapies from an assessment of his assets and liabilities; to take only a single example, the tester may discover the danger of suicide. Suitability for specific types of treatment may be ascertained, contributing to the rational selection of an optimal type of therapy. The data obtained by the psychodiagnostician and his constructed model of the personality serve also to aid various people who will be charged with responsibility for his management, custodial care, and other administrative decisions apart from therapy in the narrow sense; they are also helpful to persons who must discuss the case with the patient himself and with his relatives. If the patient enters psychotherapy, the tester's report can give an initial orientation to the therapist that will help him in his planning and in his developing understanding of the case; it can alert him to typical forms of transference and interpersonal stratagems to which the patient is accustomed. After continued contact, the subject will undoubtedly behave at times in ways that puzzle those who must deal with him; if a good psychodiagnostic test report exists, reference to it may enable the behavior to be interpreted, or the psychologist may even go back to his test data themselves and be able to reinterpret them in illuminating ways. Finally, tests given at the time of initial evaluation serve as a benchmark permitting a refined analysis of a battery given at some critical future time, such as the end of treatment or at some crisis in it.

The particular flavor of the preceding paragraph betrays the nature of the clinical setting in which I did most of my diagnostic testing; other uses have been found in other settings. As changes occur in the prevailing ways of dealing with "mental patients" in the institutions society sets up for this purpose, the values of diagnostic testing will change accordingly. Conceivably, intensive psychotherapy and psychoanalysis may be entirely

---

[3] The following paragraph is in part indebted to Thorne (1948).

supplanted by some new form of chemotherapy, behavioral shaping, or whatnot; but I find it inconceivable that any such advances will change one basic fact about people, on which the value of diagnostic testing squarely rests: *there are stable and pervasive characteristics or dispositions in personality* (generally called structural) *which enable us to predict that people will respond differently—at times in diametrically, at times in orthogonally opposed ways—to the same stimuli, press, or treatment.* The fire that melts the butter hardens the egg, a homely truth yet to be discovered by many behavior therapists who, following Skinner, believe that the laws of behavior are so general that "it is possible to obtain valid and generalizable data from single organisms" (Goldiamond, 1965). Yet Hein, Cohen, and Shmavonian (1965) have shown that groups of people who were distinguished by tests as field dependent and field independent responded entirely differently in an autonomic conditioning experiment: the extremely undifferentiated, field-oriented subjects could not be conditioned at all! There is an obvious lesson here for the enthusiast about conditioning approaches to "behavior modification," whether by classical or operant methods. (Klein and his students, inspired by the ego-psychological viewpoint of Rapaport, had made the general point a decade or more ago, that the direction of psychological effects may reverse itself entirely depending on the person's cognitive style; see Klein, 1954, and Gardner et al., 1959.)

In any situation where a person is sufficiently motivated to obtain some kind of guidance (for example, educational or vocational) or help in changing his behavior, so that he willingly undertakes the self-revelation of being tested, and when the decisions about how to treat him or what he should undertake to do are important enough, diagnostic testing may be indicated. Recent graduates of one of the country's largest clinical training programs agree that "Diagnosticians and psychotherapists are in chronically short supply in every geographical area and in every variety of clinical setting" (Pottharst & Kovacs, 1964).

Another important value of diagnostic testing has emerged from the tradition of personological research begun by Murray (1938). In much of our work at the Research Center for Mental Health, we have followed his lead of performing experiments on samples of subjects whose personalities have been assessed by means of batteries of diagnostic tests, clinically analyzed and described qualitatively and in quantitative ratings. Such ratings make it possible to examine experimental findings in a new light, which illuminates the inner sources of experimental error by revealing the kinds of personality who show a given effect most and least markedly. For example, Eagle (1962) correlated the extent of a subliminal effect, from experiments on the metacontrast or masking phenomenon, with such rated assessments of personality, and gained a new insight into the nature of the phenomenon: the correlations with modes of thinking and of dealing with impulses and intuitions suggested the hypothesis that information received without awareness is experienced as if self-generated, not coming from outside. Likewise, Linton and Langs (1962) learned from a similar application of diagnostic testing to subjects in an experiment on LSD that the nature of the drug experience differs strikingly in persons whose Rorschachs, clinically analyzed, indicate different defensive styles of ego structure.

FUTURE PATTERNS OF TRAINING AND PRACTICE

I believe, therefore, that as long as we continue to train "general practitioners" of clinical psychology, they should have thorough training in psychopathology and psychodiagnosis. In many of the kinds of jobs they are likely to be offered, such skills will be called for, and even where they are not, they will be of great value. For, whatever his function, the clinical psychologist is likely to have to deal in one way or another with more or less seriously disturbed people. If he has not had enough exposure to the pathological extremes of the major types of ego structure to be able to pick up valid diagnostic clues to the kind of person he confronts, he will make serious mistakes that are unforgivable for a professional worker in mental health. At the same time, it is unmistakably true that a large proportion of current doctoral programs approved by the APA do not give adequate training in diagnostic testing; they do not have the teaching staff to do so, and frequently their students do not have the motivation. As things stand today, there are a few programs that give intensive, rich training in diagnostic testing, while the majority offer the superficial introduction to assessment that has been described above. One of the worst aspects of this situation, as I see it, is that the latter group believe (or pretend) that they are "covering" diagnosis in all the depth it deserves, rather than explicitly announcing that they have chosen not to train people for the psychodiagnostic role.

The 1965 conference on the professional preparation of clinical psychologists (Hoch, Ross, & Winder, 1966) made one thing clear about training in clinical psychology: there are strong centripetal trends, and a growing differentiation of the doctoral programs. Clinical psychology is beginning to recognize the diversity of roles developing within its bounds, but the training institutions are reluctant to give up the pretense of providing something for everyone.

If the graduates of universities that decide to concentrate on turning out clinical personality researchers or community mental-health workers are clearly recognized as incompetent to fill psychodiagnostic roles without special postdoctoral training, and if the code of ethics is appropriately modified, it will soon develop that there is a great unmet need for skilled diagnosticians. Those who do fill that role will experience a rise in status and salary, and may be able to use the leverage of their scarcity to pry out of hospital administrators a more satisfactory diagnostic role for themselves.

I cannot forbear adding that, if enough good teaching were available, an excellent case could be made for fairly intensive training in diagnostic testing, more so than is currently available in many universities, even for graduate students who wished to specialize in clinical functions such as psychotherapy, research, or consultation. Speaking about the preparation of the psychotherapist, Kalinkowitz (in press) writes:

> If we accept the assumption that there are enduring individual qualities about human beings, and that there are central themes determining the course of human biographies, and further assume that these enduring qualities are not always manifest in behavior, then, I argue, there are sound reasons for training in diagnostic testing. . . . If we are to treat people in distress, we must know the dimensions of personality . . . the experience of administering many diagnostic batteries is an excellent way to learn about the intricate inner workings of people. . . .

I would go further: while the total case history based largely on the diagnostic and therapeutic interview is an unexcelled way of learning about the large sweep of personality development and the patterning of life's events, diagnostic tests are *the best* way of learning about the microstructure of personality, the patterning of defenses, and the interpenetration of motives and thought and affects. Just as the physician must know both gross anatomy and fine histology, any serious student of personality, whether for research and theoretical purposes or out of ameliorative intent, should be trained in both approaches to his subject matter.

Finally, a few cautious words about the future of diagnostic testing, beyond the immediate horizon. I feel reasonably confident, first, in predicting that psychodiagnosis will never be an automated function involving only clerks and computers; that dream is based on a misconception. It seems safe to say that clinical psychology will continue to be a profession of many functions; even if psychotherapy should split off as a separate professional entity in its own right, there will continue to be people making a living by applying the basic knowledge of clinical psychology to human problems in a variety of ways. I find it hard to imagine that an important part of that work will not be some form of assessment of personality and psychopathology.

In thinking about the probable future of diagnostic testing, I look for advances growing from internal changes and from changes external to testing itself. By internal changes I mean the development of new tests, new normative data, new methods of working with old instruments, and new clarifications and explications of ways to make inferences or to process qualitative data. There is plenty of room for the improvement of the reliability and validity of testing, and we can expect a good deal of assistance from our friends the statisticians and actuarial predictors; they have much to teach and many ways to help us by cutting down the routine clerical aspects of testing.

The basic orientation to diagnostic testing taught in the present book is not likely to change, however, until there are saltatory advances or breakthroughs in the theory of personality and psychopathology. It is particularly difficult to guess when such advances will come; I will be surprised to see truly radical progress in my lifetime.

It does not seem to be generally recognized that one prominent recent phenomenon in clinical psychology is bound to create a new demand for psychodiagnosis, even though it has been occurring at the expense of diagnostic involvement. I refer to the rapid development of new forms of treatment: existential approaches in individual psychotherapy, new forms of group therapy and psychodrama, milieu therapy, various forms of behavioral modification based on theories of learning, drug therapies both ataractic and psychedelic, and so forth. The medical traditions out of which psychodiagnosis grew assumed that rational treatment requires accurate diagnosis, and that a differentiated spectrum of therapeutic modalities exists, each appropriate for a determinate range of pathological conditions. When this approach was first rejected, it seemed to follow that diagnosis was useless: the people who came to psychotherapists did not have diseases, but needed help in learning to live their lives more satisfactorily, and one method was thought appropriate for all comers. As Rogers and Dymond (1954) put it, therapy—as they practiced it—was good for people, period.

This simple a view is no longer held by many experienced clinicians. There is no logical necessity to the view that if difficulties in living are not illnesses, they are all essentially the same or that all afflicted persons need the same kinds of help. Vocational uncertainty and difficulties in learning to read have hardly ever been considered diseases, but they are not therefore indistinguishable, and they call for rather specific and different kinds of help. Regrettably, all too little research in psychotherapy has tried to discover the specific conditions for which one mode of treatment is more appropriate than another. Some as yet unpublished research by Paul Bergman and by the Psychotherapy Research Project of the Menninger Foundation will throw tentative light on these matters; but they are intrinsically refractory to study. Recent years have brought a disenchantment with psychoanalysis as the ideal treatment for all neurotic conditions, while various alternatives have more or less briefly flared into prominence and subsided after initial enthusiasm and dramatic first results. Yet I believe that we shall ultimately find a residue of usefulness in many such fads, and that we shall discover the kinds of people who are best helped in each of a wide variety of techniques and methods of treatment.

According to Brill (1965), we are in a period when psychiatric nosology is being re-examined all over the world. Within psychology, one of the APA's principal boards was at the time of this writing undertaking to study the feasibility of underwriting a study of a new conceptual system for psychodiagnosis. A new international system of medical classification has recently been introduced, and the delayed decennial revision of the American Psychiatric Association's manual of diagnostic classification is getting under way. At a Conference on the Role and Methodology of Classification in Psychiatry and Psychopathology held in late November, 1965, under the auspices of the American Psychiatric Association and the NIMH Psychopharmacology Service Center, there was a refreshing emphasis on quantitative research as a partial basis for a new system, and several papers were presented on the use of psychological tests in such research. Though tests are obviously not a sufficient basis for research on diagnosis, it is hard to see how an adequate job could be done without their unique contribution of systematically assessing a number of important functions. In turn, a sophisticated revision of diagnostic terminology and concepts will probably contribute to the validity and usefulness of diagnostic testing.

Research that looks for indications that a particular form of therapy is best suited to certain kinds of people and problems should not confine itself to searching in terms of nosological categories, however expanded and refined, nor to existing diagnostic tests. I suspect that in the future, psychodiagnosis may make a good deal more use of specifically focused tests rather than relying as much as today on a few wide-band, all-purpose instruments, and that tests of the kind used by G. S. Klein and his co-workers to measure principles of cognitive control and cognitive styles may play an increasing role: situational tests, perceptual performances, judgments, and the like, which will measure aspects of ego structure that will be the major parameters determining the effectiveness of specific therapeutic interventions. To develop this kind of knowledge, we cannot proceed blindly, trying out everything; we must proceed from a firm base of the accumulated knowledge of clinical psychopathology, and from theory.

But perhaps even more important determinants of the future may be found outside of psychology, in the larger field of mental health and in the social structure itself. According to Basowitz and Speisman (1964, p. 60), "the entire mental health movement is on the threshold of drastic changes both in the conception of and approach to emotional disorder. These changes are most clearly forecast in the vast federal programs of assistance planned for the establishment of community mental health centers. They portend a much greater concern with diverse forms of treatment, with early detection and prevention of disturbance, and with early return of patients to the community and to work." The changes they refer to stem, first, from the recommendations of the Joint Commission on Mental Illness and Health, which was established by Congress in 1955 and which made its final report and recommendations in *Action for Mental Health* (Joint Commission, 1961). And second, other relevant changes grow out of social legislation introduced by the Kennedy and Johnson administration: medicare, the antipoverty programs, the new education acts, and the like. As Shakow (1965) put it: "Implicit in the legislation is the mandate that psychological principles be applied to groups (particularly the underprivileged) which have heretofore received little consideration in mental health programs. To this end psychologists will have to be most ingenious and unconventional in developing treatment and training techniques" (p. 359).

"The most general effect of *Action for mental health*," write Eagle and Wolitzky (1964), "is likely to be the encouragement of training of a greater number of mental health personnel of all kinds, including clinical psychologists. The flooding of psychology departments with clinical candidates is likely to continue in an accelerated tempo . . ." Moreover, they add, "The major foci of *Action for mental health* are treatment and research. By implication, the importance of diagnostic testing is minimized . . . the Commission's Report implies that training in diagnostic testing should emphasize selective use and should be strongly embedded in the total framework of treatment and research in mental illness."

The report faces realistically the inflexibility of the existing training institutions for psychiatrists, psychologists, and social workers, which simply cannot expand rapidly enough to supply the personnel needed. It recommends, therefore, the judicious use of subprofessionals specifically trained for limited and supervised functions, particularly in various counseling and therapeutic roles.

Psychology has reacted in predictably conservative ways to such suggestions. They are immediately taken as implying the lowering of standards, the grinding out of great numbers of M.A. clinical psychologists who by a kind of Gresham's law will downgrade the whole profession. All of the conferences on training in recent years have been faced with proposals for subdoctoral training for limited roles (see, for example, Jones, 1966), and though they have made more or less perfunctory calls to the universities to take notice and get busy, there has been little response.

When nursing and dentistry were first introduced as separate professions, medicine reacted just as psychology is reacting today: with a legitimate anxiety to protect standards, and with initial great reluctance to cooperate. This bit of parallel history should help psychologists realize that they have little to fear, realistically: there is so much more work to be done than people to do it that the established professions have only to gain by the addition of helping hands, even though trained in limited ways.

If we take as long a perspective as possible, we can see that the history of the professions generally is one of increasing specialization. With the emergence of rather clearly defined functions and of bodies of knowledge (however invalid) that provide a basis for training, new professions arise. We see the emergence of such a new profession today, I believe, in psychotherapy (see Holt, 1963a; in press); perhaps there will eventually be several psychotherapeutic professions at different levels of skill and specificity, some supervising others. There is no reason to believe that the existing pattern of professions in the mental-health field is a particularly rational one, though it is firmly entrenched and will be difficult to modify.

I can see no intrinsic reason, therefore, why there should not emerge a separate discipline of *psychometrist* or tester, trained at a subdoctoral level. Many such people already exist; we are keeping our heads in the sand not to admit the fact that a great many testers without Ph.D.'s are employed today, some of them doing diagnostic testing on a rather high level of skill. This does *not* imply that I believe that psychodiagnosis can or should be entrusted altogether to semiprofessionals. What I do believe is that there are many jobs to be done, some of them simple enough to be entrusted to well-trained technicians, freeing the doctoral-level, sophisticated diagnostic psychological tester, whom we might call *psychodiagnostician,* to concentrate upon the most interesting, subtle, and challenging aspects of his work. The X-ray technician does not threaten the radiologist, but helps him with routine chores. Would not the lot of the psychodiagnostician be a happier one if he could assign the administration, scoring, and tallying of most tests to a skilled psychometric technician? Some psychologists already function in this way (see, for example, W. G. Klopfer, 1962). In this instance, we can learn something from medical models!

What I hope to see, therefore, is the emergence of the psychodiagnostician as a more deeply and broadly trained specialist than we have today. He will be able to handle larger numbers of cases by making use of the help of technicians, and will be able to function in the kind of consultative capacity that Matarazzo (1965) has pioneered. The latter has made good use of a medical specialist as a model: "for example, a senior neurologist in a medical center or general hospital is rarely referred a patient 'for a neurological examination.' Rather, . . . he is 'called in consultation' as part of the further understanding of a patient on whom much other information already has been collected. While the neurologist undoubtedly will carry out a neurological examination . . . geared specifically to the needs of this patient . . . he is called into consultation both as a neurologist-clinician (adding his skills to the solution of a clinical problem) and as a teacher (helping other senior consultants and their residents-in-training to learn more about his specialty)." In the University of Oregon Medical School, clinical psychologists operate in precisely the same way: as consulting clinician-teachers. Matarazzo adds that ". . . one important by-product of this new model merits mention: whereas in many parts of the country (traditional) psychodiagnosis is disparaged . . . , the writer (in common with his students) finds considerable satisfaction in this type of work" (p. 72).

It may take further institutional changes to remove the remaining strains and discontents from the psychodiagnostic role, but they will be coming anyway. The day of the traditional custodial hospital, in which the job of the diagnostic tester is merely to attach diagnostic labels, is fast drawing to a close. If we do our best to train smaller numbers of psychologists—only those who are truly interested in psychodiagnosis—more intensively and well, they will have so much to offer that they will be able to make richer, more useful, and more meaningful careers for themselves.

ACKNOWLEDGMENTS

I take pleasure in the opportunity to thank the many friends who have helped with this undertaking. Roy Schafer has been generous with his wise counsel on many occasions, especially in the difficult early stages of deciding on the plan of the revision; he also read a number of sections of the manuscript and gave useful advice. A large number of colleagues have advised and contributed various kinds of help: Paul Bergman, Gerald Ehrenreich, Mary Engel, Sibylle Escalona, Leo Goldberger, Walter Kass, George Klein, Martin Mayman, Norman Prentice, Herbert Schlesinger, Sydney Segal, and David Shapiro. Mertin Gill discussed the project with me on several occasions, and I am grateful for his support and his consent to what I have done to a book that was in part his. To those friends who have critically read large parts of the final manuscript—Sidney Blatt, Philip Holzman, and especially Lloyd Silverman, who went through the entire book—the reader should be grateful, as I am, for they have improved the final product in many ways. If some of my errors remain, it is at least partly attributable to my not having accepted all of their advice. Suzette H. Annin contributed a characteristically helpful editorial reading. Several graduate students lent their statistical assistance: Joan Holt, Eli Leiter, and Judith Rabkin.

Drs. Kathleen Sinnett and Martin Mayman have my special gratitude for their kind permission to quote, in the Appendix to Chapter 3, their excellent paper (Sinnett & Mayman, 1960). The editors of the *Bulletin of the Menninger Clinic* were also gracious in allowing its reprinting.

Dr. Phebe Cramer, who was Dr. Rapaport's personal research assistant during his sabbatical year at New York University in 1959-1960, made an especially valuable contribution to Chapter 7, by allowing me to include her unpublished normative data on the Word Association Test.

Dr. A. S. Kagan and Mrs. Lottie Newman, of International Universities Press, have been ideal publishers to work with, giving me help when I asked for it and displaying enormous patience with the many delays before the book was finally delivered to them.

The typing of the manuscript has been the work of several capable pairs of hands: those of Mrs. Arthur Guilbert, Mrs. Vera van Gelder, Miss Joan Lisanti, and my invaluable secretary, Miss Dorothy Gorham.

In addition to her technical assistance, my wife Joan has made an enormous contribution to the work by her patience, support, and forbearance.

Finally, Dr. Elvira Strasser Rapaport has contributed to this book in more ways than I could enumerate. I cannot easily put into words how much it has meant to me to be able to work with her on what I hope will be something of a monument to her late husband.

All of these people have given assistance willingly and without stint, and I am glad to be able to offer in return these public thanks. But the real and lasting merits of this book are those of the man who taught all of us most of what we know about diagnostic psychological testing: David Rapaport.

CHAPTER 1

Introduction: Psychological Tests in Clinical Work

The material presented here is the outgrowth of cooperation of clinical psychologists and psychiatrists over a period of several years. It is intended to be a factual summary of experience with some of the best testing procedures psychology has to offer clinical psychiatric work. We hope it will represent a step forward in the systematization of the principles of the psychology of thinking that are part of the necessary background to a proper qualitative evaluation of these tests.

Clinical psychiatry has two basic and time-honored methods: that of the case history, and that of clinical observation. Both of these methods are powerful tools in the hands of the experienced psychiatrist; nevertheless, each has shortcomings. Historical information, whether obtained from the patient or from other informants, will have omissions and distortions. It is up to the astuteness of the psychiatrist to follow up omissions and to rectify distortions. Thus, with respect to the data on which the diagnosis is to be based, the historical case material is affected by subjective factors on the part of both informant and psychiatrist. The same is true for observational data included in the psychiatric examination and report of the psychiatrist. Such reports can do no more than pick out a few highlights of the patient's behavior which, as a time sample, may be inadequate, and, even though correct qualitatively and useful practically, are nevertheless subjectively selected by the psychiatrist.

Psychological testing is an effort to obtain whole and systematic samples of certain types of verbal, perceptual, and motor behavior in the frame of a standardized situation. The advantage of psychological tests is that little, and in many tests no, subjective selection is involved in securing the data.

In the psychiatrist's organization of the case material, his experience and knowledge, colored by subjective factors, play a considerable role. In psychological tests, more or less standard scoring systems provide for an organization of the data that is relatively free from such subjective factors.

45

It is true that subjective factors are more likely to enter the test scoring than to affect the raw test data. Nevertheless, even in the scoring organization of the test data the role of subjective judgment is definitely limited, in comparison to the psychiatrist's organization of the case history and observational material.

The last step in both the psychiatrist's and the clinical psychologist's procedure is the evaluation of the organized material, which in one case is the case history and observational records, and in the other the test protocols. Subjective judgment, based on a wealth of experience, inevitably enters the work of both psychiatrist and psychologist at this point. But the psychiatrist's organized material pertains uniquely to the individual patient in question, and resists interindividual comparison; whereas the psychologist's organized test material is in terms of scores and patterns which allow for interindividual comparison with numerical scores and score patterns of other cases. For this reason, even at the point where subjectivity enters the work of both psychiatrist and psychologist, the latter is at an advantage because the objective comparability of numerical test results delimits the role of subjective judgment.

The testing procedures of clinical psychology may be especially valuable to clinical psychiatry in certain special circumstances. When a case history is missing, insufficient, or for other reasons unsatisfactory, the possibility of obtaining the necessary information by means of tests gains in importance. When time is not sufficient, or when other limitations make the taking of a case history inadvisable, the information obtainable through tests may be invaluable. Where the scarcity of psychiatric service makes it necessary that the psychiatrist devote himself to therapeutic work, leaving relatively little time for intensive diagnostic study, testing procedures become an important adjunct in shortening laborious case history-taking and observation.

It is not our opinion that the emergency use of testing procedures is their ideal use; we are convinced that the safe and ideal use of these procedures lies in the obtaining of parallel and independent clinical and testing data.

AIMS AND APPROACH[1]

Our aims have been fourfold: (1) We have attempted to show how the six tests discussed here were welded in our clinical work into a single diag-

---

[1] For space considerations we have avoided, wherever possible, discussion of the relation of our methods and results to previous work. [There were originally summaries of the literature at the end of each volume in appendices; they have been omitted in this condensation. Excellent and comprehensive bibliographies on tests may be found in the various *Mental Measurements Yearbooks* of Buros (1938, 1941, 1949, 1953, 1959, 1965).—Ed.]

nostic tool. (2) We have attempted to develop easily handled diagnostic indicators which have been found useful in our clinical work and experience. (3) We have attempted to put to general use some tests that hitherto had been used only in the study of specific groups of cases. With these tests our effort was to develop them into tests of general diagnostic use by designing and validating new scoring and new interpretative criteria. (4) We have attempted to develop a psychological rationale for each of these tests and for the different types of responses on them; because without such a rationale the tests and test results must remain meaningless to the psychiatrist, and a matter of automatic procedure and mechanical comparison to the clinical psychologist. We shall discuss and amplify each of these aims in turn.

The Choice of Tests. In order to clarify in what sense we have attempted to weld the battery of tests into a single instrument, it will be necessary to discuss the selection of the tests and to indicate their relation to each other. The battery reported here consists of the following tests: The Wechsler-Bellevue Adult and Adolescent Intelligence Scale, part of the Babcock Deterioration Test, the Sorting Test, the Rorschach test, the Thematic Apperception Test, and the Word Association Test.[2]

The leading idea around which this battery of tests was organized is that different aspects and levels of functioning of the patient should be given a chance to manifest themselves in the tests. This idea impressed itself upon us in the course of our clinical experience. The two main points of this experience may be summed up as follows:

(a) No single test proves to yield a diagnosis in all cases, or to be in all cases correct in the diagnosis it indicates.

(b) Psychological maladjustment, whether severe or mild, may encroach on any or several of the functions tapped by these tests, leaving other functions absolutely or relatively unimpaired.

It appears worth while to expound some of the implications of these two points, because the significance attached to them implies, to a certain extent, our approach to diagnostic procedure with these tests.

The first point, that no single test is always in itself diagnostic, has several implications. First, it is possible to obtain test records that are definitely nonrepresentative of the general make-up of the subject tested, when test results are determined by a specific background, by a prevalent attitude, or by a momentary condition. Examples would be a Wechsler-Bellevue test obtained from a new immigrant, a Rorschach test of a physi-

---

[2] [In the first edition, the Szondi and Hanfmann-Kasanin tests were also included, as well as the full Babcock Test (see Editor's Foreword).—Ed.]

cian, and any test of a person in a toxic condition. It may justly be argued that such tests are nevertheless meaningful. They are; but they do not give us on these persons what they give on others—namely, a schematic picture of a personality and a general clinical diagnosis. It is in this sense that the expression "not representative" will henceforth be used. Second, the test results may appear to be inconclusive. In such cases it often remains a moot question whether this is due to a basic limitation of the test, or is inherent in the limits of the examiner's experience with the test. Third, single tests may be, and frequently are, misinterpreted; and only in subsequent clinical contact with the patient does it become clear that the test told the story truly, but that the examiner failed to grasp it in spite of adequate experience. It is, then, the responsibility of the clinical psychologist to use tools that eliminate these deficiencies of single tests. The battery here reported is an attempt to evolve such a tool. The advantages of such a battery of tests are that indicators that for some reason are absent from one or several of the tests are likely to be present in others; that indicators in the different tests are likely to support and supplement each other; and that the presence of indicators in some of the tests may call attention to more subtle indicators in others which might otherwise be overlooked.

The second point, that psychological maladjustment may encroach upon certain functions but not others, is an expression of the idea of relative autonomy[3] in the psychic make-up. It is a frequent experience that a deeply disorganized person still has enough hold on reality to maintain a part of his rational thinking intact, and to enable him to give a relatively well-organized test performance on one or more tests. It is possible, for example, that a psychotic disorganization will leave the digit span of a person not only intact, but so excellent that one may be inclined to attribute the extremely high score to a pathological shift in the functional assets of the subject. On the other hand, a state of anxiety in a maladjusted but not generally disorganized person may result in an apparently grave impairment of any of several test achievements. Thus any single test may lead to conclusions which, though correctly representing one aspect, do not take account of other aspects of the subject's make-up, and the resulting diagnosis may over- or underestimate the severity of the actual maladjustment.

In the selection of the battery of tests, then, the leading idea was to obtain material reflecting different aspects and levels of the person's psychic make-up. Experience showed that, as seen in the tests tapping one level, a temporary condition or a certain type of maladjustment may wreak havoc, making the test "nonrepresentative"; but that other levels, as seen in the tests tapping them, may remain relatively well organized, and specifically

[3] [See Hartmann (1939), and Rapaport (1951b, 1957c) on ego autonomy; also, in reference to testing, Holt (1960).—Ed.]

diagnostic. Thus, for example, in some anxiety conditions the contents of the Rorschach test may be purely anatomical and hardly distinguishable from those of some psychotics; but the Sorting Test and/or the intelligence tests are likely to remain well organized.

An intelligence test was chosen to represent intellectual functioning in general. We chose the *Wechsler-Bellevue Scale*[4] (Form I) because it is a test in which the subtests are systematically grouped and not distributed into mental age levels; accordingly, the selective impairment of the relatively autonomous functions implied in each of these subtests may be studied. One part of the *Babcock Test*—immediate and delayed recall of a story—was chosen as a necessary complement to the Wechsler-Bellevue. The *Sorting Test* was chosen on the consideration that concept formation is one of the basic components of every intellectual function. In concept formation—we assumed, and believe it to be proved by our experience—we can see one of the channels through which maladjustment encroaches upon intellectual functioning. Experience showed that the Similarities Test of the Bellevue Scale and the Sorting Test are tests of functionally autonomous, different levels of concept formation. The *Rorschach test* was chosen to obtain a scheme of personality structure, an estimate of endowment on which the concept-formation and intelligence structures are built, and a picture of the relationships of affects and anxieties to endowment and its efficacy of functioning. The *Thematic Apperception Test* was chosen to obtain a picture of the actual thought contents, attitudes, and feelings of the subjects, and to enable us to fill in the skeleton of diagnosis, personality structure, and intelligence structure with the flesh and blood of actual ideational and feeling contents. With a similar though more limited aim, the *Word Association Test* was chosen in an effort to gain material supporting that of the Thematic Apperception Test, by spotting those verbal ideas around which associative disturbances—or in other terms, conflicting attitudes—cluster. Both of these tests of content also yield direct diagnostic indicators through the disturbances of thought and of perceptual processes revealed by them.

The fact that in our clinical work we have attempted to use this battery of tests consistently, representing approximately five hours of test administration, does not imply that all of these tests are indispensable for reliable diagnosis in every case. In practice, one or two tests will often indicate which, if any, other tests are to be administered to assure a correct diagnosis. We maintain, however, that in the present state of our knowledge of personality and maladjustment—in which the interrelationships of functions are so obscure—the clinical psychologist is on much safer ground

[4] [For a discussion of the relation of this test to the now more generally used WAIS, see Appendix to Chapter 3.—Ed.]

when he has a battery of tests, rather than only a few, on which to base his diagnosis. The use of full batteries of tests is the more to be recommended since only such practice yields the kind of experience and material on which to erect a better theoretical understanding of, and better testing practices for, the interrelationships and autonomy of different functions in adjustment and maladjustment. One must remember that, while depth psychology and experimental psychology have clarified many functional-dynamic relationships, the realm of psychological functions tapped by testing procedures—and especially by the more modern procedures—has barely been touched by systematic investigation. This realm is more in the bounds of "ego psychology" than in those of "the psychology of the unconscious" explored by depth psychology. Even the "ego psychology" of psychoanalysis, with all its rapid advances, has just begun to reach this realm.[5] On the other hand, the psychological functions involved are more lifelike than those usually explored by experimental psychology. Thus psychological testing opens a new field of problems, and may become the laboratory out of which the psychology of thought processes, normal and abnormal, will issue.

The battery of tests reported here thus represents a hierarchy of testing procedures, tapping a hierarchy of psychological functions. At the base of this hierarchy are the tests that give us personality patterns and our clinical-diagnostic bearings; these are followed by tests of concept formation, this being the channel through which personality structure and maladjustment exert their formative influence on intelligence structure; these in turn are followed by intelligence and efficiency tests; and finally come the tests providing the ideational content of the formal patterns indicated by all the other tests.

Clinical Validation. It will be worth while to clarify the method we followed in studying the validity of these tests. Throughout, our guide was our clinical experience. In this experience we had come to use many tests, because the use of only a few tests frequently left us without a diagnosis, or with an incorrect diagnosis. In the course of the years we learned to look into the smallest detail of each test—into every subtest of each test, into every verbalization deviating from the usual form of each response, and even into every part of each response. We learned from clinical practice what was useful and what was not useful for clinical work. As there is generally some degree of overlap of most indicators in the different clinical groups, the presence of one indicator in most cases allows only for setting

---

[5] ["... does not quite reach this realm" in the original; but see Rapaport (1950b, 1952) and the work of his students (Schafer, 1948, 1949, 1954, 1956, 1967; Holt, 1951, 1954, 1956, 1960, 1961a; Mayman & Rapaport, 1947; Mayman, Schafer, & Rapaport, 1951; Mayman, 1960, 1963).—Ed.]

up a hypothesis about the personality diagnosis and/or clinical-nosological diagnosis. It therefore follows that only the massing of such indicators can become a basis of a reliable diagnosis. Ultimately, experience is necessary for the evaluation of what does, and what does not, constitute a massing of diagnostic indicators.

The Extension of Clinical Application. It will be necessary to survey in what respect we have developed significant but neglected features in different tests, or have brought about the possibility of a more general application of them. In the study of the Wechsler-Bellevue Scale we concentrated upon scatter analysis, believing that to use this test as a mere intelligence test is to neglect the diagnostic potentialities to be found in the dynamic relationship of its subtests to each other. In other words, we attempted to make of this test of intelligence a diagnostic clinical test. In connection with the Babcock Test, we attempted to extract its most useful features; by doing so we hoped not only to reduce the labor of administration, but to provide a psychologically meaningful and homogeneous test. In connection with the Sorting Test[6] of concept formation, our task was to expand its previously limited usage. We put it to use in diagnosing psychoses and neuroses and borderline adjustment; previously it had been limited to the study of schizophrenic and organic cases. We made the Sorting Test an effective tool for clinical diagnosis by developing a new scoring method, sensitive enough to indicate disturbances more subtle than the gross schizophrenic and organic disturbances previously studied.

In the study of the Rorschach test, we stressed the limitations of this rapidly spreading test, which is at present the most useful, and apparently the most misused, clinical tool. On the one hand, we dispensed with complicated "refinements" that proved of little significance in clinical work; on the other hand, we called attention to and created a systematic framework for the appraisal of the diagnostic significance of the patient's verbalization of his responses. In the study of the Word Association Test, our task was to revive a corpse which had been brought to an early grave by mechanical application and mechanical statistical treatment. We introduced a systematic qualitative point of view which is directly useful in evaluating individual test performance. In the use of the Thematic Apperception Test, we strove for concrete clinical applicability rather than general personality description; for this purpose we introduced a new qualitative frame of reference to spot the diagnostically significant perceptions and verbalizations, and to locate the clinically significant contents.

On the Psychological Rationale of Tests. In order to develop a psychological rationale for these tests and the types of responses on them, we

---

[6] This is the Goldstein-Weigl-Scheerer Test, which has often been erroneously referred to as B.R.L. Sorting Test [after Bolles, Rosen, and Landis (1938).—Ed.].

adopted the "projective hypothesis"[7]—namely, that every reaction of a subject is a reflection, or projection, of his private world. This approach to testing contrasts sharply with that usually characterized as "psychometric." The main aim was not to attribute to a person a percentile rank in the population or any other numerical measure allegedly representative of him. The aim was rather to understand him: to give him a chance to express himself in a sufficient number and variety of controlled situations, the nature of which has been well enough explored to enable the psychologist to infer, out of the subject's reactions, the gross outlines of his personality make-up. This expectation, however, implies the "projective hypothesis"; it implies that every action and reaction of a human being bears the characteristic features of his individual make-up.

The choice of tests on the basis of this hypothesis would favor those whose material is unconventional and not limited to eliciting habitual reactions. This hypothesis would find the Rorschach inkblot test most satisfactory; the Thematic Apperception Test less satisfactory; and the standard intelligence tests least satisfactory, because the intelligence-test questions themselves appear, at first glance, to be aimed at eliciting highly conventional responses. We included in this battery clearly projective tests; but we also attempted to demonstrate that the projective hypothesis, in generalized form, can be applied even to intelligence tests. In fact, we approached all of these tests with this hypothesis.

The projective approach is not concerned with numerical percentages or age equivalents which, in the average population, correspond to the subject's performance; its concern is to reconstruct out of features of the subject's reactions, or relationships of features in the subject's reactions, the specific individual dynamics in the living subject.

Building our rationales implied often setting up hypotheses in the field of the psychology of thinking. Though the rationales here presented are frequently tentative, the setting up of such hypotheses was indispensable in an attempt to bridge the gap between the traditionally lifeless numerical test results and the living clinical dynamics.[8] It is for this reason that: (1) we have attempted to give some rationale for the subtests of the Wechsler-Bellevue Scale; (2) we have discussed in detail some theoretical conceptions concerning memory function in connection with the Babcock Story Recall Test; (3) we have devoted considerable space to a discussion of the

[7] See Rapaport (1942b). [The term "projective" is perhaps a misnomer here, for there are many other ways in which personality affects test responses in addition to projection, even in its broadest usage. See Bellak (1950) and Holt (1951).—Ed.]

[8] The gap between clinical psychiatry with its dynamic concepts on the one hand, and mechanical testing methods lacking theoretical background and integration on the other, is one of the reasons that clinical psychology was slow to achieve professional standing.

general ideas of concept formation; (4) we have allotted a disproportionate number of pages to a relatively theoretical discussion of the different
types of verbalization on the Rorschach test; (5) we have discussed further
aspects of the theory of memory functioning in connection with the Word
Association Test; (6) we have advanced general considerations concerning
perceptual and thought processes in connection with the Thematic Apperception Test, a procedure that differs somewhat from the usual treatment
of this test.

We have limited ourselves to such theoretical considerations as are
immediately useful and necessary as background in clinical work. We attempted to remember at all times the aim of putting a useful compendium of
these modern testing procedures into the hands of psychologists in the hope
that it will prove helpful in clinical work.

General Circumstances and Procedure of Testing

The major part of our experience has been diagnosis of clinical cases
from tests alone—though in most cases the patient was diagnosed by the
same examiner who administered the tests. Useful additions to our knowledge came from experience with cases where the presenting symptom was
known to us, and from cases where the patient was not seen and the tests
were diagnosed "blind." All these conditions forced us to explore and exploit the potentialities of the tests to their utmost, and to adopt a variety
of tests to cope with the problem of diagnosing solely by test procedures.
Our usual condition of testing thus confronted us with the question, Is it
possible to find testing procedures which will correctly elicit and diagnose
personality and psychiatric status without reference to historical material?

At the Menninger Clinic, patients came for testing without the psychologist's being informed of the presenting symptoms, case history, or other
data concerning their problems. Special care was taken to avoid conversation which would have involved information about the patient's symptoms.
Clinical diagnosis, personality description, and in many cases prognosis
and treatment recommendations were made on the basis of the test results
so obtained. Only after this did the psychologist learn—for the most part
at staff conferences in which clinical material, psychological-test material,
and laboratory material were presented simultaneously—what the case was
like clinically. Less frequently, such information was obtained, after completion of the diagnosis, in discussion with the psychiatrist assigned to the
patient.

No attempt was made to test all patients in the same manner. The
requirement of "identity of conditions of testing" was interpreted to be a
requirement for the tester to adapt himself to the specific characteristics of

the patient. From an "objective" point of view, therefore, the attitude of the examiner varied from patient to patient. However, the different attitudes were necessary to arouse similar reactions in the varied patients to the testing situation.

The patients were prepared for their visits to the Psychology Department by their doctors; and when beginning the first test they were given an explanation that this was a psychological examination of a type other than the case history. Efforts were made to minimize the repugnant connotations of the concept "test." The patient was told in advance to rest whenever tired. Although cigarettes and candies were offered, no effort to create "transference"—such as has been reported by some investigators of the Thematic Apperception Test—was made.

Of the purposes for which the tests have been used by us clinically, we shall concentrate in this report upon that of clinical diagnosis and personality description. The extent of our follow-up and retest studies on cases has not been sufficiently wide or varied to warrant discussion of prognosis and treatment recommendations made on the basis of the tests. We have samples of such prognoses and treatment recommendations, and follow-ups of their success or failure; and we might have given some qualitative evaluation of this use of the tests. Again, however, we preferred to limit the extent of our discussion in order to deal intensively with the two problems of diagnosis and personality dynamics.

The premises and procedure described above imply a certain attitude toward the clinical psychologist in the psychiatric clinical setup, which crystallized in the course of the cooperation between psychologists and psychiatrists at the Menninger Clinic. Here the employment of the services of the clinical psychologist is a part of the effort to obtain maximum information about a patient, by various and independent procedures. The psychiatrist's discussions with the patient, the information from relatives and from doctors previously consulted by the patient, the hourly records of the nurses, the reports of the occupational and recreational therapists, the neurological and the general medical laboratory findings, and finally the clinical psychological information obtained by means of testing, are considered independent contributions pertinent to the understanding of the case. The clinical psychologist in this setup is engaged in work parallel to the investigative work of the psychiatrist; he also participates in the work of psychological treatment.

Nosological Considerations

In our clinical work, the emphasis is put not upon uniformity of nosological classification but rather upon expressing as sharply as possible the outstanding problems of the patient. The classificatory categories we used here were set up to divide or to unite only groups whose division or unification would clarify the validity of the test indicators. Unification and division are inevitable in clinical classification, and nosology is a fluid discipline which, in many of its parts, is open to question. The present state of knowledge about the dynamics of psychopathological conditions is such that no hard-and-fast classification system has yet been set up which is not open to question. We wish it to be clear, however, that we have avoided circularity: statements about characteristic test findings with hysterics or simple schizophrenics, for example, were always verified by reference to the test results about patients who were classified on the evidence of the clinical (i.e., nontest) findings.

We decided to eliminate from consideration all purely characterological problems, all problems of addiction, and all cases with clearly present organic features. This was necessary to keep our categories as homogeneous as possible, and to include no more than could be handled within the framework of this book.

In the following pages we shall give the general nosological classification of our material—the intensively studied patients who constitute the major part of our "clinical experience." Where our classification coincides with usual nosological concepts of psychiatry—such as the general concept of schizophrenia—we have not given specific nosological definitions. Where our material required specific delineation of groups not accepted in the general nosological literature—as in the "preschizophrenia" and the "anxiety and depression" diagnoses—we have given rather detailed descriptions of the symptoms and the characteristics of the groups so segregated. The same procedure has been followed in the case of the differential diagnostic considerations which we offer in this section. Where the basis for differential diagnosis is generally accepted in psychiatric nosological literature, we have not enlarged on the principles of differential diagnosis. But where new diagnostic categories were set up, and their differentiation from others was not immediately apparent, we have entered upon differential diagnostic discussions.

The Schizophrenic Groups. In our clinical setting, clear-cut catatonic psychoses with classical rigidity, or even with other motor symptoms approaching rigidity or waxy flexibility, are extremely rare. We were wary of diagnosing catatonic schizophrenia merely on the basis of the occurrence of catatonic excitement, as is often done. To distinguish a paranoid rage from catatonic excitement or a manic outburst, which may color even a schizophrenic psychosis, is often very difficult and may lead to nosological confusion.

Similarly rare in our clinical work is the occurrence of hebephrenia.

Partly, the cultural background of our cases may be responsible for the infrequent occurrence of this nosological entity in our work; partly, many cases diagnosed as hebephrenic schizophrenia may be the end products of deterioration in a schizophrenic process which had its earlier acute and chronic phases. In a clinical setup, where it is possible to investigate the past history of the patient, many a case diagnosed as hebephrenic schizophrenia will prove historically to be a schizophrenia of another category which was brought to a psychiatrist's attention only in a deteriorated state. Another reason we saw few hebephrenics is that, in general, relatives do not bring hopeless cases to our hospital. All schizophrenialike reactions connected with toxic conditions or even precipitated by them, all connected with post-partum conditions, all connected with even the suspicion of the presence of an organic factor, have been meticulously eliminated from our material.

After such curtailments, our schizophrenic groups comprised 75 cases. In 27 of these, paranoid delusions predominated to such a degree that the diagnosis was clearly paranoid schizophrenia. Among these there were cases of many shadings, to a discussion of which we shall turn soon. The 39 cases diagnosed as "unclassified"[9] were also clear-cut schizophrenics. In these cases the outstanding overt symptoms were inappropriateness of affect, delusions (including those of reference), withdrawal, and disorganized thinking. It should be mentioned that delusions of reference, however intense, in no case prompted us to classify a case as paranoid schizophrenia; and that some depressive coloring was present in several of the acute paranoid and a few of the acute unclassified schizophrenics.

Both the unclassified schizophrenics and the paranoid schizophrenics have been subdivided into three groups: acute, chronic, and deteriorated. The criterion of *acute* cases was primarily the occurrence of an acute break after a previous adjustment. This is not to imply that when a chronic schizophrenic adjustment on a low level broke down into a more active schizophrenic period, it was classified as acute. It does imply, however, that when a break occurred after a previously poor, though not psychotic, adjustment, it was classified as acute; and so was a second attack after an apparently complete remission. The criterion of *chronic* cases was a longstanding schizophrenic adjustment on a low level, even when no clear-cut acute schizophrenic episodes were historically demonstrable, and even when schizophrenic flare-ups were present at the time of testing and admission. In each of these cases, in the longstanding poor adjustment prior to admission, clear-cut signs of schizophrenic activity—though not necessarily with acute, full-

---

[9] The term "unclassified" here signifies that they do not belong clearly to any of the four classical schizophrenic syndromes: catatonic, hebephrenic, paranoid, and simple.

fledged schizophrenic outbreaks—had to be demonstrable before the case was classified as chronic. The criteria of *deteriorated* cases in the unclassified group were the usual ones: leveling of the psychotic process to a stationary condition with no effort to change either surroundings or self, untidiness and loss of interest in appearance, disorganization of thinking, absolute flattening of affect, irrationality and incoherence in some cases even to the point of word salad. Almost all of our deteriorated cases in the paranoid group retained, however, a semblance of interest in appearance and behavior acceptable within the confines of an institution. The leveling of the psychotic process to a stationary condition, the disorganization of thinking, absence of affective rapport, and lack of any trace of insight were for these cases the criteria of deterioration.

The group of simple schizophrenics consists of nine cases in which the most outstanding clinical feature in common was the discrepancy between the lack of affective rapport and the relatively well-retained formal front. They were all young people who had shown these characteristics all their lives with no history of an acute break. Some of this group showed antisocial behavior, but must be differentiated from psychopaths. They were not ingratiating, as psychopaths are, and committed their antisocial behavior with no planning, no excitement, and no aim of gain. As a rule they frankly confessed their antisocial acts with remarkable blandness and lack of affect. They had no insight. Of the nine simple schizophrenic cases, five were of this type; four others were merely affectless, queer, bland cases, differentiated from the other schizophrenics by a lack of rather than an inappropriateness of affect; queerness, rather than delusion, was characteristic of them; and paranoid ideas, as well as a history of acute break, were absent.

The Preschizophrenics. There were 33 cases in our material which we classified as preschizophrenic. These were cases of schizoid personalities whose adjustment was so precarious that schizophrenialike withdrawal tendencies in the guise of anxiety and inhibition, or schizophrenialike ideational productions in the guise of obsessive-phobic thought, had already penetrated into their everyday life; thus any strain or stress could precipitate a schizophrenic psychosis, but under favorable conditions they might continue with such preschizophrenic behavior or ideation without an acute break. In some of these cases we actually saw the psychotic break materialize later on.

The characteristics of this group which serve as the basis for differential diagnosis from schizophrenia are the following:

(a) These cases show a prolonged period of maladjustment, although they are able to maintain a partial adjustment in the outside world and to conceal, in some degree, their distress.

(b) These cases all suffer marked anxiety; otherwise they show considerable lack of affect in regard to object relationships.

(c) All have some degree of insight into their condition, and show some realization that their difficulty is intrapsychic, and all voluntarily sought psychiatric help.

(d) Paranoid projections are generally absent.

This group was subdivided into two categories. One of these was characterized by blocking, withdrawal, marked anxiety, feelings of strangeness, incompetence, extreme inhibition of affect, and some kind of sexual preoccupation. We call this group the inhibited preschizophrenics. The other group was characterized by an enormous wealth of fantasy, obsessive ideation, obsessions, and preoccupation with themselves and their bodies; these subjects were intensely introspective and preoccupied with their own ideas, and at first sight were often not easily distinguishable from obsessional neurotics. We call this group the overideational preschizophrenics. They were differentiated from the obsessional neurotics partly by the wide range, fluctuation, and relative instability of their obsessive ideation and obsessional thoughts, and partly by their relative lack of experiencing these ideas as ego alien.[10] The inhibited preschizophrenics were distinguished from all neurotic groups in that the tremendous amount of anxiety present was incongruous with the situations evoking it.

The Paranoid Conditions. These 14 cases, though of considerable variety, were linked together by their rigid, compulsive character structure, good general premorbid adjustment, and a varying degree of paranoid ideation, into which the majority had some degree of intellectual insight.

Four of these cases—labeled paranoid states—must be differentiated from the acute paranoid schizophrenics. Here the paranoid break was short-lived, and in a sense was a decompensation of the good compulsive adjustment shown before the paranoid break. Though clear-cut delusions and confusion were present, these people were able to go about their work, even at the time of the paranoid break and after it. In their delusions, persons helped as well as persecuted them; the paranoid break was really of an episodic character and blew over. All had some insight, and sought

---

[10] This group of preschizophrenics was diagnostically of great interest to us because the diagnosis here has prognostic, and in a sense preventive, significance. To deal with these cases as with a neurosis constitutes a misrecognition of the severity of the disorder. The unusual "psychological mindedness" of the overideational preschizophrenics is amenable to swift steps in therapy and interpretation which only facilitate the breakthrough of the schizophrenic process, rather than fortify the patient to withstand it. [Although these diagnostic categories have not been widely adopted, they have been retained because this breakdown does not correspond exactly to any other in wider current use, like "borderline case" or "schizoid character." See Schafer (1948, p. 15).—Ed.]

psychiatric help voluntarily. Primary schizophrenic thought disorder, and dissociation or flattening of affect, were absent.

The remaining 10 cases were clearly differentiated from the paranoid schizophrenics by other criteria. Four of them might be justifiably called paranoid characters. They too showed compulsive character structures; in addition, quarrelsome and suspicious traits pervaded their whole character and life history, though these never became outright delusions. These traits frequently got the patients into trouble; they were unable to make a real adjustment, and when they did they soon broke it up; but meanwhile they went on with their lives in relative calmness for long periods. The remaining five cases have one isolated delusion, either of infidelity or of erotomania. The paranoid structure of the delusion was quite clear in these cases. These patients were otherwise well ordered in their everyday life; it was relatively easy to bring them to at least an intellectual doubt of the validity of their delusions, and some of them quickly surrendered them.

The justification for lumping all these cases together is the similarity in the basic dynamics of their psychopathology, despite the fact that in one group it comes to expression as a character formation which appears as paranoid, in another as a short-lived psychotic break, in still another as an isolated delusion.

The Depressive Groups. In classifying the depressives, we excluded the very few cases of alternating elation and depression that we encountered. This left us with 33 depressives. As we already mentioned, depressions with clear-cut schizophrenic backgrounds were placed with the schizophrenias. It will be obvious, from our attitude to nosology as indicated thus far, that we had no use for such a diagnosis as "manic-depressive psychosis, depressive state"—so frequently assigned to a depression which is clearly psychotic, whether a recurring depression with no elated phase in the interim, or a single protracted period of depression. We excluded all cases where clear-cut arteriosclerotic or other palpable organic signs were present.

The depressives were divided into two main groups. One of these was psychotic, the other was not. Wherever delusions were evident, and feelings of worthlessness and of having sinned became paramount, accompanied by extreme agitation and/or psychomotor retardation, the classification into the psychotic subgroup was made (depressive psychoses). This group of 17 psychotic cases was further subdivided into two parts. We split off a subgroup of seven cases, all in the involutional age, the precipitating events in which were not very clear-cut and/or whose nature showed that declining "vital powers" made certain difficulties, which would previously have been easily surmounted, the precipitating point of the psychosis. This group was designated involutional depressives. We excluded all cases in which major arteriosclerotic changes appeared to underlie the disorder; but we did not exclude all cases where arteriosclerotic changes were present in a degree consistent with the typical physical status of persons in this age group. Drawing this line was a rather delicate task, but we feel satisfied that the group includes no case which might be designated as a "psychosis of organic etiology." The remaining 10 cases will be referred to as psychotic depressives. This group is homogeneous in so far as the presence of a depressive psychosis is concerned, but there are three cases with some paranoid coloring, two cases with some obsessive coloring, and one case with schizoid coloring. We felt justified in putting together this group, because experience with tests shows—and this is true for most of the psychological tests which we used—that psychotic depression has a paramount effect on test performance which overshadows the effects of accompanying clinical features.

The second main group of depressives was the *depressive neurotics,* who totaled 16 cases. This group was also split into two subgroups. Seven cases were clearly neurotic: that is to say, except for the strongly depressive mood and general hopelessness, tearfulness, and desperation, no ideation was present that even remotely resembled a delusion of worthlessness or sinfulness. This group will be referred to as neurotic depressives. The other nine cases did not display clear-cut delusions, but their ideation was pervaded with depressive motifs, accompanied by either a degree of agitation or of psychomotor retardation which definitely distinguished it from the neurotic depressive group. These nine cases were distinguished from the depressive psychoses by the fact that clinically they could not be considered psychotic because of the lack of delusions, the retention of contact with reality, and amenability to rapport—although some irrational features were present in their ideation. The clearly neurotic group of seven cases will be called here neurotic depressive; the nine cases just discussed will be referred to as severe neurotic depressives.

It must be clearly recognized that the nosological categorization here was based partly on the depth of the depression and partly on the extent of the departure from reality, these being the features which it can be expected will be reflected well in the tests. Thus, this exemplifies the point made in the introduction to this nosological section: we did not make a nosological categorization to have the cases fall well, and the diagnostic signs come out well in the appraisal of the test results; but we did attempt to make nosological categories so that one might reasonably expect the tests to be able to differentiate between the groups.

The Neurotic Groups. We studied 62 symptom neurotics. As already stated, we excluded all cases which may have been neurotic but whose general distortion of character stamped them as primarily character disorders with neurotic symptoms, or with addiction (whether to alcohol or to other drugs). Cases of a borderline nature, due either to predominant schizoid characteristics or to a paramount mood disorder as manifested in depressive mood coloring, were excluded from the neurotic group and were classed either with the preschizophrenics or with the neurotic depressives.

It is only natural that the two most easily identified and best-defined neuroses were hysteria and obsessive-compulsive neurosis. The former characterized 19, and the latter 17, of our cases. Of the hysterics, 11 cases were well differentiated and were spotted immediately by the presence of conversion symptoms only, or of conversions and phobic symptoms. In all the cases of conversion symptoms, careful medical and neurological examination excluded the possibility of the presence of organic disturbance, and clearly demonstrated that these symptoms were bodily expressions of emotional conflict. It should be noted here that no psychosomatic conditions were accepted as conversion symptoms. We adhered to the restriction that only bodily symptoms expressive of emotional conflict in the motor or sensory sphere were to be considered conversion symptoms. Thus, neither psychosomatic disorders such as gastrointestinal distress, colitis, and ulcers, nor cardiovascular symptoms of emotional etiology have been included in this group. Nor were the general somatic expressions of anxiety considered here as conversion symptoms.

Less clearly defined were eight other hysterical cases. In these cases hysterical character formation, mostly with minor conversion symptoms and hysterical behavior, was the criterion upon which diagnosis was based. The main features of hysterical character were impulsiveness and childish histrionic behavior. We felt justified in grouping these two kinds of cases together in the hysteric group because their psychodynamics were essentially similar, they showed the ready transference and emotional warmth of hysterics, and their course in treatment was in general favorable. No case of *grand hysterie* was encountered by us, in pure form, in three years.

The obsessive-compulsives also presented a great variety. Of the 17 cases only two had clear-cut predominant compulsions. Most of the cases showed a relative predominance of obsessional symptoms, though several showed significant compulsive symptoms also; in a couple of cases the obsessional and the compulsive symptoms were of equal weight. In six cases the diagnosis was based on the presence of obsessions, in the sense of ego-alien ideas constantly recurring in consciousness. In all these cases, the obsessive ideas were embedded in a character formation generally obsessional, overmeticulous, speculative, doubt-ridden, and consequently paralyzed for action. The differential diagnosis from overideational preschizophrenia was clear; these cases were not schizoid personalities, and the wealth and variety of pathological ideation nowhere approximated that of the preschizophrenics.

In spite of the fact that four different variants appear in these 17 cases of obsessive-compulsive neurosis, the prominence in each case of the clinical and psychodynamic features characteristic of the type of personality which develops obsessional or compulsive symptoms seemed to justify lumping these cases together.

By mixed neuroses we do not mean neuroses whose symptomatology is sufficiently unclear not to allow for categorization under any of the well-established neurotic categories. Such a usage appeared to us neither consistent with the idea of a systematic nosology, nor conducive to the statement of any results concerning test-diagnostic indicators. Thus, we excluded every case so complex that no major trend or classificatory evidence could be established. We classified as mixed neuroses only neuroses in which both hysterical (that is to say, mostly phobic) and obsessive-compulsive (that is to say, mostly obsessive) symptoms were present. A couple of cases each showed some schizoid trends, depressive characteristics, or both; but in all these cases, these features were overshadowed by the characteristics upon which mixed neurosis was diagnosed.

The anxiety and depression group is absent from the usual nosologies. This group consists of rather successful, rigid, compulsive people who, under a strain and stress that was easily identified in the case history as the precipitating event, decompensated into a condition characterized primarily by an intense anxiety and secondarily by a depressive mood. Inasmuch as none of these compulsive personalities developed an obsessional or compulsive syndrome, nor anything that might have been characterized as conversion symptoms, we were obliged to put them into a special category to indicate the main symptoms, anxiety and depression. They were differentiated from the neurotic depressions in that not the depressed mood, but rather the anxiety state with depressive coloring, was outstanding. In some nosological categorizations there appears a category called *anxiety state*. Our anxiety and depression group is distinguished from these anxiety states, into which category all kinds of obscure conditions with predominant anxiety are placed. Anxiety and depression is so named in order to indicate that the depressive characteristics were in all cases weighty. Of all the neurotics, except for the neurotic depressions, this group showed the most pronounced depressive characteristics.

The cases grouped under neurasthenia showed as presenting symptoms a general weakness with vague bodily complaints, mild hypochondriasis, and a flattened depressive mood with a generalized inadequacy and inertia. None of these cases could justifiably have been diagnosed as straight "hypochondriacal psychosis"—although this diagnosis had to be considered—because in all these cases contact with reality was retained.

In all these groups of neuroses, it is clearer than in any other category that current psychiatric nosology has many arbitrary and inadequate criteria in its groupings. It is also clear that the results achieved in the analysis of our tests for their diagnostic indicators will have to be considered as minimal. We could have laid down better diagnostic guidelines if we had had more cases and been able to work with groups having less internal variability.

Clinical experience will allow the examiner, in cases which are classified on the basis of the general indicators demonstrated in the following discussions, to point out the presence of other diagnostic indications as well, and thus to build a detailed description of the specific features which distinguish that person from other more or less typical cases, or from other variations within the same diagnostic classification. Thus, no prevalence of diagnostic signs characteristic of a nosological category should prevent further thought about the case. Minor indicators of trends demonstrated to be present in other categories should be used to understand the specificity of the case, and to specify vulnerability to other—even though minor—symptoms, and should thus enable the examiner to build up a relatively rich picture of the individual case.

FURTHER REMARKS

To systematize an accepted body of knowledge appears to be relatively easy; to describe or propound something radically new requires courage, but imposes fewer restrictions. Our task cannot be characterized as being solely either. We have attempted to weld a practical and meaningful unity out of many individually well-known phenomena and procedures. Neither novelty nor finality has encouraged us. The nature of the task has made the material to be dealt with too voluminous to afford a completely clear picture of the interrelations studied. The study of many important relationships had to be deferred because of the limited scope of our task. We do not believe that "experience" is ever the last word in scientific endeavor; it must always be followed by statistical verification, and finally by laws based on an understanding of the dynamics underlying the phenomena.[11] The considerations to follow may not be at all new to many psychologists, and in their vagueness may be unattractive. Nevertheless, we believe that to report as much of our experience as possible is better than to leave the questions untackled.

---

[11] [See the Editor's Foreword for the reasons for omitting the attempt originally made to include a statistical analysis of the tests on the available cases.—Ed.]

CHAPTER 2

The Nature of Intelligence

The days are past when a person was presumed to have been born with a certain IQ, which he bore throughout his life and died with. The Iowa studies (Wellman, 1940) and others (see Stoddard, 1943) have shattered the myth of the unchangeability of IQ.[1] The problem, "What is intelligence?," has inspired more wasted effort than almost any other problem in psychology. In a volume of practical aims such as the present one, there is no place for an extended discussion of this moot question, even if one were tempted to tackle it again.

The division of mind into sensory, cognitive, and affective spheres is a matter of past theory in psychology. But to apply recognition of this fact to a number of outstanding psychological concepts—such as memory, thinking, intelligence—is still a matter of struggling through the present and dreaming of the future. Though every modern psychologist professes that the trichotomy mentioned is outdated, memory is still being dealt with in terms of associative frequency or conditioning (Hilgard & Marquis, 1940); the psychology of thinking is still being dealt with by investigations of logic, such as those investigations referring to the rules of Mill (Long & Welch, 1942); and intelligence is still being dealt with chiefly in terms of IQ.

We do not propose to advance a concept of intelligence proper to a psychology which disclaims the trichotomy of sensation, cognition, and affection. We shall limit ourselves to giving the view of intelligence that underlies our approach to intelligence tests.

THE DETERMINANTS OF INTELLIGENCE-TEST ACHIEVEMENT

When a subject takes an intelligence test, his performance represents his efficiency of functioning then and there. This may or may not be an

[1] [For more recent studies of the question of IQ changes and their significance, see Sontag, Baker, and Nelson (1958), and Moriarty (1966).—Ed.]

adequate sample of his general efficiency, or, in other words, of the intellectual assets potentially at his disposal. His present life situation, or even the present testing situation, may temporarily encroach upon and diminish his efficiency. On the other hand, the store of intellectual assets potentially at his disposal is not necessarily a final and unchangeable characteristic. The environment in which he grew up, including home, region, and country, with its barrenness or stimulating character, had its influence. The degree of schooling and the profession chosen may have expanded or constricted the development of the endowment and range of efficiency. An emotional or organic disturbance may have caused an arrest or setback of the level of efficiency. Thus, in the intelligence-test performance, a number of influences interact, yielding the results obtained.

If one wishes to use the intelligence-test record to greatest benefit, one must make an effort to differentiate these influences as much as possible. In order to do so, we found it necessary to start out with a concept of *natural endowment*—that is, a potentiality unfolding in a process of maturation.

In the course of the maturation process this potentiality does not remain unchanged. Its psychological environs are changing, and with them the dynamic characteristics of the natural endowment also change. By "psychological environs" we mean here the psychological mechanisms internal to the subject, not the environmental conditions which will be discussed soon. What we call here "psychological environs" and "natural endowment" are not two entities; the latter is merely a part of the former, and is differently named here only for the sake of contrast. Natural endowment is the hypothesized potentiality that is specifically considered to underlie what is called intellectual maturation.

The maturation process is one in which potentialities—among them natural endowment—become differentiated and crystallized. This differentiation process is sometimes referred to as the development of the ego. In this process of unfolding, it becomes necessary for some personalities to keep a balance and adjustment by tending to avoid acquisition of new knowledge. Other personalities find it necessary to acquire knowledge, as their way of coping with new problems encountered in the process of unfolding; and some try to acquire more *concrete* knowledge, while others try to achieve more *abstract* knowledge. The psychological processes occurring in this differentiation are known clinically: repression and withdrawal in the refusal to acquire knowledge; intellectualization and rationalization in the overemphasis on acquisition of knowledge. Repression and its role in hysteria, withdrawal of interest as seen in simple schizophrenics, intellectualization and its role in obsessive-compulsive disturbances, are psychiatric commonplaces. These are but a few examples of the vicissitudes of natural endowment in the course of the maturation process. Whether the individual choice among these vicissitudes is already to some extent determined by the type of innate endowment is as yet a moot question. We do not know whether the inclination to repression rather than to intellectualization is or is not a native individual characteristic. But there can be little doubt that there is a constant interaction of the "natural endowment" and the conditions of the maturation process. A consistent follow-up of these clinically known types of development, in terms of experimentally and statistically demonstrated relationships, might serve as a basis for a psychology of thinking, and for more satisfactory diagnostic work with these disturbances than our present procedures allow. A macroscopic view of people's thinking and methods of living has usually been correlated with their disturbance and maladjustment. But a microscopic analysis of this thinking has not been compared with the *type* of maladjustment into which different types of personality are prone to decompensate. One of the ideas behind our work in intelligence testing was to trace the relationship of these general psychological reaction types and psychodynamic patterns to the most minute test findings. We realize that we have made only a short step toward this aim, but we feel that this is one of the leading ideas every clinical examiner must keep in mind if diagnostic and meaningful intelligence testing is to replace mechanical intelligence testing.

The maturation process should be viewed as guided, restrained, or fostered by environmental conditions—natural, cultural, and interpersonal "wealth" or "poverty"—which may be justly called *educational environment* in contrast to formal schooling. But educational environment crystallizes into schooling; and the influence of schooling is, in some persons, sustained in above-average cultural interests which in turn, like schooling, contribute to a systematic crystallization of intellectual assets. Endowment, degree of maturation, educational environment, schooling, and cultural predilections are the factors whose influence on intelligence must be assessed if the clinical psychologist is to understand the make-up of his subject.

But this is not all. He must know whether, maturation once achieved, there has come about an arrest of development or a setback; and, if not, whether there is present a temporary inefficiency encroaching upon and impoverishing the subject's test performance.

Different types of maladjustment tend to have different distinguishable and recognizable impairments of test performance. Nevertheless, certain deficiencies due to the educational environment, or assets due to cultural predilections, may cloud or exaggerate some of these diagnostically distinguishing features of impairment. Cultural differences and educational background will—in spite of the generality of types of impairment in the intelligence test claimed here to be characteristic of different psychiatric disturbances —still have a role in the evaluation of our material and in clinical work, especially when the question is one of differential diagnosis. Before all the diagnostic inferences from the Wechsler-Bellevue Scale have been made, the examiner must ask himself whether or not there is an educational, environmental, or cultural factor that may account for any part of the otherwise diagnostic signs, thus invalidating or making them questionable. It is for this reason that the tester must obtain a minimum of information about the patient before he can rely on his diagnosis from test findings alone. In our practice, name, age, occupation, church affiliation, schooling, present and childhood residence, occupation of parents, marital and familial status proved to be that minimum of information necessary and useful in evaluating the intelligence-test results.

An Approach to Functions Underlying Test Achievement

When one attempts to infer from the intelligence-test responses of the subject whether one is dealing with a temporary or longstanding impairment of efficiency, or good efficiency and poor endowment, or good endowment and a lack of education and schooling, and so on, one encounters new problems. We shall proceed by setting forth the premises we found to be necessary in attempting to obtain answers to these questions from the test records.

First, we found that one must consider not only every subtest score, but every single response and every part of every response, as significant and representative of the subject. Naturally, many of the intelligence-test responses are highly conventionalized; and that a subject knows who was President of the United States at a particular time merely adds to his general score. But where the response deviates from the conventional, the deviation does not merely fail to add to his score; it must also be considered as a characteristic which may give us material toward the understanding of the subject. We shall illustrate this point when we discuss one by one the different item groups of the Wechsler-Bellevue Scale and Babcock's Story Recall Test.

Second, we found that one may gain some understanding of the subject by comparing the successes and failures on a given type of test item. Thus, if a subject knows how many pints there are in a quart, but does not know what the Koran is, this will give us merely an idea of his range of information. But if he knows what the Koran is and asserts that a quart has four pints, we must consider the presence of a temporary inefficiency; and if he insists that the capital of Italy is Constantinople or that the Vatican is a robe, psychotic maladjustment will have to be considered.

Third, we found that the relationship of the score of one subtest to the scores of other subtests is also representative of the subject. Thus, if a subject demonstrates that he possesses excellent Vocabulary and Information, but is very poor on Comprehension, we must conclude that he is not able to utilize to a full extent in life situations his verbal facility and general knowledge, and we will be justified in considering that we are dealing with a case of impaired judgment. Again, we shall have to defer further illustrations of this point for a later, detailed discussion.

Fourth, we found that the relationship of all the Verbal scores to all the Performance scores is significant of the make-up of the subject. Thus, a high Verbal but low Performance score average suggests the possible presence of depression.

Fifth, we found that the data to which the above four points refer must be considered in the light of findings of tests other than those of intelligence. Thus, badly impaired intelligence-test achievement has a different diagnostic implication if the Rorschach test indicates a rich endowment or a poor endowment.

In general, one might say that this approach to intelligence testing requires a very different attitude toward tests than does routine intelligence testing, which hinges upon correct appraisal of whether a response is to be considered passing or failing. This approach implies requirements which may be condensed into two points:

(a) On the part of the tester, it requires a great deal of attention to any type of deviation from the usual run of test performances. Routine performance on tests reflects degree and ability of cultural compliance; deviation from it reflects the individual personality. Thus, the response, "Wheeled vehicles for transportation on land" to the question, "In what way are a wagon and a bicycle the same?" obtains full credit; but its deviation from the usual responses, its overexactness and relative redundancy, should raise the question in the examiner's mind, "Is this person really as doubt laden and overmeticulous as this response indicates?" One such response will not give a personality description, nor will it establish beyond doubt even a single "trait." It will, however, require the examiner to develop a personality description, first from the rest of the intelligence test and later from any other test at his disposal, which will satisfactorily explain why the test item was responded to in a manner deviating so basically from the average run of the responses.

(b) The other requirement is not limited to the individual tester, but is pertinent as a warning to clinical psychology in general: reports stating, for instance, that "The subject has good Information but his Digit Span, especially Digit Span backwards, is very poor" are psychologically meaningless, as long as the significance of a poor Digit Span for the personality make-up remains unexplained. Many have considered poor Digit Span to be a sign of poor memory; others have tried to establish the factors involved in good or poor performance on Digit Span by means of factor analysis. The former explanation was no explanation; neither the relation of Digit Span to memory nor the dynamic significance of memory and its impairment was clarified. The latter explanation yielded a number of statistically established "factors," of which neither the real existence nor the significance for personality was known. It may even be suspected that the basic assumption of most factor analysis—namely, the search for independent factors—is in sharp contrast with the basic tenets of dynamic psychology, where no factor can be considered as independent of the general drama of psychological happenings.

There are several reasons why we know so little about the psychological functions involved in the performance of simple tasks of the type included in intelligence tests. The influence of the trichotomy of sensation, affection, and cognition upon psychological thought is one of the historical reasons; the effort to correlate stimulus and response in investigating behavior while neglecting the processes that occur *between* stimulus and response is another; the enormous and forbidding complexity of functions involved in these apparently simple performances is a third. As for the failure of intelligence testers and clinical psychologists to investigate the psychological processes in question, it appears reasonably sure that although *they* were the ones to raise these problems, their failing to contribute more toward solving them was in great part due to the nature of the intelligence test that was most widely used and which served as a paradigm for most other intelligence tests—namely, the Binet, or rather its American version, the Stanford-Binet. In this test, the items are distributed over mental age levels; many items are included more because, in the standardization population, they reliably differentiated between successive age groups and were easily scorable than because the psychological functions underlying achievement on them were understood and considered sufficiently important to warrant their inclusion. Though attempts have been made (e.g., Roe & Shakow, 1942) to group the items of the Stanford-Binet into consistent groups referring to the same psychological function or group of functions, such attempts have not gained recognition. The evaluation of the clinical significance of success and failure has usually asked only, over how many age levels were successes and failures distributed? The quality of the successes and failures has not been systematically investigated. Quantitative measures of scatter of success and failure have proved to be in general nondifferentiating (see Harris & Shakow, 1937). Because of the difficulty of systematically investigating the functions involved in these successes and failures, no psychologically meaningful, theoretical rationale of the functions involved in the test performance has developed; and the clinical evaluation of the meaning of the successes and failures is usually based on "hunch" or "intuition."

Because of these difficulties in the Stanford-Binet, we sought an intelligence test in which the items were chosen and grouped to be relatively homogeneous in regard to the psychological functions involved, and the subtest scores of which were directly comparable. We have chosen the Wechsler scales and the Babcock Story Recall Test because they more or less satisfied these requirements.

CHAPTER 3

The Wechsler-Bellevue Scale

We chose the Wechsler-Bellevue Scale (Wechsler, 1939a, b)[1] for the intelligence test of our battery. This choice was dictated not merely by the fact that the standardization work on it was careful, but more by the fact that it, of all the tests extant, best meets the two criteria we described in the previous chapter for diagnostic intelligence tests: its subtests are relatively homogeneous groups of items, and the scores of all these subtests are expressed in one scale of equated and directly comparable weighted scores. The test offers the possibility for an interpersonal comparison of the subject's intelligence to that of the general population, as expressed in IQ's; and it also allows an intrapersonal comparison of the efficiency of the different functions underlying the achievements on the different subtests.

In this introductory section we shall give: (1) a description of the structure of the test; (2) a description of the administration of the test; and (3) a discussion of the diagnostic significance and value of the most general features of the distribution of the weighted subtest scores, to be referred to here as "scatter."

We shall devote to each of the 11 subtests of the W-B a special subsection: (1) describing the subtest; (2) discussing the theoretical rationale of the functions underlying achievement on the subtest; (3) presenting an analysis of the items of the subtest to establish whether, to what extent, and for which groups, success or failure on single items can be diagnostic; (4) discussing the diagnostic use of the data provided by the subtest.

A Description of the Test. The W-B consists of 11 subtests. The *Verbal* part of the scale contains six tests—Vocabulary, Comprehension, Information, Digit Span, Arithmetic, and Similarities; the *Performance* part contains

---

[1] [The original authors were exclusively concerned with the Wechsler-Bellevue Form I, which they referred to as the "Bellevue Scale." That designation has been changed to the abbreviation now commonly used, W-B, which should be taken always to mean Form I, unless otherwise specified. On the applicability of ideas and conclusions advanced here to the WAIS, see Editor's Appendix to this chapter.—Ed.]

71

five tests—Picture Arrangement, Picture Completion, Block Design, Object Assembly, and Digit Symbol.

In the Verbal part the only timed test is Arithmetic; on all of its items there is a time limit, and on two items the subject may obtain additional time credit. On the Performance part all the subtests have time limits, and on all except Picture Completion the subject may obtain additional time credit. On the Comprehension, Similarities, and Vocabulary items, both full and half credits can be obtained; no such provision is granted on the Digit Span, Arithmetic, and Information items. Picture Arrangement, Object Assembly, and to a slight degree Digit Symbol, allow for partial scores; Picture Completion and Block Design allow credit only for full accuracy of performance. On Block Design the time allowance is quite liberal; on Picture Completion the allowance is somewhat narrow (15 seconds per picture).

Wechsler's Manual (1939a) gives detailed and explicit instructions for scoring, with adequate samples of the verbal responses. The specific scoring of each subtest we shall discuss in the following subsections of this chapter. The raw scores of the subtests, once obtained, are translated into weighted scores with the help of a table. The raw scores and the corresponding weighted scores are entered in the summarizing table of the test blank. The Verbal weighted scores and Performance weighted scores are added separately, and the total of these two is also obtained. The IQ's represented by the so-obtained Verbal, Performance, and Total weighted scores are then located in the respective IQ tables in columns corresponding to the age of the subject. Special tables indicate the percentile placement in the total population of the IQ obtained and the name of the intelligence group (bright normal, superior, etc.) to which the obtained IQ belongs.

On Testing Technique. A description of some simple and yet salient features of the test's administration will be in place here. A detailed description of the general procedure of administration will be found in Wechsler's manual.

We used two technical aids in the recording of the test. In addition to the printed record blank for the W-B, we used extra mimeographed sheets to allow for the verbatim recording of *all* the subject's verbalizations, and a description of his motor and other performances on the test, and of his salient behavior in the course of the test. We believe that only beginners need be warned that record blanks are not to be used merely to record scores—however certain one may be of scoring, and however fast at looking up scores in the manual—but rather for recording what the patient actually said and did. Regrettably enough, the printed form of the "Wechsler-Bellevue Record Sheet" is conducive to the former practice because of the inadequate space allowed for entering notes.

We not only recorded the weighted scores in the summarizing table of the W-B record blank, but also used a scattergram as shown in Figure 1. This was done in order to impress upon ourselves vividly the relationships of the weighted scores to each other—that is to say, the intrapersonal relationships of the different functions underlying achievements on the subtests. After some preliminary experience, a graphically represented profile is more conducive to grasping a pattern of weighted scores, and more automatically committed to memory, than a set of 11 numbers. The scattergram card has for its horizontal axis the 18 weighted score units; and for its vertical axis the six Verbal and the five Performance subtests, and the Verbal, Performance, and Total averages in this sequence. The scattergram card then is used like a system of coordinates, on which a graph representing the weighted scores is drawn.

In introducing the test to the subject we always frankly state that it is an intelligence test. We add, however, that it is not for the intelligence quotient that we give this test, but rather to obtain certain information concerning his problems which will be used to help him. In other words, we do everything we can to diminish the anxiety of the testing situation, even though knowing that all one can hope for is a slight decrease of tension in the patient. The same attitude prevails in the course of administration of the test, where the real achievements of the patient earn approval and the failures are eased over. (We do not, however, tell the patient that his answer is correct when it is not.) We follow Wechsler's advice to allow patients to finish whatever they start, even if they exceed the time limit.

FIGURE 1

Sample Scattergram of a Deteriorated Schizophrenic

BELLEVUE SCATTERGRAM

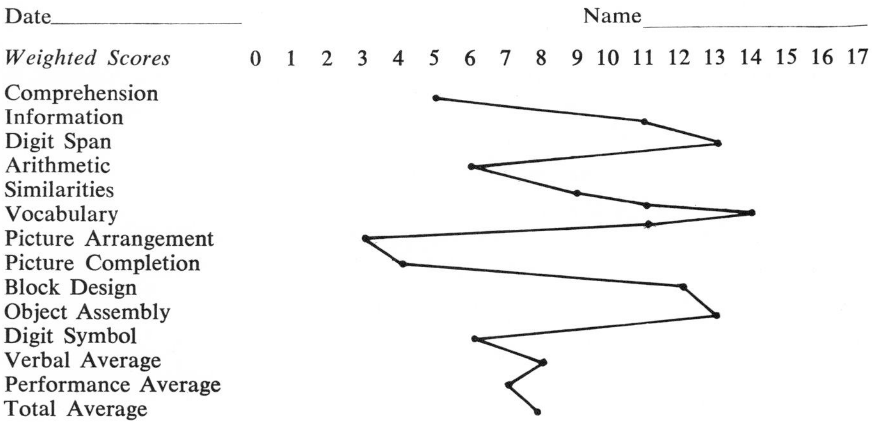

We make it a practice to adhere to the scoring standards laid down by the Manual; but after the score is established for a subtest or for an item of the subtest, if the subtest or item has something disquieting, peculiar, or vague about it, we always go back for inquiry. This inquiry has, naturally, no bearing upon the scoring itself, but frequently reveals the confusion hidden behind a stereotype. In the Performance subtests and in Arithmetic when failure is obvious, we give help again and again, once the time is up, in order to see how much help the patient needs and also to determine whether any amount of help is effective. Failure to benefit from such help must in general be considered a good basis for raising the question, Do we deal here with a psychosis? The patient's manner of dealing with such help gives additional information of clinical value.[2]

Needless to say, we do not insist upon administering the entire test in one session, but rather take the patient's tolerance into consideration; we never continue testing a patient who shows either undue apprehension or fatigue.

Real efficiency in using these tests is obtained when the general scoring scheme is so committed to memory that scoring, translation into weighted scores, entering scores into the summarizing table and scattergram, all can be done as the testing proceeds. The advantage of such procedure is partly in the time gain, as against going over the test twice for scoring and diagnostic purposes; and partly in that it makes it possible, while the patient is present, to ascertain and clarify hazy points. Furthermore, if the weighted scores on successive subtests can be determined as administration of the test proceeds, patterns of scores begin to take shape; and these patterns can serve as the basis for diagnostic hypotheses which will direct the tester's attention to special features of the performance.

THE CONCEPT OF SCATTER

The concept of scatter—that is to say, the relationship to each other of the functions underlying the person's achievements on the different subtests —is the red thread of this chapter. Instead of the customary *interindividual* comparisons, embodied in the concept of the IQ and percentile ratings, this chapter will stress the *intraindividual* comparison of functions underlying test performances as embodied in the concept of scatter. Accordingly, we devote a special section to the discussion of this concept. [See also Appendix to this chapter.]

[2] [The examiner must balance these possible gains from giving help against the additional time required, and the equivocation that is introduced into the interpretation of retesting, if it should ever be required in the future.—Ed.]

The Definition of Scatter. The scatter is the pattern or configuration formed by the distribution of the weighted subtest scores of an intelligence test in general, and here of the W-B in particular. The scatter is graphically represented by the scattergram. The relationship of any two weighted subtest scores is subsumed under the concept of scatter; moreover the relationship of any single subtest score to the central tendency of all the subtest scores—however this central tendency is determined—is also implied. The definition of scatter as a configuration or pattern of all the subtest scores implies that the final meaning of the relationship of any two scores, or of any single score to the central tendency of all the scores, is derived from the total pattern. This pattern, when inspected on a scattergram, is a visually perceived configuration: the configuration can be one where all the weighted scores cluster closely around the central tendency; it can be one where the scores are distributed somewhat loosely around this central tendency; it can be one where if one score is far above the central tendency, another is sure to be far below it, and so on down the line; it can be one where, in spite of the general clustering, one score juts out; it can be one where the first five or six scores are high above, and the rest far below, the central tendency—and so on. It is from such visually observed distributions that our concepts of scatter were abstracted.

The Assumptions Underlying Scatter Analysis. One objection to scatter analysis is that one cannot investigate the relationship of subtest scores to each other, in different clinical and control groups, without equating for age, sex, and IQ. In order to meet such objections, it becomes necessary to state two basic assumptions underlying scatter analysis.[3] (a) If one deals with differences of weighted scores, or differences of a weighted score and any kind of mean of scores, the operation of subtraction by which such differences are obtained cancels out the intelligence level which is inherent in the scores and in the means; and the differences thus obtained are directly comparable for any two persons, though one be dull normal and the other very superior in intelligence. (b) The weighted scores and their central tendency represent the general position of the person's intelligence in relation to the standardization population of the test, and thus presumably in relation to the general population. On the basis of the projective hypothesis (see Chapter 7),[4] it follows then that the deviation of some of a person's subtest scores from his central tendency of weighted scores—that is to say, from his general position relative to the total population—reveals some characteristic of his intellectual functioning and personality organization,

---

[3] [The arguments that follow cannot be considered adequate to meet the objections, in the light of work that has followed the first edition. See Editor's Foreword and Appendix to this chapter.—Ed.]

[4] [See also Rapaport (1946), and Mayman, Schafer, and Rapaport (1951).—Ed.]

whether this characteristic be an impairment or an uneven development of function.

These two assumptions are used in scatter analysis in an attempt to get away from the intelligence level of the patient—which at the time may be intact, impaired, or totally disorganized—and to try to reconstruct out of the relationships of the single subtest scores, on whatever level the whole score distribution may be, the original level of performance and the specific character of the impairment; from these, hypotheses can be derived about which diagnostic category the patient belongs in. Some limitations of the first assumption's practical application which are set by the nature of the W-B Scale must be stated. The assumption is that it makes no difference where the weighted scores of the 11 subtests of a person are distributed on the 18-point weighted score of the W-B Scale. This assumption is not entirely valid. The very fact that no lower scores than $\emptyset$, and no higher scores than 17, can be obtained on the weighted-score scale sets a limitation. In our experience, great scatter is an indicator of psychopathology: it must be noted, however, that at either extreme of the weighted-score continuum, the construction of the scale itself militates against great scatter. The feeble-minded person, even if psychotic, will not be able to register a great scatter, because his intelligence level was originally poor; and an extremely intelligent person may still remain in the uppermost ranges, even though his intellectual efficiency is actually impaired. Lack of scatter in the uppermost and lowermost ranges thus cannot be considered, without further question, as necessarily normal. In fact, *any* scatter in these extreme ranges should be looked into with more critical caution than scatter of similar extent in the middle range. In our material, subjects with originally very low IQ's are almost entirely absent, and low IQ's are as a rule the results of impairment. Nevertheless, clinically it was not the lowering of IQ's but scatter that proved to be diagnostically sensitive.

To establish statistically the relation of IQ to extent of scatter, we obtained the product moment correlation between the total IQ and total scatter rating, using a mixed group of 261 clinical and normal cases. The correlation was −.23 with a standard error of .06. This correlation is significantly different from zero ($p < .01$), which means that there is a significant but limited tendency for the IQ to be lower where the scatter is greater. This inverse relationship is easily understandable from two viewpoints: (a) great scatter in itself implies many greatly dropping scores, which in turn imply a lowered IQ; (b) clinically we rarely find *many* greatly dropping scores and at the same time an excellent achievement on the rest of the subtests. The fact is that the groups with many greatly dropping subtest scores are those which have a general impairment on all subtests, and hence show a low IQ. In our clinical work, the IQ level has proved to be of almost no diagnostic significance. Rather, the pattern of the scores of the various subtests which make up this total IQ is the diagnostically meaningful factor.

The second assumption implies that the scatter is a pattern determined by the person's development, and by his type of adjustment or maladjustment. If such scatter patterns exist, they must be somewhat influenced, but not radically changed, by age.

The Scatter Measures. Of the many possible measures, we have found two most useful: (a) the scatter from the Vocabulary; (b) the scatter from what we call the modified Verbal Mean and modified Performance Mean.

Vocabulary Scatter. The Vocabulary scatter of a subtest is the difference between its score and the score on Vocabulary. Since the average score on Vocabulary is among the highest of the subtests for all our population, it is obvious that most of these Vocabulary scatters will be negative. In the following, a Vocabulary scatter not specifically referred to as positive is to be considered negative.

The empirical basis for adopting the Vocabulary score as one basis of scatter computation is that Vocabulary has long been known to be a fair representative of the intelligence level, and to remain relatively unimpaired by maladjustment. This observation is so general as not to need specific documentation; it served as the basis for the Babcock Test, and Vocabulary has frequently been used as the sole intelligence gauge.

In our own material, we found Vocabulary to be among the three subtests that hold up best, having a mean which is exceeded only by that of Similarities. We also found that the standard deviation of the mean of Vocabulary is the lowest among the standard deviations of the means of all the subtests. Accordingly, we assume that *Vocabulary scatter measures the drop of efficiency of one or more functions below the hypothetical original level of the person.*

One of the assets of Vocabulary scatter is that the Vocabulary score and all the other subtest scores are integers: hence scatter measures are integers and are easily dealt with. But one drawback of Vocabulary scatter is that most of the scatter measures are negative, and this tends to give a somewhat one-sided picture of scatter in general.

Mean Scatter. The Mean scatter is the difference between any test score and the average of all the other subtest scores.[5] The so-obtained Mean

[5] For Verbal Mean scatter, Digit Span and Arithmetic scores are also eliminated from computation of the Verbal Mean. The exclusion of these subtests was warranted by the fact that impairments of Digit Span and Arithmetic scores are so general that their inclusion would have vitiated the representativeness of the mean as a central tendency of the scores. [What is called here "Mean scatter" is identical with the modified Mean scatter of the first edition.—Ed.]

scatter is either positive or negative. A Mean scatter not specifically referred to as positive should be assumed to be negative.

The Mean scatter represents the variation of the subtest scores away from their central tendency. Therefore, while the IQ represents the subject's achievements in relation to the general population, and the Vocabulary scatter represents the subject's achievement in relation to his own original highest achievement, the *Mean scatter measures the relationship of a subject's single achievements to the central tendency of all his achievements.*

Using the Mean scatter has two disadvantages. (1) The mean usually contains decimals; thus the Mean scatter measure will include decimals, and as a consequence is somewhat cumbersome. (2) The mean is not infrequently a dubious representative of the central tendency, especially in cases where one or two extremely low or high scores unduly displace its value. To mitigate this, in the computation of Mean scatter we always used for the Performance subtests the Performance Mean, and for the Verbal subtests the Verbal Mean; thus we took into account the difference in vulnerability to maladjustment between the Performance and the Verbal subtests.

Diagnostic Significance of Over-all Scatter. In our view, *the scatter on the W-B is not random, but follows definite rules and is diagnostically differential between kinds of clinical and normal groups.* The following discussion will not go into great detail, and will provide only a general diagnostic orientation, but a useful one. This general orientation is what the examiner must keep in mind when he first looks at a scattergram, noting the relationship of the other subtests to Vocabulary and to their own central tendency. From such considerations he can form a hypothesis about where among the clinical categories he is to place his patient. He must then go into a detailed analysis of the scatter of the single subtests, in order to find which one of the possible categories is the likeliest and to form hypotheses about supplementary diagnostic features.

Positive Vocabulary scatter is almost always much less than negative except in conditions like simple schizophrenia in which Vocabulary is specifically impaired. Negative scatter on the Performance part usually tends to be larger than on the Verbal part. In other words, the Verbal subtests are much more stable and resistive to the encroachment of maladjustment than the Performance subtests. Negative Vocabulary scatter—that is, the drop of Performance subtests below Vocabulary—is far greater in the two types of psychotic depressions than in any of the other diagnostic groups considered here. Only deteriorated unclassified schizophrenics approximate such massive impairment of Performance relative to Vocabulary.[6] Extreme predominance of negative Vocabulary scatter is an indicator of psychosis; specific predominance of negative scatter on Performance points to the presence of a depression, the severity of which can roughly be estimated by the extent of such scatter.

Another useful measure of nonspecific Vocabulary scatter may be obtained by simply counting the number of impaired subtest scores, according to the following limits. Comprehension, Information, Similarities, and Block Design are considered impaired when they are three or more weighted-score points below Vocabulary; Picture Arrangement, Picture Completion, and Digit Symbol, when the discrepancy is four or more points; and Object Assembly, when it is five or more. Digit Span and Arithmetic are disregarded for this type of analysis. A single inadequacy of this magnitude in a function underlying a subtest performance may occur—possibly as a developmental anomaly, or as an expression of limited background—in the normal population, but in general more than two extreme drops of subtest scores below the Vocabulary level indicates psychopathology, and more than five such drops suggest the presence of a depressive or schizophrenic psychosis.

The most characteristic features of the scatter of schizophrenic patients are the tendency for an impairment of verbal functions, and a tendency for the Verbal and Performance subtest scores to scatter widely from their respective means. These two tendencies differentiate schizophrenics from depressive neurotics, neurotics, and normal persons.

Depressive psychotics most characteristically have an extreme impairment of efficiency on the Performance subtests; and although their Verbal scores are also lowered, the discrepancy between their Performance level and their Verbal level remains extreme. This characteristic scatter pattern distinguishes, in general, depressive psychotics from schizophrenics, depressive and other neurotics, and normals.

The most characteristic feature of depressive neurotics is a somewhat impaired efficiency of function on the Performance subtests, while their Verbal efficiency is well retained. This scatter pattern distinguishes depressive neurotics to a certain extent from other neurotics.

Most characteristic of neurotic groups is the mild tendency to have an impaired Performance efficiency and increased Verbal scatter.

Our aim so far has been merely to present major scatter patterns. It remains then to fill in this general framework of scatter patterns with a more detailed analysis of characteristic scatter on each subtest, to the end

---

[6] [Great and generalized negative Performance scatter is also found in many organic conditions.—Ed.]

of making possible more sensitive analyses of scatter patterns for individual diagnoses.

Before turning to the analysis of individual subtests, we must point out that there are four main divisions into which the subtests fall: (1) four subtests which are essentially verbal—Vocabulary, Information, Comprehension, and Similarities; (2) two subtests measuring the related functions of attention and concentration—Digit Span and Arithmetic; (3) two subtests dependent to a large extent on visual organization—Picture Arrangement and Picture Completion; (4) three subtests which are primarily visual-motor coordination tests—Block Design, Object Assembly, and Digit Symbol. It will become clear to the reader in the following sections that there is a psychological rationale to these four major groupings.[7]

VOCABULARY

The Vocabulary subtest of the W-B consists of 42 items; each of these, if satisfactorily passed, gives a raw score of 1, and if only precariously passed, a raw score of ½. The raw scores are added, and the sum is then translated into a weighted score, as is true of all the other subtests. Under usual testing conditions the Vocabulary score is not used in calculating the IQ, which is obtained from the five Verbal and five Performance tests only. The Vocabulary test may be used, however, as a substitute for any Verbal subtest, if for special reasons one of these cannot be given or cannot be considered a fair test.

The Psychological Rationale of the Vocabulary Subtest. The special position of verbalization among, and in relation to, all psychological processes, as well as the special position of Vocabulary among all other test items applied in intelligence tests, has long been recognized. It is another question whether the implications of this recognition were conceived to constitute as serious a problem as they do. A few pertinent considerations should be gone into here.

---

[7] [This division of the subtests, arrived at on purely logical and clinical grounds, has been fairly well sustained by factor analyses. The "essentially verbal" group corresponds exactly to Cohen's (1952) Verbal Factor A; his Factor C, Distractibility, corresponds reasonably well to the second, attention-concentration, division, except that it also includes Digit Symbol in all groups of subjects and excludes Arithmetic in schizophrenics. His grouping of the Performance subtests puts Picture Arrangement and Picture Completion together with Block Design and Object Assembly as Factor B, excluding Digit Symbol. Gault's (1954) study confirms this last grouping; but his analysis (which did not include Vocabulary) puts Arithmetic with Information, Comprehension, and Similarities. Note that Cohen (1957a) did find a Factor B corresponding to the visual-motor coordination triad at ages 60-75. For further discussion of these issues, see Appendix to this chapter, below.—Ed.]

On the basis of the observation that Vocabulary seemed to be the most stable and least deteriorating aspect of intelligence yet approached in intelligence testing, Babcock (1930) built a deterioration test. In this test, the comparison of the Vocabulary level with the achievements on other types of tests yields measures by which deterioration or inefficiency can be measured. Yacorzynski (1941) suggested, and Feifel (1949) confirmed, that the nondeteriorative character of vocabulary is really an illusion, and that the basis of this illusion lies in the fact that different levels of definitions of the words are acceptable. Though a patient may use a lower level of vocabulary definition than he did originally, he can still pass. Thus, in the vocabulary misses, only the gross impairments of vocabulary will show up. The W-B Vocabulary subtest allows for half scores on primitive levels of definition, and thus to a certain extent takes into account the point objected to by Yacorzynski. It remains true, however, that the W-B Vocabulary, like other vocabulary tests, indicates on the whole only the grossest inefficiencies of vocabulary.

Though a thorough study of the structure of vocabulary and the level of verbalization used would be highly important,[8] we believe that the general method of using vocabulary as a "standard" is not a faulty one. Clinical experience teaches that vocabulary, once achieved, will be quite refractory to impairment by temporary or sustained inefficiency and deterioration, though it may change its form of functioning to levels of definition (that is, conceptualization) which are much less adequate than those used by the patient at the time when his vocabulary reached its greatest scope and efficiency. Although vocabulary-test studies tend to exaggerate the stability of the vocabulary function, they nevertheless do bring to expression its highly stable nature. In the following discussion it will be demonstrated that, on the one hand, this refractoriness to deterioration and impairment is only relative; and that, on the other hand, it is greater than that of other relatively stable groups of Verbal items, and certainly greater than that of the easily impaired Performance items.

[8] [Feifel (1949) made a useful beginning along these lines, distinguishing four types of definitions generally considered acceptable: synonyms; use, description, or a combination of these; explanation; illustration, inferior explanation, (partial) repetition, and demonstration. Regrettably, he confined his analyses to comparisons of normal and "abnormal" subjects, the latter a mixed group of schizophrenics, manic-depressives, and organics, with schizophrenics predominating; but he found that each of his four categories significantly differentiated between his groups despite the fact that they were matched for age and for over-all Stanford-Binet vocabulary score. The normal subjects gave more definitions in terms of synonyms; the abnormals gave more of the other three types, as did very young normal subjects (under nine years) and old ones with specific reference to the "use and description" category. Parallel findings appeared in a developmental study discussed below, Chapter 6: the earlier appearance of concrete and functional than of conceptual definitions in the Object Sorting Test.—Ed.]

Another point concerning the nature of vocabulary is equally important. To state it in an exaggerated form, *vocabulary is primarily dependent upon the cultural wealth of early educational environment, and is refractory to improvement by later schooling and life experience.* Clinical experience appears to show that the wealth of stimulation and width of horizon open in the childhood home and environment, rather than the extent of schooling and variety of life experience, basically influence the scope of vocabulary. These relationships are in many cases clouded, because schooling and life experience do enlarge vocabulary to some extent; but we have been impressed by the many persons of culturally poor childhood environment who remain limited in their vocabulary despite schooling and life experiences of great variety.[9] Besides original environment, schooling, and variety of life experience, there appears to be a fourth factor that influences vocabulary. This factor is concerned with the specific character of a person's intellectual functioning, and should be discussed in detail.

In our introductory discussion of intelligence, we pointed out that what is called intelligence includes an accumulation of memories of events and relationships, or data concerning relationships; and that this accumulation depends upon undisturbed functioning. We pointed out that original endowment corresponds, to an extent, to the strength of adaptive intellectual function; that progressive unhampered maturation is an expression of the absence of disturbance of function; and that in the course of maturation the undisturbed function picks up all the wealth of data and relationships, and assimilates and organizes them into the form in which they are later at the disposal of the person. This function, however, cannot be called qualitatively identical for every person and only quantitatively different in each. On the contrary, there appear to be great qualitative differences in this function. It is embedded in the personality organization, and is undiscernible in it; and the formation of personality and its characteristics is at the same time the formation of this function and its characteristics. Where a "see no evil, hear no evil, speak no evil" make-up characterizes the whole personality, it will be reflected in the function underlying intelligence. This function will be different in a personality which can be characterized by the slogan "I have to know everything in order to do the right thing." The psychological concept of repression refers to the submergence in the unconscious of information or knowledge already possessed, because of the danger hidden in that knowledge for the person's psychological equilibrium (Rapaport, 1942a, 1951a). Knowledge cannot be assimilated unless it is integrated with other freely available knowledge; and once repression plays

[9] [Dr. Lloyd Silverman points out the fact that, therefore, Vocabulary is not an appropriate base for scatter with such groups as immigrants and the culturally deprived.—Ed.]

a pathological role, it tends to become ever more extensive, and with it the accumulation of knowledge is limited. Thus, we deal here with a type of function that will tend to assimilate and accumulate less information, less cultural wealth, less vocabulary. On the other hand, when the personality make-up is such that intellectual knowledge becomes the most important conscious weapon against the onslaught of the feared unknown, a different situation is encountered. These cases characterized by intellectualization— or libidinization of thought processes, to use the psychoanalytic terminology —are on the whole found in extreme form in the groups of patients labeled as compulsive and obsessive personalities. It is these who, under stress and strain, usually decompensate into obsessional and compulsion neuroses. Similar defenses are also prominent in patients we have called overidea-tional preschizophrenics. In these cases, the functions underlying intelligence are oversharp and overkeen in picking up as much factual information, knowledge of relationships, and vocabulary as is possible.

Thus, in evaluating vocabulary achievement one must keep in mind, first, that the basic point in the psychology of vocabulary is the relatively refractory nature of vocabulary to deterioration; second, that given an undisturbed function and an unhampered process of maturation, vocabulary depends for its development more upon original wealth of educational environment than upon late schooling and variety of life experience; third, that when intellectual function is disturbed in the beginning, the lack of vocabulary attainment will reflect it; and fourth, that not only the disturbed or undisturbed condition of the function, but the specific quality of its disturbance—namely, its readiness either to accumulate or to avoid accumulating information and knowledge—also plays a crucial role in the development of vocabulary.

Administration. Whenever a peculiar verbalization—an association instead of a definition, sound alliteration, and so on—occurs, inquiry is mandatory.

When the patient flatly states, "I don't know," inquiry is superfluous; but where hesitation, hedging, embarrassment, or uncertainty are apparent, inquiry should be made. For such cases, "catacomb" may turn out to be "honeycomb," "proselyte" may be "a bad woman," "traduce" may mean "seduce," and so on.

Wherever the relationship between the word in question and its definition by the patient is unclear to the examiner, inquiry to ascertain the relationship in the mind of the patient should be made. Arbitrary nonrelated definitions are psychotic indications, and occur otherwise only in pretentious psychopaths.

Though after five missed items the examiner may correctly consider the subtest administration finished, it is advisable to check the response of the patient to a few following, but relatively easy, items, such as "harakiri." It may happen that five items are missed owing to fortuitous conditions.

Item Analysis. The basis of item analysis is the experience that the different words included as items in the Vocabulary subtest show wide discrepancies in difficulty. The *aim* of item analysis is to discover whether there are individual items on which failure is characteristic for any clinical group, and if so—as clinical experience appears to indicate—which they are.

The *reservations* the reader must keep in mind in this section are:

(a) The misses on one level of difficulty become diagnostically significant only if and when items of a higher degree of difficulty are passed by the same subject; otherwise, misses tell us only of the level of attainment.

(b) A mechanical application of the results of item analysis, without regard for the patient's general intelligence level, can only be misleading. The following rules apply to persons of at least normal intelligence.

Clinically, we usually formulated a crude item-analysis of Vocabulary in two parts. The first part of the test, 21 words, should not as a rule contain failures, as long as function is unimpaired by maladjustment. Words 14-17, 19, and 21 are, however, as difficult for many subjects as 22 and 24-28. The second part falls into two subparts. To pass approximately the first dozen words of the second part requires more information, more study, more experience than to pass the 21 words of the first part, which can easily be picked up by unimpaired function in everyday experience. To pass the last seven words of the second part usually requires special cultural pursuits, special schooling, and experiential stimulation. Thus, a failure on the first half of the test should be indicative of impairment and maladjustment, if the intelligence level is not extremely low in the first place; but failure on the second half may be an overlapping, or fusion, of maladjustment and lack of sufficient education or schooling. The last part is useful only with reference to the cultural level of the subject.

Several misses on the easy items may be expected only in depressive psychoses; one or two misses may be expected from schizophrenics, with perhaps more in the deteriorated and simple schizophrenics; and in neurotics and normals not more than one sporadic miss, explainable as a result of a relatively poor educational environment and/or a temporary inefficiency.

In addition, cases missing two or more of the 12 items of second-degree difficulty (Nos. 14-17, 19, 21, 22, 24-28) are likely to be psychotic or very depressed. A neurasthenic condition may also account for many misses on this level, and so may a precarious adjustment of a normal person with little cultural support for vocabulary achievement.

DIAGNOSTIC SUGGESTIONS

(a) Many misses on relatively easy Vocabulary items, especially if harder items are passed, are characteristic of psychotic depressives, schizophrenics, and neurasthenics. To a lesser extent, they are characteristic of precariously adjusted normals with a poor cultural background.

(b) Relatively low weighted scores are characteristic of psychotic and severely neurotic depressives, simple and deteriorated schizophrenics, neurasthenics, and precariously adjusted normals with a poor cultural background. (These conclusions are valid only if the possibility of mental deficiency has been eliminated, of course.)

(c) High weighted scores are most characteristic of patients given to intellectualization or compulsive defense mechanisms—such as overideational preschizophrenics, paranoid conditions, obsessive-compulsive neuroses, and the anxiety and depression group. These groups consistently have the fewest misses on all levels of difficulty of the Vocabulary test. Low weighted scores are extremely rare for patients of all these types.

(d) A parallel lowering of both the mean of the Verbal subtest scores (excluding Digit Span and Arithmetic) and the Vocabulary score is characteristic of simple schizophrenics and neurasthenics. A lowering of the Vocabulary score, accompanied by an even greater lowering of the Verbal mean, is characteristic of psychotic depressives and deteriorative schizophrenics.

Vocabulary does *tend* to drop with deterioration, though it remains less impaired than other functions. For the simple schizophrenics one might with some justification surmise that from the beginning their schizoid organization of personality was not conducive to developing verbal means of socialization. But low Vocabulary in neurasthenics is more difficult to understand, in the present state of our knowledge. It must be kept in mind that an acute disturbance characterized by general loss of "pep"—found also in psychotic depression—may have a specific effect on the availability of knowledge. The psychotic depressions are not deteriorative disorders but acute disturbances. In their acuteness, they seem to differ significantly from short-lived disturbances such as the acute schizophrenias. The Vocabulary level is apparently not much influenced by acute schizophrenic disturbance, but in such cases is dependent rather on the original development of intelligence.

We conclude that a parallel lowering of both the Verbal mean and the Vocabulary score is most indicative of a simple schizophrenia or a neurasthenic type of neurosis. A lowering of the Vocabulary score accompanied by an even greater lowering of the Verbal mean is most indicative of a depressive psychosis or a deteriorative schizophrenia. A Vocabulary score higher than a well-retained Verbal mean—in a case of maladjustment—is most indicative of one of the three "intellectualizing" groups (paranoid condition, overideational preschizophrenia, and obsessive-compulsive neurosis).

Here again the indicator is not in itself diagnostic; it is merely an additional diagnostic guide which can be used in conjunction with all other features of the Vocabulary subtest, with all other features of the other subtests of the W-B, and with all other indications of the other tests.

INFORMATION

The Information subtest of the W-B consists of 25 items. All but one item can and should be answered by a simply stated fact. The exception is item 23, "What is a habeas corpus?" which requires a relatively elaborate explanation. The subtest is one of the group of essentially Verbal subtests to which Comprehension, Similarities, and Vocabulary also belong. Of all these subtests, Information stands closest to Vocabulary, both requiring the statement of a piece of information; of the two, Vocabulary is the simpler, as it requires the definition of generic terms, while Information refers rather to specific facts. Regrettably, the W-B Manual does not offer correlations of Vocabulary with other subtests, by means of which the close relation of Information and Vocabulary in a large normal population could be demonstrated.[10]

The Psychological Rationale of the Information Subtest. In our introductory section we devoted considerable space to a discussion of the nature and development of intelligence. We pointed out that it is a prerequisite for systematic clinical psychological practice to look upon intelligence as a function of a natural endowment unfolding in a process of maturation, in the course of which, if the functioning of the person is unhampered, he will undergo a process of picking up information—facts and knowledge of relationships—from his educational environment, which includes the home, the relatives, their social relationships, and the geographical-cultural location and its implications. We also dwelt upon the arrests and setbacks that this function may succumb to, and the forms of its deterioration. We pointed out that the educational environment yields in part, earlier or later, to schooling and that where schooling leaves off there may or may not

---

[10] [Wechsler (1958) gives such correlations for the WAIS, however. His Table 20, p. 100, shows that Information and Vocabulary are in fact correlated more highly with one another (.81) than either is with any other subtest, despite the extensive change in the nature of the Vocabulary test, which ought to make it *less* a test of information than the one in the W-B.—Ed.]

follow special cultural predilections to complement all that the educational environment and schooling have accomplished.

In analyzing and interpreting the Information subtest, the examiner should keep in mind these considerations more than in any other of the subtests. To absorb, out of the educational and cultural environment, information or factual data is a much simpler and more direct process than to pick up knowledge of relationships. Here endowment, wealth of the educational environment, degree of schooling and of cultural predilection come more clearly to expression than in any other subtest except Vocabulary. At the same time, impairment and arrest must set in early to have a prohibiting effect upon the accumulation of information. Furthermore, deterioration, or disorganization of function by acute disturbances, must be considerable before it will encroach significantly upon the availability—in the test situation—of information, once accumulated. It is true that information, like all of memory, can become momentarily unavailable as a result of a temporary inefficiency—that is, in a situation full of anxiety where the proper attitude, which mobilizes the memory of information, may be disturbed. Such impairments are usually spotty, however, and do not cover a large part of the field of information as reflected in the responses to the 25 questions of the Information subtest. Similar spotty impairments may also be expressions of generalized repressive trends. Moreover, when invited to come back to an item later whenever he wishes and supply an answer that he says is unavailable at the moment, a temporarily inefficient subject will frequently do so.

Thus, the nature of the Information subtest allows the hope that a careful analysis of it will give a clue to the endowment, early arrest of maturation, early setbacks, wealth of the educational environment, degree of schooling and cultural interests, and finally the severity of the present maladjustment—that is, whether its effects are merely temporary inefficiencies, or essential inefficiency of function which prohibits the making available in the testing situation of information possessed.

Another aspect of the responses to Information deserves discussion here. To get credit for the Information items requires the delivery into consciousness of material acquired in the past. In other words, Information implies a memory function. It is true that some of the items are so habituated that we no longer notice that memory plays a role in them (e.g., "Who is the President of the United States?"); but other items readily show the memory function involved. A dynamic theory of memory is relevant to the background of the Information subtest.

Let us start from test observations. Information items usually elicit either a quick response—right or wrong—or a response such as "I have it on the tip of my tongue . . . I know it so well . . . I just can't say it now." Though there are cases where a number of possibilities are stated, and the wrong one is not chosen, these doubt-laden performances are relatively rare.

What is the psychological meaning of these two types of performance? We submit that memory functioning is to only a small extent directable by conscious, voluntary effort. If the information is not readily available, forcing is in most cases futile. If not forced, the answer may later, either in effortless reflection or automatically, pop into consciousness. Freud elucidated the nature of such forgetting in *The Psychopathology of Everyday Life,* and showed that the forgotten information as well as the reason for its having been forgotten can be discovered in a process of free association. The Freudian theory of forgetting has bearing on memory functioning[11] in general and on the function underlying information in particular. The availability of information is dependent upon strivings and interests which deliver the information into consciousness. Such delivery occurs on proper stimulation—in this case, the Information question—only if no other overvalent conative factors press their ideational representations into consciousness at the expense of those relevant to the stimulus, and if no generalized difficulty—repression—impedes motives from delivering the necessary information.

Thus, information is either possessed by a subject or it is not, depending upon the wealth of the educational environment from which it is picked up, and the strength of motivational function which picks it up. Information once possessed is not available if a temporary inefficiency is caused by stray overvalent conative tendencies blocking those appropriate to the stimulus question from delivering the information into consciousness. Information once possessed may become available with difficulty, by reason of strong generalized repression which affects information even distantly related to the essential repressed material. Finally, information may become unavailable when, as in schizophrenic psychoses, meanings become generalized and instead of specific information we are given symbolic substitutes, parts for wholes, and so on.

Administration. In keeping with the views advanced above, we have adopted the rule that whenever a subject claims to know the answer but to be unable to give it at the moment, we credit it with a passing score if it is offered to us in the course of the same testing session. In fact the patient is encouraged: "Skip it now, and let me know if it comes to you later."

If the patient answers a question in an either-or fashion, we insist upon

---

11 [For further discussion of topics related to the rationale of Information, including the effect of repression on the availability of information and on its original registration, see Rapaport (1942a, Chapter V; 1951a, pp. 316, 538, 42f.), and Gillespie (1937).—Ed.]

his deciding between the two, and give the correct choice a passing credit.

In questions where a quantitative latitude is allowed—such as the one on the population of the United States—if the patient states, "I don't know," or "It would be only a guess," we always encourage, and in fact insist upon, guesses. Guesses, when correct, are usually taken to imply overcaution and doubt; when incorrect, they are sometimes incongruities— such as 100 billion people in the U.S.—rarely encountered in cases other than psychotics.

On questions where explanation is needed (What is a thermometer? What does the heart do?) or where alternatives, guesses, and answers for which latitude is allowed are given, responses should be recorded verbatim, and not merely scored as passed or failed. These responses, and their relation to each other, are often qualitatively revealing. Overmeticulous and doubt-laden answers, where first one and then another answer is given, are also significant and should be recorded verbatim. Where easy items are missed, or where the answers contain peculiar features, inquiry should be made to determine whether it is the result of a temporary inefficiency or the reflection of psychotic disorganization of memory and of thought processes in general.

Item Analysis. In our clinical work we found that the 25 items of the Information subtest fall roughly into three groups. The first group consists of items the answers to which are, in the course of unhampered normal maturation, picked up by everyone with fair natural endowment. The second group consists of items the answers to which are picked up either in a fairly rich educational environment, or in the course of schooling extending over the greater part of high school. The third group consists of items the answers to which are learned only by persons who, either by profession or by special cultural interests, come into touch with them. The relationship of the achievements on these three groups of the Information items should be carefully studied. The presence of striking failures in the first group easily reveals mental defectives. Poverty of educational environment shows up in marked failures in the second group, when the first group is passed well. Attainments based on cultural predilections manifest themselves in success in the third group. Successes on the second and third groups accompanied by many and striking failures on the first group, or queer failures on the second group, are rarely found except in psychoses. Isolated misses in the first part—especially if soon corrected by the subject upon questioning—when the rest of the test is well balanced and tallies with the actual education and background of the subject, is usually a sign of temporary inefficiency; this will be found mainly in anxious or repressing subjects.

The group of first degree of difficulty, the easy items, includes the following items: 2. Where is London? 3. How many pints make a quart?

4. From what is rubber obtained? 5. What is a thermometer? 6. How many weeks are there in a year? 7. What is the capital of Italy? 10. Who invented the airplane? 12. Where is Brazil? 16. What is the capital of Japan? 17. What does the heart do?

The second, the intermediate items, includes: 1. Who was President before [current incumbent]? 8. When is Washington's birthday? 9. What is the average height of American women? 11. How far is it from Paris to New York? 13. Who wrote Hamlet? 14. Who discovered the North Pole? 15. What is the Vatican? 18. What is the population of the United States? 19. Who wrote Huckleberry Finn? 20. Where is Egypt?

The third, the difficult items, includes: 21. What is the Koran? 22. Who wrote Faust? 23. What is a habeas corpus? 24. What is ethnology? 25. What is the Apocrypha?

The examiner should set up hypotheses as soon as failures or peculiar responses occur; and he should follow these hypotheses through the rest of the Information items, to ascertain whether these failures or peculiar responses were temporary inefficiencies, or impairments, or even indicators of mental deficiency. If the Information items do not themselves make for a decision on these hypotheses, the rest of the test may give the answer. In the meantime, however, Information items will give indications of the endowment, wealth of background, schooling, and cultural predilections of the subject.

DIAGNOSTIC SUGGESTIONS

(a) To produce two or more misses on the easy Information items is most characteristic of schizophrenics and depressives; hysterics and neurasthenics may do as poorly, however.

(b) When Information is three or more points below Vocabulary, involutional depression or deteriorated schizophrenia is a likely hypothesis if the case seems psychotic; in the neurotic realm, hysteria is the outstanding possibility. The psychotic cases are likely to suffer a general impairment of Verbal scores, while the general Verbal level of hysterics is well retained.

(c) A good Information (and Vocabulary) score, associated with impairment on other Verbal subtests, is common among unclassified schizophrenics and obsessive-compulsives. Such a pattern may also be present in psychotic depressives.

(d) A relatively well-retained Information two or more points above Vocabulary is consistent with simple schizophrenia or inhibited preschizophrenia.

(e) High weighted scores on Information are most often found in intellectualizing patients, such as obsessive-compulsives and overideational preschizophrenics.

COMPREHENSION

This subtest consists of 10 items. According to the scoring instructions given in Wechsler's Manual, a complete response to each item is credited with a score of 2, an incomplete response with a score of 1, and a failed response with a score of 0. The sum of the scores thus obtained is translated into a weighted score. These weighted scores are those entered in our scattergrams and used to obtain scatter measures. In that part of our discussion which will be devoted to the items of the subtest and to their qualitative analysis, scores referred to will be the raw scores; while in that part of the discussion devoted to scatter, scores referred to will be weighted scores. The Comprehension subtest will be dealt with in the following as one of the essentially Verbal subtests, the others being Information, Similarities, and Vocabulary.

The reader may find that in the following pages we appear to devote too much space to considerations which lie rather far from our practical topic. Our only justification is in our attempt to bring the test material into some direct relationship to the everyday psychological functioning of human beings. The relationships we shall point out are based on our experience, and may be questionable; it is hoped, however, that they will interest psychologists in pursuing such considerations further, and will contribute to making intelligence tests not merely a gauge of IQ, but an experimental tool in the understanding of the everyday functioning and thought processes of human beings. Specifically in connection with the Comprehension subtest do we wish to re-emphasize this point of view. The psychology of thinking tends to be a psychology of "logical thinking" or, at its best, a psychology of "concept formation"; though very important, both of these are only parts of the psychology of everyday thinking, and do not explain the functions underlying Comprehension. It is our hope that the considerations advanced here will contribute specifically to the understanding of Comprehension, and in general will serve as a rationale to the diagnostic use of intelligence tests. The rationale advanced at this stage of our knowledge may be incorrect; but pointing out the necessity of such a rationale cannot be incorrect. The major patterns of scatter discussed in the introduction to this chapter demonstrate that there is a system in scattering. The exploration of this system, like every exploration, has as a prerequisite certain hypotheses. These hypotheses may have to be replaced later, but without initial hypotheses the examiner will not be able to organize his findings around a systematic line of thought. Further observations may in turn substantiate or refute these hypotheses, leading to new and better ones.

The Psychological Rationale of the Comprehension Subtest. It will be maintained in the following that the function underlying the Comprehension subtest is related to the function of *judgment*. The concept of judgment is frequently used in psychiatric phraseology in the form, "judgment is impaired"; this is especially the case in connection with senile, paretic, and other nonspectacular syndromes of organic etiology—in other words, where the psychiatric syndrome is characterized not by obvious and tangible symptoms but rather by an inadequacy of functioning little noticed by the subject himself, although it seriously encroaches upon his everyday existence. In the middle field of functional psychoses and of neuroses, the concept of judgment is not so generally applied, but is frequently replaced by the term "reality testing"—in other words, appropriate understanding of and reaction to reality. The concept of judgment is used also as a common-sense concept, as when we characterize someone as "a man of unusually good judgment." In such statements we do not refer merely to his intellectual attainments, nor merely to his emotional qualities as revealed in his interpersonal relationships.

It appears that judgment is one of many concepts that are used without their having attained sufficient conceptual clarification. Judgment evidently refers to a function on the borderline of intellectual and emotional functions. Though we should be inclined to state flatly that there are no emotional functions without intellectual components, and vice versa, we are accustomed to label some functions as intellectual, inasmuch as they come to consciousness mainly in intellectual terms; we label others as emotional, inasmuch as they come to consciousness more in emotional terms. Judgment appears to refer to the emotionally relevant use of one's *assets* in regard to the real situation, where intellectual and logical correctness, though implied, play a rather subordinate role. The terms "proper" and "appropriate" are other terms commonly used to indicate actions brought about by good judgment.

One might argue that good judgment is the outcome of infallibly logical thinking and conduct. It is difficult to refute such an argument. One can only reply that a conscious logical process that could prepare an action of good judgment would have to consider such an infinite multiplicity of facts and conditions pertaining to the situation that the temporal factor alone would make it impossible. Rather, the case would appear to be one in which a proper emotional orientation brings to consciousness and to execution, out of the multiplicity of logical possibilities, an action that is labeled as one of good judgment. The clinical psychologist accustomed to considerations of gestalt psychology will be at an advantage—especially when not bound by the intellectualistic terms of that school—in evaluating these problems. Not infrequently people say, "If I had just had a little more time to think it over, I would never have done that." Life, however, does not always give time allowances, and neither do psychological tests; persons of good judgment act immediately—or refrain from action—according to their own unwritten code of conduct, which is primarily emotional in nature. It is true that in some persons, especially when highly intelligent and compulsive, sharpness of logic may partially replace sound judgment; but in few cases is this successful. The majority become doubt-ridden, see too many possibilities, and the choice is very difficult for them. Good judgment is rather the efficient utilization of knowledge in a manner tuned to the whole situation.

Inasmuch as the concept of "judgment" is still undefined, we shall not attempt here to prove that the Comprehension subtest items measure it. We claim only that it is useful to think of the Comprehension subtest in the way we think of judgment. The Comprehension items, like situations requiring judgment, demand more than possession and activation of information: they demand meaningful and emotionally relevant activation, selection, and organization of those facts and relationships known to the subject. Some of them demand also a delaying of first impulses. In the question, "What should you do if, while sitting in the movies, you were the first person to discover a fire?" the impulsive response, "Holler 'fire!' " must be suppressed if a good response is to be achieved. Many self-controlling impulsive people will begin, "I wouldn't holler 'fire,' but rather . . ."; others, who are less contained, will say: "I know one shouldn't holler 'fire' but I am afraid that's what I'd do . . ." The Comprehension items, like situations calling for judgment, also require more than merely a delay of impulse and enumeration of possibilities. To the question, "Why does the state require people to get a license in order to be married?" references to license revenue, legality of children, health examination, age requirements, or prevention of venereal disease do not improve the response; rather, they call for an appropriate selection.[12]

The information possessed and the relationships known must be so structured as to meet the questions' requirements. This is thus a complex function, which can be expected to be neither so refractory to impairment as Vocabulary nor so highly developed as Vocabulary in the intellectualizing clinical groups. As a matter of fact, the defense of intellectualization

[12] [This sense of what is appropriate, of which one of many possible answers is the expected one, is a subtle matter to measure, but one that is clinically most relevant, since *inappropriateness* is a hallmark of schizophrenia. It is so difficult to define the principles that underlie common sense because they are largely determined by convention—by social consensus. For this reason, Comprehension is vulnerable to social withdrawal, negativism, rebellion, or other trends interfering with contact with and acceptance of social reality.—Ed.]

may be considered to have been developed to replace judgment because of the presence of doubt.

The vulnerability of the Comprehension subtest to impairment can be readily understood from another point of view. While in an Information problem the answer is known or not known, in a Comprehension question a myriad of items of information and knowledge are activated—brought into or near consciousness—by the question. Thus not merely the grasp of information and knowledge but also their proper selection and emphasis can become impaired. Information can be learned and retained; but balance of the varied factors that go into good comprehension and judgment can be acquired progressively only by prototype and interpersonal experience, and cannot be taught. The relationships of information, knowledge, and comprehension here discussed have played a considerable role in giving many an educator a feeling of the futility of all education.[13]

These discussions, however, may give a distorted view of the relationship of the Comprehension subtest to the function of judgment. To obtain a more adequate view of this relationship, it should be remembered that good judgment, once developed, may achieve a stereotyped verbal form which will survive long after the function has been distorted and rendered ineffective by maladjustment. In these cases, passing Comprehension responses are empty skins of a once live function of judgment. Such cases are quite frequent, especially in chronic schizophrenic conditions which are characterized clinically as "able to put up a good front." To the development of such an apparent good front, commonplace stereotypes which society creates for itself contribute more than is obvious. A very characteristic stereotype of the contemporary American scene is the response to the question, "Why should people pay taxes?"—"To support the government." Another factor which frequently contributes to the maintenance of this kind of good front is a strict moralistic education, which communicates as dogmatic information what otherwise would be a result of judgment; thus the person's attitude toward judgments renders them "objective laws" which become unchangeable. This is not infrequently the effect of conservative Catholic education. Poor judgment will be manifested by such persons mainly in the form of inflexibility.

In the following we shall attempt to indicate in which groups of patients judgment is impaired and in which groups it is well retained. It is not enough, however, to estimate only quantitative trends. Much can be learned about the patient by a qualitative analysis of the answers, especially of the unscored aspects of them.

The examiner will segregate in his thinking those persons who answer

[13] It is worth while in this connection to remember the Socratic discussions with Sophists on the "teachability of virtue."

the questions squarely, and those who amass a great variety of possibilities. The former, whether of poor or good judgment, will differ by their decisiveness from the latter, who see too many possibilities and cannot make up their minds. The examiner will segregate those who, without hesitancy, reply, "I would yell 'fire,' " and those who say, "I certainly should not yell 'fire,' I hope I would not yell 'fire'; I don't know what I would do; I know I *shouldn't* yell 'fire,' but I am not certain that I wouldn't." The former probably will be the impulse-ridden persons; the latter, obsessional persons whose "better judgment" is in constant struggle with their impulses.

The examiner will distinguish between persons who "keep away from bad company because it is a bad influence"; those who do not want to keep away from bad company because they consider themselves not so weak as to yield to bad influence, or because one can have fun with or "learn a lot" from them; and those who consider bad company as uninteresting or uninspiring. In making such a segregation, he will again differentiate between persons of judgment, persons of sophistication of a kind that encroaches upon judgment, and persons in whose judgment—however rigid it may be —the vestiges of a moral code are effective.

Administration. We have already stated that the responses to Comprehension questions may be merely verbal stereotypes, instead of expressions of good judgment. This obliges the examiner to watch every response carefully; and wherever a peculiar verbalization occurs, or the structure of the response is unusual, he should inquire into what the subject meant, in order to discover whether an utterly inadequate judgment hides behind a well-sounding stereotype. Thus, one schizophrenic responded to the question on movie-fire as follows: "I'd shout out 'fire' and then notify the management." This might have been considered a mixture of good judgment and impulsiveness. The inquiry, however, gave evidence in another direction: the patient said, "I'd notify the management so that the ushers could tell it to those who didn't hear me."

Wherever a response is failed in a not too usual manner, inquiry is also in place for two reasons: first, it will yield material on the basis of which the degree of distortion of judgment (neurotic—psychotic) can be estimated; and second, it will familiarize the tester with the thought processes of the maladjusted person. Only the accumulation of such material will lead to a psychology of thinking which will be more than an investigation of logical thinking.

It is important with every subtest to take verbatim notes of the subject's verbalization; and this is particularly so in regard to Comprehension. Without full notes, a restudy and qualitative evaluation is impossible.

Concerning scoring, our experience shows that no amount of scoring samples and instructions will embrace the enormous variety of responses.

It will be necessary for the tester to use his own judgment. We proceed by equalizing scores; that is, if three responses each barely suffice for a score of 2, we give two of them this score and the weakest of the three a score of 1. We use this principle generally. Nonsensical response features are sufficient for us to score as 0 a response which otherwise would have passed. If inquiry into a passing initial response goes beyond what the W-B Manual prescribes, it should never affect the scoring.

Item Analysis. We divided the Comprehension items into two groups: easy items (Nos. 1, 2, 3, 4, 5, 7, and 8) and difficult ones (Nos. 6, 9, and 10).

Questions in the first group presuppose not an extensive education, but an unhampered receptiveness to everyday experiences; the second group implies some breadth of information and appreciation of relationships. In the group of easy items there are two which, at first glance, do not seem to fit the characteristics of this group. These are: "Why are laws necessary?" and "Why should people pay taxes?" These questions appear to be more abstract and complicated than the rest, and do not refer as directly to practical life experiences. Nevertheless, a survey of the answers indicates that the average, normal American has a pat answer to these questions. Moreover, these stereotyped answers are apparently as much a matter of commonplace information as any direct life experience is.

A complete miss on one of the easy items is most characteristic of schizophrenics and depressive psychotics. Such complete failures are very rare in neurotics and normals, but may sometimes occur as a result of temporary inefficiency. Here again it should be emphasized that one cannot rely on a single indication, whether in the item breakdown, such as that given here, or in analysis of a full subtest score; but the piling up of evidence in the eyes of the careful examiner will indicate in a great percentage of cases the lines on which the diagnosis must be drawn.

The first group of seven questions—even by the mere form of presentation in several items, "What should you do?"—makes the judgmental character of the Comprehension subtest and its reference to life situations reasonably clear. Failure on one or several of these seven questions must be considered an indication of impaired judgment. Whether this impairment is a general one, or one to be referred to as temporary inefficiency is a matter that must be decided by the examiner in each case, considering the quality of the failure, the total number of items failed in this group, and the quality of the responses to the other group. Thus, bizarre verbalizations and judgments on any of the Comprehension items will indicate that the failure is probably not one of temporary inefficiency, but is to be viewed as pathological. Differentiation from low level of intelligence or feeble-mindedness is achieved by the observation that subjects who fail on one or several of the seven easy items, and pass any of the more difficult items, are most likely not feeble-minded. Passing difficult and failing easy items is one of the important diagnostic indications on the Comprehension subtest.

Failure on the second group of three questions, as stated above, does not necessarily imply impairment of judgment; persons coming from certain educational and social settings may be prevented by limited knowledge from adequately answering some of these questions. But a majority of 0 scores even on these questions should raise the possibility of the presence of impaired judgment. In order to evaluate failures on this second part, one will usually turn to the total score on the Comprehension group, and compare it with other scores such as the Vocabulary or the Information scores, or the mean of the Verbal subtest scores.

Comprehension and Information. The outstanding relationship of the Comprehension subtest is to the Information subtest. The first reason for discussing this relationship is found in our discussion of the psychology of judgment. There we pointed out the relationship of information and judgment; it would follow from this that intelligence is harmoniously structured if information and its appropriate application in reality—that is to say, judgment—are equally well developed. The second reason for discussing this relationship is that Comprehension and Information are usually the first two subtests given; thus the understanding of their relationship gives the examiner a direction of expectancy for the rest of the test. In this connection it is important to note that Information is about as stable as Vocabulary; and where Vocabulary suffers under maladjustment—as in simple schizophrenia—Information may stand up.

In order to have a proper perspective for the evaluation of the relationship of Comprehension and Information in our material, let us first inspect the relation of these two subtests in Wechsler's standardization population. The correlation coefficient of these subtests is .68 to .71 for the standardization population, which is among the very highest correlations in Wechsler's tables. Furthermore, if we turn our attention to the mean scores of these two subtests in the different age groups of the standardization population— as represented in Wechsler's Table 40 (1939a, p. 214)—we also find a remarkable parallel between the two. Up to about 10 years of age, Comprehension scores are higher and Information lags somewhat; from 11 years on to 16-19 years, Information tends to be higher, though the two scores become progressively equalized; and a remarkable equality is achieved above that age. Thus, both the correlation coefficient and the score comparison lead us to expect that disparity of Information and Comprehension scores will prove an indicator of psychopathology; and, specifically, that a greater lagging of Comprehension behind Information than is shown by the standardization population will be indicative of impaired judgment.[14]

Clinical experience indicates that Comprehension is impaired in all psychoses, and drops below Vocabulary and even below Information, which tend to stand up. Furthermore, obsessional persons tend to behave like psychotics in this relationship; while hysteroid neurotics tend to have Information impaired, which presumably is referable to repression. Therefore, a great drop of the Comprehension score below the Information score raises the suspicion of psychosis, or of neurosis with obsessional features. In psychoses, Information dropping below Comprehension is an involutional or chronic paranoid indication; in neuroses, it is a hysteroid indication referable to repression.

DIAGNOSTIC SUGGESTIONS

(a) Complete failures on any (especially on more than one) of the seven easy Comprehension items are most characteristic of schizophrenics and psychotic depressives. Such misses are almost nonexistent in normal persons (except for impulsive "Yell 'fire!' " failures on No. 2), and are to be considered indicative of impaired judgment. If easy items are failed and difficult items are passed, the question of psychosis arises.

(b) A Comprehension score two or more points below the Information score indicates that one's knowledge is not being used effectively in dealing with problems, and therefore is indicative of impaired judgment (unless Comprehension is at a good level and Information atypically high). This pattern is characteristic of psychotics and, to a lesser extent, obsessive-compulsive neurotics. Hysterics tend to have a Comprehension score higher than their impaired Information score.

(c) A Comprehension score three or more points below the Vocabulary score (or below the mean of the other verbal subtests: Information, Similarities, and Vocabulary) is characteristic of schizophrenics (especially chronic and deteriorated cases) and depressives (especially psychotic cases). Even preschizophrenics, who are in general well preserved, tend to have impaired judgment as estimated by this measure. Normal and neurotic persons (with the exception of obsessive-compulsives) have relatively few such cases (only about 10%).

(d) Great positive Comprehension scatter (two or more points superior to Vocabulary) is not to be expected in depressives or schizophrenics; it is most likely to occur in neurotics and normal persons. Among schizophrenics, if Comprehension is well retained, the case is most likely to be a *paranoid* schizophrenic.

[14] [In the WAIS, the correlation is again .70 (Wechsler, 1958). Moreover, in factor analyses, these two consistently turn up in the same factor, which Wechsler calls "verbal comprehension."—Ed.]

SIMILARITIES

The Similarities subtest of the W-B consists of 12 items. Successful performance on these items implies *verbal concept formation*. Responses on a high conceptual level merit a raw score of 2, those on a lower conceptual level a score of 1, and failure a score of 0. The Similarities subtest belongs to the group of essentially Verbal subtests. It stands somewhere between Information and Comprehension as far as its vulnerability is concerned, and consequently it is diagnostically very significant, showing neither a generalized impairment nor a general refractoriness to impairment.

The Similarities subtest is also one of the three concept-formation tests of our battery, and will be dealt with again in the section on the diagnostic testing of concept formation. It is necessary, however, to present here some considerations concerning concept formation underlying responses to the Similarities subtest and advance some reasons for and some consequences of so doing. A general discussion of the psychology of concept formation will be found in Chapter 5 below.

The Psychological Rationale of Similarities. Concept formation is the function which informs the human being about the "belonging together" of the objects and events of his everyday world. Each word with which one names an object implies an automatic concept formation, a placing of the object where it belongs in one's world. Every percept implies concept formation, because to identify anything implies determining where it belongs. Consequently every thought process, the most simple and the most complicated, implies concept formation in the sense that our looking upon, and mode of discerning, thought processes is such that concept formation always appears to be one aspect of them. Concept formation as a conscious, voluntary, effortful process is experienced in all systematic scientific endeavor; but even here it may occur in an automatic, effortless manner in the form of hunches, experience, and so on. In everyday thought processes, where not too much of the unknown or the emotionally difficult is encountered, concept formation is mainly automatic and effortless.

Affective orientations and attitudes help to build the world of the individual—that is, structure it in patterns of conceptual coherence, into which he organizes new experience automatically when the patterns are not disrupted by the encroachment of maladjustment. Symbolism and physiognomic characters (Werner, 1940, Chapter IX) are the most primitive patterns, and here the affective nature of conceptual organization is clearly perceptible. Symbols, physiognomic impressions, and most of the patterns of belonging together and meaning that are characteristic of unconscious processes (Freud, 1900, Chapter VII) are organized around affects. The development of conscious thinking, however, tends to replace these idiosyncratic, affective conceptual organizations by verbal abstract and communicable ones, common to the social group and attuned to reality. Yet this process of replacement never exorcises the idiosyncratic, affective origin of conceptualization. The assumption that concepts are commonly accepted is shattered when one puts questions like those of the Similarities subtest to many normal subjects, or inquires—as in the Sorting Test, to be discussed later—which of a set of objects they would consider as belonging together.

Concept formation is one of the aspects of every thought process, and experience shows that it is one of the main channels through which maladjustment encroaches upon intellection. To state this in more operational terms, the effect of maladjustment on intellection can be discovered earlier in concept formation than in other aspects of thought processes. In *verbal* concept formation, however, impairment may be disguised, for reasons soon to be seen.

The pairs of objects whose similarity must be conceived are to be each considered as constituting a conceptual *realm*, the conceptual content[15] of which must be discovered and stated. There are several qualitatively different levels of concept formation on which the content of these realms can be defined. We shall distinguish here only three: the concrete, the functional, and the conceptual.

Let us take, for instance, the pair *dog—lion*. A subject whose thinking is entirely concrete and who is unable to make abstractions, and the subject for whom *lion* is merely a carrier of threatening physiognomic quality, will refuse to answer the test question, stating that the two are not similar. Subjects who are concretistic, though not to this extreme, state that dogs and lions are similar because both have legs, or tails, or hair. Here concrete detail is taken as the content of the realm, although such details are inessential if we deal with concepts of any complexity.[16] In this response, a great number of common concrete features of dogs and lions are neglected, and not even a complete enumeration of all such details would "cover" or communicate the concept. Besides being too limited, a concrete definition is also too inclusive: tables too have legs, people have hair, and so on. As a matter of fact, the concrete definition in some cases may be pathologically inclusive, as in the response that dogs and lions are similar because both

---

15 For a detailed definition of the terms *realm* and *content* of concepts see pp. 191ff. The *realm* is all the objects to which the concept pertains (e.g., all tables); the *content* is what all the objects of the *realm* have in common (the "tableness").

16 The degree to which a concrete detail can become the essential content of a concept is necessarily relative. Thus, for a statistician persons may become differentiated merely in terms of income-tax blanks—for him a very concrete and single characteristic. If he attempts to use this criterion outside of his office ("every inch a statistician") he will inevitably be dubbed "queer."

have cells. Such generalization is characteristic of schizophrenic conceptualization. Concrete definitions are therefore inadequate.

Another way to define the similarity of a pair such as *wagon—bicycle* is to say, "You ride them both." This definition refers to a function of the objects; that they have other functions, and conceptually more general characteristics, is not taken into consideration by such a definition. Although it is possible in some cases for a functional concept to be completely adequate, in general it will be partial and not exhaustive.

A third way to define the similarity of dogs and lions is to say that both are animals. This is the abstract-conceptual level of concept formation: that is, the subsuming of items of the realm in question under a general term, the complex content of which is so clearly defined that it is the common treasure of our vocabulary and thinking. Yet not even on this level is there an unequivocally specific answer to the question, "How are they similar?" The responses "mammals," "quadrupeds," "carnivora" are just as much on the abstract-conceptual level as is "animals." In other words, a degree of freedom is present in concept formation in the Similarities subtest. The response "animals" is a relatively lax one, but implies common sense; the responses "mammals" and "carnivora" imply sophistication, ostentatious show of information, or overmeticulousness, but each is within normal limits, and indicates character trends rather than the presence of maladjustment.

A cursory survey shows that the norms Wechsler gives for scoring the Similarities items—in other words, the enumeration of what types of response should be scored 2, 1, or 0—in general follow the sequence: conceptual, functional, and concrete level; though not infrequently some concretistic responses will obtain a score of 1, and some functional definitions will obtain a score of 2. As scoring norms are established by statistical frequency, we may look upon this sequence of scores as evidence in support of our theoretical differentiation of conceptualization into these three levels. The exceptions to the sequence of scores may be considered as the statistical reflection partly of the difficulty of some of the Similarities items, and partly of the fact that the abstract-conceptual level of concept formation is the ideal rather than the general rule for the cross section of the population.

No one of these levels alone dominates a test. Even though one or another level may predominate, the more difficult a question becomes and the less firmly established the subject's level of concept formation is—or the more maladjustment has weakened an established abstract-conceptual level—the more frequently do we find functional and concretistic responses cropping up. The examiner sometimes obtains, to the *dog—lion* pair, such a response as, "They are four-legged, mammalian, carnivorous animals covered with hair." Such definitions not only are redundant, but also show that on the abstract-conceptual level functional and concrete concepts survive and are relied upon, presumably because confidence in the abstract concept is absent. The compulsive meticulousness of such definitions is essentially the expression of the weakening of the abstractive and generalizing abilities of the subject, and points up the presence of pathological doubt, vacillation, overintellectualization, and indecision in the clinical picture of the subject.

Where responses are obtained to the Similarities items, the verbalization and content can be scrutinized and understood. But where the items are flatly failed ("I don't know," or "They are not similar"), the basis of the failure must be inferred partly from the specific nature of the item and partly from the general level of conceptualization manifested in the other responses. To give a foundation for such inferences, we shall discuss some characteristics of the 12 Similarities items.

There are considerable differences among the conceptual demands made by each of the 12 Similarities items. For instance, *orange—banana, coat—dress, dog—lion* are pairs to which the abstract-conceptual responses have become a verbal convention. But the similarity of *air—water* or *egg—seed* must be more or less inferred on the basis of information; while those of *wood—alcohol, praise—punishment,* and *fly—tree* require technical information, a considerable degree of ability for abstraction, or both.

First, it will be obvious that such relations as *orange—banana: fruit,* and *dog—lion: animal* have achieved such a degree of verbal coherence or conventionalization that these abstract-conceptual responses are not sufficient evidence of a high level of concept formation. In fact, these responses may survive as empty shells even when concept formation is disorganized. As in Comprehension, so in Similarities verbalization has the tendency to survive the function that created it; thus, the examiner must be cautious, because in *all* Similarities responses he may be dealing with a well-retained front covering a disorganized function.

Second, where items to which conceptual response has become verbal convention are answered on a functional or concrete level, either original poverty of concept formation or impairment of verbal concepts due to maladjustment is present.

Third, some of the items can be acceptably responded to on a functional level (as *orange—banana: You eat both; coat—dress: You wear both*); but a functional response to others *(egg—seed: You eat both)* cannot obtain a passing score. Similarly with concretistic responses: *orange—banana: peels,* is scored as passing; but *egg—seed: round,* is not. Such failures should be understood as evidence of the subject's clinging to either a functional or a concrete level.

The differences between the conceptual demands of the Similarities items may be illustrated by other instances. It is rather easy to respond to *wood—alcohol* on a functional level: *they burn.* It is not so easy to give an acceptable answer on a functional level to *praise—punishment.* Here the response *methods of discipline* or *motivations* can hardly be replaced by adequate functional descriptions, and a concretistic definition is altogether unacceptable. It is possible to give an acceptable concretistic response to *coat—dress: they are made from cloth;* but it is almost impossible to give one to *poem—statue.* The examiner accordingly should try to see what type of response a subject gives to the items he passes, in order to infer the reason for his failures. Subjects who get by with concretistic definitions will fall down on items where such definitions are difficult or impossible. An analysis of the responses from this point of view is quite fruitful, and gives a qualitative understanding of the nature of the patient's verbal concept formation.

It should be re-emphasized that the Similarities subtest refers to verbal concepts and can be responded to merely by virtue of verbal convention, and on several levels of conceptualization. Thus it is understandable that in general Similarities will keep up in spite of maladjustment, even though other forms of concept formation may have already become impaired.

Administration. Subjects who state that they do not know the answer to an item should be encouraged to think about it longer, but should not be pressed unreasonably hard. In cases where the other subtests or other Similarities items show queernesses, however, we usually insist upon the subject's making a response, because these are the very points where material revealing psychopathology usually appears.

Subjects who give differences instead of similarities must be held to giving a response in terms of similarities. Adults who are *not able* to understand that the question is one of similarities are usually feeble-minded, and those who *refuse* to give similarities are likely to be psychotic.

If a subject states there is no similarity, caution is in place; negativism or projective-paranoid trends may be thus indicated. Our practice is to explain to the subject directly that our asking for a similarity implies that similarities exist.

Every examiner meets subjects who insist on pinning the examiner down to "just what he means by similarities." We consistently refuse to give any explanation on this point, assuming from experience that the question is clearly understood by these subjects and that the inquiry is an expression of doubt and/or suspiciousness.

When a subject gives several responses at once—especially if these responses are of varying importance, and on varying conceptual levels—we usually ask the subject to indicate the essential similarity. This becomes the basis of our scoring, and we lessen the score only if some of the other alternatives are decidedly poor.

Here again it can hardly be overemphasized that verbatim recording of the total verbalization of the subject for every item is important, because frequently the examiner must fall back upon the verbalizations in order to be able properly to evaluate the subject's total achievement on verbal concepts.

Item Analysis. Clinical experience suggests a division of the 12 Similarities items into three subgroups, according to the degree of conventionality of the correct response, the degree of specific information implied, and the degree of abstract conceptualizing ability required. The easy items are: 1. Orange—banana. 2. Coat—dress. 3. Dog—lion. 4. Wagon—bicycle. 5. Daily paper—radio. 8. Eye—ear. The second group, items of intermediate difficulty, includes: 6. Air—water. 9. Egg—seed. 10. Poem—statue. The difficult items are: 7. Wood—alcohol. 11. Praise—punishment. 12. Fly—tree.

Additional information is obtained if one considers in each group the item which shows the greatest frequency of failures. We found that in the easy group it is item No. 8 *(eye—ear);* in the intermediate group item No. 6 *(air—water);* and in the difficult group item No. 11 *(praise—punishment).* The examiner should keep these in mind, and even in passing responses should look for the subject's difficulties in answering them. The difficulty with all three items is that though the terms are only too well-known to the subject, their similarity lies on a quite abstract level. Thus the subject is usually tempted to describe them, or to deny their similarity by pointing out their differences.

The theoretical import of this point is that it is not unknown to these subjects that *eye* and *ear* are parts of the body or organism, and it is not usually a lack of knowledge that underlies failure, but rather the difficulty of achieving an adequate generalization. It is true that in *air—water* proper information can be—at least theoretically—helpful, and subjects frequently will say that "both have hydrogen," in an effort to replace their inadequacy of conceptualization by equally inadequate information. Persons of great intelligence and wealth of information will sometimes state, "They both contain oxygen, but that cannot be the similarity between them. That cannot be what you want." The most obvious and simple response, "Both are necessities of life," is known to all but unavailable to most subjects because the way to it lies in proper abstract conceptual analysis. Concept formation is thus not simply a matter of information or of good logic. Information may be present, and yet the proper conceptual response may still not be obtained; logic may be operating, and yet be errant if the point to which it is applied is not correctly chosen. Passing responses to Similarities are dependent either upon well-automatized verbal convention or, where the items are more difficult, upon an appropriate organization of attitudes which, in turn, organize the available information and conceptual coherence patterns in the most economical way, striking a balance between concretistically narrow and loosely wide concepts in establishing the appropriate conceptual content.

Thus, concept formation is based on something that transcends formal information and formal logic. Since the item analysis shows that it is not a lack of information or of logic that is the basis of failures and low scores on Similarities, the examiner can with assurance conclude that, if failures occur, there is a disturbance of the automatic balance in thought processes that allows for good mobilization of attitudes summoning up information and logic in an appropriate manner; and that maladjustment is encroaching upon concept formation. This is the true diagnostic significance of verbal concept formation, though the examiner must remember that impaired concept formation may be disguised by verbal convention.

DIAGNOSTIC SUGGESTIONS

(a) Failures on the easy Similarities items are most widespread in depressive psychotics and simple schizophrenics. To a lesser extent, these failures occur in unclassified and paranoid schizophrenics, and severe neurotic depression. Few or no misses occur in neurotics and normals.

(b) A Similarities score three points below Vocabulary is suggestive of psychosis [or brain damage], a scatter of five points strongly so, either full-blown schizophrenia or depression.

(c) If a patient seems clinically depressed and his Similarities is three or more points below Vocabulary, psychotic depression is likely, especially if Similarities is also below the Verbal mean; if it is a point or so *above* Vocabulary, neurotic depression is likely.

(d) Paranoid trends are often indicated (except in chronic and deteriorated schizophrenics) by well-retained Similarities, rising above Vocabulary and the Verbal mean.

(e) High weighted scores (14 or better) are most likely to occur in neurotics, especially in intellectualizers even of psychotic degree (such as those with overideational preschizophrenia or paranoid condition). High scores are rare in depressive psychotics, deteriorated paranoid schizophrenics, and precariously adjusted normal persons of poor cultural background, of which Similarities is a more sensitive indicator than any of the other essentially verbal subtests.

ATTENTION AND CONCENTRATION: DIGIT SPAN AND ARITHMETIC

Comparison with the Verbal Subtests. In this section we shall advance some theoretical considerations which pertain to the two subtests—Digit

Span and Arithmetic—to which the following sections will be devoted. In the W-B [and the WAIS] these are subsumed under the Verbal subtests. They differ radically from the four essentially Verbal subtests thus far discussed, however. First, they are by far more vulnerable to maladjustment than the other Verbal subtests. Second, in these subtests verbalization plays a quite different role than in the others. In Vocabulary, Comprehension, Information, and Similarities, the words carry the essential meaning of the response; in Digit Span and Arithmetic this is by no means true. The real distinction between the significance of the verbalization on the other Verbal subtests and of that on the two here segregated is hard to define at present. It appears that in the first four subtests more *verbalization,* and in the latter two subtests more *vocalization,* is involved. In other words, it seems that in the essentially Verbal subtests the essence of the response is the communication of content which is inseparable from the verbalization which communicates it. This is not the case for Digit Span, where visual and/or auditory imagery may replace verbal imagery, and where no content specific to the subject or to the verbalization is communicated. It is also not the case for Arithmetic, where formal relationships, for some persons in the form of abstract spatial images, are the content and are not necessarily bound up with verbal images and verbal communication.

General Considerations. In our opinion, one can most fully exploit intelligence tests neither by stating merely that the patient was poor on some and good on other subtests, nor by trying to connect directly the impairments of certain subtest scores with certain clinical-nosological categories; but rather only by attempting to understand and describe the psychological functions whose impairment or change brings about the impairment of scores. One reason is that there is no one-to-one relationship between any subtest achievement and the nosological category to which the maladjustment impairing that achievement belongs. Every nosological category is an isolation—in a sense arbitrary—of a complicated, dynamic equilibrium of psychological functions. Every subtest score—and especially the relationship of every subtest score to the other subtest scores—has a multitude of determinants. If we are able to establish the main psychological function underlying the achievements on the subtests, and to infer from the impairment of the achievement an impairment or change of the function underlying the achievement, then we can hope to construct a complex psychodynamic and structural picture out of the interrelationships of these achievements and impairments of functions; this in turn can be brought into relationship with a specific clinical picture, conceived of as a variant of the typical picture of a nosological category. It is on the basis of such considerations that we are in a position to draw diagnostic conclusions from the relationships of achievements and impairments on the subtests of an intelligence test.

This is the reason for devoting so much space to even a tentative construction of the rationale of the functions underlying subtest achievements. The present section will be especially extensive because it deals with functions which are neglected and in disrepute in current psychology, although they were considered to be of great significance in the early Wundtian and Titchenerian days.[17] No effort will be made to clarify the relation of the concepts of *attention* and *concentration* here advanced to their historical predecessors; but no identity is presumed.

The Definitions of Attention and Concentration. Attention and concentration are ill-defined concepts. We propose to give here a working definition of them without attempting to penetrate to a full theoretical clarification of their nature.[18]

(a) Attention. If a person can devote himself freely to obtaining impressions, if he can read so that he goes with the stream of the book without being carried into other streams of thought or fantasy, if he can listen to and absorb a lecture without effort and without suddenly discovering that he has been "absent," if he can participate in the flow of a conversation without again and again discovering that he has missed a part of it, then we may call his attention excellent and unimpaired.

This type of attention is to be distinguished from what frequently goes under the same name. There is a difference between "absorbing freely without effort" and "being absorbed," between "going with the stream" and "being carried away by the stream." In being absorbed or carried away, the interests or affects or strivings of the person are intensely mobilized; in what is referred to here as attention, this need not be the case. Many persons who are able to be absorbed or carried away are unable to attend.

In the terminology of psychoanalytic psychology, one might formulate this state of affairs as follows: attention corresponds to the ready mobilizability of energies that are not specifically tied up with any particular affect, emotion, interest, or drive, but are at the free disposal of the ego to be utilized in thinking and in dealing with reality.[19] Being absorbed or being

[17] [This statement is far less true today than it was when it was originally written. Indeed, this book's impact may have been one of a number of historical factors that have brought about an awakened interest in the "mentalistic" concepts discussed here. See Holt (1964a, b).—Ed.]

[18] [For further discussion of these concepts, and a guide to further relevant literature, see Rapaport (1951a), index entries under Attention and Concentration.—Ed.]

[19] [These (hypothetical) energies freely available to the ego Rapaport later (e.g., 1959a, 1959b, 1960a) identified with hypercathexis or attention cathexis. The corresponding term used in the first edition of the present work was "not-specifically-

carried away is also a receptive form of psychological activity, but is characterized by the fact that the material is being taken in by virtue of its appeal to a strong specific affect, drive, or interest of the subject. In other words, it is much more a selective and less flexible type of receptiveness than is attention; and this selectiveness hampers the intake of everything that does not have an affinity to these selecting factors.

Attention is considered here an effortless, passive, unhampered contact with outside reality—a free receptiveness. This free receptiveness appears to be hampered if the subject's affects and anxieties are not well controlled and get out of balance.

The hypotheses that underlie this view of attention are: (1) all psychological energies derive from instinctual sources;[20] (2) part of these— affects, drives, strivings, impulses—bear the mark of their instinctual origin, and these will be herein referred to as drive cathexes; (3) another part of the psychological energies, having lost in the course of development the marks of their instinctual origin, become freely available to the ego for its purposes, and these will be herein referred to as hypercathexes; (4) attention depends upon the strength of the ego, by which is meant that the drive cathexes are kept in balance and control, harmonizing with and not encroaching upon the ego's functions, nor demanding that it employ its hypercathexes to curb them.

From these hypotheses, it becomes understandable that not only unbalanced affects and anxieties, but also overvalent (emotionally overloaded) ideas—such as fantasies, obsessions, delusions—may be able to encroach upon attention, because in them the ideas are bound up with drive cathexes.

(b) Concentration. In terms of the above hypotheses, concentration would mean employing hypercathexes in order to control the drive cathexes, and to keep out of consciousness the ideational representations of the latter which interfere with attending.

In contrast to attention, concentration may be characterized as an active[21] relationship to outside reality. When one finds himself unable to

---

deployed energies"; the contrasting term, "specifically-deployed energies," referred to instinctual drive energies. I was reluctant to change this terminology because I have tried not to alter the text so far as it represents the status of Rapaport's theoretical thinking in the mid-1940's. But the replaced terms are cumbersome and involve an incorrect metaphorical usage; moreover, Rapaport never used them in this way again. In the end, therefore, I replaced "not-specifically-deployed energies" by hypercathexes, and "specifically-deployed energies" by drive cathexes.—Ed.]

[20] [Rapaport was later (1960a) less certain of this proposition, which leans on the hypothesis of neutralization of drive energies (Hartmann, 1939). For a cogent argument against neutralization, see White (1963); for a case against energy concepts altogether, see Holt (1965a, 1967a).—Ed.]

[21] [For Rapaport's later views on activity and passivity, see Rapaport (1953b); for tangentially relevant considerations on the "relationship to outside reality," see Rapaport (1957c).—Ed.]

take in freely what the flow of a book, a lecture, or a conversation brings to him, he may exert a conscious effort to keep out of consciousness all material that is not directly pertinent. This focusing of consciousness upon the current topic, by exclusion of other emotional or thought contents, we shall designate as concentration.

The effortful character of concentration, as contrasted with the effortless character of attention, is a conscious experience. It may be well to remind ourselves that not even receptive thinking is always effortless attending; and also that reproductive or productive thinking, as soon as its material becomes complex or the context in which it is called forth is not in itself conducive to its being remembered, usually becomes a voluntary effort—that is, concentration. Complexity of material generally arouses such a variety of ideas and affects that only an active conscious selective control of these—concentration—allows for coping with it.

Attention then may be regarded as automatic, concentration as a voluntary effort. It should be clear that in using the expression "voluntary," we do not imply here an independent psychological force, such as in the past has been termed will.[22] We refer rather to the energy freely available to the person for disposal in intellectual processes, in contrast to drive cathexes which are not available. From this point of view, attention has already been characterized above as an expression of, or as a function of, the equilibrium of these drive cathexes. That is, attention is a function of the ego's efficacy in controlling these emotional and intellectual energies so that their ideational representations enter consciousness at appropriate times only. In a strong ego, this control is not experienced consciously. In a weak ego, or when the material being dealt with is complex, hyper-cathexes must be available to control and limit the field of consciousness. This control or concentration is experienced consciously. Where the ego has more or less disintegrated, as in some schizophrenics, these hyper-cathexes are no longer available, and concentration becomes almost impossible. Furthermore, concentration, with its role of voluntary selection, implies pre-existing patterns within the person that enable appropriate selection to occur. Where, however, pre-existing patterns do not exist, as for instance in regard to the Digit Span material, voluntary effort is of little avail, and straining improves the score little, if at all. This statement does not apply when the digits are transformed by voluntary effort into meaningful numbers or are made meaningful by a grouping procedure.

The Relation of Digit Span and Arithmetic Scatter. In the following discussion of the Digit Span and Arithmetic subtests it will be maintained

[22] [For further discussion of this concept, see index entries under Will in Rapaport (1951a); see also Holt (1965b).—Ed.]

that the Digit Span may be considered a test of attention and Arithmetic a test of concentration. We do not maintain that no other functions underlie achievements on these two subtests: what is implied is rather that attention plays the major role in the Digit Span, and concentration in the Arithmetic, achievements; that relatively poor scores on these subtests most frequently are understandable as impairments of these functions; and that no other subtest of the W-B is related more clearly to these functions. (See below for discussion of the role of concentration in Picture Completion.)

Whether or not these hypotheses are correct, we have leaned heavily upon them in the analysis of these two subtests and their relationship, and they have seemed useful. It is possible that our attempts at developing psychological rationales for the subtests, more than the specific hypotheses employed, will in the long run prove clinically useful; while the hypotheses themselves may prove useful more in a theoretical psychology of thinking. There also, whether correct or not, these hypotheses may reopen the field for investigation and lead to new and more correct hypotheses.[23]

Among neurotics, as well as in most normal subjects we have tested, Digit Span is usually poorer than Arithmetic. In other words, the Vocabulary scatter of Arithmetic—that is, the drop of the Arithmetic scores below the Vocabulary level—is less than that of the Digit Span scores. This state of affairs is true even in depressives. The situation is different in schizophrenic patients who tend to have a Digit Span scatter equal to or less than the Arithmetic scatter.

Moreover, the low average Vocabulary scatter of Digit Span in schizophrenics cannot be explained by assuming that Digit Span drops less than Arithmetic. In a number of schizophrenic cases we have seen not only high positive Vocabulary scatter of Digit Span, but also high weighted scores, which are quite out of keeping with the general score level of these cases. The evidence of the case histories makes it seem quite unlikely that some of these people ever had a general intelligence level corresponding to their high score on Digit Span. We have seen two unclassified schizophrenias, two paranoid schizophrenias, and one paranoid condition with weighted scores of 14 on Digit Span.

At this point, the meaning of scatter should be rediscussed. The weighted score equalizes the subtest achievements of the standardization population—that is, creates statistically an "ideal" person who would show equal weighted scores on each of the subtests. A subject's deviations from identical or nearly identical weighted scores on each subtest must thus be considered characteristic of him as an individual. This does not imply that

_____

[23] [Years after he wrote these words, Rapaport began his final program of research in an attempt to sharpen and test such hypotheses. See Rapaport (1959b, 1960a), Schwartz and Rouse (1961), and Schwartz and Schiller (1967).—Ed.]

every subject should conform to the average performance of the standardization group by whose scores the weighted scale was determined. It implies that the deviation from the average carries a meaning, and that this
meaning is revealing not only in terms of depth of maladjustment and impairment of function, but also in terms of the specific nature of personality
make-up and type of maladjustment. Thus, if a subject has a Digit Span
score far above his present general level, or even far above what is inferred as his original level, this disparity must be meaningful.

If we assume that Digit Span is a test of attention and that Arithmetic
is a test of concentration, then the fact that normal, neurotic, depressive,
and even preschizophrenic subjects show a greater drop in Digit Span than
in Arithmetic could be explained as follows: attention suffers first under
the blows of anxiety, affect, and overvalent ideas; as long as concentration
is relatively well preserved and the person's ego has hypercathexes at its
disposal, he is able to replace the impaired free receptiveness by voluntary
effort, or concentration. This assumption is corroborated by experience; it
is only too common for human beings of our civilization to replace natural
effortless living by effortful concentration upon achievement.

But what happens in the schizophrenic? We would like to formulate the
hypothesis—which we believe is in harmony with clinical observation—that
the schizophrenic loses his ability to summon up voluntary effort to cope
with a situation; and this would correspond to the impairment of concentration, seen in Arithmetic. Nevertheless, he may or may not be able to
show free receptiveness to incoming stimuli. The free receptiveness manifested in high Digit Span scores may be tentatively explained as due to two
factors. (a) In teleological terms, the aim of the schizophrenic psychosis is
to rid the patient of anxiety; if it is true that attention suffers, as in neuroses, from the effects of anxiety, getting rid of anxieties should leave attention unimpaired. (b) The incoming stimulation may find an open door
in some schizophrenics; that is, it will not be really attended to, but rather
taken in by virtue of its appeal to specific trends in the schizophrenic.[24]

Other schizophrenics, however, show deep disturbances of attention, as
indicated by very poor Digit Span scores. This fact could be explained
tentatively as follows: (a) the acute storm of the schizophrenic psychosis
may create a situation loaded with anxiety; (b) total withdrawal of interest
may shatter the surface of consciousness turned toward the outside—that
surface which, created by the stable balance of the drive cathexes, affects,
or strivings, gives the person a prerequisite sensitivity and reactivity to any
stimulation.

[24] [The loss of autonomy with respect to the environment that Rapaport (1957c)
described as characterizing chronic schizophrenics might also be relevant in some
relatively dilapidated cases with high Digit Span.—Ed.]

From here on we shall call the reversal of the usual Digit Span-Arithmetic relationship an "out-of-pattern" relationship. Schizoid subjects who are still within the normal range show this "out-of-pattern" tendency by keeping both Digit Span and Arithmetic high and nearly equal. A schizoid person appears to develop a type of thinking of which one expression is the tendency to have higher Digit Span and Arithmetic scores—that is, a sharpened attention and a sharpened concentration. If the schizoid person is not able to cope with reality and a breakdown occurs, concentration is likely to suffer first and only afterwards—if at all—attention. Nevertheless, it must be understood that there are many factors present in any stress and any maladjustment; and thus the rule here arrived at is not without exception.

Diagnostically, then, any superiority—especially a significant superiority—of the Digit Span score over the Arithmetic score should be taken as a schizoid or schizophrenic indication. Inasmuch as some degree of anxiety is to be expected even in normal populations, any equality—especially if on a high level, and if Digit Span and Arithmetic are above the general level of the other weighted scores of the subject—must raise a suspicion of schizoid trends. Obsessive character formation also may lead to high Digit Span and Arithmetic scores, and even to an out-of-pattern relationship on that level.

DIGIT SPAN

The Digit Span subtest consists of two parts: the first requires repetition of series ranging from three to nine digits in length, as called out by the examiner, the second requires repetition in a *backwards* sequence of series from three to eight digits in length. On any missed series an alternate is given, and if passed the item is credited. The raw score on this subtest is the sum of the number of digits in the longest series passed forward and backward.

The Psychological Rationale of the Digit Span Subtest. As the general theoretical considerations concerning attention have already been advanced in the preceding section, we shall present here only some additional considerations on the rationale of the Digit Span subtest.

Digit Span has usually been assumed to be a test of memory in general, and of "memory span" in particular. In our theoretical understanding and clinical experience this assumption is incorrect. Theoretically, the function of memory refers to logically meaningful[25] and emotionally relevant ma-

[25] This point constitutes the focal point of gestalt psychological theory, and its point of attack against the memory theory of association psychology and conditioned-response psychology. See, e.g., Köhler (1929), Koffka (1935), and Katona (1940).

terial which has been assimilated in reference to interests, attitudes, affects, and strivings of the person; it is organized in the course of the retention period according to developmental changes and relations of these same dynamic factors; and this material is brought into consciousness again as "remembering" when these dynamic factors require it, or make it relevant in a new context.[26] How the *facts* of conditioning, habit formation, and association by contiguity are coordinated with this conception of memory is as yet an unsolved problem.[27]

The difficulty of memory theory is reflected in the fact that the literature—as well as clinical practice—repeatedly makes a distinction between learning and incidental learning, and between immediate (recent) and delayed (remote) memory. It is highly questionable whether the immediate and delayed memory phenomena of the laboratory, and the recent and remote memory phenomena of clinical and life observation, are altogether comparable entities. Clinical experience shows that a high Digit Span score does not assure that the recent memory of a patient is intact, nor does a very low Digit Span score warrant the conclusion that recent memory is impaired. On the one hand, there is a distinct group of schizophrenics in whom, although memory is disorganized, the Digit Span score is extremely high. Except for certain organic cases, memory impairment as seen clinically may accompany a relatively or absolutely intact Digit Span score. On the other hand, there are normal and neurotic people with impaired Digit Span whose recent memory as seen clinically is excellent.

It would be difficult to offer conclusive clinical evidence—rather than merely statements of clinical experience—in support of these contentions. The clinical concept of "recent memory" is a very indefinite one, referring sometimes to the patient's own complaints, sometimes to an absurd forgetting of what happened the day before, sometimes to memory lapses in the course of a single conversation, and sometimes to the patient's recall of a story told by the examiner. For these reasons, any comparisons of our results with clinical observation would be inconclusive. Rather, we will give some evidence in the form of examples.

Let us take three cases in which Digit Span is badly impaired: Case 1, an anxious and depressed, somewhat decompensated, compulsive man, has a weighted score of 7 with a Vocabulary scatter of -5; Case 2, a woman with a paranoid condition, has a weighted score of 4 and Vocabulary Scatter

[26] See in this respect Rapaport (1942a), particularly Chapters I and X [and Rapaport, 1951a, *passim*.].

[27] [At the time of his death, Rapaport was working on problems of this kind, and had moved away from the aggressively progestalt position of this text. For some of the later work on memory done under his aegis, see Paul (1959) and Schwartz and Rouse (1961).—Ed.]

of -10; and Case 3, an obsessional housewife, has a weighted score of 7 and a Vocabulary Scatter of -7. Let us turn now to data which may give us some estimate of these patients' memory functioning.

In the section on the Information subtest, the memory function implicit in that subtest was discussed; thus here we shall take the Information scores as one of the indicators of memory efficiency. The memory function in this subtest would usually be designated as "remote memory." The first case has an Information weighted score of 15, the second of 14, and the third of 16. Thus, although Digit Span is very low, the memory function implied in Information remains intact. Let us now turn to the immediate and delayed repetition of a story (see below, Chapter 4). The first case was not given a Story Recall test. The score of the second case on the immediate recall is 12, on the delayed recall 17; that of the third case on the immediate recall is 15, on the delayed recall 16. Thus we see that in both the immediate and delayed recall of a story, these cases achieve adequate scores. In these cases, low Digit Span goes with high Information and good memory for meaningful material.

Let us now take two cases with very high Digit Span scores. Cases 4 and 5, young, acutely schizophrenic women, have Digit Span scores of 13 and 17, respectively. The Information scores of these cases are 8 and 10, respectively. The immediate and delayed recall scores for the Story Recall test are, for Case No. 4, 7 and 5; for Case No. 5, 11 and 6. In all four of the recalls, there were also more errors than creditable memories.

If the Digit Span measured immediate memory or memory in any real sense, it would be difficult to explain why we find on all these three types of memory tests—Information, and Immediate and Delayed Recall of a story—such divergent scores: high Digit Span score accompanied by low scores on these memory tests, and low Digit Span score accompanied by high scores on these memory tests.

Thus far the argument has been in terms of why Digit Span is not a test of memory.[28] We shall now advance a few qualitative considerations, in terms of Digit Span as a test of attention.

[28] In order to point up the fact that our treatment of the issues here involved simplifies matters too much and avoids coming to grips with a number of thorny problems, we shall quote part of a communication from David Shakow. Quoting it does not imply agreement with his points, but is rather an effort to make the complexity of the situation clear. We agree with his statements concerning the difference between Digits Forward and Digits Backward, and concerning paretics whose attention disturbance is certainly not caused by anxiety. The correlations he quotes may or may not be indications of a common attention factor in the tests correlated. At any rate, his comments are of importance in indicating that further theoretical clarification is urgently needed: "I must point out again the great weakness of dealing with Digits Forward and Digits Backward together. You save the situation somewhat by putting the two in the 'attention-concentration' group—Digits Backward

First, there is the qualitative similarity of the subjective experience in Digit Span performance to that described in the preceding section as typical for attention and its failures. Digit Span achievement is highest if intake is effortless and free. Patients who take it in a matter-of-fact way pass better than those who try very hard. Failure having once occurred, and the alternate series being passed with much effort, full failure is likely to occur on the series following: effort does not help on Digit Span beyond a very narrow margin.

Second, the device of grouping the digits, which helps to extend the subject's digit span, changes its nature: it introduces "meaning" into it—in the sense of patterning the numbers, with intervals of hundreds, tens, and units, and with awareness of rises and falls in magnitude. These groupings may even give rise to past connotations. Such grouping is radically different from the visual, auditory, or vocal-motor imagery of the digit series which usually occurs. The introduction of meaning changes the function underlying Digit Span performance and in part makes it dependent on concentration.

The extent of impairment of Digit Span appears to indicate the presence and degree of anxiety; drops occur in anxious normal persons, and great drops occur in neurotics and depressives. Great positive Vocabulary scatter usually indicates the presence of schizoid features or schizophrenia proper.[29] Extreme impairment of Digit Span may occur in schizophrenic cases also; this indicates in some cases that the break with reality has not succeeded in

---

certainly involves the latter more. But there is something more to be said about the way in which you look at digit repetition. In the first place consider these correlations, which come from a group of some 180 normals on whom our memory test is standardized: Digits Forward/Sentences .47; Digits Forward/Digits Backward .57; Digits Forward/Immediate Recall of Story .38; Digits Backward/Sentences .46; Digits Backward/Immediate Recall of Story .50; Sentences/Immediate Recall of Story .52. So you see, at least according to our data, there is some relationship among items involving the recall of new material. The correlations with old recall are, with few exceptions, much lower. What I am getting at is that I believe that you are oversimplifying the situation. By emphasizing your point in an all-or-none way you weaken your argument. It is possible that Digits Backward is a test of immediate learning primarily and attention secondarily and Digits Forward is a test of attention primarily and learning secondarily; but, except in very extreme instances, both are involved. (You see that I am taking your anxiety component of attention seriously into account.) Some evidence for what I say comes from our data on general paretics who show their greatest disturbances on Digits Forward and I am very doubtful if this difficulty could be accounted for on any anxiety basis. I believe that the anxiety element here is very minor and that the difficulty is almost entirely one of the 'impression' phase of learning. Of course one can define memory or learning in a number of ways but for me memory deals with non-sensical as well as with sensical material and covers all the range between them. I have a suspicion that in different groups different ratios of learning and anxiety are involved—which only makes the problem so much more complicated!"

[29] [Except that, as Schafer (1948) points out, their use of isolation enables some obsessive-compulsive persons to achieve unusually high scores on Digit Span.—Ed.]

eliminating anxiety—and these cases usually have a better prognosis—and in others that deteriorative withdrawal has already set in, impairing attention.

Administration. Clinical experience seems to show a characteristic rhythm of intake for each person. This rhythm comes to expression in highly organized form in the splitting of Digit Span series into groups, and in the fluctuation in speed in serial performances of tasks such as Digit Symbol. In each individual there seems to be present a certain flexibility of this rhythm, which allows him to adapt to the rhythm of the examiner. A striking example of the decrease of this flexibility is found in those neurotics who comment that if the examiner were only a bit slower, or a bit faster, they could get it. On trial, they prove to be right. A striking example of the rigidity of such rhythm in some neurotics is seen when, if the examiner inadvertently delays for a second in giving one digit or otherwise changes speed, certain subjects become confused and lose the series. An extreme impairment of rhythm—which may be due to great rigidity or disorganization of the rhythm, two alternate possibilities which one cannot decide between at present—is found in cases where more or fewer digits than given by the examiner are recalled. Quite possibly the disturbance of attention seen in failures on the Digit Span subtest is intimately linked to this matter of rhythm, though at present nothing further can be said with any certainty.

In line with these considerations the tester should keep in mind the following three administrative rules: (a) The necessity of keeping strictly to a stop-watch-timed presentation of digits at one-second intervals increases in significance with the degree of maladjustment in the subject. (b) It is useful to note whether or not a subject groups the digits, and thus alters the nature of the task. (c) When a subject in repeating the digits gives more or fewer digits than actually called out by the examiner, this fact should be noted.

It is worth while to inquire, "How did you go about remembering them?" and to record whether, for example, the patient visualized the digits and read them off from his visual image, or whether he muttered them to himself and reproduced them with the help of verbal-motor or auditory techniques.

It is generally advisable to watch for the types of errors that occur in repetition of digits. Failure of attention may manifest itself in several ways. (a) The patient may state, "I lost it," or may indicate by voice or statement that he is not sure of certain digits. In this case we may be dealing either with a disorganization or temporary inefficiency making for failure, or with the subject's limit of attention; and the subsequent series will tell which is the case. Temporary and generalized inefficiency imperceptibly shade into each other here. (b) The patient may reverse the position of two digits, or displace a digit to another position. This procedure usually indicates temporary inefficiency; and though no general rule can be set down, such persons are frequently negativistic, harbor hidden antagonisms, and not infrequently prove better on Digits Backward than on Digits Forward. (c) Indicative of considerable personality disorganization are misses on the three-, four-, or five-digit series, especially when these misses are accompanied by giving more or fewer digits than called out by the examiner, or by missing the first digit of a series. (d) A markedly lower score on Digits Backward than on Digits Forward (a discrepancy greater than two) is a sign of seriously impaired attention, notwithstanding a high total score. (e) Very few (three) digits passed forward or backward appears to be in itself a very pathological indicator, and always raises the suspicion of psychosis or organic disorder.

The Relation of Digits Forward to Digits Backward. Among normal and neurotic people, eight or nine out of every 10 give either one or two more digits forward than backward or else the same number. More digits backward than forward are given by an occasional normal person, but mostly by schizophrenics, particularly acute and chronic paranoid schizophrenics. An exaggeration of the usual relationship—that is to say, a raw score on Digits Forward *much* better than on Digits Backward—will most likely occur in depressive psychotics and schizophrenics, though this relationship can occur in almost any kind of psychopathological condition.

Drops of the Digit Span score four or more points below the Vocabulary level are those here considered significant; and a Digit Span score two or more points above the Vocabulary score is considered high positive scatter.

DIAGNOSTIC SUGGESTIONS

(a) The extent to which Digit Span is impaired appears to indicate the presence and degree of anxiety. A weighted score four or more points below Vocabulary indicates an appreciable amount such as may be found in anxious normal persons; greater drops in score occur in neurotics and depressives.

(b) Since anxiety is a common feature of most clinical groups, a lowered Digit Span is generally not a diagnostic indicator. But if the Digit Span score is extremely low both absolutely (e.g., weighted score no more than 5) and in relation to the other scores, the possibility of a depressive psychosis or deteriorated schizophrenia must be considered.

(c) Extreme impairment of Digit Span in schizophrenia indicates in some cases that the break with reality has not succeeded in eliminating anxiety—and these cases usually have a better prognosis—and in others that deteriorative withdrawal has already set in, impairing attention.

(d) A Digit Span score two or more points above Vocabulary or the Verbal mean is generally characteristic of nondeteriorated schizophrenics among the psychotics, and of schizoid adjustment among normals. Among schizoid normals, a high Digit Span score does not mean an absence of anxiety: anxiety in such people seems not to affect their Digit Span scores.

ARITHMETIC

The Arithmetic subtest of the W-B consists of 10 timed items. If answered within 15 seconds, the last two items merit an additional credit. The problems come for the most part from daily life. Their solutions require that the subject have available to him the standard arithmetical operations, and that he do them "in his head"—without the aid of pencil and paper.

The Psychological Rationale of the Arithmetic Subtest. The usual psychometric assumption is that Arithmetic is a good test of "g"; and, in fact, it correlates highly according to Wechsler's tables with most of the subtests, except for Picture Arrangement and Object Assembly. Arithmetic is here considered a test of concentration, because to pass the items of this subtest which, excepting perhaps the last two, consist of the four basic calculations, the subject—the average person of our civilization—must utilize patterns of arithmetical relations ingrained in him. He must reflect on and deliver the answers from the patterns that he possesses. Such focusing upon internal or external, actual or potentially existing patterns, to discover and amend them, is concentration. Two questions emerge here: (a) Are not all the subtests of the W-B such that concentration is necessary to their performance? And if so, why should Arithmetic specifically be considered a test of concentration? (b) Is it not possible to assume that the Arithmetic scores correlate so highly with most of the other subtests because it tests mainly concentration, and concentration is implied in the performance of the other subtests also?

To answer these two questions we must first examine the process of concentration. Concentration is a voluntary effort made in terms of either receptive or productive psychological activities. In *receptive* activity such voluntary effort can be made in order to insure intake of outside stimulation either when preoccupation with intrapsychic processes would encroach upon and make difficult the intake of such stimulation, or when the multiplicity of the outside stimuli is such that automatic effortless organization of the momentary intake becomes inefficient and must be replaced by voluntary selective effort. There are two conditions in external stimulation that interfere with attending and necessitate concentration: (a) interference of simultaneous stimuli in the same or in different sensory fields; (b) a more complicated and important type of interference, based on the fact that the person, when stimulated, takes in not the stimulus but its meaning. Frequently, when the stimulus pattern becomes complicated, the meaning does not reveal itself automatically to the effortless attention. In such cases concentration, focused upon discovery of the meaning of the stimulus pattern, becomes necessary. One might sum up by stating that in the *receptive* processes, concentration becomes necessary when external and/or internal stimuli interfere with each other, and when as a consequence of this or of the complexity of material, meaning is hidden.

At first glance the situation seems somewhat different for concentration in *productive* activity. Productive activity is considered here to be any activity that brings to consciousness memories, information, and knowledge of facts, events, and relationships that have once been experienced and now belong to the armamentarium of the person's thinking. As a rule, such assets at the disposal of the person come into his consciousness in an effortless manner. This ceases to be the case under certain conditions. If an idea, emotion, or general restlessness (anxiety) dominates consciousness, such effortless productive activity is hampered. Such might also be the case when the productive activity becomes quite complex and the production must take a systematized form. The person then must scrutinize, select, and correct the results of his effortless productive activity. Such scrutiny is reflection, or turning back upon, one's thoughts. Scientific reasoning usually consists of both effortless productive activity and reflection or turning back upon it, scrutinizing, selecting, and organizing it. As a rule, if the effortless productive activity is to supply ideas to fit a complex ideational pattern already in consciousness, the effortless character of production ceases, and effortful concentration takes its place in order to assure lack of contradiction and homogeneity of conscious thought contents.

Thus, productive and receptive concentration fulfill essentially the same function. Both consist of seizing with conscious effort material at the person's disposal, either in the external or in his internal psychological world. Both are called upon to function selectively, either when externally or internally interfering factors make free receptiveness or productivity difficult, or when the complexity of the material to be received or produced requires critical scrutiny and selection not supplied by effortless attention.

After these considerations we may return to the two questions raised in the opening of this section. Undoubtedly, concentration becomes a factor in every one of the Verbal subtests as soon as any degree of difficulty—which will be individually variable—is encountered; in other words, as soon as verbal convention and automatic memory function fail to supply the pat answers. Yet Arithmetic will be considered here as a direct test of concentration.

To demonstrate the reasons for this conclusion, let us consider each sub-test of the W-B from the point of view of concentration:

(a) Digit Span is a test of attention. Concentration, as was already stated in the section on Digit Span, does not help the subject to attain a good score on Digit Span once attention is impaired.

(b) Information is an untimed test; the subject is not under a psycho-logical time-pressure symbolized by the stop watch, and is not penalized for slowness. It might be held that concentration is important in helping to de-cide which of several available responses should be given. The material of these decisions is still supplied by automatic effortless memory function, which is hardly replaceable by concentration. As a matter of fact, people rarely call upon concentration in answering the Information questions. They give answers, both good and absurd, rather quickly and without too much deliberation, even when they have doubts about it: "Wasn't it Wilson?" would be a typical example of the form the response takes. Or one gets answers like this: "I am sure I know it. May I tell it to you later? It must come to me." It is here to a certain extent as with Digit Span and with the memories of our experiences in everyday life. Conscious effort is much less likely to bring back a name or a fact than free automatic memory func-tioning.

(c) In the Comprehension items, the most that concentration might do is to collect a number of possibilities as pertinent responses. But in this test many possibilities make it not easier but rather more difficult to answer. If, in connection with the letter found in the street, one considers the possi-bilities of the post office, of the mailbox, of deriving some advantage from opening the letter, of the legal consequences of opening it, of consulting someone who walked by, of finding the owner of the letter among passers-by, of the letter's being some kind of a trap, and innumerable other vari-ants—all of which are "logically" possible, and thus can be made available by sufficient concentration—one does not make judgment easier but more difficult.

(d) The Similarities subtest is a test of comparisons—that is, of con-cept formation. As most of the Similarities items may be responded to with well-established generic verbal terms, concentration enters only when the subject's verbal concepts are too weak to make these generic verbal forms easily available. In these cases, concentration is more likely to deliver par-tial concrete or functional similarities—for example, a visual image of the objects to be compared, or some memories concerning them—thus making for an inadequate response.

(e) In the Performance subtests, Block Design, Object Assembly, and Picture Arrangement are psychologically highly complicated; partly visual organization and visual-motor coordination, and partly planning and anticipation, enter into their performance. Although concentration is certainly required by them, their complexity clouds its role, and thus they cannot serve as concentration tests. In the Digit Symbol subtest, motor speed, absence or presence of motor inhibition or retardation, and a process of learning are all involved, and again the role of concentration is clouded and becomes partial.

(f) The situation is different in the Picture Completion subtest. Here all the materials necessary for achieving a good response are put before the subject, and he works under the instructions to find what is missing; thus, his task is explicitly one of concentration. Knowledge or judgment for the most part do not enter these Picture Completion tasks. To illustrate this point, let us take the picture of the crab one of whose legs is missing on one side. One need not know what animal it is or how many legs it is supposed to have; consideration of these is rather a sign of impairment. All one need notice is that there is an asymmetry in an otherwise symmetrical animal. This example brings into relief that the task is one of systematic search for inconsistency in pattern—that is, concentration on the parts and whole of the picture. Perhaps this is even clearer when one compares the Picture Completion subtest with the Picture Arrangement subtest. This comparison is facilitated by the fact that, in both, small cards with similar types of drawings constitute the material of the test. In Picture Arrangement, a comparison of the pictures to each other and, on the basis of the general characteristics of one picture, an anticipation of the next step—that is, the step toward the picture that should follow—is the basis of performance. Where concentration is focused on parts of an individual picture, it usually indicates to the examiner that the general survey of the pictures is faulty and that the subject is about to start off on a tangent suggested by some inconspicuous and irrelevant detail in a picture. In Picture Arrangement the trend in meaning of the individual pictures is conveyed to the subject by a free automatic attention and, if it fails, concentration usually leads to worse failure; while in Picture Completion the gap in pattern can only be perceived by concentration on parts of the pictures. In addition, the Picture Completion subtest is worked under time pressure, the presence of which always emphasizes the role of concentration.

It should be noted that in Picture Completion concentration takes place on visually presented material; thus visual organization plays a great role in the successful performance of the subtest, and concentration is not the sole factor involved—though the visual factor is not so potent as to overshadow the concentration factor totally, as happens in Digit Symbol, Block Design, and Object Assembly.

Thus far we have advanced reasons why we consider only one subtest to be a test of concentration, even though concentration plays a role in others. We should like to add a further statement of why the Arithmetic subtest is eminently a test of concentration. The subject matter of all the tests discussed—except, to a degree, Picture Completion—is multidimensional in character. In contrast, the subject matter of Arithmetic is a unidimensional continuum of numbers. In Arithmetic, all the material necessary for the response is before the subject, as in Picture Completion, as soon as the numbers in question are mentioned. It is true that in Arithmetic the numbers are embedded in verbal formulations; it is true that, in the last two Arithmetic items, lack of experience with the type of task may make concentration insufficient for coping with the problem, and a complicated process of reasoning and concept formation may become a part of solving the task. Therefore, cultural background may enter the response to the last two items and influence the achievement. The effects of this lack of familiarity on these two items in the average population may obtain on more of the items for subjects of below average intelligence. But on the level of the first eight items, nothing is required but concentration on and utilization of patterns which the average American adult may reasonably be expected to possess.[30] It is a test of the patient's ability to concentrate and, with this concentration, to summon up knowledge he has, within the limits of a given time. We do not wish to identify all kinds of arithmetic or mathematics as concentration proper; but on this level the necessary arithmetic knowledge is so ingrained that merely concentration comes into play in delivering it to consciousness.

The psychology of arithmetic is not a sufficiently explored territory. Nevertheless, it is clear that it is one of the purest forms of abstract thinking which follows most closely and is virtually the prototype of the rules of the secondary process,[31] and which, once obtained, does not have reference to any kind of past experience in its application. Thus its application is referable more to concentration proper than to any other aspect of psychological functioning. Every process of *ordered* thinking presupposes concentration, voluntary effort, employment of hypercathexes at the disposal of the ego. But in much of ordered thinking the material upon which concentration is required is not available to the subject's consciousness, as are either the Picture Completion drawings through perception or the Arithmetical basic relations through introspection; the material of most ordered

[30] We do not maintain that there are no individual differences in mathematical ability, or, in terms of our analysis, in the ability to establish and maintain sets of relationships that are necessary for arithmetic achievement. Our point is that most items of this subtest involve a group of basic and elementary relationships which are essential to everyday business transactions such as shopping, and which are to be expected of the average adult.

[31] "Secondary process" is the psychoanalytic term for conscious and ordered thought processes.

thinking must be first delivered automatically by memory, anticipation, and so on. Thus concentration comes into play as a secondary function only, even though its role may be crucial in organizing complex material; while in the simple processes of ordered thinking implied in these arithmetic problems, concentration is the primary function at play.

Inasmuch as concentration replaces free attention if the latter is impaired, we would expect Arithmetic to be better preserved in neurotic persons who, in spite of impairment of effortless attention, keep contact with reality and perform, usually with great effort, their everyday tasks. Analysis of the "out-of-pattern" relationship given in a previous section on Attention and Concentration shows that this is really the case; Arithmetic scores are better than Digit Span scores in neurotics. On the other hand, we find that schizophrenics who cease effort to keep contact with reality, and who do not have sufficient hypercathexes available to control their impulses or ideation, earn lower scores on Arithmetic than do the neurotics, and even tend to get lower Arithmetic (concentration) scores than Digit Span (attention) scores.

Administration. Wechsler suggests that in general a subject should be allowed to finish an item even though the time limit expires. We suggest that failures due merely to overstepping the time limit, and particularly when overstepping it by only a few seconds, be taken into consideration in the *qualitative* evaluation of the weighted score.

We recommend that those subjects who give quick erroneous responses should be told they are wrong; and if the correct response is forthcoming within the time limit, it should be credited with a half score. If the error is an error in principle, or due to a basic impairment, no correction will be forthcoming; but if temporary inefficiency is present, the correction merits some credit.

We recommend that help be given to failing subjects, and that either the degree of help necessary for success or the inability to succeed in spite of help be established; thus it may be decided whether poor achievement is due to "temporary inefficiency" or to basic impairment. (No credit is given in the quantitative scoring for items on which help has been given, of course.)

Erroneous results should be inquired into, to see whether they come from temporary inefficiency or error in principle.

In contrast to Wechsler's recommendation, we suggest that no Arithmetic item, not even the easiest, be omitted in administering the test to any subject; temporary inefficiency of concentration shows up most clearly on the easiest items.

"Thinking out loud" on all the more difficult items should be encouraged, so that errors of principle, methods of thinking, and solidity or disintegration of patterns may be better perceived by the examiner.

Item Analysis. In the analysis of the 10 items of Arithmetic, we will keep in mind the theses that misses on the easiest items are of diagnostic significance, and that misses on difficult items are meaningful in terms of educational background.

The items fall into three groups. The five easy problems are:

1. How much is four dollars and five dollars? (time limit: 15″).

2. If a man buys six cents worth of stamps and gives the clerk ten cents, how much change should he get back? (15″).

5. How many hours will it take a man to walk twenty-four miles at the rate of three miles an hour? (30″).

6. If a man buys seven two-cent stamps and gives the clerk a half dollar, how much change should he get back? (30″).

7. If seven pounds of sugar cost twenty-five cents, how many pounds can you get for a dollar? (60″).

The three intermediate items are:

3. If a man buys eight cents worth of stamps and gives the clerk twenty-five cents, how much change should he get back? (15″).

4. How many oranges can you buy for thirty-six cents if one orange costs four cents? (30″).

8. A man bought a secondhand car for two thirds of what it cost new. He paid $400 for it. How much did it cost new? (60″).

The two difficult items have time limits of two minutes each:

9. If a train goes 150 yards in ten seconds, how many feet can it go in one fifth of a second?

10. Eight men can finish a job in six days. How many men will be needed to finish it in a half day?

DIAGNOSTIC SUGGESTIONS

(a) Failures on the easy Arithmetic items are most frequent in deteriorated schizophrenics and depressive psychotics. To a lesser extent, such misses occur in other schizophrenics and depressives, and are rare or absent in normals and neurotics. These same trends hold true in general for the Arithmetic items of intermediate difficulty.

(b) Great drops of the Arithmetic score (four or more points below the Vocabulary score) are most frequent in deteriorated schizophrenics and depressives. It appears to be a special feature of the unclassified schizophrenics that they tend to have greater impairment of Arithmetic than of Digit Span.

(c) Arithmetic appears not to be as vulnerable to impairment by normal and neurotic anxiety as Digit Span.

(d) Schizoid normals tend to do better on Arithmetic than nonschizoid persons. Relatively high scores are also earned by intellectualizers (obsessive neurotics and overideational preschizophrenics, for example), concentration being an especially favored and highly developed function among intellectualizers.

PICTURE ARRANGEMENT

The Picture Arrangement subtest is a Performance subtest; that is to say, in it the test problem is not merely verbally put and verbally answered. The motor action is of a nonessential kind, however, requiring merely a change of position of cardboard squares so that the pictures on them make a meaningful story sequence. The visual presentation of the material is, however, an integral part of the nonverbal or performance nature of the subtest. In this respect it is similar to the Picture Completion subtest. The pairing of these two subtests is justified by their sharing, of all subtests, the greatest vulnerability to maladjustment.

The Psychological Rationale of Picture Arrangement. (a) Planning and Anticipation. Planning ability is a concept very rarely used in psychiatric or psychological terminology. Even in common-sense usage it is a rather infrequent term. Only in the assessment of executive abilities are this or equivalent terms used with relative frequency. It is rather surprising that the concept and its psychological implications have been so little explored, especially since the function referred to appears to be one of our most human qualities. K. Bühler (1919), endeavoring in his volume on child development to characterize human thinking as contrasted with that of animals, uses the following illustration: we do not build bridges and then test whether or not they can carry the weight we want them to; rather, we sit down at our desk and plan how to build a bridge that will carry that weight. We might paraphrase Bühler's idea as follows: we do not build bridges by trial and error, but by anticipating and planning the future.

This most human ability of anticipating and planning was found clinically, for instance, to be strikingly deficient in the Korsakoff syndrome (Buerger-Prinz & Kaila, 1930). Anticipation is a central concept in Selz's (1913) rarely read and otherwise outdated work on "ordered thinking." Otherwise, the concept of *Einstellung,* of the German schools of the psychology of thinking, is the only concept developed by psychologists which is analogous and pertinent to the concept of planning ability.[32] It is well-

[32] [Except for the contemporary concept of *set* (see Gibson, 1941). Again, the polemical tone of this passage sounds dated by developments in a vigorously growing cognitive psychology and in psycholinguistics (see Miller, Galanter, & Pribram, 1960; Holt, 1964b).—Ed.]

known that these schools of the psychology of thinking were the first to declare war upon association psychology in their explanation of the nature of thinking. They first realized that the emergence of the next link in a chain of thoughts is not due to a process of mechanical association, in which the earlier link in the chain brings the next one into consciousness by virtue of having frequently occurred together with it in the past, in spatial or temporal contiguity; but rather to an *Einstellung* which is activated by the earlier link in a chain of thought and which performs a function of selecting, out of all the available memory material, that which is most appropriate in the situation. In other words, the sequence of ideas in ordered thinking is determined by selective anticipation and not by mechanical association.[33]

The existence and significance of the function of *Einstellung* or anticipation is vouched for by common human experience in the process of reasoning or even of free conversation, when although we do not yet have the next idea in consciousness we nonetheless feel in what direction it lies.

Like the concept of judgment discussed in the section on the Comprehension subtest, the concept of planning ability is also one on the borderline of the concepts couched in intellectual and those couched in emotional terms. The difference appears to be that while judgment appears to refer more to a situation here and now given, planning ability and anticipation appear to refer rather to a *sequence* extending into the future; thus they imply a temporal factor.[34] *Einstellung,* a concept analogous with that of attitude or set, is of a more clearly emotional and less rationalistic character than the latter.[35] Further, the efficacy of *Einstellung* or anticipation is dependent upon the person's width of experience over which the *Einstellung* or anticipation exerts its selective function.

Planning ability is thus partly a function of emotional adjustment, mak-

---

[33] It appears superfluous to demonstrate here that the concept of anticipatory response in conditioning (see Hilgard & Marquis, 1940) is a mechanical conception only very indirectly pertinent to the function discussed here.

[34] There appears to be an intimate relationship between the temporal factor implied in anticipation and what has been called *time perspective* (Lewin, 1935; Frank, 1939a). Particularly in connection with level of aspiration experiments (see Lewin, Dembo, Festinger, & Sears, 1944; Escalona, 1940, 1948) the concept of time perspective has become significant. Both anticipation and time perspective appear to be intimately connected with the general problem of time experience, a problem of psychology which is of utmost importance and has been badly neglected. For a summary of the contributions of psychopathology to the understanding of the background of functioning of time sense, see Rapaport (1942a), Chapter IX [and Rapaport, 1951a, pp. 87, 360-361].

[35] The role of *Einstellung,* attitude, and emotional factors in general has been discussed by Rapaport (1942a) in reference to memory functioning. Indications will be found there concerning the applicability to thought processes generally of the considerations which were advanced concerning memory. A theoretical exploration or, even more, systematization of the role of such factors in thought processes is still lacking. [See, however, Rapaport (1951a) and Holt (1967b).—Ed.]

ing for emergence of the proper anticipation or *Einstellung;* and partly of the width of experience at the disposal of the person, which is to be mobilized by these anticipations.

(b) The Role of Planning Ability and Anticipation in Picture Arrangement: Examples. The relationship of the Picture Arrangement subtest to planning ability is in need of clarification. No doubt there is a great difference between arranging a series of pictures into a story sequence and planning one's own life endeavors, the layout of a business organization, or only a day's overfilled schedule or one's moves in a chess game. But if we recall what is requisite to a simple conversation—which might well serve as the simplest pattern of planning—we are much reminded of organizing a series of isolated pictures into a sequence. For a conversation between two persons not to become stagnant, the prerequisite is that each person get the implications of the other's statements and anticipate the direction his ideas are taking. This is true not only for conversation, but even for the simple reading of a sentence. We read not by reading every word singly and putting them together; rather, when a sentence starts with a "though," it awakes in us an anticipation of a sentence structure or pattern of antithesis, into which we shall integrate—or which shall define our integrating, organizing, and giving meaning to—the verbal content of the rest of the sentence. If we do not anticipate, we do not understand what we read.

On the Picture Arrangement subtest, we submit that the subject's achievement is a reflection of his ability to anticipate the consequences of initial acts or situations, and hence is a reflection of his planning ability.

A few examples will show clearly how disturbances in anticipation make planning impossible, and result in failures on Picture Arrangement. These failures may be due either to lack of anticipation and/or to false anticipation determined by overvalent ideas.

First we shall give a full presentation of the Picture Arrangement performance of an ambulatory schizophrenic, who at first sight presented an obsessional picture. After the sample "bird's-nest" series was shown to him, the three pictures of building a house were put before him; the patient then asked, "Can I switch them around?"—indicating that from the sample demonstration he had formed no anticipation of the test proper.

In the first and easiest item—the building of a house—he was not able to anticipate the story, and actually tried all possible combinations of sequence before he was able to decide on the correct one. The inability to plan or to anticipate was thus again indicated.

The second item—the story of the thief—took the patient two minutes, and finally he decided on an incorrect sequence; that is, he put the picture of the thief imprisoned before the picture of the courtroom trial. Since those rare normals who fail this item produce this sequence, one would be tempted to pass this patient's failure lightly. But, encouraged by the examiner's general attitude, the patient gave further significant information: "A man sitting on a bench outside . . . shooting another man . . ." That is, even at the end the patient was not able to explain his arrangement of the pictures. The verbalization shows that there was no anticipation from the act of shooting—to begin with a misinterpretation of the picture—to give meaning to the prisoner's striped uniform. Consequently the court scene remained entirely uncomprehended ("a man sitting on a bench outside . . .") and dangled at the end of the series as a meaningless appendage. The pictures remained isolated.

In the third series of pictures—the scene of a rising elevator—the patient came to the right solution, but so late that he did not get credit for it; and with some disgust he said, "I don't know what it is," completely failing to recognize that he had reached a solution and that the solution was correct. This series of pictures can be arranged simply by following the gradual rising of the angle of the door of the elevator from one picture to another, without reference to the meaning of the picture. Some feeble-minded persons and some children do verbalize this procedure clearly. In this patient the procedure remained unverbalized, and we find only the negative of it: "I don't know what it is."

The fourth series—the car ride and flirtation of the Little King—brought to expression certain devious anticipations rooted in the pathological ideas of the patient. He came to no arrangement, failing the item totally; but while working he said, "What is it? . . . Negro riding in a motorcar? . . . or getting married? . . . a policeman? . . . I can't make it out." There are three features in this verbalization: the first and most outstanding is that the car ride in the presence of a woman makes for the anticipation of "getting married"; the second is the direct failure to identify the man's figure, but rather the black hair of the woman is misidentified as that of a Negro and the anticipation makes the Little King a Negro; the third is that the chauffeur's uniform cap is misidentified as a policeman's cap, either contributing an anticipation resulting in the misidentification of the Little King or being itself determined by an anticipation based on this misidentification. It is understandable that under such conditions, where ideas, percepts, and anticipations are present in isolated, piecemeal form without integration, no order can be brought into the series of pictures.

Devious anticipations became even clearer in the last two series. In the fifth series the patient, who is very familiar with fishing, said, "Fishing obviously . . . looking very much alike, all of these . . . don't see much difference in them." The familiar idea of fishing was so rigidly associated with all the pictures that it made superfluous any further connections or anticipation of any progression: all the pictures appeared alike to him, because only one idea was mobilized by them—that of his favorite sport, fishing.

Finally, the sixth series—the car ride with a statue—was put into a sequence which was a partial solution, meriting a score of 1. This score was spurious because the patient said, "Riding—kissing, this is obviously a petting . . . whatever these eyes in the back of his head mean . . ." The overvalent idea of the patient—sexual preoccupation—and lack of anticipation from one picture to another made it impossible for him to recognize that the figure seen with the man in the car is the statue he carried in the street, or that the man is looking back over his shoulder rather than that he has eyes in the back of his head.

We have described in detail the Picture Arrangement performance of this patient, because it shows a variety of forms in which lack of anticipation, or devious anticipations due to overvalent ideas, make for failure.

The influence of projective false anticipations, rooted in the patient's own problems and character, is shown in the responses of one very despondent and dependent schizophrenic. In the fishing pictures this patient failed altogether, and said, "He [the King] is discouraged . . . tries again . . . has a bite . . . quits." This is the type of patient who in his own life always tries again, always fails, and readily quits. In his everyday anticipations failure looms large, and the actions of the Little King are regarded by him accordingly.

The lack of unifying anticipations is seen in the responses of a deteriorated schizophrenic to the sixth series, the taxi ride with the statue: "He didn't like the lady so well . . . he got out to take the statue with him . . . his lady friend was in the taxi with him." The statue and the figure in the car are not identified with each other, which makes for a reversal of the events pictured.

We believe that these examples help bring into relief the role of anticipation and planning as the underlying psychological functions in the Picture Arrangement items. They also show some of the patterns of the pathology of anticipation and planning.

(c) The Relation of Picture Arrangement to Attention and Judgment. The planning on the Picture Arrangement subtest implies both attention and judgment. Attention should effortlessly convey to the subject the essential features of the individual pictures, or the deviations of the pictures from each other. An effortful concentration usually becomes necessary only when the patient's sense for the outstanding is weakened, and the essential and the nonessential are apperceived with the same emphasis. It is then that effortful selective search for meaning starts. When this is the case, the patient usually gets lost in the single pictures of a series, does not come to an arrangement, comes to one late or to a wrong one predicated upon some unimportant feature of the pictures. Nevertheless, there is no notable impairment of Picture Arrangement by anxiety, as in Digit Span. At present we have no explanation for this fact.

We cannot analyze here the visual organization process entering the Picture Arrangement performance; partly because it is so highly stereotyped that only in borderline defective, culturally alien, and psychotically maladjusted cases are obvious variants to the stereotypes seen; partly because the visual organization of complex meaningful material is a little-explored problem; and partly because the interlacing of those processes called here visual organization and those called here attention is at present entirely beyond our knowledge.

We must discuss, however, the role that judgment plays in the performance of Picture Arrangement. It is probable that acting upon any anticipation implies judgment. But the function in Picture Arrangement performance is more complex than that of judgment; it implies the time perspective of anticipation.

Logically one is tempted to assume that as soon as judgment is impaired, planning ability will be impaired too. This is not always the case. Psychopaths may have Comprehension scores much inferior to their Picture Arrangement scores. Several recent authors have attributed this finding to the psychopath's superior "social understanding." It is difficult to see clinically what is meant by this; but we might judge that, as far as the Picture Arrangement subtest is concerned, what is meant is good anticipation. It is possible that planning here becomes scheming and, as in dealing with specific life situations, the psychopath may here be quite shrewd. This is not contradictory to the finding that more general life-planning and long-range anticipations of the psychopath are poor or absent.

Administration. Not only failures, but also partially correct arrangements made by the subject should be recorded.

The subject should not only be allowed to finish if he oversteps the time limit, but should also be encouraged to try again (without credit) after failure.

In all failed items the story or anticipations conceived by the subject should be inquired into; even the passed items should be inquired into if any peculiarity of performance is seen.

The stories conceived by the subject on the last two items should always be inquired into; incorrect anticipations or lack of understanding frequently underlies a passing arrangement.

The patient should be asked in advance to indicate when he is finished with an item; thus the examiner may be sure that he is neither arbitrarily interrupting him nor giving him a clue that he has successfully completed the item.

Item Analysis. The item analysis of the Picture Arrangement subtest, consisting of only six items, naturally cannot be as revealing as the item analyses of the Verbal subtests, which have from 10 to 42 items. Items 1-3 constitute the easy group, and Items 4-6 the difficult group.

In evaluating failures one must keep in mind an objection which has repeatedly been raised against the Picture Arrangement subtest. For our usual clinical population it is a fair test; but for a large part of the general population it is too sophisticated, requiring anticipations of a type that are familiar to readers of such publications as *The New Yorker*. Intelligent persons from a different subcultural background, being unaccustomed to the conventions and devices of wordless cartoon sequences, may therefore be slow in grasping items of this type.

DIAGNOSTIC SUGGESTIONS

(a) Depressive psychotics and deteriorated schizophrenics do very badly on Picture Arrangement, in terms of failing easy items, obtaining weighted scores below 6, and four or more points below Vocabulary. A similar trend characterizes other schizophrenics and depressives, but poor performance on this subtest is commonly enough encountered in most diagnostic groups to make it not a very differentiating indicator.

(b) Nevertheless, schizophrenics may often be distinguished by the fact that they tend to show a special impairment of Picture Arrangement in comparison to the other Performance subtests; depressives in particular show no such trend.

(c) Neurotics who are given to intellectualizing often do badly on this subtest (as do such psychotic intellectualizers as paranoiacs and overideational preschizophrenics).

(d) Among nonpsychotic patients, hysterics[36] tend not to have notable negative Vocabulary scatter or mean scatter on Picture Arrangement.

PICTURE COMPLETION

The Picture Completion subtest of the W-B consists of 15 drawings; an important element is missing in each drawing. The task of the subject is to discover what is missing. The time limit on all of these items, although they are of varying difficulty, is 15 seconds. Only the correct answer gets credit.

Vulnerability appears to be a more prominent feature of Performance subtests than of Verbal subtests; this is certainly true for Picture Comple-

[36] [Plus character disorders, particularly when psychopathic trends are present.— Ed.]

tion. Qualitative analysis of these subtests points to the performance nature of the tasks, since verbalization plays no significant role.

The Psychological Rationale of Picture Completion. We attempted to show in the section on Arithmetic that the function underlying achievement on Picture Completion is concentration acting upon visually perceived material.

It could be argued that the function involved is merely effortless attention. The time pressure is an argument against this. Furthermore, given the meaning of the pictures, which of course are recognizable to the average subject of our civilization, the task is to discover an inconsistency or deficiency in this meaning. The discovery of inconsistency or consistency— the appraisal of *relationships* in a limited time—is one essential characteristic of the function here referred to as concentration.

It could be argued that this is merely another type of information test, depending on the patient's intimate and accurate knowledge of the pictured objects. But for the average person of our civilization most of these items do not require any special kind of information, but rather *common* information from everyday life. Experience indicates that reference to lack of information by the subject is a disguise for faltering concentration, and is usually not to be taken seriously. A survey of the pertinent experience will elucidate the point. Reference to lack of knowledge is made by patients almost exclusively on No. 4 (the playing card), No. 5 (the crab), No. 7 (the ship), and No. 13 (the light bulb). About the crab some patients say, "I wouldn't know—I never saw a crab"; but the fact is that living creatures are as a rule symmetrical, and a concentration on the picture readily shows the asymmetry caused by the missing leg of the crab; and inquiry about playing cards usually reveals that the subject knows that the dots and numbers on them are supposed to correspond to each other. In other words, checking of parts of the picture with available knowledge would have brought about the solution.

It is likely that many psychologists will consider the deficient function here to be reasoning. It is difficult to argue against this point of view, because what is here called concentration is the kernel of all reasoning. We prefer to consider reference to inconsistencies in common patterns as concentration, and to reserve the concept of reasoning for the more complex processes which are characterized by the interaction of attention, concentration, possibly anticipation, concept formation, and so on.

The importance of information in connection with the light bulb and the ship usually is of a different character. The patients will say, "There seems to be something wrong with the filament—but I never did look carefully at one"; or "The sails are funny, but I don't know enough about sailboats." Here the reference to lack of knowledge is a source of their failure. They really believe that they have found *where* something is missing but do not know *what* it is. It is true that knowledge of bulbs or sailboats would help in such cases by telling the patient that he is on a wrong track, but this role of information is of a definitely secondary nature: many people who have never seen a real boat and know little about filaments do pass these items by discovering the obviously missing threading and the missing smokestacks indicated by the smoke line.

How a query for information replaces concentration and defeats the subject is clearly shown in an obsessional patient of orthodox Jewish rearing who on No. 6 asked, "Do pigs have tails?" Apparently he had discovered that the missing element was the tail; but instead of relying on the result of this scrutiny, as a good obsessive doubter he wanted the approval of information—which probably due to his rearing he did not have.

The consideration of the role of information in the performance on this subtest leads us to the description of other types of failure. It will be of interest to analyze these because Picture Completion is the first subtest we have considered of a type to which the Rorschach test and, to some extent, the Thematic Apperception Test also belong—that is, tests where the identifying of visually perceived material plays a role.

In general, the failures can be divided into two groups.[37] The first is characterized by the subject's experiencing the picture as unfamiliar, strange, or incorrect. We shall term this type of difficulty "increase of distance" from the picture. The failures are verbalized thus: "I don't know what it (crab) is supposed to be," or "Is it a light bulb or what?" If it is conceded that concentration is an effort at meaningful intake of stimulation from the outside world—that is to say, a safeguard for keeping contact with reality— then impairment of concentration is impaired contact with reality. Familiarity with things is a sign of contact; an ability to recognize some familiar features in the unfamiliar is one of the main characteristics of the human being, as long as his contact with reality is unimpaired. A psychotic expression of increase in distance from the picture was given by a schizophrenic young man who had fought with the Commandos in Crete and had been evacuated to Egypt. On the fifteenth picture—the man facing a sun setting behind mountains—he said, "Sun setting by the pyramids." Here it is probable that overvalent affects and ideas so encroached upon visual organization that the picture itself was not correctly apperceived and understood; or in other words, the subject had not actually come to grips with the objective meaning of the picture. The loss of reality testing in this patient came to clear expression in this response.

The second type of failure is characterized by the subject's loss of ap-

---

[37] [For an independent verification of the main hypotheses advanced here, see Saunders (1960b) and fn. 6 in the Appendix to this chapter.—Ed.]

preciation that he is dealing with a *sketched* picture and not with the real thing; here the picture is taken too literally. Accordingly the question, "What is missing?" is taken to refer not to a missing element of a drawing but rather to reality as the subject would imagine or want to have it; in other words, he is considering as missing something that was not *intended* to be in the drawing, but which he would have to have there in a corresponding real situation. We shall refer to this type of failure as "loss of distance" from the card.

Thus a chronic paranoid schizophrenic, with an otherwise well-retained "front," said about the pig, "No food in the pen." Another chronic unclassified schizophrenic said about the man without the shadow, "The road is missing." Another schizophrenic said about item No. 7, "No crew on the ship." An extreme form given by very disorganized subjects is to state of any profile that "the other eye is missing"—a response that is the pathological counterpart of those drawings of preliterate peoples and children who put both eyes into the profile drawing (see Werner, 1940). A mild and, even in normals, frequent abortive form of this type of failure occurs when the subject responds to the picture of the woman at the mirror by naming missing parts which obviously were not intended to be drawn there. Other forms of this type of failure, which may occur on a low cultural level, but which sometimes serve as psychotic indicators, are the pointing out of minute gaps in the sketch lines or of the undrawn bodies of heads as the missing parts.

Administration. The handling of the stop watch should be such that— although no verbal instruction to this effect is given—the subject will have no doubt that he is being timed, and that speed is expected. The examiner can ascertain the correctness of his technique by inquiring after completion of the test into the subject's impression of what was expected of him. If the technique is correct, such reports of subjective experience will include the idea of expected speed. The examiner's certainty of the correctness of his technique is of great importance, because it can serve as a baseline for considering *characteristic* all performances that reveal a disregard for speed.

Wechsler's instruction to allow patients to finish the items even if the time limit is overstepped should be interpreted to mean not only that some answer should be obtained, but also that false answers should not be accepted and that new answers should be asked for. Such a procedure, as well as inquiry into peculiar answers, will bring to the fore many characteristic features of the subject's perception and its elaboration, which will be diagnostically useful, and will generally develop the examiner's frame of reference for qualitative appraisal.

It should be noted that the weighted-score scale of Picture Completion extends only from 0 to 15, and not over the whole weighted-score scale from 0 to 17. This is not only a structural shortcoming of the W-B but may to some degree vitiate the general equivalence of weighted scores when the subject is in the highest weighted-score range.

It is recommended that the verbalization of each response, except those consisting of the standard one- or two-word answers ("smokestack," "doorknob") be recorded, whether or not the response seems correct.[38] A similar procedure for time recording is also recommended, partly because responses given in one to five seconds reveal a personal characteristic, and partly because responses missing by a few seconds are likely to be temporary inefficiencies, in which case a low score should not be evaluated as though it were caused by full failure.

Item Analysis. The easy items are Nos. 1, 2, 3, 6, 8, 9, 10, and 12; the difficult items, Nos. 4, 5, 7, 11, 13, 14, and 15. If a subject quickly gives a false answer, it is recommended that the examiner wait silently until the end of the 15 seconds; this may indicate to the subject that he is wrong, and corrections should obtain full credit.

When misses occur in clinical subjects on the easy items, they are most likely to occur on Nos. 3 (the missing ear), 8 (the missing doorknob), and 10 (the missing flow of water). The relative difficulty in visual organization of these three items becomes clear when they are compared with the missing half moustache (No. 2) or missing nose (No. 1).

The most difficult items of all are Nos. 5 (the crab with the missing leg), 11 (the missing reflection in the mirror), and 14 (the missing eyebrow). It will be recognized that the failures on the latter two are connected with relatively greater difficulties in visual organization. The difficulty associated with No. 5, the crab picture, is harder to understand. It appears to be a most sensitive item for a test of concentration. Superficial information cannot supplant concentration; many persons do not know how crabs really look, and the effort to replace concentration by calling upon memory and information merely slows up the subject and makes him fail, while some subjects who call it a lobster nevertheless spot the missing leg.

DIAGNOSTIC SUGGESTIONS

(a) There is a rather clear hierarchy of groups in respect to failures on the easy as well as on the difficult items of Picture Completion, although the failures on the easy items are more diagnostically significant. The hierarchy is as follows: deteriorated unclassified schizophrenics and depressive psy-

---

[38] [Occasionally, brain-injured patients with word-finding difficulty have trouble with the specifically verbal aspect of the test. It may be used even with severely aphasic persons, however, by changing the instructions so that the task is merely to "point to the missing part."—Ed.]

chotics have the most failures; acute and chronic schizophrenics have somewhat fewer failures; neurotics (including the depressive neurotics) do relatively well in this respect.

(b) The relation of the Picture Completion score to both the Vocabulary and Mean levels is of importance in differentiating schizophrenics from depressives. Both groups tend to have scores five or more points below the Vocabulary level, reflecting their impairment of visual concentration, but for depressives this impairment is merely one segment of a general impairment of all the Performance subtests, and the scatter from the Performance mean is insignificant; while for schizophrenics there appears to be a tendency for other Performance subtests to be better retained than Picture Completion, and hence the scatter below the Performance mean remains generally significant. In other words, schizophrenics tend more than any other group to suffer special impairment on this subtest.

(c) Preschizophrenia and paranoid conditions—the intellectualizing psychoses—often produce some impairment on Picture Completion in comparison to well-retained Vocabulary and Verbal subtest scores.

(d) Obsessive-compulsives and hysterics at times show impairment relative to Vocabulary and to the performance mean on Picture Completion; for the obsessive-compulsives this is but another indication of their tendency to have a scatter pattern similar to schizophrenics', while for hysterics the impairment appears to be specifically isolated.

(e) A characteristic manifestation of a paranoid ego structure is a perceptual overalertness that lends itself to good performance on Picture Completion. When this subtest score is higher than those of the other Performance subtests in an otherwise schizophrenic record, it is an indicator of paranoid trends, like an elevated Similarities score. In paranoid schizophrenics, even deterioration often does not seriously impair Picture Completion; indeed, it may eliminate the tendency of some paranoid psychotics to seize upon some tiny or peculiar detail of the picture as significant and thus to lose the broad survey necessary for a good response.

(f) Weighted scores of 7 or less should be expected only[39] in schizo-

---

[39] ["Only," it should be reiterated, means in this book: "among the diagnostic groupings considered here, only . . ." Organic brain lesions can produce severe impairment on this as well as other Performance subtests, sometimes in the context of relatively unimpaired achievements on Verbal subtests; and it must be kept in mind throughout that mental deficiency should be ruled out before specific diagnostic significance is sought for extremely low scores on *any* subtest. Because of their relative inability to muster intellectual effort and concentrate on nonmanipulative tasks, persons suffering from character disorders (most notably those with psychopathic and addictive features) often miss easy items and obtain low scores on Picture Completion, particularly relative to Picture Arrangement (as they tend to do also on Arithmetic, because of the same inability to tolerate the tension of sustained effort). —Ed.]

phrenics or depressive psychotics. Cultural factors appear to play no significant role in this subtest; rather, a normal adjustment and no impairment of concentration are the important factors in efficient achievement.

VISUAL-MOTOR COORDINATION

In the sections to follow we shall deal with the remaining three performance subtests of the W-B: Object Assembly, Block Design, and Digit Symbol. These tests must be segregated because they differ from the two other performance subtests, Picture Arrangement and Picture Completion, as well as from all the Verbal subtests. They will be referred to as tests of visual-motor coordination.[40] This was the common psychological denominator by which these three tests could be referred to, although visual-motor coordination, visual organization, and speed of motor action play such varied roles in these three subtests that it is somewhat arbitrary to refer to them under one heading. Nevertheless, they all involve essential motor activity guided by visual organization; that is, they imply visual direction in their execution.

Visual-motor coordination is a term implying that our motor actions are not executions of mental decisions which precede them in time, but rather are initiated by a general decision, which in the course of the motor action is modified step by step to meet the specific situation partly encountered by and partly created by the motor action in progress, as this situation is revealed to us by the visual function—and in more complex situations by other functions too.

In everyday life, for reasons to be discussed below, this visual-motor

[40] In order to underscore the great importance we attach to the role of visual-motor coordination in the performance of psychiatric patients in these tests, we wish to quote here the more usually accepted view. In our treatment of the Block Design test we have made a point similar to the one to be quoted. The relationship of the more customary view to the one crystallized out of our clinical experience is not as yet clear to us. The following quotation is given here to indicate to the reader the need for further theoretical clarification: "In your characterization of this group as involving 'visual motor coordination' I have the feeling that you have avoided getting to grips with the essential character of the material and have compromised on a rather superficial description. The visual part is to a considerable extent irrelevant, isn't it? Wouldn't the same general principles be true if you were dealing with material in the auditory sphere? And is the coordination being tested particularly here? Except in extreme instances it appears to me that it probably plays little special role except in Digit Symbol. The important things after all would seem to be the analytic and synthetic processes involved in achieving relevant assembly. In giving it the name which you have, haven't you led yourself astray somewhat and haven't you drawn the reader's attention away from the more essential aspects? To some extent what I say here also holds for the 'visual organization' items." (Quoted from a letter of David Shakow.)

interaction rarely becomes easily perceptible. But in learning new functions implying motor action, or handling delicate or dangerous objects, we become keenly conscious of this interaction. The impairment of this coordination may remain veiled by habituated movements; but the results of it are seen in the avoidance of new activities requiring such coordination. Visual-motor coordination, though hardly noticed in everyday life, is a very sensitive indicator of maladjustment.

Only since Goldstein and Scheerer's (1941) studies has interest in visual-motor coordination been revived in modern psychopathology. The investigations concerning drawing and sculpture in comparative developmental psychology (Werner, 1940) scarcely pay attention to analysis of integration of visual and motor functions in the creative activities of children, primitives, and brain-injured and psychiatric cases. Interest in visual-motor coordination came most to expression in the work of Schilder (1935) and Loretta Bender (1938), both of whom put to use in their investigations the experimental methods of Wertheimer and Lewin. We do not feel in a position to evaluate either the clinical or the theoretical significance of the investigations that culminated in Bender's Visual Motor Gestalt Test. It appears certain, however, that this work more than any other brought to the fore in psychology the problem of visual-motor coordination.

This problem remains veiled to psychologists mainly as a consequence of two circumstances. First, a great sector of motor-executive action is very much habituated and thus stereotyped.[41] Just as in tests like Comprehension, where verbal convention veils and replaces judgment, so in motor action the delicate interplay of visual and motor functions is disguised and made imperceptible by its habituated, automatic character. Second, many of our actions occur in a situation so simple that its visual organization presents no problem. In other words, the spatial situation is such that it lends itself easily to visual organization, and as a result it appears that we have consciously decided, before the motor action occurs, the course the motor action should take. As a consequence, visual organization and motor action do not appear to interact, and motor action seems to be only a servile executor of the directives of visual organization.

But the space of visual organization and the space of motor actions are not two psychologically independent spaces. We create the space in which we live by a delicate interaction of many factors, of which visual organization and motor action are probably the most predominant; and the interaction of these is one of our most finely tuned functions. It is possible that one of the reasons for the inclination of Performance subtests to be

41 [See the discussion of automatization in Rapaport (1951a).—Ed.]

more vulnerable than Verbal subtests is the delicacy of this interaction, which is so easily disturbed by maladjustment.

We are still far from the time when knowledge of the rules governing visual-motor coordination will be sufficient to serve us as the basis for judging achievements on tests. The effort to offer at least some tentative framework within which the performance of the following three subtests can be judged appears to justify our putting forth here some considerations concerning visual-motor coordination.

The role of visual organization in each of these three subtests is different. In Digit Symbol, its role consists mainly of the same guiding action which visual organization plays in every kind of writing or drawing; the extent of this will be appreciated by anyone who has attempted to have a variety of subjects draw familiar patterns or write more than a few words blindfolded. Closer consideration, however, shows that the symbols to be copied in this subtest are not quite as well habituated as those of handwriting. Furthermore, it will be noticed that in Digit Symbol visual organization has the additional role of being the channel of *learning* the proper symbols, as well as of their correct reproduction.

The role of visual organization is quite different in Object Assembly, the most vulnerable of the three. Here jigsaw parts must be put together into a form familiar in everyday life. The essential motor action consists here of juxtaposing the different parts so that a visual process of "clicking together" of the parts into a meaningful pattern may occur. If the pieces are shifted too quickly, there is no time for such a process to occur. If it is done too slowly, the subject either gives himself no chance to try the possibilities of different combinations, or the slowness, accompanied by doubt or lack of interest, prevents the clicking-together experience. Each subject appears to have an optimum speed at which this experience can come about; and once he has lost this speed he achieves the solution with difficulty or not at all.

One who administers Object Assembly often enough will see cases in which it becomes clear that the random moving of the parts suddenly brings one part into a relation to another, by which a familiar configuration is brought to the subject's mind and reveals to him the meaning of the entire mix-up of parts. At such times the subject behaves as though in that moment the pieces were magnetic and pulled each other together.

In the Block Design subtest the material is quite different, and the visual organization pertains to geometrical patterns. The pattern is given on the sample card, and must be broken down and built up again out of block faces. The work of visual organization here seems to be first analytic and then progressively synthetic, but in reality the two interlace. On the one hand, the Block Design patterns are much less familiar to the subject than the patterns of Object Assembly; on the other hand, the subject is guided here by a pattern, kept before him as he works, of straight lines that obey definite recognizable rules, and can be followed logically to a completion of the task. Yet it would be an error to consider the whole performance a matter of logic. This is clearly shown in the fact that persons superior in logical reasoning may fail badly on Block Design.

Thus far we have not discussed the role of motor action in these subtests, which may have given the impression that we consider motor action to be of secondary significance. That motor action is of primary significance in the Digit Symbol subtest is well-known to anyone who ever tested a case in which brain injury has impaired motor action. Such a subject may well see, and may well verbalize, the symbol he wants to write, and nevertheless the hand may not obey. Similarly, the occurrence of cases in which motor-habituated forms, similar to one of the sample symbols given to the subject, distort the reproduction of that symbol, shows one aspect of the role of motor action in this test. This is a test of speed of both writing and ocular shifts, though the learning process may cloud the motor action. In this subtest individual examiners may be tempted to think less about the role of visual organization and more about that of motor action and its speed. In earlier paragraphs we have attempted to show that this assumption is detrimental to the proper understanding of the achievement.

Escalona (1940), in her "level of aspiration" studies on depressives, has adduced some evidence that their motor retardation may be of two types: either a retardation of *decision,* or an essentially *motor* retardation. In the former, it takes a long time for a decision to come about, but as soon as the decision is made the action is carried out; in the latter, the execution as well as the decision takes a long time. The examiner will find these same conditions present in the Digit Symbol achievement of slow cases. Hesitation, and the necessity of studying and relearning the symbols again and again, show the disharmony of visual and motor organization in these cases. Such an initial retardation may be followed either by a quick and correct writing of the symbol, or by a slow, hesitant, poorly shaped writing of it. On the other hand, the retardation may consist of slow laborious writing, without loss of time from excessive hesitation or the need to make special decisions about the symbol.

The role of the motor factor is quite different in Block Design and Object Assembly. From the initial description of these subtests, it may seem that motor activity is subordinated to visual organization. It is quite probable that visual organization plays a primary role, but the essential role of motor action should not be forgotten, especially when we except the "manikin" from Object Assembly and the first two items from the

Block Design, and when it is clear that the subject has difficulty in immediately deciding what the Object Assembly tasks should result in, or exactly
how one should go about building the required type of pattern with the
blocks. The blocks or the jigsaw parts must be brought near to each other,
and then put distant from each other, in order to allow for proper combinations, on the basis of which visual organization can make clear the
meaning of what is to be constructed and how it can be constructed.

It is difficult to put into words what every experienced examiner notices
about the character of this motor action. In some very keen subjects it can
be replaced by acute reasoning and unusually alert spatial organization.
They decide promptly what is to be put together and how, and the motor
action becomes merely one of placing the parts. In the majority of cases,
the motor action remains more important. Sometimes in the last three or
four seconds, the examiner is expecting the subject to put the last block into
place, and it may even already be in place; yet the subject, not giving himself time for the visual clicking together to occur, will remove the block
from its place, and may even remove several other blocks with it, thereby
failing the item.

Acute tension, anxiety, and hyperactivity are some of the factors whose
impact on motor action prevents whatever visual organization would bring
about. On the other hand, schizophrenic chronicity and deterioration may
result in visual disorganization, preventing the breakdown of visual patterns
into parts.

Object Assembly

Object Assembly consists of three items, each of which is a simple jigsaw problem: a manikin, a profile, and a hand. The manikin consists of
six pieces, the others of seven pieces each. If all the pieces are correctly
placed, a raw score of 6 is credited. One raw score unit is deducted for
each misplaced or unplaced part.

The time allowances are generous, being two minutes on the first item
and three minutes on the other items. If five or six raw score units are
achieved on the last two items in less than 65 seconds, time credits are
given, ranging from one to four raw score units.

Clinical experience shows that the vulnerability of this subtest is in considerable part due to the fact that, on the one hand, the highest weighted
score obtainable without time credits is 10, and on the other, no time scores
are given on an item if a raw score below 5 is obtained. Thus, a reversed
ear in the profile item, or an exchanged position of two fingers on the

hand—which in themselves may be temporary inefficiencies—will not only decrease the raw score of the subject by two units, but will also eliminate the possibility of acquiring time credits. The significance of this point for the administration and the theoretical background of the subtest will be discussed in the appropriate sections.

The Psychological Rationale of Object Assembly: The Role of Visual-Motor Coordination. The manikin has many painted markings on the limbs, body, and head which make it relatively easy to identify the parts, especially since they are cut up in conformity with the natural articulation of the human body. The situation is different for the profile. On the manikin, the natural articulation and the painted lines both serve as clues; on the profile, the six parts to be fitted to the large skull part do not follow the articulation of the human head, and thus the painted lines of features become of crucial significance as clues. The hand is even more difficult: it has no markings, and though the finger parts are separated roughly in conformity with the natural articulation of the hand, the thumb part and its adjoining wrist area are not so well articulated, and—what is more important—the palm character of the main part can hardly be discovered on first sight. Since there are only three items, a quantitative item analysis hardly seems expedient.

The concept of *visual organization* is in need of discussion, because it will be referred to repeatedly. The most common role of visual organization lies in the perception of objects, where it plays the role of identifying—supplying us with the meaning of—the objects. We are so accustomed to it in this role that we do not even notice it. But when objects are seen under conditions adverse to "perception as usual"—such as when partly covered, or moving with great speed, or in dim light, or at an unusual angle or distance—the role of visual organization becomes clear. In misrecognitions and in individual differences in apperception of the meaning of the object and its properties, it becomes clear that visual percepts are not passive copies of the world but rather are actively structured by a visual organizing process. That the visual organization process is determined in final analysis by the affective organization of the subject, as in the case of memory organization, will become clear in the discussion of the Rorschach and Thematic Apperception Tests. Here, however, we are concerned with the structural rather than with the affective aspect of visual organization.

Another everyday form in which we encounter visual organization is in visual memory as expressed in imagery. Any person who has attempted to get subjects to describe their visual memories of an object or person they are very familiar with, knows that the visual memories in question vary from extreme vagueness to crystal-clear detail. It goes without saying that characterization of persons as "good observers" and "visual types" refers to sharpness of visual organization.[42]

Visual organization as a dynamic entity becomes clear when we see a part of something usually seen as a whole. Thus, in the Incomplete Pictures subtest of the Minnesota Preschool Scale, one series of pictures presents on its first card one line of a shoe, on the second card more lines of the shoe, and so forth, until the last card represents the total shoe. The aim is to learn how much must be presented before the visual organization of "shoe" comes about. The individual variations are very great. A sharply accurate and differentiated visual organization will deliver correct images on few clues, while a vague, indefinite visual organization will need many clues. A rigid visual organization will stick to a once-conceived interpretation of a clue without allowing for change; a flexible visual organization will quickly integrate new clues and adapt itself to them by restructuring the visual image.

In this connection one could talk about concept formation present in visual organization, about visual anticipation, about the role attention and concentration appear to play here, about the relationship of visual organization to the concept of closure (*Prägnanz*) of gestalt psychology—but at the present stage of our knowledge such discussions would lead us too far into speculation. It will be seen below that visual organization plays a very considerable role in Object Assembly achievement—in fact, much more so than in Block Design and Digit Symbol, because in the latter subtests samples are put before the subject, while in Object Assembly he must rely more on visual organization unguided by samples.

To clarify the role of visual-motor coordination in Object Assembly, let us examine the performance on the manikin item. On the basis of our experience, the course of a normal, successful, and speedy performance can be described as follows. Inspecting the pieces put before him, the subject sees one which identifies the item for him; he states to himself, and frequently even aloud, "It is a man." Most frequently it is the head part from which this recognition emanates. Subjects of the keenest visual organization (observation) are by this time clearly aware that there are arms and legs before them, and have also noticed the difference between those limbs which have a curved and those which have a cornered joint. For these cases the rest of the performance—that is, the motor activity—is purely executive; its role is merely to move the parts into the places clearly defined by the specific and correct visual organization. Other subjects, when they

---

[42] [Though this proposition sounds self-evident, recent evidence indicates that visual organization in memory images and in the observation of an immediate display may be quite different matters (Holt, 1964a).—Ed.]

recognize that the object is a man, may not apprehend at all the significance of the shape of the joints and other features of the limbs. Some
subjects of this type will leave the rest of the performance to a trial-and-
error motor activity; they will try the round-ended arm into the angular arm
base, and only then will place it correctly. Some subjects even among the
adult population will try the legs in the arm sockets; this is most frequent in
psychotics. Some subjects will not learn by trial, probably because their
visual guiding image is very vague; they will leave the round-ended arm in
the angular arm base and vice versa, or even the legs in the place of the
arms. Other subjects resort to trial motor activity, but have sufficiently clear
visual-motor coordination that while moving the parts, and before actually
trying the rounded arm in the angular arm base, they recognize the situation; thus without having lost time in this trial, they will shift the piece into
its right place.

We see here a continuum: visual organizations that are sharp and fully
anticipating; those that come into full play only after some trial motor
activity; those that are mobilized only after considerable trying and erring;
those that are so vague that only the general idea of dealing with a human
figure is crystallized, and it makes no difference to them whether the arms
are in the proper joints or even in the place of the legs; and finally, those
where no visual organization is initiated, and no recognition of what they
are dealing with comes about. We also see that the less crystallized and keen
the visual organization is, the more important is the role given to trial
motor activity. The extreme end of this continuum of increasing significance
of trial motor activity is seen in those psychotic cases—mainly deteriorated
ones—where by trial and error all the pieces are fitted into their right place,
and only then, if at all, do these subjects recognize it is a man's figure. The
principle underlying such performance will be called *pattern coherence*.[43]

Here we shall devote only a short discussion to it. Pattern coherence is
a term describing a regulative principle of motor performance other than

[43] Martin Scheerer calls our attention to the fact that Goldstein and he described
this state of affairs using almost the same term that we have proposed here. We are
glad to give them here full credit of priority by quoting Dr. Scheerer's letter: "I think
there are certain correspondences between your findings and ours, and I wonder
whether you perhaps could point out these similarities in your publication. When you
read Goldstein's and my monograph, you will find that we speak of a 'matching' in
fitting angles or line-continuation instead of grouping in terms of the meaning of the
object parts or objects (pp. 32, 33). Correspondingly, we found on the Kohs [blocks]
a very similar procedure which you describe as: 'the subject is guided in his placement of each block by the perceptual agreement of his construction with the sample
design. In some cases upon completion of the design the agreement might really
click . . . for both the object assembly and the block design subtests we have used
the term "pattern coherence." ' We have described the same approach and procedure
and speak of concrete matching of patterns without abstract conception of the design construction" (Goldstein & Scheerer, 1941, pp. 113-115).

the one referred to as visual organization. When visual organization is impaired, and no visual anticipating image is formed, motor trial-and-error attempts are usually made. These trials and errors are characterized by fitting of edges and finding continuations of lines; that is, by *concrete,* piecemeal, partial characteristics rather than by over-all guiding organization, image, meaning, or plan. One could argue that this is still visual organization in a primitive or fragmented form. This would be correct in so far as the fitting and continuation of pieces, once achieved or failed, is approved or disapproved by visual organization; and when a figure is completed, visual organization may lead to its recognition. But the significance of the motor feeling that "it fits" should not be underestimated, and the fact that even finished figures may be unrecognized is also an aspect of performance by pattern coherence.

Motor *speed* does not play a great role in completing these items, because the time allowance of two minutes is ample to finish the manikin even by trial and error. Motor speed does play a role when action in moving the parts is too fast or too slow, and prevents the subject from restructuring his visual organization.

In visual-motor coordination, the motor action is, on the one hand, guided by the existing visual organization, and on the other, gives clues and opportunities for restructuring of visual organization by bringing pieces into relationships conducive to closure—recognition of a familiar pattern. Motor inefficiency itself, besides making for low motor speed of performance, may result in careless and not-quite-fitting placement of the parts into their right places; this is considered a temporary inefficiency, and is penalized by subtracting one raw score unit from the total raw score.

Similar considerations hold true for the role of visual-motor coordination in the second item, the profile. The difference between the manikin and the profile is that with the latter most subjects obtain in the beginning a vaguer visual organization of what they are dealing with, and even many normal subjects will not at first realize at all the object they are piecing together. The painted hair lines and eye lines, continuing from one fragment to another, have influence here. This influence can be of two kinds. On the one hand, the painted lines may lead to visual organization; on the other, where pattern coherence is the guide, the lines may prompt only a search for continuation, and may lead to total confusion by joining pieces which are entirely unrelated. Taking these facts into consideration, it is obvious that on the profile item we shall see fewer performances where visual organization directs the motor action in the assembling of the pieces, and more performances where visual-motor coordination—an attuning of motor speed and the restructuring of visual organization—will be the basis of the performance. Experience shows that the less familiar and the less clearly structured the task, the more the test becomes one not of visual organization with subsequent motor execution, but of visual-motor coordination. Still, on this item we do encounter performances based on immediate and correct visual organization.

The sawed-in-two rectangle of the ear is frequently placed in upside down. In doing so, the subject displays a weakness ("carelessness") of visual organization, and sometimes even an absence of it. In the latter case, the subjects go merely by pattern coherence in fitting together the two parts of the rectangle and in placing them in the rectangular hole in the skull; and upon questioning, it may be found that they do not realize that it is an ear. In many subjects, however, it is a temporary inefficiency that causes the reversal of the ear and the consequent loss of two raw score units with the additional loss of possible time credits. Here again it is obvious that the test is not one of motor speed, and that as far as motor function plays an essential role, it is by virtue of the necessary visual-motor coordination.

The considerations for the third item, the hand, are again similar, though pattern coherence may play a much greater role in its performance than in the first two items. The reason is that there are no markings, and only a partially natural, anatomical division of the parts to be pieced together. That pattern coherence often takes the place of visual organization in this item is seen by the fact that the fingers are frequently placed upside down into the interfinger spaces on the palm, and that the thumb is often fitted in correctly only by virtue of the angle at which it meets the palm part, without recognition by the subject that it is a palm and a thumb. The interchange of the fingers is also a sign of weakness of visual organization, though usually a temporary inefficiency.

On both the profile and the hand items, a placing of the pieces around the periphery of the main part is frequently seen. This is characteristic of visual disorganization, and is frequently seen in people characterized by overwhelming anxiety and in clear-cut psychotic cases.

Thus, visual-motor coordination is the underlying process of Object Assembly; it consists of a visual guidance of motor action which in turn, if of proper speed, gives an opportunity for restructuring the initial visual organization. Abortive forms of this coordination occur when the visual organization is fully crystallized at the beginning, and the motor action appears to play the role of the executing servant; or when visual organization is extremely weak or absent, and trial motor activity and pattern coherence appear to determine the performance.

Administration. Low weighted scores may be due to temporary inefficiency, as manifested by reversing the ear or interchanging two fingers, each resulting in the loss of two raw score units and possible time credits.

Thus the examiner should establish whether or not losses are due to temporary inefficiency; if this is the case, in evaluating the scatter of the subtest he should refrain from inferring the presence of profound impairment.

Since assessing temporary inefficiency may be of crucial significance for the evaluation of the scatter, it is necessary that the examiner record the subject's procedure in working on the items of the subtest, and inquire into and record the patient's subjective experience of his performance. It is particularly important to find out whether, when, and how the subject discovered what object he was piecing together. Needless to say, the rationale of queer constructions particularly must be inquired into.

As in the other subtests, here also it is necessary to ask the subject to indicate when he is finished, so that he gets no clue of approval or disapproval from the examiner. It is also important to test whether an erroneous solution can be corrected, or a slow performance completed; furthermore with how much help, if any, the patient can reach a solution.

Qualitative Features of Performance as Diagnostic Aids. Depressive retardation of motor speed and/or decision time results in poor achievement, since it reduces the possibility of getting extra time credit and even the possibility of completing the tasks within the time limits.

Random motor activity, free from emotional turmoil of the impulse-ridden or anxious type, may improve the schizophrenic patient's achievement. This is not to say that the solution is reached in the normal manner; rather, close observation of deteriorated and chronic schizophrenics' performance shows that in many of them coordination between motor activity and visual organization is absent, as is any basic understanding of the achievement. In other words, the blandness of deteriorated and some chronic cases results in good achievements on this test because the restlessness or bizarre impulsiveness of some of anxious acute cases is no longer present, and the hurried planless trial-and-error performance and preoccupation with small details of the jigsaw pieces no longer occur. Deteriorated schizophrenics tend to move the pieces around somewhat aimlessly and casually, and when one of the fragments is more or less accidentally held near its correct position, gross appreciation of the fitting together occurs with little understanding of why the piece belongs there or what it represents. Such understanding generally becomes conscious only near the end or sometimes after the end of a successful performance, or even not at all. Many reservations must be made concerning these observations. Nevertheless, they merit attention because they offer some evidence concerning the striking variations of visual-motor function in schizophrenia, and may contribute to the understanding of the change in functioning that takes place in deterioration.

DIAGNOSTIC SUGGESTIONS

(a) Impaired efficiency on the Object Assembly subtest may reflect depressive or neurasthenic retardation or anxiety.[44] If the impaired efficiency is essentially the consequence of depression, the score on this subtest will be much below the Vocabulary level but will not differ from the other Performance subtest scores, as depression tends to lower all these rather uniformly. If the impaired efficiency is essentially the consequence of anxiety, especially neurotic anxiety, the scores will not only be significantly below the Vocabulary level but also below the level of the other Performance subtest scores, which do not appear especially vulnerable to encroachment by anxiety. If anxiety and depression are both present, the Object Assembly score will, because of the additional anxiety factor, be even lower than the other Performance subtest scores, which have been lowered mainly by the depressive trend alone.

(b) Among schizophrenics, as one progresses from the acute delusional disorientation, panic, and anxiety of acute schizophrenics to the increasing blandness in chronic and deteriorated schizophrenics, one finds less and less encroachment upon the efficiency of Object Assembly. The Object Assembly score in deteriorated cases will not only be on the same level as the Vocabulary score, but will be two or more points above the level of the other Performance subtest scores, which in general are lowered by the increasing schizophrenic deterioration. The blandness of simple schizophrenics, similar to that of deteriorated schizophrenics, results in their also doing relatively well on this subtest. In other words, if the Object Assembly score is well retained while the other Performance subtest scores show considerable impairment, it is likely that one is dealing with a chronic or deteriorated schizophrenic.

(c) The Object Assembly subtest appears to be especially sensitive and vulnerable, and therefore one may find impaired efficiency on it in many different kinds of disturbances, even in normals who show anxious, schizoid, or depressive trends.

(d) These considerations hold true even on the absolute weighted score level. Many deteriorated schizophrenics have good or excellent scores on this subtest; depressive psychotics often have weighted scores of 4 or less.

---

[44] [Further rationale for the impairing effects of such affects as anxiety and depression is suggested by the work of Blatt, Allison, and Baker (1965): the fact that the items all represent parts of the body may make this subtest particularly vulnerable to preoccupation with bodily intactness.—Ed.]

BLOCK DESIGN

The Block Design subtest consists of seven items; these are preceded by two sample items which, if difficult for the subject, are demonstrated to him.

The two sample items and the first four test items consist of four blocks each to be juxtaposed so as to form a given design; the next two items consist of nine blocks each; the last item consists of 16 blocks. The blocks are those used in the Kohs Block Test, each having a blue, a white, a red, a yellow, a blue/yellow, and a red/white side; only the red, white, and red/white sides are used in this subtest. The blocks in each completed design constitute a square, and all the designs show some symmetry. In items No. 1, No. 3, and No. 5, it is easy for the subject to infer which block-faces should be juxtaposed. The designs of items No. 2, No. 4, and No. 6 give no such help. The design of No. 7 occupies a middle position, giving vague indications of the block-faces to be used.

The items are timed, but the time allowances are quite liberal, though not so liberal as on Object Assembly. The passing of each item within the time limit is credited with three raw score units, and additional time credits from one to three are awarded for speedy performance. Successful performance on all items without time credits—21 raw score units—yields a weighted score of 10; thus it is identical with that obtainable on a completely correct Object Assembly performance without time credit. It is true that partially correct performances on Object Assembly obtain partial credit, while on Block Design only flawless performance gets credit; but the fact that the obtaining of a weighted score of 10 depends in Object Assembly on success on three items, and in Block Design on seven items— on several of which time credit is easily obtained—makes Block Design much more refractory to impairment than Object Assembly.

The Psychological Rationale of the Block Design Subtest: The Role of Visual-Motor Coordination. Visual-motor coordination in the Block Design subtest can be characterized as occupying a middle position between its role in Object Assembly and its role in Digit Symbol.

In Object Assembly, individually different pieces with predetermined roles are to be put together into a pattern inherent to these parts. Thus visual-motor coordination, and particularly visual organization, play a *productive* role, in the sense that indications of the parts must be developed into an anticipatory image of the whole and this whole be put together out of the parts given.

In Digit Symbol, the role of visual-motor coordination is an *imitative* one; that is, visual organization is concerned with samples given to be copied, though the motor action of copying some symbols can be expedited by the subject's breaking them down into units of motor performance.

In Block Design, the role of visual-motor coordination is *reproductive*. On the one hand, the patterns to be recreated are kept before the subject, somewhat as in Digit Symbol; on the other hand, they are to be put together from parts, somewhat as in Object Assembly.

Unlike Digit Symbol, however, the given sample patterns on Block Design must always be differentiated into their parts, which are to correspond not to units of ease of motor performance but rather to units equal to those found among the block faces. Unlike the Object Assembly subtest, the pattern that must be constructed in Block Design is given visually and is to be reproduced out of blocks which are identical, interchangeable, and not inherently carriers of the meaning of the pattern to be constructed; that is, a red/white block face in the stripe pattern of No. 6 is not a carrier of the meaning "stripes" in the same sense that a leg is a carrier of the meaning "man" or a nose is a carrier of the meaning "face."[45]

Thus, Object Assembly being constructed out of units not interchangeable and hence inflexible, and Digit Symbol allowing for quite flexible drawings which need convey only the salient features of the configuration of the symbols, we may say that the interchangeable but precise units of Block Design place it in a middle position with regard to flexibility.

The role of visual-motor coordination in Block Design will become clearer if we consider the steps usually taken in the course of performance. The first step is the inspection of the item design. Here only visual organization comes into play. Its function and achievement in this first phase depend upon two factors.

The first factor is the acuity of visual organization in the subject, which (a) may immediately differentiate the pattern into its parts, and prescribe a priori how the pattern can be reproduced out of the blocks given; or (b) may give only a vague idea of the pattern as a whole, with the concrete realization of one or two isolated parts and the blocks to be used in reproducing these parts—that is, give a crystallized idea only of a starting point; or (c) may give no ideas of either whole or parts, whereupon the subject turns to the blocks to find in them some reminder of the pattern which will offer a starting point.

---

[45] It was Goldstein (see Goldstein & Scheerer, 1941) who emphasized first that a job of breaking down the pattern into its constituent parts is a matter of abstract attitude—the same function which he identified as underlying performance on any kind of sorting behavior, whether it is that on the Weigl Color-Form Test, the Sorting Test, or the Hanfmann-Kasanin Test. These tests which Goldstein considers tests of abstract attitude are considered by the present authors as tests of concept formation. The analytic and synthetic task implied by Block Design is related to the conceptual analysis underlying successful performance of concept-formation tests.

The second factor is the patterns themselves; some—1, 3, 5—lend themselves easily to differentiation in terms of block-face units, while others—2, 4, 6—convey only general impressions.

The second step is usually to turn to the blocks. Those subjects who have visually differentiated the pattern into its parts will turn to the blocks to execute their visual plans. Even here there will be great individual variation. On a pattern requiring only red/white faces, some of these subjects will turn all the blocks to red/white before proceeding; others will use first random blocks which are turned to that face. In both cases the security of approach will reveal to the examiner the superior visual organization; the latter subjects will usually be more flexible and economical, the former more systematic and rigid.

Superiority of visual organization does not always indicate superiority of visual-motor *coordination*. The differentiation of the parts to be used may be excellent, yet the handling of the blocks in an effort to find the right face can be fumbling and time wasting; or the certainty of the visual pattern may lead to hasty motor action which is not guided and corrected in its course by the visual organization, and which may result either in wrongly placed blocks or in the removal of rightly placed ones. Both an insecure performance which repeatedly compares the constructed parts with the pattern, and an overconfident performance which does not make such comparisons often enough are detrimental to efficiency. The efficient performance is an even balance of regard for the pattern, for the parts already constructed, and for the number, character, and position of the remaining spaces and blocks.

The role of visual-motor coordination becomes most obvious in those subjects who in the beginning form only a vague undifferentiated idea of the structure of the pattern and who isolate a secure starting point. By their handling of the blocks one can note the tacit problems, such as, "Are all red/white block faces congruent?" or "Does it make a difference which one I choose?" Once they find the block that will do as a starting point, we see them turning back to the pattern, and from this vantage point another—usually adjacent—part of the pattern becomes better differentiated for them; they turn back to the blocks again, manipulating them until they seem to click. In this manipulation they will repeatedly bring the new block with the desirable face up, but will turn to the wrong face because their movements are too rash for them to notice that it clicks; that is, they move the blocks too fast for the visual organizing process to get hold of it. Blocks once in the right position are often kept moving, for the same reason. Often the failure to fall back at the right moment upon the pattern for guidance will be the cause of such fumbling. A lucky coincidence of correct pace, right position, and checking with the pattern will clinch the point. *Good visual-motor coordination provides the maximum likelihood for such "coin-cidences."*

Insufficient interaction between pattern and blocks may be seen at times when in items No. 2, No. 3, or No. 5 the white-face blocks are not used, and the spaces where they belong are left empty. In this example visual organization is rather keen, but the blocks are disregarded. Cases where visual organization is vague and, at the same time, the blocks are not sufficiently taken into consideration, are seen when the stripes of item No. 6 become two thin stripes and one thick stripe, or even two thick stripes, or when the middle white square of item No. 7 is represented by the white face of one block or of four.

Subjects who form no visual organization of the pattern turn, for better or worse, to the blocks for a clue. Some of these subjects, by progressive visual differentiation, soon arrive at the same position as the subjects last described; others get nowhere. Random beginnings characterize them, and some of them come neither to a crystallization of the visual organization nor to any results. Others, by trial and error, may reproduce the pattern piece by piece without at any time—or even at the end—having an or-ganized picture of other than isolated parts, and steps in construction, of the pattern. This procedure is again governed by the pattern coherence dis-cussed in connection with Object Assembly. When such procedures prevail in his approach, the subject may construct out of the blocks a pattern whose contour is other than square, where the relation of any two blocks may be as required by the pattern but where the total pattern has not been experi-enced. Such a solution, as the result of persevering—that is, not as a result of vague visual organization which progressively crystallizes, but rather of absence of over-all visual organization—is rarely found in cases other than psychotics.[46]

Our emphasis on visual-motor coordination should not veil the fact that the work of visual organization in this test implies concept formation as evidenced in the analytic and synthetic phases of performance.[47]

[46] It should be made explicit that these conclusions do not take account of the achievements of children, mental defectives, and organic cases, which we have not studied.

[47] It will be worth while to mention here one more facet of such blind procedure by quoting a passage from a letter from Martin Scheerer: "I think it would be very desirable if you could call attention to the congruencies between your and our find-ings wherever they occur. It is so unnecessarily often that disagreements have been stressed in science and agreements have been neglected because of prestige factors overshadowing the common interest in the nature of the problem that I think we should be glad to announce agreements if they have been found in different methods of investigation. You mention, for instance, 'Another form of apparent success with-out understanding that we observed was a lack of recognition in some subjects as to the fact that different portions of design could be identically constructed.' You

Administration. The subject is to be told to indicate to the examiner when he is finished. In successful performance, however, the time credit is given according to the time of actual completion and not the time of indication of completion. Completion is defined as a solution not afterwards changed.

After a subject has stated that he is finished when his design is not correct, or that he cannot do the item, indication that he is wrong or help in proceeding should be given by the examiner; and it should be tested how much help, if any, brings completion. Such performances are not credited. If the error is minute—the design complete but erroneous in the orientation of one or two blocks—no help should be given and the subject should have a chance to infer from the examiner's silence that a recheck is necessary. If this is successfully done within the time limit, the item should be considered passed, though no extra time credit should be given.

Understanding and restudy of the visual-motor coordination underlying the Block Design performance is not possible without careful recording of the procedure the subject follows.

Item Analysis. Even on the sample items, indications which arouse suspicion of the presence of psychotic or prepsychotic conditions may be observed: as for instance, if the first sample is considered performed by the subject when he has turned one block red face up instead of four, or if he attempts to place the four blocks on the pattern card, or if he claims that solution is impossible "because these blocks do not have a black line" (referring to the black dividing lines on the pattern). The second sample also gives such indications if the square outline of the pattern is disregarded, and the subject thinks that the task is solved. Other difficulties on the second sample are frequent enough not to be suspicious unless they remain uncorrected after help showing the use of one red/white face in a corner.

The seven test items divide into three groups: (a) No. 1, No. 3, and No. 5, on which it is relatively easy to differentiate the block faces out of which it is to be constructed; (b) No. 2, No. 4, and No. 6, on which it is difficult to differentiate the block faces; (c) No. 7, on which the difficulty is intermediate, partly because it has misleading areas which look like differentiated block faces, and partly because the differentiation of block faces is by no means as difficult as on Nos. 4 and 6.

---

have here on a higher level (because of the 16-block design) what we found on a lower level in using four blocks where the patient is unable to conceive that the same distribution of colors occurs on all of the four blocks; he therefore looks for a third block and fourth if he can't find the particular color on the second block, to repeat that color which he found successfully on the first block." (See also Goldstein & Scheerer, 1941, pp. 43–48.)

One might formulate that these differences of difficulty are based on the extent to which the block-face elements lose their independence and submerge in the pattern of which they are parts. In group (a) the perceptual differentiation of the patterns coincides grossly with their block structure; in group (b) the patterns, while not less differentiated perceptually, are not identical with the single block faces, and can be duplicated only by more or less complex combinations of parts of block faces.

In group (a) the items show an increasing order of difficulty, because only No. 1 is unequivocally differentiated into block faces, and the white spaces in No. 5 are not. Failing items No. 1 or No. 3, or even having a prolonged solution time on them, suggests severe psychopathology—though there is one exception, that persons with very rigid visual organization may carry over to No. 1 the use of the red/white faces they learned on Sample 2. This may occur even in normal subjects. No. 5 may be missed merely as a result of temporary inefficiency. Particularly frequent is the correct placing of the cross consisting of one red and four white faces, while orienting the red/white faces offers great difficulty. This difficulty is usually connected with the aspect of visual-motor coordination that is frequently referred to as spatial orientation. Attempts to construct the middle red face in No. 5 out of four red block faces constitute a psychopathological indication.

Similar increase of difficulty is seen in group (b) where in No. 2 the blocks only partly lose their contours, while in No. 4 they lose considerably more, and in No. 6—with the exception of the somewhat perceptible corner blocks—they lose their contours almost entirely. No. 2 should not be missed, because its principle was present in Sample 2. No. 4 can be missed as a result of temporary inefficiency. No. 6 can be missed simply because a normal subject's function of visual organization is not specifically developed. In both No. 4 and No. 6 the corners serve as rather easily differentiated elements for the starting points of performance. For a subject to disregard the square contour of the pattern, and nevertheless show evident confidence and anticipation of success, is a psychotic indication. Constructions made of red-face rows and white-face rows placed at a 45° angle are similarly suggestive.

Item No. 7 is the most complex item, though from the point of view of visual organization not the most difficult one. The difficulty here is frequently the same as that encountered in the four corner blocks of No. 5— the direction of red/white faces. Temporary inefficiency can be so massed as to become easily defeating. Only queer constructions, disregarding length of rows and contour of pattern, can be considered strong evidence for the presence of psychosis. Depressive patients tend to be so overwhelmed by the amount of work required on this item that they usually are distinguished by their early attempts to give up.

DIAGNOSTIC SUGGESTIONS

(a) Depression is the most potent factor making for impairment of efficiency on the Block Design subtest.[48] All types of depressives, and neurotics with noteworthy degrees of depression or sluggishness, show great impairment of Block Design score (three or more points below the Vocabulary level); and psychotic depressives may even show a drop of Block Design score below their extremely impaired Performance means. The extent of impairment roughly parallels the depth of depression.

(b) The Block Design score of schizophrenics usually does not show any significant impairment from their Vocabulary level, and tends to be above their Performance mean. In some schizophrenics, however, psychotic disorientation and confusion may cause extreme impairment on this visual-motor subtest. The relatively superior efficiency found in most schizophrenics occurs not only in the full-blown cases, but also in preschizophrenics and even in schizoid persons in the normal range. Deteriorated schizophrenics may do well on this visual-motor subtest by a method of achievement very different from the normal. They proceed by means of a random and casual shifting of the blocks, putting two blocks together where they click grossly with a part of the pattern presented, so that in an inefficient and aimless manner the piecemeal visual impressions become a guide to a gradual reconstruction of the pattern. Inasmuch as on Block Design, unlike Object Assembly, partial scores are not given and time allowances are more strict, the achievements of deteriorated schizophrenics are less striking.

(c) The sharp contrast between depressives and schizophrenics is crucial for differential diagnosis on the basis of scatter patterns: extreme impairment is characteristic of depressives, and striking retention of efficiency, of schizophrenics.

(d) Weighted scores of 7 or less are extremely rare in normal or in nondepressed neurotic persons of above-average intelligence; this attests to the great stability of Block Design when depressive trends or psychotic confusion are absent.

DIGIT SYMBOL

The Digit Symbol subtest presents the subject with a sample line of nine simple symbols, each printed below a number from 1 to 9; also given are 67 empty squares, each under one of these numbers in a random sequence. The test requires that the subject write, in the empty square below each number, the symbol associated with that number in the sample line.

[48] [This subtest is also sensitive to brain damage.—Ed.]

The symbols are familiar to the people of our civilization, except possibly for No. 3. They are, however, of several kinds: No. 1, No. 3, No. 7, and No. 9 do not resemble letters; No. 4, No. 5, No. 6, and No. 8 strongly resemble letters, No. 2, somewhat so.

The subject is allowed 90 seconds for work, and each symbol correctly copied is credited with one raw-score unit. Correct copying implies that the symbol be drawn recognizably. The writing of a regular N instead of a reversed N (No. 2) merits a half raw-score unit. The highest weighted score obtainable is 16, which marks the second of the two systematic deficiencies of Wechsler's weighted-score scale.

The Psychological Rationale of Digit Symbol. The performance on Digit Symbol implies visual activity, motor activity, and a learning process.

The motor activity is of two kinds: first, the head and eye movements used in falling back upon the samples; second, the writing and drawing movements used in the reproduction of the symbols.

The learning process is always abortive, because of the nonsense connection between digit and symbol. Even if learning is stressed by the subject, the performance usually remains of an attentional character; that is, it exists—as in Digit Span—as a momentary noting rather than being integrated with the subject's interests and general frame of reference. This learning itself may be of three kinds. First, it may imply, "What symbol goes with this digit?" Second, it may be of a more spatial-motor type and imply, "Whereabouts on the sample line is the digit whose symbol I must look up, and whereabouts in the line of empty squares do I have to return to go on working?" The latter type of learning is really a structuralization of the motor task under visual guidance. It frequently replaces the first type of learning, since very efficient people will refrain from any effort to remember which symbol goes with which digit, and rather organize well for an efficient copying job by learning merely the spatial position of the material to be copied. A very efficient variation of this method, involving considerable concentration, consists of not falling back systematically upon the samples, but rather using the nearest identical copied symbol as a sample. The third kind of learning is present in both of the first two; it involves the efficient writing of the nine symbols which are, in great part, habituated anyway.

The visual organizing function plays two different roles: first, as the channel of learning and remembering the digits and associated symbols;[49] second, as a guide in both the spatial-motor learning and the executive actions of drawing and writing.

[49] The verbal-motor function may also become the channel of a type of learning seen when the patient mutters to himself while working. This type, however, is error producing; verbalization of certain symbols often changes them to nonidentical letters.

The Digit Symbol subtest is generally, and with considerable justification, regarded as a test of psychomotor speed. In point of fact, motor retardation shows up more clearly on this subtest than on any other, with perhaps the exception of Block Design. But psychomotor speed is not a function in the sense in which "function" is used in these pages. Psychomotor speed appears rather as a complex effect of a variety of interesting functions, an expression of a relatively undisturbed working of the organism. It may remain very good in strongly habituated tasks—as seen in stenographers—or in some chronic and deteriorative cases where the disturbing acute storms of psychosis have subsided and automatism prevails.

The visual-motor coordination in this subtest is expressed in the tuning together of the visual percept (or memory) of the symbol and digit, the spatial-visual and spatial-motor orientation, and the executive half-habituated action of drawing. It is small wonder that such a delicate interaction is easily disturbed from any side.

First of all, anxious hesitancy and obsessive doubt impair the stability of visual organization and the percept of what is to be looked for, and where. Meanwhile, motor action becomes hesitant; and while, if the percept had been quickly acted upon, it would have served its purpose, in the course of hesitant movements preparatory to action the visual guiding percept all but disintegrates, and time-consuming checks and rechecks follow. At times we see subjects, especially those whose anxiety and attention disturbance are considerable, compensate for a labile visual organization by jotting down the symbols with a jerky rapidity, in order not to lose them. Thus not only visual and motor efficiencies are attuned, but also their inefficiencies.

Visual and motor disorganization can be profound enough to distort the symbols so much that it becomes difficult to decide whether the disorganization is essentially visual or affects the total coordination whereby motor action is guided by visual organization.

Some meticulous people, in spite of the obvious stress on speed, proceed very slowly and draw the symbols with painstaking exactitude. The instructions—uniform for every subject—are apparently understood by these people as requiring exact rather than extensive copying. The result is a low score on psychomotor speed, which should not be interpreted as a depressive indication. Otherwise, a general extreme slowness without hesitation, doubt, meticulousness, or distortion of the symbols is rarely seen, and then only in depressives. Such essential retardation of psychomotor speed is a part of the generalized depressive retardation, and as yet we have no testing data that would contribute to its explanation.

Administration. We find it useful to insert into the standard instruction: "Take each in order as it comes." Subjects who are inclined inadvertently to skip a space here and there or to shift from one line to another, or to fill in first the squares underneath one given digit, will do so in spite of the added instruction, and the examiner will know that this is not a result of misunderstanding the instruction.

We find it useful to inquire into any repeated peculiar writing of a symbol; such peculiarities are sometimes due to a schizophrenic misinterpretation of the symbol.

Whenever a subject starts erasing we in part give "time out"—without crediting the symbol, if it was originally unacceptable—and in part discourage such corrections. Our attitude is conditioned by our desire to have a test performance as little distorted as possible by disturbances other than those of visual-motor coordination.

It is recommended that the examiner note and record changes in speed of performance. In particular, general trends of increasing or decreasing speed, as measures of both readiness of adjustment to a task and fatiguability, as well as wavering attention deserve consideration.

DIAGNOSTIC SUGGESTIONS

(a) Greatly impaired psychomotor speed as reflected in the Digit Symbol score is most directly related to the presence of depressive trends or schizophrenic deterioration. Increasing severity of depression results in increasing impairment of visual-motor speed; and therefore, diagnostically, one may estimate the severity of the depression from the impairment of the Digit Symbol score, with reference to both the Vocabulary level and the weighted score itself. A score six or more points below Vocabulary indicates depression of psychotic degree.

(b) Schizophrenics often show some impairment on the Digit Symbol subtest, probably reflecting their impairment of concentration; but some bland schizophrenics may do exceedingly well on this subtest.

(c) Weighted scores of 7 or less are practically absent in intelligent normals, even those inclined toward depressive mood swings. This gives emphasis to the point that a relatively poor performance on Digit Symbol is generally a sign of pathological depression or, less frequently, of some schizophrenic disturbance.

CONCLUSION

Having reached the end of these analyses, we are obliged to ask ourselves, What have we found? The existence of clinically characteristic scatter patterns is not demonstrated merely by finding quantitative differences in over-all impairment on the subtests more or less proportionate to the extent of maladjustment, but rather by the selective impairment of single subtests or subtest groups in specific clinical groups.

We attempted to find in our material individual scattergrams for each clinical group which would contain all the features we found characteristic of that group. No such typical individual scattergrams were found. We must ask ourselves whether the absence in our material of such typical cases implies that the general patterns we have described are illusory. The answer is definitely in the negative. It has to be kept in mind that psychological functions and their impairments are subject to many influences specific to the person and to the testing situation; and accordingly general idealized patterns, like those of nosological categories found in textbooks of psychiatry, appear only with individual variations. It is our experience that the scattergram of the W-B is definitely diagnostic in 30-40% of the cases; in another 30-40% the scattergram, though by no means conclusive, offers indications about the diagnostic direction; in the rest of the cases the scattergram is inconclusive.

Here a new question arises. Is it worth while to work with a diagnostic test if the examiner must keep in mind general scatter patterns, specific subtest scatter distributions, results of item analysis, and many cumbersome instructions concerning administration, only to obtain diagnoses in 30-40% of the cases, and diagnostic hints in another 30-40%? Without attempting to answer this question directly, the following considerations are offered:

(1) In clinical testing work as practiced at present, some kind of intelligence test is always given. The results obtained in analysis of the W-B suggest that, in using it, one uses a two-purpose tool instead of a one-purpose tool. That is to say, in addition to the intelligence measures one can obtain indications of ego structure.

(2) The efficiency of other diagnostic procedures is not far superior to the percentages stated for the W-B.

(3) Where other clinical or testing data are at the disposal of the examiner, both the overlapping and the mutual exclusiveness of diagnostic indications will make the W-B scatter more valuable than it appears at first sight.

(4) Granted that in the beginning the examiner finds the procedure of using item analysis and scatter analysis very cumbersome; still, after some experience neither the recording nor the analysis requires any more effort than the usual administration of the test. For the experienced examiner, the significant parts of the W-B stand out against the routine stereotyped parts so sharply that the evaluation becomes, in a sense, automatic.

(5) The examiner must keep in mind that the subtests do not tap all the functions that can be tapped by intelligence testing. It is hoped that systematic, widespread work in scatter diagnosis will encourage exploration

of scatter of tests tapping other functions than those tapped by the W-B, and will lead to a more intimate knowledge of selective impairments of intellectual functioning and finally to the construction of intelligence tests specifically for the purpose of diagnostic scatter analysis, with the yield of an IQ a matter-of-course side issue.[50]

[50] [A sixth point might be added, that the W-B also yields another type of diagnostic information, from the qualitative analysis of verbalization and test behavior. The two relatively independent types of analysis, quantitative and qualitative, helpfully check and complement each other.—Ed.]

Concerning Scatter and the WAIS

THE PROBLEM OF SCATTER ANALYSIS

As Chapter 3 has shown, an excellent a priori and theoretical case can be made for the proposition that variations in the patterning of abilities ought to yield diagnostically and personologically relevant information. True, psychometric considerations limit what can be expected of any specific instrument. An ideal test for scatter analysis should contain perfectly reliable subtests, completely homogeneous and factorially simple, each of which would be as independent as possible of the others. Moreover, they should be standardized so well that a flat average profile of weighted scores would be obtained for reasonably large random samples of normal persons.

Some of the publications that have appeared during the past 20 years concerning the W-B and the Wechsler Adult Intelligence Scale (WAIS; see below) have shown how far from this ideal either of the Wechsler tests is. The standardization of the W-B left a great deal to be desired, so that the average scattergrams of normal college students, Kansas Highway Patrolmen (the control group of the original Menninger research study), and applicants to the Menninger School of Psychiatry (Holt & Luborsky, unpublished data) all deviated from a straight line in just about the same ways.[1] The WAIS seems to be better in this respect, and the reliabilities of

---

[1] Specifically, the 11 subtest mean scores were ranked for each of the following three groups and were correlated: (a) Harvard students (Estes, 1946), (b) physicians applying to the Menninger School of Psychiatry (Holt & Luborsky, 1958), (c) Kansas Highway Patrolmen. The rhos between successive pairs were: $rho_{ab}=.97$; $rho_{bc}=.87$; $rho_{ac}=.89$.

Lloyd Silverman, in a personal communication, suggests that a flat baseline is not in principle attainable anyway, except as a group mean. He argues that the "analysis of scatter is based on the assumption of equality in the innate capacities underlying different functions" for everyone, from which inherited baseline the effects of psychopathology would push the various subtests up or down. This objection is, however, based on a misconception of Rapaport's assumption about the nature of abilities and their relation to psychopathology (see Mayman, Schafer, & Rapaport, 1951). Scatter

its subtests are higher, so that errors of measurement alone should not give rise to as much substantial but diagnostically meaningless scatter. Jones (1956) and McNemar (1957) have pointed out the fact that difference scores (e.g., Vocabulary scatter) are even more unreliable than the subtests on which they are based, so that according to Field (1960), a WAIS subtest weighted score should differ from the mean of all the others by at least 5.75 for the difference to be significant at the .05 level! His calculations also indicate that a 10-point difference (or larger) between Verbal and Performance IQ is likely to arise from errors of measurement alone in almost 5% of the cases.

Further intrinsic limitations on scatter analysis are suggested by factorial studies of the W-B and WAIS. By conventional means, both have been shown to have large general factors (which is necessary for an intelligence test), and in addition a limited number of group factors. For example, using a variety of subject samples, Cohen (1952, 1957a, b) has found that the W-B and WAIS have similar factorial structures: he calls the group factors verbal comprehension, perceptual organization, and memory, and finds relatively little factorial specificity of subtests.[2] He found, in addition,

---

analysis does not require us to assume that individual differences in the pattern of achievements on the subtests are entirely the product of psychopathological experience. Indeed, in the Rapaport tradition it has been left an open question whether there might not be genetic "diatheses" in the form of innately given types of ego structure. Thus, if a person is born with especially keen abilities along the lines of concept formation and concentration, outrunning his judgment and other functions, this state of affairs might predispose him to develop projective types of defenses, which if decompensated under the impact of life stress might lead to paranoid symptoms. It must be conceded, however, that the emphasis of the text upon the differential diagnosis of a set group of psychopathological conditions lends itself to Silverman's interpretation.

[2] In a personal communication, Lloyd Silverman suggests that the conflict between Cohen's results and Rapaport's rationales is only apparent, and may be resolved as follows: "In certain instances, there is no conflict. For example, the finding that Block Design and Object Assembly have the same factor loadings is in keeping with Rapaport's formulation that these subtests both tap visual organization, visual-motor coordination, and motor speed. In other instances, however, there was no such congruence, and some psychologists have taken this fact as invalidating Rapaport's formulations. While modifications in certain of his formulations may well be warranted, two points should be kept in mind:

"(1) Cohen's patient population was, in many respects, very different from the Menninger population and these differences often make comprehensible the lack of congruence between Rapaport's rationale and the factor-analytic results. For example, Cohen's studies have failed to show that Information and Comprehension load different factors to any noteworthy degree. This finding might be thought of as contradicting Rapaport's conclusion that subjects who rely heavily on repression show a notably higher score on Comprehension than Information. Such a use of repression would be expected primarily from hysterics, a sizable patient group at Menningers. Not only was there no hysteric group in Cohen's population, but the subjects he utilized were all males. This is important since hysterical characteristics are much

that the W-B Picture Completion was factorially complex, with sizable loadings on both of the first two factors mentioned above (Cohen, 1952). Saunders (1960b) followed up with a factorial study of the *items* of this subtest on the WAIS, and discovered three distinct factors within it. In a parallel study (Saunders, 1960a) he found no less than six factors in the items of the WAIS Information and Arithmetic items! In an earlier study (Saunders, 1959), he reported a factorial structure for the WAIS subtest scores similar to that of Cohen, and concluded: "The results are consistent with the efforts of some clinical psychologists to interpret the Wechsler 'psychogram' as a personality measure provided attention is given to individual items of Comprehension and Picture Completion."[3]

The results actually obtained by Rapaport, Gill, and Schafer (1945-1946) and their successors must be viewed against these intrinsic limitations. In a way, it could be argued that the results are better than they have any psychometric right to be. Even though the poor reliabilities of the individual W-B subtests ought to give rise to considerable random variation on retesting, Griffith and Yamahiro (1958) found rather impressive repeat reliability of scatter. With a mixed group of 55 patients, some of whom were given different forms of the test after varying intervals of time averaging 42 months, they found an average rho of .51. The rank ordering of the subtests was even more stable when the same form was used on both occasions, and when shorter time lapses were involved. When one reflects

---

more apt to be found among females. As another example, Cohen's studies have failed to reveal any noteworthy unique variance for the Similarities subtest, which instead heavily loads the 'verbal' factor together with Information, Comprehension, and Vocabulary. Rapaport, although recognizing the verbal component in this subtest, also saw it as tapping concept formation and pointed out that this ego function can be expected to show impairment primarily in depressive psychotics, deteriorated schizophrenics, and chronic schizophrenics. In Cohen's studies there were no patients of these kinds, the schizophrenics who were used mainly being early and acute cases. [See, however, text below.]

"(2) In those instances in which differences in population cannot account for the discrepancy, Rapaport's conclusions, rather than being invalid, may simply be of more limited scope than he originally believed. For example, Rapaport discusses at length the difference between Arithmetic and Digit Span in terms of the degree to which concentration and attention are involved in each. Cohen's finding that these two heavily load the same factor and contain little unique variance has led me to modify (rather than discard) Rapaport's formulation in the following way. It seems likely that each of these subtests demands *both* concentration and attention, though Arithmetic demands more of the former and Digit Span more of the latter. For this reason, and also because concentration and attention usually vary together, the weighted scores on these two subtests are usually quite close. In the relatively unusual case when a sizable discrepancy *does* exist, however, it is not out of keeping with Cohen's results to interpret this as a function of differential impairments of attention and concentration, for the particular individual involved."

[3] See below for discussion of internal differences within Comprehension and Picture Completion subtests.

that differences of a single point can determine the ranking of subtests, and that many of the patients had probably undergone a good deal of therapy, this is an impressive result.

If nothing else, the first volume of Rapaport's work stimulated a flood of research on scatter patterns. This literature has been reviewed in several places (Rabin, 1945; Watson, 1946; Rabin & Guertin, 1951; Guertin, Frank, & Rabin, 1956; Guertin, Rabin, Frank, & Ladd, 1962; Guertin, Ladd, Frank, Rabin, & Hiester, 1966) to which the interested reader is referred. The story is a rather dismal one: despite occasional verification of the Rapaport hypotheses, there are predominantly negative findings— from badly designed studies, most of which ignore the advice about clinical research given by Rapaport et al., though a number of them have done a good job of controlling the variance due to age, sex, social class, etc., which the pioneering study neglected. Some studies (e.g., Wittenborn, 1949) re-analyzed the original Menninger data and concluded that the groups could not be differentiated in terms of their W-B subtest scores, nor were the patients within groups more alike than they were like those in other groups.

It is difficult to remain cheerful about research and practice in clinical psychology after plowing through a good deal of this literature. So much effort has been wasted by so many, by the application of inappropriate research design! In summarizing one of their reviews of published research, Guertin et al. (1962), who are anything but uncritical enthusiasts for scatter or pattern analysis, conclude that, despite the predominance of negative findings, "the frequent occurrence of positive studies may be regarded as evidence that analysis of patterns can be meaningful and that something other than the tool itself might account for the failure of the research to provide consistent and definitive answers" (p. 19). They point out the general methodological inadequacy of most studies in this area: above all, the failure to use homogeneous diagnostic groups, but also the oversimplicity of research designs and of the statistics used to cope with an intrinsically multivariate problem, and the tendency to sacrifice clinical considerations for statistical ones.

Let us consider one of the best studies, one of the few that have not simply compared means of subtest scores in different groups. Cohen (1955) allowed seven clinicians with from four to 14 years of diagnostic experience with the W-B to use any cues they could extract from the profile of subtest scores, plus the three IQ's, to diagnose 300 VA patients. In some respects, the test data were carefully selected: they were the first 100 consecutive admissions who received unambiguous "neuropsychiatric" diagnoses of, respectively, schizophrenia, psychoneurosis, and brain damage, who also satisfied the following criteria: the groups were all white male veterans between ages 20 and 40, with nonsignificantly differing means and standard deviations on age, education, and Full Scale IQ.

Yet the three major groupings were internally quite heterogeneous. The organics included 66 with focal lesions (but with no further specification of the *location* of the lesion!), 20 with generalized ones, and 14 "focal-diffuse." The neurotics included 34 "anxiety states," 25 conversion hysterias, 14 mixed neuroses and the rest miscellaneous; the schizophrenics were equally diverse: 56 paranoid, 12 simple, seven hebephrenic, four catatonic, and 21 mixed or unclassified. In an earlier study which used the same subjects, Cohen (1952) comments that they could all be considered "early or acute . . . the 'back wards' type not being represented." This statement is difficult to square with the experience of most psychologists in the VA that true acute schizophrenics are not often seen, the predominant types on admission being flare-ups or exacerbations of longstanding chronic schizophrenias; the fact that seven were diagnosed as hebephrenic also clashes with his characterization of the schizophrenic sample.

Aside from this internal heterogeneity, note that the author merely accepted the "neuropsychiatric" diagnosis given in the VA hospital, despite ample evidence that such routine diagnoses are quite unreliable, and are often based on superficial study. Compare this insouciant attitude toward the criterion with the diagnostic care used by Rapaport and Gill in their original research (Rapaport, Gill, & Schafer, 1945-1946, Vol. 1, pp. 16-31).

Despite these inherent limitations, the findings were statistically significant. The best judge's over-all results considerably exceeded chance ($p < .001$), and his ability to diagnose neurosis and brain damage separately was also at that level. Two others could also significantly select the brain-damaged cases. True, the strength of the relationships was not great: the corrected contingency coefficient for the best judge's total performance was .31, and he and the next best obtained phi coefficients of .22 for the diagnosis of organic damage. Cohen remarks: "The conclusion that some experienced psychologists can make diagnoses from Wechsler-Bellevue patterns significantly better than chance is inescapable." He is not impressed with the size of the coefficients, however, and the tone of his evaluation is that scatter analysis has not yielded a useful level of discrimination.

In an earlier review, Rabin and Guertin (1951) also judged that "the mountain of scatter analysis brought forth a mouse." Yet if one looks again at Rapaport's original claims for scatter analysis, they are modest rather than mountainous, though more optimistic than mousy: "the scattergram . . . is definitely diagnostic in 30-40% of the cases; in another 30-40% the scattergram, though by no means conclusive, offers indications about the diagnostic direction; in the rest of the cases the scattergram is inconclusive" (above, p. 159).

In clinical practice, no one worthy of the name of psychologist attempts to do a diagnostic job of any kind from the scattergram *alone,* any more than he does by means of any single test score or sign. Despite the bad example set by his own research (see Editor's Foreword), Rapaport was clear enough that scatter analysis was not the be-all and end-all of psychodiagnosis: it was an attempt to make some use of an easily available set of data as a source of hypotheses to be checked against other test data. To check claims like those quoted in the previous paragraph, one would need to design research on the *incremental validity* contributed to a battery of tests by the scattergram, when analyzed by trained clinicians. The criterion, moreover, should not be a set of psychiatric diagnoses, however carefully established. Scatter analysis suggests hypotheses (primary inferences) about various aspects of personality, thought organization, defenses, etc., and it should be validated in terms of such constructs, with the most convincingly face-valid assays that can be obtained.

With the field in this ambiguous state, it seemed to me best to let the text of Chapter 3 stand essentially as it was, so far as diagnostic leads from W-B scatter were concerned. They need to be taken *cum grano salis,* and used in the way recommended in the Editor's Foreword and in Chapter 3's concluding remarks.

In his clinical practice, the reader will probably find that he is grateful for any ready source of hypotheses, to guide his qualitative analysis of test data; hence he will be well advised to pay some attention to the quantitative findings of the Wechsler scales as he does to those of the Rorschach. But neither of these sets of numbers will prove valuable if they are taken too seriously. They are only sources for hypotheses, which need internal verification just as badly as hypotheses based on the most qualitative analysis of test behavior or verbalization. Occasionally, he will encounter an anomalous case in which a false lead given by scatter analysis produces serious error because it seems verified by one or two other types of information in the test battery and the available clinical data, or by secondary inference based on the over-all picture suggested by well-founded primary inferences. As his experience grows, however, he will find, strangely enough, that such cases seem to grow fewer; he will learn when to disregard certain suggestions from the scatter and when to listen to them. Depending on his personal talents and inclinations, he may find that he pays less and less attention to scatter, or that it retains enough suggestiveness for the diagnostic process so that he would feel handicapped without it. As long as he uses it in the spirit advocated in this book, however, he is not likely to fall into serious error with it.

The Wechsler-Bellevue and the
Wechsler Adult Intelligence Scale

In 1955, David Wechsler published the Wechsler Adult Intelligence Scale (WAIS), after some years of research and development. It was quickly adopted by clinicians, and is now the most widely used test of intelligence with adults. The old W-B (Form II, and record blanks for Form I) can still be purchased, a substantial amount of research using it continues to be published, and it remains in fairly wide clinical use. In all likelihood, however, it will drop quietly out of the picture during the second decade of its younger sibling's life. The latter has several advantages: it is better standardized, it is less handicapped by out-of-date items, and it is improved in many details, as we shall shortly see.

The question arose, therefore, in the course of the revision of this book, whether to try to modify the text to take into consideration the specific differences between the two scales. For many reasons, it seemed best to keep essentially intact the original text with its explicit reference to the old items, and to add the following discussion as a general guide to aid the reader in adapting the discussions to the newer test.

The best discussions of the two tests I know of, from the point of view of the present book, are in a paper by Sinnett and Mayman (1960), and a review by Schafer (1956). With the kind permission of these authors, the former paper is reprinted here in slightly abridged form, supplemented by passages from Schafer's review put in as footnotes with the initials R. S.

The WAIS Compared to the W-B As a Clinical Diagnostic Tool
By Kathleen Sinnett, Ph.D. and Martin Mayman, Ph.D.

The Wechsler Adult Intelligence Scale is an extensive revision of the original Wechsler-Bellevue Intelligence Scale Form I first published in 1939. The WAIS is in many ways a new test and, for the most part, a distinct improvement over the original. It is likely that the clinician who has heretofore relied upon the Wechsler-Bellevue in routine clinical work will gradually adopt the WAIS in its place, but this will require that he revise his "apperceptive mass" of experience with the test.

Wechsler made good use of the two decades of experience with the original form of the test, and has tried with remarkable success to clear up many of its faults. The changes are many, some of them major ones affecting subtest rationale,[4] others more trivial and likely to have little

---

[4] Information now contains two items that overlap Comprehension ("Why are dark clothes warmer than light-colored clothes?" and "How does yeast cause dough to rise?"); also Comprehension now contains three items that overlap tests of concept formation (three proverbs). Thus, not all the changes are in the direction of greater homogeneity within the subtests.—R.S. [The same point about the inclusion of proverbs in Comprehension was made in personal communications by Sidney Blatt and Lloyd Silverman.—Ed.]

effect on the significance of subtest scores or item content. Yet, every sub-test has been altered in some significant ways, some of them in the method of administration, some in the adjustment of scoring criteria for retained items, and some in the addition of new items and deletion of old ones.[5]

The addition of new items over a wide range of difficulty, and a re-arrangement in the order of presentation of old items serves to eliminate abrupt discontinuities in the level of item difficulty as one proceeds through each subtest. Each subtest is now more discriminating over a wider range of accomplishment than was true in the original Wechsler-Bellevue.

Probably the most radical general overhauling of the test was done with the Performance subtests. For example, in the Picture Completion subtest, of the 11 items which are carried over from the Wechsler-Bellevue, nine are redrawn in a fashion which makes this a quite different kind of task.[6] The sketches are now less "sketchy," the drawings are larger, drawn more boldly with the lines carefully completed; the pattern includes many distracting details so that the task becomes more difficult on each of the new or redrawn items. What seems to be required now of the subject is a more meticulous searching of the design, where previously a quick scan-ning of the Gestalt would have provided the correct answer.

Another major change was made in the scoring of the more motor performance tasks. On Block Design there are far fewer time credits (allowed on only the last four of the 10 problems), so that if we consider the maximum attainable Block Design score, only 17% is contributed by time bonuses on the WAIS, whereas 50% of the maximum score is con-tributed by time bonuses on the W-B. Nevertheless, speed remains an im-portant factor because the time limits have become more stringent so that one now fails an item 15 to 30 seconds sooner (even on new items which are much more difficult than any on the W-B), and one must work con-

---

[5] The WAIS seems to be a more efficient machine than the W-B. Because of this, it seems reasonable to expect that temporary inefficiencies and other deviations of response will be even more diagnostically significant on the WAIS than the W-B.—R.S.

[6] [In three of these redrawn items, however, the changes introduced are minimal. Note that Saunders (1960b), in a factorial item analysis of the Picture Completion subtest, found three factors: "I. Maintenance of Contact; II. Maintenance of Perspec-tive; and III. Effect of Uncertainty." These factors do not clearly distinguish between the old and new (or redrawn) items, though only Factor II is not heavily loaded by one of the original, sketchy items. "Factor I is most highly correlated with item 18, which is the same item [old item 15, redrawn] used by Rapaport to illustrate what he termed 'increase of distance from the picture' or 'impaired contact with reality' as one of three major sources of failure on PC items." It also includes items 16 (old item 11) and 12. "Factor II is most highly correlated with items 8 and 9. The most com-mon wrong responses to these items are 'Bow' and 'Oarsman,' respectively, and such responses may be judged to be psychologically similar to what Rapaport termed 'loss of distance' as a second source of failure." Also prominent in this factor is item 13. "Factor III is most highly loaded by items 2 [old item 6], 10 [old item 13, redrawn], and 14 [old item 7], which are precisely the items used by Rapaport to illustrate failure in PC when a 'query for information replaces concentration,' his remaining major source of failure." It is amusing that factor analysis, an approach for which Rapaport never had sympathy, has provided such an impressive and quite inde-pendent confirmation of his rationale for this subtest!—Ed.]

siderably faster to earn any time credits at all. Similar, though not so drastic, changes in the other Performance subtests make them, too, more sensitive speed tests. The net effect of these changes has been to make the Performance battery an apparently more sensitive measure of retardation and confusion such as may be found in severe depressions, schizophrenia, and brain-damaged conditions.

The greatest change in the verbal battery is in the treatment of the Vocabulary subtest. For one thing, it is no longer an optional subtest, but rather adds its full weight routinely to the total IQ score. It is also an entirely new test, administered differently and comprising an entirely new series of words. The various parts of speech are much better represented in the new test: there are 15 verbs, 17 nouns,[7] one adverb, and seven adjectives; the W-B list consisted of 33 nouns, seven verbs, two adverbs, and no adjectives. In effect, we now have a more genuine "vocabulary" test and less a test of general information than the original W-B Vocabulary Test. It is our impression that the WAIS Vocabulary is more sensitive to disruptive influences; it is probably no longer the most stable of the verbal subtests. But we will probably be well compensated for this loss, for the new Vocabulary test is a better tool with which to assess the clarity, conciseness, and subtlety of a subject's thought processes, and his facility in communicating his thoughts—cognitive functions which are of central importance to the assessment of ego organization and adaptive behavior.[8]

A number of interesting possibilities for content analysis of responses suggest themselves. The new Vocabulary list contains words touching upon a variety of important realms of human experience: there are words that refer to the subject's awareness of intrapsychic states *(remorse, compassion, ominous)* and others referring to alloplastic action [i.e., acting out] tendencies *(hasten, commence);* words that touch upon latent expectations concerning nurture, care, or protection *(consume, sanctuary, tranquil);* and others that refer to hostile destructive actions, either directly or in more modulated form *(slice, tirade, obstruct, impale);* words referring to the control of action tendencies, in the sense of the modulation, inhibition, or the facilitation of impulse discharge *(regulate, terminate, repair);* and words that describe forms of interpersonal relationship *(conceal, reluctant).* The ease and clarity with which a person can articulate ideas in one category as compared with another may become a significant indicator of his capacity for impulse modulation, particularly with respect to oral needs and aggressive impulses; his capacity for empathy; and his capacity to grasp subtle subjective processes in himself and others.

A question that is bound to arise when one begins using the WAIS in place of the W-B concerns the actual equivalence of IQ scores and weighted scores of the two tests; particularly will this affect the significance

[7] Many of these are abstract or "literary" nouns (like *compassion, calamity,* and *fortitude*).—R.S.

[8] [In a personal communication, Lloyd Silverman points out another advantage of the WAIS vocabulary: even its most difficult words are encountered in the conversation of highly intelligent and literate persons, as those in the W-B are not. Thus, it is less dependent on vagaries of sampling, and is a better measure of what it is intended to measure.—Ed.]

that attaches to IQ differences and scatter differences found in test-retest studies in which the first IQ was based on the W-B and the second IQ on the WAIS. An analysis of the various conversion tables offered by Wechsler indicates a number of significant differences between the two tests. A given weighted score total is worth more (sometimes as much as eight IQ points more) on the WAIS than on the W-B in the lower intelligence range. Similarly, on the WAIS a raw score is converted into a somewhat lower weighted score at the upper end of the continuum. Perhaps the intent was for these changes in the conversion value of raw scores into weighted scores and of weighted scores into IQ's to cancel each other out so that the final IQ's obtained from a WAIS and W-B would be virtually equivalent. We have found, however, that 22 of 26 subjects (average W-B Full Scale IQ = 118) scored higher Full Scale IQ's on the W-B than they did on the WAIS; 25 of the 26 scored higher Performance IQ's on the W-B than they did on the WAIS.[9]

The noncomparability of the two tests affects also the inferences which can be drawn from an analysis of an individual scattergram. Not only is the nature of the task on some subtests of the WAIS considerably different, as has already been indicated, but the weighted scores have new normative-statistical meanings. With the increased discriminating power in the upper levels, one can now obtain a top weighted score of 19 where in the previous editions of the W-B the top limits were 18 and 17. With respect to scatter analysis, one would have wished that in this new revision all of the subtests had been made commensurable with each other over the entire range of weighted scores. This has not been accomplished; we find that once again the highest weighted score obtainable varies from subtest to subtest.

An allowance for deterioration with increasing age is once again built

---

[9] In our opinion, clinicians should use great caution in accepting the suggestion made by the Psychological Corporation in their description of the WAIS, that Wechsler-Bellevue II is the retest instrument for the WAIS as well as for the Wechsler-Bellevue I. We use the WAIS as its own retest instrument, just as for many years we have used the W-B I as its own retest instrument.—K. S. & M. M. [So far, throughout this book the abbreviation "W-B" has been used to stand for Wechsler-Bellevue, Form I. Form II, which was published a few years later as an equivalent alternate form, never achieved wide adoption; relatively little research with it has been published, and I have been able to find no specific review of it. It is only in part a separate form, containing many of the same items, and it was not thoroughly standardized. A good deal of recent research has backed up Sinnett and Mayman in their conclusion that neither form of the W-B is a satisfactory alternative to the WAIS for use in retesting, and in their impression that Performance and Full Scale IQ's tend to be higher on the W-B than on the WAIS. Cole and Weleba (1956), Cook and Hirt (1961), Goolishian and Ramsay (1956), Neuringer (1956), and Prado and Schnadt (1965) have all made comparisons of the WAIS and W-B I which differ in their designs and adequacy, but on the whole support the above conclusions. The consensus seems to be that Block Design, Object Assembly (see also Garfield, 1960), and Digit Symbol were easier on the W-B, and Comprehension and Digit Span are easier on the WAIS. Light and Chambers (1958) found Verbal and Full Scale IQ's to be *higher* on the WAIS, but with a population of mental defectives; this result may merely reflect the superiority of the WAIS as a test for the lower ranges of intelligence, since it contains more very easy items and thus may not only measure low IQ's more reliably but less traumatically.—Ed.]

into the IQ conversion tables. Just as with the W-B, this gross effect of age on performance seems a little hard to believe.

In view of Wechsler's emphasis upon the effects of aging in the preparation of his standardization norms, it is a surprise (though a pleasant one) to find that he has changed the age limits on his IQ conversion tables in a direction which assumes homogeneity within a 10-year span rather than the W-B's five-year span. Now all subjects between ages 25 and 34 form a single normative subgroup, as do subjects aged 35 to 44 and 45 to 54. This change seems appropriate, according to our own clinical experience, particularly because it will help eliminate abrupt shifts in the normative base line in test-retest studies.

On the whole, therefore, it seems advisable to keep as much of Rapaport's W-B rationale as one's clinical experience with the WAIS supports. His discussions may not apply equally well to all items in each subtest, but they are the best starting point for any more refined analysis. Likewise, an attitude of skeptical optimism is recommended for the diagnostic use of W-B scatter patterns with the WAIS, with a reminder that the qualitative interpretation of individual verbalizations and performances is more intrinsically valid anyway.

CHAPTER 4

The Babcock Story Recall Test

Perhaps the most serious shortcoming of the W-B [and WAIS] is the lack of a subtest that tests memory functioning in a more direct way than the Information subtest. Experience shows that an adequate assessment of the subject's intelligence is not possible without a test of his memory. Furthermore, for clinical work we have found disturbances of memory to be of diagnostic significance. Therefore, we included the Story Recall subtest of the Babcock Test (Babcock & Levy, 1940) in our battery.

Our inclusion of this part of the Babcock Test in our battery does not imply agreement with the notions advanced by Babcock about the nature of intelligence and the nature of her test. We came to the view that the hope of being able to measure "deterioration" by a single number should be abandoned; rather, patterns of performance on several kinds of tests should be used as the basis for inferring the extent of deterioration or of lowered efficiency.

The Babcock Test in its original form had 24 subtests; a "short form" was also standardized, consisting of only nine of these. We used this short form, finally narrowing it down to one subtest, Story Recall.[1]

The following story is read to the subject by the examiner: "December 6. / Last week / a river / overflowed / in a small town / ten miles / from Albany. / Water covered the streets / and entered the houses. / Fourteen persons / were drowned / and 600 persons / caught cold / because of the dampness / and cold weather. / In saving / a boy / who was caught / under a bridge, / a man / cut his hands."

The subject is then told, "Begin at the beginning and tell me all you remember of it." After the subject has given the Immediate Recall, the examiner says, "Later, I will want to see how much of it you can still remember"; he pauses, as if giving the subject a chance to think over the

---

[1] [Or "Learning Efficiency," in Babcock's phrase. This is the title by which the test is referred to by Schafer (1948). In the way it is used, however, this is a misnomer.—Ed.]

story, and continues, "I will read it to you again"; he then does so. The delayed recall of the story is given by the subject after about 10 minutes of work on other tests.[2]

Scoring. There are 21 unit memories that can be credited in each recall as indicated by slant lines, above. The score is the number of correct memories minus the number of penalties (see below). In order to eliminate the advantage of the rereading for the Delayed Recall and to make the two scores comparable, four extra credits are added to the score on Immediate Recall.

The subject is required to grasp the meaning of the story, which he may retell in his own words. In general, the exchange of one expression for another is not penalized, so long as the change does not alter the general meaning of the story or its details. Thus, what is being tested here is the accuracy of meaningful memories, relatively independent of exact verbal reproduction. Lack of accuracy is penalized; saying "in Albany" instead of "10 miles from Albany" is penalized by loss of both scores that would have been obtained for "10 miles" and for "from Albany." Memories such as "near Albany" or "in the neighborhood of Albany" are not especially penalized, however; the omission of "10 miles" merely loses one unit. According to Babcock's scoring, one unit is subtracted from the score for each bizarre detail introduced.

We differentiated four degrees of increasing distortion, and numbered them 1, 2, 3, and 4, respectively. Only those distortions worthy of a score of 4 were penalized in the actual scoring of the subtest by the subtraction of one unit. We also subdifferentiated two distinct types of errors—out-of-place memories (OP), and fragmentation of memories (Frag). The criteria for, and examples of, each of the four error scores are the following:

Distortion Score 1: This score was given (a) for the substitution of words with allied but not synonymous meaning; (b) for the use of a vague term to represent a specific part of the story; (c) for the introduction of mild, "appropriate" material to accompany some of the nouns. Examples: (a) "injured" for *cut,* "arm" or "wrist" for *hand,* "village" for *town,* "a week ago" for *last week;* (b) "exposure" for *dampness and cold weather,* "flood" for *the river overflowed,* "lost lives" for *drowned;* (c) "little boy" for *boy,* "small river" for *river.*

Distortion Score 2: This score was given (a) for false memories; (b) for introduction of new elements. That is, this score was given for more serious distortions of the story than those in Score 1, provided they did not

---

[2] [It is useful to interpolate the Immediate Recall after the first two or three subtests of W-B or WAIS. After three more of the Wechsler subtests, the Delayed Recall is asked for: "Now let's go back to that story I read you—tell me all you can remember of it."—Ed.]

become bizarre. Examples: (a) the wrong number of people drowned or catching cold (provided that the distortion is not unreasonable), "injured" for *caught cold,* "killed" for *drowned,* "in Albany," "Albany, N. Y.," giving the wrong date, "on" *Dec. 6;* (b) *the river overflowed* "its banks," *the river overflowed* "the town," *the man cut* "both" *hands.*

Distortion Score 3: This score was given (a) for serious distortions of content; (b) for recombination of parts of the story without resulting queerness; (c) for the introduction of new material, usually of an emotional nature, with no specific source in the original story. Examples: (a) a grossly inaccurate recall of the number of persons drowned and/or catching cold, a reversal in the proportion of the number drowning and catching cold, "last year," "two weeks ago," "last winter," "south of Albany," "north of Albany," "the water entered shops" or "basements"; (b) "the boy cut his hand," "the man was caught under the bridge," the boy was caught "on" the bridge; (c) "the boy drowned," "the man drowned," "killed and wounded (or injured)" for *drowned and caught cold,* "the bridge was overflowed," "people were left out in the cold," "the water was so high it flooded the streets," "the town the water damaged," "the man seriously (or severely) cut his hands" or "smashed his hands."

Distortion Score 4: This score was given for (a) introduction of *new* material of a strong emotional tone; (b) introduction of arbitrary material, relatively unrelated to the original story; (c) a recombination of the elements of the original story making the story entirely different, though perhaps involving the same events. Examples: (a) *the people were* "homeless," *the bridge was* "washed away" or "fell," *the boy was* "washed downstream," *the people got* "pneumonia"; (b) giving the boy a specific age, "there was a storm," "it rained," "December 6, 1942"; (c) "a man saved 14 people from drowning under a bridge."

Out-of-Place Memories: It frequently occurs that some segment of the story is recalled out of its correct sequence in the story. Where this segment is separated from its original place by a complete thought, a distortion score of 2 is given.

Fragmentary Memories: It happens, especially in schizophrenics, that a phrase or even part of a phrase is remembered but its relation to the story is lost. The subject might recall, "A boy . . . something about boy." Each such *fragmentation* was scored 4, and one point was subtracted from the total score accordingly.

In addition to the procedure of correcting the sum of memories for these qualitative errors, we make some use of an additional score, called "error percent." First the errors are added up, each being given its score value; thus, for example, a Distortion Score 3 contributes three units, an

Out-of-Place Memory two units, and a Fragmentary Memory four units. This sum is then divided by the number of correct memories, to take the amount of recall into account; the quotient can exceed 100%.

RATIONALE

In *Emotions and Memory* (Rapaport, 1942a), it is suggested that the organization and distortion of memory material in recall give clues to what happens in the everyday memory functioning of the subject, and that memory should be looked upon as one aspect of our thought processes. Thus, the recall of meaningless material, which is most frequently tested by academic psychologists in their efforts to study memory, cannot give information about the organization of memories that is characteristic of memory functioning as we experience it, use it, and observe it in our everyday life. Our discussion of Digit Span in the Wechsler-Bellevue Scale attempted to shed some light on one of the psychological functions—attention—involved in the immediate recall of meaningless material. It is demonstrable that, in learning nonsense syllables or digits for delayed recall, not only attention but also concentration is called into play. The role of concentration would be to introduce subjective meaning, by some act of organization or association, into the meaningless material. The examiner or experimenter is thus never quite sure of what his results mean, in terms of everyday memory functioning.

The only test in our whole battery that measures memory functioning directly is this Story Recall subtest of the Babcock Test.[3] In it we see the memory function in a reproductive, rather than a productive, role. The greater a person's original natural endowment and its efficiency, and the less his conscious thought processes—including attention and concentration—are encroached upon by maladjustment, the more likely it is that the aspect of thought processes called memory will function freely and efficiently, and bring about good story reproductions. A freely receptive, unhampered attention will facilitate intake; concentration will be crucial in extracting the essential meaning and pattern of the story. A good span of attention is not in itself sufficient, since the story is relatively long; omissions will consequently occur in the subject's reproductions. But the examiner tells the subject that he will want to hear the story again; and the

[3] In our minds, the Word Association and Thematic Apperception Tests are indirect approaches to memory functioning. In both these tests, the patterns of memory functioning are tested in their productive aspects. The organizing, affective, attitudinal factors mobilized by a stimulus word or picture deliver to consciousness reaction words, or story-pattern material, which are expressions of these factors as well as of the memory content associated with pathological disorganizing factors.

subject has a chance to think over what he has retained of the story, before the examiner rereads it. The normal subject's reaction is usually a gesture implying, "Oh, now I know what I left out," or "How stupid I am to have left this out." Such subjective experiences help to lock the previously omitted material firmly into the structure of the story, and thus to make the story more complete in the Delayed Recall.

Very frequently the subject, in his Immediate Recall, remarks that he knows something is missing but cannot recapture it; this would indicate that the pattern of meaning and sequence is felt by him. Before the rereading of the story, he has another chance to think it over, which re-emphasizes the gaps or at least summarizes the retained material; he can then measure this against the complete story as repeated by the examiner. A normal subject easily makes a comparison between his version and the complete version, and fills in his version or corrects it if there were distortions. This comparison requires the capacity for a well-organized intake of the story, and a relative independence of the memory function from strong personal affects which tend to distort it. If the dominance of drives and affects results in a disorganized intake and retention of the material, the gaps will not be noticed by the subject, and the difference between the original version, as repeated by the examiner, and the subject's version will not be apparent to him. Both are organized for him in terms of the paramount drive or affect; if a strong distorting idea or affect influences the intake the first time, it is likely to influence it the second time also, and the original distortion will persist in the Delayed Recall.

We expect normal subjects to have a relative autonomy of ego functions, free from strong affects and drives distorting or warping thought organization and the specific aspect of it that we are accustomed to refer to as memory organization. As soon as such distorting affects, or strivings, or attitudes become apparent in the recall of the story—especially in the Delayed Recall—we have evidence of considerable impairment of the ego's ability to keep its autonomy and to protect thought and memory organization from the encroachments of maladjustment. This type of memory disorganization does not become as tangible in any other test of our battery as in the Story Recall. Such memory disorganization is one of the most acute indicators of maladjustment approaching or reaching the psychotic degree.

Omissions, or minor errors such as "in Albany" instead of "10 miles from Albany," are expressions of temporary inefficiency, and are attributable to a limited span of attention in intake. But distortions to the effect that "1400 people were drowned and 1600 caught cold" are manifestations of affective interference with memory organization and memory function. An even higher degree of disorganization is indicated when the parts of the story are given in an incorrect sequence. This occurs in normal people also, as when a subject suddenly remembers something which belongs to a previous part of the story; but normal subjects interrupt their narratives, and either by a tone of voice or by explanation indicate that they are filling in a previous gap. The situation is different when, instead of a story, only fragments are recalled by the subject, and these in a completely different sequence from the correct one, with a consequent loss of cause-and-effect relationships. This is the case even if the subject superficially gives the impression that he is simply trying to assemble the material before he forgets it. Such a disintegration of the story's structure is important evidence of near-psychotic or psychotic conditions. In such cases the organization, coherence, and meaning of the story are lost, and correction after the second reading of the story becomes impossible. The subject's procedure in such cases becomes similar to that described in connection with the "pattern coherence" of motor action in the Object Assembly subtest of the W-B where guiding visual organization is absent. In memory performances, however, we see "verbal-motor coherence" replacing meaningful interrelated memories. When such a disorganization of memory is present, the experience of "aha, now I have it"—so characteristic for the discovery of omissions in normal people who give well-structured Immediate Recall—is necessarily absent. The Delayed Recall, instead of becoming more efficient than the Immediate Recall, becomes, if possible, worse. The total disorganization of the story brings about emergence of snowstorms, fires, rains, and other disasters instead of the flood. That is, there occurs a rearrangement of the details of the story not in terms of its *objective* meaning, but in terms of its *affective* meaning to the individual subject. This process may go even further, and recalls may be offered which have almost no resemblance to the original story.

Thus, in these two memory performances, as soon as the autonomy of thought functioning is encroached upon, we see the unconscious drive factors distorting and disorganizing memory functioning. As our experience indicates that disorganization of patterns of thought processes is among the earliest and most crucial signs of severe maladjustment, Story Recall becomes a potent diagnostic indicator. Not only is it of great importance qualitatively, but quantitatively also it is a help in diagnosis.

The examiner who will look upon disturbances in this test as expressions of the forces that organize memory in everyday life, cause slips of tongue, accidental forgettings, persistently recurring memories, and deficiencies in the availability of memories when they are needed, will find Story Recall instructive for understanding memory as it actually operates in living persons, and for understanding the state of organization and degree of coherence of the patient's thought processes.

Administration

It is essential that the subject's recall should be recorded verbatim. On the Stanford-Binet this technique is not provided for, as that story is written out on the blank and the examiner in one way or another checks off the correct memories offered by the subject. Such a recording technique neglects almost completely the significance of the quality of memory performance, since the exact verbalization of the subject, the exact sequence of memories, the fragmentary memories, the introduction of bizarre material, and so on, are not recorded. We have found a consideration of these features of recall necessary for correct and meaningful interpretation of the subject's performance. The verbatim recording which we consistently follow allows for an evaluation of the extent to which the structure of the story and the sequence of ideas with cause-effect relationships were retained. It is important to follow Babcock's instructions here: after the Immediate Recall is given, one does not at once reread the story, but rather tells the subject that later he will be asked how much of the story he still remembers; a pause of a few seconds before rereading the story is necessary to allow him to crystallize the retained memories and to re-emphasize to himself significant omissions. It is true that such a technique offers a special advantage to normal subjects, who in general are able to take advantage of this opportunity and who therefore derive maximum benefit from the rereading; but this is the essential reason for following this technique: It is always the normals or the well-preserved neurotics who are able to benefit from it, and the more disorganized, psychotic, or near-psychotic patients who cannot. In other words, this technique results in a sharper differentiation of organized and disorganized memory functioning.

Diagnostic Implications

Quantitative Analysis. Although Story Recall is most directly a test of immediate recall for meaningful material, satisfactory performance also requires adequate attention and concentration, the capacity to maintain sets or anticipations, and intactness of linguistic function generally. Therefore, poor performance can occur in a variety of conditions in which these various functions are impaired.[4] The examiner will be most interested, usually, in what Story Recall can contribute as a supplement to the Wechsler tests.

[To begin with, both Immediate and Delayed Recall are moderately

---

[4] [Most obviously, aphasic brain-damaged patients will perform badly, as will persons with generalized intellectual deficit; but in these respects, the test gives no special information beyond that furnished by a test of verbal intelligence.—Ed.]

correlated with the essentially verbal subtests of the W-B (except Comprehension) and with both Verbal and Total IQ's (see Table 1).[5] As a rough rule of thumb, the data in Table 2 mean that the expected scores on Story Recall for persons in the Average range of intelligence are from 12 to 16; for those in the Bright Normal range, 12 to 18; in the Superior and Very Superior range, 13 to 20. A mildly impaired Story Recall, therefore, is one at the lower end of the interquartile ranges just given; below the first quartile point, we may speak of serious impairment.]

TABLE 1

Correlations between Scores from Wechsler-Bellevue
and Story Recall (Babcock) Tests

Wechsler-Bellevue Score	Correlates of Immediate Recall			Correlates of Delayed Recall		
	Normals	Neurotics	Preschiz.	Normals	Neurotics	Preschiz.
Vocabulary	.47	.32	.36	.27	.37	.55
Comprehension	.26	−.08	.26	.07	−.06	.48
Information	.43	.20	.15	.25	.23	.18
Similarities	.48	.28	.40	.18	.40	.57
Digit Span	.31	.46	.10	.19	.32	.13
Arithmetic	.08	.30	.24	.08	.43	.36
Verbal IQ	.41	.32	.30	.22	.42	.46
Total IQ	.50	.34	.56	.31	.48	.48
Numbers of cases	54	44	23	54	44	23

(Figures in *italics* are significant at the 5% level; figures in **bold face** are significant at the 1% level.)

TABLE 2

Expected Values (Ranges and Quartile Points) for Story Recall Scores
in Subjects of Various Intellectual Levels

Intellectual Level	Immediate Recall				Delayed Recall				Numbers of Cases
	Range	Q_1	Q_2	Q_3	Range	Q_1	Q_2	Q_3	
Normal (IQ 90–109)	8—18	12	13	14	8—20	13	15	16	27
Bright (IQ 110–119)	6—21	12	14.5	17	7—21	16	17	19	41
Superior (IQ 120–129)	8—21	13	15	18	11—21	15	17	19	45
Very Superior (IQ 130 and over)	15—21		(18*)		17—20		(18.4*)		5

* Means.
Note: These figures are based on 118 normal, neurotic, and preschizophrenic subjects.

[5] [The analysis summarized in Tables 1 and 2 was prepared for this edition, using the raw data originally published in appendices. I am grateful to Joan Holt, Eli Leiter, Harvey Nightingale, and Judith Rabkin for assistance with the statistical computations. For this purpose we used the normal sample of the original research, the Kansas Highway Patrol, plus the patients whose scores were least impaired: the neurotics (including neurotic depressives) and preschizophrenics.—Ed.]

In general, the quantitative results alone have little diagnostic significance, because of the diverse reasons for impairments. Marked deficits do, however, suggest a psychotic condition, usually schizophrenia or depressive psychosis. Depression of a neurotic degree makes for a milder impairment of Story Recall. In these same diagnostic groups, the Delayed Recall is somewhat more likely than usual to be inferior to Immediate Recall; a discrepancy in this direction of more than four points (after correction) should always raise the question of a serious disorder, because of the usual tendency to profit from the second reading of the story. A qualitative analysis of the recalls is, however, indispensable.

In the performance of schizophrenics, the impairment of performance seems to be attributable largely to a failure of synthetic functioning, producing a disorganization of the memory process. It may be assumed, tentatively, that the synthetic and organizing function is related to the function of concentration. When the material to be reproduced markedly exceeds the normal attention span (as is true of this story), it must be organized by a process of directed, concentrated effort in order to be retained. One could say that when the process of organization is no longer automatic and effortless, concentration begins to operate. Although some bits of this story may be delivered into consciousness by pure reproductive attention, their consistency with the meaning of the total story, as well as their sequential organization, may well be a function of the voluntary effort of concentration, in which parts are tested against each other and against the total story schema.

We believe that the poor performance of schizophrenics on both the Arithmetic subtest of the W-B and on Story Recall results from their inability to concentrate, to turn back voluntarily upon their own reasoning. Moreover, in our experience the most frequently encountered nonorganic condition in which this type of impaired functioning occurs is schizophrenia.

Another way of looking at impairment of memory is to examine the types and quantity of errors in Immediate and Delayed Recall. In Immediate Recall, schizophrenics (including preschizophrenics, incipient and ambulatory cases) exceed all other patients in incidence of extreme and bizarre distortions, and are approached only by other psychotics. A great incidence of severe distortions—two or more—may therefore be taken as an indication of a schizophrenic disorder, especially when accompanied by the peculiar tone that characterizes the verbalizations of schizophrenics in any test. Such peculiarities of verbalization are somewhat more likely to occur in Story Recall than in the more disciplined and structured answers called for by the Wechsler tests, so that well-preserved acute or incipient cases may at times be spotted by a distorted Story Recall in the setting of a relatively well-ordered performance on the W-B [or WAIS]. In addition, the occurrence of several memories out of their correct sequence may be the first sign of a schizophrenic disorganization of memory.

A high incidence of affectively toned serious distortions (scored 3), which, however, are not bizarre, appears to be associated with great affective lability and impulsiveness such as is found in hysterics [and certain character disorders]. The incidence of bizarre distortions and fragmentary memories is very low in all neurotic and normal cases.

In the Delayed Recall, full-blown schizophrenics tend to produce as many serious and bizarre errors as in the Immediate Recall, or more; whereas the kind of adaptive façade that makes us characterize other cases as preschizophrenic (ambulatory, pseudoneurotic, or latent schizophrenics) shows itself in a tendency to produce a less error-filled recall on the second trial. The poorer the patient's contact with reality, the less able will he be to profit from the rereading of the story by the examiner. Consequently, depressions of psychotic and near-psychotic degree are also characterized by serious distortions and the loss of feeling for the structure and sequence of the story on Delayed Recall. Other types of patients tend to produce Delayed Recalls with fewer serious distortions and to retain the sense of the story's organization. A relatively reliable sign of functional psychosis is a sum of serious and bizarre errors (of the types scored 3 and 4) as large as or larger than the number of correct memories, especially when this sum is larger in Delayed than in Immediate Recall.

The picture is quite similar if we consider *all* types of error, as measured by the "error percent" described above. A great massing of errors in the Immediate Recall is most likely to occur in schizophrenics' records, though by no means exclusively; but if on the Delayed Recall the error percentage is above 100, the likelihood is that we are dealing with a schizophrenic or a depressive. An increase in the error percent on Delayed Recall is commonest in schizophrenia, and appears to be a feature of the type of memory disorganization found in that disorder. Neurotic and normal subjects typically have a relatively low error percent to begin with, one that furthermore decreases in the Delayed Recall.

Qualitative Analysis. The Immediate and Delayed Story Recalls allow for a quantitative analysis of the qualitative features of the recall. This analysis can be done in terms of the amount and the kinds of errors in the recall of the story.

To elucidate the meaning of errors, it seems advisable to give full story samples here. With these examples it can be demonstrated how the errors can be evaluated qualitatively.

A clear example of affect and attitude shaping the memory distortion is given in the Immediate Recall of a mixed-neurotic housewife. This woman ended an otherwise fairly good recall as follows: "In rescuing a boy from a bridge . . . somebody must have been drowned." It is obvious that she had forgotten exactly what happened to the person who rescued the boy, although she remembered that something did happen to the rescuer; and what she finally offers can be assumed to be a direct consequence of the whole feeling tone elicited in her by the story—namely, that related to the ideas of death and misfortune.

Perhaps an even clearer example of affective reorganization of the story is seen in a woman in whom a paranoid condition and hysterical symptoms both were present, and whose violent aggressions against males in general, and her husband in particular, were outstanding. Her second recall reads: "December 6, a river overflowed in the town of Albany. *1400 men* were drowned and 600. . . . In saving a boy who was drowning a man was injured. I think he *has his hand smashed.*" The first major distortion is "1400" instead of "14." This seems related to her changing "persons" to "men," thereby achieving a great destruction of men. The second major distortion is "he had his hand smashed." At first she said merely "injured," but apparently the influence of her intense hostility upon the vague memory that the injury was more specific elaborated it in tune with her prevalent affective attitude, and as a result she had the man's hand "smashed."

In general, these errors may all be characterized as emotional elaborations of implicit or direct statements of the original story. Emotional elaboration is obvious in such expressions as "many people were left homeless," "great damage was done," "the man cut his hand severely," "a terrible flood," and so on—where it is apparent that the elaborations are based on the feeling tone usually accompanying ideas of great destruction and catastrophe, and elicited in the subject by the story.

Where affects corresponding to intense aggressions or to destructive fantasies are well controlled—as in many normals—the mere reading of a story will not elicit these affects in such force that they may distort the recall. It is for this reason that these distortions become diagnostically significant. It is interesting to note here that hysterics, characterized clinically by their affective lability and impulsiveness, are prone to produce such distortions, especially in their Immediate Recall. The extremes of this type of emotional distortion in recall are such expressions as "carrying trees and roads away," "washing the bridge down," and so on. The weakening control of affects can progress so far that not only affective elaborations and distortions occur in the recall, but the affects elicited push their ideational representations, foreign to the logical meaning and structure of the story, into consciousness; thus new material is introduced that is not at all justified by anything in the story. This is no longer modification of memories by emotions but an expression of a complete and far-reaching breakdown of the subjective distinction between memories of reality and memories of fantasy.

There also occur mild forms of these distortions to which proportionately less significance is to be attached. For instance, *boy* will become "a little boy"; the river may be called "a small river." The fact that it was a child to whom this happened, or that it happened in the vicinity of a small town, has in these cases introduced a modification which appears as a displacement of an adjective; this modification may be understood to be the effect of an attitude elicited in the subject by one part of the story, upon other parts of it in recall.[6]

A few examples will be given here to illustrate, first, that not *only* in schizophrenics or in other psychotics do great distortions occur, and second, that the quality of distortions and the ways they occur allow for some differentiation between psychotics and nonpsychotics.

The following is the Immediate Recall given by an able, well-adjusted highway patrolman: "December 6, last week, a *terrible* flood *14* miles from Albany. Water covered the streets and *lawns* and 14 people were drowned and 600 *injured*. A man cut his hand rescuing a boy who was caught *on a fence*." *Lawns* and *fence* are complete departures from the story, while *terrible* and *injured* are both distortions referable to his affect-dominated recall. Nevertheless, in the evaluation of the memory efficiency of this case, it must be noted that he had an almost flawless Delayed Recall, a feature militating against the pathological implications of the previous distortions.

Contrast the recall of a schizophrenic chemist. Immediate Recall: "December 6, a small boy was saved when the weather was damp from drowning." Delayed Recall: "December 6, a small boy saved 600 people from drowning. The weather was damp." The first example illustrates a feature common to many schizophrenics' records—a recombination of isolated fragments into a superficially meaningful-looking recall. This becomes even more striking in the Delayed Recall, where four isolated parts of the story are remembered as fragments and reintegrated into a new story, and a fifth fragment is left hanging: "the weather was damp." The recombination involved a boy, saving, 600 people, and drowning; these elements were not immediately related to each other in the actual story. The sentence structure itself is a clue to the schizophrenic character of these recalls, which were given quite glibly without pause and without much searching for other memories.

Another kind of schizophrenic recall pattern is seen in the following, given by a young but deteriorated man. Immediate Recall: "December 6, last week, 14 people were drowned when the river overflowed in a small

---

[6] [This is only one of various possibilities; see Paul (1959) for an experimental treatment of distortions in memory, carried out under Rapaport's guidance.—Ed.]

town . . . a hundred . . . or 400 . . . most of them were saved . . . some 400 people because one man rescued a 14-year old boy was saved." Of striking interest here are the recombination of elements into the idea that most of the people were saved; the contamination and/or perseveration, as in the use of the number 4, in 14 as the age of the boy and in 400 as the number of people; and, worst of all, the incoherence resulting from the causal connection implied in *"because* a man rescued a boy." The Delayed Recall, as in most far-gone schizophrenics, is much worse: "Last week there were in a town about 40 miles from Albany, or was it 1400 miles, when the river overflowed. . . . There was much confusion. . . . For when 14 people were drowned and 600 were ill. . . . The town was over-flowed with water. . . . The water was very deep, wasn't it? Much concern was caused when one boy risked his . . . no, yes, 14 years old risked his life saving people under a bridge. . . . Cut his hand. . . . Must have lost his life." Incoherence, recombination of elements of the story, the distor-tions resulting from affective attitudinal reactions to the original material, mixing up of and perseverative use of the numbers involved in the story, are the salient characteristics of this recall.

Such bizarre distortions of the story are not limited to far-gone schizo-phrenics, however. Cases from other nosological categories may produce distortions that are sometimes hard to differentiate from those of schizo-phrenics. For instance, here is the recall of an overideational pre-schizophrenic woman. Immediate Recall: "December 6. A river overflowed its banks in Albany and entered the streets and houses. 14 persons drowned and 600 were sick, no . . . The boy . . . I have forgotten it . . . *hanging on with his hand on the bridge, trying to save the bridge, caught cold."* The absurdity of this recombination at the end of the story needs little discus-sion. The structure and sequence, however, have been otherwise relatively well preserved. Another instance is that of a markedly schizoid late-ado-lescent girl diagnosed as obsessive-compulsive. Delayed Recall: "December 6. In a small town the river flooded over, I think it was washing trees and roads. . . . 14 people were drowned. . . . Something in between there but I can't figure it. . . . 600 people caught cold. A man while trying to save the life of a small boy. . . . Oh, there is a. . . . Wait a minute. . . . Who was caught under a bridge. . . . Or bridge falling in . . . bridge collapsed . . . cut his hand." The conscious effort to reconstruct the story accurately and the feeling for gaps in it are of course not characteristically psychotic; but the extent of distortion is suggestive. Diagnostically, the experienced examiner will sense that such a recall might indicate a near-psychotic condition retaining enough integration to sense the gaps and distortion; this was actually the case here.

The next example is that of a man with a severe neurotic depression, a kind of patient who as a rule stumbles on Story Recall. Delayed Recall: "December 6. A big rain came and flooded the streets. 600 houses and 1400 people. . . . One boy nine years old was taken down the stream, caught by the bridge, cut both hands." Obviously distortions and fragmentation are present, similar to those seen in schizophrenics.

The next case is that of a man whose neurasthenia was described clinically as his last defense against a depressive psychotic break. Immediate Recall: "Last Wednesday on December 6 there was a heavy rain. . . . Overflowed a bridge six miles from Albany. . . . A boat overturned in which there were 14 people and in trying to rescue them a man cut his hands." Here again emotional elaboration, introduction of strange new material, and a general disorganization of the structure of the story are present. There were no signs in the recall that he was conscious of gaps and distortions. His Delayed Recall was nearly perfect, which distinguished his performance from the usual schizophrenic and depressive type: he gave 17 correct memories, with no distortions.

CHAPTER **5**

Introduction to the Testing of Concept Formation

The illusion that human thinking consists of associations, in which the idea comes to consciousness that has the strongest associative bond to the one preceding it—the strength of the associative bond being determined by the frequency of contiguous occurrence—faded when subjected to careful psychological analysis. As far as "public opinion" in psychology is concerned, the death blow was dealt by the discoveries of gestalt psychology. Even earlier, however, the German schools of *Denk-Psychologie* had shifted attention to the role of attitudes and to the logical make-up of human thinking, and thus inevitably came to the problem of concepts.[1] Genetic psychology and ethnopsychology used the analysis of the concepts of children and of primitive peoples[2] in an effort to understand the development of thought organization.

In the last 50 years there has been a steady growth of the recognition that human thinking is determined by the strivings, affects, wishes, and interests of the person.[3] Regrettably enough, there has been little quest

[1] [Much of the relevant literature is translated or summarized in Rapaport (1951a). For an influential modern statement of many related issues, see Bruner, Goodnow, and Austin (1956), and Rapaport's review (1957b).—Ed.]

[2] See Werner (1940), Chapter IX.

[3] [This view, which Rapaport himself was later to call the "seething-caldron" conception of thinking, gave way rapidly in his theorizing after 1945, as he increasingly emphasized the role of structures—enduring dispositions—in thought organization. This book was part of the turning of the tide; though it provides much evidence for a structural conception, it still contains a good deal more emphasis on the determination of thought by affect and drive than Rapaport would have used today. In the 1940's, his thinking paralleled that of psychoanalysts generally; see Gill (1959) for an appraisal of the "reductionism to motivation" prevailing in psychoanalysis until recent years (and see also Holt, 1967b). Rapaport was probably as responsible as any other single person for bringing about the change toward an appreciation of the prominence due to structural considerations, along with the adaptive ones urged by Hartmann (1939) and Erikson (1950). Nevertheless, the notion that cognition was

after the missing link between concept formation, as one of the intrinsic formal characteristics of human thinking, and the determination of thinking by the person's strivings and interests.

It is a generally assumed fact that emotional disturbances and personality disorders—maladjustment in general—encroach upon thinking. *How* this happens remains a great unknown. Yet a beginning must be made sometime. It is necessary to create a frame of reference, however hypothetical and vague, within which the observations and inferences concerning the nature of thought processes can be ordered and brought into relationship with each other. Only the ordering of the phenomena of thinking into a single frame of reference, and the assessment of relationships between them, can lead to new, fruitful questions and hypotheses, and through these to a clarification of the dynamics of thought processes and an understanding of how maladjustment encroaches upon them. Without such a frame of reference, even an attempt at coordinating the testing of concept formation with general diagnostic testing is doomed to failure. Thus we shall advance a tentative one, with the understanding that at present there is no proof of the *necessity* of just this specific frame of reference, nor of the *existence* as dynamic entities of the functions hypothesized by it, nor of the *exclusiveness* of these hypothesized functions in the construction of a well-balanced frame of reference into which all phenomena of human thinking can be ordered.

We shall temporarily bypass the dependence of the ideas emerging into consciousness upon emotions, affects, attitudes, interests, etc. This dependence of all ideas upon "psychodynamics" is a relationship sufficiently accepted; what is not clear about it are the rules of dynamics governing this dependence. We suggest that this relationship will remain unexplored until we have much more knowledge about the phenomenological characteristics of ideas. Thus, in our view, the first step toward the understanding of the ways ideas depend upon emotional dynamics is a *phenomenological* frame of reference for the understanding of the characteristics of ideas. It is not the single isolated idea, but rather the general phenomenological framework of ideas whose interrelation with emotional dynamics can be attacked with any hope of success. We submit the following framework for consideration.

An idea once in consciousness can be characterized by its identifiability. Identifiability has three facets. The first is that an idea is identifiable if it has reference to ideas that have been previously in consciousness and were

---

shaped by drives and affects was one of the key concepts in the "New Look" movement that helped put cognition on the contemporary map in psychology; see Bruner and Klein (1960), Solley and Murphy (1960), and Holt (1964b). As Heider (1957) has pointed out, *Diagnostic Psychological Testing* was itself one of the important influences that brought the "New Look" into being.—Ed.]

either identical with or meaningfully related to the idea whose identifiability is in question. This facet of identifiability we refer to as memory—
though this formulation of memory is a sweepingly general one.

The second facet of the identifiability of an idea is its similarity to,
dissimilarity from, or belonging with other ideas. That is, for an idea to be
identifiable it is not sufficient that it should have some meaningful connection to another idea which *before* has been in consciousness, but that this
connection should also be clear. This facet of identifiability is usually referred to as concept formation—though, again, this view of concept formation is sweepingly generalized.

The third facet of identifiability is in a sense a quantitative one, and
implies the ease or difficulty of identifying. Ideas whose past references and
belongingness are clear emerge into and are apperceived in consciousness
without effort or selection, and in a sense passively. But when the past
references of ideas must be deciphered, and their belongingness decided,
effort, selection, and active orientation are required. In other words, the
meaning of ideas either emerges effortlessly into consciousness, or must be
deciphered by voluntary effort. In previous chapters we considered these
two types of functions of consciousness, and called the former *attention* and
the latter *concentration*.[4] Extending our discussion from single ideas to
chains of ideas—that is, to ideas embedded in the continuous flow of conscious happening—it must be clear that the prevailing flow of ideas sets or
prepares our consciousness for the reception of the new idea. Such a
preparation obviously facilitates effortless apperception of the meaning of
the emerging idea. This getting set for the apperception of an oncoming
idea was referred to as *anticipation*. The third facet of identifiability then
divides into the functions of attention, concentration, and anticipation.

Thus, within this frame of reference, an idea can be investigated phe-
nomenologically from three points of view: (1) memory; (2) concept formation; (3) attention-concentration-anticipation. We propose to deal with
these as functions, but we shall not forget that they represent only a tentative structure for the phenomenological systematization of the outstanding
characteristics of thought processes; and that for all we know they are
merely three different ways in which human beings are accustomed to think
about their thought processes. It should also be remembered that thought
processes are such that they induce us to look at them now from one of
these aspects, now from another. When our experience of a thought is, "I
have heard this before," then the memory aspect is in the foreground,
though here too it is possible and profitable to look at this thought from
both other aspects also. When the experience is, "What could it be? It is a

---

4 [See also Rapaport's paper on activity and passivity (1953b).—Ed.]

ship," then the concept-formation aspect is in the foreground. When the experience is, "The boss is smiling at me; it must be a promotion he is going to inform me about," then the anticipation aspect is in the foreground. It is more difficult to give such sharply defined examples for the processes of attention and concentration, but it is evident that in any recognition of a known object or known idea there is an attentional aspect, and in any solving of a problem an aspect of concentration, in the foreground.

These different aspects are present in all thought processes, even though one may seem outstanding and thereby conceal the presence of the others. Accordingly, impairment of any of these aspects may also encroach upon the others. This is especially true of attention-concentration-anticipation, the disturbance of which is usually demonstrable even when memory or concept formation is the aspect in the foreground.

Here we are particularly interested in that aspect of thought processes referred to as concept formation, and which determines the belongingness of our ideas—that is, of the objects of *our world*—to each other. The meaning of concept formation that usually comes to mind is taken from the point of view of logic—that is, the relationship between the concept "table" and the actually existing tables of our world. In introducing the tests of concept formation, we shall open with a discussion of this logical view of concepts. This, however, is only a limited view; although it must be remembered that, if one draws the last conclusions from the logical viewpoint, the naming or identifying of anything must be considered conceptualization. If we call to mind that language consists of a manipulation of such namings, it becomes obvious that the very realm of language, in all its nooks and crannies, is pervaded by conceptualization. If we further remind ourselves that verbal thinking has been accepted as abstract-symbolic thinking, words being considered symbols for things, we must realize that any symbolization is, in a sense, conceptualization. If we turn our attention to symbols in a narrower sense—such as religious, ethnic, superstitious, and dream symbols, and perhaps even the symbols manifest in the bodily expression of certain unconscious ideas as conversion symptoms—we must realize that concept formation is by no means merely the highly developed abstract conceptualization investigated by logic: its roots go far back, and are demonstrable in all thinking, whether it finds expression in bodily manifestations, in dreams, in superstitions, in national ideas, or in religious beliefs.[5]

---

[5] We cannot go further here into the discussion of concept formation as present in the form of symbolism in the narrower sense. We should like to refer the interested reader to Cassirer's admirable three volumes on the philosophy of symbolic forms (1925). Nor can we consider the conceptualization of children, discussed by Piaget (1927); nor that of "preliterate" people, discussed by Lévy-Bruhl (1921); nor that of mentally deficient and brain-injured persons, reviewed by Werner (1940). We do wish to point out that the thought processes usually referred to as "unconscious ideas" or

Present-day dynamic psychiatry considers different syndromes to be, in large part, the results of encroachments of unconscious ideas upon consciousness (or upon the ego), and/or as a defense of consciousness against such encroachments. We might thus expect to find, in the aspect of conscious thought processes we know as concept formation, either traces of the encroachment of the unconscious and its type of concept formation, or the traces of the defense of consciousness against the encroachment. This is the justification of the statement, advanced in the introduction to this volume, that *concept formation is one of the main channels through which maladjustment encroaches upon thinking, and that in it we may be able to discover early traces of impending maladjustment.* We shall remind ourselves in this connection that, in analyzing such memory tests as Information in the W-B and Story Recall, we followed a similar reasoning. On the one hand, we considered the poverty of information in hysterics, and the wealth of it in obsessive-compulsives, as different types of defenses of the ego against the encroachment of unconscious ideas; and on the other hand, distortions in Story Recall were considered as an encroachment of unconscious ideas upon conscious thinking.[6]

It should be remembered that not only the direct encroachment of unconscious thinking can impoverish concept formation; it is also prey to the impairments and disturbances of the other aspects of thought processes—especially those of attention and concentration, and also memory.

Concept Formation From the Point of View of Logic

The aim of testing concept formation is to discover and diagnose *in statu nascendi* the encroachment of maladjustment upon conscious thinking. We have pointed out that the influence of unconscious processes upon consciousness (or the defense agaiust it) is considered by psychoanalytic psychiatry to be the principal basis of all maladjustment. These unconscious

---

"unconscious thinking" represent forms of concept formation which are closer to those present in preliterates and children—that is, present in symbolic form—than to those present in conscious ordered thinking as represented by logic. These two types of thinking are referred to in psychoanalytic writings as primary processes and secondary processes respectively. For their discussion see Freud (1900, 1911). [See also Rapaport (1950a, 1951a, 1957a, 1960b); Langer (1942); Holt (1967b), especially articles by Gill, Wolff, and Holt.—Ed.]

[6] [The above two paragraphs are good examples of the overemphasis on dynamic factors in Rapaport's thinking in the 1940's. Today, he would have emphasized the role of different styles of thought organization and of defense, and of different states of consciousness (Rapaport, 1951a, 1957a) in determining the special features of diagnostic groups. He would also undoubtedly have eschewed the terminology of the topographic model, following Gill (1963).—Ed.]

processes employ a different type of concept formation than do conscious processes. In order to discover whether this other type of concept formation encroaches upon that proper to conscious thinking, we must first turn our attention to the concept formation of conscious (secondary-process) thinking, the ideal of which is outlined for us by logic.

Every concept has a *content:* this is the sum total of the characteristics that are common to all the objects subsumed under that concept. Every concept has a *realm:* these are all the objects that are subsumed under that concept by virtue of having its content in common. Thus, for instance, the realm of the concept "table" is all the tables that exist or can be thought of, irrespective of their material, shape, color, number of legs, or use. The content of the concept "table," which may be referred to as "tableness," is the elusive common characteristic of all tables. "Tableness" exists nowhere, but still is inherent to all tables. "Table" is here a verbal symbol which, according to logic and our usual expectation of the average person of our civilization, stands for *all* the characteristics embodied in the content of this concept. The word "table" does not expound all these content characteristics, but only implies them. Though we all use the word "table," we do not all necessarily imply thereby exactly the same kind and number of content characteristics; actually, using the same word conceals individual differences in connotation.

Anyone who tests the concept formation of a variety of subjects within the normal range soon discovers that our expectation of the average person is too great, and though we all use the same abstract verbal symbols, they mean different things to different people; and contrary to the expectations of logic, they are by no means for everybody generalizations that exhaust all possible content characteristics. The variability even within the normal range is enormous. Thus tests of concept formation measure not only the encroachment of maladjustment upon conscious thinking, but also the varieties of "normal" concept formation corresponding to different modes of adjustment and to the types of intelligence functioning they imply.

Still, the view of logic concerning concept formation is the conceptual ideal of our civilization. "Table" should not mean for us merely "a place to eat at" or "the thing that has legs and a plate" or "the thing that the carpenter makes," but a composite of all these and more. Yet we expect the average person of our civilization to use this composite flexibly, and not to think always of *one* certain table or tables *in general,* but in different situations to think relevantly of tables and to be able to segregate from the all-exhaustive *content* of the concept more narrowly defined contents also. We expect the average person of our civilization not to bring a tiny shred of paper if somebody wrapping up a good-sized package calls for paper. Everyday expectations thus are much less rigid than those of logic concerning concept formation. This will become even clearer if we consider the process of concept formation itself.

From the point of view of logic, a concept has two variables, realm and content. To use a metaphor from mathematics, two types of problems can be set up, each solvable for one of the variables as an unknown. In the first problem, the realm of the concept can be given and the content is the unknown for which the problem is to be solved: as when many objects are given, and their *identical color* is to be discovered. In the second problem, the content is given and the realm is the unknown to be found: as when many objects are given from which only the *tools* are to be selected. The first problem is described by logic as one requiring *induction,* and the second as one requiring *deduction.* In the first, one must reason from the actual individual cases to their common uniting principles, which should be an eminently empirical-inductive procedure; in the second, a principle must be applied to find a result that fits it.

In a system of logic that operates in a world of abstract ideas, the first task can be solved purely by induction and the second purely by deduction; but in everyday life, this is not the case. Realms are never given alone but rather intermingled with other realms, and we usually want to determine content for the purpose of segregating realms. Thus, the content should not only unite all the objects of the realm but also segregate them from objects not belonging to it; and since to exhaust all the common features of the objects of a realm is a task without end, usually only those common features necessary and sufficient for segregating the realm from the not-realm are included in the content. Thus, in practice we always make some kind of an induction on the basis of the objects of the realm; the resulting content can be then immediately used for deduction to ascertain whether the content arrived at covers all the objects of the realm and whether or not it includes objects that do not belong to that realm. In either case, the omitted or added objects, as well as the objects to be omitted or added, are taken into consideration in a new induction; and this process of interchange continues so long as an adequate concept is not arrived at. This process is very clear in the development of any science; it is also encountered in everyday life situations, but as a rule it is an automatic process of concept formation which goes on unnoticed, and of which we become conscious only when the conceptual problem confronting us becomes too difficult. The situation is similar with the problem whose solution starts as a deductive process. The interaction of induction and deduction is so universal that it appears to justify the contention that the elementary units of thought processes are not induction and deduction; these are rather artifacts of abstraction isolated out of concept formation, which appears to be the basic unit of thought processes, in which induction and deduction occur indivisibly integrated with each other.

The balance of inductive and deductive steps—or the balance of the regard for the objects of the realm and for the content of the concept—cannot be treated by means of mechanical rules, and has to be conceived of as a dynamic equilibrium which changes with the changing context in which concept formation occurs. A content as expressed in a verbal abstract symbol is dependent on the constellation in which it is called upon to play a role, and is not a rigid pre-existing archetype. A steady approximation to each other of the objects of the realm and the content is the life of a concept, or of concept formation. If this were not the case, everything could belong with everything, since each thing has so many features that some similarity can be found between any two; or only identical things could belong with each other, since things have so many features that some dissimilarity can be found between any two. In this case, no concepts at all would be formed, everything would remain isolated, and different names for each and every single object would render thinking cumbersome and dead. The former extreme is approached in the schizophrenic process, the latter in mental deficiencies of various origins.

CHAPTER 6

The Sorting Test

The clinical application of the Sorting Test (Goldstein & Scheerer, 1941) has been in general limited in the past to the study of the impairment of "abstract attitudes" in organic and schizophrenic cases. These investigations have presented only qualitative analyses of the characteristic performances of these two types of subjects. The test appeared to us to have potentialities as a diagnostic tool, within the framework of the understanding of thought processes and their impairment by maladjustment discussed above. We attempted to put it to such use.

In order to use any test as a diagnostic tool, the following criteria must be met: (a) a scoring system must be devised which will allow for direct comparison of a subject's achievements on the different items, as well as of the achievements of one person with those of others; (b) the scoring system must be shown to differentiate between different types of maladjustment and adjustment, or in other words, its clinical validation must be undertaken. These were the two major tasks confronting us. In the course of validating this test we undertook a developmental study of concept formation using this test as a tool; this study shed light on the test and helped to develop the scoring system. To this developmental study (Reichard, Schneider, & Rapaport, 1944) we shall refer repeatedly.[1]

A Description of the Test. The test materials consist of 33 objects common in everyday experience. These objects are: a real knife, fork, and spoon; a miniature knife, fork, and spoon; a real screwdriver and pair of pliers; a miniature screwdriver, pair of pliers, hammer, and hatchet; two nails; a block of wood with a nail in the center of it; two bottle corks; two sugar cubes; a pipe; a real cigar and a cigarette; an imitation cigar and cigarette; an empty matchbook; a rubber ball; a rubber eraser; a rubber sink

---

[1] [Because this paper was not included in Rapaport's *Collected Papers* (1967), the data of principal interest have been reproduced here as Tables 1 and 2.—Ed.]

stopper; a white filing card; a green cardboard square; a red paper circle; a lock; and a bicycle bell.[2]

The test is divided into two parts, each presenting the subject with a different type of conceptual problem. Part I consists of seven items. In each of these, one object is put before the subject and he is asked to find which of all the remaining objects "belong with it." In all but the first of these items a standard initial object is placed before the subject by the examiner; in the first item the subject is asked to pick any of the objects at random. After the subject finishes his grouping he is asked, "Why do all these belong together?" Thus, in Part I the subject's task is to form conceptual groups (realms) and define them (state their content).

Part II consists of 12 items. In each item the examiner places before the subject a group of chosen objects and asks, "Why do all these belong together?" Each such grouping implies an abstract-conceptual definition of the objects in it, such as "eating utensils," "smoking equipment," "toys," and the "rubber" objects. Thus, in Part II the subject's task is to define groups (state the conceptual content of realms) put before him by the examiner. The implications of the difference between the types of problem in Part I and Part II will be discussed in the section on rationale.

The subject's groupings and his verbalizations are recorded completely on a blank which has ample space for detailed notes on both his behavior and side comments. The groupings and the definitions are both evaluated, and the scores are written alongside the responses. No total score has been developed by us; there are only 19 items on the entire test, and our scoring system is designed simply to make the scores easily surveyable at one glance down the scoring column.

The Psychological Rationale of Sorting Behavior

Sorting behavior, in response to the instruction to "put together those that belong together," is an expression of concept formation. It may take both the form of actively putting together those objects that belong together, and the form of discovering why the objects put together belong together.

Sorting behavior can be understood only by reference to both the actual sorting (whether by examiner or by the subject) and its verbalization (by the subject); impairment may encroach either on verbalization or sorting,

[2] [This list of objects differs somewhat from the contents of the Object Sorting Test currently sold by the Psychological Corporation. It is not usually difficult to assemble one's own set, and once the rationale of the test and its scoring is mastered, the same principles can easily be applied despite differences in objects.—Ed.]

and is usually a disturbance of the relationship between the two. This is precisely what makes the Sorting Test a more sensitive test of concept formation than Similarities: it makes possible a comparison between sorting and verbalization (the realms created and the definition of their content). In purely verbal tests of concept formation, the actual realm of the concepts in question is present only in the mind of the subject: thus on the one hand, memory and attention-concentration-anticipation play a strong role together with concept formation; and on the other, the comparison of the realm with the content is more difficult.

Sorting behavior, wherein the subject compares objects that belong to the realm and objects that do not belong to the realm, gives the examiner an opportunity to assess how rigid and concrete (narrow), or how fluid, vague, and overgeneralizing (loose) the concept formation of the subject is.

Finally, sorting behavior and its verbalization indicate whether the subject's concept formation is on a concrete, functional, or abstract-conceptual level.

In so far as sorting behavior pertains to the belonging together of objects in terms of their objective characteristics, it reflects the concept formation proper to conscious ordered thinking. The pathological variations of this kind of sorting behavior we shall discuss below in detail. In so far as sorting behavior pertains to the belonging together of objects in terms of value judgment (useful—useless) or of affective value judgments (good—bad, pleasant—unpleasant, liked—disliked) or of aesthetic value judgments (beautiful—ugly, tasteful—disgusting), it approaches the type of concept formation proper to unconscious processes.[3] Signs of this kind of sorting behavior in the course of performance are conspicuous and in adults are to be considered as diagnostic signs, indicative of either queer and rarely encountered adjustments or of deteriorative maladjustment; in children, however, they may occur at preschool age with considerable frequency. But the genetic relationship between these two types of sorting behavior should be recognized: the steps between something which is "good" or "no good," and something which is "good for playing with" or "no good for playing with," and something which is "toy" or "not toy," are indeed short; and observation of young children shows that this is not merely a logical connection, created a posteriori, but rather corresponds to developmental stages.

THE PSYCHOLOGICAL RATIONALE OF THE SORTING TEST

By virtue of the nature of the material it uses, the Sorting Test pertains to concept formation as exercised every day by the human being of our

[3] [I.e., the drive organization of memory; see Rapaport (1951a).—Ed.]

civilization. As a matter of fact, the test shows how a person sees the segment of the world of objects that surrounds him daily, and the interrelationships therein. For this reason, the concept formation tested by the Sorting Test is referred to here as "everyday concept formation." All human beings call objects by generic names: a knife a knife, a fork a fork, and a spade a spade. Whether, and to what extent, the concepts behind these generic names are identical for all human beings, and, if not identical, in what respects they are interindividually different, can be assessed only by creating a map of the actual interrelationships of objects as seen by different subjects. The Sorting Test charts this kind of map of the interrelationships of 33 objects.

Part I of the Sorting Test pertains to *active* (sorting) concept formation; Part II to *passive* (understanding) concept formation. In Part I the subject actively displays how *he* sees the conceptual interrelationships of objects; in Part II, where the common conceptual content of a group of objects must be determined, the conventionalized "understanding" factor plays the main role, and we are much nearer the verbal concepts. In Similarities we derive the common content from verbal *abstractions,* but in the Sorting Test the *objects* with their manifold properties are before the subject; accordingly, there is a greater chance for him to bog down among the many attributes of the objects. The Sorting Test is thus more vulnerable to maladjustment.

TABLE 1

Mean Scores on Sorting Test in Developmental Study

| | Part I | | | | | | | | | Part II | | | | |
| | Grouping | | | | | Verbalization | | | | | | | | |
Age	+	L	(L)	N	(N)	+	CD	FD	In[1]	M[2]	+	CD	FD	In[1]	M[2]
4	2.0	1.1	.3	3.2	.9	1.0	.1	.8	2.6	3.7	1.4	.7	.6	3.3	7.5
5	5.1	.7	1.4	1.4	2.8	3.8	2.5	.8	2.2	1.3	3.6	2.9	.7	7.3	1.1
6	4.4	.2	.2	4.0	2.1	2.9	1.4	1.7	1.5	2.4	4.1	2.5	1.6	6.1	1.8
7	4.7	.6	.5	2.7	1.1	4.4	2.2	1.9	2.1	.8	5.8	3.7	1.8	5.6	.9
8	5.1	.1	.3	2.7	2.0	4.9	2.0	2.6	1.1	1.3	6.4	4.3	1.7	5.1	1.1
9	5.7	.4	.6	2.0	2.1	5.5	2.8	2.4	.9	.8	6.6	4.3	2.0	4.3	1.4
10	5.7	.5	1.0	1.4	1.9	5.6	3.1	2.1	1.1	.7	7.0	4.8	1.7	4.4	1.0
11	5.7	.1	.9	1.6	1.2	5.4	3.1	1.7	1.3	.6	8.0	6.5	1.2	2.8	1.4
12	5.8	.3	1.2	1.4	1.9	5.5	2.9	2.2	1.5	.4	8.0	6.4	1.6	2.6	1.5
13	5.9	.3	1.5	1.1	2.0	5.8	3.2	1.9	1.1	.7	8.3	6.5	1.6	2.3	1.7
14	5.5	.5	1.5	2.2	.9	5.2	3.2	1.4	1.6	.8	10.3	8.6	1.5	.7	1.2

[1] In—inadequate responses
[2] M—missed, i.e., failure to respond
(For numbers of subjects, see Table 2)

TABLE 2

Percentages of Each Age Group Attaining Particular
Scores on Sorting Test

| | | Part I | | | | | | Part II | | | | |
| | | Grouping | Verbalization | | | | | | | | | |
Age	N[1]	+	+	CD	FD	In	M	+	CD	FD	In	M
4	10	29	14	1	11	37	53	12	6	5	28	63
5	25	73	54	36	11	31	19	30	24	6	61	9
6	24	63	41	20	24	21	34	34	21	13	51	15
7	27	67	63	31	27	30	11	48	31	15	47	8
8	19	73	70	29	37	16	19	53	36	14	43	9
9	24	81	79	40	34	13	11	56	36	17	36	12
10	22	81	80	44	30	16	10	58	40	14	37	8
11	27	81	77	44	24	19	9	67	54	10	23	12
12	25	83	79	41	31	21	6	67	53	13	22	13
13	23	84	83	46	27	16	10	69	54	13	23	14
14	13	79	74	46	20	23	11	86	72	13	6	10

[1] N = Number of children in each age group (total N = 239).
Note: For legend, see Table I. Both tables reprinted unchanged from Reichard, Schneider, and Rapaport (1944). Percentages do not always add to 100, partly because of rounding error.

Reichard et al. (1944; see Tables 1 and 2) showed that, in the course of childhood and adolescence, the accuracy of active (sorting) concept formation develops earlier than the accuracy of definition in passive (understanding) concept formation; but the quality of sorting tends to remain on a more primitive conceptual level in the active part of the test than the quality of definitions in the passive, compliant part. Apparently, Part I is more like a map of the conceptual relationships as subjectively experienced by the subject; and in Part II, concept formation tries to meet the logical ideals of our society, which requires highly conventionalized concepts in harmony with the conceptual standards of our society. These conceptual standards apparently remain confined to passive understanding, while our everyday actions are directed by an active concept formation which is conceptually on a lower level.

On Part I the active sorting process begins on the sample object. The subject determines its conceptual content. On the one hand, this process may have abstractive, inductive characteristics, as when the sample object is "green and cardboard and square"; on the other hand, it may be merely a process of subsuming the sample under its generic term, as when "tool" covers the sample object, pliers. Once the conceptual content is established by either process, the next step is deductive. That is, the conceptual content arrived at is applied as a selective principle upon the other objects, to segregate from them those that fit the content best. In the course of this deductive process, the subject may encounter three situations: (a) The content defined for the sample selects a well-defined and sizable realm of objects, well differentiated from all the other objects. (b) The subject finds that few or no objects fit the conceptual content in question; consequently he either fails, or makes a narrow concrete grouping, or finds other objects from which, by inductive reference to the sample, he derives a more inclusive or different conceptual content, which is then applied deductively to all the objects of the test and yields a satisfactory sorting. (c) He may hit immediately upon test objects which, in conjunction with the sample, appear to make a more relevant sorting; this leads to an inductive process out of which a new conceptual content, either radically different from or merely a modification of the original one, may issue, and the subject then applies this deductively to the objects of the test. These processes may occur repeatedly, with an interchange of deductions and inductions, before a final sorting is arrived at. It is always the interaction of the apparent conceptual content of the sample and the test objects that determines the final sorting.

Similarly, in Part II, the first attempt at a definition is based on one of the common features of the group itself; this conceptual content is then checked against the other test objects to see whether it sufficiently excludes them. In the determination of the conceptual content of the group, interacting processes of induction and deduction have already taken place. The more homogeneous the group is at first glance—that is, the more familiar and stereotyped its conceptual content—the less consciously perceived these processes become.

THE PSYCHOLOGICAL RATIONALE OF SCORING

In the attempt to make the Sorting Test a diagnostic tool, we developed a scoring system to take account of both *sorting* and *verbalization*. Specifically, we scored: (a) the *adequacy* of sorting and verbalization—that is, to what degree the sortings or verbalizations approximate or deviate from the norm on that item; (b) the *conceptual level* of the verbalizations—that is, whether the definition of the group was on an abstract, functional, or concrete level; (c) the *concept span*—that is, the patient's regard for all the objects in the test, and whether he omitted or included too many objects in the group he sorted, or whether his definition of a group did account for all the objects in it or accounted for objects not in it.

We attempted to make our scoring such that Part I, involving active concept formation, and Part II, involving passive concept formation, should be directly comparable. On Part I the sorting itself is scored both for its adequacy and its span, and the verbalization is scored for its adequacy and its conceptual level. The scoring of "adequacy of verbalization" was introduced here in order to obtain an adequacy score which would be directly comparable to the adequacy score of verbalization on Part II. Statistical analysis shows that the adequacy of sorting and the adequacy of verbalization on Part I do not essentially deviate from each other.[4] On Part II, where no sorting performance by the subject is required, only the adequacy of the verbalization, the conceptual level, and the concept span are scored. The concept span is here a much more limited scoring category than in Part I.

The Adequacy of Sorting and Verbalization

A sorting is adequate if all the objects put with the sample object are relevant to it. The verbalization of a sorting is adequate if it gives a sufficiently inclusive and exclusive definition of the group of objects to which it refers, whether this group was selected by the subject or the examiner.

Adequate Sorting. If the sample is a rubber ball, and the subject puts all the rubber objects (rubber cigar, rubber cigarette, rubber sink stopper, and rubber eraser) with the sample, the sorting is adequate. It is quite unusual to group all the round objects with the rubber ball; nevertheless, this also is considered an adequate sorting, because it segregates a well-defined, sufficiently large realm. Thus, adequate sorting is a grouping which is (a) usual and relevant to the sample object; (b) so common that it must be accepted as normal; or (c) though rare, clearly intelligible and based on a well-accepted concept which clearly segregates a sufficient number of objects. Such adequate sortings are allotted the score "+."

Inadequate Sorting. In the discussion of this category, we shall omit inadequate sortings referable to disturbances in the concept span or conceptual level. An inadequate sorting is in some way faulty in its relevance to the sample object. An example is grouping the small silverware with the big table fork and omitting the rest of the big silverware; this disregards the differences in size and "purpose" between the sample and the sorted objects. Grouping the green cardboard square with the small green-handled hatchet is also an inadequate sorting; it disregards the fact that the sizable group of cardboard and paper objects would make a more appropriate grouping. In other words, an inadequate grouping is one not relevant to the sample object, too large or too small, and not taking into account the other objects at the subject's disposal. Inadequate sortings are allotted the score "—."

---

[4] [The adequacy of verbalization need not be scored, therefore, in routine clinical work.—Ed.]

If an adequate sorting is made, but an essential object is omitted or an irrelevant object added without affecting the general idea of the sorting—as established from the verbalization—the sorting is scored "±."

Adequate Verbalization. A verbalization is adequate if it covers correctly the group sorted. If a subject groups the green square with the green-handled hatchet—though an inadequate sorting—the verbalization that "both have the same color" is considered adequate. Thus, the adequacy of verbalization may be distinguished from the adequacy of sorting. This is an unusual case; usually adequate verbalizations match adequate sortings.

Inadequate Verbalization. Definition of all the rubber objects as "all having some red on them" is an inadequate verbalization; reference to the other objects would have shown red objects outside the group, and indicated the necessity of a different principle. In the majority of cases, where the sorting is inadequate the definition will be inadequate also. Nevertheless, there are cases where the grouping will be adequate and the verbalization inadequate; these may indicate severe disorganization. A relatively mild instance of this type is grouping all the toys with the definition that "they are all small," or with the more pathological definition (because of the intrusion of drive organization) that "they are all used to break something."

The adequate verbalizations are scored "+"; the inadequate ones are scored "−"; small peculiarities or deviations in otherwise adequate definitions are scored "±"; inadequate verbalizations with some glimmer of the correct idea are scored "∓."

The Conceptual Level of Sorting

The notion of conceptual levels has already been advanced in the discussion of the Similarities subtest. There we discussed the concrete, functional, and abstract-conceptual levels in verbal concept formation. We shall not duplicate that discussion, beyond stating that on the first level the subject considers things as belonging together because of a concrete attribute they have in common; on the second level the subject considers things as belonging together because of a function they have in common, or because of a common function performed with or on them by human beings; on the third level the subject expresses their essential abstract-conceptual common content in a generic term.

The conceptual level in the Sorting Test is determined mainly on the basis of the subject's verbalization. The subject who groups the tablespoon and the table knife with the big fork appears to be operating on an abstract-conceptual level; but by verbalizing this sorting as "we eat with them" or "they are all on the table" he reveals that his concept formation really lies on the functional or concrete level. At times, however, the sorting itself will be more revealing than the verbalization. Thus a subject who groups the sugar with the table utensils, and defines them all as "tableware," reveals by the grouping rather than by the verbalization that his abstract-conceptual level of concept formation is not at the highest level.

Definitions on the concrete level of concept formation are scored *C* (concrete), on the functional level *FD* (functional definitions), and on the abstract-conceptual level *CD* (conceptual definitions).

Four other types of definitions, which are more or less related to the functional and concretistic levels of concept formation, but which are definitely pathological indicators, should be discussed separately. These are the syncretistic *(S)*, the fabulated *(Fab)*, the symbolic *(Symb)*, and chain *(Ch)* definitions.

Syncretistic definitions may use a functional or a concrete attribute common to the objects of the group to be defined, and thus may be similar to functional and concrete definitions. On closer scrutiny, however, the function or attribute in a syncretistic definition is so vague and generalized that it includes many other test objects not present in the group. Syncretistic definitions of the functional type are: "We use them all," "They all give us pleasure." Syncretistic definitions of a concrete type can be divided into several groups; those referring to location, to origin, or to the belonging to something or someone, are the most frequent. Examples are: "They can all be found in the house"; "They all come from plants"; "They all belong to men." It is characteristic of all the syncretistic forms of concept formation that the concept basis or common link becomes tremendously extended so that everything may belong with everything.

In the syncretistic groups there are other types of conceptualization also, which are more difficult to label systematically. One of these is seen when the subject groups a number of unrelated objects by reinterpreting several of them into things which they are not, and thus creating some kind of set. Such sets lead us, partly by their fabulated character and partly by the symbolic meaning given to the objects, to two other types of definition.

Fabulated definitions start out with one attribute of one object, and make it the starting point of a story which then unwinds so that in its course reference is made to all the other objects in the group. Thus, it is not *common* conceptual content which unites the objects, but rather attributes in which they *differ* from each other and which figure as different parts of one story. Thus, a subject will start out with the sample "big screwdriver" as belonging to a workman, and will add the rest of the tools, relating the different kinds of work he does with them; then the sugar and eating utensils are added with the explanation that the workman went to lunch; the lock is added, because he locked up his tool kit with it while lunching; and finally all the smoking utensils end up in the group, either by way of giving the workman a choice, or because he likes to smoke a cigarette when he does heavy work, a cigar when he does easy work, and his pipe after lunch. Sometimes fabulations are innocuous looking, but their presence should always be considered a serious pathological indicator. Fabulated sorting usually appears similar to definitions on the functional level, but can be distinguished from them by the fact that it is not identical functions of the objects but a narrative into which they are woven that unites them. Fabulatory concept formation is an extreme of the concrete type, however functional it may look. In it all the objects are isolated and lack any relationship to conceptual contents of other objects; they are chained together only by extraneous stories.

Symbolic definitions radically reinterpret the meaning of the objects, and make an arbitrary symbolic meaning the basis of sorting. This type of sorting not only interprets a round piece of paper as an ashtray and a square piece of paper as a table, but will join the large and small silverware under the verbalization, "mother and child." Symbolic sorting is a sign of the encroachment upon consciousness of the affective-evaluative type of concept formation.

In *Chain* definitions the sample object may be red, and another red object is put with it; this being rectangular, a rectangular wooden block is then added; then a tool which has a wooden part is put in; this induces the addition of another tool; and so on. Here concepts are formed, in a sense, on a concrete level of concept formation, but because of a generalized disturbance the concept becomes fluid; from one moment to the next there is no retention of the conceptual frame of reference, and perhaps not even of the memory of the first principle. The result is a chainlike performance which, though resembling the fabulated performance, reveals even more warped characteristics of thinking.

Concept Span

A working definition for adequate sorting and verbalization might state that adequate sorting includes all the objects that belong with the sample, and excludes all the objects that do not belong with it. Sorting that includes objects that do not strictly belong will be considered as *loose,* and sorting that does not include objects that do belong will be considered as *narrow.* Subjects who sort *narrowly* usually arrive at their conceptual content on the basis of the sample, and even if they find few or no objects which fit this content, they will not modify it but will rigidly stick to their deduction. Thus, they may decide that the ball is "red, round, and rubber"; consequently they will group only the sink stopper with it. Those subjects who sort loosely usually let themselves be led to inductions by the objects of the test, and their urge extends to further and further inclusions. Thus, they may find other small tools to go with the small pliers, then the big tools, then the nails and the block of wood, and finally even the lock.

Ideal conceptual behavior, as already stated, unites inductive and deductive processes, because neither alone will make for adequate concept formation. Conceptual balance between inductive and deductive processes is seen in sorting behavior when equal weight is given to the available objects and to the sample. This is implied in the testing situation as a *tacit* instruction, and though it is never made explicit, normal subjects understand it. The deviations from this balance are significant; and the test behavior of the subject—his centering upon the sample alone, or always discovering additional objects to be sorted—in itself expresses his tendency to deviate from the balance in one or the other direction.

Narrow sorting may result from a rigid adherence to a preconceived decision, or from the logical-deductive rigidity frequently seen in compulsive, overmeticulous, pedantic persons who find that most or all of the other objects do not fit the sample because of small but to them significant differences. A different origin of narrow sorting—the extreme of concretistic thought, sheer inertia and/or uninterestedness—is seen in some depressive psychoses, in deteriorated schizophrenia, and in neurasthenia. It is not possible for an objective scoring to differentiate the types of narrow sorting, but the test behavior and verbalizations of the patient often reveal which it is.

Loose Sorting. We differentiate three degrees of looseness. The score *l* is given to mild looseness, such as grouping the sugar with the silverware. In these cases it is stipulated that the looseness should not be sufficient to disrupt the conceptual level of the verbalization. This type of sorting occurs so frequently in normal subjects that it cannot be considered to have pathological significance.

The score *(L)* is given to loose groupings where the conceptual character of the verbalization has suffered under the loosening of the concept, but is not altogether out of bounds. An instance is the grouping of the lock with the tools, "to lock the tool kit."

The score *L* is given for essential looseness. An example is the procedure of a preschizophrenic who grouped with the ball all objects which had the slightest roundness. Thus, the knife was included because its end was rounded, the nail was included because its head was rounded, and so on; and so almost all the test objects were put with the ball. A loose grouping need not consist of a great number of objects: if the fork and the small pliers are placed together because "you pick things up with both," that is also an essentially loose sorting. In other words, the looseness of the sorting is determined not only by the number of objects, but also by the lack of their belonging together. The more flagrantly the sorting departs from the usual sorting, and the more the verbal definition departs from the usual verbal definition, the looser the sorting must be considered. Sortings on any conceptual level may be loose, but only the active sorting (Part I) may be scored *l, (L),* and *L.*

Narrow Sorting. The score *N* is given essentially narrow sorting. This is the case when the concept derived from the sample excludes all or all but one or two objects, even though with less rigidity, or more interest in searching, others could have been included.

The score *(N)* is given to sortings where the grouping is good and its definition relevant, but one or two objects which should have been included were omitted. The cause is usually carelessness, unconcern, or over-meticulousness.

N scores are most frequently obtained where the sample object is the bell. *(N)* scores are most frequently obtained where the adequate sorting should include imitations—such as the rubber cigar and cigarette with the smoking equipment—and the subject omits them.

These scores pertain to active concept formation, and thus are given only on Part I. On Part II, narrowing of the concept span results in splitting the groups sorted by the examiner, and in defining the subgroups separately. This procedure is labeled "split-narrow," and scored *S/N.*

THE ADMINISTRATION OF THE TEST

The administration of this test may be discussed under two headings: instructions, and inquiry. In the instructions, the essential point is a strict adherence to the formulation presented below. In the inquiry, the essential points are caution, a noncommittal tone of voice, and the avoidance of any leading questions.

Instructions and Recording. On the first item of Part I, the examiner says, "Pick out any one of these objects; it doesn't matter which one you choose." When this has been done, the examiner notes what it was on his recording form and continues, "Now pick out all objects that belong with it, and tell me when you are finished." This latter point precludes subjects' inferring from the examiner's demeanor whether or not they have correctly finished the task, and enables him to refrain from influencing the narrowness or looseness of the sorting. When the subject announces that he is finished, the examiner records the choices and inquires, "Why do they all belong together?" On the second to seventh items, the examiner selects the sample object[5] for the subject and instructs him, "Put with it all the

[5] For the sequence of the sample objects, see the section on item analysis.

things that belong with it." Subjects' verbalizations are of course recorded verbatim.

On Part II the examiner puts a group of selected objects before the subject with the instruction, "Now tell me why all these belong together." The procedure for all 12 items is the same.[6]

Inquiry. Inquiry should be restricted to a minimum sufficient to clarify the subject's response. Questioning frequently gives the subject the feeling that something is wrong, and he may then change his grouping, alter his response, or offer several alternative responses; the result will be an unscorable tangle of the correct response in a variety of irrelevancies. Where questioning is necessary, the wording and the tone of the question should give the subject the impression that what is wanted is merely amplification and clarification of what he has said, not modifications, corrections, or rejection of the original response.

It would be ideal if inquiry could be postponed until the test is done,[7] because inquiry may not only induce modification of the response but influence the subsequent sortings and verbalizations. On the other hand, it is often quite difficult to find out later what the subject had in mind. It is up to the examiner to strike a balance between these advantages and disadvantages.

Inquiry is usually necessary on the following occasions: (a) When the definition of the group obviously does not take into account all the objects in the group, the examiner should ask the subject, "What have these objects to do with it?" (b) When the definition remains vague in relationship to the group or is contradictory to it, the examiner should ask, "It is not quite clear to me what you mean; would you explain it?" (c) When the subject subdivides a group put before him and defines the subgroups separately, the examiner should ask, "But why do they *all* belong together?" (d) When subjects state that they see nothing that belongs with the sample object, the routine procedure is to say, "My question was which of these objects *do* belong with it." The item is considered failed only if the subject refuses to respond after such a suggestive instruction. (e) When subjects state on Part II, "They do not belong together," the routine procedure is to say, "My question was why *do* they belong together." The item is considered failed only if the subject still finds no answer. (f) Responses which appear to be nonsensical should not be inquired into until after the test has been

---

[6] [Again, all remarks of the subject are written down, along with notes on all behavior that is at all unusual. It facilitates recording if the examiner adopts and memorizes a set of abbreviations for the objects, so that he can effortlessly jot down a notation for each object selected while the subject is sorting.—Ed.]

[7] Inquiry about Part I cannot be postponed until Part II is completed, because the latter contains some of the answers to the former.

completed. It should be determined whether the nonsensical response can be satisfactorily rationalized, or whether it is completely indefensible; and whether the subject can be made aware by questioning that his solution was wrong, or whether he will stick to his bizarre response. Results of such inquiry should not influence the scoring, which is always based on the spontaneous definition given by the subject. Such questioning should not be done during the test because it may put the patient on his guard, make him realize his verbalizations are not correct, coherent, or acceptable, and result in a covering up of his pathological thinking; thus the test results will be meaningless. (g) The subject frequently asks, "Is that right?" In such cases the examiner should say that it is not a question of right or wrong, but that he is interested rather in which objects the subject considers to belong together and why. In general, the examiner should not indicate during the course of the test whether a response was satisfactory or not; this may not only give the subject clues to the preferable kind of response, but may preclude the possibility of retesting at a later date when correct answers may be remembered.[8]

Further Remarks on Administration. Subjects often make a grouping with their chosen sample that will later be required of them again. Thus, a subject may pick the large screwdriver as the sample object, and make a grouping of tools, and later another "tool" grouping is required. The examiner should not yield to the temptation to forego the later item, but if time permits should administer it to determine how flexible is the concept formation of the subject—whether he considers this an encouragement to form a different grouping, or whether he regards the repetition suspiciously and looks for a "catch," or whether he reacts to it with the idea that his former group was incorrect, and so on. The responses to this repetition frequently give indications of the stability, flexibility, or insecurity of the subject's attitude toward his own thinking and reasoning.[9] If the subject forms one of

[8] [If the subject's behavior and remarks do not clarify the basis on which he produced a sorting or a definition, the examiner should wait until that part of the test is over, lay the relevant objects out again, and inquire. For example, to elucidate the basis for a narrow sorting, he can indicate other objects besides those sorted that fit the subject's definition and ask, "Why didn't you include these?" Or if he is uncertain whether a syncretistic definition was given out of disinclination to work actively at the task or out of a schizoid overexpansiveness of conceptual boundaries, he might ask, "Couldn't that be true of other items here, too?—Then see if you can find something these things have in common that could not be said about any of the other things." If the subject gives several alternative answers, he should be asked which of his responses he considers best.—Ed.]

[9] [If the subject happens to choose for Item 1 the large fork, however, it is best not to present him with this same object immediately afterwards as the usual Item 2, since that would seem to call unmistakably for a different response. In such a case, the order of the second and third objects may be reversed; or the subject may be given a free choice to start with on Item 2, also.—Ed.]

the Part II groups on Part I and defines it on an abstract-conceptual level, however, the examiner may forego the administration of that item on Part II and score it as on Part I. But if the first grouping was either narrow or loose, or if the definition was not on an abstract-conceptual level, the corresponding item on Part II should be administered. The subject's reaction to the recurrence with modifications of a grouping he has already made is frequently significant of his thinking; it gives clues especially about whether his concept formation is flexible enough to allow him to appreciate his mistakes and the examiner's correctness, or so rigid that he will criticize the group put before him by the examiner if it does not accord with his own concepts.

Item Analysis

PART I OF THE SORTING TEST

Item 1. This item varies from subject to subject, since they choose the sample object.

Item 2. The sample here is the *large fork*. The adequate sorting includes the large knife and spoon, and the miniature fork, knife, and spoon. The most frequent deviations from this grouping are either to exclude the miniature silverware, which is a mild narrowing, or to include the sugar cubes, which is a mild loosening. It is also acceptable to group all the metal objects with the fork under the definition "metal," though an inkling of loosening is here implied.

The definition on the abstract-conceptual level is "silverware" or "eating utensils"; on the functional level, "you eat with them" or "used for eating"; and on the concrete level, "you find them on the table" or "in the kitchen." The definition "a table setting" should be inquired into, because it may be either a concretistic definition or a misleading formulation of an abstract-conceptual definition.

Item 3. The sample here is the *pipe*. The adequate sorting includes the real cigar and cigarette, the imitation (toy) cigar and cigarette, and the matchbook. Omission of the two imitations, or the inclusion of only the matchbook, are both frequent. Loose groupings on this item are extremely rare, and should be considered a sign of psychopathology. The definition on the abstract-conceptual level is "smoking equipment" or "smoking utensils"; on the functional level, "you smoke them" or "used in smoking"; on the concrete level—usually when only the matches are added to the pipe— "you use the matches to light the pipe." The response "smoking set" should be inquired into, to determine whether it is a concrete or an abstract-conceptual definition.

Item 4. The sample here is the *bicycle bell*. The adequate sorting includes the round objects, or the metal objects, or the toys. All of these are rare even in normal cases, and most frequently the lock and/or one or more tools are put with the bell. This item is the one most frequently failed. The abstract-conceptual definition is "round," "metal," or "toys"; the functional definition—when the lock is included—"used on a bicycle"; the concretistic definition—usually when the tools are included—"with them you put the bell on the bicycle," or "tools and the bell belong with a bicycle." Frequently the subject, especially when functioning on a good conceptual level, is unable to find anything to group satisfactorily with the bell. Failures on this item, either through achieving no sorting or achieving a concretistic sorting, should not be looked at askance, and only loose sortings with far-fetched definitions are diagnostically significant.

Item 5. The sample here is the *red paper circle*. The adequate sortings include all the red objects, or all the round objects, or all the paper objects. The most frequent is the paper grouping, including filing card, green cardboard rectangle, matchbook, and real cigarette. No significance should be attached to the frequent omission of the cigarette. Abstract-conceptual definitions of these adequate sortings are "paper," "round," "red"; adequate functional definitions do not occur on this item; concretistic definitions are frequently given when the eraser is included, such as "if you write on the paper, you might need an eraser." Of all the items of Part I, syncretistic and fabulated responses are perhaps most frequently given on this; hence this item should be watched carefully. The usual syncretistic response is to put various objects with the circle, and define them as "all geometric shapes." In the fabulated responses, the circle is usually given the significance of a table mat and the miniature silverware and sugar are grouped with it.

Item 6. The sample here is the *toy pliers*. The adequate sorting includes four miniature tools and two large tools. Other frequent sortings are (a) only the miniature tools; (b) all tools, the nails, and the block with the nail in it; (c) all toys, including miniature tools and tableware, ball, and imitation cigar and cigarette. These variations have no special diagnostic significance. The abstract-conceptual definition is "tools" or "toys"; the functional definition is "you use them to make something" or "fix something," or "used in carpenter work"; the concretistic definition is "found in a tool chest." On the concrete level the grouping may become very narrow, as when only the large pliers is added to the sample and the definition is "pliers," or when only the block with the nail in it is added and the definition is "you use the pliers to pull the nail out of the wood."

Item 7. The sample here is the *red rubber ball*. The adequate sortings are rubber objects (eraser, sink stopper, rubber cigar, and rubber cigarette), round objects (two corks, bell, the paper circle), red objects, or toys. The most frequent is the rubber grouping. The omission of the imitation cigar and cigarette is a relatively innocuous temporary inefficiency; but the inclusion of corks, with a modification of the concept to "rubbery" or "spongy," represents loosening of the concept basis. The adequate abstract-conceptual definition is "rubber," "round," "red," or "toys"; functional definitions occur mostly in the case of the toys, such as "to play with"; and similarly with concretistic definitions, such as "you find them in a child's playroom," or "child's." In some disorganized cases nothing is grouped with the ball, and the subject's verbalizations are pathologically concrete, such as "there is no bat to hit it with," or "no glove to catch it with." Such concrete attitudes in disorganized people will on occasion lead to fabulated responses, such as putting the paper circle with the ball and defining it as "a sidewalk to bounce the ball on," or defining the cardboard square as a "baseball diamond."

Item 3 (pipe) and Item 6 (pliers) are the two easiest items on Part I; Item 2 (fork), Item 5 (red paper circle), and Item 7 (ball) are the three items of intermediate difficulty; Item 4 (bell) is so difficult that no diagnostic weight should be attached to failure on it.

Consequently, an inadequate grouping on Items 3 or 6 indicates maladjustment beyond the normal range; failures on Items 2, 5, and 7 are of dubious significance, although in our experience a massing of misses is generally indicative of severe maladjustment; and failures on Item 4 can be disregarded, unless they are farfetched or bizarre in character.

PART II OF THE SORTING TEST

Item 1. The examiner sorts the ball, the paper circle, the matchbook, the sink stopper, and the eraser. The abstract-conceptual definition is "all red." The examiner does not include any objects that are only partly red, such as the tools. Functional and concretistic definitions are inadequate for this sorting, and the failures are usually one of the following: (a) *no response;* (b) a *split-narrow* response, where the group is split into two parts separately defined, such as rubber and paper subgroups; (c) *false* definitions, such as "for a child to play with"; and (d) *syncretistic* definitions, such as "all manufactured" or "all come from plants." This is one of the more difficult items of Part II, probably due in large part to its being the first item. That is, later items are more easily and more frequently passed than earlier ones of comparable difficulty, because of learning.

Item 2. The examiner sorts the large silverware, the small silverware, the bell, the lock, the two nails, and the two pairs of pliers. The examiner does not include objects that are only partly metal. The abstract-conceptual definition is "all metal." Definitions such as "all steel" or "all iron" are also considered abstract-conceptual, though with some concretistic tinge, since only a specific kind of metal comes to mind. There is no adequate functional definition for this sorting; subjects who attempt such usually give syncretistic definitions, such as "all used by man," or "all used in our everyday life." There is no satisfactory concrete definition. The failures are usually *split-narrow,* as when the subject separates the silverware and the toys, or *syncretistic,* as exemplified above.

In cases of serious disorganization of thinking, such as that present in schizophrenics, this item lends itself to *fabulation:* "With these you eat your breakfast, and then you go to work with these, and this is a lock for your tool chest, and this is a warning bell." Fabulation in this case appears to be an attempt to deal with an originally split-narrow reaction based on a concrete attitude to the objects, by uniting the split-narrow subgroups in a story.

Item 3. The examiner sorts the ball, sink stopper, two corks, bicycle bell, and paper circle. The abstract-conceptual response is "all round." Functional and concretistic definitions are unusual with this sorting, and failures are usually of the following types: *split-narrow,* as when the rubber objects of the group are distinguished from the nonrubber objects, or the red objects from the nonred objects; *false,* as in the definition that "a child plays with them all"; *syncretistic,* as in "all found in a house," or "all used by man"; *fabulated,* as when the subject relates them all specifically to the everyday activities of a person; and finally, *no response.* This is one of the hardest items on Part II.

Item 4. The examiner sorts the large screwdriver and pliers, small screwdriver and pliers, small hammer and small hatchet. The abstract-conceptual definition is "all tools." A functional definition is "you use them to make things"; a concretistic definition is "all in the tool kit." This is one of the easiest items on Part II and definitions deviating from abstract, functional, or concrete levels are rare. Sometimes one gets *split-narrow* definitions within a conceptual definition, such as "all tools, but these are real tools and these are imitation tools." Where thinking is already disorganized, this split-narrow reaction may develop into a *fabulation:* "These are for the father in his work, and these are for his child who is imitating him."

Item 5. The examiner sorts the red paper circle, green cardboard square, white filing card, matchbook, and real cigarette. The abstract-conceptual definition is "all paper." A functional definition of this group is all but impossible, the nearest being "all used to write on"; but this is actually a *false* definition. Even concretistic definitions, such as "you find them all on a desk," contain an element of falseness. *Split-narrow* responses sometimes occur when the subject is doubtful about the cigarette because it contains tobacco, but this is so rare that its occurrence indicates an overmeticulous mode of thinking. This item also lends itself to *fabulation:* "a man working at a desk (the filing card), smoking (the matchbook and cigarette)," and so on. *Syncretistic* definitions, such as "all come from plants," also occur.

Item 6. The examiner sorts all the items of which there are two, whether real or imitation; that is, the forks, knives, spoons, corks, nails, sugar cubes, screwdrivers, pliers, cigars, cigarettes. The abstract-conceptual response is "all pairs." In administering this item, each pair should be put close together and separated from other pairs on the table, and the two items of a pair should be put out in sequence. Contrary to expectation, this does not give away the answer; and Item 6 is actually one of the difficult items of Part II. The subject clinging to a functional level will usually give a *syncretistic* definition, "We use them all." Even concretistic responses are actually syncretistic on this item, such as "You find them all in the house." The great variety of objects prevents the subject from finding any more specific function or location for these objects, either of which would make it a functional or concretistic definition. *Fabulations,* especially about a father and son or even a whole family, are frequent on this item, because it presents such great difficulty and so many different objects. A frequent response is "a real and imitation (or miniature) of each"; this response has an element of abstract-conceptual thinking, since "two of each" is implicit in it. However, such a definition is partly *false,* because of the inclusion of the two identical sugar cubes, two identical nails, and two identical corks, and partly has an element of the *split-narrow* meticulousness in it, because the subject will not accept the real and the imitation as both possibly representing a "pair."

Item 7. The examiner sorts the real cigarette, the two sugar cubes, the filing card, and the green rectangle turned on its reverse (white) side. The abstract-conceptual definition is "all white." As on previous items, attempts at functional or concretistic definitions usually prove essentially *syncretistic* or *fabulatory.* Meticulousness also is seen when the subject has difficulty because of the brown tobacco in the cigarette, and gives a partly *split-narrow* definition. This too is one of the difficult items on Part II, as was the "red" first item.

Item 8. The examiner sorts the sink stopper, imitation cigar, imitation cigarette, ball, and eraser. The abstract-conceptual definition is "all rubber." This item and Item 9 are the easiest on Part II. Functional and concretistic definitions are also well-nigh impossible, and poor responses are usually *syncretistic, fabulatory,* or *split-narrow.*

Item 9. The examiner sorts the pipe, real cigar and cigarette, imitation cigar and cigarette, and matchbook. The abstract-conceptual response is "all smoking material (or equipment)." Functional definitions are usually "You use them to smoke with," or "You smoke them"; a concretistic definition is "You find them on a smoking stand." *Split-narrow* responses occur when the subject cannot integrate the two imitations with the real objects. Responses to this item are generally on either the abstract-conceptual, functional, or concretistic levels; any other type of response on this easy item is usually indicative of profound pathology.

Item 10. The examiner sorts the large silverware and the miniature silverware. The abstract-conceptual definition is "all silverware," or "all eating utensils." Functional definitions are "You eat with them," or "used in eating"; a concretistic definition is "found on the table." This also is one of the easy items. Any definition departing from these three levels is indicative of disorganized concept formation. *Split-narrow* responses do occur, as the subject may not be able to reconcile the real and imitation utensils; in schizophrenics especially, this split-narrow perception may lead to *fabulatory* or *symbolic* connections in terms of "parent's" and "child's."

Item 11. The examiner sorts the four miniature tools, three miniature eating utensils, imitation cigar, imitation cigarette, and ball. The abstract-conceptual definition is "toys," or "playthings." A functional definition is "You play with them all"; concretistic definitions are "for a child," or "you find them in a child's room." This is an item of intermediate difficulty, and any definition departing from these three levels usually becomes a diagnostic indicator.

Item 12. The examiner sorts the filing card, green cardboard rectangle, block of wood with the nail in it, matchbook, and two sugar cubes. The abstract-conceptual definition is "all rectangles." Attempts at functional or concretistic definitions usually turn out to be *syncretistic*, or *fabulatory*, or simply *false*. This is one of the most difficult items on the test. Definitions such as "all have right angles," or "all squares," are not quite as accurate "all rectangles," but are acceptable as abstract-conceptual.

Items 2, 4, 5, 8, 9, and 10 of Part II are easy, being failed (scored other than *FD* or *CD*) by no more than one normal person in 10. Items 1, 3, 6, 7, and 12 are difficult. The two levels of difficulty on Part II are sharply distinguished, with Item 11 falling in between. The examiner should therefore keep in mind that failures on the easy items of Part II should be considered as indicative of impairment or disorganization of concept formation; this is especially the case if failures on the easy items are massed. Of course, any failure that contains a fabulatory or otherwise bizarre element, regardless of the item's difficulty, is also an indicator of psychopathology.

In this discussion of the items and the types of responses to them, we have indicated only briefly the variety of sortings and definitions possible. In the course of testing many hundreds of patients, the examiner comes across many unique definitions or sortings, and the scoring and interpretation of the response must be left to his judgment. One sometimes finds unusual but nevertheless correct sortings; but very unusual definitions, especially on Part II, are rarely adequate. Such responses, in our experience, can be scored and understood in terms of the rationale of the test we have advanced.

DIAGNOSTIC SUGGESTIONS

To begin with, it is important to point out that some of the diagnostic indicators we used do not necessarily increase in frequency with increasing profundity of maladjustment or decompensation. Some of these diagnostic indicators show their greatest predominance in the less serious forms of the maladjustment of which they are characteristic. In clinical practice, they are good indicators of impending severe maladjustment; thus, in special circumstances they may be used to identify persons likely to break down under stress.

Adequacy of Sorting (Part I) and Verbalization (Part II). Although the developmental study (Reichard et al., 1944) showed an earlier maturation of adequacy on Part I, by age 14 the adequacy of socially compliant conceptual thinking surpasses that of active concept formation, a relationship that obtains in most normal adults and clinical groups with which we have had experience. Moreover, active concept formation is more vulnerable to impairment by maladjustment than is compliant concept formation. This relationship is reversed only in some of the most incapacitating disorders, wherein even compliant concept formation is encroached upon; three or more inadequacies on Part I tend to be found in some schizophrenics, in depressive psychotics, and in neurasthenics [also in brain-damaged cases]. Extreme inadequacy of active concept formation—four or more minus sortings—is a sign of profound maladjustment, usually of longstanding schizophrenia [or an organic lesion]. In many chronic schizophrenics, the adequacy of compliant concept formation tends to be fairly well retained. If the presence of schizophrenia has been indicated by other tests, and if compliant concept formation is markedly superior to active concept formation (Part II much better than Part I), the likelihood is that we are dealing with a psychosis settling into an ambulatory, chronic condition. Among neurotics, depressionlike conditions such as neurasthenia or anxiety and depression show the greatest impairment of compliant concept formation; six to eight minus scores on Part II are not uncommon.

A poor cultural background in a normal person often results in a limited adequacy of active concept formation (e.g., four plus scores on Part I), especially if some trends toward maladjustment are present. This cultural factor has little effect upon compliant concept formation; yet well-adjusted normal persons without any particular intellectual interests or capacities beyond the average may occasionally—especially if anxious—do badly at compliant concept formation, even producing as many inadequate verbalizations on Part II as adequate ones. This fact points up the danger of blind reliance on such quantitative diagnostic indicators as are given here without careful qualitative analysis, particularly of the tone of the verbalization.

The Concept Span on Part I. We defined the concept span of active sorting as the extent to which the sorting of the subject approximates the inclusiveness of the correct (normative) one: when too few objects are included, the sorting is considered narrow; when more than or other than the appropriate objects are included, the sorting is considered loose.

Loosening of the concept span, except of a mild degree, rarely occurred in the developmental study (Reichard et al., 1944); except in children under eight years, more than one L score is a significant deviation from the norm, though mildly loose sortings were fairly common at most age levels. In normal or neurotic adults, the presence of one or more L scores indicates schizoid or paranoid trends. Three or more L scores are very rarely found except in schizophrenia. Moreover, the presence of one L sorting or more will not infrequently differentiate a schizophrenic from a depressive psychotic whom he otherwise resembles, especially in the presence of some N. Although the weakening of the boundaries of concepts with a resulting loosening of their span is virtually a hallmark of schizoid disorganization of thinking, a significant amount of mild loosening (the l and (L) scores) can be produced by anxiety or depressive trends, probably because these trends interfere with attention and concentration, with a consequent haphazardness of sorting.

Narrowing of the concept span may also occur for various reasons, which can be partly distinguished by careful analysis of verbalization or by discreet inquiry. Direct observation of test behavior will often attest to the lethargy, sluggishness, and psychomotor retardation that produce the characteristic narrowness of sortings by depressives. Thus, although deteriorated schizophrenics have a high incidence of N scores, it is usually uninterestedness or inability to concentrate that prevents them from even considering other objects to put with the sample. In depression, however, either the above-described type of retardation can be seen to be responsible, or a characteristic blocking or "true narrowing" of thought so that the subject conscientiously tries but concludes that there is nothing that belongs with the sample. Also, when a deteriorated schizophrenic can be momentarily interested in the task, he will usually respond with an arbitrary and bland overinclusiveness, which is never found in nonschizoid depressions.

Two or more N scores are enough to raise the question of depression, and four or more of these essential narrowings of concept span on Part I strongly indicate depressive trends [or organic impairment], retarding the ease and flexibility of the interaction of inductions and deductions necessary to form an adequate sorting. Schizophrenic impairment of attention and concentration, with a consequent inability to make systematic and relevant inductions and deductions, may also result in the accumulation of two or more essential narrowings. Inhibition, paranoid suspiciousness and rigidity, and lack of interest in the test also may be responsible for a couple of N scores in almost any subject, so that no great diagnostic weight should be given to this indicator unless it is found on most of the items of Part I.

Mild narrowing, as reflected in the (N) score, can occur through carelessness, inattention, or lack of effort, which cause the overlooking of one or two relevant objects, and is therefore likely to occur in almost any diagnostic category. It can also occur, however, as a result of compulsive meticulousness or extreme inhibition; in the former case, the subject will characteristically look over and often pick up to examine minutely many of the objects, sometimes offering spontaneous comments indicating that he is overconcerned with minute differences, whereas the inhibited subject will declare himself finished after considering only a few objects. Again, the quality—and quantity—of the verbalization when the subject is asked to justify his grouping will usually enable the examiner to identify the basis on which the narrowing occurred.

The Conceptual Level. In this section we shall be concerned with the different levels of conceptualization on both parts of the test: the abstract-conceptual definitions *(CD)*, functional *(FD)*, and concretistic *(C)* ones, and also syncretistic *(S)*, fabulatory *(Fab)*, split-narrow *(S/N)*, symbolic *(Symb)*, and chain *(Ch)* concepts as well as complete *failures* when no response is offered. There will be no discussion of *false* definitions, since they tend to occur spottily in all diagnostic groups and do not appear to have any regular psychological meaning.

In the normal adult, at least half the definitions on Part I and two thirds of those on Part II should be scored *CD* (*abstract-conceptual definitions*). Intellectualizers and highly intelligent subjects or those with rich cultural backgrounds will tend to have higher proportions; since the test has relatively little "top," it does not take an outstandingly gifted person to get all or nearly all *CD*'s, especially on Part II. On Part I, two *CD*'s or less are likely to occur in schizophrenics (especially chronic and deteriorated cases), depressive patients of either neurotic or psychotic degree, and in other neuroses with depressive trends. The same trends hold in Part II, except that many chronic schizophrenics and anxious, depressed neurotics show up much better; 10 or more *CD*'s are not uncommon. Even in the normal range, however, anxiety and other signs of maladjustment, or cultural deprivation, can result in only six or seven *CD* responses on Part II.

Functional definitions, which represent a lower developmental level of concept formation, tend to be more frequent on Part I than on Part II; *FD's* are almost always less frequent than *CD's*. No clinical groups seem to be characterized by any particular frequency of *FD* on Part II, but moderately regressed psychotics (notably simple schizophrenics) at times produce about as many *FD's* as *CD's*.

From one to three *concretistic definitions* on Part I are not uncommon among normal persons of limited cultural background and intellectual interests, but even a single *C* on Part II is unusual except among culturally and educationally deprived adults. A greater incidence of *C's* is found in depressives (including neurotics with depressive trends) and schizophrenics, especially paranoid schizophrenics.[10]

Syncretistic definitions manifest a characteristically schizoid type of thinking, but they do not carry much diagnostic weight unless massed: five or more *S* scores on Part II strongly suggest a schizophrenic process. One or more *S* scores on Part I are often found in early stages of schizophrenic disorder, accompanied by loose sortings. Note, however, that certain weak, innocuous types of responses ("all found in the household"; "all come from trees"; "all made by man") may be given to one or two of the difficult items on either part of the test by almost any patient who is not mustering much interest or effort, and is groping for an answer. These types of responses are an easy way out, and may have little more pathological significance than intellectual laziness. The *S* scores with more pathological implications are more peculiar in wording, fantastically overgeneralized ("all made of atoms"), or betray the breakthrough of strong drive preoccupations ("they will all burn"); any *S* response carries more psychopathological weight when given with a sense of conviction that "this must be it."

An item is scored as a *failure* on Part I if no sorting is made (since it is very rare for the subject to sort and then be unable to explain why he put objects together), and on Part II if no definition is offered. Because some of the items are difficult, one or two failures on either part are not to be taken as a very untoward indication if on difficult items; an amassing of failures is most frequent where depressive trends or a simple or deteriorated schizophrenia are present. Neurotic subjects with depressive trends often fail several items on Part II. They do not give wild or incorrect definitions;

[10] [A high incidence of this least advanced type of adequate conceptualization, particularly in Part II, should raise a serious question of brain damage. In such cases, it will be particularly important to look for the other kinds of organic indicators described by Goldstein and Scheerer (1941).—Ed.]

it may be that their hold on reality prevents their doing so while the manifold properties of the objects set out by the examiner confuse them hopelessly, and consequently they do not offer any definition.

Fabulations are like syncretistic definitions in the sense that they are characteristic of schizophrenic thought disorder, yet certain weak and benign forms of them tend to occur on difficult items in almost any diagnostic category. More than two fabulized responses on either Part I or Part II—especially when on items of intermediate or less difficulty—strongly raise the question of psychosis, and specifically of a schizophrenic process.[11]

The *split-narrow* response predominantly characterizes depressive psychosis, though in general any of the psychopathological trends that produce narrowing of the concept span on Part I can produce S/N responses on Part II: overmeticulousness, inertia, blocking, pathological concreteness, and constricted inhibition. Again, observation of test behavior and study of the subject's verbalizations are essential for this discrimination.

Symbolic definitions are quite rare, and follow the general pattern of symbolic responses to the Rorschach inkblots: they are given either by pretentious, overintellectual people who self-consciously present them as "creative," "sophisticated" productions which they can easily abandon when asked to do so, or by full-blown schizophrenics. It is a question of a (somewhat inappropriate) regression in the service of the ego versus maladaptive regression to the direct emergence of the primary process.[12]

---

11 [Or organic damage to the central nervous system. Because fabulations and syncretistic responses are pseudo definitions which superficially appear to be attempts to cope with the task without really facing it squarely, they may be produced in quantity by subjects with character disorders marked by avoidance and intolerance of sustained effort at intellectual tasks. For this reason, it is desirable to vary the administrative procedure if a patient begins to give one fabulized response after another, particularly on easy items, to make it clear that this is not an acceptable solution: Interrupt the patient, saying: "No, don't do it that way; look at this object, then examine the others and put with it only the ones that belong with it." If the subject protests that the things he has sorted do belong together because one person could use them all in the sequence he has described ("He eats his dinner, has sugar in his coffee, then he smokes his cigar . . ."), tell him: "You are supposed to put together only things that are similar or alike in some way, things that have something in common." Or, on Part II: "I put these particular things out because they all have something in common that the others don't have—they are alike in some way. See if you can figure out what that point of similarity is, and tell me." If after such clarification the subject still persists in fabulations, the quality of his behavior and remarks will usually give away the basis on which he does so: stubbornly and negativistically (as in a rebellious, passively aggressive, or psychopathic character disorder), blandly disregarding or failing to comprehend your words, or with a peculiar, autistic rationalization (as in chronic schizophrenia), perplexedly and hesitantly, indicating pathological concreteness that allows no other possible solution (brain damage or mental deficiency).—Ed.]

12 [See Kris (1932-1952); Rapaport (1951a); Holt and Havel (1960).—Ed.]

Chain responses are likewise very unusual, appearing very occasionally in Part I of the test records of schizophrenics.[13]

THE RELATIONSHIP BETWEEN SIMILARITIES AND THE SORTING TEST

On the average, these two tests of concept formation tend to give similar results. In a research population of 41 schizophrenic cases, we examined the relationship between impairments on these two tests as follows. We considered Similarities impaired when the weighted score was either three or more units below the Vocabulary level *or* was at an absolute level of 9 or lower. Impairment of the Sorting Test performance was measured in terms of the following signs of psychopathology:

(1) Fewer than five adequate or nearly adequate (+ or ±) sortings on Part I.

(2) Two or more loose sortings on Part I.

(3) Fewer than three abstract-conceptual definitions on Part I.

(4) One or more syncretistic definitions on Part I.

(5) More than one fabulated or symbolic definition on Part I.

(6) Fewer than eight adequate or nearly adequate definitions on Part II.

(7) Fewer than six conceptual definitions on Part II.

(8) More than two syncretistic definitions on Part II.

(9) More than two fabulated or symbolic definitions on Part II.

In our schizophrenic sample, the 16 with impaired Similarities had an average of 4.3 pathological signs on the Sorting Test, while the 25 with unimpaired Similarities yielded a mean of .9 signs; t=3.87, p<.01. The corresponding biserial correlation is .69, indicating not only a highly significant but a strong relationship. (Similar but weaker findings obtained in other diagnostic groups.)

Let us also examine this relationship theoretically. In Similarities, the questions imply that the subject is to state the common *content* of only two objects of a realm. This narrowness of the realm is such that the process of concept formation requires only a minimum of interaction of inductions and deductions, and is experienced as automatically occurring. Thus, in this test we should expect concept formation to take place smoothly, with a minimum of doubt and a maximum of precision. But the very limited range of the *realm* hinders success; it is conducive to functional or concretistic definitions, by including points of similarity that would be excluded by the presence of a greater number and variety of objects of the realm. That is,

[13] [They are most often given by manic patients, since they can be a rather direct and "pure" expression of the distinctive form of manic thought disorder.—Ed.]

dog—lion—whale would not allow such responses as "have legs," "walk," "bark." Where a greater number of objects must be dealt with, as in the Sorting Test, the average subject is driven to take a more and more abstract attitude toward them, and is less likely to be struck by immediately apparent concrete relationships.

The concept formation required by Similarities is on a purely verbal level; that is, no reference to specific samples of the objects takes place and the definitions offered are usually based on the verbal coherence established in everyday experience between the objects and their generic terms (*coat— dress:* "clothing"). The subject has a relatively simple task as long as this verbal coherence is operating. If, however, it has never been created or is weakened, the subject may follow either of two courses. First, he may take reference to images of the objects, which generally results in concretistic or at best functional definitions. Or he may attempt generalizations. In this second case the situation is quite unlike that in the Sorting Test, in the second part of which the realm of objects whose conceptual content is to be defined is juxtaposed with other objects outside this realm: generalization is limited by the fact that the subject can always ask himself, "Do the other objects not fall within this generalization?" In Similarities there is no such limitation, and generalizations may accordingly become farfetched. Thus, where the automatic verbal coherence of the names of the objects with their generic terms is lost, search and effort drive one away from the abstract-conceptual level rather than toward it.

These verbal coherences become so stereotyped and ingrained in a person's thinking that profound impairment or even deterioration of active concept formation may leave them untouched; thus, a good score on Similarities may well be the result of the perseverance of these empty shells of concepts. But in such cases the absence of underlying comprehension of the verbal coherences makes the formulations rigid, inflexible, and easily broken by questioning. If a deteriorated subject responds to *orange— banana* with "fruit," the question, "What do you mean by fruit?" will quickly reveal an inability to define adequately the content of this concept, and the subject will say, "Well, you eat them," or "They have peels."

We conclude that the passive and automatic delivery of ingrained verbal stereotypes is to be expected, and deviation therefrom is likely to be a diagnostic indicator; furthermore, that the retention of these stereotypes may obscure a disorganization of active concept formation.

Not *all* verbal coherences are retained in *all* cases of profound maladjustment, however. Where impairment is evident even on easy items, active concept formation—such as that on the Sorting Test—will be even more impaired. Thus, it is insufficient in testing clinical cases to accept verbal clichés at face value; one must go beyond that, and see what happens when active grouping and conceptualizing, with little help from clichés, is required. This further step is especially crucial for detecting preschizophrenics—overideational ones in particular—because the high premium they put on verbal formulations results in good achievement on Similarities; but the beginning encroachment of the schizophrenic process upon the organization of thought processes becomes apparent when they are placed in a situation where they must make independent conceptualizations, as on Part I of the Sorting Test. If a full-blown schizophrenic has a good verbal front and his Similarities is unimpaired, even though he is most likely to do relatively well on the Sorting Test, if the psychosis shows itself it will be in both Parts I and II. Some psychotics, such as simple schizophrenics, may do poorly at verbal conceptual thinking, since verbal formulation of ideas is one of their essential weaknesses, and at the same time they do better when the actual things are put before them, as in Part II of the Sorting Test, where everyday experiential coherence helps them.

CHAPTER 7

Diagnostic Testing of Personality and Ideational Content

Diagnostic testing of intelligence and concept formation scrutinizes the extent and quality of a subject's *achievements*. From the relationships between different achievements, and from the types of falling short of or deviation from expected achievements, we infer the maturity and strength, as well as the degrees and kinds of impairments, of the functions underlying the achievements—and the personality structure or type of maladjustment in which these would be likely to occur.

Diagnostic testing of personality and ideational content, on the other hand, is not concerned with achievements, but rather with the *different types of organizations* of the subject's spontaneous thought processes, and attempts to infer from their course and characteristics the nature of his personality and maladjustment. In the former, the subject is required to live up to a standard, and his type of deviation from it becomes a basis of his diagnosis; in the latter, the basis of diagnosis is the characteristic course of the subject's own spontaneous thought processes—his own reactions to, understanding and organization of, and selective choice from, different more or less complex stimulations.

But this distinction is not hard and fast. First, the diagnostic testing of personality and ideational content is also concerned with standards. These are not like the intelligence-test standards, subject to factual or logical verification; they are rather standards indicated by trends in large segments of the population. No logical necessity or explicit social agreement in everyday life vouches for these standards, and yet there is a trend in the general population to agree on them. Thus, there are "popular" responses to the Rorschach test which are given on the average by at least one—and some by three—out of five subjects. Second, even in the tests of intelligence and concept formation the rigid expectation or standard refers only to the achievement per se: the pathways for reaching identical achievements are not restricted. The verbalizations of passing as well as failing performances carry signs of the great variety of ways in which success or failure can be reached, and many of these signs are diagnostically useful. And yet, although the divisions are not hard and fast, the principles underlying the two types of procedures here discussed are strikingly different.

From this distinction, some of the principles of diagnostic tests of personality and ideational content may be derived.[1] The material of these tests must be unstructured to such an extent that the subject in responding will not find support in superficial formal information and conventional, traditional procedures. This is necessary because the human being of any society, but especially of our society, is so fenced in with formal information, conventions, and traditions as to display his undisguised individuality but rarely. Thus these tests seek to obtain reactions that are sufficiently unstilted to be able to serve as the subject matter for reconstructing some general patterns of the individual personality.

Unstructuredness is achieved in the Association Test by the demand in the instructions, "React with the very first word that comes to your mind," which leaves the manner of reaction up to the subject. (A comparison with any vocabulary test makes the issue of structuredness versus unstructuredness very clear.) Unstructuredness is achieved in the Rorschach test through the inkblot character of the test material, which offers well-nigh infinite possibilities for structuring and organizing it. Even if it were claimed that no real organizing process occurs in reacting to the Rorschach test—that there is merely choice between a lot of hazy possibilities—then the choice itself would amount to a structuring of the different possibilities into acceptable and unacceptable ones. The material of the Thematic Apperception Test (pictures of people and situations) is structured in the same sense as is that of the Word Association Test (meaningful stimulus words). But as in the Word Association Test, where the reaction is dependent upon the connotations the stimulus word has for the subject, so in the Thematic Apperception Test the choice of story—past, present, future, feeling tone, and thoughts of characters—depends upon the subject's mode of understanding the pictured situation; the story is made up by the subject, and thus reflects his bents. The lack of time limitation on the test, however, and the chance for the subject to check the internal logical consistency of the stories and their verbalization as well as their consistency with the picture, obviously allow more conventional and concealing responses to be introduced than in the Rorschach or Word Association Test. Thus, there are apparently many degrees to which the requirement of "unstructuredness" may be fulfilled by any single test.

[1] [On this topic, see also Rapaport (1952).—Ed.]

In this connection, another advantage—and requirement—of these tests should be stated. Here the subject is résponding to the test materials and instructions without any idea of how or from what point of view his productions will be evaluated. When he does have an idea, it is most likely to be wrong. The significance of the procedures is thus essentially unknown to the subject, and he cannot influence his productions in any systematic way.

Such procedures have come to be called "projective techniques" or "projective tests." In them the subjects are presumed to project their "private worlds" (Frank, 1939b) into the unstructured test material.

PROJECTIVE TESTING: CONCEPTS AND CRITERIA

The concept of projective testing has been overused, and yet limited to a relatively small set of procedures in the minds of those working in this field. It is sometimes forgotten that the central and time-honored procedure of personality study—namely, the case history—is a projective procedure too. The tendency is to forget that the term "projection" in connection with projective tests is not identical with the psychoanalytic concept of projection as a defense mechanism central to the nosological picture of paranoid disorders, nor even with the popularized and emasculated version of that concept denoting any attribution of one's own intents, thoughts, and feelings to another person.

Consequently it will be important to describe (1) the procedures to be rightfully considered projective; (2) the concept of projection implied here; and (3) the criteria of a projective test.

The Projective Hypothesis and Projective Procedures. Projective procedures imply a general projective hypothesis (see Rapaport, 1942b): manifestations of the human being's behavior,[2] from the least to the most significant ones, are revealing of his personality—that is, the individual principle of which he is the carrier. The projective hypothesis can therefore be applied to any segment of human behavior; and in earlier chapters we have shown that it can be applied profitably to the diagnostic analysis of intelligence-test results. Therefore the projective hypothesis, far from differentiating projective from nonprojective procedures, implies rather that

[2] The concept of behavior here implied includes all of the following aspects: (a) behavior historically viewed in the life history; (b) behavior statically viewed in the environment with which the subject surrounds himself, such as the furniture of his house, the clothes he wears, etc.; (c) bodily behavior, or the patterns of voluntary, habitual, and expressive movements; (d) internal behavior, including percepts, fantasies, thoughts.

any procedure investigating human behavior can be looked upon from this point of view.

What then is characteristic of projective procedures proper? They are procedures in which the subject actively and spontaneously structures unstructured material, and in so doing reveals his structuring principles—which are the principles of his psychological structure.[3]

It is assumed that the psychological structure of the person is a principle governing all his behavior; and by vigorously applying this hypothesis one may succeed—more likely by intuitive than by systematic approach—in discovering some facets of the structure of a person in any of his life manifestations, in spite of the fact that life manifestations, through their conformity to rules of conduct and conventions, conceal as much as they reveal our psychological structure. Projective procedures elicit life manifestations (play, perceptual-associative organizing, associative structuring, drawing, modeling) in material that is not conventionalized, where the person's psychological structure is no longer indicated merely as a "peculiarity" deviating from the conventional, but as a characteristic essence of the behavior and its creations. In usual life manifestations, the projective hypothesis *may* be applied; in projective procedures, the test behavior and the final product *cannot* be understood without it.

The Concept of Projection. The concept of projection as used in projective procedures is one formed on the pattern of projector and screen. In this sense, a projection has occurred when the psychological structure of the subject becomes palpable in his actions, choices, products, and creations. Therefore, when a procedure is so designed as to enable the subject to demonstrate his psychological structure unstilted by conventional modes, it is projective. The subject matter used in the procedure serves as a lens of projection, and the recorded material of elicited behavior is the screen with the picture projected on it.

The process of projection itself is no enigma, though only fragments of the rules governing it are known to us. It is known that the mind does not receive stimulations in the way a movie screen receives pictures projected on it, but rather acts like marble which breaks under a blow in the direction of its own grain and veins; thus it can be no surprise that even simple perception, when closely scrutinized, will bear characteristics not only of the perceived object but also of the perceiving subject. The more difficult the conditions of perceiving the object, the more clearly the percept bears characteristics of the perceiving subject (mishearing weak voices, misseeing swiftly passing objects, seeing trees in a dark forest as stalking

---

[3] [In this context "psychological structure" is used quite inclusively, to comprise what are usually called dynamic as well as structural aspects of personality.—Ed.]

enemies). The process of projection is given in the nature of human reaction.

The Criteria of Projective Tests. Intuition and diligent scrutiny of vast amounts of conventional manifestations—as in the life history—can arrange these manifestations into patterns giving an inkling of the "leitmotiv" of the life underlying the facts. Projective *tests* seek to avoid the necessity of scrutinizing vast amounts of life data, and of relying upon intuition. Successful or not, projective tests have the boldly proclaimed aim to *elicit,* to *render observable,* to *record,* and to *communicate* the psychological structure of the subject, as inherent to him at any given moment, and without study of historical antecedents. The mode of achieving these aims distinguishes the projective tests from projective procedures at large.

The *eliciting* procedure must be (a) economical—i.e., not time consuming; (b) simple—i.e., feasible for an examining office, and not requiring complicated or bulky apparatus; (c) impersonal—i.e., not involving the need for building up time-consuming transference relationships, nor complex and intense interpersonal relationships such as are present in psychodrama; (d) limited to one segment of behavior; (e) standard, in the sense that all subjects face the same materials and the same degree of cooperation by the examiner. All these are *necessary* criteria, which establish the *test* character of the projective tests. The aim of the tests is to allow for predictions on the basis of samples; and the smaller the samples which allow for reliable prediction, the better the test. Meeting these criteria assures the applicability and practicability of a projective test. Where tests are most needed, economic limitations are the greatest; psychological testing must be economically feasible in order to have a justification for existence. These criteria preclude the introduction of any factor which by its presence will make the test situation one that changes the subject's condition or grossly influences it. Furthermore, they preclude all variables that may obscure the results and their comparability. They make interindividual comparison possible. They limit observation and recording to one layer of behavior, the total recording of which is at least a possibility, while total behavior is a continuum, and as such is not subject to complete recording.

Let us turn now to *observing.* The procedure must be such that its subject matter and starting point—the stimulus word, the inkblot—is objectively given and observable to the examiner, and its end point fixed by the instructions. To make up any story or to do anything with toys provides no basis for *test* observations, because the segment of behavior to be considered is not delimited in advance, nor is the whole behavior defined by a beginning and end point. Total observation is feasible only within such limitations; and valid observation requires them because otherwise the distinction between test behavior and general behavior cannot be made by either examiner or subject.

The segment of behavior to be elicited must be amenable to full *recording*. Any and all arbitrary selection of the material to be recorded—as is common in clinical observations and recordings—must be avoided, if projective tests are to remain tests. Therefore, projective-test procedures early in their development limited the test behavior to verbalizations of the subject, or to simple choices. In contrast, finger painting—the total recording of which is very complicated (photographic), and the end result of which is by no means representative of the total behavior invested in it—remains a projective procedure far from constituting a test.

Finally, *meaningful verbal communication*—descriptive of a psychological structure, and not mere paraphrasing of the raw material of observation—requires that the recorded material of the tests be amenable to objective systematization in terms of an exhaustive scoring system, which will embrace the total record and express its qualities in quantitative terms allowing for inter- and intrapersonal comparisons. To describe a personality structure verbally, one must first state the next of kind, which implies an interpersonal comparison; and second, designate the features specifically differentiating each, which implies intrapersonal comparisons as well. This is difficult to do systematically without quantitative means of comparison.

The final interpretation of all the data is a matter of verbalization by the examiner, and thus inevitably implies subjectivity. Therefore, the standardization nature of the eliciting test material, the standardized limited field of observation, the total and nonselective recording, and the all-embracing quantitative scoring system, are the real advantages of a projective test and the safeguards of its objectivity.

These ideals are closely approached by the Rorschach, and claimed to some extent for the Word Association Test that we present in this volume. The Thematic Apperception Test—in spite of the ingenious efforts of Murray and his collaborators—remains far short of this ideal, although in practice it is none the less extremely useful.

PERSONALITY AND THE PROCESSES UNDERLYING REACTIONS IN THE PROJECTIVE TESTS DESCRIBED HERE

The use of projective tests assumes that the examiner is after something in the subject which the subject does not know about or is unable to communicate; otherwise the examiner would ask him about it directly. Projective tests are indirect questions, and the responses to them are indirect answers, pertaining to the psychological structure of the subject, and their use implies a theory of personality which assumes that much of this psychological structure is not consciously experienced by the subject. By means of projective tests we discover tremendous aggressions in persons who appear meek, or great dependent needs in suspicious and manly-appearing persons who deny having any such inclinations. If taken seriously, these tests therefore refer to unconscious *motivation* of action and behavior, and necessitate a personality theory that assumes the existence of, and accounts for, these motivations. The most extensive and consistent personality theory of this type is the psychoanalytic theory; and the projective tester must lean heavily on it to find relationships and analogies which will help him in his thinking about the material.

Here certain dangers arise. First, it may become difficult to decide whether any test indication refers to a conscious overt trend or to an unconscious latent trend. Second, glib analogies and direct transposition of psychoanalytic concepts to projective-test data become a great temptation, and may often replace independent thinking appropriate to the projective-test material. Such independent thinking utilizes modes of thought parallel with the modes of psychoanalytic thinking, but does not borrow concepts from it uncritically. The effects of both of these dangers have become manifest in the work of some projective testers.

One can cope with the first danger only if one uses several tests and can securely diagnose clinical-nosological entities; then, at least in great part, one can infer from the context of all the tests whether "impulsive colors" on the Rorschach test refer to destructiveness, torpid flat affects, impulsiveness proper, or affects that are latent determiners of a general tenseness. We have found no simpler way to cope with this danger. Not to cope with it leads to such a ludicrous diagnosis as the following: many color responses in a compulsive character, meek in bearing, with psychosomatic (arthritic) difficulties, interpreted as "in general rigid, but has violent destructive outbursts."

The second danger—uncritical use of psychoanalytic concepts—demands a scrutiny of the relation of psychoanalytic theory to the processes that occur in the subject during the course of the test. This relationship is very obscure, and there is no agreement about what it is or should be; therefore, we shall advance here our view of it. When the subject is asked to respond to a given test item, a thought process is set off; and when a reaction is obtained it represents the end point of a thought process. This process may be of a purely associative character, as in the Word Association Test; or of an intertwined associative and perceptual organizing character, as in the Rorschach test; or of a complex, intertwined, perceptual and

logical, narrative and organizing character, as in the Thematic Apperception Test. In all of them, however, personality manifests itself through a
thought process or through the product of such a process.

In presenting the tests of intelligence and concept formation, we have
shown how different aspects of the conscious thought process predominate
in different achievements of intelligence. In virtually all projective tests,
all aspects of thought processes come into play; and we do not test the
strength or impairment of these aspects, but rather trace the course that
thought processes take as a result of the strength or impairment, and interrelation, of their different aspects. While in the above chapters we were
concerned to some extent with component aspects of the thought process,
in the following we shall be concerned with the resultant: the spontaneous
course which thought processes take. Hereby a link is created between the
tests discussed thus far and those to be discussed below; and this link will
be useful to the diagnostician who grasps it and constantly bears it in mind.

Consistent exploration of projective tests is exploration of thought
processes. In these tests the ego, the carrier of conscious thinking, demonstrates its bent and its proclivities. The unconscious makings of the thought
process will occasionally become palpable, especially when thinking is disorganized; but in the main, projective tests are concerned with the type of
organization of thinking palpable in the course of the spontaneous thought
processes, and characteristic of the person and his ego.

The psychology of thought processes is a part of ego psychology. If a
breakthrough of unconscious modes of thinking occurs, it should prompt
the projective tester to draw on psychoanalytic theory concerning such a
breakthrough and the nature of unconscious processes. But the patterns
characteristic of conscious thought processes are unexplored by psychoanalysis, and the next of kind to them are defense mechanisms—the subject
matter of psychoanalytic ego psychology. To draw on the theory of the
latter with the utmost caution, and to attempt to mold a theory of observed
thought patterns so that they and the known patterns of defense mechanisms will elucidate each other and be welded into one common theoretical
framework, is the great unsolved task of projective testing.

Here we may state the picture of personality structure implied in the
projective-test procedure as it appears to us. The subject has an ego which
is the *recipient of outside stimulation,* and which may be inclined to take,
to avoid, or incessantly to invoke stimulations. This ego is also the *executor of the intentions of the unconscious strivings,* which in their particular
constellation and strength are specific to the person; as executor of these
intents, the ego may oppose them, subserve them without delay, or post-
pone them and by thinking prepare for their optimal realization. The ego

has a certain autonomy:[4] autonomous energy (bound cathexes), autonomous behavior (defense mechanisms), and autonomous thought patterns— to govern perception, execution, and thought. The reception of stimulation by the ego is not automatic but selective, and to some extent distorts the stimulation to meet the needs of the subject. The execution of intentions by the ego is likewise not an automatic discharge of internal tensions, but an adaptation to the nature of the objects in reality which these intentions are aimed at or must cope with.

[4] [The conception of the ego and of autonomy expressed here shows its age somewhat. For his later views on ego autonomy, see Rapaport (1951b, 1957c).—Ed.]

CHAPTER **8**

The Word Association Test

From the tests thus far described, we are able to assess the functioning of the subject's intelligence and concept formation. The Word Association Test indicates to some extent the ideational content of the problems which stand in the focus of the maladjustment. The test was first included in the battery on the assumption that disturbing areas of ideation could be inferred from associative disturbances on specific stimulus words. In actual use, however, the test has turned out to be of limited significance in this respect, and its use must not be restricted to such content information. The formal characteristics of the associative reaction have been found to be in themselves diagnostically significant. These formal characteristics, to which the greater part of this chapter will be devoted, are partly relationships of reaction time to reproduction time, partly relationships of reaction, stimulus, and reproduction words to each other, and partly relationships of the reaction word to the popular trend of reaction in the population. Many of these formal characteristics have been mentioned in previous literature as complex indicators. We have attempted to evaluate these, to treat them from a unified point of view (rationale), and to complement them wherever it seemed necessary.

Description of the Test. The Word Association Test we used contains 60 stimulus words (see Table 1). We preferred this set of words[1] to that of Jung (1906-1915), or Kent and Rosanoff (1910), because of its content and brevity. This set of stimulus words includes words of familial,[2] household and home,[3] oral,[4] anal,[5] aggressive,[6] phobic,[7] and quite varied

[1] This list of stimulus words is a revision of one originally compiled by William D. Orbison, Ph.D.
[2] Nos. 5, 30, 49, 55.
[3] Nos. 2, 8, 14, 16, 19, 24, 31, 35, 45.
[4] Nos. 7, 10, 11, 27, 33, 34, 38, 44, 48, 53, 60.
[5] Nos. 13, 40, 50.
[6] Nos. 21, 32, 41, 44, 47.
[7] Nos. 23, 43.

sexual[8] connotations. Therefore, it taps a great variety of areas of ideation, conflicts in which are likely to be prominent in the different types of maladjustments. One of the advantages of this list is that it consists entirely of nouns (about a dozen of which can also be taken to be verbs); therefore it facilitates gathering clinical experience by providing the examiner with the frame of reference, "associative reactions to nouns." Nouns embedded in a stimulus list of other nouns usually draw noun reactions, and other reactions to them are to be considered associative disturbances. It will be seen below that the relationships between stimulus and reaction words lend themselves to a rather clear categorization in terms applicable only to noun-to-noun relationships. To what terms of analysis reactions to verb or adjective stimuli would lend themselves is an issue we have not sufficiently explored, though it is of great importance for the psychology of thinking as well as for that of language.

The test consists of two parts: in the first part, the subject is told to give quickly the first word that comes to his mind after hearing each stimulus word; in the second part, the stimulus word is read to him again, and he is asked to reproduce his original response to each stimulus.

TABLE 1

Most Frequent Reactions, Word Association Test

Stimulus Words	Normal College Students' Reactions*	Schizophrenics' Reactions*	Rapaport's Mixed Original Norms
1. Hat	coat (44%) head (33)	coat (58%) head (12)	coat (37%) cap (14) head (10)
2. Lamp	light (56) shade (18)	shade (32) light (29)	light (67)
3. Love (t)	hate (24) marriage (17) girl/boy (16)	hate (45)	hate (46)
4. Book	read(ing) (39)	read(ing) (24)	read(ing) (44)
5. Father (t)	mother (72) man (4) son (2)	mother (61) son (12)	mother (56) parent (9) son (6)
6. Paper	pencil (26) pen (26) write(ing) (8)	pencil (22) pen (11)	pen/pencil (15) news (14) write(ing) (11)
7. Breast** (t)	woman (14) milk (12)	woman (22)	chest (18) woman (8)

[8] Indirect: Nos. 3, 15, 36, 51, 57; Intermediate: Nos. 7, 38; Direct: Nos. 18, 25, 29, 59.

Stimulus Words	*Normal College Students' Reactions**	*Schizophrenics' Reactions**	*Rapaport's Mixed Original Norms*
8. Curtain(s)**	window (47) drapes/drapery (10) rod (9)	window (31) rod (19) shade (11)	window (33) shade (17) drapes/drapery (14)
9. Trunk	elephant (21) car (11) tree (10) clothes/clothing (9)	suitcase (12) tree (10)	suitcase (29) clothes/clothing (9)
10. Drink (t)	water (29) liquor (8)	water (18) glass (11)	water (43) liquor (10)
11. Party (t)	fun (32) dance(ing) (11)	fun (19) people (13)	fun (22) people (7)
12. Spring	flowers (18) summer (16) love (10)	fall (17) summer (14) water (10)	summer/fall (32) water (13)
13. Bowel movement (t)	bathroom (26) toilet (23)	toilet (14)	shit (18) toilet/bathroom (15)
14. Rug	floor (44) carpet (28)	floor (41) carpet (19)	floor (48) carpet (17)
15. Boy friend (t)	girl friend (40) love (19)	girl friend (62)	girl/girl friend (51)
16. Chair	sit (36) table (30)	table (33) sit (19)	sit/seat (43) table (18)
17. Screen**	movies (29) window (17) picture (7) door (7)	window (39)	window (36) fly (12) door (10)
18. Penis** (t)	boy (22) male (17) man (14) sex (13)	man (16)	man (15) prick (14)
19. Radiator	heat (61) steam (14) car (4)	heat (59)	heat (42) car (18) water (9)
20. Frame**	picture (66) window (7)	picture (58) window (12)	picture (44) window (14)
21. Suicide (t)	death (50) kill (11) murder (7)	death (40) kill (13)	death (35) kill/murder (23)
22. Mountain**	high (24) climb(ing) (14) hill (11)	hill (19) valley (11)	hill (31) high/height (15) climb (13)
23. Snake‡ (t)	bite (11) grass (5)	grass (19) bite (10)	

Stimulus Words	Normal College Students' Reactions*	Schizophrenics' Reactions*	Rapaport's Mixed Original Norms
24. House** (t)	home (46) live (12)	home (19)	home (22) dwelling (11) barn (9)
25. Vagina** (t)	woman (24) girl (20) female (14)	woman (27) penis (10)	woman (29)
26. Tobacco**	smoke(ing) (50) cigarette (29) pipe (7)	smoke (46) cigarette (23) pipe (10)	smoke(ing) (60) cigarette (15)
27. Mouth‡ (t)	kiss(ing) (20) nose (13) tongue (11) lip(s) (11) eat (11)	teeth (19) eat (10)	
28. Horse	ride(ing) (32) animal (11) cow (4)	cow (15) ride (13) animal (10)	cow (35) animal (21) ride(ing) (7)
29. Masturbation (t)	sex (20) boy (11)	sex (7)†	jack off (15)†
30. Wife‡ (t)	husband (60) mother (13)	husband (49)	
31. Table**	chair (65) food (7) eat (7)	chair (58)	chair (44) eat/food (15)
32. Fight‡ (t)	argue (10) win (5)	win (8)	
33. Beef	meat (29) steak (20) food (10)	cow (16) steak (16) meat (10)	meat (24) cow (20) eat/food (8)
34. Stomach**‡ (t)	ache (21) food (13) ulcer (1)	ulcer (10)	
35. Farm**	animal (32) cow (15) house (12)	animal (12) cow (12)	land (18) country (13) home (7)
36. Man**	woman (77)	woman (67)	woman (58) male (8)
37. Taxes	[omitted]	money (28) government (16) pay (11)	money (28) pay (11)
38. Nipple (t)	bottle (32) breast (30) suck (13)	breast (51) bottle (18)	bottle (26) breast (23) baby (10)

Stimulus Words	Normal College Students' Reactions*	Schizophrenics' Reactions*	Rapaport's Mixed Original Norms
39. Doctor	nurse (28) sick (10) lawyer (4)	lawyer (21) nurse (13)	nurse (21) lawyer (9) sick/ill (8)
40. Dirt‡ (t)	filth (19) clean (17) mud (11) ground (4)	filth (18) ground (12)	
41. Cut (t)	bleed (15) knife (10) blood (9) hurt (8)	blood (18) wound (14)	blood/bleed (18) wound (11) knife (11) hurt (11)
42. Movies**	picture (22) theatre (8) show (6)	picture (11)	picture/show/ theatre (68)
43. Cockroach‡	bug (35) insect (10)	bug (21) insect (17)	
44. Bite** (t)	dog (19) hurt (17) tooth (11) chew (11)	teeth (19) chew (11)	teeth (19) chew (17) hurt (11)
45. Dog**	cat (53) animal (8)	cat (59)	cat (54) animal (15)
46. Dance	fun (17) sing (11) twist (10)	fun (11)	music (18) fun/pleasure (12)
47. Gun‡ (t)	shoot (41) kill (14)	shoot (36) kill (11)	
48. Water	drink (39)	drink (19)	drink (42)
49. Husband‡ (t)	wife (75)	wife (78)	
50. Mud‡ (t)	dirt (50) dirty (14)	dirt (39)	
51. Woman** (t)	man (64) female (4)	man (60)	man (46) female (15)
52. Fire** (t)	hot (14) burn(s)(ing) (13) smoke (10) flame (10)	water (18) heat (12) burn (10)	water (26) burn (12) heat (11)
53. Suck** (t)	nipple (22) baby (10) bottle (9) breast (7)	breast (13) nipple (12)	baby (13) nipple (11) breast (6)
54. Money**‡	spend(ing) (14) dollar (7)	dollar (7)	

Stimulus Words	Normal College Students' Reactions*	Schizophrenics' Reactions*	Rapaport's Mixed Original Norms
55. Mother (t)	father (65)	father (47)	father (48)
56. Hospital	sick (35) bed (10) sickness (10)	sick (17)	sick/ill (46)
57. Girl friend (t)	boy friend (55)	boy friend (60)	boy/boy friend (45)
58. Taxi**	cab (41) driver (10) car (7)	car (15) cab (14) ride (13)	car/automobile (41) cab (17)
59. Intercourse (t)	sex (37) love (14) marriage (13)	sex (24)	fuck (18) sex (13) women (6)
60. Hunger**‡	thirst (31) food (20) eat (11) pain (10)	thirst (23) food (17) pain (12)	
Number of subjects	167	200	151

(t) "Traumatic" words (see p. 257).

* These data are used with the kind permission of Phebe Cramer. They are taken from a research project supported by NIMH Grant No. MH 10504-01.

** Totals for some reaction words include plurals also.

† In these groups, the stimulus word used was "masturbate."

‡ These words were not contained in the list used at the time the Rapaport norms were accumulated.

Note: The normal students' data were obtained by a self-administering, written version of the test. All reaction words with frequencies of 10% or more are included, plus a few others for comparative purposes.

THE PSYCHOLOGICAL RATIONALE OF THE WORD ASSOCIATION TEST

"Content" and "Formal Characteristics" of the Associative Reaction. The Word Association Test in its clinical application supplies two types of information. On the one hand, a reaction word may be so specific, so deviant from the usual, that in itself it will indicate that the stimulus word has touched a conflictful area of ideation, and its meaning in relation to the meaning of the stimulus word will be so patent that it will give information concerning the nature of the conflict present—e.g., *father*—"tyrant"; *intercourse*—"trouble." On the other hand, the stimulus word may elicit an associative disturbance which in some instances will indicate that the stimulus word is touching on a conflictful area, but in others will prove to be merely a part of a generalized disturbance of the associative process— leaving the connection between the stimulus word and a conflictful area of

ideation unclear, and mostly unclarifiable because of the extreme remoteness of the word. Thus, if the stimulus word *wife* is responded to by the reaction word "suspicion," not only the presence of a conflict but something of its nature is revealed. Failure to react to the stimulus word *wife*, however, will indicate only the presence of a conflict connected with the area of ideation denoted by the word *wife*. If the stimulus word *wife* is responded to by the reaction word "house," the distance between the stimulus and reaction words may indicate a conflict connected with the area of ideation denoted by *wife*, without revealing anything of its nature; or it may be only a part of a generalized inclination to give distant or other disturbed associative reactions, in which case it need have no implication of a conflict connected with the area of ideation denoted by *wife*.

The associative disturbances to be dealt with may be summarily classified as: (1) reactions not in conformity with the instructions; (2) reactions significantly deviating from the usual ones; (3) deviations from the instructions on the Reproduction Test.

Our treatment here will deal little with the content information to be derived directly from the Word Association Test. It must not be forgotten, however, that the formal characteristics of associative reactions, with which we shall deal extensively, always point to the stimulus word, and always indicate at least the possibility that the stimulus word stands for a conflictful area of ideation. Thus, the discussion of the formal characteristics here does not replace, but rather implements, the quest for content information expected from the test.

Analysis of the psychological nature of the Word Association Test opens up the following questions: What psychological process delivers a reaction to a given stimulus word so that this reaction, in conformity with the instructions, takes the form of *one word quickly given?* What psychological process determines the choice of the reaction word? Finally, what encroachments upon the process in question result in associative disturbances?

Our attempts to clarify the psychological process underlying associative reactions will proceed on the lines of the general view of the thought process outlined in Chapter 5. Accordingly, we shall discuss three aspects of the associative reaction considered as a thought process: *memory, concept formation,* and *anticipation.*[9]

The Memorial Aspect of the Associative Reaction. Associationist psychology taught that the functioning of memory is determined by the strength

[9] The *attention* and *concentration* aspects of the associative reaction will not be treated here, partly because their role is not well enough understood by us, and partly because we have insufficient data to discuss what we do understand about them (e.g., the failure to apprehend and the misapprehension of stimulus words).

of associations, and that strength is determined by the frequency of contiguous appearance in the subject's consciousness of the "mental elements" involved. In other words, it was claimed that an idea will be followed in one's mind by the idea which has most often appeared contiguously with it before. This view still persists in the "conditioning" theories of memory and learning, the more clearly so the less sophisticated they are.

The Word Association Test—or Association Experiment, as Jung (1906-1915) called it—was born amid such views of memory's functioning. Its original idea may be summed up as follows: *experiments on memory and learning study how associations come about by frequent contiguous repetitions, how long a life they have, and to what interferences the process of association is subject; let us now investigate not how associations come about, but rather what associations or their residual dispositions are actually present in the person.* The Diagnostic Association Experiment presumed that those stimulus words for which no, or delayed, or particular types of reactions were found were connected with emotionally charged "complexes" which interfered with the associative process.

However, psychoanalytic psychology—and, partly under its influence, general psychology also—progressively developed a new view of memory functioning (see Rapaport, 1942a [see also Paul, 1967]). According to this view, ideas are apperceived in terms of the emotions, affects, strivings, wishes, attitudes of the person; they become preserved or distorted—that is, organized—according to these; they are delivered into consciousness—that is, reproduced—when the affects or attitudes which were responsible for their apperception are again brought into play by a situation. For such a view, memories of words, images, bodily movements are but representatives of emotions, or affects, or attitudes. This view recognizes a whole hierarchy of organizing motives ("forces") in memory functioning, ranging from the instinctive unconscious ones, such as drives and wishes, through their derivatives, such as affects and emotions, to more or less conscious ones, such as strivings, interests, and attitudes. The simple variants of forgetting and memory distortion are explained by the process of repression, which attempts to keep out of consciousness all ideas connected with unacceptable preconscious and unconscious wishes, affects, or strivings—in order that these may not themselves enter consciousness.

How do these views of memory function apply to the Word Association Test? Reaction-time disturbances may be accounted for easily in terms of an associationist theory of memory, by reference to conflicting associative connections—that is, by a clash of associations of about equal strength; but not the other associative disturbances. We shall forego analysis of the inadequacy of the associationist theory to account for reactions which repeat the stimulus words, or perseverate with one reaction word, or create neologistic reaction words, and for the other varieties of stimulus-reaction relationships to be treated below. These difficulties will become obvious as we discuss these forms. We shall here endeavor only to describe the view of the process underlying the associative reaction that crystallized in the course of our work; this view was based on the dynamic theory referred to above, and has come to serve more and more as the basis of our work with the test.

For our dynamic theory, memory is merely one aspect of or one way of looking at thought processes. In terms of this theory (see Chapter 5), the associative reaction must be considered an artifact—a segment isolated out of the flow of the usual thought process by means of the test instructions. The associative reaction has its memory aspect, like all thought processes, since the reaction word has been in consciousness prior to its present occurrence. What then is the dynamic factor that delivers it to consciousness? We conceive it to be the *attitude* of conforming with the directions of the test. Attitudes are distant derivatives of the instincts or drives lying at the base of the hierarchy of the dynamic factors which organize thought processes. The more distant from the base of the hierarchy, and the more intellectualized these dynamic factors are, the more clearly they pertain to the ego—and not to the id—and the more nearly conscious or available for becoming conscious they are. The nearer the base of the hierarchy these dynamic factors lie, the more idiosyncratic their representations are; the more remote from the base the dynamic factors lie—and attitudes are far removed—the more their representations conform with logic and social convention, and the more stereotyped and interindividually similar they become.[10] The result of an attitude's being the dynamic factor that brings into consciousness the associative reactions is a great interindividual consistency in the reactions of normal subjects to stimulus words; unusual reaction words become more frequent with more profound maladjustment. The general prevalence of commonplace reactions and the pathological character of deviant ones have been demonstrated by Kent and Rosanoff (1910), and is confirmed by our experience. When an attitude of conforming does not come about at all, or on certain words is rendered ineffective by more deep-lying dynamic factors—emotions, affects, etc.—which do not make for interindividual conformity, psychopathology is present. The more solid the organization of the ego, the more surely will the

[10] It must not be forgotten that, in final analysis, all the peripheral dynamic factors—to which attitudes also belong—develop out of the basic ones in a process which from one point of view may be referred to as the development of the control of drives, from another as the development of the ego, and from still another as the process of socialization. [In Hartmann's (1939) terms, all autonomy is relative, a point stressed by Rapaport in later years, but along with the recognition that attitudes and memory do have considerable autonomy despite their links to drive.—Ed.]

associative reactions be delivered by and be consistent with the attitude of conforming with the instructions; and the weaker the ego, the more will affects or repression directed against affects disrupt this attitude. This is to be expected, if we keep in mind that in good adjustment, personal and/or traumatic material is not mobilized easily, either in life or in the testing situation; while in maladjustment, such material is often mobilized even by situations which are only remotely relevant. In other words, the usual associative reaction is delivered into consciousness by the "attitude of conformity with the test instructions"; the associative disturbances are delivered into consciousness by dynamic forces other than such an attitude.

The task to react in the test situation is not unlike many tasks in life situations, and thus it should be no surprise that the test instructions elicit predictable reactions which show interindividual consistency. The situation is different when maladjustment is present, because maladjustment disrupts such consistency and allows affects and emotions and their inhibitions to dictate reactions in life situations, and to dictate or prevent delivery of reaction words in the testing situation. The simplest forms of interference with the reaction are those usually described as repression, inhibition, and their extreme, blocking. In mild cases a delay of reaction time, and in more severe ones no reaction or no reproduction in the Reproduction Test, are the effects. While these forms of associative disturbance have been studied repeatedly, the effect of maladjustment upon the reaction-word choice has been little investigated. The early analyses of the Association Experiment looked mainly for extension of reaction time or blocking, reflecting the effect of repression emanating from the complex which the stimulus word touched upon; it also looked for the reaction words singled out by reaction time or reproduction disturbance, which would give a clue to the *content* of the complex. Although there are instances where this is possible, they are sufficiently few—in our experience—not to warrant our troubling to hunt for them by giving every patient a Word Association Test. They are no more frequent than the responses on the Rorschach test that reveal the nature of a facet of the patient's problem by content symbolism. For the theoretical understanding of these, we must keep in mind that these are cases in which a central dynamic factor—affect, emotion—delivers into consciousness its direct representative. Thus the association *suck*—"disgust," coming from a rather poorly integrated woman in whose marital life the husband's recurring demands for fellatio were one of the serious difficulties, is such a case. In better integrated patients, or in cases where the problem touched upon by the stimulus word is less intense, the difficulty may be indicated merely by a delay of reaction time or a reproduction difficulty. Thus, both the intensity of the conflict touched upon and the degree of weakness of ego organization are responsible for such reactions. If the intensity of the conflict is the major factor, the associative disturbances will be spotty; if disorganization, the associative disturbances will more likely be widespread. Some types of associative disturbance in themselves indicate far-reaching disorganization, however, even though the Word Association Test is otherwise "clean."

For the evaluation of associative reactions, it must therefore be kept in mind that, when the ego is strong, the reaction word will only rarely reveal the nature of the conflict; and when the disorganization becomes extensive, the associative disturbances become generalized, and the reaction word is *no longer* representative of the conflict. Our experience then is that the affect-laden areas of ideation can be inferred more from the stimulus word on which the associative disturbance occurred than from the content of the reaction word. That is, we find in the Word Association Test the *traces of interference* by affects or emotions, rather than their direct representation in the reaction words. What is interfered with is the associative reaction dictated by the "attitude to comply with instructions," which if unhampered would result in near-popular or popular responses related to the stimulus word in conventional conceptual terms. (Popular responses for each word are listed in Table 1.) Or, as Lipmann (1911) would have put it, we find symptoms of the presence of rather than the direct representation of affects in the Word Association Test (see also Rapaport, 1942a, p. 54). As in all ego functions, we observe the defenses against encroachment of unconscious ideas, rather than the unconscious ideas themselves (see Anna Freud, 1936, pp. 8-10).[11]

One more point revealing of the memory aspect of the associative reaction needs to be touched on here: namely, what happens in the Reproduction Test. First of all, there are few patients who do not begin this part with such statements as, "How could I?", "How can you expect me to remember all that?" or "I don't remember any of it." Yet it is amazing how many reaction words are correctly reproduced. Second, when subjects who claim not to remember are encouraged to give again the first thing that comes to mind, they reproduce correctly a great many of their original reaction words. Third, a number of clearly introspective patients who did perfectly in reproducing their original reaction words stated afterwards that "it just came" to them, that they did not "remember" them, and that only after they uttered them did they feel, "That's it." What occurs in the Reproduction Test is a true re-production process, and not mechanical recall. Finally, the better the adjustment, the better the reproduction. This shows strikingly the dynamic nature of recall, and the memorial character of at

[11] [As P. S. Holzman points out (personal communication), a contemporary formulation would be that we see "compromise formations which contain *both defense and impulse* aspects" in ego functions.—Ed.]

least one aspect of the associative reaction. In the Reproduction Test the same *attitude* is brought into play as in the test proper, and this is how the surprising accuracy of reproduction is accounted for.

The Concept-Formation Aspect of the Associative Reaction. It appears, then, that the attitude mobilized by the instructions of the test is one which makes for reacting with words conceptually related to the stimulus word. This is in a sense amazing, if we keep in mind that all thought processes have preparatory phases in which multitudes of possibilities offer themselves to consciousness (see Stekel, 1924; Freud, 1900; Varendonck, 1921; and Schilder, 1920). These preparatory phases are, in the average subject, preconscious; in introspective or obsessive people, however, the inquiring examiner often obtains reports on what happens in the brief interval between the stimulus and reaction words—how definitions, images, clang and other deviant associations occurred and were rejected, though the result came out quickly and as a popular reaction.[12] Apparently the well-adjusted ego provides for emergence of an attitude in response to the instructions— and probably in response to any task *(Aufgabe)*—which prompts the coming to consciousness of ideas related to the stimulus in conventional conceptual terms. Thus, not only the memorial aspect of the thought process, but also its conceptual aspect plays a decisive role in determining the associative reaction.

This set of ideas provides the examiner with a frame of reference for judging which associations embody an associative disturbance and which do not. The more the relation of stimulus and reaction words approaches a coordinate conceptual one, the more the association can be considered neutral; the more it departs from this—in the subordinate or the superordinate direction, or by abandonment of conceptual relation—the more it can be considered an associative disturbance. The association disturbances that entail an abandonment of conceptual relation between stimulus and reaction words will be treated later. Here more needs to be said about the various conceptual relations of the stimulus and reaction words.

We have pointed out (see Chapter 6) that formation of concepts is the outcome of a preparatory process of interchanging inductive and deductive steps, which come to a balance in the actual content or realm of the concept

---

[12] It might be argued that what happens in obsessive cases cannot be construed as a proof for the general existence of a complex preparatory process to all thought and all associative reaction, but only as an obsessive disorder. Such an argument, however, disregards the principle that pathological manifestations usually represent an exaggeration of conditions normally existing. The obsessive cases differ from the others by the fact that at least part of this complex preparatory phase of ideas becomes conscious. Such coming to consciousness of ideas usually unconscious or preconscious is the focal clinical characteristic of obsessive cases, as well as of many preschizophrenic conditions.

formed. Whenever this balance is disturbed, narrow or loose concepts come about, according as the shift is more in the deductive or the inductive direction.[13] We may formulate it thus: in disturbances of concept formation, *preparatory* phases of the concept present themselves as though they were *final* conceptual forms.

The disturbances of association may be similarly described: they are preparatory phases of thought in which the process has halted, and they come to consciousness instead of the more or less "popular" response which would result if the process were completed. Furthermore, a parallel to narrow and loose concepts may be drawn: in associative disturbances the thought process may halt either close to or distant from the stimulus word. "Closeness" and "distance" are here defined as symptoms of the interference with the associative process, and are in need of clarification. How it comes about that the symptoms of interference take just these forms is a question to which we have no answer. The question itself is of the same order as that on the relationship of different types of ego development to different psychiatric nosological entities, and to the differential development or impairment of the partial functions comprising the achievement called intelligence. All these will have to be answered before a theory of thinking and its development can get out of its infancy. Some further understanding of close and distant reactions can be gained if we consider the anticipation aspect of the associative reaction.

The Anticipation Aspect of the Associative Reaction. A thought process, once started, is represented by one or more ideas clearly in consciousness, and more or less vague directedness which we have termed "anticipation."[14] The "idea clearly in consciousness" is usually represented by a word (at times by an image or a relationship of words); in the Word Association Test, this is the stimulus word. The directedness termed anticipation is set up by the context in which the idea has emerged in consciousness; in the Word Association Test, this context is determined by the test instructions. The idea once in consciousness modifies the context, and thus also to some extent the anticipation; similarly, the general anticipation set up by the test instructions is specified by every stimulus word. The usual experience is that once an idea is in consciousness (stimulus word), the idea subsequently entering consciousness and becoming verbalized (reaction word) is such as more or less to fulfill the anticipation accompanying the initial idea. About how this happens—how the selective function of

[13] It is patent that subordinate relationships correspond to a deductive, superordinate relationships to an inductive, direction of conceptualization.

[14] See the discussion of the Picture Arrangement subtest of the W-B, Chapter 3, above.

the anticipation works—we know little more[15] than that it occurs more or less outside our consciousness, preconsciously or unconsciously. From investigations of dreams (see Freud, 1900) and daydreams (see Varendonck, 1921 [also Rapaport, 1951a, 1957a]), where this selective function does not operate in the same sense as in waking thought, we have some hypotheses about what subject matter the selection acts upon. According to Freud (1915b), the conscious, verbally represented idea always refers to objects —or sets or relationships of objects; and these are not objects in general, but objects actually experienced in the past by the person. The word expressing the idea, though in its form a generic term, implies *all* the specific connotations of the objects experienced in the past to which it refers. The thought process does not operate with the *word* as such, though it may appear to us to do so; instead, it falls back on those specific aspects of the object experiences which are expedient and helpful in finding ideas to fulfill the anticipation. If the word *table* is used in a context referring to "discussion," our thought process will traverse *round table* and its allied connotations in a search for the idea which is to fulfill the anticipation; in the context of "dinner," it will be *dining table;* in the context of "living room," it may be *end table.* Further, the verbal expression of an idea is linked with a multitude of visual images, memories, concepts, subjective feeling experiences, self-references, clang associations, which are all represented by the idea, and which derive from the life experiences in the course of which the idea and its relation to its verbal expression have crystallized. The thought process, in the search for an idea to fulfill the anticipation, may fall back on any of these; and may proceed to any of the ideas connected with these, until an idea fulfilling the anticipation is arrived at. Even in conscious *reasoning* it is most common to fall back upon the definition of a verbal idea if its usage or meaning offers any difficulty. In the thought process, we usually fall back beyond the *definition* itself, and this occurs effortlessly and usually not consciously. The idea arrived at may be reached through one of its component images' being connected with an imaginal component of the initial idea, or through any similar relationship in any phase of the thought process. From the component which is the link to the initial idea's corresponding component, the thought process proceeds

[15] The Sentence Completion Test [of which Buros (1965) lists seven currently published versions] sheds some light on the role of anticipation in the Word Association Test. In the former test, truncated sentences of the following type have to be completed: "I am best when. . . . . . ," "I feel. . . . . . ," "My father. . . . . . ," etc. These truncated sentences set up a frame of reference which excludes all except a certain grammatical type of completion; and this exclusion and the direction it sets for the response are the essence of anticipation. In this test, the major part of the anticipation is set up by the trunk sentence; in the Word Association Test, the major part is set up by the test instructions.

then through other components to the appropriate verbal expression of the idea arrived at. It is as though this thought process consists of an "analytic" (decompository) and a "synthetic" (compository) phase. In the analytic phase, the thought process falls back upon one of the components of the idea in consciousness, one which appears to promise to fulfill the anticipation, or at least not to clash with it; in the synthetic phase, another idea which the component is also part of is progressively reached, the choice of this second idea being dictated by the anticipation it is to fulfill.

The character of the usual anticipation in the associative reaction has already been discussed. It is apparently dictated by the test instructions, and results in a conventionally and conceptually related reaction word. How generally true this is for the thought process in any association test cannot be decided; but it is likely that our noun stimulus list and our instructions play a decisive role in setting up this anticipation, and that under other instructions with grammatically different stimulus words, other results would be forthcoming and other aspects of the thought process would be elucidated.[16]

The anticipation aspect of the Word Association Test, as already stated, comes clearly to expression in the uniformity of "popular," conceptually related reactions, as can be seen in Table 1, above. The anticipation aspect is seen more directly in those reactions where the subject corrects himself (*girl friend*—"boy friend—rather, boy"); and most directly in more far-reaching corrections. One preschizophrenic gave the association *fire*—"flee" and added, "But the meaning I was trying to get were flames rising into the air." Here the anticipation is consciously experienced, and comes into relief clearly because the reaction word that came did not fulfill it. Obviously, "flame" was a conceptually related idea, while "flee" was not. Such examples could be marshaled in great quantity to demonstrate the role of anticipation.

Formal Characteristics of the Associative Reaction. The previous three sections have advanced the general rationale of the psychological processes underlying associative reactions. The present section will advance the rationale of specific associative reactions, in an attempt to discriminate theoretically and understand the formal characteristics by which they can be classified, easily spotted, and understood. We shall discuss mainly the close and distant reactions, and their subvariations.

(a) Close Reaction. We consider close reactions to be associative disturbances due to halting of the underlying process in its analytic phase.

---

[16] Tentative experimentation appears to show that lists composed entirely of verbs or of adjectives as stimuli tend to elicit verb and adjective reactions, respectively.

This comes to expression in reactions which stick close to the stimulus word, since in the analytic phase the process passes through components of the stimulus idea and has not yet passed on to other ideas.

The responses labeled close can be set into the following hierarchic series: (1) When the subject offers the stimulus word as his response; in some cases where no response is forthcoming, there is also a sticking to the stimulus-word.[17] (2) When a multiword definition is given as a reaction. A multiword definition differs from a synonym in that the latter complies with the test instructions ("give another word") and is a discrete concept, while the former merely paraphrases the stimulus word itself (*boy friend*— "male acquaintance," *house*—"to live in"). (3) When the reaction is the stimulus word with self-reference attached to it, or merely a self-reference (*house*—"my house," *suicide*—"me"). (4) When the reaction is the stimulus word repeated in a word combination, or in a shortened form (*fire*— "forest fire," *fire*—"fireman," *doctor*—"doc," *boy friend*—"boy"). (5) When the subject states that he did not get a reaction word but an image, which may be an image representing the stimulus word (*house*—image of a house), or related to it (image of a door), or unrelated to it (image of a tree).[18] (6) When the subject gives a reaction word related arbitrarily or in an unusual way to the stimulus word (*house*—"white"), and the inquiry shows that the reaction word refers to an attribute of the image experienced by him. (7) When the subject reacts with a senseless or sense-changing distortion or amendment of the stimulus word (*suicide*—"wooicide," *taxi*— "dermist"). (8) When clang associations or alliterations are given (*suck* —"fuck," *vagina*—"Virginia"). (9) When the subject responds by naming random objects in the examiner's office.

The category "close" is not exhausted by these nine types; in fact, it is less a category than a point of view from which the examiner may look upon associative reactions. There is a related class of reactions which is hard to describe. If one takes the popular reactions as a baseline—that is, using the conventional conceptual connections as a yardstick of distance— then between these and the close reactions described above, there stretches a whole continuum of reactions, some of which are near to popular reactions and acceptable. Thus many subordinate connections belong to this category: *house*—"door," *window*—"glass" (in contrast to coordinate relationships, like *rug*—"floor," *house*—"home"; or supraordinate relation-

---

[17] In other cases, failure to respond may be due to sticking to a conscious but suppressed reaction (that is, the subject hides his reaction from the examiner), or to sticking to a repressed reaction word of which the subject is not aware. In both these cases, the disturbance emanates from the reaction word.

[18] In the last case, it may happen that the reaction is a distant one. These cases are rare, however; we preferred to classify all image reactions here, and only point out this alternative possibility.

ships, like *breast*—"body," *water*—"liquid"). Yet certain subordinate relationships are rather close reactions, especially if they are of the *lamp*
—"shade" or *mountain*—"peak" type which approximates the completion
responses. These can be judged only by the experienced examiner who will
easily get the "feel" of the subject's tendency to stick to the stimulus word.
A reaction like *man*—"finger," which may appear to be a subordinate and
thus close reaction, must be carefully inquired into: in the case we obtained
it in, it proved to be a distant reaction. The apparent subordinate conceptual relation is *not always* a yardstick of closeness.

Like the narrow responses on the Sorting Test, the close reactions here
may result from a variety of conditions. Rigid compulsive character make-
up may produce as many definitions as the general lassitude of depressives
or aged people will—although repeated instructions will more easily induce
the former to give responses sufficiently independent from the stimulus
word. Psychotic blocking may produce failure or repetition of the stimulus word as much as intense repression in a hysterical case. Flighty super-
ficiality may fasten on phrase completions and obvious clang associations
(*drink*—"drunk") as much as psychotic conditions of blocking (*doctor*—
"daughter"), though their repeated occurrence will usually be referable to
the latter. Images occur in many normal subjects, though their interference
with conventional associative responses will be mostly referable to schizoid
and at times to obsessive trends. Reacting by naming objects in the examining room occurs in children, and in evasive and negativistic normals
seeking to escape the emotional implications of the stimulus words—
though their persistent recurrence in spite of warnings is referable to prepsychotic or psychotic psychopathology. Only the distortions and neologisms described under point (7) occur in virtually no cases other than prepsychotic and psychotic.

Between the stimulus and reaction words a relatively complex psychological process occurs. In close reactions, this process is, as it were, short-
circuited, and components which are *usually* present in its unconscious
preparatory (analytic) phase enter consciousness. What might be the conditions under which such short-circuiting occurs? From a purely formal
point of view, it could be hypothesized that the stimulus word is rigidly
embedded into a cognitive system[19] that prohibits the initiation or completion of the decompository or compository phase of the process. For example, complete or partial blocking would be an expression of difficulty in
initiating the process; visual images and definitions would be expressions of
difficulty in completing it, the patient offering only a preparatory component. This formal approach, though providing the clinical psychologist

[19] The term "system" is used here in a formal way not unlike that used by Lewin
(1935) in reference to tension systems.

with a schematic framework which is helpful in dealing with associative reactions, is not sufficient for a thorough understanding of the close reactions. It appears that a clinical approach in terms of the various types of psychopathology may be more helpful.

From clinical experience, one might hypothesize that in rigid, compulsive people the structure of the ego—and within it, of the thought process—is such that ideas once in consciousness have a general inclination to decompose into their formal meaning connotations. As a consequence, the thought process remains formalistic and shows a lack of flexibility in passing from old to new ideas—that is, from the analytic to the synthetic phase.[20] In depressions, partly an exaggeration of the compulsive meticulousness, and partly a general sluggishness of all processes, may be considered to account for the short-circuiting of the analytic phase or its failure to come about.

To understand the close reactions in schizophrenics requires a consideration of characteristics of schizophrenic thinking other than rigidity. Freud (1915a) discussed the nature of dereistic thinking—one aspect of schizophrenic thinking—and maintained that, dynamically, dereistic thinking is characterized by the libidinal cathexis of words instead of objects; that is, the words themselves become cathected, and their relationship to the objects proper is severed. In the Word Association Test we get a taste of this cathexis of words when a schizophrenic responds to the stimulus word *lamp* with "Just a lamp." In such cases the analytic phase of the process—at least, as it is assumed to exist in normal subjects—probably never comes about. The words do not refer to objects, their images, their conceptual relationships, or their emotional connotations, but rather carry a self-meaning. However, this point—as can be inferred from the material we shall present on Rorschach verbalization referred to as "increase of distance" and "loss of distance"—is true for only some schizophrenics, and only for a part of their thought processes.

Even in these clinical categories, the conditions described do not alone determine all thought processes and all associative reactions. These conditions are even less generalized in hysterical and most other neurotic cases, and the close reactions are usually not referable to a general characteristic of the subject's thinking, but directly to the stimulus words. In such instances, isolated failures or repetitions of the stimulus word usually refer to a set of

[20] The analytic phase, when it occurs to its full extent, mobilizes a side variety of conceptual, formal, emotional, and other connotations, and sets the stage for the synthetic phase, which is the basis of what is usually called imaginative or creative thinking. The wealth, variability, flexibility of the analytic phase are prerequisites to the coming about of the synthetic phase; but the analytic phase may be all this and yet of such a nature—as in sterile encyclopedic minds—that no transition to a synthetic phase of any wealth will occur.

affects and conflicts[21] which, being repressed, are prohibitive of the smooth production of an associative reaction.

One type of close reaction in particular should be discussed here—the recurrence, or perseveration, of the same reaction word to several stimulus words. This may be of several kinds. A subject who will invariably react to the stimulus words *bowel movement, masturbation, vagina,* and *intercourse* with the reaction word "embarrassment" indicates an inhibition extending over this whole rather unitary system of ideas. Such perseveration rarely indicates a psychosis. The likelihood of psychosis increases the more generalized and loose-knit the field of ideas becomes. If all the stimulus words referring to human beings—*man, woman, father, mother,* etc.—or to parts of the human body elicit the reaction word "person," more serious psychopathology is likely.

Another type of such perseveration is the carry-over of the disturbed reaction to subsequent stimulus words. The mildest form of this is manifest in reaction times, when a stimulus word which may or may not have caused an extended reaction time on its reaction word causes extended reaction time on one or more following reaction words. Such carry-over is a frequent neurotic phenomenon, and at times is seen even in normal subjects. A severe form of perseveration, the inappropriate repetition of a just-given reaction word to the following stimulus word, is rarely encountered in others than psychotics. Serial occurrence of such perseveration is definitely a psychotic indication, making for many apparently distant reactions which are merely effects of perseveration—that is, of a tendency to give close reactions. These perseverative reactions appear to show that, as discussed earlier, an affect elicited by the stimulus word may push its own representative into consciousness as a reaction word; this same affect also may chain into one system a series of stimulus words relevant to it, throughout which a perseveration may spread. On the other hand, the perseveration may spread through stimulus words that are contiguous only in the sequence of the stimulus list. Therefore, we may conclude that the ideas in the course of a thought process in general—and an association test in particular—may be connected on the lines of both *meaning* and *contiguity.*

(b) Distant Reaction. The distant reactions are here considered to be due to interference with the "synthetic phase" of the thought process underlying associative reactions. In distant reactions, it is open to question whether the instruction to "give the first word that comes to mind" was closely adhered to; and the subject's anticipation is usually not fulfilled, as is sometimes shown by his surprise over his own reaction.

[21] Such connections are those referred to by Jung (1906-1915) as "complexes."

In order to construct a rationale for the distant reactions, let us classify them into a hierarchic order: (1) The most extreme distant reactions are those which show no apparent connection between stimulus and reaction words (*book*—"turkey," *lamp*—"shuttle"), and on inquiry the subject states, "I don't know why—it just came to me." (2) Less extreme are those where some faint connection seems discernible to the examiner, but the subject claims unawareness of any connection (*suicide*—"wooicide," with the implication of womancide). (3) Still less extreme are those where the apparently faint connection is explained upon inquiry by a vague, arbitrary, and sometimes absurd chain of connections (*dance*—"eat— people sometimes eat at dances"). (4) Next in sequence is what proves upon inquiry to be an idiosyncratic reaction (*house*—"empty," *masturbation*—"loss"). (5) From these a continuum of reactions stretches to the popular reactions; and next in line are the loosely coordinated and super-ordinate, generalizing reactions. Examples of the latter with pathological implications are *chair*—"house," and *taxes*—"war."

The reactions described under (1) we shall refer to as "unrelated" reactions, and they are with few exceptions indicators of schizophrenic psychopathology, but they must be so classified only after careful inquiry. The reactions described under (2), (3), and (4) will be referred to as "distant" reactions: (2) and (3) usually indicate some degree of schizophrenic psychopathology, while (4) may occur in depressives and neurotics, as well as in original and flexible normal persons of exceptionally vivid thinking. The reactions described under (5) we shall refer to as "mildly distant."

In attempting to understand the nature of these distant reactions, one must keep one consideration in mind: Any systematic psychology of thought processes must first of all postulate a thoroughgoing causality in the thought processes, and must therefore assume a definite connection between any stimulus word and the reaction to it. This applies even when a schizophrenic cannot rationalize his reaction into any acceptable connection. When schizophrenics do give explanations, these are often of the character which in the chapter on the Rorschach test is described as "autistic logic." From their explanations it becomes obvious that the distant reactions result when the thought process takes a devious course over very distantly related but still connected systems of ideas, without regard for conventional conceptual relationships.[22] In the coming about of the close reactions, the thought process appears to have been short-circuited and stuck in its first analytic (decompository) phase; the coming about of

---

[22] Compare with the loose sortings in Chapter 6. [In a personal communication, Lloyd H. Silverman points out the fact that sorting involves reality testing, while remote associations violate no external constraints; therefore, nonpsychotic people who think loosely occasionally give distant reactions.—Ed.]

these distant reactions may be conceived of as a luxuriant development of the synthetic (compository) phase. It is as though after the analytic phase, when from a component of the initial idea a connection to a component of another idea has been found, the synthetic process does not drive to the composition of an adequate verbal expression of the new idea fulfilling the anticipation set by the instructions and the stimulus word; rather, it uses the component of the new idea arrived at as a mediating link to another, and that again as a link to components of even further ideas. When this process is finally consummated, therefore, and an adequate verbal expression is synthesized, the product appears quite distant from the initial idea. An example of a relatively brief process of this type, with a resulting reaction of an intermediate distance, is *suck*—"air." The usual or popular reactions to *suck* are "nipple," "breast," "baby," or "draw." On rare occasions the mildly distant reaction "vacuum" is obtained. Upon inquiry, the chronic schizophrenic who gave this reaction described the following sequence of ideas: *suck* made him think of "vacuum," and "vacuum sucks air." The patient stated that the first *word* that came to him was "air"— and the connecting link, "vacuum," was only "felt" vaguely by him. We must conclude that the component of "vacuum" arrived at in the course of the analytic process was not used as a basis for a compository process, but rather as a link to the component, "air." Mediating links are often reported "felt" by the subjects without their being able to compose this feeling into a verbal expression. The same schizophrenic gave the reaction *party*—"home," and could only explain, "It just felt like home." A more extreme distant reaction is: *lamp*—"pencil." The overwhelmingly frequent reaction is *lamp*—"light." Upon inquiry the subject explained that lamp made him think of "light, the long rays of light it throws," which led him to think of "reading" and in turn of "writing," which with the "long rays of light" led to "pencil." Here again the mediating links did not lead to reaction words even though the reaction time was only 2.4 seconds.

From a formal point of view, one might characterize this state of affairs as one in which the thought process occurs within very fluid cognitive systems which overlap and are without firm boundaries.

One must remember, however, that isolated idiosyncratic connections determined by specific neurotic (or depressive psychotic) problems may bring about such distant relationships as much as may the genuinely weakened boundaries seen in schizophrenics. Only careful inquiry can establish the differentiation here, on the basis of distance and clarity of connections.

These considerations, like those concerning close reactions, contribute merely to a systematic phenomenology of the thought processes and their psychopathology, and specifically to the phenomenology of schizophrenic thinking; however, they reveal little concerning the dynamics which allow two apparent antipodes such as closeness and distance to coexist in the schizophrenic thought disturbance. The study of close and distant reactions suggests that the usual characteristics of the thought process—to fulfill the anticipation set by the immediate context—is lost in schizophrenics. The compelling character of the anticipation is gone, and other forces determining the reaction come into play.

The Content of the Associative Reaction. The rationale of the content analysis of the Word Association Test needs no specific discussion, because the treatment of the memory aspect has covered the relevant points. The following discussion will systematize only the phenomenology of the associative content, and the reasoning behind our clinical analysis.

From the point of view of content analysis, association disturbances may refer to either the stimulus or reaction words. In the former, they consist of one of the following: (a) The subject may profess not to know the stimulus word. This may be the truth, or merely a guise for avoidance of words whose exact denotation the subject has never established for himself and only some of whose connotations he is dimly aware of. This is usually not a matter of chance, but is referable to the centering of serious difficulties and repression in the system of ideas whose meaning clarification is thereby avoided (for example, *vagina, masturbate*). (b) The stimulus word may be misunderstood. This is rarely due to poor pronunciation by the examiner. In rare cases, such misunderstanding is massed in a record and is due to a generalized disturbance of attention, but most frequently it occurs on specific words because of a specific affective difficulty centered in their connotations. For example, *suck* (sock)—"hit" was given by a subject who compensated for his strong oral passive-dependent trends by a show of independent, aggressive, manly bearing.[23] (c) Finally, any other associative disturbance may indicate that the *stimulus word* refers to a conflictual set of ideas, although many of these disturbances are due to a generalized or perseverating disturbance.

In content analysis of the *reaction word,* proper names and vulgar reactions stand out. Reacting with names is to some extent related to the close reactions. It must be established whether the name is drawn from the subject's personal world, however; at times distant reactions take this obscure form, and a completely irrelevant name may occur as the reaction word. Vulgar reactions, except to stimulus words of sexual and anal connotation, are extremely rare and occur only in psychotics. We have not

---

[23] This explanation is given here not as a sample of interpretation, but rather as an example of this type of "misunderstanding." The rest of the Word Association Test, as well as the other tests and the clinical story, confirmed these characteristics of the patient. No single associative reaction, and not even a Word Association Test as a whole, can be the basis for such far-reaching inference.

seen vulgar reactions given by women, except a very few psychotics and promiscuous libertines who could be designated either as prepsychotics or as character disorders with prostitution as the social diagnosis.[24] In men of lower-middle-class or working-class background and/or mediocre cultural achievements, appropriate vulgar reactions are not rare; however, in members of the upper middle class or in intellectuals of any significant cultural achievements, such vulgar reactions are so rare that they usually raise the question of psychopathology going beyond the neurotic range.

The usual method of content analysis in the clinical diagnostic use of the test is to establish whether associative disturbances have accumulated on any specific group of stimulus words, and whether there are unusual reaction words which (in relation to the stimulus words) are so meaningful that they may be considered revealing of the subject. The first procedure will usually pick out alcoholics, drug addicts, and other patients of strong passive-dependent leanings, by a massing of reactions with associative disturbances on stimuli of oral connotations. The second procedure will pick out reactions like *intercourse*—"fear" or *mother*—"sweetheart," and use them as material for building a picture of the person and his difficulties. In the first procedure, it is necessary that either the majority of the words of the connotation in question elicit associative disturbances, or that there be few associative disturbances in the whole test and a considerable part of those concentrated on the words in question; otherwise, diffuse associative disturbances could be misinterpreted as specific ones. In the second procedure, it is usually necessary that other disturbances—besides the unique reaction word—be attached to these associations, in order to be safe in using them as a basis for interpretation.

The clinician versed in clinical problems and their psychodynamics will be able to use the test beyond these points. Not only the massing of disturbances on one association, or on stimulus words of a certain connotation, but also dynamically interrelated mild disturbances will become useful to him, and a series of associations such as *suicide*—"me," *man*—"beast," *husband*—"brute," *intercourse*—"terrible," will click together into a meaningful picture. One cannot warn enough against hasty constructions of this type; one must underline the necessity for the clinical psychologist to obtain training in clinical problems, psychiatric and psychoanalytic theory, and testing work, to enable him to make such guarded inferences.

---

[24] We once tested a woman who received psychotherapy of a rather erratic type for a serious disturbance in her sexual life. On two of the stimulus words of sexual connotation, the patient stated that the doctor who sent her to us had told her to be frank, but that she could not say the words that came to her mind, and asked for permission to spell them. Not even psychiatric permission appears to lift the taboo for vulgar words in women. [This generalization now seems specific to the time and place of its making.—Ed.]

Disturbances in the Reproduction of the Associative Reactions. The basis of the rationale of the reproduction disturbances is given in our treatment of the memory aspect of the associative reaction. The following discussion only systematizes the different types of such disturbances, and amplifies the general rationale of the memory aspect to clarify them.

Reproduction disturbances may be: (a) failure to reproduce; (b) delay in reproduction; (c) a false reproduction distant from the original reaction word; (d) a false reproduction similar or related to, yet different from, the original reaction word; (e) a variation of the original reaction word; (f) a false reproduction immediately corrected. Failures and delays of reproduction are to be evaluated as on the Word Association Test proper. A massing of false reproductions distant from the original reaction words, or any false reproduction distant from both stimulus and original reaction words, is to be considered a disturbance of thought organization in general and memory frame of reference in particular. Under usual conditions, what happens in reproduction is similar to what happens in any meaningful remembering. If one loses his keys somewhere in his apartment, he traces his steps from where he still had them to the other places passed through, in order to get a clue. In the Reproduction Test, the clue is given by the re-presentation of the stimulus word, and the thought process under usual conditions takes the same course it took originally. This would appear to explain the high percentage (about 80% for our mixed clinical population) of correct reproductions. We have occasionally encountered subjects who consciously experienced instances of such retracing and reported some of them in the inquiry. Inasmuch as there is no reason to expect a realignment of the conditions that determine the course of a thought process in a reasonably stable thought organization, one would justifiably expect such a very high proportion of correct reproductions: but this is not always the case where considerable lability of thought organization is an expression of far-reaching maladjustment.

The rationale of failures and delays in reproduction time might be conceived of as follows: if the stimulus word touches upon a repressed set of ideas, many potential reactions connected thereto become subject to repression also; and when the thought process passes through them, it becomes delayed until a relatively neutral reaction word is found. In the time between reaction and reproduction this reaction word, owing to the emotional setting in which it was first seized, may become subject to the same repressive process. This may manifest itself either in failure to reproduce or—if the repression has been only partially successful—in delayed reproduction. Not infrequently the stimulus word is quickly reacted to with a popular reaction, and the reproduction is nevertheless delayed. In these cases it appears that, in the course of the Word Association Test proper or the Reproduction Test, an emotionally loaded meaning which was originally bypassed has shifted more to the fore and caused the delay. In other words, subjects are frequently able to "put up a front"[25] upon first contact with the traumatic idea, but on second contact the disturbance gives them away. In cases of failure of reproduction, these processes have taken place in a more exaggerated form, and effect a realignment of conditions for the associative process; the reaction word becomes more closely tied up with the emotionally loaded connotations of the stimulus word, and is consequently no longer remembered. Another manifestation of the activity of the repressive forces—which here are quickly overcome—is seen when a false recall is quickly corrected.

The situation is different when words distant from the original reaction word are offered as reproductions. Here the realignment of conditions for the associative process appears to be radical, especially if all awareness that the reproduction is incorrect is lost. A variety of conditions may account for such false reproductions. In some cases an affect mobilized by the stimulus word, but originally unable to press its own ideational representative into consciousness as the reaction word, manages to do so in the Reproduction Test. Conversely, a disturbing affect may in the Word Association Test press its ideational representative into consciousness, while in the reproduction its representation becomes repressed and replaced by a neutral or popular reaction word. Of the two, the former suggests more serious psychopathology because as a rule in the course of time more control over affects is established, and the realignments that occur are directed toward eliminating the intrusion of disturbing affective connotations into consciousness. Especially strong affective connotations even in normal people may disturb reproduction; these connotations are sometimes discernible in the content of the reaction word. For instance, vulgar reactions are frequently replaced in reproduction by more acceptable words.

When the reproduction is distant from both the original reaction word and the stimulus word, however, the disturbance is more generalized; in the reproduction the associative process traverses routes very different from its original course, indicating an instability of thought organization. *The degree of stability of thought organization is what is being tested by the Reproduction Test.*

A very mild manifestation of instability is seen when the subject offers a false reproduction which is meaningfully related to both the stimulus word and the original reaction. Such false reproductions, unless extremely massed, have minimal psychopathological implications. In the same class

---

[25] To "put up a front" does not designate here a conscious effort. It is rather an expression for a fairly successful repression, which in the course of the test may spread to the reaction word.

are the reproductions which are mere variations of—parts or extensions of—the original reaction word.

The Rationale of the Diagnostic Significance of Associative Disturbances. A great multitude of so-called "complex indicators" cropped up after the Association Experiment was first propounded as a diagnostic tool. Attempts at statistical validation[26] of these "complex indicators" have tended to invalidate rather than validate most of them. The fact is that the symptom of a disturbance in the associative processes may be any one of many: delayed reaction, failure to react, any variety of close or distant reaction; any type of reproduction disturbance, etc. Several of these may simultaneously occur, and any one may replace another. Thus validation which attacks them one by one must of necessity fall short of evaluating their real significance. For these reasons we do not concern ourselves in the main with the evaluation of associative disturbances as complex indicators; nor do we try to evaluate associative disturbances either by matching them against known "problems" of subjects, or by seeking—as Hull and Lugoff did—to establish the correlations of different complex indicators in order to infer a single complex underlying two highly correlated indicators. Since associative disturbances may *replace* as well as *accompany* each other, one could select two groups of subjects in one of which two complex indicators are highly correlated positively, while in the other they are highly correlated negatively. The explanation would be that in the first group the associative disturbance was so intense that it showed up by the presence of both of these complex indicators, while in the other group either it was mild enough to be adequately represented by one disturbance, or the single indicator which occurred was expressive enough for even a severe disturbance. We have found that, with increasing severity of maladjustment, the various formal symptoms of associative disturbance tend to increase in number; we shall further attempt to indicate the nosological groups that show this tendency for all the indicators in general, and those that show it for a specific indicator in particular.

One of our central conclusions is: The more symptoms of associative disturbance are concentrated on one association (reaction and reproduction), the more it is likely that the realm of ideas referred to by the stimulus word is one of great emotional significance for the subject, and that the degree of maladjustment and instability of thought organization is great. Furthermore, the greater the accumulation of symptoms of associative disturbance in a record, and the more they take the form of disturbances other than those of reaction time, reproduction time, or failure of reproduction,

---

[26] See, for example, Hull and Lugoff (1921). [For more modern references on this and other issues, and for an excellent historical review, see Wiggins (1965).—Ed.]

the more likely it is that maladjustment is profound and thought organization impaired.

The administration of the test consists of three parts, the Word Association Test proper, the reproduction, and the detailed inquiry. The administration begins with the instructions: "I am going to read you a series of words one by one. I want you to respond to each word with *one* other word. It does not make any difference what your word is, but it should be the very first word that comes to your mind *after* you hear my word. I will time you because I want you to be just as fast as you can. When some people take this test they have a tendency not to hear some of the words the examiner calls out. I want you to resist this tendency: I am not to repeat the words." The reaction words and reaction times are recorded. In the course of administration, brief inquiries are made solely to establish whether the subject correctly understood the stimulus word ("What was my word?") or to ascertain the reaction word if not clearly heard by the examiner ("What was your word?"). The patient's misunderstanding of a stimulus word is not communicated to him; rather, the misunderstood stimulus word is given again after four or five others, preferably not close to a usually "traumatic" stimulus word. We use the term *traumatic* for words that are likely to touch upon sensitive personal material according to clinical experience, and also words that attract associative disturbances. Traumatic stimulus words are indicated by "(t)" in Table 1.

In the course of the test, additional instructions or pressure to obtain conformity with the original instructions may become necessary in order to distinguish whether the subject misunderstood the instructions, is disregarding them, or is unable to comply with them. This may occur in several ways:

(1) The subject may *consistently* give multiword reactions or multiword definitions instead of single words. In such cases the examiner intervenes: "One word, please." Such additional pressure is applied only after a sequence of about 10 multiword reactions and not if single-word reactions are interspersed.

(2) The subject may be consistently slow. In such cases, the examiner first attempts to speed him up by accelerating the tempo of the administration, pronouncing the next stimulus word quickly and immediately after the subject gives his reaction word. Where this is not effective, the examiner reminds him: "Remember, I am timing you." If necessary, he will once interject: "Quickly, please." Steady prodding, however, is useless and ill-advised.

(3) The subject may react with the names of objects in the room; as soon as a single such instance is noted, the subject is told: "Don't pick

objects in the room; wait for something to come to your mind." If he finds it difficult to do this, he may be instructed to close his eyes.

(4) The subject may react with words unrelated to the stimulus word and obviously—by the speed of reaction—decided upon in advance; the examiner in this case intervenes: "Remember, you should give the first word that comes to your mind *after* you hear my word."

If the reactions to several stimulus words appear to suggest an idea that is not directly raised by any of these stimulus words, and yet they point to one word that may elicit it, it is advisable to add that word to the list. Thus, if several reactions point to marital difficulties, the stimulus word *marriage* may be added to the list. Furthermore, it is useful to add as a stimulus word any word that appears—in the course of intelligence tests, concept-formation tests, and even the Thematic Apperception Test or Rorschach—to stand for emotionally important content. Such additions should, however, be made sparingly. For these purposes, and because this test is best administered when the examiner has the confidence of the patient and each is at ease with the other, it is most practical to administer the Word Association Test as one of the last tests of the battery.

The second part begins with the instruction: "Now I am going to call out the same words again, and I want you to respond with the very same words you did before. Please try to be quick: I will again time you." Reproductions are recorded only if they deviate from the original reaction words. Reaction times are recorded only if they exceed two seconds in otherwise quick subjects, and three to four seconds in otherwise slow subjects. Correct and quick recall is recorded with a plus sign; inability to recall with a minus sign; spontaneously corrected recall is also recorded with a plus sign, together with the erroneous reproduction. No inquiries, other than those occasioned by possible mishearing of the stimulus word by the subject or of the reaction word by the examiner, are made in the course of this part. Both the misunderstood and correct forms of an originally misunderstood stimulus word are presented in the Reproduction Test. If the subject persists in giving false reproductions over a series of stimulus words, he is reminded: "Give the same words as before."

Whenever the Word Association Test is given in a battery, the examiner should keep in mind the possible influence of the preceding tests upon the associative reactions, and their possible influence on succeeding tests. Thus, in compulsive persons, to administer a vocabulary test immediately before the Word Association Test frequently conduces to definitions instead of associations on the latter. In schizophrenics, the Word Association Test, if it precedes the vocabulary test, may elicit associations to the latter instead of definitions. When given before the Rorschach test, the Word Association Test may encourage schizoid persons to associate instead of verbalizing perceptions in the Rorschach, and may also encourage sexual responses. These influences will affect only persons showing such inclinations in the first place; but the inexperienced tester will do well to avoid such complications until he becomes sufficiently assured about the effects of his own technique.

A few comments about timing and recording should be added. The stop watch is started when, and not after, the stimulus word is called out; and it is stopped when the subject begins to call out the reaction word, not when he starts to make some advance comments or has finished the reaction word. If the subject gives several reaction words, all of these are recorded; but the reaction time refers to the first one. Proper administration is one in which everything fosters an attitude of compliance with the instructions, once it is assumed by the subject. Interruptions, fumblings, side comments, and discussions divert attention and interfere with this attitude. The examiner must handle the stop watch and note taking so smoothly that they do not make for interruptions of the testing.

The attitude of the examiner throughout this test is perhaps more important than in any other test. All approval, disapproval, surprise, amusement, or impatience in giving additional instructions, *must* be avoided. An even, generally approving attitude, without stern or machinelike shouting of stimulus words, must be maintained. It is advisable to watch the patient in the course of the test, and to record signs, grimaces, and other expressive manifestations. The patient also watches; thus this test can be given well only if the examiner is at ease with his job and the patient.

Inquiry. Inquiry is to be recorded in full.[27] Its objectives are the following:

[27] [Inquiry immediately follows the Reproduction Test. It is well to begin and to end the inquiry by asking about reactions that do not appear highly personal or deviant, for purposes of rapport. The inquiry may be introduced by some remarks such as these: "All right, now I want to ask you a few questions. You gave your answers quickly on many of the words, but I noticed that on a few of them you were somewhat delayed. I'd like to have you think back to those instances and tell me what went through your mind during the few seconds between my word and your response. For example [naming a nontraumatic word with moderate reaction time]—can you recall the first thing that came to mind when you heard me say that?"

In general, the emphasis of the inquiry is on getting the subject to introspect and to reconstruct the unverbalized train of thoughts, images, words, etc., that intervened between stimulus and response words. Two purposes are thereby served: First, the examiner ascertains the degree to which the subject can tolerate self-awareness, his capacity to reflect on his own thought processes, which is of considerable diagnostic import in identifying the intolerance for introspection found in many character disorders, or the excessive awareness of the preparatory stages of thought in obsessional states (especially decompensated ones). Second, this procedure matter-of-factly encourages the subject to bring out into the open both personally meaningful content and formal properties of his thinking that enable the examiner to clarify (and classify) the nature of the associative disturbances involved.—Ed.]

(a) To clarify whether the subject misunderstood the stimulus word, and, if so, what word he heard. This inquiry is made immediately after the stimulus word is reacted to. Any apparently unrelated reaction word raises the possibility of such misunderstanding. The need for such immediate inquiry is obvious; the labeling of a reaction word as distant is correct only if it can be safely assumed that the stimulus word was accurately understood.

(b) To clarify the relationship between the stimulus and reaction words not only where this is unclear to the examiner, but also where the relationship deviates markedly from the conventional conceptual norms—that is, the popular reactions. Frequently such inquiry will be revealing of the close or distant character of the reaction, and sometimes it will also bring forth clearly schizophrenic forms of reasoning or visual images which have come to consciousness, disrupted the association process, and led to the deviant reaction. Where the subject cannot offer any explanation of the relationship between the stimulus and reaction words, the presence of a psychotic or near-psychotic condition can be safely hypothesized.

Inquiry to establish the occurrence of visual images should follow these steps: the subject should first be asked whether anything went through his mind between hearing the stimulus word and giving his reaction. Initially direct or leading questions should be avoided. The starting point of inquiry should be where the reaction has definite implications of some visual experience. If the subject seems doubtful about his image he may be asked to describe it, in order to establish its existence and degree of vividness. If the subject does not understand the question or denies any intervening experience, he may be asked more directly whether he had some kind of "mental picture" after hearing the stimulus word. This, however, should only be done after all reactions possibly involving imagery have been *indirectly* inquired into. Once an image has been established, the subject should be asked to enumerate all other stimulus words which provoked images and to describe these images; only finally should suggestive instances not mentioned by the subject be inquired into again.

Inquiry into the possible mediating links of other apparently deviant reactions starts out by citing the stimulus and reaction words in question, and continuing: "Did anything go through your mind between the times you heard my word and gave yours?" If nothing is learned hereby, one proceeds: "Any connection between these two *you* had in mind?" If still no explanation comes forth: "What *could be* the connection between them?" If the subject professes ignorance, he is encouraged to make a guess. The judicious and experienced examiner will know which of these steps he can bypass in inquiry. Any peculiarity of the explanation should be further inquired into, in the fashion to be described concerning the Rorschach verbalizations (see pp. 426ff. below).

(c) To clarify the background of extended reaction times and failures, by seeking to establish whether any conscious idea which the patient wished not to communicate is the cause of the delayed reaction or the failure. Some bring to the fore sexual or other material that is not usually acceptable socially; if this occurs on nonsexual stimulus words, it is to be considered a symptom of far-reaching pathology. If it occurs on stimulus words of sexual connotation, the considerations advanced in the preceding discussion of vulgar reaction words apply. Inquiries into these disturbances also not rarely reveal the presence of interfering images and peculiar alternatives or connections.

(d) To establish whether false reproductions on a number of consecutive stimuli are real failures, or disregard of the instructions, or the subject's attempt to "improve" on his reactions.

SCORING

The kinds of associative disturbances we have differentiated in our everyday clinical work, though treated here under "scoring," are not scores in the sense we use scores on other tests. In everyday practice we *notice* these types, but do not score them since it would be too cumbersome to do so. The beginner in the field may prefer to score them for his own sake, because test scores help in accumulating and systematizing experience.[28]

We differentiate the following kinds of associative disturbance:

(a) Blocking—offering no reaction word.

(b) Object naming—naming objects in the examiner's office. This is usually an expression of blocking, but sometimes of evasiveness.

(c) Definitions—a *multiword* definition of the stimulus word.

(d) Attempted definitions—subjects inclined to offer definitions sometimes, in their haste, offer poor ones (*rug*—"to walk on").

(e) Repetitions—of the stimulus word (*breast*—"breast").

(f) Partial repetitions—the stimulus word is included in, or part of it constitutes, the reaction (*boy friend*—"boy"; *taxi*—"taxicab").

(g) Clang associations—only where no sense relationship can be established. Thus *breast*—"chest" is not considered a clang association, while *man*—"can" or *beef*—"weef" is so considered.

---

[28] [The first step in identifying associative disturbances is to identify the popular and near-popular reactions, with the aid of norms like those in Table 1; none of them is to be considered distant, close, or disturbed in other semantic respects. They have the same general interpretive significance as popular responses to the Rorschach (see below, pp. 419ff.).—Ed.]

(h) Phrase completion—the reaction completes a word or phrase of which the stimulus word is part, usually the first part. These may vary between two extremes: from *table*—"cloth" and *fire*—"place," to *taxi*—"dermist," *spring*—"is here," and *man*—"a big."

(i) Close reaction proper—no significant departure from the stimulus word and relevant only if the stimulus word is kept in mind (*screen*—"through"; *breast*—"two").

(j) Attributes—an adjectival association modifying the noun stimulus word, or naming a component of the object referred to by it (*woman*—"pretty"; *table*—"wood").

(k) Images—the first and sometimes only reaction to the stimulus word is a visual image, spontaneously reported by the subject or elicited by inquiry.

(l) Suspected images—the reaction word, and sometimes a delay in reaction, suggest the presence of an image which is not confirmed by the subject.

(m) Self-references—such as *father*—"mine"; *girl friend*—"I have none."

(n) Perseveration—(1) repeating the same reaction inappropriately on successive stimulus words; (2) repeating the same reaction on most or all stimulus words having some link between them (*father*—"person," *boy friend*—"person," *mother*—"person"); (3) reacting to a stimulus word with a word appropriate to the previous stimulus word (*beef*—"food," *stomach*—"roast"); (4) reacting to a stimulus word with a word appropriate to the previous reaction word (*water*—"spring," *husband*—"autumn").

(o) Multiword reaction—excluding multiword definitions, which are classified separately (*party*—"lots of friends").

(p) Unrelated reactions—no connection can be established between the stimulus and reaction words (*book*—"turkey").

(q) Distant reactions—related to the stimulus word in a farfetched manner (*masturbation*—"loss"; *party*—"funeral"; *breast*—"frankness"; *man*—"creature"; *boy friend*—"strength").

(r) Mildly distant reactions—not farfetched but outside the usual run of reactions (*trunk*—"lock"; *bowel movement*—"passage"; *rug*—"dirt"; *intercourse*—"breed").

(s) Neologisms—such as *suicide*—"wooicide"; or *intercourse*—"reproduct."

(t) Affective reactions—value judgments, usually adjectives (*mother*—"nice"; *bowel movement*—"disgusting").

(u) Alternatives—more than one reaction (*suck*—"baby or bottle").

(v) Proper nouns—*boy friend*—"John"; *horse*—"Seabiscuit."

(w) Vulgar reactions—ranging from more or less socially acceptable colloquial reactions to completely unacceptable ones (*intercourse*—"fuck").

(x) Mishearing the stimulus word—hearing *scream* for *screen* or *gladiator* for *radiator*.

(y) Not knowing the stimulus word—either spontaneously admitted by the patient, or established by inquiry into peculiar-appearing reactions.

We have also distinguished the following types of reproduction disturbance:

(a) False unrelated recall—in any of the following forms: (1) great distance between the original reaction and the recall, such as *love*—"life," then "woman"; (2) a reversal of the sex implied in the original reaction—mostly on the familial and interpersonal words such as *father, mother, woman, man;* (3) a shift in the interpretation of ambiguous words such as *breast*—"shirt"—"woman"; *spring*—"flexible"—"water"; (4) a reversal of mood, such as *laugh*—"cry"—"smile"; (5) abandonment of a multiword reaction, or definition, or any other type of unusual reaction; (6) abandonment of, or switch to, a vulgar word, such as *bowel movement*—"shit"—"toilet," or *penis*—"man"—"prick."

(b) False related recall (*chair*—"sit"—"seat"; *spring*—"water"—"fountain."

(c) No recall.

(d) Delay in recall.

(e) Partial recall (*cut*—"healing"—"to heal").

(f) Spontaneously corrected false recall (*dog*—"cat"—"animal . . . No! cat").

In scoring associative reactions for any purpose, do not hesitate to give more than one qualitative score to a reaction. Thus *father*—"our father in heaven" may be considered as a multiword, repetitious, distant reaction. The significance of such reactions for the disorganization of thinking is such as to warrant highlighting the reaction with every score applicable to it. One exception might be made: the direct communication of an image experience is *necessarily* multiword in character, and frequently involves self-reference, attribute, etc. In these cases it is reasonable to score only the occurrence of an image.

DIAGNOSTIC SUGGESTIONS

Significance of the Various Types of Associative Disturbance

In the following discussion, it should be assumed that unless otherwise specified, a single instance of any of the following types of associative disturbances is not to be given much weight as a diagnostic indicator, since normal subjects do occasionally produce a lone disturbance of almost any one of these types.

(1) *Blocking* shows its greatest incidence (among the types of cases considered here) in deteriorated unclassified schizophrenics and in inhibited preschizophrenics. In general, blocking is most suggestive of schizophrenia. Strikingly, however, overideational preschizophrenics do not block on the Word Association Test, nor do many acute unclassified schizophrenics. Although depressives do not often accumulate many blockings, the latter are to some extent replaced by object naming.

(2) *Object naming* (naming objects present in the room) is rare in our experience, largely because of the pressure we apply as soon as it becomes evident. Nevertheless, it does occur occasionally in depressive psychotics and inhibited preschizophrenics. A single clear occurrence after it has been made clear that this reaction is unwanted should be considered of pathological significance.

(3) *Repetition and partial repetition* occur most frequently in acute and deteriorated unclassified schizophrenics and in inhibited preschizophrenics. Paranoiacs, depressive psychotics, and neurotics with anxiety and depression have some tendency in this direction.

(4) *Definitions and attempted definitions* occur with a very high incidence in depressives and deteriorated unclassified schizophrenics. They are rarely encountered in the absence of psychosis except in persons of little education or sophistication.

(5) *Close reactions proper* are outstandingly often encountered in simple schizophrenia and in no other diagnostic category (among those considered here), but even then rarely more than one per case.

(6) *Self-references* are not very frequent in our diagnostic groups. They occur at times in chronic and deteriorated unclassified schizophrenics and depressive neurotics.

(7) *Perseverations* are very rare in the kinds of cases considered here. Including the doubtful instances, they do, however, crop up in chronic schizophrenics, acute paranoid schizophrenics, and simple schizophrenics; also in overideational preschizophrenics and mixed neurotics. A single instance carries pathological weight.

(8) *Clang associations* are present in schizophrenics and preschizophrenics, most in overideational preschizophrenia and least in acute schizophrenia. They are practically absent in depressions, neuroses, and normality. If bizarre and neologistic (e.g., *suicide*—"wooicide"), even a single clang should raise the question of schizophrenia.

(9) *Phrase completion* occurs most in chronic unclassified schizophrenia, acute paranoid schizophrenia, and overideational preschizophrenia.

In general, other subgroups of schizophrenics come next. Some incidence in depressives, and little in neurotic and normal persons, is to be expected.[29]

(10) *Images and suspected images* occur most often in preschizophrenics and obsessive-compulsives.

(11) *Attributes* appear at a maximum in chronic and deteriorated schizophrenics, and are also common in paranoid conditions. In obsessive-compulsives and anxious depressed neurotics, the relatively high incidence of attributes reflects merely their accumulation of suspected images.

(12) *Unrelated reactions* are commonest in deteriorated unclassified schizophrenics; in second place come chronic unclassified schizophrenics and simple schizophrenics; and in third place overideational preschizophrenics and acute paranoid schizophrenics.

(13) *Distant reactions* are given most numerously by deteriorated unclassified schizophrenics. They are usually present in chronic unclassified schizophrenics' records and those of overideational preschizophrenics and simple schizophrenics. Some noticeable incidence occurs in other schizophrenics and depressive psychotics; in other diagnostic groups it is rare to find more than one.

(14) *Mildly distant reactions* occur most often in simple schizophrenics, but also in depressive psychotics, overideational preschizophrenics, neurotics of all kinds, paranoid conditions, and chronic unclassified schizophrenics. One or even two instances carry no pathological significance.

(15) *Multiword reactions* have by far the highest frequency in deteriorated unclassified schizophrenics, followed by acute unclassified schizophrenics, paranoid conditions, and depressions; but depressed patients are more likely to produce a few of these reactions than any other kind.

(16) *Emotional reactions* are seldom encountered (even in hysterics), but they turn up most frequently in the tests of overideational preschizophrenics and acute unclassified schizophrenics.

(17) *Alternate reactions* are not often given except by some schizophrenics (not including preschizophrenics, however). Depressives produce a few at times.

(18) *Vulgar responses* are most prevalent in men of relatively little education and limited cultural background, especially if impulsive and not inhibited; otherwise they are prominent only in mixed neurotics and inhibited preschizophrenics.

(19) *Subtotal of close reactions* (the sum of definitions, repetitions, blocking, object naming, clangs, self-references, and close reactions proper): Up to six can be given by almost any kind of case, but more than that is characteristic of depression, with some incidence in schizophrenia also.

---

[29] [They are most common in character disorders and addictions.—Ed.]

Summary of Diagnostic Suggestions

(a) *Schizophrenics:* Unclassified, paranoid, and simple schizophrenics together may be grossly characterized as usually having more than one clearly distant reaction. Schizophrenics also show a significant tendency toward clang associations and phrase completions. Although both of these are close rather than distant, they appear to be more prevalent in schizophrenic thinking than in that of the other groups; they may be taken as indicators of a flightiness and irrational impulsiveness which allow for a preparatory phase of the associative reaction to enter consciousness. In this respect they differ from the close reaction of depressives, who *cannot get past* the preparatory components. Multiword reactions and blocking (in the form of failure to react, or of repetition of the stimulus word) are also frequent in schizophrenics. Their reaction times show great variability; many are quite long, in contrast to their generally quick reactions. Of special importance is the relative speed with which they offer their distant reactions; this speed serves to distinguish them to a large extent from depressives, who are prone to give their distant reactions slowly. In their reproductions schizophrenics tend to have more serious distortions than neurotics or normals.

Among schizophrenics, deteriorated unclassified schizophrenics stand out by reason of unrelated, distant, blocked, clang, multiword, and definition reactions; by their extreme variability of reaction time; and by their very inefficient reproduction, including many false and unrelated reproduction attempts which tend to be even more unacceptable than the original reactions. Chronic schizophrenics tend to exceed the acute ones in their number of distant, clang, and self-reference reactions. In simple schizophrenics there are special tendencies to give unrelated, clang, and perseverative responses.

(b) *Paranoid Conditions:* Here the incidence of distant reactions is relatively high, exceeding that of neurotics. Their tendency to accumulate definitions and repetitions is probably referable to their rigid, compulsive personality structure. Images also occur, though not in large amounts. Their reaction times and reproductions are in general not conspicuously disturbed.

(c) *Preschizophrenics:* Inhibited preschizophrenics somewhat resemble depressives in their high incidence of close reactions, but they are distinguished from them by not showing a generalized slowness of reaction, by not massing as many close reactions of the definition type, by better reproductions, and by accumulation of images. As regards distance, overideational preschizophrenics resemble full-blown schizophrenics; they do not accumulate any of the various forms of blocking or closeness, however, and tend to have idiosyncratic, mildly distant reaction words rather than unrelated ones. Thus, inhibited preschizophrenics in many respects differ markedly from overideational preschizophrenics. The inhibited group shows an accumulation of the close type of reaction; blocking, images, and repetitions are outstanding. In contrast, overideational preschizophrenics give distant and mildly distant responses, with clang associations, phrase completions, and emotional reactions; blocking and repetition are practically absent. They also have poorer reproduction, and show a great prevalence of serious reproduction disturbances; while the inhibition of the other preschizophrenics apparently serves as a rigid system, more effective for the retention of reactions once given.

(d) *Depressives* are best distinguished from other groups by their generalized slowness of reaction and by their massing of all types of close reactions, particularly definitions. Their reaction times are quite variable but, unlike those of the schizophrenics, include few quick reactions. Psychotic depressives are distinguished from neurotic depressives by having a greater incidence of both close and distant reactions; they also accumulate more of the various forms of blocking. Slowness of reaction in the distant reactions usually distinguishes depressives from schizophrenics.

(e) *Neurotics: Hysterics* are distinguished from other neurotics mainly by the greater incidence of blocking, expressed mainly in a few extremely long reaction times—usually to words of sexual connotation—but also somewhat in failure to react and in giving definitions. Otherwise their associative and reproductive reactions show little qualitative disturbance. *Anxiety and depression* appears to differ most crucially from neurotic depression by a low incidence of close reactions (except for repetitions). In general, associative and reproduction reactions are orderly, and reaction time—again in contrast to neurotic depression—does not appear to suffer markedly in this disorder. Such patients have a tendency to accumulate mildly distant reactions—idiosyncratic but not farfetched associations. *Obsessive-compulsives* are set off from other neurotics by their relatively high incidence of images; however, they do not manifest the many disturbances shown by inhibited preschizophrenics, who also produce many images. The many idiosyncratic ideas of obsessive-compulsives are expressed in the form of mildly distant reactions. *Mixed neurotics* appear to give the greatest number of distant reactions among the neurotic groups. A tendency toward images, similar to that in obsessives, and a tendency toward definitions, similar to that in hysterics, are also indicated. In summary, *neurotics* in general appear to differ from the various types of schizophrenics and depressives by a low incidence of distant reactions, of close reactions, and of elongation or variability of reaction time.

CHAPTER 9

The Rorschach Test

With the advent of the Rorschach test (Rorschach, 1921) the door to projective testing of personality and maladjustment was for the first time boldly thrown open. Today this test still stands as the most useful tool of its kind, and as the most widely used tool in diagnostic personality testing.[1]

An outstanding advantage of the Rorschach test, and one which has been fundamental in maintaining its eminence among clinical psychological tools, is its ease of handling. This ease has been to some extent obscured by the many intended refinements and extensions in its application which have been developed since the appearance of Rorschach's original publication (Rorschach, 1921). As soon as one gets behind the conditions making for the apparent complexity of the test, however, and becomes aware also of the fallacies and hazards of a mechanical use of it without a comprehensive and meaningful psychological rationale, the fundamental simplicity of its application becomes clear. But it is then also seen that the most fruitful application of the Rorschach test lies in its use as one test in a comprehensive battery; in such a setting it can make a fundamental contribution to the psychological understanding of the individual case, without the hazard of attempting to stretch the test's potentialities beyond its intrinsic limitations.

In its history, the Rorschach test has undergone a variety of vicissitudes. Extensive revisions of its scoring were introduced (Binder, 1932-1933; Beck, 1937; Klopfer & Kelley, 1942), new methods of inquiry were recommended (Klopfer & Kelley, 1942), methods of group administration were developed (Harrower & Steiner, 1943; Munroe, 1942), a "multiple-choice"

---

[1] There have been more publications dealing with the Rorschach test than with all other projective personality tests taken together. Many of these publications have appeared in the *Rorschach Research Exchange* [later called *Journal of Projective Techniques and Personality Assessment.* Complete bibliographies may be found in Buros's *Mental Measurements Yearbooks* (1938, 1941, 1949, 1953, 1959, 1965).— Ed.].

variation was introduced (Harrower & Steiner, 1945a), parallel sets of blots were developed (Zulliger, 1941; Harrower & Steiner, 1945b). None of these, however, has solved the formidable problem in the application of the Rorschach test: its standardization and validation (Rapaport, 1939). The development of a rationale of the test and its tie-up with the theoretical development in general psychology and psychology of personality has also lagged. In consequence of these deficiencies, the reputation of the test has not been unequivocally positive. In spite of its great impact, the Rorschach test has failed to fulfill the job of breaking through the wall of statistical security behind which the "IQ intelligence testers" and the champions of personality questionnaires withdrew to defend themselves against the entrance of dynamic psychological thinking into clinical psychology. Doubtless the difficulties in the way of standardizing and validating the Rorschach test are extreme. The published comparisons of blind diagnoses with clinical histories and symptomatology, however successful, do not standardize or validate the test; they merely demonstrate its usefulness and potentialities. Nor can the answer to the problem of validation be found in studies dealing with single nosological groups. Such studies may find indicators which distinguish their experimental clinical group from a group of normal cases, but they cannot make clear to what extent those indicators would distinguish any or all other clinical groups from the normal population. Furthermore, they do not meet the problem of distinguishing one clinical group from another, a problem always in the foreground of clinical psychological practice. The characteristic patterns of a single nosological group thus discovered cannot be used as diagnostic indicators; they may or may not be necessary parts of the diagnostic picture of the group in question, but are generally far from sufficiently describing it and differentiating it from other nosological groups. Nor do the studies which lump together all kind of "neuroses" or "depressions" or "schizophrenias"—useful as they may be as first approximations—attempt to cope with the problem of validation of the test.

It appears to us that several requirements must be met by any attempt at validation and clinical standardization of the Rorschach test. First, the study must seek to include all major psychopathological groups within the psychotic and neurotic ranges, and as many types of normal adjustment as possible. Second, a unitary set of nosological criteria should be used in setting up the experimental clinical groups and these criteria should be put forth clearly, so that the reader will know by what criteria certain cases were considered obsessional neurosis and others acute schizophrenia. Clear statement of and rigorous adherence to clinical diagnostic criteria will provide an internal consistency of the case material which, for a meaningful study, is as necessary as the internal consistency of administration and scoring. Third, the most frequently neglected clinical consideration has been a concern with the nature of the "normal" control group: its geographical-cultural background, the different kinds of psychological adjustments its members have made, specific maladjustment tendencies in each case, recognition of the more and less successful adjustments within the control group and a segregation of these according to clearly stated criteria —all are as fundamental to a clinical psychological study as the diagnosis of the subjects of the experimental groups. Fourth, all of the tests to be used in the study should be administered and scored according to a single set of criteria and practices, so that the experimental data will have an internal consistency.

It is little wonder, then, that the published clinical studies have been almost entirely restricted to standardizing certain diagnostic indicators, and have usually been unable to tackle the problem of validating the significance of the different types of responses on the Rorschach test: because without a clinically well-explored control group, in which manifestations of psychopathology do not obscure the test record, one cannot even hope to be able to track down the psychological significance of different types of responses. It is obvious that such an investigation implies a large-scale comparative clinical and normal Rorschach test study, with consequent difficulties in the way of time, adequate personnel, adequate financial support, availability of case material representing a great variety of forms and degrees of maladjustment and adjustment, etc.

One must not be surprised, then, that isolated attempts at mechanical-statistical standardization have not taken all these complexities into consideration; nor that the attempt to standardize signs of maladjustment in the Rorschach test in the Armed Forces was not successful, and that the test was abandoned as useless for military selection purposes; nor that a critical reaction against the test persists with a consequent defensiveness among its proponents, and that in general a somewhat unhealthy atmosphere has begun to surround the Rorschach test in which its diagnostic limitations have not been sufficiently emphasized, looked for, taught, or kept in the foreground of investigation.[2]

Aims and Approach. Our aims in this study of the Rorschach test will be, first, to clarify to what psychological processes, normal or pathological, the different types of responses refer. In this connection, it will be necessary to clarify somewhat the psychological processes involved in reactions to Rorschach cards in general, and in specific types of responses in particular. Secondly, our aim will be to state as well as our clinical experience permits the differential diagnostic indications provided by the Rorschach test. Our

[2] [Or else (more recently) they are stressed exclusively and the test's clinically demonstrated merits completely discounted.—Ed.]

third major aim will be to systematize a manner of analyzing the *verbaliza-tion* of Rorschach responses, a task which has been thus far neglected in the main, to the detriment of the test's diagnostic potency. It is our hope that our analysis of different kinds of verbalization will also contribute to the understanding of schizophrenic thinking.

The material of this study was obtained using the cards of the original Rorschach test. Our method of administration and inquiry and our cate-gories of scoring deviate as little as possible from those described in Rorschach's *Psychodiagnostics* (1921). This procedure is not dictated by distrust of innovations, which we believe are basically necessary to keep the Rorschach test a live diagnostic tool. Rather, it is dictated by the same necessities which we believe prompted Rorschach himself in his original attempt: the necessity for a simple method of administration and scoring which would allow for an adequate survey of records obtained from any kind of maladjustment or adjustment. To facilitate such a survey, both in our everyday work and in the organization of the material of this study, scoring categories and their arithmetic derivatives (e.g., ratios) had to be kept to a minimum; and time-consuming, complicated inquiry had to be avoided as much as possible. Only by such an approach did we find it possible for the novice to crystallize, and for the experienced tester to retain, a helpful frame of reference derived from cumulative experience which would be easily applicable to each new case. And only with such an approach could we avoid the temptation—especially for the beginner—to translate a multitude of highly refined scores into psychological statements with the help of a source book of interpretations, and then to throw these psychological "dream-book" statements together in an interpretative hash. Regrettably enough, the literature is replete with interpretations in which "significance of a score" has replaced clinical-psychological thinking and understanding of subjects. By keeping the administration and scoring as simple as possible, we find that the Rorschach record lends itself more easily to a focusing upon its implications, and makes a relevant and valid personality description and diagnosis possible.

It is to a large extent inevitable that further refinements of scoring lead the tester, and especially the novice, to the dream-book type of interpreta-tion. These refinements also obscure the fact that scoring categories are merely aids to facilitate an appraisal of what has happened in the course of the test, and that a "correct" set of scores is not an end in itself. Such a preoccupation can easily blunt any appreciation of the psychological proces-ses active in the subject taking the test, and can lead only to mechanical application and interpretation. The examiner will be able to avoid the dream-book type of interpretation, the mechanical attitude toward the test, and the idolizing of scoring only if he has a sound background of psychological and psychiatric theory. Clinical psychologists often have the misconception that to do a better job they need more testing tools; but what needs improvement is the training of clinical psychologists and the exploration of testing tools now at their disposal.

Simple methods of administration, inquiry, and scoring cut down on time expenditure, to the greater justification of the everyday clinical use of the test.

A GENERAL RATIONALE OF THE PSYCHOLOGICAL PROCESSES UNDERLYING RORSCHACH RESPONSES

The question of what happens psychologically within the subject between the time he is confronted by a Rorschach card and the time he gives one or more responses can at present be answered best by calling to our assistance the facts that are known about perceptual and associative processes.

From the perceptual point of view it *appears* that the Rorschach ink-blots are "unstructured" perceptual raw material, in contrast to the familiar animate and inanimate objects of our world which are considered "structured." But this appearance is deceptive. Let us remind ourselves for a moment of the processes involved in the perception of these so-called structured materials. The days are past when visual perceiving was considered to be a photographic process. It is clear now that no sensory stimulation falls on an empty, passive-receptive organ but that all stimuli are taken in by a complicated receiving system, and that this receiving system is structured and directed by basic needs and interests of the organism, modified by experiences long past and "set"[3] by experiences of the recent past. At a time when these facts were only dimly recognized, it was necessary to account for the meaning of a perceived object by differentiating perception and apperception—perception referring to the direct sensory experiences, and apperception to those perceptions which were given meaning by the organism. At present, however, all perception is recognized to be an elaboration of the "pure sensory experience"—which is an abstraction never available to conscious experience—in terms of needs, drives, interests, attitudes, and the experiences of past and present related to them. The present view, therefore, invalidates any sharp distinction between "structured" and

---

[3] The "set" of this receiving system refers to the anticipations (see above, pp. 125f.) that are active in the present life of the subject. The quest for these may be paraphrased as follows: what is the subject ready (and eager) to see? [In addition to the dynamic emphasis of this passage, Rapaport would have added a greater stress on structural features of the person, if he had been writing at the time of his death.—Ed.]

"unstructured" perceptual raw material. According to this view, the perceptual process only becomes more extensive and conspicuous in its organizing aspect when dealing with so-called unstructured material.

Let us leave for a moment the intentionally unstructured Rorschach inkblots, and consider perceptual experiences in everyday life. There we find a continuum of degrees of structuredness of perceptual experiences. On the one hand, a familiar object seen from a familiar view under normal conditions gives rise to an instantaneous and effortless recognition (meaning-giving organization) of the object; on the other hand, under certain disadvantageous conditions of lighting, or hampered by strange angles of perceiving, the recognition of objects is a more effortful and consciously experienced organizing process. Certain febrile, toxic, dreamlike, and other pathological processes also have this effect on the perceptual process. All along the continuum of greater or lesser structuredness, the importance of different aspects of thought processes shifts to meet the situation most adequately. When a familiar object is seen from a familiar view, well-established *memories* play the prominent role in quick recognition; as the perceptual material becomes more unfamiliar, clear-cut memories are few, other memories are called up for assistance, and now *concept formation* becomes important in establishing differences and similarities; and finally, it appears that under difficult conditions a shift from *attention* to *concentration* must occur, and that the guidance of both organization and interpretation by the subject's own *anticipations*—i.e., expectations—also becomes prominent (see Rapaport, 1942a). Such anticipations vary from those determined by a context or setting to more subjective ones.

These considerations may prompt the examiner to see in the subject's reaction to the Rorschach inkblots a perceptual organizing process which has a fundamental continuity with perception in everyday life. But while everyday perceptions allow conventions, specific memories, and familiarities to obscure the active nature of the perceptual process, the Rorschach inkblots bring the active organizing aspect of perception into the foreground and provide the examiner with much insight into hidden aspects of a person's adjustment or maladjustment.

Thus far the discussion has centered around the perceptual aspect of the Rorschach responses; but for a more complete understanding of the coming about of a Rorschach response, it is necessary to consider the role played in it by the subject's associative processes. Our manner of looking upon association has been extensively described in the previous chapter dealing with the Word Association Test. We pointed out that the stimulus word sets off an associative process of considerable complexity, largely guided and limited by the test situation and instructions, the outstanding feature of which is the demand for a termination of the process in a one-word reaction. Now, it is likely that if the stimuli were pictures instead of words, and if the instructions were for the subject to react with the first word coming to mind other than the name of the pictured object, the results would not differ significantly from those reported in the previous chapter. The psychological processes in such a test would in many ways be similar to those in the Rorschach test, and would differ mainly in that the stimulus material was familiar or structured. Our Rorschach test instructions— "What could this be?" "What does this suggest to you?"—definitely discourage the response, "An inkblot"; that is to say, they discourage responding with the name of the object just as the hypothetical test would. In the Rorschach test, the subject must draw new ideas relevant to the stimulus from internal ideas, images, and relationships; thus the coming about of a Rorschach response requires an associative process leading to it, since the response content is not given in the inkblot.

These considerations may prompt the examiner to see in the subject's reaction to the inkblots an associative process initiated by the inkblots as stimuli.

As with the perceptual aspect, so with the associative aspect: the inkblot stimuli are unfamiliar in contrast to the stimuli in everyday life, and they bring much more clearly to the foreground the subject's own patterns and difficulties of associative thinking.

Each of these points of view—perceptual organization and associative process—has been advanced in the past separately as the rationale of the test. Our thesis here is that both processes are always implied in every Rorschach response; but that one can learn more about the subject sometimes by looking at a response from the point of view of its perceptual organization, and at other times by looking at it from the point of view of the associative process that brought it forth. However, one must never neglect the essential integration of the two processes.

But how are we to conceive of this integration? We have already indicated that there is no perceptual organization that does not imply associative processes; and we have implied, especially in the chapter on the Word Association Test, that in many associative processes there occurs a phase of visual imagery, drawing on percepts which have been at one time in consciousness. Percepts derive their meaning from the associative processes in which they become embedded; and associative processes cogwheel into reality by weaving percepts, or imagery aroused by percepts, into their course. These percepts and images are clues or points of orientation for the thought processes: they indicate necessary changes of direction and points of termination, they bind the associative process to the necessities of reality, they prevent them from running wild and being directed only by subjective wishes. Thus percepts and associations in the smoothly functioning organism are mutually dependent upon each other, mutually stimulate, guide, and limit each other.

Let us now turn specifically to the processes occurring in the subject when facing a Rorschach inkblot. It appears that the process of responding to the "unstructured" inkblots begins with vague perceptual experiences, which then set off associative processes. These, like all thought processes, can be approached from the point of view of concept formation, of memory, and of the triad of attention, concentration, and anticipation. It appears that for the purpose of analyzing the Rorschach test, concept formation is the conspicuous aspect. The process starts with the query, "What could this be?" which implies, "Where does this belong?" or "To what is this similar?" The associative processes take as their starting point some salient feature of the vague perceptual impression of the inkblot, and mobilize such memories as show some congruence with the percept. These memories are largely ideas and, most important, imagery related to these ideas; but rarely is the latter consciously experienced by the subject. In the smoothly functioning person there appears to occur a fusing of perceptual impressions, ideas, and images, so that what becomes conscious is a possibility for a response—i.e., an idea with the feeling tone of "this is *possibly* it" or "this *may* do."

The ideas aroused by virtue of some congruence with the salient features of the first vague perceptual impression have an obviously memorial character, but this recedes in significance so much that it is extremely rare to obtain Rorschach responses in terms of personal memories of the subject.[4] The occurrence of such personal responses is an indication either of severe psychopathology or, sometimes, of an idiosyncratic originality.

Thus it appears to be congruence and fusion between perceptual impression and image that normally stand in the foreground of the process underlying the responses; and the establishment of this congruence by the subject is concept formation. The associative process initiated by the perceptual impression, and progressing in quest of an idea which is to fulfill the anticipation set up by the question "What could it be?" will terminate when it arrives at an idea whose corresponding image is sufficiently congruous with the perceptual impression of the inkblot. The criteria for congruence vary greatly from person to person, and even within the same person in different settings. It is clinically crucial that these criteria vary from one psychiatric disorder to another, and thus become important sources for differential diagnostic signs. We shall discuss this matter in detail in the sections concerned with "form-level" and "absurd" responses.

---

[4] [This fact may remind us of the important distinction Rapaport made (above, pp. 87f.; see also 1951a) between *personal memory* and *information*. The latter type of memory is involved in the Rorschach response process.—Ed.]

In the course of the associative process, once stimulated by the perceptual impression, changes in perceptual organization occur. The associative process may push into the foreground either the total contour of the blot or only a part of it; it may focus on an isolated part of the blot and never depart from it, or it may proceed to integrate it with all the other parts of the blot. Thus, in the course of the associative process, a structuring or articulation of the perceptual raw material occurs, which goes beyond the first vague perceptual impression of its salient features. Unification, architectonic combination, and figure-background elaboration of the total material may all ensue. They can often be inferred if the examiner carefully observes the wandering of the subject's gaze over the inkblot; and such a process is demonstrable, under certain pathological or other extreme conditions, when one or another of the steps in it becomes conscious and is verbalized by the subject.

At this point, we must swing our attention back to the perceptual aspect of the process. Although the associative process may articulate and integrate different aspects of the inkblot in different ways, it must always contend with its reality. This reality includes a welter of potentialities for associative elaboration, but at the same time sets definite limitations. The perceptual material and the perceptual processes themselves have intrinsic laws, many of which have been explored by gestalt psychology—those referring to *Prägnanz,* "closure," "figure-background," and so forth. These laws of perception, which to a large extent function independently of the inclinations of the subject, regulate and limit the associative process once it has been initiated. If this process takes too few clues from the perceptual raw material, it either results in extremely vague generalities or becomes very specific; in either case, the limitations and potentialities of the inkblot are violated.

At this point, we see three prominent phases in the process of the coming about of a Rorschach response: in the first phase, the salient perceptual features of the blot initiate the associative process; in the second, this process pushes beyond these partial perceptual impressions and effects a more or less intensive organization and elaboration of the inkblot; in the third, the perceptual potentialities and limitations of the inkblot act as a regulating reality for the associative process itself. Clearly, then, it would not be correct to reason that the Rorschach response is to be considered mainly either a perceptual product or one of free association. Either view would fail to reflect the cogwheeling of the progress of perceptual organization with the associative process.

Clinically, this cogwheeling is a primary concern of the examiner in the appraisal of the freedom and mobility of the associative processes, and of the flexibility and firmness of perceptual organization, which constitute the basis for judging the quality of the responses, for reflecting these qualities in the scores, and for inferring diagnoses.

This cogwheeling, and the preparatory phases which it implies, rarely become conscious to the subject, but frequently and in many ways they are apparent in the responses. One expression of them is the range of responses from popular to original, and from sharp form to absurd. In fragmentary percepts—Do^5 responses usually—we see how the process has stopped at a preparatory phase, so that only part of a response commonly covering a larger area is offered while the rest of the area remains without perceptual articulation or associative links. Another of the preparatory phases becomes clear when affective responses to the inkblots, such as pleasure or disgust, are verbalized: in such instances it must be presumed that somewhere in the associative material clustering around the percept, strong affective components have been aroused although not discriminated by the subject. Sometimes personal memories emerging in the associative train, and sometimes such abstract qualities of the perceptual mass as symmetry or architectonic relationships, may be verbalized. We shall touch upon many other manifestations of preparatory phases of responses in discussing the individual scores.

ADMINISTRATION

A great deal has been written about the technique of Rorschach testing since the appearance of Rorschach's *Psychodiagnostics*. Yet, for two reasons we feel it is indispensable for us to describe the general manner in which we administer the Rorschach test. (a) Our method has been to a large extent dictated by the fact that we use this test in a clinical setting where the establishment of correct diagnoses is crucial, and where the necessity for integrating the administration and results of the Rorschach test with those of a battery of tests is a prime one. (b) We feel that the implications of certain techniques and problems of administration require discussion beyond that found in previous publications. In this connection we shall attempt to make clear the advantages for clinical diagnosis of certain variations of administrative technique. We shall stress especially the problem of inquiry, which for clinical diagnosis is the most crucial and delicate aspect of test administration.

Beginning the Test. The patient, seated facing the examiner, is shown the first card and asked: "Tell me, please, what could this be? What might it be?" He does not sit with his back turned to the examiner, but takes this test in the manner in which he has taken and will take all the other tests

---

^{5} Oligophrenic detail; for explanation, see pp. 321f.

of the battery. This not only dispels any special significance which the subject might attribute to the test, but allows for careful observation of his face and expressive movements; and it permits a secure contact with the subject, so that difficulties in the course of the test, particularly the appearance of negativism, may be more easily coped with.

The test is usually not given as the first in the battery. No explanation of the test is offered. Our aim is to leave the subject with as few bearings as possible: with the entire testing situation as unstructured as possible, the thoughts and reactions of the subject become very much more revealing and diagnostically more useful. The majority of clinical subjects will not be very much upset by the vagueness of the situation, nor press the examiner for a more explicit statement of what is required; it is rather the obsessive, doubt-ridden characters or the overcautious paranoid patients who will press for clarification. The examiner must state only that he will explain the test more fully after the subject has completed all 10 cards. Only when there have been many failures will it be necessary to explain the nature of the inkblots and the kind of production expected by the examiner. In general, this method of beginning the test is designed to meet two main problems of clinical testing: first, how to bring into sharp relief the inability or unwillingness to comply with the test instructions which are present in a large portion of the psychiatric population; second, how to avoid giving too much orientation to subjects, most of whom are on the lookout for hints about what kind of performance will be most acceptable and least revealing.

After the First Response. If the patient indicates that he thinks the first response is all that is required, the examiner should ask, "Anything else?" The examiner should repeat the question after each response to Card I, until the subject states that there is nothing else. If the subject spontaneously offers more than one interpretation, he should be allowed to continue until he himself announces that he can see no more. Once the subject is finished and the card removed, the examiner explains, "You see how it goes: it will be the same with all the rest of the cards. You will take your time, you will tell me everything you think they might be or could be, and when you are finished, tell me and I will take the card away." Thus, as the subject has not been told that people see all kinds of possibilities in each card, his own inclination to productivity usually becomes quite clear on the first card. The brief explanation about the rest of the cards also leaves the subject on his own; he has no idea what the rest of the population does and is not set the task of meeting their productivity; the entire problem is posed as one specific to him, and his idea of what others would do reflects his own expectations.

In the Course of the Test. Answers to questions about the nature of the test should be deferred until it is completed; no hints or explanation should be given until then, even if the subject fails most or all of the cards. If the subject asks whether he may interpret parts alone of the inkblot, he should be told, "It's up to you"—or if the situation is such that this may be taken as a reproof, "As you like," or "Tell me anything it could be." Only if there are many failures, or if the record is entirely perseverative (usually with anatomical responses), should the nature of the inkblots be explained *at the end*. The explanation is followed up by a readministration of the test.

If the subject wants to reject the card with no response, he should be encouraged to keep trying for at least two minutes, and preferably three, before the examiner removes the card and records a failure. In such cases the examiner should repeat and vary the test instructions. "What could it be?" "What might it be?" "What does it look like to you?" "What does it resemble?" "What does it suggest or call to your mind?" "Isn't there anything on this card which reminds you of something?" Although this sequence of increasing pressure by questioning makes the problem somewhat more explicit, experience indicates that little "suggestion" is involved in any of them; they merely put the subject more at ease about his responses, indicating that he can be freer and less critical about the possibilities he entertains. If a subject has offered responses before having great difficulty on a particular card, the examiner may state, "You noticed different kinds of things on the other cards: those are the kinds of things I want you to look for."

In general, conversation in the course of the test should be avoided. If it becomes clear that the patient needs to be put at ease, the examiner may comment after a card is finished, "Good!"—or may even converse briefly with the patient. However, the offering of reassurance and the establishment of rapport should occur mainly during the initial recording of personal data. At that time there is ample opportunity to show interest in, express appreciation for, and arouse confidence in the patient. Yet a too rigid administration of the test, with little concern for the difficulties of and exacerbation of anxiety in the patient, is poor technique; it only appears to keep the test administration a homogeneous procedure.

All interchange of comments and all conspicuous behavior of the patient should be recorded, such as expressive movements and all indications of affect.

Inquiry. Two main problems arise in connection with inquiry: when should it be made, and how far should it go? The usual procedure described in the literature is to conduct inquiry into the subject's responses only after all 10 cards have been interpreted by the subject.

We do not follow this procedure: for purposes of diagnostic testing, it has proved expedient to do the bulk of inquiry after each card is finished.

One might object that inquiry in the course of the test administration prejudices the rest of the test results by revealing to the subject not only those aspects of the inkblot in which we are particularly interested, but also his poor responses. We shall discuss the validity of this objection below. Furthermore, we found it necessary to conduct the inquiry as far as possible with the inkblot removed from the sight of the subject; and under this condition, to delay inquiry until the end of the testing makes it so dependent on memory that it becomes unreliable. If the subject's response has been determined by a color or a shading in the inkblot, it will easily be discovered in this "blindfold" inquiry, which throws the subject back upon images of the inkblot which he has retained; in such inquiry only those determinants which were most influential in the coming about of the response will be conspicuous. But if the card is kept before the subject during inquiry, such questions as "Was there anything else that suggested the response to you?" might intimate that aspects of the inkblot were neglected; and subjects who were not influenced by color or shading might re-examine the inkblot and discover these or other aspects which are compatible with their response. This method of inquiry will obscure those aspects which the subject spontaneously responded to, by mixing them with the results of a direct checkup on the reality of the inkblot. This danger is present even when the inkblot has been removed, but much less so. It must be understood that we all *can* perceive what there is on the cards, and the issue is not what is *perceptible,* but what is *spontaneously perceived*—that is, what features of the perceptual mass initiate associative processes spontaneously and influence their course.

Combating the suggestive influence of inquiry means restricting questions to the absolute minimum, and always inquiring indirectly so that even the possibility of giving clues is absent. Questions should be asked only to clarify the scoring of the response, to insure that the scores represent all its important aspects. Inquiry into most responses, even those given by clinical cases, is uninstructive and superfluous. Minimum inquiry achieves three purposes. First, it keeps the record maximally free from speculation, rationalization, and secondary elaboration. Too many questions may direct the attention of the subject to aspects which he has been relatively insensitive to; and soon it becomes unclear which aspects of the response stem from the original perceptual organizing and associative processes, and which from speculation stimulated by unnecessary inquiry. Second, minimal inquiry does not prepare the subject to fear that every response he offers will be inquired into; the apparently irregular incidence of inquiry allows many cases a greater freedom of response, and thereby facilitates diagnosis. A further advantage, especially relevant to the diagnosis of schizophrenic psychopathology in patients with a well-preserved front, is that unexpected inquiry following a peculiar response may catch the patient off his guard before he himself has become too aware of its aberrant nature and has consolidated a halfway acceptable rationalization. Third, minimal inquiry is a timesaver which is not detrimental to the clarity of the test, and such timesavers are precious to the clinician.

Normally, the only time inquiry is made in the course of the test, with the inkblot in front of the subject, it is for the purpose of establishing the exact area the response refers to. But even this is an infrequent necessity for the experienced examiner, and it is mainly in the most disorganized cases, in confusional conditions, that he will need to check the area chosen.

There are two main occasions when it becomes necessary to delay inquiry until the test is completed. The first is when peculiar responses are offered by a subject who appears generally cautious and not at ease with any of his responses; here inquiry early in the administration might not only dismay the patient, but heighten his caution to the point where only the most obvious responses would be subsequently given, with a minimum of verbalization. The second occasion is when the examiner believes that a certain aspect of the inkblot has been influential in the coming about of the response, although the usual indirect inquiry has been unable to elicit this fact. When testing is over, the examiner may return to these responses and ask more direct and leading questions; but the significance of the information he elicits must be interpreted with added caution.

Ideally, the examiner should be able to score the subject's responses as he records them. The advantage of this procedure is that any difficulty experienced in scoring a response on the spot will make the necessity for inquiry apparent. After completion of each card, the gaps in the scoring column will direct attention immediately to those points where inquiry is necessary, and will eliminate the awkward delays required for a complete rereading of the subject's responses.

Recording. All the subject's verbalizations—and not merely the response proper—should be recorded verbatim. The time that elapses between the presentation of the card to the subject and his first response should be recorded, as well as the time between the presentation of the card and his returning it. In those cases where the subject has been encouraged to continue working on the card, only the initial reaction time is significant. Pauses between responses or in the course of the verbalization of a response should be indicated by an appropriate sequence of dash marks. Upon returning to the record, the examiner can thus easily reconstruct the fluid or blocked character of the test performance. The subject's rotations of the cards and the position of the card at the time of each response should be indicated by a wedge with its top pointing in the same direction as the top of the card. We have found it convenient to number the responses to each card.

Tabulation of Scores. The *formal psychogram,* the summarized account of all the scores, should be prepared as soon after the administration of the test as possible. This helps the examiner to discover gaps, omissions, or inconsistencies, which he may try to correct when he next sees the patient. The *formal psychogram* includes the frequency of each score in the record, and certain percentages calculated therefrom—to be discussed below.

Additional Problems and Cautions. It is inexpedient to administer the Rorschach test as either the first or last test in the battery. Preferably, it should follow the intelligence test. The advantage of this procedure is that before the Rorschach test is begun, the subject can be reassured, "Now this will not be an intelligence test; you need not be concerned about doing well or doing badly." The intelligence test also usually establishes the proper testing relationship between examiner and subject. Such a relationship should be one of friendly, interested, appreciative, but firm and unostentatious authority. This relationship cannot be established by a stereotyped attitude identical for all patients, or identical for the same patient in all situations; rather, the examiner must adapt himself specifically to each patient and to each extreme reaction—that is, showing friendliness with a panicky subject, firmness with one who attempts to disrupt the testing situation by verbal aggression or passive resistance, a self-assured handling of the haughty and supercilious subject, and so on.[6]

If the subject has taken the Rorschach test before, it is advisable to state: "You have had this test before; it does not matter to us whether you see now the same things you saw before; tell me everything it looks like to you now." When the test is completed, it is instructive to compare the patient's recollection of the responses he gave previously with those he actually gave.

The examiner will be more efficient and at ease if he always gives the test in a standard place, situation, and position; but the test may be given in the examiner's office, or on the ward, or even at the bedside of a restrained patient. There must be no minimizing of the importance of the fact that it is given only in a *testing situation,* however. This implies that it must be clear to the subject why he should cooperate, so that any noncooperation can then be evaluated with proper weight. Any "party demonstration" and any glib interpretation of a person's casual comments while skimming through the cards should therefore be conscientiously avoided and strongly discouraged.

[6] [For a detailed and insightful treatment of these issues, see Schafer (1954), Chapter 2.—Ed.]

In the remainder of the chapter, we shall first describe the general scoring system of the Rorschach test, elaborating somewhat upon the five aspects of each response which are separately scored. We shall attempt to show how each of these aspects relates to the perceptual and associative processes. We shall then briefly discuss the "major dimensions" of the test —that is, those major aspects which may be dilated or constricted, enriched or impoverished, etc., with relative independence from each other.

Second, we shall devote to each of the five general scoring categories a section in which we shall discuss, one by one, the individual scores subsumed under that category. We shall describe the kinds of responses which obtain that score; we shall discuss problems of administration and inquiry centering on it; we shall offer some psychological rationale of it in conjunction with whatever data we have that can validate its psychological "meaning" (significance); and we shall indicate the diagnostic implications of each score.

The Major Scoring Categories

Discussion of the psychological significance and diagnostic indications of the individual scores must be prefaced by describing the general derivation of the major scoring categories and their interrelationships, as well as the greater or lesser role played by each in the dimensions of the test. To put it more concretely, first we must acknowledge the fact that the individual scores refer to psychological functions of the subject, and that just as all of his functions are interrelated and in constant interplay, so of necessity are the Rorschach scores; and second, the interrelationships of these scores—i.e., the psychological functions they refer to—must be clarified. Validation and standardization of the single scores do not make the Rorschach test a machine to be used by examiners ignorant of the psychology and psychopathology of personality. Personality is not compartmental, but consists of continua of a great variety in extent and shadings. Standardized diagnostic indicators and validated score significances in themselves will therefore be useful for only the crudest and most obvious diagnostic problems, where any or all of the tests can be unequivocal. But for more adequate, definitive, and subtle diagnoses, the examiner must understand the dynamic relationships underlying personality make-up and maladjustment. Only thus can he, in his test report, transcend a haphazard enumeration of personality characteristics or a mere statement of a diagnostic label. To facilitate and foster this understanding is our aim in this section and the rationale sections presented for the individual scores.

In general, the Rorschach scoring system allots five scores to a response

—or, in other words, assesses and summarizes the response from five points of view. It must first be made clear that all the scores pertain to *formal* aspects of the response; they are not intended to convey what the subject saw or said, but represent *a set of abstractions* about the response offered.

An example will make this clear. On the first Rorschach card the subject may state that it looks like a butterfly because of its shape. The scoring of this response would indicate that the *whole inkblot (W)* was the area interpreted; that the response was determined by the *form (F)* of the inkblot; that the inkblot shows enough points of congruence to a butterfly shape for the response's form accuracy to be considered *acceptable* (+); that the conceptual category under which the response may be grossly subsumed is *animal (A);* and finally, that as this response is very frequently given by subjects, it can be considered a highly conventional or *popular* response *(P)*. In Rorschach's symbols, this response would therefore be scored *WF + A P.*

It became clear in our treatment of the Word Association Test that for diagnostic purposes it was necessary to emphasize the *formal* characteristics of the responses, as against their *content*. This necessity is even more extreme in the Rorschach test. The psychologist who expects to find in it direct manifestations—projections—of the content of the patient's problems will be sorely disappointed. Only in very sick patients, or in cases with acute isolated problems, does the content become directly revealing; but then it reveals nothing of which the patient is not conscious or could not tell us in a few moments without the test.[7]

The formal characteristics, in contrast, give information about the patient of which he is hardly or not at all aware. They indicate the function patterns of his awareness, rather than its content—that is, in what way he tends to become aware of situations, or experiences his affects, or avoids or elaborates on them. The content of a response can be controlled by the subjects, modified by speculation, or even suppressed; but the formal characteristics are expressions of perceptual organizing and associative processes which are usually not consciously experienced, and hence are not amenable to conscious censorship.

These formal characteristics are of the greatest significance, in that they reduce the response material to inter- and intrapersonally comparable common denominators.

Let us consider now each of the five major scoring categories, enumerating the various aspects of responses subsumed under each and their relation to the perceptual and associative processes.

---

[7] [The point of view expressed here is obviously an extreme one; it was overstated for polemical purposes, because at the time the prevailing tradition was heavily overweighted in the direction of "deep" interpretations of content.—Ed.]

THE AREA CHOSEN

The subject's response may include the entire inkblot, or only a part of it; if only a part, it may be a large section or quite small; it may be well defined or an arbitrary, unconvincing fragment; it may even be a white space within the inkblot. The area chosen has reference mainly to the perceptual organizing process, although implicitly we must acknowledge the guiding and supporting role played by the associative processes. Thus, the relative weights of the different scores in this category indicate to what extent the subject's perceptual organization is geared to hold together a total complex impression; to what extent it is limited to larger or smaller details in its integrative scope; to what extent the perceptual impression remains a global one or becomes articulated; and how well the associative process can supply appropriate content for each shift in the perceptual organization. The examiner will often see that a subject has a clear impression of the inkblot and its articulation, but cannot summon up any content from the associative process and hence cannot offer a response. For example, a subject stated in reference to Card IX, "I see how three symmetrical parts tower over each other in a pleasing balance . . . but I don't know what it could be." Another subject stated with much vexation, "This part! I don't quite know what it could be." In such instances, the cogwheeling of the perceptual and associative processes is impaired, and frequently the slowing down of the associative processes is to be blamed. But often a weakness of perceptual organization is to blame, as in a response on Card II, "I have an impression of a leering face but I can't put my finger on it." It may be inferred that the usual, apparently spontaneous, and easily given response must emerge from a smooth cogwheeling of the perceptual and associative processes, which in these examples appear to be out of gear. It seems to be a general rule that a subject or an observer can become aware of the complexities involved in apparently simple human functions only under pathological or other extreme conditions.

The scores of areas chosen also offer information about the flexibility of the subject's perceptual organization. That is to say, when the associative processes are unable to offer content for an interpretation of the whole inkblot, the question is, how ready is the perceptual organization to break down the blot into parts and to work on each of them separately? and to what extent will perceptual organization cling to the entire inkblot even if it necessitates delivering a response of vague content? The formal aspects of these problems are essentially the same as those occurring in everyday life when one is confronted with a task of large scope: the person may be able to cope successfully with the necessity for a clear survey, or he may find the survey and integration too difficult and decide that he is competent to tackle only a part of the job, or he may persist in working on the whole job even though his efforts and thinking about it become vague and unproductive.

The scores of areas chosen also indicate the stability of the perceptual process—that is, the extent to which its breakdown of the blot into parts follows or defies the natural articulation of the blot. Two questions must be answered here: what are the criteria for the natural articulation of the inkblot? and how does it come about that the perceptual organization clings to or departs from it? In regard to the first question: our knowledge about perceptual organization is based upon social agreement. Social agreement about the Rorschach inkblots is indicated by the statistical frequency of responses to the various parts of the inkblots, as well as by general agreement among judges who have inspected them. Just as perceptual disorganization is indicated by a departure from the perceptual norm of a society, so on the Rorschach test it may be indicated by a predominance of responses to areas of the inkblots very rarely responded to by the general population. In regard to the second question: an instability of the perceptual organizing processes may make them ignore the press from the natural articulation of the blot and fasten upon some unusual area or combination of areas. But also the pressure of associative material may be strong enough to make the perceptual organizing processes subservient to it, and to overrule the press of the natural articulation of the blot; the content of the associative processes may be such as to require the perceptual processes to fasten upon rarely used areas of the inkblot before a response can come about. For example, a frequent tendency among subjects who are unable to tolerate anxiety in consciousness is to interpret only the edge contours of the heavily shaded inkblots. Such cases avoid the heavily shaded bulk of the blot by taking flight to small parts of the inkblot contour and leaving the shading in the vague background of perception.

We see then that the scores of the areas chosen provide many indications about the kind of cogwheeling of perceptual and associative processes characteristic of the subject.

THE CONTENT CHOSEN

This scoring category has reference to the final product—the response —offered by the associative process, but implicitly recognizes the regulative effect exerted by perceptual organization. In general, these scores do not attempt to convey the concrete content of each response, but rather the conceptual category under which it may be subsumed. This conceptual abstraction in the scoring stresses the fact that it is the concept-formation aspect of the associative process which plays the prominent role in determining the final content of the response. If the final response is "a bear," it appears that the associative process has worked its way through the realm of the concept "animal life" until this appropriate concrete instance is hit upon. The scoring system attempts to indicate those very realms through which the associative process passes in a search for a response. The final tabulation of the number of *animals* seen, *humans* seen, *objects* seen, then becomes indicative of the wealth, availability, and flexibility of conceptual realms from which the subject chooses his responses. Perseveration and stereotypy of the content chosen are just as characteristic a formal property of the content as its singularity or extravagance, and all these are at least as important—from the point of view of psychopathology—as a response of directly informative content. This approach to the content of the subject's productions should strike us as neither arbitrary nor strange. In a conversation in everyday life, the variety and color of references introduced by any participant indicate how free he is in use of his experiences and ideas— or, to put it in psychological terms, the range and availability of the conceptual realms of ideas from which he can draw.

THE DETERMINANTS

This scoring category indicates which perceptual qualities of the ink-blots determine the response, by initiating and influencing the associative process producing it. Thus, the determinant of a response may be the form of the area chosen, its color, its shading, or any combination of these. The determinant scores indicate the strength of the impact of each of the perceptual qualities of the inkblots on the subject. They indicate which of these perceptual qualities are to a greater and which to a lesser extent so experienced by the subject as to initiate an associative process, and to compel it to offer as a response suitable content, harmonious with the perceptual impression. From this point of view, the perceptual process appears to retain a dominating role throughout the course of the associative process; but this is a one-sided view. All subjects[8] see, for example, the different colors of the cards, yet only some of the responses are initiated or brought to their final crystallization by colors. It is not the perception, but rather its impact upon the associative process, that matters here. It would appear then that the associative processes exert a selective influence on the choice of determinants; in other words, the perceptual impressions can initiate associative processes only when there are associative processes available in the subject which have an affinity to them, have a readiness to respond to them; and they can guide the associative processes they initiated to a

[8] [Except, of course, the rare ones with color blindness; yet the significance of color responses does not seem much altered by common protanopia.—Ed.]

crystallized response which expresses them only if the associative processes available in the subject are conceptually and otherwise able to cope with any and all of the perceptual impressions that initiate them. Certain pathological conditions are distinguished by an inability to supply content to match certain perceptual impressions; thus, for example, persons characterized by paramount inhibition rarely give color responses.

The determinants are the justification for the response. Perceptual qualities of the inkblot become determinants in so far as they determine (regulate) what content can be given by the associative process to an area chosen. We do not mean to imply here a temporal sequence of processes—first choosing an area, then giving it a content—but rather simultaneously occurring and interacting processes. There are, however, cases in which there is such an apparent temporal sequence. The patient may state on Card II, "This white space in the middle reminds me of something . . . What could it be? . . . I know! A turnip!" This difficulty may come about when the sharp articulation of the area chosen is extremely compelling. In general, however, we may formulate that this is the case whenever the perceptual process is a jump ahead of the associative process; and it is this temporal disharmony that becomes apparent above in the subject's verbalization. We have cited examples above in which the perceptual process lagged behind the associative process.[9] In the coming about of the usual response, the articulation of the area chosen and the formulation of an appropriate content occur simultaneously and influence each other. Such interaction frequently becomes conscious in obsessively inclined intelligent subjects. A subject states on Card I, "This form . . . a wing effect here . . . let's see . . . oh, the whole thing . . . winged . . . these forms . . . it must be something animate . . . it looks more like a body in the middle . . . the whole side affair is the wing . . . but still it is not birdlike . . . this center figure is like human . . . a human being with wings . . . an angel."

Rarely do the determinants become the subject of conscious speculation, and often they remain entirely unverbalized and are established only on inquiry. This freedom from the fetters of conscious speculation and control makes the determinants the most significant aspects of the responses. When a single determinant has initiated the associative process and remained dominant all through it, it can easily be established and scored. Other than in the very frequent pure form responses, additional determinants also usually come into play in the course of the associative process, and at

---

[9] It makes a difference whether the perceptual process is a jump ahead of the associative process, or the associative process a step behind the perceptual process. In the first instance, the temporal disharmony is referable to some catalyzing influence upon the perceptual organizing processes; in the latter instance, the temporal disharmony springs from a slowing down or inertia of the associative processes.

times achieve equal significance with or even overshadow the originally active determinant. For example, a color may initiate the associative process, but in its course some form characteristic of the area chosen may come into the foreground and influence the formulation of the final response. In such instances, decision as to which should be considered the major determinant is often difficult; all active determinants should be scored, but inquiry should be made to clear up their relative weight.

THE FORM LEVEL

The scores pertaining to the form level refer mainly to the perceptual process. They indicate how accurately or arbitrarily, or how definitely or vaguely, the form of the response is conceived. They also implicitly recognize that, and reflect how, perceptual organization copes with the abundance or paucity of possibilities offered by the associative processes.

In dealing with the form level, a function heretofore inconspicuous in our considerations comes into the foreground. This is the critical controlling function inherent to all conscious thinking which is here, as it were, responsible to the reality of the inkblot, and accepts or rejects response possibilities on the basis of their congruence with the perceptual characteristics of the area chosen. It should be apparent that concept formation is crucially involved in this critical control. It is through concept formation that sufficient identity is established between, on the one hand, the idea and the corresponding image offered by the associative processes and, on the other hand, the structural characteristics of the inkblot. We frequently see this critical function at work when subjects verbalize their dissatisfaction with a response possibility. For example, a subject states in reference to the upper two thirds of Card VII, "It could be a rabbit . . . It doesn't really look like one."

There are several reasons why responses which show little congruence with the inkblot, and hence are considered as of "poor form," come about. First of all, the associative processes may foist a specific content arbitrarily upon the inkblot, overriding both the regulating function of the perceptual process and the influence of the critical function. Such instances are always indicative of psychopathology. Second, even in cases where the articulations which the inkblot easily lends itself to grossly guide the associative process, the perceptual organizing processes may be too impaired to bring these articulations into relief. This can be seen most clearly in confusional conditions, where the subject may offer a very common response but be unable quickly and accurately to point out its different parts. Third, several response possibilities may emerge and the final choice be a poor one. Here an impairment of the critical contact with the reality of the inkblot, and of the concept formation which it implies, appears responsible. Fourth, vague forms may come about when the associative processes are impoverished, so that a sufficient variety neither of conceptual realms nor of individual instances is traversed by them. Vague responses refer to concepts with extremely wide realms and very meager content or distinguishing signs (e.g., maps have an infinite number of forms and there are very few signs that distinguish between "map" and "not map"). This associative impoverishment—a frequent consequence even of anxiety— alone does not bring forth poor forms. For these to come about, the critical function which rejects responses of poor form and leads rather to complete failure, must also be impaired. Inasmuch as the form level, and especially the number of arbitrary form responses, refers to the subject's regard for an adherence to the perceptual reality of the inkblot, it reflects his ability to meet reality's demands by formal reasoning. In everyday life, when a person clings to arbitrary statements in the absence of support from reality, or even in contradiction to it, he is considered "odd"—that is, his attitude toward and ability to comply with the reality situation is estimated as impaired.

THE FIFTH CATEGORY

There is no summary title for the scores subsumed in this category, since there is little unity among them. First, it scores whether a response is extremely frequent ("popular") or extremely rare ("original"). These scores refer in the main to the associative process. In the previous chapter, the popular reactions on the Word Association Test were said to be expressions of a socially stereotyped course of associations—that is, a compliance with "the conventional" in the choice of associative pathways. This holds true here too. The "original" responses reflect choice of the opposite associative pathway, one which is individually characteristic, and dictated by the individual make-up, unique past experience, and idiosyncratic inclinations.

Also scored in this fifth category is the presence of combinations and constructions. Here parts of the blot which are essentially unrelated to each other in an abstract conceptual way are linked together in the response. For example, on Card VIII an "animal" and a "tree" may be seen, and the animal may then be seen as climbing the tree. These scores also refer more to the associative than to the perceptual processes, because although the perceptual process is responsible for breaking down the blot into its parts, combination and construction depend upon flexible, vigorous, and rapid associative processes; only these will offer sufficient material and appropriate links leading to a reuniting of what has been perceptually articulated, and which a less vigorous associative process might have left as a series of independent responses.

There is a last gross subgroup of scores in this fifth category. To enumerate only some of them, we might mention queer, peculiar, absurd, confabulated, and contaminated responses. We cannot go into an explanation of each of these scores here; we shall mention merely that they too refer mainly to the associative process, but always have reference to its verbalization and/or its cogwheeling with the perceptual process. In the responses scored "absurd," for example, the associative process flouts the perceptual process by offering responses completely unsupported by the inkblot; or, in the fabulized combination response to Card VIII, "An animal stepping from a flower to a tree," animal, flower, and tree are perceived, but their relation is associatively elaborated in an unrealistic manner. Peculiar and queer verbalizations and neologisms refer directly to the verbalization of the response emerging from the associative process.

In general, then, the scores of the fifth category evaluate the responses from several points of view, all referring mainly to the associative processes. They are concerned with stereotypy versus originality, elaboration and synthesis of responses versus a passive-realistic attitude toward them, verbalization of and about responses, and so on.

If the examiner keeps in mind these general points about the significance of the five scoring categories, he will not view the recording and scoring as merely a necessary nuisance; nor need he be inclined merely to count up totals, calculate percentages, and establish ratios which may then be looked up in a source book of diagnostic indicators, or one which translates these scores into a "personality description" restricted to an esoteric terminology. Rather, he will gain an impression of his subject's manner of functioning, which will lead him to assumptions about where in a diagnostic or descriptive scheme he may most meaningfully and simply locate the subject; and he will then use the summary of the scores for substantiating his impressions and hunches.

THE MAJOR DIMENSIONS OF THE TEST

In integrating the test indications into a psychologically meaningful picture, we find it most useful to follow a scheme that is not fully congruent with the categories discussed above. Let us call the lines along which the examiner should organize the scores *dimensions* of the test, considering them as though they were a system of coordinates within which the individual case can be located. The term *dimensions* implies that the scores grouped in each dimension are all pertinent to some major aspect[10] of the

[10] More accurately, the scores grouped in each dimension are pertinent to one of our ways of looking at personality make-up.

subject's psychological make-up which may be considered as relatively independent from other major aspects of it. This point should become clear in the following discussion. In this sense the major dimensions of the test are: the quantitative wealth, the qualitative wealth, the form level, and the verbalization of the record.

THE QUANTITATIVE WEALTH OF THE RECORD

This dimension refers to the amount and kind of productivity the subject shows. We gain our first impression about his quantitative productivity by the number of responses he gives, the speed with which they are given, and the duration of his spontaneous application (without pressure from the examiner) to each card. But this quantitative wealth may be of many kinds. A first appraisal can be gained by inspecting the percentage of responses having animals as their content, and the percentage of responses frequently given by the general population (popular responses). The higher the animal percentage, the greater the degree of stereotypy of the output, whether great or small. The higher the popular percentage, the more the productivity is ruled by common-sense considerations; so that at one extreme it may lack all common sense and at the other be completely dominated by ordinary triteness. Thus, both the animal and popular percentages indicate the extent to which the subject's productivity is conventional or variable, reflecting the wealth or shallowness of his personality.

But most revealing of the kind of productivity are the areas chosen—in other words, the relative weight given to whole responses, large detail responses, or small detail responses. When an undue number of small and tiny areas have been interpreted, the subject's productivity—regardless of quantity—is probably of a quibbling, anxious, "small-time" nature. When undue emphasis is placed on the large and obvious details of the inkblot, the productivity is rather of the practical kind, too much rooted in actualities. When responses referring to the whole inkblots prevail, the productivity is of the kind concerned with survey, generalization, integration. The problem is not how often one kind of area is chosen, but rather what balance the subject strikes among them. No one always generalizes, and no one always quibbles. It is around this balance that the dimension of quantitative wealth is really organized.

Analysis of this first dimension does not usually indicate what specific pathological condition or personality trend has heightened or lowered the inclination toward productivity; it does not reveal under what conditions productivity will especially increase or decrease, nor in what segments of psychological functioning it will increase or decrease; and it tells us nothing of the quality of the subject's output, whether great or little. In a sense, then, this first dimension does not get close to the dynamics of the subject's personality or pathology, and it is not among the most stable features of the Rorschach test. For further information we must turn to the other dimensions of the test.

THE QUALITATIVE WEALTH OF THE RECORD

The qualitative wealth of the record represents the variability of the subject's reactions—in thinking, affective life, and action—to the many kinds of stimulation we are all subject to. At the core of the qualitative wealth of the record stands the relationship between the number of responses involving human movement and the number of responses in which the bright colors of the cards are used. The balance between these indicates the potentialities of the subject for ideational and affective intake and output. Records with few human movement and color responses are usually referred to as coarctated; those with many human movement and color responses are usually referred to as dilated.

In general, the qualitative poverty of the record is indicated by the prevalence of pure form responses. These involve neither kinesthetic, color, nor shading impressions; hence the percentage of pure forms in the entire record indicates at a glance the variability of ideational and affective intake and output. At the opposite extreme are responses in which many determinants have been integrated in a well-organized, convincing manner. The wealth of determinants other than pure form provides a general picture of the reactivity of the subject, of the kinds of stimulation most likely to initiate productive associative processes in him, and of the affective and ideational intensity of his productions.

An analysis of the number of original responses, of carefully articulated observations, and of combinations and constructions is also relevant to the qualitative wealth of the protocol. These aspects indicate not so much the reactivity of the subject as his manner of responding to stimulation. That is to say, they indicate that once the associative process has been touched off by the impact of one or another determinant, it may follow a free and unstereotyped course, drawing material from many conceptual realms, elaborating upon the ideas that suggest themselves, going beyond what is merely seen, and attributing convincing and imaginative relationships to the sections of the inkblot.

Thus, analysis of the qualitative wealth of the protocol adds considerable body to the picture supplied by analysis of its quantitative wealth. This analysis goes beyond the amount and scope of productivity, and indicates the stimulations to which the subject's productivity is most reactive and his specific manner of coping with them. For example, the subject's sensitivity may be intense and varied but his consequent responsiveness to stimulation may be weak, so that although many determinants will be used, little originality or imaginative constructiveness comes into play; or his sensitivity may be limited but his responsiveness to a few stimulations may be quite varied and rich, etc.

THE FORM LEVEL OF THE RECORD

The form level indicates the sharpness of judgment exercised in selecting from the possibilities offered by the associative process the one that represents the most convincing response. The form level is, however, to a large extent also dependent upon the quality of the subject's perceptual organizing abilities, and upon the availability of a sufficient number of associations.

The key measure of this dimension is the percentage of acceptable (or better) forms in the whole record: the form-plus percent $(F+\%)$. This percentage allows for further refinement, and we distinguish four different levels of form response. Form responses may be extremely sharp; they may show little congruence with the part of the inkblot interpreted; they may leave the area almost unarticulated and therefore vague; or they may—and this is seen most frequently—show sufficient articulation and congruence to be convincing, but be neither excellently conceived, nor poorly, nor vaguely. We have described the significance of each of these kinds of form response in the previous section on the five major scoring categories. Here we must point out that this selective judgment, this critical controlling attitude toward the responses, is not divorced from the associative and perceptual processes that offer the response possibilities; that is to say, this attitude must cope with weaknesses of perceptual organization which may limit the subject to poorly conceived or vague perceptual material and with limitations of associative material which may result in only a few poor possibilities from among which the subject must choose. On the other hand, this critical controlling attitude to a large extent retains independence from the perceptual and associative processes. One evidence for this is that neurotic depressives, in whom the quantity and quality of associative material is characteristically poor, are conspicuous by the absence of poor form responses in their records. Anxious but generally normal people may suffer some weakening of their perceptual organizing abilities, but still not introduce many arbitrary form responses, clinging rather to the more innocuous vague responses. Thus, the form-level dimension contributes further to the picture of the person's adjustment or maladjustment, by indicating to what extent a critical controlling attitude is able to pass good judgment upon the congruence of his productions with the reality of the inkblot form.

THE VERBALIZATION OF THE RECORD

The subject's verbalization of his responses constitutes the fourth major dimension of the Rorschach record. This dimension is concerned with the relationship to each other of the end products of the perceptual and associative processes. It is mainly through an analysis of verbalizations that we are able to make inferences about the processes underlying the coming about of Rorschach responses.

Verbalization does more than communicate the response and at times shed light on the process of its making; it also indicates the subject's attitude toward the Rorschach cards as objects. That is to say, through analysis of the subject's verbalizations it can be seen whether he has kept the necessary and proper distance from the cards and been fully aware of the nature of his relationship to them, or has misestimated the realistic significance of the inkblots and of his responses. This dimension is thus far the least explored, and we shall devote a large portion of our space to discussing the significance of many different verbalizations.

Having thus briefly surveyed each of the major dimensions, let us attempt to trace their interlocking implications. In everyday clinical work, the examiner infers the general pattern of the subject's psychological functioning and the most likely diagnosis from this type of survey of the entire record. Usually such a review takes as its starting point whichever dimension is conspicuous—for example, an unusually great or unusually meager quantitative production, or an emphasis upon a certain determinant or certain combination of determinants. For the present, however, let us follow the sequence of presentation used above. Quantitatively the record may be rich or impoverished. From this dimension we gain an impression of the extent of the subject's output, the scope of the problems it encompasses, and the degree of stereotypy of approach. It then becomes necessary to ask such questions as, "To what extent is this output stimulated by anxieties? To what extent by the press of emotion-laden situations? And whatever the amount of output and the sources that stimulated it, to what extent is the subject's coping with these stimulations rich, imaginative, and variable?" The answers to all of these questions must be sought in those scoring categories subsumed in the second major dimension, and must help to clarify the dynamic interplay of the subject's quantitative productiveness and his ideational and affective intake and output. However, further questions must be answered: "To what extent is the subject's responsiveness geared to meet the reality of the stimulating situations? and just how does he cope with this reality? are his reactions fitting and appropriate?" For an answer to these questions, the examiner must turn to an analysis of the form level of the subject's responses. There is still another question: "How can we sufficiently penetrate the subject's thought processes to detect disharmonies between the perceptual and associative processes underlying his responses, disharmonies indicative of his specific maladjustment?" In search of an answer, we must turn to the fourth major dimension, the subject's verbalization of and around his responses. These verbalizations do not always give us an answer to the question, and quite frequently they do not even provide clues; however, there are many cases, especially among the schizophrenics, who will let us know—if we are sensitive enough to the implications of verbalization—where and what these disharmonies are. We are not restricted in these analyses to psychiatric cases; some normal subjects, especially those obsessively inclined or highly introspective, provide us with an abundance of information about the nature of the harmony and disharmony of the perceptual and associative processes.

In the bulk of the following discussions, we shall rarely refer back to this necessity for surveying an entire Rorschach record in terms of the relationships of these four major dimensions. In fact, it may appear at times that we have fallen into the old rut of evaluating each score quite independently of all the others—of attempting to develop a source book of discrete interpretations. This is emphatically not our aim, but an artifact of any presentation that avoids becoming unduly repetitious and lengthy.

THE VOLUME AND SPEED OF PRODUCTION

Before discussing any of the five major scoring categories, we shall deal with the simplest quantitative aspect of the records: the number of responses *(R)*, the number of failures *(Fail.)*, and the reaction times *(R.T.)*.

THE NUMBER OF RESPONSES: *R*

Rorschach's experience indicated that there were about 30 responses in the average-sized record. Our patient population shows extreme variability, but an average of between 23 and 24 responses. Our experience with various layers of the normal population has been that the average number of responses is somewhere around 24.[11] In any range, *R* is characteristic of the subject's general productivity rather than specifically diagnostic.

---

[11] If we consider the Rorschach records of 47 applicants for stenographic jobs at the Menninger Clinic, the average response number is around 26. Of these applicants, 6% had less than 15 responses, 30% had from 15 to 22 responses, 36% had from 23 to 29 responses, 19% had from 30 to 37 responses, and 8% had more than 37 responses. [It must be remembered that the technique of administration outlined here tends to discourage long records, and the definition of a scorable response is narrower than that of many.—Ed.]

Scoring and Inquiry

The main problem in scoring is, what constitutes a response? A scorable response is one that refers to a definite area of the inkblot, has a definite conceptual content, reveals its determinant either spontaneously or in inquiry, and can be evaluated for its form level if form is involved as a determinant. Thus, naming the colors on the card, describing its abstract geometrical properties, expressing an affective reaction ("Beautiful!"), describing vague perceptual impressions such as "It seems to have an upward thrusting quality," do not constitute responses. These all remain on the level of description, either of perceptual aspects of the inkblot or of feeling reactions of the subject; they do not answer the question, "What might it be?"

Moreover, sometimes full responses are given that are not scored by us: If the subject gives in sequence these four responses to Card I, "Bat . . . butterfly . . . insect . . . bird," only one score is allotted to the four responses. Our justification for this procedure is that none of these responses differs in any of the five scores allotted to them; they refer to only one perceptual organization of the blot, and to only one very limited conceptual realm of content. Similarly, when a subject gives a sequence of vague responses, such as "X-ray picture . . . microscopic slide," they are scored separately only when inquiry establishes the fact that there is some feature distinguishing between them, either in their perceptual articulation or in their use of determinants. Thus, the inkblot may look like a microscopic slide "because it is so irregular," and like an X-ray film "because of the shadings."

If the subject elaborates connections between sections of the inkblot which he has interpreted independently, the combination does not constitute a new response: each element in the combination should be scored separately, "additional whole response" should be credited in the first scoring column, and a "combination" should be credited in the fifth scoring column. Each of the parts is thus counted separately in obtaining the total number of responses, but the additional whole response is not.

New responses obtained during inquiry should not be counted in the total number of responses proper, but should be indicated as "additional responses." These additional responses are usually not given equal weight with the responses which were spontaneously given. Only in those few cases where an extreme misconception about the nature of the test has resulted in many failures and few—or solely anatomical—responses, and it has become necessary to readminister the test with a clear explanation of it, do the new responses constitute primary material for interpretation. Correct administration and careful inquiry will elicit no, or occasionally one or two, additional responses.

In the course of the test proper it is permissible, and often advisable, to press for further responses when only one response is obtained to any card and the subject wants to give it up in less than two minutes. The sequence of pressure should be, "Anything else?"; then, "Is there nothing else it might be?"; and finally, "Would you take one more look at it just to make sure that there are no other possibilities?" The examiner may also exert pressure if he notices that the subject has fixed his gaze on a specific part of the card for a relatively long time, yet gives no response. In such cases the examiner may ask, "What do you have on your mind?" He may even stress that the subject must tell *all* that the cards suggest to him; he may call attention to the fact that the subject was really working on a specific part of the card, and inquire whether he had entertained any possibilities which he rejected as "no good" or "too farfetched." Such pressure should be applied judiciously, and kept to an absolute minimum. It is advisable only when the subject has been giving few responses, or when some facial play indicates that pressure may elicit a withheld response.

The Rationale of R

The number of responses, R, reflects the quantitative productivity of the subject. This productivity depends upon the flexibility of the perceptual processes, and the wealth and pliancy of the associative processes. If the perceptual organizing processes become rigid, the subject may be unable to look at the inkblot from different points of view, to shift the figure-background relationships of it, to shift from a greater to a lesser articulation of it. Thus, the subject may complain, "Once it looks like one thing to me, I can't get away from that and make it look like anything else." Even if the perceptual organizing processes are flexible, they require a rich and extensive support from the associative processes before a large number of responses can be worked out. In this connection, the number of responses appears related to both the intelligence level and the range of interests of the subject. Only with a sufficiently large homogeneous population, however, could one expect to demonstrate that within certain limits there exists a positive relation between R and IQ.

What are the characteristics of adjustment and maladjustment that influence R? The extent of maladjustment has little to do with the R score. Personality characteristics making for a relative wealth of ideational and affective output increase R, while those that inhibit such output decrease R. Rorschach contended, and our experience corroborates, that within the normal range a large number of responses refers to an "ambition for quantity of production"; and that whatever dynamics may underlie this ambition, it is usually apparent in the subject's everyday activity, in the general volume and expansiveness of his ideational productions. The quality of this "quantity ambition" may of course vary, so that in everyday life it may come to expression in empty verbosity, persistent and plodding but unimaginative output, or in a free and versatile creative productivity. Which of these it will be we can largely infer from the qualitative wealth of the record. Empty verbosity as the basis for great productivity may be indicated by a superficially elaborate record which is poor in quality; productivity based on persistent plodding may be indicated by a slow, careful, and persistent application to each of the parts, which usually results in flat, uninspired, and uninteresting responses; free creative productivity may be indicated by a considerable variability of content and of use and combination of determinants, and by convincing elaboration and integration of responses.

If we consider people in the normal range who have a low number of responses, we cannot always conclude that inhibition or extreme paucity of associative material is responsible. "Quality ambition" may also result in a low R. Poor responses may be withheld by pressure from a highly self-critical attitude; long delays may occur until a possibility that has presented itself is sufficiently articulated and elaborated; the separate details interpreted may again and again be integrated into one internally consistent response. Inquiry in such cases easily shows that many possibilities were noted, but discarded as "poor." At its extreme, such quality ambition results in the offering of only one response to a card, which, however, will be an excellently construed interpretation of the entire inkblot. A low R associated with quality ambition can easily be distinguished from one associated with inhibition; inhibition shows not only little quantitative but little qualitative wealth.

R as a Diagnostic Indicator

A low R is most clearly and definitely associated with depression; even in the neurotic range, depressionlike conditions reveal this inclination. The most severely depressed patients average from 11 to 15, and the less depressed from 16 to 18, while nondepressed neurotics average between 22 and 28 responses.

There are two groups in which depression does not play a role but which nevertheless stand out with a low average R: these are simple schizophrenics and deteriorated paranoid schizophrenics. The low average of the simple schizophrenics is no surprise, since clinically the flatness and poverty of their ideation is a crucial diagnostic feature. Deteriorated paranoid schizophrenics lag far behind other deteriorated schizophrenics; apparently the retention of coherence in deteriorated paranoid schizophrenics, together with an extreme devastation of ideation, results in a fairly low number of responses, while the incoherence and flightiness of deteriorated unclassified schizophrenics allow much more for an accumulation of meaningless and confused responses.

Overideational preschizophrenics stand out with high average R. This finding is readily understandable, since they are characterized by intense ideational productivity. Less striking, but of the same meaning, is the high R of acute unclassified schizophrenics, mixed neurotics, and obsessive-compulsives—all characterized specifically by ideational symptom formation. Acute paranoid schizophrenia and the paranoid conditions are also characterized by active delusions and yet their average R is relatively low. This is far from being an inconsistency, however: both of these disorders are characterized clinically by considerable inhibition, rigidity, and suspicious caution, and these qualities are reflected in the somewhat low average number of responses.

Conclusions: Degree of inhibition and R appear to be negatively correlated, even in the normal range. In the pathological range, a low R is suggestive of depression or neurosis with strong depressive coloring, or of a flat but coherent simple or deteriorated schizophrenia.[12] A high R suggests intense ideational activity and, where specific signs of psychopathology are present, indicates pathological ideation, whether psychotic or neurotic.

FAILURES

A full failure is scored when the subject is unable to offer a response to a card; "conditional failure" is scored if the subject cannot offer a response until two minutes after the presentation of the card, or is able to give a response only when the card is again shown to him at the end of the test. Rorschach considered failures to indicate blocking and to be a feature of serious maladjustment. We have found, however, that even in well-adjusted normals inhibition results in the occurrence of a full failure in about one out of every three cases, and that one out of eight may have even more than one failure.

Scoring and Inquiry

If the kinds of pressure described above elicit no response to a given card, it should be presented again to the subject at the end of the test, and inquiry should be made in the following sequence: "Will you please try this one again?"; then "Is there anything it even faintly suggests?"; then "You saw different things on the other cards: can't you see anything of

---

[12] Many cases of addiction or of character disorder have a low R [because of their poor tolerance for unpleasure and corresponding inability to exert prolonged effort.—Ed.]

that sort on this one?"; and finally the inkblot character of the test should be made clear to the subject and "making something of it" should be encouraged and insisted upon. If a response is then obtained, a "conditional" failure must still be scored.

The Rationale of Failures

In general, the failure score correlates negatively with the number of responses, and indicates a paucity of ideomotor activity. It represents the subject's failure to organize the perceptual raw material to an extent where it can initiate and guide to consummation an associative process; and it indicates a failure of the associative processes to supply a sufficient variety of possibilities to further the perceptual organizing process. Inhibition, which clinically and in everyday life is detected at least partly by its limiting effect upon ideational productivity, is a factor making for failures.

The incidence of failures varies on the different cards. The incidence of failures is highest on Cards VII and IX; Cards VI and II follow. The diffuseness of the colors on Card IX and the diffuseness of the shading on Card VII appear to be disturbing to the majority of subjects, normal or otherwise—although the disturbance usually comes to expression in other ways. Card II combines many disturbing features, being the first card with heavy shading and colors, bright red colors at that; Card VI is conspicuous for its strong shading. The great incidence of failures on Cards VII and IX, even within the normal range, leads to the conclusion that failures on these need not have strong pathological implications; but on such Cards as I, III, and VIII—on which normal subjects almost never fail—they must be considered an indicator of psychopathology.

The Failure Score as a Diagnostic Indication

Inhibitory factors, even within the normal range, are likely to cause failures. In the psychopathological range, depression appears to be the outstanding cause of failures, although the inhibition of ideation in inhibited preschizophrenics and the poverty and flatness of ideation in simple schizophrenics are also potent factors. Failures also appear to occur frequently in paranoid and neurasthenic conditions. On the other hand, the clinical cases characterized by excessive ideational productivity—obsessive-compulsives and overideational preschizophrenics—almost never fail on any of the inkblots.

REACTION TIME

Reaction time is defined as the time that elapses between the presentation of a card and the offering of the first scorable response. Although we systematically record the total time spent on each card, we cannot use this as a reliable measure since we usually encourage second responses, thereby artificially extending the time; and the necessities of verbatim recording sometimes require the subject to "hold it" until the examiner can catch up. The reaction time is subject to no such extensions, and remains reliable.

The two main problems of recording reaction time are: (1) What is a scorable response? (2) When does the reaction time terminate—when the subject begins to verbalize his response, or when he has finished? Our answer to the first question was presented in the discussion of R. As to the second question, the reaction time terminates when the subject utters the first word that makes it unequivocally clear that a scorable response is being verbalized. This working rule avoids the hazards created by subjects who launch into a description of a part of the card which sounds as though they are leading up to a response—which they never reach—and by subjects who may give a response, but dwell on it for an unduly long time, elaborating and criticizing it.

The Rationale of Variations in Reaction Time

Variability of reaction time must be evaluated both intra- and interpersonally. That is, how does the average reaction time of a subject compare to that of the general population? and to what extent and on which cards are his reaction times fast or slow *for him?*

In the normal subject, the reaction time may be long (over one minute) for any of several reasons: (1) if the card is difficult to grasp or to organize perceptually on the level set by the subject as his standard—as found in meticulous people; (2) if the card elicits a multitude of simultaneous impressions, so that the associative processes need time for the necessary abstractions from or integration of these impressions; (3) if the subject's specific mode of adjustment is such that actively and successfully coping with anxiety-arousing situations is difficult.

In the normal subject, the reaction time may be quite short (under 20 seconds): (1) if the perceptual grasp of the card is acute and secure, and the wealth and versatility of the associative processes quickly supplies response possibilities; (2) if the subject's mode of adjustment is such that he sets his standards of production at a low level with little critical appraisal of his productions, and therefore verbalizes the first possibilities he thinks of; (3) if a high degree of stereotypy of the associative pathways is present, resulting in the obvious popular responses; (4) if the subject's versatility allows him to offer as his first response an easy and obvious one, thereby gaining time to consolidate more complex and original responses.

In pathological cases, long reaction times may result from: (1) psychomotor retardation or blocking; (2) doubt or overmeticulousness; (3) an anxious reluctance to tackle the problem of articulating what appears at first glance to be an amorphous perceptual mass; (4) fascination with a part of a card, especially of a colored card, which attracts the subject and holds his attention without his being able to produce a response. This may happen particularly on the bright red parts of Cards II and III. More versatile and less anxious subjects on encountering such a difficulty will soon recognize that *for them* there is nothing to find in that area, and turn to happier hunting grounds; strong anxiety restricts this freedom.

In the pathological range, very short reaction times usually occur: (1) when vague or arbitrary responses are glibly offered, with little or no interference from any critical attitude; (2) when a heightened psychomotor speed is present—which does not necessarily exclude good responses; (3) when some aspect of the inkblot offers ready support for an overvalent idea of the subject, as in many responses of sexual or aggressive connotations.

Any evaluation of the reaction times of a subject must take into account not only his own difficulties in offering responses, but also the varying degrees of difficulty presented by different cards. Card IX offers the greatest difficulty. It is followed by Cards VI, VII, and X. On the other hand, Cards I, V, and VIII seem seldom to produce long reaction times.

The long reaction-time tendency on Card IX is to be expected; the diffuseness of the colors, and the difficulty both of breaking down the blot into details and of integrating the whole blot, serve to delay the first response. On Cards VI and VII the diffuse shadings seem to make for delay of reaction time. That Card X should permit few quick reaction times is somewhat of a surprise: though this card usually defies attempts at a whole response, it lends itself easily to detail responses, being the most articulated inkblot of all. The core of the difficulty here appears to be the brightness of its colors, and the scattered and confused appearance it has at first glance. We have already indicated how reaction time may be lengthened when a multitude of impressions crowd in upon consciousness, and delay a response until the subject can make sufficient abstractions or integrations or can settle down to a single aspect of the card. But there appears to exist also a rather general difficulty of coping with bright colors in themselves, and this too may make for some of the delay.

The prevalence of quick reaction times on Card I and V is readily understandable by the unitary structure of these cards, which readily lends itself to an interpretation of some flying creature. The many short reaction times on Card VIII are due to a well-articulated portion of this inkblot, which even the most cautious subject will admit looks like a "four-legged animal of some kind." This response is actually the easiest response in the entire test, the most popular of all the popular responses; it is so compelling that even at two and a half years of age it may be obtained—often as the only response to the entire Rorschach test.

Reaction Time as a Diagnostic Indicator

Within the normal range, slow reaction times are referable mainly to the effects of inhibition. In the psychopathological range, the presence of long reaction times is usually indicative of depressive psychomotor retardation or pathological inhibition (as in inhibited preschizophrenics); and very short reaction times frequently indicate extensive ideational productivity.

THE AREA CHOSEN

The subject's approach to the inkblots of the Rorschach test is grossly parallel to, and has a fundamental continuity with, his manner of approaching situations in everyday life. Different persons react differently to new situations, and the same person reacts differently to situations of different kinds. One will be more inclined to strive for a general survey of the situation confronting him; another may concentrate on the separate details of outstanding significance; others may become overconcerned with outlandish, unimportant trifles. In everyday life, the advantages of familiarity and experience, and the possibility of falling back upon convention and stereotype, often obscure this characteristic "manner of approach." The strangeness and difficulty of the inkblots of the Rorschach test help bring it more clearly into relief.

The examiner must determine what balance the subject strikes between different kinds of approach to situations, and just how this specific balance differentiates him from the rest of the population. It is here that one of the basic advantages of the Rorschach test comes to the fore: as each response can be scored and these scores totaled, intratest relationships can be quantitatively established and intertest comparison becomes possible.

The examiner who relies solely upon the scores, however, and does not try to empathize with the difficulties and inclinations of the subject as he attempts to organize the inkblot, will not derive from a Rorschach record its full implications. That is to say, it should be a primary striving of the examiner to put himself into the frame of mind of his subject by following with him the sequence of areas chosen. None of the other major scoring categories lends itself so easily to empathy and understanding as this. In general, the tendency of the subject to comply with the obvious unity or articulation of the inkblot may obscure the significance of the final score totals. Only by carefully observing the sequence and smoothness of choice of areas will the examiner grasp the full significance of the scores.

Nevertheless, the relative weight given by the subject to the different areas of choice—as indicated by his score totals—remains a salient and revealing aspect of the Rorschach record. It appears from experience with large populations that there is a rough norm, or expected balance between whole and detail responses, to be met. This balance is roughly two detail responses for each whole response.

We have pointed out that a deviation from an expected score may reflect a personality characteristic rather than a feature of maladjustment, and that only extreme deviations become suggestive of maladjustment. This must be kept in mind especially in evaluating the balance of areas chosen by a subject, because in this respect we rarely encounter extremes that are characteristic of a specific disorder.

It is also important to know that deviations from this norm take on a different significance in different kinds of adjustments and maladjustments. The balance struck is an important indicator of the subject's endowment; and the inclinations of the subject within his range of endowment have a bearing on the significance and kind of psychopathology present. Thus, in the low-grade feeble-minded whose natural endowment is extremely poor, many arbitrary whole responses crop up; in the high-grade feeble-minded a very low incidence of whole responses is what indicates poverty of endowment, while the occurrence of good large detail responses refers to some ability to comply with accepted standards of thinking. In the range of average or better-than-average endowment, the relationship between whole responses and detail responses generally indicates the subject's proclivity to theoretical or practical pursuits, respectively. In the range of maladjustments, though these individual proclivities may still be partly preserved, a specific kind of extreme balance (or imbalance) may be struck which will be diagnostically suggestive by reflecting the impact of the maladjustment on the subject's thought processes. A schizophrenia characterized by an inclination to grandiose theoretical constructions may show up in an extreme prevalence of whole responses, while the extreme impairment of survey and integrative abilities in a depression may show up in an emphasis almost completely on detail responses with few or no whole responses.

To put it in terms of our general rationale, the perceptual organizing processes and the associative processes have a general trend in structuring a situation, and it is according to this trend that the emphasis divides between a general grasp and survey (W) and a concentration upon concrete detail (D). The fact that some kind of gross norm exists indicates that there is a significant amount of interindividual or social agreement as regards manner of approach. More specifically, there appears to be a somewhat uniform responsiveness in the normal population to the limitations and regulating effect of the perceptual raw material. The usual subject will "survey" when the difficulties the card offers to perceptual organizing and to finding suitable associative content are not too great; he will become concrete and practical when these difficulties necessitate it. To a large extent, then, it is the nature of the inkblots of the Rorschach test that sets the expected balance between whole and detail responses.

Therefore, when a subject strikingly deviates from the balance defined by social agreement, he is letting us know of a strong proclivity or pathological tendency of his own. Naturally, the limitations of endowment discussed above must be kept in mind.

In assessing the balance struck between whole and detail responses, it becomes necessary to consider *how* each kind of area is chosen. Tiny extravagant details may be given by the subject after prolonged effort has not resulted in a more usual response, or they may be given quickly, carelessly, and in masses. Thus, an analysis of the *sequence* of areas chosen is an important supplementary procedure in evaluating the record. It is also a very different matter whether the prevalence of whole responses is the result of sharp and well-structured responses or of vague, unarticulated ones. Thus, it is also important to analyze the *form level,* especially of the whole responses, so that the quality of the subject's abstractions or concrete considerations may become clear. Here too sequence is important: the examiner should note whether vague or arbitrary whole responses only follow well-articulated ones, precede them, or generally replace them.

Although the remainder of this section will treat the scores pertaining to "area chosen" individually, the reader should remember that the full meaning of the individual scores derives only from their interrelationships with the other scores. Our emphasis in the following, however, will be mainly upon the variants of each score pertaining to area chosen, variants which are not conveyed in the scores—for example, well-articulated versus vague whole responses. We shall try to understand the genesis of each of these variants, and to elaborate upon the significance each variant has for the kind of adjustment or maladjustment of the subject.

THE WHOLE RESPONSE: *W*

A response is scored *W* when the area chosen refers to all or almost all of an inkblot. This definition does not imply that the response must necessarily penetrate into and interpret all facets of the entire inkblot, and it therefore becomes apparent that we may obtain a wide variety of *W*'s: they may range from responses that are based on a clear or vague single impression of part of the blot, through those that are based on a well-articulated series of impressions, to those that account for too many partial impressions with painful meticulousness.

Scoring and Inquiry

It is usually clear whether or not the response extends to the whole inkblot. If doubt arises, the examiner should inquire after removing the card, "How much of it was the............?" Establishing the intensity of a *W* is usually more difficult than establishing its extension. The clue to its intensity is the degree of articulation achieved in it. In our scoring we designate all kinds of whole responses by the score *W*; but in our thinking about the records we make many distinctions among them. We shall attempt here to outline these distinctions, indicate briefly the justification for making them, and describe the problems of administration and inquiry which arise in connection with each.

W +. These are the intensely and sharply articulated whole responses, and include the tightly-knit combinatory *W*'s as well as the finely differentiated but unitary (abstract) *W*'s. As an example of the former, we may take the response to Card II: "A large courtyard surrounded by dark hedges leading up to the castle in the distance with red sunset clouds in the sky." As an example of the latter, we may take the response to Card IV: "A man sitting on a stool, seen from a worm's-eye view, and his boots are worn and muddy." The subject's spontaneous verbalization usually makes clear the sharpness of articulation and validity of integration. If not, one very general inquiry will usually clarify the intensity of the response. The number of such whole responses is an indication of the subject's intellectual assets.

Wo. These *W*'s are the average (*o* for ordinary) responses based on a gross abstraction from, or generalization about, the entire inkblot. Thus, the response "bat" to Card I may be a *W* based on the perception of a body in the center and winglike sides. But this response on Card I may refer merely to approximately the upper one third of the card, with the wings represented by the upper side projections and the body by the upper central area: this is a detail response. The eyes and ears of the experienced examiner will detect those responses which sound like but may not be the customary *W* response; he will then make inquiry. Steady and too intensive inquiry, however, reduces the significance of the test findings. If the examiner shows too much concern about "how much" was used, the subject may infer the desirability of whole responses; he may also become overcritical in regard to the exact areas he chooses for a response, and make all kinds of meticulous exclusions in defense against discrepancies that may be brought out in inquiry. Therefore, outlining the area or pointing out crucial parts of the figure, rather than questions of "how much," is the form the inquiry should generally take.

Wv. These responses are based on a vague general impression with a corresponding vagueness of content—X-ray films, islands, microscopic slides, etc. There is little reason to inquire about the localization of such responses or the degree of articulation present: unless inquiry after determinants, especially shading, indicates a convincing and sufficient amount of articulation, the response is a *Wv*. It might be contended that what we have subsumed in *Wv* is as much an abstraction as that subsumed in *Wo*. The essential distinction is that the abstraction made in the *Wo* response is strictly regulated by the perceptual structure of the card, so that the final content fuses with the structure; in the *Wv* response, almost any structure of the inkblot would serve satisfactorily. For example, butterflies have a standard shape, but islands do not.

W—. These responses are *W*'s which, while showing a perceptual articulation, involve considerable arbitrariness in it or in the assignment of content to the *W*. Such is the response to Card VII: "An animal, its head is this whole bottom part, the forelegs are these side projections, and the hind legs are these top projections." Inasmuch as the *W—* response shows little congruence with the inkblot, it is frequently necessary to establish that the entire inkblot was involved, and to ask the subject to point out one or two specific parts of this response. With these two inquiries answered, the arbitrariness of the *W* almost always becomes clear.

These then are the four major kinds of *W* which we distinguish. There are two other kinds of whole responses which should be mentioned here.

DW. These are a subgroup of *W* responses which the subject can justify only by referring to a detail—that is, they represent a conclusion from a detail to a whole. An example would be "cat" on Card VI, if on inquiry the subject says "These two projections on the side of the top looked like whiskers so I thought the whole thing must be kind of a cat." Such responses may originate from a larger *(D)* or a quite small *(Dr)* area of the card, and hence we have *DW* responses and *DrW* responses. In order to detect these pathological *W* responses, the examiner must be alert to the general character of the subject's responses: when it appears by other indicators that his perceptual organization is weak and arbitrary, or that the associative content is uncritically delivered, the examiner may reasonably suspect any of the subject's *W* responses and should inquire into them: "What made it look like a............?"—and, if only a limited segment of the inkblot is referred to: "Nothing else?" It is incorrect to pursue this inquiry too far, because the subject may feel threatened by his inability to justify his response.

Cut-off W. Klopfer and his co-workers have suggested that *W* responses which explicitly exclude a minor portion of the inkblot—for example, an interpretation of Card III which does not include the red areas, or of Card IV which excludes the upper side projections—should be called and scored "cut-off W" responses. An inspection of the inkblots shows that exclusions on certain cards are more acceptable, and to a large extent more inevitable, than on others. We have not found this extra score necessary in our work, although we do systematically note and interpret this tendency if it grows strong. It is an expression of meticulousness and rigidity indicating a limitation of the scope of abstractions the subject can make; such meticulousness demands that all minor segments of the blot not entirely consonant with the abstraction be specifically excluded.

The Rationale of the W Score

In the Rorschach literature, ever since the publication of Rorschach's *Psychodiagnostics,* the W responses have been considered to represent the abstracting, surveying, and integrating abilities of the subject. It stands to reason that the more the whole of the inkblot is coped with, the more elements or segments of it must be either integrated or brought into harmony by a selective abstraction. It is necessary to go beyond this gross formulation, however, and examine more closely the processes out of which W responses in general, and the different kinds of W responses in particular, emerge.

In general, both abstraction and integration are involved in the coming about of the W response. The multiplicity of perceptual impacts emanating from an entire inkblot is such that a synthesis of only certain of these impressions, and an abstractive disregarding of others, are prerequisite for the coming about of a response. All of the elements of the blot can never be encompassed by one meaningful association. The only response which really encompasses all of them is "an inkblot"—but this is merely a statement about the reality of the test material, involving no perceptual articulation of the inkblot, no initiation of associative processes in connection with it, and hence no interpretation—i.e., no conceptual shift from its reality. The more the subject attempts to cope with every fine aspect of the inkblot, the emptier the content of his responses becomes and the more he approaches the "inkblot" formulation.[13] Thus, in order to give any W response the subject must disregard certain aspects of the inkblot: but this disregarding, or abstraction, must strike a balance between the two poles

[13] This is essentially a problem in concept formation. We know that the greater the multiplicity of instances subsumed by the concept, the emptier the content of the concept becomes. A concept such as "things made up of cells," while it includes a wide realm of instances, is very empty in content; things made up of cells have only one common feature, that they are made up of cells.

of accounting for everything and accounting for nothing. At either extreme the responses have no meaning. Subjects experience varying degrees of difficulty in their efforts at abstracting. Some will squint at the inkblot, in order that only its grossest perceptual features need to be coped with; this is merely an instance of artificial abstraction, a reflection of some impairment of the subject's own abstracting ability. Others may attempt to cope with all the discrepant features of the inkblot; in these cases we usually have a spectacle of uncertainly, doubt, self-criticism, and rejection of response possibilities or actual responses. Still others may cope with the entirety of the inkblot by retreating from or not even attempting abstractions; these subjects will work out different interpretations to different areas of the entire inkblot, and will then combine or integrate these into a full response. Here too a balance must be struck between interpreting every fine detail of the inkblot, a procedure which precludes any successful final integration, and interpreting sections so large or occupying such a place in the structure of the inkblot that responses are offered such as, "one half of the card is a reflection of the other." Abstraction, then, represents a process leading away from too many specific details; while integration represents a process attempting to account for details. These two processes, of course, follow the patterns of the logical processes of deduction and induction, respectively, and much can be inferred about the subject's manner of reasoning from his manner of working out W responses.

But let us turn now to the four major kinds of W response, and attempt to understand the specific qualities and underlying processes of each.

$W+$. Most of these are combination responses—integrations of separately perceived details, sharply seen and integrated in a convincing way. (On Card I, "two angels carrying a headless woman to heaven.") Emphasis on these responses reflects careful induction as the subject's method of choice for coping with complex situations. And a $W+$ response may also be an abstraction which is very finely articulated (on Card V, "a dancer, at a Mardi Gras, rabbit mask and wings"). In these, the emphasis swings over to deduction, though deduction which is thoroughly responsible for its implications. In the integrated $W+$ responses, the associative processes are apparently unable to offer material to support a major abstraction, but are competent to support detail responses and to elaborate links between them. In the abstract $W+$ responses, the associative processes rise to their greatest height by offering material not only to support a major abstraction, but to elaborate upon and articulate the parts of this abstraction in an entirely harmonious and imaginative way.[14]

14 [Compare the concepts of "$W+$" and "$W++$" in the developmental scoring of Werner's students (Friedman, 1953; Hemmendinger, 1960). In that scoring system, the concept of "Wv" is the same as the score introduced here by Rapaport; "Wm"

Wo. These responses are largely abstractions which have struck an adequate balance with the inkblot's complexity of detail, so that neither too many nor too few details are neglected (on Card V, "a bat"). Some articulation may be present in these gross abstractions; here the associative processes support the gross perceptual impression, and the latter is regulated sufficiently by the structural characteristics of the inkblot. The kind of abstraction they imply is one of validity, but with little impressiveness, imaginativeness, or importance.

Wv. In these responses the abstraction appears to have been made too quickly and haphazardly; that is to say, insufficient account was taken of the multitude of features, and the final response implies little or no articulation ("map," "cloud"). This very restricted grasp of the perceptual material, as well as the possible limitations of the underlying associative processes, occur in most records; only a great accumulation of these is suggestive of psychopathology. We shall discuss below what factors in the normal range appear to be responsible for their occurrence.

W—. Here an abstraction has been made which, although it has not taken into account enough of the details, appears sufficiently convincing to the subject for him to accept the response and then attempt to work out its articulation: this articulation can only be arbitrary, except by a stroke of good luck, since a minimum of responsibility to the actual perceptual features of the inkblot regulated the coming about of the response (on Card III, "a crab"). In these responses, either the pressure of associative material appears to override the perceptual limitations of the inkblot and the perceptual organizing ability of the subject, or the associative process lags far behind the perceptual impressions. The first of these possibilities partially explains the tendency of schizophrenics to have a preponderance of *W*. The incidence of vague and arbitrary whole responses is strikingly high in schizophrenics, indicating their predilection for farfetched generalizations. The extreme of such generalizations becomes apparent in that the *DW* responses occur frequently in schizophrenics only, and that in them often an irresponsible and farfetched generalization is made from a single detail to the entire inkblot.

In assessing the record the examiner must survey the balance struck between the different kinds of *W* responses. If *W*+ responses are conspicuous, the indication is for the presence of excellent integrative as well as abstractive abilities; if *Wo*'s are dominant, the indications are for a merely adequate survey and generalizing ability; if *W*— and *Wv* stand out, the

is virtually identical with *Wo*, and "*W*—" with *W*—. In general, it is valuable to learn the distinctions presented here among various types of *W* responses, but few clinicians routinely score in this way.—Ed.]

indications are for haphazard, arbitrary generalizations in the subject's thinking.

There is a popular W response on each of the first six cards, which probably accounts for the fact that the most frequently encountered type of whole response on each of these is Wo. On the other hand, Wv responses appear to predominate on the last four cards. Perceptually they are the least unitary of all, and an attempt to cope with the entirety of these four blots will drive the subject toward such typical vague responses as "smoke" or "anatomical chart," particularly if he is of only average intellectual and cultural achievement.

These considerations are usefully amplified by an analysis of which cards are most likely to elicit W responses of any kind. For subjects of all types, Card I has the strongest pull for W. To be sure, the instructions accompanying the presentation of the first card are merely, "What could this be?"—a question that tends to drive the subject more to a total interpretation; and Card I has a unitary character which supports the implication of the opening question. The popular response "butterfly" or "bat" is extremely frequent, and it is also frequent to obtain a second whole response, although this one is usually vague and in the direction of "anatomy" or "map." When the subjects reach Card II—which is much more difficult to interpret in its entirety, but easily lends itself to the interpretation of only the black areas—they are driven to become more flexible in their understanding of the instructions. With or without asking whether it is permissible, they will interpret only a part of the blot. From this point on, the pressure—of both the testing situation and the inkblots—toward W interpretations is weakened. Cards IV, V, VI, and VII cluster around or slightly above the 10% incidence ("chance"); Cards II, III, VIII, IX, and especially X stand out by the generally low incidence of W's.

It will be of great help to the examiner to keep these gross trends on each card in mind; striking deviations from them should put him on his guard in the course of the test, and a consequently sharper inquiry into the responses or verbalizations may greatly clarify the diagnostic implications. Thus, a W response on Card X, in a record in which many of the "easier" W's have been passed by, may be capitalized upon; similarly may the absence of a W response to Card I if on usually more difficult cards a W response has been given. In regard to the form level of the W's, a $W-$ on Card V or a Wv on Card II may point up psychopathology or pathological trends, since these responses are rare or absent in the usual normal subject.

W as a Diagnostic Indicator

$W+$ responses are not common in any disorder, but seem to reflect mainly the effects of superior intelligence and intellectualizing trends. Thus, even within a normal group of mediocre attainments, those with cultural interests or idealistic conceptions of their work will generally produce at least one $W+$, which is not otherwise to be expected.

$W+$ is so uncommon in severe depressions as to be a basis for ruling out the depressive possibility in favor of schizophrenia or paranoia if even a single response of this type occurs.

Wv responses are a good index of general maladjustment within the normal range; more than two Wv's strongly suggest a borderline adjustment in a nonpatient. The same tends to be true of $W-$ within the normal range. Wv carries a specific implication of anxiety, however, especially when present in force (more than five in a record of 20 R, for example). Schizophrenics tend to exceed the normal expectancy of W, but by virtue of having more than the usual number of Wv and $W-$, which accumulate with chronicity and deterioration. Thus, if schizophrenia is otherwise indicated, and more than four Wv's are present, there is strong likelihood that the case is *not* acute. The incidence of Wv's is slightly less in paranoid schizophrenia, as is consistent with the clinical picture of paranoid patients as rigid, constricted, cautious personalities. Similarly, obsessive-compulsives tend to have fewer Wv's than other neurotics; not only their rigidity, but also their excessive doubting and critical attitude concerning their own productions, militate against Wv's.

DW (or DrW) is given by approximately one schizophrenic in four, but is extremely rare in other conditions.

Depression appears to interfere with an initial perceptual structuring of the inkblot, and hence with the initiation of associative processes; thus, few W's in general, almost no $W+$, and a tendency toward Wv responses, characterize the depressives. On the other hand, schizophrenia does not prevent the forming of W responses but, because of a lack of cogwheeling of the perceptual and associative processes, impairs the quality of the W responses; so that not only Wv but $W-$ responses occur with significant frequency. $W+$ responses are not altogether eliminated, however, and the coexistence of both very good and very bad W's is frequently a diagnostic indication of schizophrenia.

THE DETAIL RESPONSE: D

The "normal detail" (D) response refers to a part of a card which is conspicuous by its size, its isolation, and the frequency of responses it draws. The D responses stem from, and are regulated by, the perceptual structure of the inkblots, and our discussion of the rationale of the D response will be essentially concerned with its significance for the perceptual organization of the subject. We shall also attempt to show how the place of the *D* responses in the sequence of areas chosen on each card becomes revealing of the subject.

Inquiry and Scoring

A major problem in scoring the Rorschach test is the establishing of criteria for what should be considered a *D*. The criteria we used were given above. In the Rorschach literature there has been much discussion about which of these criteria must be met. In our practice, if any one of these three criteria is clearly met, and if none of the other criteria is clearly flouted, we consider a *D* score justified. Our justification for this rule of thumb is rooted in the perceptual basis of the *D* response: a portion of the inkblot which is conspicuous in size, as well as clearly delineated by its insular or peninsular position, of necessity has a regulating influence upon perceptual organization; it thus appears to represent the most likely starting point for an associative process if and when no—or no further— *W*'s can be given. The compelling character of an area is not, however, necessarily based upon its isolation; there are articulations not externally conspicuous that can be quite compelling—for example, the rabbit frequently seen in the middle of Card V, where a perceptual link or continuity appears to be established between the upper and lower middle projections on Card V. Thus, a *D* response may come about also by reason of the internal dynamics of the perceptual process which drives the subject toward continuations or closures within the perceptual raw material. As to the role played by the position of an area within the whole, areas in the center of the inkblot appear to be most compelling, but areas at the top or at the extremes may be also.[15] The compelling character of such closure can be established only by a high frequency of the response in the general population. Thus, not merely the obvious geometrical articulations of the inkblot, but also regard for statistical frequency should guide the scoring of *D* responses.

In general, our inquiry is usually limited to asking the subject to trace quickly the area used. With progressively increasing experience of the examiner, the need for such inquiry will diminish. It must be stressed that the score *D* refers only to the area chosen, and should in no way be influenced by considerations of peculiarity of content or formulation. But the presence of peculiarities or choice of tiny or arbitrary areas elsewhere in the record indicate that the examiner should check into responses which sound like usual *D* responses; frequently such inquiry uncovers significant

---

[15] The determination of such compelling locations may arise from unconscious sources, as, for example, in the case analyzed by Rorschach and Oberholzer (1923). The issue of compelling position is one common in painting and architecture. [See Zener & Gaffron, 1962.]

and striking deviations from the usual area chosen. Although omissions or additions to the usual area may be tolerated, any striking departure from the area must change the score to *Dr*. If two clear-cut *D* responses are integrated into one response, the score in general remains *D*. For example, on Card IX the response to the pink and green might be "Fire and smoke." But not all combinations of *D* responses necessarily remain *D*. A combination of the lower and upper side projections on Card IV involves considerable perceptual strain to achieve any "closure," though either of these *D*'s interpreted alone can be easily grasped and is quite convincing. Another example of unacceptably strained combination of *D*'s is that of the lower green areas on Card X: either of the darker green areas or the lighter green area intepreted alone is an acceptable *D*, if the subject combines one side of the dark green area with the light green area, this is a strained response in which the associative process has forced two areas arbitrarily together. Combinations of *D*'s involving such strain should be scored *Dr*. On the other hand, the yellow and gray-brown areas on Card X interpreted as a branch with a budding flower constitute a good *D*. Finally, the examiner should carefully note the degree of articulation of the *D* responses; this becomes important in connection with the evaluation of the form level of the record.

The following are the areas on each inkblot which we consider to meet the criteria for the *D* score:

Card I. The entire side area ("wings") or only the upper half of the side area; the entire middle area (the "person") or the upper or lower halves of this middle area. The lower half of the middle area consists of a darker central portion and a light shaded outer portion, and if only the darker portions are interpreted the response should be scored *Dr;* if the entire middle area is interpreted but the lighter shadings of the lower half are omitted, the score may remain *D*, but a tendency toward *Dr* is implied by this exclusion.

Card II. One or both of the black areas; one or both of the upper red areas; the lower middle red area. Sometimes only the upper half of one of the black areas is interpreted, usually as a "dog's head," and the score for this response may remain *D;* however, any peculiarity in the tracing of this area by the subject or in its articulation indicates that a score of *Dr* is more appropriate.

Card III. Each side of the black area without the lower middle area ("persons bending"); the black area usually interpreted as "men" but with the leg excluded; this "leg" by itself; the lower middle black areas in themselves; one or both upper side red areas; the middle red area. Sometimes the area of the frequently seen "man," referring only to his torso and arm, is interpreted ("a bird"), and this may be scored *D;* but it leans toward the *Dr* response, and any peculiarity in the tracing of this area, or any omissions or further inclusions, indicate that the *Dr* score is appropriate.

Card IV. The entire lower side projections ("boots"); the upper side projections ("snakes"); the lower middle projection ("animal head"); the solid black areas in the lower side projections (upside down, frequently as "witches"). If the three lower projections are excluded and only the upper half of the inkblot is used, the score remains *D;* but this response tends to be a *Dr* and may be so scored if irregularities are present.

Card V. The middle portion ("rabbit"); the entire side areas including the extreme side projections; the larger of the two extreme side projections. If the area chosen is one of the side portions, and if the extreme side projections are excluded, a tendency to *Dr* is present. Sometimes the outer half of the side area together with the extreme side projections are seen as a "reclining figure," and this area also tends to be a *Dr*. If either of these two areas described shows any significant extensions or exclusions, the *Dr* score is indicated.

Card VI. The upper middle projection with or without the top side embellishments; the upper side areas ("wings"); the upper projection with the stumplike base ("candle in a candle holder"); either half of the card with or without a division through the middle of the upper projection; the lower bulk of the inkblot without the top projection; the entire middle area ("river and its bank"). This last area inclines toward *Dr,* and the examiner should carefully note its exact delimitations before deciding the score.

Card VII. The upper third of one side ("hand"); the middle third ("animal head"); these two thirds together; the entire lower area ("butterfly"); or half of this lower area in combination with the areas above it.

Card VIII. The side pink area; one or both halves of the middle blue area; the entire upper gray area; the entire pink and orange lower area; the white area above the center of the inkblot ("ribs"; scored *DS*. See below, p. 330.)

Card IX. The upper orange area; the middle green area; one or both halves of the lower pink area; the lateral part of one of the lower pink areas ("head"); the mid-line area ("spine"); and the area where the green fuses with the upper orange ("deer head"). This latter response tends toward *Dr,* and should be scored as such if any peculiarities so indicate.

Card X. Any of the single colored areas; the upper gray areas ("insects") with or without the shaftlike center.

The Rationale of the D Score

It is customary to view the *D* score as an indicator of interest in and responsiveness to the obvious, the practical, and the concrete. This is in contrast to the abstractive and integrative inclinations and abilities indicated by the W score.[16]

Within the framework of this general understanding of the D response, a number of crucial questions arise. How great a share should the D responses have in the average-sized record? What conditions are especially conducive to the coming about of D responses? What are the implications of the place of D responses in the sequence of areas chosen? What is the significance of the quality (form level) of the responses given to the areas scored D? The problem of amount will be taken up in the section on our clinical data, and the question of the quality of the D responses will be considered in our discussion of the form level and determinants. Our emphasis here will be mainly upon the sequence of areas chosen and, in this connection, upon the conditions making for the coming about of D responses.

Usually the D responses follow one or more W responses on each card, excepting perhaps the last four. It appears that once the subject has spent his first efforts at generalizing or integrating, he turns to the obvious details or articulations of the inkblot and responds to these separately. The strain on both the associative and the perceptual organizing processes is much less when the subject is coping only with parts of the inkblot. This tendency in the general population was described by Rorschach himself, and has been corroborated by all subsequent investigators. Common-sense reasoning tells us that persons of quick grasp and wide scope should survey the entire situation that confronts them first, and later turn to its specific details. But this analogy to everyday life must be modified: otherwise it would mean that a subject who had once interpreted an entire inkblot as a "butterfly" would then proceed to elaborate upon its wing structure, its body structure, its kind of antennae. If this happens in the Rorschach test, it is usually an indication of overmeticulousness and circumstantiality. Rather, in going from the whole inkblot to a part of it the subject makes a conceptual shift, so that his next response has an essentially independent existence and usually refers to another realm of ideas. Thus, after a "butterfly," the next response might be "rabbit." In everyday life also a conceptual shift occurs to some extent when a person turns his attention from a survey of a situation to one of its specific details; however,

[16] Although clinical experience provides ample evidence in support of this contention, a full demonstration of its validity could best be accomplished by a careful study in the field of vocational choice and achievement. Such a study would have to encompass both the persons who do the strategic generalizing and those who do the tactical, prosaic work in a variety of vocations; the study would of course need to be controlled by some psychiatric appraisal of the subjects, so that personality factors extraneous to the choice of the vocation and their influence on the D and W scores would be known and included in the interpretation.

the criterion of independent existence is not met in such instances. Furthermore, in interpreting a segment of the inkblot, the resulting background position of the remainder of the inkblot appears to have little influence upon the coming about of a response, whereas in everyday situations, problems of context and interrelationships are obviously crucial. At any rate, it appears that the subject's ability to make such a conceptual shift corresponds to his ability in everyday life to follow an abstract survey through to concrete practical detail.

The usual case is that more D's than W's are obtained, the proportion being roughly two to one. This to a large extent is a consequence of the kind of inkblots used: while the entire inkblots, especially the last three, do not allow a wide range of generalizations (W responses), the range of possibilities for the separate details (D responses) is great. On the other hand, most of the Rorschach inkblots have a sufficiently unitary character that W responses are not severely restricted or completely precluded. When the size of the record increases, the number of D responses usually increases much more rapidly than the number of W's. An anxiety state, or the bland condition of simple schizophrenia, all too frequently prevents any articulation of the inkblot into the areas scored D.

It frequently happens that on a certain inkblot the subject is suddenly able to produce only D responses. This may be due to the structure of the inkblot, as can be established from the trend of the general population, or it may be due to some specific aspect of the inkblot which, for this subject, precludes giving W's. Thus, to give a good W, or for that matter any W, on Card X is far more difficult than on Card I, and the converse is true with respect to D responses. Card I is a unit and is easy to grasp as such; Card X is extremely fragmentary, and easy to grasp only in its separate parts. D responses as emanating from the difficulties of a specific subject may be seen when, for example, he can give only D responses to Card IV even though he has given W responses for the previous three cards. Here it seems that the amount of anxiety in the subject is great enough for the diffuse quality of Card IV to disturb him, and he is unable to grasp the whole card. The subject may express his difficulty in other ways, such as in complete failure, Wv responses, tiny (Dr), peripheral (De), or arbitrary $(W-)$ responses. This multiplicity of ways in which anxiety may be expressed makes it difficult to validate statistically the role played by anxiety in limiting the subject to D responses; in everyday practice it frequently becomes obvious, however.

Conditions other than the nature of the inkblots or the presence of anxiety may also restrict the subject to D responses. A subject may be overmeticulous and dissatisfied with the abstractions he makes in reference to the entire inkblot, inasmuch as *for him* there are too many discrepancies between the blot and his abstraction. Or a subject may be too practical or too inert, and will on any or all of the inkblots grasp at only the simplest and most obvious areas for his responses. High-grade feeble-minded subjects and psychopathic personalities, particularly the younger ones, also appear very prone to focus on the D areas: the impairment of surveying and abstracting ability in these groups needs no elaboration here. This finding is not true for all such subjects, some of whom may resort to vague or arbitrary whole responses. In general, then, a restriction of areas chosen to the most obvious ones may result from an extremely practical orientation toward new situations, from an impairment of abstractive or integrative ability by the impact of strong anxiety, from inertia of the type frequently found in depressives, from overmeticulousness which does not permit and cannot accept abstractions or complex integrations, from a native limitation of endowment such as is found in feeble-minded subjects, or from a pathological impairment of abstractive and survey abilities characteristic of many psychopathic maladjustments.

Although progressing from W to D responses is usual, the reverse sequence sometimes occurs—that is, only after one or more secure D responses does the subject attempt interpretation of the whole inkblot. Common-sense reasoning leads one to expect, and clinical experience corroborates, that if this sequence is followed on several different cards we are probably dealing with a plodding kind of intelligence which looks first for the most obvious details and only afterwards makes generalizations. This tendency of the subject becomes most manifest on cards with strong colors, or with clear-cut piecemeal articulation, or with intense diffuse shadings. In general, however, even the plodding person will begin a number of the cards with a response on the Wo level. But if this D to W sequence is systematically followed on all cards, we have a fairly reliable indication of a personality which is pedantic, overcautious, lacking in spontaneity and boldness, and annoyingly "logical."

In the pathological range, a shift of sequence from $W \rightarrow D$ to $D \rightarrow W$ always derives its meaning from the card upon which the reversal occurs. On the strongly colored cards, this impairment in quality of approach appears to stem from disturbing affects; on strongly shaded cards, it stems from strong anxiety; on the cards where a movement response is compelling (Card III), it stems from ideational symptoms. When the reversal is extended to all the cards, an obstreperous, self-righteous, merciless, paranoid logic is suggested.

We have attempted to show here some of the ways in which the location of the D responses in the sequence of areas chosen allows for a further understanding of the subject's manner of approach to situations in everyday life. A number of problems connected with "sequence analysis" must be highlighted here. First of all, in clinical work the number of responses in the average record is usually so low that the consistency or inconsistency of sequence is difficult to evaluate. Furthermore, analyzing the sequence of areas chosen is almost always more relevant to constructing a personality picture than to the establishment of a diagnosis. In general, a too strong emphasis upon sequence analysis would appear to make the test overcomplicated and be detrimental to its practical application. The clinical examiner need have only a general understanding of the idea itself.

Theoretically, we are on unsure footing with regard to sequence analysis. It seems relatively easy to understand that when anxiety prevents perceptual articulation of diffuse shading, the associative process may start out from, and center on, a well-articulated detail in which the impact of diffuse shading is not too great. It is possible to understand that an articulation of the rest of the card may progressively develop to the point where the subject can turn back to the entire inkblot and give a W response. It may be conjectured that in the usual sequence of giving a W response first, we have an indication that the associative processes have started out from several points of the perceptual raw material and converged to a synthesizing or abstracting response—and that the stages passed through in the course of this synthesis are picked up only later as D responses. There is, however, much arbitrariness in such conjectures, and until crucial experiments have taught us more about these processes, the examiner should pursue a sequence analysis cautiously.

D as a Diagnostic Indicator

There is little to be said diagnostically about this very common score. The kinds of patients we see have average percentages of D that cluster between 45% and 55%. This is somewhat lower than what would appear to be the expectancy (60% to 65%), and is referable largely to the generally low number of responses given by our subjects. In a record with a low number of responses, the D's usually bear the brunt of the decrease; that is to say, a good share of the popular whole responses remain, a number of vague or arbitrary W's usually appear, and an occasional Dr or Dd or S response may come into the record. When R is low, therefore, the $D\%$ may be expected to drop to 45 or 50. Chronic and deteriorated schizophrenics fairly often show a marked underemphasis on D (less than 30%), a reflection of their loss of feel for the obvious; this loss is usually clear in clinical appraisal of these cases. Many simple schizophrenics show this same extreme tendency, and clinically this group shows many points of similarity with other chronic schizophrenics. $D\%$ tends to run low (under 50%) in some neurotics: in those suffering from anxiety and depression the D's are replaced largely by vague Wv's, and in neurasthenics by $W—$'s, probably because of anxiety in the former group and general inadequacy in the latter.

THE Dd SCORE

The areas in responses scored Dd stand out by reason of their clarity, in spite of their small size. The small size makes them unlike the D responses; yet they are not too tiny like some Dr responses, nor perceptually unbalanced like those Dr responses that cover large areas. Almost all of the areas scored Dd have a peninsular relationship to the bulk of the ink-blot. Examples are: the upper middle projections in Card I, "hands"; the upper middle projection in Card II, "castle" or "hands"; the side projection from the lower orange in Card VIII, "dog head." Although the Dd score is determined only by the choice of area, almost all Dd's given show a sharp perceptual articulation and hence are usually on a high form level. These responses are usually given with an air of pleasure by the subject, and appear to indicate an interest in the fine details of situations, without finickiness or overconcern with them. A few such responses in a record point to a person with sharp observation and a sense for the aesthetic. They appear to occur in highly productive patients (e.g., overideational preschizophrenics), and to decrease when inhibition becomes strong or when visual organizing ability becomes sluggish, as in neurasthenics.

THE Do SCORE[17]

Strictly speaking, a Do response does not refer to a specific kind of area chosen. It refers to the segregation of an area which is usually seen as a part of a common W or D response of good form level: the specific justification for the Do score is that the area retains the same interpretation as in the larger area. For example, if a subject sees only the heads of two men on Card III and does not see at least their trunks and arms, the score is Do. The implication is that some inhibitory factor has overruled the compelling cohesive power of an entire area of the inkblot, and limited the response to only a portion.

To a large extent, the need for inquiry and the correctness of scoring will hinge upon the examiner's familiarity with what are the common— though not necessarily popular—responses. With progressive experience the examiner becomes sensitive to the presence of Do responses, or tendencies toward them. Some difficulty may arise in differentiating a series of Do

---

[17] The score Do is the symbol for "oligophrenic detail," the name given by Rorschach to this type of response because he encountered it most frequently in feeble-minded cases.

responses from a progressive description of an integrated response. In such cases it is practical to delay inquiry until the card has been removed from the subject's sight, and then to ask the subject to relate what he saw. If the subject's verbalizations were communicating merely a progressive description, a concise statement of an integrated response usually emerges in inquiry; but if the subject was giving rather a series of *Do* responses ("a leg . . . and here's a hand . . . and this could be a head"), inquiry will again elicit an enumeration of the same responses, and at most the statement, "It could have been a man but I could not quite make it out." If an isolated *Do* occurs, it is frequently helpful to inquire into whether doubt about the rest of the figure or absence of its perception lay behind the response: the differentiation of an essentially perceptual from an essentially associative disturbance usually becomes clear upon such inquiry.

This statement implies our view of the psychological processes underlying the *Do* response: such a response may be due either to fragmentary perceptual organization, or to a failure of the associative processes to pave the way for integrations by supplying connections or elaborating the areas surrounding the *Do* area. Fragmentary percepts appear most frequently in psychotically disorganized and in feeble-minded subjects; poor integrative support by the associative processes appears most frequently and clearly in blocked psychotics and in compulsive neurotics; both fragmentation and weakness of integration seem to account for some incidence of *Do* responses in depressives. It is impressive and instructive to see a compulsive person describe on Card III a head, a leg, and an arm, and later comment, "But the whole thing just does not make a whole figure." Generally the response "man" on Card III represents a quick abstraction—that is, the response emerges into consciousness in full-fledged form. If such quick abstractions are not the specific subject's manner of approach to situations, a detailed perceptual articulation with a subsequent integration into a complete figure may occur; in the compulsive's difficulty described above, however, we see how both abstraction and integration are weakened as an expression of compulsive meticulousness, rigidity, doubt, or self-criticism. It is similarly impressive to hear a feeble-minded subject or a completely disorganized schizophrenic point out "a beak" (the usual head) on Card III, without even reaching the idea of a head. In the blocked schizophrenics the case is somewhat different: here the fragmentation occurs in the associative process, which is jumpy, and parts of its content may be tossed into consciousness and verbalized prematurely. In these cases, a simple question about the response usually catalyzes the process and elicits the answer, "Some kind of a bird, I suppose."

The specific interpretation, diagnostic or otherwise, to be given to *Do* responses hinges on several considerations. It is important to know on which cards the *Do* responses occurred: thus, the presence of strong anxiety in a subject, and especially in a child, can give rise to *Do* responses to the heavily shaded cards. We have seen in discussing the *Wv* responses that strong anxiety may impair both perceptual organizing abilities and smoothness of the stream of associative content; experience shows that *Do* responses may also be manifestations of strong anxiety. If anxiety is the underlying factor making for *Do* responses in a subject, we will usually also find an abundance of *Dr* responses on the heavily shaded cards. When the general picture supplied by the record is that of a severe depression, the occurrence of *Do* responses refers to an inertness and incapacitation of the entire psychological functioning, but specifically of the perceptual organization and wealth and vitality of associative content. If the *Do* responses occur in a record in which schizophrenic indications are abundant, they imply a poor prognosis because of disintegrative tendencies in the psychological functioning of the schizophrenic. If they occur in a record with a great prevalence of movement responses over color responses, with a high and quite sharp form level, and with no peculiarities, the diagnosis of an obsessive-compulsive neurosis is suggested. If they occur in a record characterized by great quantitative productivity, they indicate an inclination in the subject to lose sight of connections, to be unable or disinclined to follow through ideas once conceived, and lead to the final inference that his productivity is an expression of great pressure rather than a free flow of ideational content.

THE TOTAL AMOUNT OF OTHER AREAS CHOSEN: *DR*

We have segregated for general consideration the total amount of the other kinds of areas used by the subjects in their responses, besides *W, D, Dd,* and *Do.* The pathological significance of the choice of some of the remaining areas is greater than that of others, but all of them can carry some. Four major kinds of response are subsumed for this purpose under the symbol *DR*: those using a very small or perceptually unbalanced area (scored *Dr*), those which interpret only the contour of the inkblot and hence not really an area (*De*), and those using a white space, either large (*S*) or small (*s*). Diagnostically it appears that a great massing of such responses is definitely limited to those clinical groups in which ideational (especially obsessional) symptom formation is outstanding: foremost, over-ideational preschizophrenics, who often accumulate 10 or more *DR*'s, but also mixed neurotics and obsessive-compulsives. Their absence may point to inhibition, depression, or some neurasthenialike condition.

THE *De* SCORE

The symbol *De* means "edge detail"—in other words, the area chosen is not really an area but only part of the contour lines of an inkblot. Rorschach included this kind of response under the general heading *Dd*, together with the responses we score *Dr* and *Dd*. Recent investigators have found it practical to differentiate between these.[18] In our experience, a specific significance seemed to accrue to the *De* response, and we consequently scored it separately. Typical *De* responses are those given to the upper and lower contours on Card V: "profiles, faces." The majority of *De* responses will be profiles or faces, but "coastlines" are also frequent.

Usually no inquiry is necessary to establish this score. Sometimes it becomes necessary, however, to distinguish *De* responses from *Dr* responses. This is easily done by determining whether there is any surface differentiation of the blot proper implied in the response. The examiner should not be misled into giving a *Dr* score when in addition to the profile the subject points out a speck which might be an eye, or when a coastline response includes a very thin "beach" area. In these cases the amount of surface differentiation of the blot is so meager that the *De* score will best convey the nature of the response.

In our experience, *De* responses occur most frequently on strongly shaded cards, and there in a setting of poor, vague, or no other responses. In such settings it becomes clear that the subject is unable to penetrate the heavily shaded areas perceptually, and it is *as if* a swing of attention to the outer edges of the blot constituted a way out, an escape from a situation in which articulation is prevented by anxiety.[19] This is especially indicated if after a long reaction time the subject offers as his first responses *De*'s which are, in addition, small in size and not frequently given. Thus, this manner of approach to the inkblots allows for the characterological inference of a specific defensive tendency: escape reaction to anxiety-arousing situations.[20] We find this manner of approach in some subjects' coping with the colored cards; the inference here is that the escape reaction is to situations likely to arouse strong affect.[21]

De responses may also appear in the rich protocols of introspective, highly intelligent normal subjects, as well as in those of patients with ideational symptoms; here they may result from the subject's systematic

[18] See, e.g., Klopfer and Kelley (1942) [and Klopfer et al., 1954].

[19] For an amplification of this point, see the discussion of the relationship between shading and anxiety, pp. 397-401.

[20] This is frequently encountered in cases of addiction [and character disorder generally.—Ed.]

[21] For an amplification of this point, see the discussion of the relation between colors and affect, pp. 376-383.

search for more and more response possibilities. In this setting the *De* responses will more likely occur late among the responses to the card. Finally, experience seems to indicate that in meager records the occurrence of a few obvious *De* responses—such as those on the upper and lower edges of Card V and on the side green edge on Card IX—are an indication of a more or less structuralized and stabilized character pattern of avoidance. If other—particularly if unusual—*De* responses appear in a meager record, however, they represent the threat of strong anxiety and an attempt to escape.

For clinical application of the test, it is always important to know on which cards a specific type of response tends to accumulate in the general population. Card V is striking in its pre-eminent tendency to pull *De* responses. Most of these are either an interpretation of the entire upper half of the contour as the profile of a face, or of a small section of the upper contour near the center as a "devil's profile." Accordingly, the pathological implications of these two *De* responses on Card V should be minimized. In contrast, Cards II, III, VI, and VIII elicit the fewest *De* responses, and their presence on any of these cards should be considered to be of pathological weight. In general, however, one *De* response can occur in almost any record.

THE *Dr* SCORE

When the area chosen is small, perceptually unbalanced, or arbitrarily delimited, the *Dr* score is in place.

Scoring and Inquiry

When tiny areas are chosen, the differentiation from *D* is simple; it becomes more difficult when the area chosen is sizable. Here one must be guided by the rule that in a *D* score there must be a convincing perceptual balance (closure) within the area chosen, and that if this balance is lacking the score must be *Dr*.[22] It often becomes necessary to inquire into the outline of the subject's response. Such inquiry will establish whether there is an unsatisfactory, haphazard delimitation of the area chosen. A danger arises only when the subject is in a confusional or disoriented condition: good (*D*) responses may then be so haphazardly pointed out that the examiner is tempted to score a *Dr*. Confusional and disoriented patients will be the least likely to give *Dr* responses. It is better in such cases to score by inference and experience, rather than by the subject's inadequate responses to inquiry.

---

[22] Balance or closure should not be confused with *Prägnanz,* which corresponds on the Rorschach test to "goodness of form": the form level may be high or low in *Dr* responses, and should never decide the score for the area chosen.

In this connection an important principle of scoring and inquiry may well be formulated: the subject's statements in the inquiry should never be taken at face value. The examiner must always evaluate these statements against what his experience has shown to be the usual response to the area in question; this cross-evaluation is the basis for security and consistency of scoring. This principle of inquiry has its greatest relevance to the scoring of determinants, form level, and the scores subsumed in the fifth major scoring category: in connection with the area chosen its significance is usually limited to appraising the responses of confused and disoriented subjects.

If the subject is giving a quantitatively rich record which includes many quickly given *Dr* responses, the examiner will find it helpful to ask him to point out the area as each response is verbalized. Subjects who give many *Dr* responses almost always have difficulty in relocating all of them if inquiry is delayed, even if only until the card in question is completed. However, the experienced examiner will be acquainted with a great many of the *Dr* responses, and can save considerable time in these cases by being able to skim briefly over the familiar ones.

The Rationale of the Dr Score

Clinically, it is important to recognize that *Dr* responses may emanate from different sources and, from the context in which they appear, to infer these sources. In introducing this discussion we may advance the following gross formulation: *Dr* responses may stem from the impairment by strong anxiety of perceptual organizing ability, or from an intensity and over-activity of the associative process in conditions characterized by excessive ideational activity, pathological or otherwise. To clarify this formulation, we shall organize the following discussion around those clinical groups in which the *Dr* responses carry most clearly the indications of the processes giving rise to them.

How can we characterize the perceptual difficulties which may give rise to *Dr* responses? It appears that anxiety may prevent the subject from penetrating and articulating the inkblot as a whole, and making an abstraction about it; it may prevent him from sufficiently articulating the entire inkblot into its prominent segments. Consequently the subject may be driven to vague generalizations based on associative processes set off by few perceptual features of the blot, or he may resort to areas which are unusually small and which are "torn out" of the inkblot. In other words, the perceptual organization remains piecemeal and the associative processes set off by the inkblot are kept isolated by the subject's anxiety; in a sense, the choice and interpretation of the tiny areas are so conceived as to force them to remain independent of the rest of the inkblot, and not support any spread of the response to further portions. If a tendency to extend the response is encountered in a setting where anxiety drives the subject toward tiny *Dr* responses, the result may be a larger *Dr* or a *D* or *W* response which is completely vague, or even a *DrW* response. Thus, when anxiety severely restricts the perceptual organizing processes and isolates the associative processes, any attempt to get beyond the restrictions usually ends only in further difficulties or in an increase of vagueness and arbitrariness.

But further considerations are necessary for establishing the connection between anxiety and *Dr* responses. Experience indicates that cases of anxiety hysteria are prone to give a noticeable number of them; and it seems reasonable to conclude that their intense anxiety is responsible for the weakening of perceptual organization which comes to expression partly in these *Dr* responses. However, an analysis of the content assigned to these *Dr* areas frequently reveals it to be significant of the subject's symptoms. This significance may be immediately grasped through the nature of the content, may be suggested by a perseveration of content all through the subject's *Dr* responses, or may be uncovered only by the psychiatric study of the case. It appears that because of the weakness and lability of perceptual organization, the overvalent ideas or symbols of the subject can find or force their way through perceptually weak spots to more or less hidden symbolic expression (cliffs, towers, teeth, tweezers). Yet this pressure of pathological associative material need not be successful in connection with all *Dr*'s based on perceptual difficulty: our point is that, if anxiety does impair perceptual organizing ability and drives the subject to very small areas of the card, his regard for the objective reality of the inkblot becomes considerably lessened—that is, he can fall back upon any number of possibilities offered by the associative processes, and easily foist them upon a tiny simple area which requires neither genuine abstraction, integration, nor articulation. These considerations summarize to some extent what experience suggests: the occurrence of *Dr* responses in a setting of intense anxiety indicates that the subject, instead of attempting to work them out, is attempting to escape situations in the articulation of which he is handicapped by his anxieties. He is driven to an overalertness which no longer distinguishes important stimulations from unimportant ones, and leaves him overresponsive to too many irrelevant stimulations. The overt clinical picture will be one of generalized restlessness.

Thus far we have limited our discussion to the perceptual difficulties leading to *Dr* responses; let us turn now to those *Dr* responses which appear to emanate more from characteristic trends or psychopathology of the associative processes. If we turn to our clinical cases, it appears that obsessive-compulsive neurotics, overideational preschizophrenics, and acute schizophrenics amass this second kind. These are the ideationally most productive of all our clinical groups, those in whom the associative processes show the greatest quantitative—if not qualitative—wealth and flexibility. It appears that these subjects search for such responses *to begin with,* and quite frequently produce them in great quantities—often sharp, excellently conceived, and original—with little or no experience of perceptual difficulty. In cases with acute anxiety, the reverse is rather the rule. Thus, the perceptual organization of these ideationally productive groups is in general unimpaired, but is subservient to the pressure of the associative processes. It is true that in some members of the ideationally productive group, perceptual organization may be weak either because of the great anxiety which may be present as in anxiety hysterics, or because of a general psychotic disorganization, as in acute schizophrenics. If we go more specifically into the *Dr* responses of these groups, and especially of overideational preschizophrenics, we discover that if sexual preoccupation is clinically overwhelming every peninsular area may become a "penis" and every invagination of the contour may become a "vagina." This observation suggests a similarity between the symbollike *Dr*'s of anxiety hysterics and those of preschizophrenics or even obsessives. This similarity suggests the possibility that the *Dr*'s of anxiety hysterics originating in anxiety-weakened perceptual organization, and those of the groups of intense ideational activity (obsessive-compulsives, overideational preschizophrenics) originating in a search for a greater quantity of responses, are not radically different. It is possible that in the latter group also the *Dr*'s are expressions of anxiety, but anxiety is turned into channels of intellectualizing, into a pressure of ideational output. The fact is that many clinically very anxious preschizophrenics and acute schizophrenics have none of the usual indications of anxiety in the Rorschach test, but tend to mass *Dr* responses. Zulliger (1933) contended that *Dr*'s indicate anxiety. Our experience with children bears this out.

The summary inference from a massing of *Dr*'s thrown up by associative processes appears to be that they refer to a divorce of ideation from reality; whether this split is accepted (psychosis) or considered ego alien (obsessional neurosis) is indicated in the subject's attitude toward and elaboration of his *Dr* responses.

It is clear that nonanxious cases can also give *Dr* responses; any inclination to quibbling, any interest in the extravagant, any interference with perceptual organization stemming from sources other than anxiety, may give rise to them. Here one of the characteristic features of the Rorschach test comes into relief which plagues attempts at statistical validation: there are no one-to-one relationships between scores and specific psychological trends, even if mainly one psychological trend accounts for the prevalence of a specific score. The need for clearly segregated experimental standardization groups is apparent. But such groups can practically never be clearly segregated with respect to all the relationships to be investigated; attempts at segregation make for only small groups, and even these, at the present stage of clinical psychiatric theory and nosology, may have a dubious clarity of delineation. We have dwelt here upon the complexities of a validational study in order to make it clear why it is in many instances difficult to obtain clear-cut statistical differentiations.

Let us again remember that the different cards offer different amounts of resistance to perceptual organization; hence, certain cards may be more likely to elicit *Dr* responses than others. Four cards stand out in accumulation of *Dr* responses: VI, VII, IX, and X. Cards VI and VII (but also IV) are the most strongly shaded, and Cards IX and X are the most strongly colored of all. Later on we shall attempt to establish a specific relationship between shading and anxiety indications, and between colors and affect indications. With these relationships in mind, it could be argued that the *Dr*'s tend to accumulate on the anxiety-indicating cards, but also on the cards likely to elicit affect indications. Cards III and V appear to attract the fewest *Dr* responses (5% or less of all *Dr*'s are given for each). *Dr* responses occurring on cards where they are usually infrequent must be given more pathological weight; and any peculiarity about a *Dr* response, or any symbolic content in it, increases its pathological weight. But in addition, a subject who accumulates many *Dr* responses by giving them on many cards, regardless of the perceptual difficulty offered by the specific card, is revealing a pathological trend in his associative processes indicative of the presence of a great extent and variety of ideational symptoms. One *Dr* response in each record is well within the normal range. It must be stressed, however, that the quality of a single *Dr*—its location, extravagance, unusual sharpness, or absurdity—may carry more pathological weight than an accumulation of several nondescript *Dr* responses.

Dr *as a Diagnostic Indicator*

(1) Concentration of *Dr* responses in the main implies that ideational symptoms are prominent; it is most notable in overideational preschizophrenics but the trend is also apparent in obsessive-compulsives, mixed neurotics, and acute schizophrenics. (2) The lowest concentration of *Dr*'s in general coincides with clinical groups with the least ideational productivity or greatest monotony of ideation; *Dr* responses tend to be absent in depressive psychoses, simple schizophrenias, and depressionlike neuroses (anxiety and depression, and neurasthenia). (3) One or two (less than 10%) *Dr* responses without peculiarities may occur in the record of any normal subject; strong anxiety within the normal range may find expression

in the choice of *Dr* areas to a slightly greater extent than the usual. (4) When *Dr*'s are given to unusual places, and especially on Card X, they have more pathological significance than usual; this is often one of the indications of acute schizophrenia.

THE *S* AND *s* SCORES

The symbols *S* and *s* indicate that the area chosen for response was part of the white background rather than the inkblot proper. *S* refers to large white areas, *s* refers to smaller white areas.

Inquiry and Scoring

If the area of a response is only a white space, a full *S* or *s* score is given; if a space response is given in connection with a *W, D,* or *Dr* response, the *S* score is represented as additional (*WS, DS, DrS*). Inquiry is almost never necessary to locate these responses, but sometimes is to establish whether any areas surrounding the white space are involved.

We shall present here a description of the outstanding space responses which can be considered of good form level. The possibilities for poor space responses are practically infinite.

Card I. The upper of the inner white spaces interpreted as some figure, human or bearlike, in a sheet.

Card II. The central white space seen as a "top" or "dancer" or, with the card turned upside down, as a "turnip"; with the card turned upside down the space between the two red splotches seen as a front view of a cat's head and shoulders; with the card in its normal position, the space between the two upper red splotches and between the splotches and the black areas seen as "feet (Charlie Chaplin's)"; with the card upside down, the spaces between the two red splotches and the black area seen as the profiles of two women looking up.

Card III. The space between the two black areas seen as the outline of a vase or as a "shirt front" (usually with the central red area as a "bow tie"); the space above the lowest central dark areas seen as a "delicate butterfly" with the light gray streaks usually indicating wing articulation; with the card turned upside down, the entire central white area seen as some kind of "piece of porcelain," sometimes of the type found on electrical transmission poles.

Card IV. The three white spaces adjoining the lower middle area seen as "the figure of a woman holding a baby" or "woman with her arm upraised and a loose sleeve hanging down"; the lowermost of these three spaces seen as a profile view of a dog looking upward; with the card held sideways, the middle of these white spaces seen as a "duck."

Card V. The white space adjoining the lower middle projection seen as the "figure of a reclining woman (Queen Victoria).".

Card VI. There are no acceptable space responses on this card given with any frequency.

Card VII. The central white space seen as an "arrowhead"; with the card upside down, the central white space seen as the front-view outline of a "head" ("George Washington," "the Sphinx") or as a "lamp."

Card VIII. The upper central white space seen as some kind of "insignia (caduceus)"; this same space seen as "a devil's face" or "mandarin-like face"; with the card turned sideways, half of this space seen as the figure of a "resting camel" or as "teeth"; with the card turned upside down, this same space seen as the figures of two people kneeling and facing each other; the white space between the central pink and blue areas seen as a figure of a "bird or bat."

Card IX. The upper central white space extending down into the brownish areas seen as a "vase" or "light bulb"; with the card upside down, the same area seen as "a form used for fitting dresses"; with the card upside down, the small white space between the pink and green areas seen as the "figure of a kneeling man (Jesus)" or the "figure of a man walking along holding up the skirt of his robe."

Card X. The white space under the middle blue area seen as "some goddesslike figure (Hindu)" or as an "owl"; the white space above the middle blue area and extending up between the upper gray areas seen as the "head and trunk of a person" or as a "Buddha squatting"; with the card upside down, the white spaces on the outside of the large pink areas seen as the "profile of a woman."

These space responses are all of good form level, but nevertheless do not lack pathological implication. The reader may also notice, if he checks these responses on the cards, that many of them can easily be integrated with some area adjoining them. For example, the Buddhalike figure described on Card X might become an "oriental prince with a high and elaborate headdress" (the upper gray). When such integrations are achieved, the *S* is scored only as an additional area chosen; but it must not be lost sight of that the white space itself bears the major emphasis. Hence the additional score should in no way tone down its significance in the evaluation of the record. This point must be especially stressed, because there are other additional space responses which carry much less significance. If a subject says on Card VII, "It looks like a string of islands and this space in the middle could be a kind of bay they form or a harbor," there is essentially no articulation of this white area; it represents rather an elaboration of the response to the gray areas. Thus, the examiner will have to keep in mind—since the scoring system does not directly convey it to him—whether space responses are sharply articulated or vague; it is the sharply articulated white spaces that carry the full significance of the score.

In evaluating space responses the examiner must be familiar with the tendency of the different cards to elicit them. Cards II, VII, and IX—with large, clear-cut spaces in their centers—are most likely to elicit space responses. In contrast, Cards IV and V show a very low incidence of space responses; accordingly, their occurrence on these two cards should be interpreted with full emphasis. The significance of those occurring on Cards II, VII, or IX should not be overemphasized unless there is an unusual twist or peculiarity to the response, a sequence of separate responses to the same white area, or a general accumulation of S responses in the record. In general, also, S responses have less significance when given after a number of usual responses to a card.

The Rationale of the Space Responses

Rorschach stated in his *Psychodiagnostics,* and our experience corroborates, that space responses refer to some kind of oppositional tendency of the subject. No statistical validation of this contention was offered by him; there are several reasons why such a validation constitutes a difficult problem. Persons who are prone to give a great many responses, and among them especially Dr's, are also inclined to give S responses in abundance. It might well be argued that this type of productivity is always a consequence of doubt (opposition directed toward one's own thinking). This type of record usually includes a prevalence of movement responses; and Rorschach suggested, and our experience corroborates, that in a setting of movement prevalence, the occurrence of space responses indicates that the opposition tendency is directed toward the subject's own self and thinking. The significance of space responses in a record where colors are prevalent changes to opposition directed outward in the form of negativism and stubbornness. In short, the many possible clinical expressions of such an opposition tendency seriously hamper any attempt at validation.

Furthermore, not all definitely negativistic or doubt-ridden people have space responses in their records; oppositional tendencies may find other or no avenues of expression in the test. In order for a sharply articulated space response to come about, the subject must have considerable perceptual versatility and associative freedom. Thus, poor endowment may preclude the occurrence of the significant space responses; or inhibition may block them out while driving the subject to the most obvious and popular responses, and forcing him to give up the cards quickly.

How is it that space responses seem to refer to an opposition tendency? The first answer appears to lie in the common-sense consideration that a subject who interprets the white spaces is actually doing the reverse of what the instructions imply. This rationale is, however, in dire need of verification by means of figure-ground experiments, in which the ease of reversal of the figure-ground relationship is systematically varied, and the findings are integrated with the clinical evaluation of the subjects' personality make-up.

Actually, the highest relative incidence of space responses occurs in paranoid conditions; and clinically, the oppositional implications of projective delusions are relatively clear in such cases. Otherwise, a large number of *S* responses appear most frequently in the clinical groups showing the greatest wealth and intensity of associative processes; e.g., overideational preschizophrenics and mixed neurotics. Frequently the record of a paranoid patient is markedly coarctated with few responses or determinants, but still with a great number of space responses. In such a rigid, inhibitory setting, the occurrence of many space responses of good quality should always put the examiner on the alert for the possible presence of projective-paranoid trends.

THE INTERRELATIONSHIPS OF THE SCORES REFERRING TO THE
AREA CHOSEN: THE MANNER OF APPROACH

If the average-sized record contains 25 responses, seven or eight will be expected to be *W,* 14 to 16 *D,* and the remaining two or three responses an occasional *Dr, Dd, S,* or *s.* This 1:2 relationship between the *W* and *D* responses is subject to considerable change when *R* greatly increases or decreases, since *W* usually changes at a slower rate. To a large extent, this is attributable to the perceptual characteristics of the inkblots, and to some extent to the nature of the instructions. Thus, in the larger records a prevalence of *D* responses (1:3), and in the smaller records a relative prevalence of *W* responses (1:1), is to be expected. In the case of meager records, any deviation from an approximately 1:1 ratio may be considered the person's characteristic manner of approach, although not necessarily indicative of any specific disorder. In a setting of few responses, the retention of the 1:2 ratio indicates that most likely the generalizing, surveying, and integrative abilities of the subject—and not merely his quantitative productivity—are poor. Whether this poverty stems from poor endowment or poor cultural background, or from a rigid meticulousness, or from any pathological process, cannot be decided from this dimension of the test alone. If the presence of a neurosis is established by other indications, the retention of the 1:2 ratio in a record with few responses suggests the presence of great anxiety and strong inhibition; if the presence of a psychosis is indicated by other signs, the preservation of this 1:2 ratio suggests the presence of a depressive psychosis. If the ratio shifts to 1:2 or 1:4 in a record which has fewer than 14 or 15 responses, these indications become still more forceful.

When R is low and the W's prevail over the D's in a 2:1 relationship, two inferences are possible for the normal range: this may be a sign of quality ambition, which will be confirmed by a prevalence of $W+$ responses, or it may be a sign of an anxious adjustment which will be confirmed by a prevalence of Wv responses. The presence of clinical psychopathology cannot be decided from this dimension alone; yet the possibility of a schizoid disorder or an anxiety state will be supported by this 2:1 relationship if other signs of a maladjustment of either kind are also present.

When R is high and the relationship of the W's to the D's is less than 1:3—for example, 1:4 or 1:5—and if at the same time the absolute number of W's falls below eight to 10, some kind of pathology is suggested. The ratio may, for example, indicate a very productive psychopath in whom survey ability is characteristically quite impaired. In records with a very large number of responses (e.g., around 100), a 1:2 or 1:1 relationship is also frequently a pathological indicator. It may occur in normal subjects given to overgeneralizing, however, or in unusually able people. In the pathological range, such a ratio usually refers to especially able preschizophrenics or to schizophrenics with expansive delusional ideation, present or potential.

Before leaving the $W:D$ relationship, it must be stated that whether the responses are many or few, the location of the D responses on the different cards must always be noted. If special prevalence of D over W responses occurs because of a concentration of D on the last three (colored) cards, it cannot be considered as strong as one sustained throughout: the last three cards, especially VIII and X, lend themselves easily to many D responses and offer little opportunity for W responses. Conversely, a W prevalence sustained through the last three cards must be considered much stronger than one abandoned on them.

There is no expected frequency of Dd responses, nor do they carry any pathological weight. Nevertheless, too many in an average or small-sized record indicate a tendency toward Dr responses, as well as an escape from coping with the larger areas of the inkblot and hence some impairment of surveying and abstractive abilities.

No Do response should occur in the average-sized record. If Do's are present in a record with a low number of responses, with a decrease of W and an absence of $W+$, the presence of a depression must be considered. At the other extreme, if the number of responses increases above the average, and if the Dr responses also increase, the occurrence of Do usually refers to an obsessional neurosis.

The responses included in the general heading *DR* should not exceed 10% of the record. In general, their absolute incidence increases where the total number of responses shows a sharp rise. Their number should not be proportionate with the increase in *R,* however; rather, the *DR%* should preferably fall below 10%. Thus, in a record of 20 responses, one or two *Dr* or *S* responses may not carry special significance; nor in a record of 40 responses, will two to three. If *DR* responses increase faster than *R,* the presence of pathological ideation is indicated. Some of these *DR* responses may occur under the pressure of strong anxiety, but even in this case the indication is that the anxiety drives the subject toward greater ideational productivity.[23] Space responses, if massed in a small to average-sized record, raise the question of paranoid involvement. If a few space responses occur in a large-sized record, they refer rather to general ideational productivity, although the implication for the presence of some oppositional tendency is present.

Of course, the examiner will always need to turn to other aspects of the record to confirm the leads given by this analysis of the manner of approach.

THE DETERMINANTS

The determinants are those perceptual qualities of the areas chosen which initiate and regulate the associative processes underlying the response, and justify the assignment of a specific content to a specific area. These qualities may be the *form* of the area, its *shading,* its *color,* its characteristics which give the impression of *movement*—or any combination of these qualities. The scrutiny of these determinants lies at the core of any evaluation of the qualitative richness of the record. Furthermore, they are often considered the test's best indicators of personality characteristics and of psychopathology.

Since the publication of Rorschach's *Psychodiagnostics* (1921), the number of determinants which are separately scored has greatly increased. Such refinements make sense in so far as they call attention to qualitative features of the record not thus far systematized, but only if the psychological significance of these new determinants and a reasonable frequency can be established. But the psychological meaning of the majority of the added scores that have been promulgated has been even less validly established than those of the scores originally introduced by Rorschach; they refer mainly to features by no means as conspicuous as those the original

---

[23] In children, however, the usual implication of a high incidence of *DR* responses is one of strong anxiety only, excepting in certain high-grade mental defectives.

scores refer to, and their relation to major characteristics of adjustment and maladjustment is harder to assess by experience or to capture by statistics. Furthermore, too much refinement of scoring gives the impression that interpretation can be achieved by consulting a handbook of scores, and without genuine understanding of the theory of personality and psychopathology. The use of the test in this manner becomes mechanical and out of touch with clinical reality; and the psychologically meaningful relations of the scores become reduced to echoing the magic words, "A Rorschach record is a configuration (or gestalt) in which the meanings of the different scores are interdependent."

This approach has its crucial test in the following problem: What if one obtains a Rorschach record which has a widespread paucity of all determinants other than form, or a specific paucity of one or another of the major determinants? Many investigators have been concerned with this difficulty. Several answers to it have been proffered. Some investigators have attempted to extend the scoring system still further in order to differentiate very fine nuances of responses and to represent these in quantitative form in the formal psychogram, where they are subject to analysis in terms of quantitative interrelationships. This introduces scores for some "subliminal" determinants, as it were.

A second method was to extend the inquiry into every response given by the subject, and even to introduce a "testing of limits" in which the examiner puts pressure on the subject to give responses using those determinants which hitherto he has largely ignored. This method obviously aims to unearth "subliminal" determinants. Upon the disadvantages of too extensive inquiry we have already commented. It is possible by means of it to collect more material concerning the subject, but it is inadvisable because it disrupts the unity, internal consistency, and objectivity of the test, and makes it a cumbersome and time-consuming clinical tool. Furthermore, such inquiry is superfluous if the Rorschach test is used in conjunction with other tests. This practice avoids the necessity for *stretching* its limits. The essential simplicity of the test is retained only if the examiner sticks to the spontaneous productions of the subject, and gathers additional material only in connection with certain responses not fully understood by him. These spontaneous productions constitute the crucial and revealing material of the test record.

This statement is in need of amplification. Perceptual and associative processes have not only a certain spontaneity, but a considerable flexibility in response to external pressure. We usually see and think in our own way but, being socialized, we are able to assume more or less the position of other persons and understand how *they* see and think. There is a wide range of possible balances to be struck between the extremes of complete spontaneity and flexible responsiveness to pressure; and the specific balance struck by the subject in question is always characteristic of him. But the relationship between spontaneous and forced productivity is not well understood. We have some evidence that certain kinds of responses cannot be elicited even under pressure, but this is by no means true for all; the total number of responses, or the use of color and shading as determinants, can be so increased. Thus a new unknown is introduced by this testing of limits into a test already abounding in unknowns. There is no way of defining what an inquiry means to the subject as long as the card is before him to inspect, and before the psychological conditions established by this technique and the kinds of reactions it elicits are fully explored. Therefore in our practice we limit our consideration of a test record as much as possible to the spontaneous productions of the subjects. This procedure places more or less homogeneous material at our disposal which is not complicated by the presence of any more complex anticipations in the subject than those aroused by the original instructions, or by the inevitable minimum of inquiry. Perceptual and associative processes are hereby kept at an optimal simplicity.

A third method of coping, or rather of not coping, with the difficulty is to declare the entire test invalid or at least not very helpful. In its mildest form, this approach declares the meager records noninterpretable. It is true that the difficulties of interpreting extremely coarctated records are great, and this constitutes a limitation of the Rorschach test. This limitation can to some extent be bypassed by careful psychological thinking about, and qualitative analysis of, the subjects' responses, especially their verbalizations. Furthermore, this never becomes a crucial problem if the test is used in conjunction with a battery of tests: the others, if carefully selected, can shed much light upon trends in the subject which are never, or at best indirectly, indicated by the Rorschach test. Finally, inferences derived from other tests in this battery may be used to understand more fully the implications of the meager Rorschach record. Many such records allow for negative diagnostic statements only; they exclude certain diagnostic possibilities, and narrow the diagnostic problem. If the examiner is working with a battery of tests, he may then turn to the others for positive evidence. Any comprehensive view of the complexities of the psychological functioning of a single person obliges one to acknowledge that, although the Rorschach test tells much, it is not in itself sufficient for constructing the total picture of a personality.

A reconsideration of the dimension of "qualitative wealth" is in place here. The kinds and amounts of determinants used by the subject are crucial indications of the qualitative wealth of his psychological experiencing; in addition: (a) The qualitative wealth depends upon the presence of other than form determinants. (b) Nevertheless, the form level of all the responses, and especially of the pure form responses, will play a considerable role in determining the qualitative wealth of the record. (c) Furthermore, it is not justified to conclude, from a record with an overwhelming prevalence of pure form responses on a high form level, that dullness and poverty of inner experiences characterize the subject. The more coarctated a protocol is, the greater must be the weight attached to the slightest indication of variability or wealth. It must not be forgotten that a person who is inhibited or inclined to block will react accordingly to the new and ambiguous situation of testing in general and of the inkblot in particular. Hence, a certain leeway must be allowed for the subject who shows strong inhibitory or blocking tendencies, and any breach in these must be taken to indicate potentialities and variability which in a less constrained situation might come to expression more freely. (d) Other aspects of the record besides the determinants must also be evaluated in connection with establishing its qualitative wealth: the number of combinations and constructions, the number of original responses in contrast to that of popular responses, the variability of the content of responses in contrast to the $A\%$, etc.

The determinants are psychologically the least understood of any of the aspects of the Rorschach responses. This is especially true for those determinants other than form. The relationship of colors, shadings, and movement impressions to intrapsychic processes is weak and unintegrated, and does not represent a source of material on which the Rorschach tester can freely and easily draw. We do not fully understand how it happens—even though our experience and statistical data demonstrate that it does happen —that subjects behave toward the colored inkblots as toward affective stimuli, toward the shaded inkblots as toward anxiety-arousing stimuli, and toward movement impressions in the inkblots as toward ideation-mobilizing stimuli. Considering this state of affairs, all we can do is to attempt to work out psychological rationales which seem to fit in with our experience.

THE FORM RESPONSES: F

The form responses are determined only by the contour and articulations of the area chosen. In almost any record, the number of times form alone is used as the determinant by far exceeds the number of times any other determinant is used; in fact, the number of F responses usually exceeds the total of responses which include other determinants. Thus, a detailed and careful consideration of the subject's use of form plays a crucial role in the evaluation of any Rorschach record. The subject's F responses may be "good" or "bad," sharp and definitive or vague and inconclusive, or of any degree of arbitrariness. Obviously, form may also be used as a codeterminant, that is to say, not alone but together with some other quality of the area chosen, such as color. But in whatever setting it occurs, the use of form as a determinant appears to relate to the subject's formal reasoning and his adherence to the demands of reality.

Thus, four general problems arise: (1) What is the relation between form responses and the subject's formal reasoning and contact with reality? (2) What implications for the subject's adjustment or maladjustment derive from an overabundance or paucity of form responses? (3) Similarly, what implications derive from the quality of the form responses? (4) What is the significance of the number and quality of those form responses that involve other determinants?

Scoring and Inquiry

(1) The first task of inquiry is usually to ascertain whether other determinants are also involved in the response. The problems and techniques of such inquiry can be more profitably discussed in connection with the treatment of the other determinants, and will be deferred until then.

(2) The first score percentage which is crucial in the evaluation of the Rorschach record is the $F\%$:[24] it indicates what percentage of all the responses given were pure form responses. This is obtained by totaling the pure form responses—regardless of their quality—and determining what percentage of R they constitute. As already indicated, responses may occur in which other determinants such as color or shading may accompany the form. In everyday clinical work, our considerations about the $F\%$ are always modified by considering how strong the form element is in these other responses. For the purposes of this presentation, we thought it necessary to communicate in quantitative form how these considerations amplify or modify the implications of the $F\%$ alone. Hence, we have introduced the *new F%,* which expresses the share among all responses of all those responses in which F is either the sole or the principal determinant.

(3) The main problem in scoring and inquiry is to establish the "form level" of the response. In his scoring system, Rorschach distinguished only between good ($F+$) and poor ($F-$) forms, rating thus all responses which involved the use of form as a determinant. Rorschach also calculated the $F+\%$, that is, the percentage of "good" forms in all the F responses. But what are the criteria for "good" and "bad" form? There are two trends of thought on this issue: one considers all responses which can be readily em-

[24] Systematically introduced into the literature by Klopfer. [Since Rapaport did not consider animal movement to be a separate determinant, however, his $F\%$ includes such responses and thus runs considerably higher than Klopfer's (see Klopfer et al., 1954).—Ed.]

pathized with as being of good form; the other considers all responses which occur with frequency in the general population as being of good form. Rorschach himself used a combination of the two criteria, and we adhere to this usage. A response which is given with great frequency must be considered one of good form, even though the examiner himself cannot readily empathize with it. In turn, responses that are convincing and easy to empathize with must be considered good forms, even though not frequent. Thus, the popular response "butterfly" on Card I may appear to the examiner as a very poor abstraction from the whole inkblot, and yet he will have to consider it as a good form; and at the other extreme, the response "skating woman" to the orange projections toward the middle of Card IX, held sideways, must be considered as a good form. One caution must be stated here: there are many people, psychologists as well as laymen, who empathize too readily with certain kinds of productions. The examiner who himself tends to give certain types of response (e.g., Dr responses) will usually empathize with such responses; for the inverse reason, other examiners will be too unprepared to empathize with these responses. Examiners using the Rorschach test should be aware of their tendencies to bias, and should attempt to make the necessary corrections. This problem arises mainly in the evaluation of F responses pertaining to tiny portions of the inkblot. As a matter of regulative principle, the examiner should ask himself in such cases, "How many other such tiny areas or projections will I have to admit as being of good form level, if I admit this tiny figure of a person, profile of a face, outline of a nose, penis, or vagina, to be of good form?"

(4) In the course of application of the Rorschach test, it became apparent that the average examiner would be more at ease in evaluating a record if further distinctions were drawn in connection with the form level. The need was for categories that would allow the examiner to record quantitatively, instead of evaluating qualitatively, the form level of each subject. Rorschach's dichotomy results in including a variety of different good and bad forms in each of the two categories. Klopfer introduced a new scoring procedure which scored as $F+$ only the excellent and sharply conceived form responses, and as $F-$ only the grossly arbitrary form responses; the remaining form responses were scored F without any sign of evaluation. Thus three kinds of forms were distinguished, and this radically changed the size and clinical significance of the $F+\%$; it also left the bulk of the form responses without any evaluation, so that both a fairly good and frequent form response and a vague, noncommittal form response were scored F.

In our practice we adhered rather to Rorschach's method of scoring, but with some modifications. We found it helpful to use four scoring categories: $F+$, $F\pm$, $F\mp$, $F-$. The $F\pm$ score refers to an essentially good response, with some traces of weakness of perceptual organization in it; the $F \mp$ score refers to an essentially poor response, but with some traces of good perceptual organization. We assigned these ratings to all responses in which the form determinant was prevalent, whether alone or combined with another determinant (*FC, FCh, M,* etc.). Unlike Rorschach, we did not assign such scores to *CF* or other comparable responses. We too calculated an $F+\%$, but with some slight modification. Our $F+\%$ has two parts, which are entered in the formal psychogram as a ratio. First, we calculate the sum of $F+$ and $F\pm$ responses and its percentage in all the pure form responses: this percentage is entered as the numerator, and indicates the quality of the subject's use of pure form as a determinant. Next, we total all form-prevalent responses (*F, FC,* etc.); of this total, we calculate the percentage of all those scored $+$ or $\pm$; this percentage is entered as the denominator and, when compared with the numerator, indicates the effect on the form level of the subject's coping with other determinants.[25]

(5) In everyday clinical practice we go beyond this scoring system, and pursue a qualitative analysis of the form responses.[26] In general, four kinds of form responses may occur: the form may be quite sharp, well articulated, and definitive; it may be frequent and undistinguished, but adequate; it may be vague; or it may be definitive but arbitrary. Although we leave such distinctions to qualitative analysis, their importance in diagnostic work is great enough to necessitate here a detailed presentation of form analysis from this point of view also. We use the following scores: *special F+* for the sharp, definitive, and convincing form responses; *special F—* for the definitive but arbitrary and unconvincing form responses; *Fv* for the vague form responses; *Fo* for the mediocre but acceptable form responses. As a consequence, certain problems in inquiry arise. Inquiry is directed to establishing exactly the location and articulation of responses which are new to the examiner, as well as to determining whether the familiar responses are seen in the usual acceptable manner. The first task is usually the more meticulous one: inquiry should provide a sufficiently clear picture of the form to allow for the passing of judgment about its quality. Most of us are inclined

[25] For example, if the subject gave 10 pure form responses, five of which were scored $F+$ or $F\pm$, the numerator of the $F+\%$ would be 50%; if the subject also gave five *FC* responses, all of which were *FC+* or *FC±*, the number of form-prevalent responses is 15, and the denominator would be 67%. ["Numerator" and "denominator" are used simply descriptively, without any implication that one is to be divided by the other. Thus, in the example just given, the figures are written 50/67.—Ed.]

[26] [The additional scores presented here formed the basis for an even more highly differentiated scoring system with eight categories, which Martin Mayman has been developing over the course of a decade. He has prepared a detailed scoring manual, with many examples of each form-level score, and it has proved itself valuable in several research projects though it is as yet unpublished. It is a necessary adjunct to my own primary-process scoring system.—Ed.]

to consider the new as not so good, and it frequently takes considerable effort to empathize with a new response, however shrewd. The second task does not require meticulous inquiry, but rather good insight into verbalization and perceptual organization. Such inquiry should be made only if something in the subject's verbalizations—such as a vague reference to the area—indicates that the percept may be divergent from the familiar one. The inquiry here will consist in asking for a quick outlining of the area referred to, or for a quick pointing out of a perceptually salient or questionable point in the area (nose, legs, etc.). Only by a demand for speed will the examiner be able to detect weakness or absurdity of the perceptual organization of the response: the subject who is able to take his time will take the inquiry as a clue to improve upon or sharpen his response, and proceed to do so.

Aside from establishing the general form level, inquiry also attempts to establish the clarity or vagueness of the articulation of the response. For example, inquiry may be directed into a usually vague response ("X ray," "map") to establish whether specific articulations are present; these will decrease its vagueness and allow for considering it either as arbitrarily or acceptably articulated. Conversely, inquiry may attempt to establish whether a response which is usually seen clearly has any vagueness about it. The type of inquiry discussed in this paragraph should be extensively practiced by the student, who must familiarize himself with the fact that usual responses are not always seen in the usual way, and that the examiner's own anticipations may make for inaccuracies in the scoring. In everyday clinical work, the experienced examiner will pursue such inquiry only where the subject's verbalization indicates the presence of some deviation from what is expected.

Rationale of the Form Responses

In most records, at least two thirds of the responses are pure F; this fact has cultural as well as ego-psychological implications. The primitive and the child tend to apperceive objects of their environment in terms of physiognomic characteristics,[27] affective characteristics, and usefulness; but our culture apparently has forced adults to apperceive objects of the environment in terms of their formal characteristics. That is to say, formal characteristics and their relationships become our guide in life, and not our affective reactions to the things about us: we are trained from childhood on to be objective.

[27] A term coined by Heinz Werner (1940) to express the preliterate's undifferentiated, diffuse mode of apperception, in which formal and affective features are indivisibly fused.

From the ego-psychological point of view, the form responses refer to processes of formal reasoning which should pursue their course without anxiety and affects intruding into and disrupting them. Form responses apparently represent what Hartmann (1939) calls the conflict-free sphere of the ego. Therefore, they stand for the autonomy of the perceptual and thought processes from encroachments by unconscious factors. Finally, as we shall attempt to show below, the coming about of form responses represents a capacity for delay of discharge of impulses—or, as it could be phrased in psychoanalytic terminology, for a delay of gratification of instinctual needs and their derivatives. It is obvious that inhibition, with its implied renunciation of gratification, tends to increase the area of this autonomous segment of ego functions. It seems too that impulsiveness implies a limitation of this autonomous sector, since in an impulsive person the unconscious factors are only precariously subjected to regulation by conscious thinking in terms of formal characteristics.

Civilization does not demand that all psychological experience be strictly limited to such guidance by formal characteristics; it allows also for guidance by intuition, for appropriate display of affect and anxiety. The emphasis upon appropriateness, however, indicates that any such display must be in accord with the formal characteristics and relationships of the real situation in which it occurs. Thus, even those form-prevalent responses in which the form is accompanied by another determinant indicate an ability to delay impulses[28] until they can be integrated with the dictates of the formal rules of thinking.

The cultural pressure for formal logical thinking as the basis of action is two-edged: too much yielding to it leads to undue inhibition, while gross rejection of it leads to impulsive, ill-considered behavior. The smoothly functioning person must strike a balance between too much and too little delay of impulse (inhibition); thus, on the one hand his thinking and acting will be essentially in conformity with the demands of reality, and on the other he will not sacrifice too much spontaneity. In the Rorschach test, the $F\%$ indicates the degree to which the subject yields to this strong cultural pressure.

But this formulation is in need of some correction and some amplification. First of all, certain kinds of form responses (absurd) may occur which themselves indicate an inability for delay of impulses and an impoverishment of the critical attitude implicit in formal logical reasoning. Second, the circumstance that we have a variety of form responses reflects the fact

[28] The concept "delay of impulse" will become clearer in the discussion of the color response (pp. 372ff.). It refers to the conditions under which formal characteristics of reality can be regarded and unconscious impulses constrained from discharge to allow testing of reality. See Freud (1911) [and Rapaport (1960b)].

that different people achieve different degrees of delay and use the delay differently.

For assessing the effectiveness and quality of the subject's response to the cultural pressure in question, we must turn to a consideration of the quality of the F responses. The form level of a response indicates the extent to which there has been a balanced interplay or cogwheeling of the perceptual and associative processes. This statement directly implies the necessity for some delay before a satisfactory response can be worked out.[29] The subject's mode of functioning should allow for the delay necessary for a perceptual articulation of the inkblot, for an initiation of associative processes on the basis of the initial perceptual impressions, for a consequent reorganization of the perceptual material to obtain a congruence with the possibilities offered by the associative processes, and finally for a critical appraisal of the response which came forth; otherwise the form level of the response will be poor. The occurrence of any form response implies some delay, however, while in contrast a pure color response implies its absence. For example, a subject may say on Card X, "This yellow could be a urine stain" (a relatively frequent schizophrenic response); here only a gross color perception has initiated the associative process, and this process did not run a long course to lend a complex elaboration to the original perceptual impression and thus was not regulated by formal considerations. Such a response is usually verbalized almost as if the subject has lost sight of the fact that he is dealing with inkblots, and not with any directly meaningful piece of reality.

The process underlying the coming about of a response is usually set off by a specific perceptual impression from some part of the inkblot. If the subject is unable to get beyond this starting point, for reasons of difficulty of perceptual organization or of meagerness of associative content, a dilution of the response occurs in which any attempt to interpret a larger area can be made only by giving a vague form response. If the interplay between the spread of perceptual articulation to a larger area and the possibilities offered by the associative process is smooth but without too much sharpness or wealth, an adequately abstractive and acceptable form response usually results. If this development of the response is accompanied by a considerable sharpness of perceptual articulation and by a wealth of associative processes, very definitive, convincing, and well-integrated form responses come about. If the subject pursues a course of ex-

---

[29] By "delay" we do not imply any quantitative temporal factor, but rather that a process responsible to many influences is successfully consummated. In quick and alert subjects the amount of temporal delay may be almost negligible; nevertheless, a complete and responsible psychological process has occurred.

tensive perceptual articulation and integration of associative content, without subjecting the process to critical conscious control, arbitrary, incorrectly definitive form responses result.

Let us consider the vague form response *(Fv)* first. It appears that when the subject cannot perceptually articulate the area he is dealing with, it remains vague, and he falls back on and uses this real vagueness of the blot. Part of the difficulty may stem from a poverty of associations which fails to supply adequate subject matter taking account of a variety of initial perceptual impressions; thus what is finally offered as a response is based on only a few partial perceptual impressions and a few associative contents which are diluted to refer to the whole area, e.g., the responses "dough," "something anatomical." We have already shown that the presence of strong anxiety may account for the occurrence of *Wv* responses; in general, it appears that anxiety can underlie all vague responses, however large or small the area. That is to say, anxiety may prevent penetration of the indistinct perceptual mass, even though distinct features that might serve as suitable starting points are present and noticed.

We have stated too that *Dr, De,* and *Do* responses may also be anxiety indicators. If anxiety blocks an articulating penetration of the perceptual mass, the process leading to a generalizing *(W)* response is short-circuited; no further associative productions result, and the subject gives a *Dr* response. This short-circuiting brings to the surface a preparatory phase of an *Fv* response: the vague responses emanate from the same difficulties as the anxious *Dr*'s, except that in the former the products of the associative process initiated by a few small areas are applied to a larger area, and we experience this dilution of content as vagueness. In a sense, the occurrence of a large *Fv* is an indication of more "daring" than the occurrence of the *Dr* and *De* responses. In the latter, peripheral minor impressions are not used as leads into a *W* or *D* response because anxiety is prohibitive to coping with such a vague and shady mass. Clinically it is almost always a more encouraging sign if the subject attempts to cope with the larger areas of the inkblot and gives *Wv* responses rather than *Dr, De,* and *Do* responses. This daring sometimes has its rewards, although not rich ones: when anxiety is mild, the usual and popular whole responses may come about—even though they are generalizations from only a few perceptual clues and are not based upon a thorough penetration of the perceptual mass. These considerations hold more for the heavily shaded than for the other cards.

Let us turn now to the opposite extreme and consider the sharp, definitive, and correct form responses *(special F+)*. Three main factors appear to make for these: (1) a wealth of past experiences, which supplies an abundance of variegated associative possibilities to match the perceptual impressions; (2) a sharpness and daring of perceptual articulation, which necessitates a coping with a great variety of features of the inkblot; (3) a strict critical assessment of the degree of congruence between the possibilities offered by the associative processes and the formal articulations of the area.

But articulated and definitive form responses may come about in which there is a serious discrepancy between the content of the response and the perceptual configuration it refers to (*special F—*). In such responses the perceptual and associative processes have not come to an equilibrium: either the parts of the perceptual mass that initiated the associative process did not lend themselves to integration by this process whose critical censorship was weak enough to allow delivery of haphazard or arbitrary responses; or the presence of an overvalent emotional and ideational content overruled both the regulating effect of the perceptual impressions and the critical censorship of the associative process. The latter type of *F—* response may abandon all regard for the form of the inkblot, and appear completely incomprehensible to the examiner. A *form* response which becomes this arbitrary merits the score "absurd" in the fifth scoring category.[30]

Finally, let us consider the ordinary form response *(Fo)* which is neither too vague, nor too arbitrary, nor too sharply articulated. Here a few definite form characteristics of the area chosen[31] initiate an associative process, which proceeds along lines of correct generalization from these few features to a superficial balance and harmony with the gross articulations of the area. Such responses are those most readily agreed upon and given by the general population. While the *special F+* responses indicate the maximum efficiency of delay, the *Fo* responses indicate merely an adequate effectiveness of it. The *special F+* responses indicate that in the course of delay, ideation has reached a peak of productivity where the associative process could integrate an optimum of perceptual impressions; while the *Fo* responses indicate that the delay has allowed only for sufficient ideation for the associative process to integrate the necessary minimum of perceptual impressions that could support a response.

Thus, the $F+\%$ indicates the general effectiveness of delay of impulse in the subject, and the sharpness of critical control which is exercised in this delay. This sharpness of critical appraisal depends first of all on endowment and wealth of past experiences, and second upon the prompt availability of appropriate associative material. Hence it is a function of

[30] Such responses show many similarities to the distant reactions of the Word Association Test.

[31] It must be understood that the area chosen itself crystallizes in the course of the interaction of progressive perceptual articulation and the associative process.

judgmental nature, which even with good endowment may become impaired.[32]

When tendencies toward maladjustment are present within the normal range, the form level tends to drop, and an increase of vague form responses is to be expected. More specifically, the presence of strong anxiety within the normal range appears to disrupt the form level and make for vagueness; good normal adjustment, and especially some cultural interests, appear to make for increase of sharp form responses and a generally high form level.

As was the case for the $F\%$, we must keep in mind that the $F+\%$ should not be too high. When the $F\%$ is too high, inhibition and a decrease of spontaneity and affective reactivity appear; when the $F+\%$ is too high, the critical controlling processes may have become rigid and intolerably accurate, making for meagerness of productivity and for rigidity in thinking and behavior.

The norm for the $F\%$ is to be set approximately between 67% and 75%, with the minimum around 60% and the maximum around 80%; the new $F\%$ should be between 73% and 87%; the $F+\%$ should fall between 65% as the minimum and 80% as the maximum. Within the normal range, an increase in the $F\%$ refers to the presence of strong inhibition, while a decrease is referable more to the presence of impulsiveness. Scores beyond the extreme limits given here point to the presence of pathology.

The F% as a Diagnostic Indicator

The $F\%$ reaches its greatest height in the groups characterized by extremely rigid or compulsive character formation or by extreme inhibition, depressive or otherwise. Outstandingly high $F\%$'s are found among depressives especially, but also in paranoid schizophrenics (usually rigid personalities prior to break), simple schizophrenics (in whom flattening of ideation and affect and absence of anxiety are clinically outstanding), and inhibited preschizophrenics (who are generally constricted). If we consider the new $F\%$, depressives yield even higher figures; the same is true for paranoid schizophrenics; and now the obsessive-compulsive group stands out among other neurotics. Neurasthenics also have very high new $F\%$'s, reflecting their general poverty of affective and ideational output.

Acute schizophrenics show a greater degree of control, as indicated by the new $F\%$, than chronic and deteriorated schizophrenics. It is also significant to note that depressive neuroses exceed depressive psychoses in the prevalence of the form determinant; this is understandable in terms of

---

[32] See the discussion of the Comprehension subtest of the Bellevue Scale in Chapter 3, above. [Note that in this paragraph, $F+$ refers to all responses of acceptable form, whether scored special $F+$, $F+$, Fo, or $F\pm$.—Ed.]

the clinically observable affect storms occurring in depressive psychoses. Among neurotics, the hysterics stand out with the lowest average $F\%$, in accord with the clinical picture of hysteria, of which intense affects and anxieties with a minimum of control are characteristic. Obsessive-compulsives have a quite high *new* $F\%$, and it may be noted why they are not outstanding on the usual $F\%$. Clinical experience indicates that the obsessive-compulsive *neurosis,* in full-fledged form, represents a breakdown of a previous compulsive *adjustment;* if such cases are tested while this adjustment is still fairly well preserved, the $F\%$ will almost always be considerably higher than after a decompensation of the adjustment has occurred and symptom formation begun. Nevertheless, we have seen many obsessive-compulsive neurotics with exceptionally high $F\%$ and *new* $F\%$ reflecting the retention of the premorbid pattern. Finally, paranoid schizophrenics stand out from other schizophrenics by their number of pure form responses; this is frequently a helpful diagnostic indication of the originally rigid, often compulsive personality make-up of the paranoid patient.

The F+% as a Diagnostic Indicator

Within the schizophrenic range, both paranoid and unclassified, the $F+\%$ should be expected to be relatively high in the acute cases and show a significant drop in the chronic and deteriorated cases. That is, clinically the crucial signs of the *acuteness* of a schizophrenia are the vestiges of the patient's attempt to keep a hold on reality, which in later phases is usually abandoned. Thus, in schizophrenia a very low $F+\%$ is suggestive of an advanced stage of the process.

In paranoid conditions, the $F+\%$ remains reasonably high by virtue both of their similarity to acute schizophrenia and the vestiges of an originally rigid, compulsive personality make-up. In contrast, simple schizophrenics, who clinically resemble the chronic and whose reality testing is seriously impaired, show an average $F+\%$.

Preschizophrenics were described as cases of longstanding maladjustment in whom poor reality testing is conspicuous. Inhibited preschizophrenics are characterized further by blocking and intense anxiety, which we would expect to make for a disharmony between the perceptual and associative processes. Overideational preschizophrenics are characterized by an overabundance of associative content and ideational symptom formation, which we would expect to make for a pressure of associative content and a disregard of perceptual organization. Thus, in both groups, though for somewhat different reasons, the average $F+\%$ falls below the acceptable minimum.

Depressive paucity or monotony of ideational content implies that the associative processes lag behind the perceptual organization, which is itself slowed down. The lag of the associative process when pronounced makes for an increase of vagueness; but the perceptual organizing processes have sufficient time—if the examiner is patient enough—to form abstractions from the blot and thus result in an adequate or even high $F+\%$. Depressives form only the grossest and most obvious ones, however, consisting largely of the popular responses with scarcely any sharp form responses. In fact, where the critical function is not impaired, as in some depressive psychoses, generalized slowness and paucity of associations makes for a picture resembling that of overcautious people characterized by a high form level. Therefore, as we progress from psychotic depressives through severe neurotic to milder neurotic depressives, the impairment of the form level diminishes and the $F+\%$ reaches its peak in depressive neurosis. Neurasthenics' weakness of perceptual organizing ability and poverty of associative content are clinically outstanding and their $F+\%$ is correspondingly impaired, partly because bodily preoccupation leads them to anatomical responses of poor form level. Hysterics do not show weakness of perceptual organizing abilities and are not usually subject to the pressure of overvalent ideational content; hence they have a good $F+\%$. The contrast between a generally impoverished form level and the retention of a few very sharp form responses can suggest the presence of schizophrenia. In contrast, depressives, who have high form levels in general, stand out with their very low *special* $F+\%$. In preschizophrenics, particularly overideational ones, the contrast of the great number of very good form responses with the generally poor form level is especially great. Paranoid conditions, however, have both a good form level and a fairly high *special* $F+\%$. This is sometimes helpful in differentiating a paranoid condition from an acute paranoid schizophrenia; even schizophrenics of an excellent form level weaken in a few places and give absurd form responses.

Within the neurotic range, the anxiety and depression group follows the depressive pattern with fairly good $F+\%$ and a low *special* $F+\%$; neurasthenics follow their general pattern of having both a low form level and a low *special* $F+\%$; obsessive-compulsives follow overideational preschizophrenics and schizophrenics by having a low average form level but a high incidence of excellent form responses—although the low form level of obsessive-compulsives rarely stems from an abundance of absurd and arbitrary forms, as in schizophrenics.

Turning to the *special* $F-\%$ which refers to the definitive but arbitrary form responses, we find that their incidence is outstandingly high in chronic and deteriorated schizophrenics, in preschizophrenics, especially overideational ones, and, within the neurotic range, in neurasthenics. Even acute schizophrenics, who have a relatively high incidence of very good form responses, also have a very high incidence of quite poor form responses; again we emphasize that the contrast is frequently an important diagnostic aid. Within the depressive range, only psychotic depressives have a high *special F—%*, while other depressive groups have exceptionally low average *special F—%*.

Turning finally to the incidence of vague form responses *(Fv)* which principally indicate strong anxiety, we find that their incidence can run high in almost any diagnostic group. But the high average *Fv%* in the ideationally flat simple schizophrenics, in the blocked, and extremely narrow anxious inhibited preschizophrenics, and within the neurotic range in the generally impoverished neurasthenics, seems consistent with our rationale. Acute paranoid schizophrenics frequently show a complete or almost complete *absence* of vagueness in their records. In general, the absence of vague form responses in an average-sized record in the pathological range usually indicates considerable rigidity, compulsive meticulousness, and caution.

MOVEMENT RESPONSES: *M*

"Movement" responses were defined by Rorschach as responses in which a human form is seen in motion or in some posture isolated out of a process of motion. Later, Rorschach and Oberholzer (1923) pointed out that responses in which animals are seen in motion indicate some tendency of the same kind. In *Psychodiagnostics* Rorschach also notes that sensitivity to dynamic movementlike characteristics of lines, or to architectonics of an inkblot, also represents such a tendency. He did not give these responses any *M* score, however, and evaluated them only qualitatively in his interpretation of the record. In our scoring we followed Rorschach's procedure closely. Movements of inanimate objects, and expressive movements such as facial grimaces, we did not consider related to *M* responses, although in other connections we evaluated them qualitatively.[33]

Scoring and Inquiry

It is crucial for correct inquiry into and scoring of movement responses to know where they usually occur; such knowledge simplifies the recognition of *M* responses and directs the inquiry. The most frequent *M* responses are as follows:

Card I. The entire side area ("hovering angels," "Santa Claus"); the entire middle area with the two upper middle projections as hands ("pray-

---

[33] See section below on fabulized responses. [Subsequent research has not supported Rapaport's position on animal movement and *m*—Ed.]

ing"); the entire middle area seen as two figures standing back to back but again with the "hands."

Card II. An entire half of the card including the upper red ("people dancing or drinking or playing pat-a-cake"); each black area ("people with their hands together but hiding their heads behind their shoulders"); the central white space ("a ballerina doing a pirouette"); the upper middle black projection ("two little elves sitting back to back with cone-shaped hats").

Card III. Each half of the black area ("two people bending over bowing or dancing")—the most frequent movement response on the test; with the card upside down, each half of the black area ("cannibals with upraised arms"); with the card upside down, the entire black area ("an orchestra conductor from the waist up with his hands raised"); with the card upside down, the outer red area ("dancers leaping").

Card IV. The entire inkblot with or without the lower middle projection ("a man sitting on a stool" or "a giant walking toward you but foreshortened by perspective"); the three white spaces around the lower middle projection ("a woman holding a baby"); the upper side projection ("acrobat doing a backbend or swan dive"); with the card upside down, the solid black areas in what are now the upper side projections ("two women with veils" or "two witches"); with the card held sideways the light gray area ("Santa Claus with a bundle on his hunched back").

Card V. The entire inkblot seen as the figure of a person in the center with big wings attached ("masquerade costume"); the lateral half of each wing area including the extreme side projections ("two reclining figures with their arms folded"); the white space on the outside of the lower middle projections ("the figure of a woman sitting: Queen Victoria"); with the card held sideways, the entire inkblot ("a dancer in a violent stretching movement" or "an old woman bent over with an umbrella under her arm").

Card VI. The upper projection with its winglike extensions ("man hanging on a cross" or "a Hindu standing with outstretched arms"); with the card upside down, each half of the inkblot ("English trumpeters with horns, they are standing back to back"); with the card held sideways, the large upper projection ("a prophet with one arm outstretched and his cloak hanging down from it and the other arm uplifted to heaven").

Card VII. Each complete half of the inkblot ("two ladies fighting or dancing or gossiping and pointing away from each other"); the very small light gray-white area ("two people standing, holding hands or with their arms across shoulders"); with the card upside down, each entire half of the card ("two figures in a dance with their heads touching"); with the card upside down, the lower two thirds of the inkblot ("two figures jumping or dancing with their heads hidden behind their shoulders").

Card VIII. There is no frequent movement response on this card, and only a few infrequent ones. The halves of the lower middle pink-orange area ("Arab women sitting back to back at the foot of a tree bent, mourning"); upside down, the white area between the two blue areas ("two knights in armor kneeling—fence between them").

Card IX. The upper orange areas ("two clowns or witches with their hands in front of them, maybe in a sword fight"); with the card turned sideways, the green area ("a woman housecleaning or chasing a child" or "a bicyclist" or "a hunter broiling his meal"); with the card held sideways, the finely articulated orange projections above and toward the midline of the inkblot ("a lady doing a jig") or these same projections but below the mid-line ("two people standing by a tree"); with the card upside down, the entire inkblot ("Cyrano de Bergerac with spread legs and a huge hat"); with the card upside down, each half of the inkblot ("two figures leaning back to back with their legs forward" or "two figures dressed for Mardi Gras with their noses together").

Card X. The pink and upper gray areas ("two firemen with their helmets on"); the pink areas and the middle blue areas ("two people sucking on something"); the side brown-gray areas with or without the yellow areas on the outside of the large pink areas ("a woman swimming"); with the card upside down, the pink area ("a cat-faced woman in a pink tulle dress looking very haughty"); with the card upside down, the central blue areas together with the pink ("two people on cliffs holding hands over a chasm"). In the upper side blue areas manifold but often very arbitrary movements may be seen in the branchlike articulations surrounding the core of that area.

There are, of course, many more possible movement responses, but it is unlikely that these would be given by subjects who do not also give a good number of those described.

The task of the movement-response inquiry and scoring is to discover (a) where the verbalization is merely a secondary elaboration not really referring to a movement impression, and (b) where the verbalization fails to indicate a movement impression even though one is present.

When a subject clearly verbalizes a frequent movement response, and no suspicion of queerness or arbitrariness derives from the rest of the test and its verbalization, the examiner will score the response *M* without further ado or inquiry. The less stress placed upon determinants in inquiry, the more valid the record usually is. Inquiry becomes necessary when a figure usually seen in motion is not so described in the subject's spontaneous verbalizations. Frequently it is sufficient to ask the subject to trace quickly the area of the response; the inclusion of armlike or leglike extensions, or the bridging of gaps as on Card III, make it clear that a movement impression was the determinant—since such inclusions and bridgings do not occur in static perception of the blots—and that the score M is justified. Further inquiry must be made with the inkblot removed, and should proceed in the following sequence until sufficient evidence for the presence or absence of a movement impression is found: (1) "Describe this figure to me." (2) "Anything noteworthy about it?" (3) "Was he (she) doing anything?" (4) "Anything you noticed about his (her) posture?" The score M should be used only if the answers to the first questions establish the presence of a movement impression. If the last two—quite leading—questions elicit a probable movement impression, the score FM should be used. This score indicates a movement tendency, and quantitatively carries only half of the weight of a full movement response.[34] If what is usually seen as a human form in motion is seen as an animal form in humanlike motion, the score FM should be given.

Inquiry must also be made, and very carefully, where an unusual area elicits movement impressions. Movements are relatively limited to certain configurations of the inkblot, except in the most versatile and productive subjects. Furthermore, most areas seen as animals are given no FM score, whatever elaboration of movement the subject may advance—such as the "kissing bears" on Card II and the "stalking wolf" on Card VIII. There are a few exceptions. If the whole of Card II is seen as "dressed-up" or "dancing" bears with the upper red area as their heads, the fact that the gap between the black and the red is bridged points to the presence of a movement impression; similarly with the figure in Card III seen as (for example) "Donald Duck," if the subject indicates that he has bridged the gap between the body area and the leg area. The justification for this procedure will be advanced in the section on rationale. However, any emphasis on the disjointed character of either of these two responses indicates a weakness of the movement impression.

The main problem in scoring is to establish consistent criteria for movement responses. Here the examiner's own tendencies play a crucial role. One who is inclined to see many movements himself will tend to accept too many from his subjects, while another may be more inclined to reject too many; the examiner always must know his own bias, and attempt to make corrections for it. Still, extremely rare movement responses occur which are difficult for any examiner to judge. Some of these are movement impressions derived from very small areas (Dr responses). Here the examiner must first attempt as adequate a critical appraisal of the movement impression as possible, asking himself: "If I admit that this tiny projection

[34] This FM score has no relationship to the FM score used by Klopfer: in his use the score is reserved for responses in which animals are seen in movement, and also has a different interpretative significance.

with its slender curve looks like a bent-over person, how many other such responses will it become necessary to accept at face value?" Second, the examiner must find some yardstick in the rest of the record for evaluating these rare and usually tiny movement responses. If the subject has given with great smoothness the most familiar movement responses, and has in addition given a number of more unusual but convincing movement responses, then the few others which are difficult to judge probably also represent some movement impression. On the other hand, subjects who bungle even the most common movement responses can rarely be trusted to have had vivid movement impressions on original responses. This is a general principle of inquiry into the role played by determinants, in clinical practice especially: *there are instances where it cannot be decided from the response itself, nor from the subject's verbalizations around the response and inquiry, what the most appropriate score is; and in such cases the examiner must turn to the rest of the record for decision.*

When it is difficult to empathize with a movement response that is merely a deviation from a familiar one, the score *M*— is in place if careful inquiry indicates a poor percept by the subject. *M*— scores have great pathological weight. Delirious and confusional cases which are not deteriorated tend to give many movement responses, often very sharp ones. Such patients will not be able to point out accurately what they saw or where, however; their responses must be scored by inference, and should be sharply distinguished from *M*— responses which have an entirely different diagnostic significance.

Movement responses to small areas are scored *Ms,* "small movement." These responses have a special significance and must be discriminated in the scoring system. The areas need not be very small to merit the score *Ms:* in our scoring only large areas of the inkblot are given a regular *M* score. In contrast to the *FM* score, the *Ms* score counts with full weight alongside the regular *M* responses. But when the areas chosen get too small, the score *M* should almost never be given, even though the indications of some *M*— tendency may be present. Similarly, parts of human forms do not merit the score *M,* although an *FM* score may be in place if the part figure is large and the *M* tendency clear; but the smaller the area thus chosen, the more the attribution of movement by the subject to that area becomes independent of the percept and the more it represents merely an associative elaboration not based on an actual movement impression. Finally, descriptions of the general architectonics of the inkblot parts and of the dynamic qualities of the internal lines or outside contours are never given the score *M,* and are not even counted as responses. The examiner merely notes a movement tendency: these responses too have a special significance, which will be elaborated on later.

Rationale of the Movement Responses

Rorschach assumed that the *M* responses stand for the subject's natural endowment, for the potentialities for and inclination toward achievements in culture and thought: the greater the number of movement responses, the higher the level of endowment. Rorschach discussed the significance of the *M* responses in the context of "introversive" versus "extratensive" tendencies in the subject. We shall consider this issue after a discussion of the psychological processes through which movement responses come about.

What role is played by the perceptual and associative processes, and the nature of the inkblots, in the coming about of *M* responses? As defined above, the movement responses consist essentially of experiencing an actually static area as moving or being at some point in the process of motion. These movement impressions have been referred to as "kinesthetic" responses, because it was assumed that such experiences have some connection with the kinesthetic experiences of our own body. It is apparently implied that it is these bodily experiences which allow us to empathize with movement impressions in static visual pictures, and that these kinesthetic experiences actually occur in the subject when he gives movement responses. For these reasons it was assumed that the greatest likelihood is that such impressions will be most vividly experienced in connection with responses involving human figures. No evidence was put forth, however, to support the assumption that any kinesthetic experience actually takes place in the subject as the prerequisite for the coming about of a movement response. What the process bringing about the movement responses actually is, has not been explored; but from some of Rorschach's comments, from what other Rorschach test investigators have since written, from subjects' verbalizations, and from general psychological facts and theories, the following assumption may be drawn: movement impressions come about from perceptual raw material that somehow is unbalanced—that is, by some change of position in a part or aspect it would become more balanced, would show a better closure. For example, in the figures of the two persons on Card III, the formal spatial relationship between the upper and larger area ("trunk and head") and the lower slender area ("leg") seems to be experienced as an imbalance, strong enough to cause the two areas to be linked together in the subject's response as though the gap between them did not exist; thus an impression of bending arises.

So far it would appear that a perceptual sensitivity to formal imbalance enters into the movement responses, as well as a flexibility of the perceptual organizing processes which allows for articulating the inkblot. But once the perceptual imbalance has made its impact, not only the perceptual organization but also the associative process needs to be flexible and rich enough to cope with it. From gestalt psychology we have learned that there is a tendency toward balance in the perceptual field; that is, an imbalance in the perceptual field elicits a tendency in the organism to reorganize the portions of the field so as to bring about more stable relationships in the field. An example of such activity of the perceptual field is the phenomenon of apparent movement (see Wertheimer, 1912),[35] which may have an even more intrinsic relation to these movement responses.

The coming about of a human-movement response seems to represent the most successful coping with the impact of this imbalance, as shown in the following considerations. (1) It indicates that the course of the associative process has sufficiently great variability, can draw on such rich associative resources, and is regulated by the perceptual imbalance so flexibly, that it is able to offer a content for the area which implies a resolution of the imbalance. In terms of the human body: any outstretching of arms or bending of waist is not the most stable spatial configuration of the body; and thus the response content "a man bending" implicitly indicates where the different parts of the whole area should be for the most stable balance, and implies not merely a static position but a process of motion which will lead to a more stable configuration. In other words, the response is a high integrative achievement. (2) It indicates that subjects with vivid movement impressions are able actually to achieve a resolution of this imbalance rather than merely implying one. Specifically, in some subjects there occurs intrapsychically a shift from the actual perceptual imbalance toward an imagelike internal experience of the balanced position of the figure. As a consequence of this shift, an experience of apparent movement, such as is seen on moving arrow advertisements, occurs. In the apparent-movement experiments, the starting and end positions of the shift occur within the external visual field; but in the present instance the shift is between a

[35] [Experimental attempts to test this hypothesized relationship have not been notably successful. Altogether, my impression is that this rationale for M is the weakest and least plausible of Rapaport's contributions to the Rorschach, and that the M response remains shrouded in mystery. The continued failure of attempts to test many theories about movement responses may well be attributable to the lack of internal unity or psychological consistency in the various responses so scored. To see the popular M on Card III can hardly be considered a creative, integrative achievement simply because it is so common; and yet the rationale advanced here is more suitable for this response than for many others. The fascination of M and persisting clinical impressions of its significance may be traced to the fact that it entails the following *as well as* movement impression or kinesthesis: human content, and some degree of thematic (or, in Rapaport's term, fabulized) elaboration. The former may account for whatever aspects of empathy are involved, the latter for implications about fantasy or ideational activity. Then, since it is difficult to give a creatively ingenious, well-elaborated response without involving figures in motion (except for certain kinds of mechanical and technical responses), it is not surprising that M becomes associated with creativity. Yet the fact remains that this type of creativity has no *demonstrated* relevance to productive and original work in the arts and sciences.—Ed.]

starting position which is in the visual field, and an assumed end position which is an internal imagelike experience. Thus, on Card III some subjects may not see the bent-over figures per se, but rather will see them—and clearly verbalize this experience—*straightening up* or *bending over* so that the "body" part is in a more consistent relationship with the "leg" part. We are not in a position to maintain that this latter explanation obtains in all cases; nevertheless, the fact that it occurs in people with very vivid movement impressions, and many movement responses in general, makes it likely that this shift may underlie the coming about of all movement responses whether or not the subject is aware of the occurrence of the shift.

At any rate, the indications are that movement responses reflect a considerable flexibility, versatility, and wealth of both associative resources and processes and perceptual organizing abilities. Furthermore, it appears that no actual kinesthetic experience need be invoked to explain the coming about of M responses. In these, then, many form elements and their spatial relationship must be integrated by the associative process, and configurations other than those perceptually given in the inkblot must be anticipated. It is then obvious that, for such a complex perceptual anticipatory and associative integration to come about, considerable delay[36] is a prerequisite.

Rorschach emphasized that the subject must be able to draw from a wealth of associations and memory images in order to derive a movement experience. He considered this associative wealth representative of the subject's general endowment, and thus for him the flexibility of these associations made the M responses representative of psychomotility.[37] We should like to add only that the associative processes do not work alone, but must be stimulated by, regulated by, and integrated with sensitive and versatile perceptual organizing processes.

There is another aspect of Rorschach's rationale of the M responses that must be taken up here. Rorschach quantitatively compared the weight of movement responses with the weight of color responses; he considered the prevalence of movement over color as a sign of introversive personality make-up, and a prevalence of color over M responses as a sign of extratensive personality make-up.[38] Even though in Rorschach's usage the terms

[36] [See fn. 29, above.—Ed.]

[37] [The flexibility of cognitive processes.—Ed.]

[38] In Jung's sense. [According to many other Rorschach workers (e.g., Ainsworth & Klopfer, 1954), "introversive" and "intratensive" are *not* to be considered synonymous with Jung's concepts of introversion and extraversion, at least not as popularly understood. It is hard to suppress the cynical reflection that this denial may have been motivated by a desire to explain away the failure of attempts to correlate M and C with other measures of Jung's constructs. Surely no useful purpose is served by retaining these variant terms if they do not mean what they seem to and cannot be given operational definitions except by reference to Rorschach scores.—Ed.]

referred to tendencies rather than to absolute personality types, the intro-duction of this dichotomous thinking seems to have caused much confusion in Rorschach test interpretation. In the following we shall avoid as much as possible any such dichotomy.

The fact that certain people are more inclined to think things out, and others more to follow their impulses and act out, seems to have served as the basis for the introvert-extravert dichotomy. Such dichotomous thinking neglects the fact that any delay of impulse, whether instinctual or affective, is the fundamental condition for human thinking; it is the prerequisite of every thought, and indeed gave birth to thought (see Freud, 1900, 1911). In other words, the development of the ego and thought processes repre-sents a progressive mastery over impulses. A delay between impulse and its discharge must come about so that during this delay the reality of a situation may be tested, and the least dangerous way of reaching the goal be discovered. Thus, thought serves the impulse but is rendered possible only by a delay of its discharge. When the ego is more fully developed and the person is able to think beyond the immediate tension experience, an impulse may be not only delayed but curbed and deflected from its goal, or even totally rejected, for the benefit of the organism as a whole.

From a description of the persons in whom M responses are found to prevail, it would appear that they excel in this ability for delay—and might even show pathological extremes of delay in the form of action-paralyzing obsessive doubts or fantasies. Thus the process presumed to lead to the M response parallels the process that actually leads to the type of behavior in everyday life to which the response apparently refers. We have also pointed out that the M response implies an anticipation of the most stable spatial relationships of the areas chosen, and this characteristic also is shared by thought processes in general, whose function is to anticipate vari-ous pathways toward the object of the impulse and the dangers implied in pursuing them.

Therefore, in normal subjects the M response should be considered to indicate the level of natural endowment—in so far as natural endowment comes to expression in a wealth and vividness of ideation—a readiness to make anticipations, and a versatility and flexibility of perceptual and asso-ciative processes in general. In different normal contexts, these may show up as creativeness or as an inclination to be ruminative; in different neu-rotic contexts, they may show up in the form of obsessions and/or phobias; in the context of psychoses, they may show up as delusion formation. A too-great prevalence of M responses indicates a decline of spontaneity, an abating of the intensity of drives and their striving for expression; with too much delay the impulse is impoverished. It is also patent that the M re-sponse does not refer to a category of psychic make-up, or to a reaction tendency present in some people but absent in others: movement responses refer rather to a propensity present in all people, and varying only in its strength and the context in which it is set. With these views accepted, the term *introversion* can be forgotten.

Within the normal range, therefore, we should expect *M*'s to be more abundant in subjects who show cultural interests, and less so where these are absent and where normal inhibition increases.[39]

It is of great diagnostic significance that *M* responses are vulnerable to maladjustment, and especially to inhibitive tendencies. It does not follow, however, that the greater the impulsiveness of the subject the more *M* responses result. *M* responses flourish neither in inhibition nor in impulsiveness, but in that middle ground where there is a freedom of impulse from inhibition and yet a capacity for drive delay preventing impulsiveness.

Because the *M* responses are so vulnerable, it often becomes necessary to look for signs in the record indicating *M* tendencies or residual indications of movements—in other words, signs showing that at one time movement responses might have been given. Some of these signs derive from the statistical frequency with which *M* responses are given to different cards and to the different parts of each card; others derive from an implicit interrelationship between the actual response and the *M* response usually given to the area. Rorschach referred to these as signs of "repression" of *M* responses. We shall list here the most outstanding ones.

(1) The subject may see animals in motion where usually humans in motion are seen. This must not be extended to include all responses of animals in motion; these are indicators of *M* tendencies only where other *M* responses are present, and merely reflect the pervading tendency to actual *M* responses. (2) The subject may see human figures, or parts of them, as not in motion where they are usually seen in motion. As the definition of the area and its parts is intimately linked with the movement impression emanating from it, seeing such figures or parts of figures is a sign of some movement tendency. But this indication must not be extended to include any and all fragments of a human figure, because many of these can emanate from a pure form perception alone. (3) The subject may get a movement impression from the architectonics of the inkblot and its lines, without being able to mold his impression into any response. That such an impression comes about at all indicates considerable flexibility of the perceptual and associative processes; actually, such responses usually occur only in highly intellectualizing and aesthetic people. If, however, a person is restricted to such a vague movement impression without definite content,

---

[39] It must be remembered that the concept of inhibition does not refer merely to interpersonal relationships; clinically, inhibition implies a general lack of productiveness, ideational as well as affective.

his associative processes are probably inhibited. (4) The subject is able to give M responses in connection with unusual areas or on more difficult cards, but one or more of the most common M responses may be absent. The overwhelmingly frequent M responses are those given to Card III (the two black figures); next come Card II (the clowns) and Card IX (the witches); then come Card I (the middle figure with upraised hands) and Card VII (the two gossiping women). In contrast, Cards V, VI, and especially VIII, offer the greatest difficulty. Thus, no M on Card III but one on Card II or Card IX—or an M on Card III, none on II or IX, and an M on V—represent deviations from the expectancy. A difficulty in giving common M responses usually refers to some type of ideational symptom.

Finally, there are a few signs for which only our experience vouches. Persons who see the cards as "mirror images," or are overconcerned with the symmetry and/or asymmetry of the cards, or discuss the spatial relationships of the different parts of any card—in general, persons concerned with the formal abstract characteristics of the inkblots—show characteristics of personality and maladjustment similar to those of persons with an M prevalence. Under the influence of sodium amytal, some of these subjects may give full M responses in those places where previously they had discussed the formal relationships. Such discussions in a record appear, therefore, to carry some indications for the "repression" of M responses.

In the average-sized record of 20 to 25 responses, two or three M responses should occur. When R increases, M should increase to some degree also. If R grows disproportionately large relative to M, it is indicated that the subject's productivity exceeds what would be justified by his native endowment, and becomes an expression of factors other than endowment. If R remains too low in relation to M, either a strong quality ambition may be present or productivity commensurate to the subject's endowment is not fully achieved; the latter is almost always a sign of psychopathology. In regard to the areas chosen, there should be about two W responses for every M; in addition, the number of well-integrated whole responses ($W+$) should roughly equal the number of M's. If W's are more abundant, this suggests the subject's attempt to extend his abstractions and integrations beyond the range justified by his endowment; if W is significantly low with respect to M, it suggests impaired survey ability or a fabulatory, unrealistic tendency. Such a relationship is frequently found in some varieties of psychopaths and juvenile delinquents.

As the number of M responses increases, we should expect an increase of the $F+\%$ toward the optimum. If the $F+\%$ is low in a setting of many M responses, it constitutes a serious pathological indication, usually found in prepsychotic or psychotic conditions. This indication becomes especially conclusive if the form level of the M responses themselves is poor.

In connection with the other determinants, the number of *M* responses should be equaled by the number of form-color responses, to be described below; if the form-color responses are significantly fewer than the *M* responses, the possible presence of psychopathology is indicated. Following the section on color responses, we shall devote a special section to the diagnostic significance of the relationship between the number of *M* responses and the number and kind of color responses.

M *as a Diagnostic Indicator*

In general, the greatest accumulation of *M* responses is found in those records of persons who have ideational symptoms; conversely, the incidence of *M* responses decreases in conditions characterized by flattening, inertia, or monotony or inhibition of ideation. Among schizophrenics, we find the most *M* responses in acute cases, in whom active delusional thinking is clinically outstanding. In contrast, chronic and deteriorated schizophrenics show considerable flattening of ideation; even if they remain delusional, their delusions become unsystematized and transient. Furthermore, their capacity for "delay" of impulse has been so extensively impaired that the coming about of *M* responses, even with the presence of clear-cut delusions, is largely limited.

With regard to *M,* paranoid conditions resemble acute paranoid schizophrenia, and simple schizophrenia resembles other chronic schizophrenias. The constrictive rigidity that is part of paranoid ego structure works against the production of *M* responses, however, so that even highly deluded patients with one or another type of paranoid psychosis seldom produce more than a single *M.*

Overideational preschizophrenics tend to produce many *M* responses (four or more), or very few (one or none), depending largely on their premorbid make-up. On the other hand, the low incidence of *M* in inhibited preschizophrenics reflects their generalized inhibition, in which at best excessive sexual preoccupation represents an ideational symptom formation, but of a very meager and unimaginative kind. One might argue that the delusional condition of psychotic depressives should foster an accumulation of *M* responses; but this argument overlooks the fact that the generalized retardation characterizing these cases almost prohibits the coming about of *M* responses, which imply considerable perceptual mobility and associative versatility. Even a mild depression lowers the incidence of *M* responses; it is rare for any depressed patient to produce more than one *M.*

Within the neurotic range, we find the highest incidence of *M* responses in obsessive-compulsive cases. On the other hand, the anxiety and depression group, being similar to depressives, shows the lowest incidence of *M* responses. The incidence of *M* responses is also quite low in hysterics whose use of repression and inability to control impulses are clinically outstanding. Mixed neurotics, who clinically fall between obsessive-compulsives and hysterics, show up accordingly in regard to the incidence of *M* responses. Neurasthenics usually give very few *M* responses.

When other signs of pathology are present, a high incidence of *M* responses points to the presence of ideational symptom formation. Whether this symptom formation is obsessional, delusional, or mixed obsessional-phobic, can be determined only by reference to other aspects of the record. When signs of psychopathology are present, and *M* responses are absent or limited to one, a restriction of ideational output or an inability for delay is implied. This ideational limitation may be referable to generalized schizophrenic impairment, of the type seen in simple, chronic, and deteriorated schizophrenics; or to general retardation and inertia, as found in depressives and in neurasthenics; or to the presence of strong repressive trends and/or impulsiveness, as seen in hysterics.

We have already indicated that the location of the *M* responses on the different cards, or parts of cards, can be significant. The movement response to Card III is the most frequent universally, even where a striking poverty of *M* responses is the rule. This *M* response thus loses much of its significance, as compared to the others, and becomes conspicuous only if absent. It is also striking that depressives, excepting neurotic depressives, are limited almost exclusively to the *M* response on Card III if they achieve even that. Therefore, if a meager record which resembles that of severely depressed patients contains an *M* response to cards other than III—and, to some extent, II and IX—a depression is strongly contraindicated. This differential diagnostic issue frequently arises in connection with paranoid schizophrenics, some of whose Rorschach tests closely resemble those of depressives in general coarctation; schizophrenics, however, will probably give an *M* response other than on Card III. Finally, diagnostic groups we have characterized as being ideationally flat, impoverished, or inhibited are most likely to miss the *M* response on Card III and to give *M* responses elsewhere: chronic and deteriorated schizophrenics, simple schizophrenics, and inhibited preschizophrenics. Another factor besides depression of *M* responses may enter here: the residue of an inclination to give *M* responses, which persists in some chronic, deteriorated, or simple schizophrenics, may manifest itself in this irregular way. Hence, such irregularity frequently becomes indicative of a longstanding schizophrenic maladjustment which has devastated the patient's ideational output and organization.

COLOR RESPONSES

A color response is defined as one in which a color other than black, gray, or white has played a determining role. In other words, color was at

least part of the perceptual impression which set off the associative processes, regulated them in their course, and was integrated with them in the
final response. It is apparent that color responses can be given only on
Cards II, III, VIII, IX, and X.

The number and kind of color responses a subject gives constitute a
most significant aspect of the entire Rorschach record. The general population—and especially the general clinical population—uses *color* as a determinant more frequently than any other perceptual quality of the inkblot
excepting form. Further, the subject's use of *color* appears to reflect his
handling of affects, impulses, and actions. For both these reasons, the color
responses assume great significance in any test evaluation, and we shall
devote to them a proportionately detailed section. Finally, the emphasis
placed by Rorschach and all subsequent investigators on the relationship
between color and movement response appears to be a valid one, especially
for clinical diagnostic work; thus, following the analysis of color responses,
we shall devote a section to analyzing the diagnostic significance of the
relationship between movement and color scores.

The Three Basic Color Responses

The three basic color responses are: pure color responses, scored *C,*
in which the color impression is the sole determinant ("blood, because it
is red"); color-form responses, scored *CF,* in which the color plays the predominant role, but where some form elements are also involved ("flames:
the color of flame and these tonguelike projections"); and form-color responses, scored *FC,* in which the color contributes to the response but is
contained within a definitive form response, and is only of equal or subordinate significance to the form determinant ("tomato worm: shaped like a
worm and it is green"). It is obvious that the intensity and regulative effect
of the color impression decrease as one proceeds from *C* through *CF* to *FC.*
One of the crucial quantitative scores is that designated as *sum C.* In this
sum, a pure *C* response merits 1½ units, a *CF* response merits 1 unit, and
an *FC* response merits only ½ unit. Thus, a subject with one *FC,* one *CF,*
and two *C* responses will have a *sum C* of ½ + 1 + 3, or a total of 4.5.
Although a gross quantitative measure, the *sum C* is important because it
indicates the intensity of the subject's affective life, although it tells nothing
about its quality.

General Problems of Inquiry

The real issues of inquiry are: (a) when not to make it, and still be
safe in scoring; (b) how to make it without arousing the critical awareness
of the patient, and thereby disrupting the homogeneity of the record; (c)

how to use its results not merely to give a score but also—and mainly—to assess the quality of the response behind the score.

Let us first re-emphasize that the examiner must use as little inquiry as possible. Even though the card is removed from sight, the subject under pressure of inquiry may invoke an image, visual or verbal, of the area in question, and start a logical exploration of it for further justification of his response. Once aroused, this reflective attitude will basically change the usual conditions of the test administration, and limit the discriminating effect of the test. The existence of these critical and logical attitudes, aroused by too much inquiry, can easily be ascertained by the examiner, especially in introspective and intelligent subjects. In cases where the inquiry has made the subject overready to verbalize about some aspect of the inkblot, it becomes necessary to ask, "Did you have that in mind when you first looked at the inkblot and gave your response?" and also, "Why did you not mention that aspect of your response when I first asked you about it?"

It could be argued that, as long as the subject is able to invoke a specific aspect in the course of a series of inquiries, the score of that response should take into account all the information elicited; and that, in general, inquiry should consist of a thorough questioning concerning all aspects of every response. The experience countermanding this argument and defining the general ideas of inquiry may be summed up as follows: First of all, extensive questioning makes the administration time-consuming and generally impractical. Second, overdone inquiry relies upon the ability of all subjects to give a correct account of their conscious experiences, which actually few have. Third, if extensive questioning were pursued after each card, the subject would grow alert to features of the inkblots previously ignored and equally alert to his own conscious experiences—both changes of attitude being detrimental to a correct administration of the Rorschach test. The subject should take the test directed only by his own spontaneous attitude toward the inkblots, with whatever spontaneous changes occur in this attitude in the course of the test. Fourth, if inquiry were started after all 10 cards have been completed, and during it the cards were not shown to the subject, the inquiries would rely on his memory of a mass of vaguely structured impressions, and the results could not be considered reliable; and if this delayed inquiry were pursued with the cards before the subject, the critical and logical attitude fostered by the inquiry would now find concrete support for its speculations, and homogeneity within the test would be lost. Of course, the material thereby obtained would lend itself to interpretation, since there are individual limitations imposed even on such speculation. But there is no end to the mass of material inquiry can bring out if pursued extensively, and since there can be no objective measure of the amount of pressure imposed by the examiner or experienced by the subject, the material obtained would of necessity lose homogeneity.

In connection with the color responses, inquiry should be made only if one of two basic requirements is met: when the subject's spontaneous verbalizations indicate that color has played a role in his response, without indicating the strength of this role; or when the content of the response given appears congruous with the color of the area chosen, although the subject has not specifically mentioned the color. An example of the first would be, "A red rose"; an example of the second would be, "Caterpillars" to the lower green areas on Card X. Some subjects even after inquiry have not made it clear whether a response was an *FC,* a *CF,* or a *C.* The subject should not be pressed too far to elicit a clear statement; not only will his final conclusion frequently be arbitrary—due to the fallible character of introspective reports in general—but the persistent inquiry will make him alert as to what the examiner is after, and confusing and deceptive verbalizations may result. The statement in the response and the reaction to a not-leading inquiry are likely to be spontaneous reactions, and thus objective material for interpretation. Further inquiry elicits reactions not only to the card, but to the examiner's questions as well, and thus cannot be considered to be of the same quality as the test responses proper. If the subject cannot be pinned down, this elusiveness should be considered characteristic of his responses and of him; and establishing such characteristics is, after all, the purpose of inquiry. With these general considerations in mind, let us turn to the specific problems that arise in connection with each of the varieties of color responses.

The Pure Color Response: C. If the subject says, "Blood because it is red," obviously no inquiry is needed. In such a response, the content itself shows that no form can be involved; thus a score of *C* is proper. Specific inquiry into a pure color response is made where the content of the response does not seem congruent with the color of the area chosen: e.g., if the subject says "grass" to the brown-orange area at the lower side of Card X. The schizophrenic who gave this response explained, "It looked like dried grass."

The main problem in scoring *C* responses is to differentiate them from *CF* responses. Inquiry should be aimed at eliciting the presence of form elements. A subject's spontaneous verbalization is frequently conclusive in this respect: the response "Red-hot explosion" to the central red area on Card II shows that form elements, though relatively indistinct and diffuse, are present; this response is explicitly *CF.* The response "Fire" to the same area leaves the issue open, however; and inquiry will be necessary to determine whether tonguelike flames were included in the impression, or whether it was "Fire because it is red." The response "Blood" is explicitly a pure *C*, as is clear when the examiner compares it with "Red-hot explosion." Such a comparative procedure is of considerable importance in scoring and evaluating Rorschach records: examiners may thereby counter-weigh their own bias.

If the first question of inquiry, "What made you think it was fire?", elicits only a mention of the color of the area, the inquiry should be pursued further: "Was there anything else that made you think that?" Whatever the outcome of this second inquiry may be, the response must be scored pure *C*, and only an inclination to *CF* should be qualitatively noted if, after the second or third question, the subject introduces some form element into his response.

There is a further consideration relevant to the distinction between *C* and *CF* responses: if such a response as "Blood" occurs embedded in a more complex response with a clear-cut form prevalence—Card II, "Two bears fighting, there's blood on them"—the score of pure *C* for the blood is not warranted. Here the associative process has not been ruled solely by the color impression, the impact of the color has not prevented a sharp perceptual organization of the area chosen, and thus *CF* is the correct score. The response should be broken down into two parts—the bears and the blood—to be scored separately.

The Color-Form Response: CF. As the *CF* response falls between the *FC* and *C* responses, the inquiry is aimed at distinguishing it from these. We have already discussed the differentiation from *C*. The differentiation from *FC* becomes a problem mainly in connection with responses whose content is some very colorful animal, plant, scene, etc. Frequently the subject's spontaneous verbalization decides the issue. If the subject says to Card X, "All these five colors—the same on both sides—remind me of the brightly colored wings of a butterfly," *CF* is the score. If he says to the lower middle area of Card VIII, "A colorful butterfly," or to one side of the lower green area on Card X, "A green caterpillar," the likelihood is that we are dealing with an *FC* response. In these latter instances, inquiry should be pursued only if the record shows a preponderance of *CF* responses, especially if *FC* responses are usually given to the area in question.[40]

But a great proportion of *CF* responses are not so explicitly verbalized. It is erroneous to give an *FC* score automatically when a subject says, "Flower" to an area which is usually seen as a flower of good form: this

---

[40] [According to the logic of Rapaport's definitions, no such problem exists: a butterfly and a caterpillar both have definitive forms, and both of these would have been routinely scored *FC* without further ado in the years following publication of this book, especially in view of the remarks on inquiry two paragraphs below. See Editor's Foreword.—Ed.]

response may be a *CF,* and in some schizophrenics even a pure *C.* The examiner should first ask, "What made it look like a flower?" and only a clear-cut form articulation of the area justifies the score *FC.* Sometimes this first question elicits only an ambiguous answer, or merely a reference to the colors; the examiner should inquire further, "Was there anything else that made it look like a flower?" If a clear-cut answer is obtained it is practical to ask the question once again, to avoid intimating to the subject that the examiner "got what he wanted." If no clear-cut answer is obtained then, the examiner should, as a last resort, ask the question Rorschach made specific use of: "Do you think it might have looked like a flower if it were gray?" If the subject says he thinks so, and is able to offer sufficient justification, the score *FC* is correct. It is advisable to avoid this question as much as possible, because it makes clear to the subject that the examiner is especially interested in his use of color and then he may artificially increase or decrease the number of color responses.

Another problem of differentiation arises in such responses as that frequently given to Card X, "A collection of bugs." If inquiry elicits only the statement, "Well, the general colorfulness of it and the many small longish shapes," with no further form specifications, the score *CF* is warranted. If, however, the subject proceeds to enumerate specific forms, the *FC* score is correct.

Finally, a caution about inquiry. We have mentioned that there is no need to inquire into the relatively clear-cut *FC* response, "A green caterpillar," to the lower middle area of Card X. If one does inquire into this response, one frequently gets the answer, "Mainly because it was green, but also the shape of it." It may then be argued that the subject was most impressed by the color, as indicated by the sequence in his verbalization; but such scoring solely in reference to verbalization would be erroneous. The scoring must consider the subject's verbalization in relationship to the area chosen. In this example, the form of the area is so close to that of a caterpillar that the subject's verbalizations cannot be trusted to communicate the processes that led to his response; whatever the impact of the color was, a correct form perception came about: the color was merely an amplification of it, making it a "caterpillar" rather than a "snake." Thus, too much inquiry may weaken the examiner's sense for the relationship between the area chosen and the verbalization of the response, and may prompt him to rely too much on the subject's explanation. These explanations are frequently mere rationalizations or arbitrary conclusions, without support from careful and correct introspections. On the other hand, as we pointed out, it is erroneous to score a response solely in reference to the area chosen, especially when such responses as "flower" or "butterfly" are in question.

The Form-Color Response: FC. It remains to take up the problems of distinguishing the *FC* from the pure *F* response—in other words, of deciding whether a response of a clear-cut definitive form was influenced by a color percept. The problem does not arise when the response is explicit— "a green caterpillar"—or when its content is such as to exclude the color of the area as a determinant, as in "sheep" to the upper green areas on Card X. But when the area chosen bears a color consonant with the content of the response and no mention is spontaneously made of color, inquiry must be made. Here too the examiner cannot be guided by the area alone; the response "caterpillar" need have no reference to the greenness of the area, although that greenness is quite consistent with the response. The examiner must make explicit inquiry: "What made you think it was a caterpillar?" If the subject answers, "The form and the color of it," the score is *FC*. To be sure, this *FC* does not bear as strong a color impression as that conveyed by the spontaneous verbalization, "A green caterpillar." If color is not emphasized by the subject in response to inquiry, if he delays any mention of it until the form aspect has been extensively elaborated upon or until a second question has been asked, the value of the *FC* score is decreased; and even though explicit mention of color may be made eventually, it is our practice to put a tacit question mark over the letter *C* in the *FC* score.

The examiner should be careful to avoid giving *FC* scores on the basis of such verbalizations as, "This green here looks like a caterpillar." Frequently the reference to the color is merely a means of identifying the area, and has no implication that the color was a determinant. As a matter of fact, experience indicates that an excessive use of such identification rarely goes with good color responses (especially not with *FC* responses) and usually indicates a weakening of the impact of the color as an agent setting off associative processes. Nevertheless, inquiry must be made in these instances if the color designation is compatible with the content of the response. There is one exception to this: "This red here is blood" is usually a pure *C* response in no need of further inquiry. Thus, this problem arises mainly in connection with *FC* responses that can usually stand up without the integration of color, even though the color may be appropriate.

We shall turn now to the six variations of these three basic color responses, and indicate briefly their definition, differentiation, and scores; plus four color-relevant notations.

The F/C *Response.* In these the colors are used merely to distinguish areas having specific form connotations. Thus, the response "Anatomical drawing" with specific organs pointed out, and the different colors used to contrast these different organs, warrants this *F/C* score. Furthermore, responses in which colors are "put on" or "painted on" or "used as a mark," in reference to or in the framework of specific forms, are F/C responses. These must be segregated from the regular FC responses, because here the color impression has barely been integrated with the content in the associative process. The problem of inquiry into F/C is to determine whether specific forms were involved at all; if they were not, the score C/F is in place.

The C/F Response. Responses scored C/F may at first glance appear quite similar to those scored F/C since in neither has the color impression stimulated or become integrated with specific associative processes; but actually C/F indicates a much stronger impact of color. An example of a C/F is, "Some kind of medical drawing: they have all those different colors on them—but I don't know what it is meant to show." A lack of specificity, in contrast to the F/C responses, serves as a distinguishing sign. Not only anatomical drawings, but "maps" and "diseased conditions" are relevant in this connection.[41]

The Form-Color Response by Denial: $F\bar{C}$. Here the influence of color on the associative process is indicated in the response only by a negation of the color of the area chosen. For example, on Card VIII in reference to the side pink figures, "A bear: but it's the wrong color." This score never requires inquiry, for its verification is given by the spontaneous verbalization. The subject may introduce some such comment in the course of other inquiry about the response; this rejection of the color should not be taken into account in the score, because it is the result of the mobilization of critical or speculative attitudes during inquiry. Such additional reference to the inappropriate color should not be taken to indicate an impact of color upon the associative process underlying the response.

The Arbitrary Form-Color Responses: FC arb. Here the use of color is obviously incompatible with the content of the response, but the subject clings to its arbitrary inclusion. This response indicates an integration difficulty similar to that described in the previous paragraph, except that here the critical attitude toward the response is entirely lost. For example, the subject may see "green sheep" or "blue monkeys." By definition, these are in the range of FC responses; the discrepancy exists only by virtue of the presence of a definitive form. Almost always these responses are spontaneously verbalized so clearly that inquiry is not necessary. However, there are subjects who will have idiosyncratic memories of "blue monkeys" or a fairy tale about a "green rabbit"; the task of inquiry will be to ascertain the possible presence of these (which are then scored F/C). There are

[41] The scores F/C and C/F were systematically introduced into the literature by Klopfer (Klopfer & Kelley, 1942) [see also Klopfer et al., 1954].

other subjects who in a humorous vein will use such descriptions, but the entire context of the record and the verbalization will aid in recognizing these. The inquiry, "Blue monkeys? What do you mean?" will immediately elicit a jocular explanation.[42]

The examiner must proceed cautiously because *FC arb* responses are given almost exclusively by preschizophrenic or schizophrenic subjects. Here the inquiry should be, "I am sorry, I do not know much about monkeys (or sheep): are there blue monkeys?" Whether the subject denies their reality or not the score *FC arb* is in place; if he believes in their existence, but does not give an idiosyncratic explanation, the presence of a schizophrenic process is established.

The Color-Form Response with Texture: (C)F. These responses differ from the ordinary color-form responses only in that the texture of the color plays a role in setting off the associative processes. For example, the subject may say in connection with the lower pink areas on Card IX, "Lumps of strawberry ice cream; it's pink and it has that kind of soft grainy texture that cold ice cream has." Such responses represent a perceptual penetration of the color itself, which, however, does not lead to a more definitive form in the response. Nevertheless *(C)F* has milder implications that *CF*. Other such responses are usually on the order of "A piece of pink silk or gauze," or "A strip of muscle tissue with that fleshlike texture." The examiner need not inquire into such color experiences; they do not occur very frequently, and the subject's spontaneous verbalization, or his answer to some general question in the inquiry, will provide the indication for this score.[43]

The Symbolic Pure Color Response: C sym. A subject may say to Card III, "Two people, and this red here in the middle stands for an attraction between them"; or to the whole of Card VIII, "An animal because it is colorful, because colorful things are mobile, because mobile things are alive and animals are both alive and mobile: therefore, this must represent an animal." Such responses do not require inquiry, because their derivation is apparent in the verbalization itself. Sometimes they may be obtained in the course of a general inquiry: the second example was derived thus. There will be a few instances where the subject's verbalization more or less indicates that a single inquiry may elicit color symbolism. On Card III

[42] [Such responses are to be scored *FC arb* but do not carry as much pathological weight; they are common in character disorders.—Ed.]

[43] [In the tradition that developed, such responses in which both the hue and the texture or diffusion of the colored ink play a part were scored *C(C)F,* and the score *(C)F* reserved for similar use of shading in colored areas when the color itself was *not* used or was explicitly called irrelevant by the subject. See discussion of *F(C),* below. Responses in which both *C* and *(C)* are determinants may have specific value as an indicator of suicidal tendencies; see Appelbaum and Holzman (1962).—Ed.]

the subject may say, "Two people being attracted to each other," and only by inquiry will it become clear that the central red area symbolizes attraction.

The Deterioration Pure Color Response: C det. The word "deterioration" is included here because of the diagnostic connotations of the response. In these pure color responses, the interpretation of the color is either gory or uncanny, or gives the impression of an extreme haphazardness of association with something (even an object) colored like the area in question. An example of the former, to Card IX, "Some kind of malignant condition; the pink is like inflammation and it has that gangrenous green quality"; an example of the latter, to the yellow areas on Card X, "Egg yolk" or "Urine stain." These responses may take a form which combines both gore and extreme haphazardness, and is often seen in hebephrenic schizophrenics: "Blue blood, green blood, yellow blood." All these usually require inquiry, because the spontaneous verbalization, "This is tissue," may hide a gory elaboration; or because in the "egg yolk" kind of response some form element may be present. Inquiry almost always brings to the fore the deteriorative implications of these responses.

The Color-Naming Response. This consists of a mere naming of colors. It is a response in so far as the subject names the colors with an air of complying with the test instruction, "What could this be?" It is relatively infrequent in routine clinical work, and is seen mostly in certain organic disorders.

Color Denomination. This is color naming as a mere reference to the inkblot, and is not given by the subject as a response—nor should it be considered such by the examiner. Whenever a color is referred to specifically, but not for the purpose of locating the area chosen for a response, or in any other relation to a response, this notation is in place.

Color Description. References to the beauty or colorfulness of the cards which are not intended as responses should not be considered as such, and only the notation "color description" is in place.

Color denomination and color description do not involve any inquiry: they refer to spontaneous verbalization. If they are verbalized in the course of other inquiry, they should be disregarded.

Some Further Qualitative Indications. The examiner should note whether the subject's color responses are given in reaction to the green-blue-grayish areas, the yellow-brown-orange areas, or the red-pink areas. He should also qualitatively note whether the color responses accumulate early in the test, or only on the last one or two cards; whether one kind of color response is given on each of the colored cards; and other aspects of the place of color responses in the general sequence of responses.

The Psychological Rationale of the Color Responses[44]

In the literature on the Rorschach test, the color responses have been considered representative of (a) the subject's prevailing mode of affective expression and responsiveness, (b) the mode of control of impulse and action, and (c) "extraversion" or "extratensive tendencies." In the current theory of personality, the relationship between these three concepts is unclear and the concepts themselves are quite vague. Accordingly, much of our rationale will consist of stating our empirical impression regarding what aspects of the subject's psychological experiencing correspond to the color responses and their varieties; and in this connection we shall need to elaborate somewhat on that concept of affect which we have found useful in our clinical work. But it must be stated in advance that, just as with introversion, we shall not concern ourselves with extraversion either as a tendency or as a personality type. Methodological difficulties of the extraversion-introversion dichotomy cannot be discussed here; nor can we attempt to demonstrate that considering two such categories or tendencies as basic human characteristics leads to dismaying and insoluble contradictions in the course of clinical work. These contradictions will become apparent to any examiner who insists upon the internal consistency of his diagnosis, the internal consistency of his theoretical assumptions, and the consistency between the two. To cite an example, any attempt to explain the marked decrease of movement responses and increase of color responses accompanying schizophrenic deterioration as representing an increase of "extratensive tendencies" would entirely miss the point of the psychological changes which have occurred in these cases, and would amount to psychological nonsense.

The Impact of Color upon the Perceptual and Associative Processes. When a response includes as one of its determinants the color of the area chosen, it is apparent that the perceptual impact of the color has initiated an associative process in the subject, a process which has been more or less controlled in its course by the color impression and more or less successful

[44] [Rapaport's continuing concern with understanding the nature of controlling processes and the phenomenon here called "delay" led him to an exploration of the related issues of autonomy (1951b, 1957c) and of activity and passivity (1953b). In these later papers, he laid down the beginnings of a new basis for understanding the relations between control of drive and control over environmental press: they could be understood in terms of the growth of structures that subserved the person's way of defending himself against both types of threats to ego autonomy. The implications of these ideas for understanding responses to color in the Rorschach test were taken up and developed by Shapiro (1956, 1960). His papers represent the furthest extension of Rapaport's ideas on the rationale of color responses, and are recommended for study to supplement the basic themes presented here. See also Miller (1962) and Holt (1960, 1965b).—Ed.]

in integrating it into the final response. The questions the examiner must answer, from the subject's spontaneous verbalizations and from inquiry, are: How strong an impact did the color have upon the subject, and to what extent did this impact restrain him from perceptually articulating the form of that area? How far, if at all, was the subject thus prevented from integrating the color impression with the form characteristics of the area chosen? How much integrative effort to achieve unified whole responses was possible? In terms of the intensity of this effort, how successful was the final integration of color, form, and other perceptual qualities of the blot area? To answer these questions, we shall here outline briefly the implications each variety of color response has as to the associative and perceptual processes underlying it.

The *pure color response* in its usual form ("blood," "grass," or "water") appears to come about when there is a "short-circuiting" (see Chapter 8) of the associative process so that it does not reach any definitive content, and instead produces as a response possibility a content which shows only a very slight conceptual distance from the concrete color impression. In turn, this short-circuiting precludes any return to the area chosen which could lead to a perceptual articulation and structuring of that area, and to an integration of it with the rest of the blot. Thus, the pure color responses represent an absence of the delay which would have allowed for a further development of associations and their integration with other qualities of the blot. It must be presumed here, as well as in connection with the following responses, that it is the color impression itself which disrupts the course of the perceptual and associative processes; later on we shall attempt to explain why this should be the effect of the color impact.

The *color-form response* appears to come about when there has been more delay possible than that found for the pure color responses. Yet the delay is only minimally effective, as the form aspects of the area chosen are barely integrated with the color impressions in the course of the associative process. We have explained in our rationale of the form responses the necessity for delay in the emergence of adequate or good form responses. In the course of this delay, the perceptual impact initiates associative processes; these in turn lead to perceptual reorganizations of the ink-blot which, in turn, are brought to a focus in the course of the associative process and modify it; this process repeats itself until the final result is an integration of a clear-cut percept with a definite content. The weakness of the form element in the color-form (CF) response indicates the insufficiency of whatever delay is achieved, and gives this response an impulsive character—though a complete abandonment of control or delay, as in the pure C response, is not indicated.

The *form-color response* requires the greatest delay of all the color responses, as it represents an integration of an appropriate color with a definitive form. In other words, the impacts of both the color and form of the area chosen were worked through in the course of the associative process. This associative process, in interaction with the progressive perceptual reorganization of the inkblot, progressed to a vantage point from which the final articulation of the area chosen, its form and its color, appeared in a harmonious integration, and was so verbalized. Consequently flexible control and careful regulation of the perceptual and associative processes are indicated by these responses.

Let us turn to the less frequent variants of these three basic color responses. The F/C response indicates that the regulating effect on the associative process was exerted exclusively by the form aspect of the area chosen; the inclusion of color in the response, for the purpose of differentiating areas ("anatomical chart"), does not represent an integration of color and form by the associative process, but rather an arbitrary addition. The C/F response represents a similar but more extensive difficulty: not only a genuine integration of the color impression, but a genuine form integration is absent. That is to say, neither the specific articulations of the area chosen nor the specific colors included in that area have set off any extensive associative process; the subject was therefore limited to giving a response based on the vagueness of his initial impressions. Here not only arbitrary use of color, but a vagueness of form perception characterizes the response: associative and perceptual elaborations are meager.

The $F\bar{C}$ (by denial) response has a background similar in some respects to that of the F/C response. The form of the area chosen initiates an associative process which leads to a considerable articulation of the area; the colors have an impact too, but not sufficient to influence the associative process, which leads to a response in terms of the form determinant. The color impact remains present, as in the F/C responses, but the subject retains a sufficiently critical attitude toward his productions to exclude arbitrary color impressions. Thus, the $F\bar{C}$ response indicates a weakness of the ability to integrate colors in the course of the associative process— probably due at least partly to weakness of impact of the color impression— although this process is not entirely able to reject the color impression.

The *FC arb* response represents a complete loss of the critical attitude toward the response, which otherwise is like the $F\bar{C}$: the subject will see a "blue monkey," not even excused as a "monkey painted blue." As in the F/C response, there is no real integration of the color into the final response, nor has the color exerted any steering effect upon the associative processes giving rise to the response: the color was there, and simply had to be included.[45]

The *C sym* responses are a special case of the pure *C* responses. In the symbolic responses we usually have an obvious communication of overvalent ideational content; its pressure may be so great that the associative processes need progress only minimally before the content emerges, or the symbolic interpretation may emanate after a reasonable course of associative pathways has been traversed. The former is the more usual in schizophrenics, to whose *C sym* responses a considerable air of reality attaches ("This red in the middle *must* stand for some attraction between them"); the latter case is the more usual in normals, by whom the response is given with an air of "fancy" (*"Let's say* that this red in the middle stands for the love they bear for each other"). In either case, this is a pure color response, and indicates that there was no return of the associative processes to the inkblot itself to articulate it and influence the progressive perceptual reorganization of it leading to more definitive forms.

The *C det* responses are another special case of pure *C* responses. But such responses as "urine stain" indicate the lack not only of any perceptual reorganization of the inkblot, but also of any associative re-evaluation of the response possibility which comes to mind. As a result, these responses have the strongest "reality" taint of all, and amount merely to a conceptual subsumption of the color in question with practically no associative play around the original color impression. The other variety of *C det* responses —endowed with the qualities of gore and the uncanny—must be considered, like the *C sym* responses, to be products of some overvalent morbid content of the subject's associative processes. Thus, either an extreme inertia or an extreme fluidity of the associative processes may give rise to the *C det* responses.

The *color-naming* response represents no associative departure from the color impression itself, and indicates—by the misunderstanding of the test instructions—that the subject's anticipatory abilities are impaired. *Color denominations* and *color descriptions* are not responses proper, but indicate that the colors on the inkblot have had an impact upon the subject; this impact neither sets off any associative processes nor leads to any perceptual articulation of the area in question. Thus, if not followed by true color responses, both these references to the colors represent an es-

---

[45] The *FC arb* responses, looked at from another point of view, indicate an extensive impairment of the subject's ability to make abstractions; that is to say, the area chosen is taken as an indivisible unit in which the color given *must* be accepted and used because it is there. In this respect, the *FC arb* responses show much similarity to the responses which we shall describe later as *confabulations.*

sential inadequacy of the subject's ability to cope with color impressions.

This completes our survey of the role played by the perceptual and associative processes in the coming about of the different varieties of color responses. Before going further, we must consider the problem of the relationship between the colors of the inkblots and affects.

The Relationship of Color to Affect. Experience appears to show that the subject's use of the colors as determinants in some way refers to his characteristic expression and control of affects, impulses, and actions. Attempts have been made to explain why this relationship should obtain. Comparisons to the role of colors in affective display in the phylogenetic series (mating colors), in different ethnological groups (colors of sorrow and joy), in figures of speech ("rose-colored glasses" or "dark glasses"), are suggestive but weak analogies. Furthermore, all of these may be merely different manifestations of the same underlying relationship between colors and affect. Thus, these analogical statements do not represent any real explanation.

Another attempt to understand this relationship posits some intrinsic relationship between colors and affects, and rests merely with the statement that the colors have an impact upon the associative processes similar to that of affects in everyday life. But this formulation also does not represent a real answer to the problem: it offers no explanation of the relationship, but merely asserts its existence and attempts to describe its manifestations.

We feel that the following formulation of the relationship goes as far as one can go at the present state of knowledge: it appears that, dependent upon their organization of affects and impulses and their modes of control of these, people have associative processes that allow for dealing with the color impressions in a specific manner characteristic of their affective life. For example, persons prone to quick and violent emotional outbursts bring to the testing situation a make-up which has its characteristic associative processes: these processes are such that they will be greatly stimulated by, and will cling to, the colored areas of the inkblots. More generally, the subject's characteristic organization of his associative processes will exercise a selective effect over the stimulations emanating from each inkblot. Thus it may deal sufficiently or too much or too little with the color impressions, and it may deal with them in a way which leads to responses through associative short-circuiting or any other pathological or characteristic associative course. But in order to make this formulation more explicit, we must now outline briefly the view of affects and actions which we have found useful in our personality and diagnostic interpretations of Rorschach records. Then we may consider again the specific variants of the color responses in relation to these theoretical considerations, as well as to the previous considerations of perceptual and associative processes.

A Clinical View of Affects and Actions.[46] Let us take it for granted that human action issues out of needs which are instinctual in their roots, which set up tensions within the person, and which require release. The infant is quite limited in the choice of ways in which he may achieve such release, but in the course of development, a variety of definite channels of discharge is established. While finding and setting up such channels for discharge as will secure in a safe way the different kinds of satisfactions, one must institute a delay of discharge of the tensions themselves. In other words, discharge of the original impulse which was directed toward a specific goal —an object satisfying it—becomes delayed; methods of probing for, ascertaining, selecting, and grasping the satisfying objects with least risk are developed, but only at the expense of delaying immediate action toward the goal. In turn, these selective probings make for more and more delay of action, inasmuch as the ensuing differentiation of the psychological environment makes the search for satisfaction much more complex. Thus a kind of self-perpetuating system of probing and delay comes about, which extends its scope to wider and wider areas of the person's functioning. The various methods of selective probing derive their driving power from the original instinctual source; but as development proceeds they become relatively independent of this source and are able to regulate autonomously the availability and mode of expenditure of these instinctual energies. For example, we learn to look for food even though not ravenously hungry, and we may feel and think about things other than hunger and food even when our thoughts may be ultimately subservient to the goal of getting food. Thus, relatively autonomous derivatives of the original drive are built up. These derivatives are partly in the nature of ideation or thought processes, and partly more of an impulsive character like their instinctual sources. The latter derivatives are those that supply the energy for action, and give rise to specific manifestations of their momentary status which we refer to as affects.

The smoother the control of the delay and satisfaction of the instinctual impulses, the more varied and rich their derivatives become. If the delay cannot be achieved smoothly, repressive measures become necessary, with a consequent impoverishment of the derivatives. But the repressive measures are not always successful and do not always result in smooth control, and their inability for achieving delay will be indicated by the appearance of affects in spite of the repression: in this case, the affects will not manifest themselves in mild, smooth, and richly variable forms, but rather in spasmodic and explosive forms, with little variation or modulation of feeling tones. The more widespread and successful the use of repressive meas-

[46] [See also Rapaport (1953a, 1959a).—Ed.]

ures to achieve control over instinctual strivings, the more impoverished becomes the variability of affective experience, and the more gross and violent the affective expressions will be when they do break through the repression.

Thus, affects are manometers and vents of the state of tension of the instinctual needs from which they were derived.[47] They are also indicators of the smoothness or spasmodicity of control of action. We are not referring here to affective expression merely in the sense of expressive movements, or of those physiological changes described by Cannon. Affects may find their expression in physiological changes, in actions and their planning, and in structure and mode of thought processes and their disturbances generally. In all these spheres the affective expression may be of normal or pathological character, momentary or chronic. In brief, affects may find expression in any and all of these functions in the course of their normal discharge.[48]

The color response and its variants are considered to be representatives of these affects and modes of controlling actions. That is, they represent (1) the degree to which repressive control of instinctual needs has impoverished the affective and feeling output of the subject; (2) the degree to which the control of these impulses functions smoothly, allowing for delay and at the same time for vigor and free availability of the impulses; (3) the degree to which control is not achieved and the instinctual tensions manifest themselves in violent affective display; (4) the degree to which all attempt at control is abandoned, with consequent flouting of the usual channels of probing for and finding satisfaction, and abandonment of affects as indicators of conflict tensions—a state of affairs that obtains conspicuously in chronic and deteriorated schizophrenic conditions;[49] (5) the extent and mode of control over actions, which runs grossly parallel to the forms of affective experience and display described here.

But this discussion would not be complete without a discussion of the form determinant, which so overwhelmingly often is intertwined with color as a determinant. A further elaboration on the significance of the form

[47] This view of affective experience should not be construed as a rejection of the view that affects come to expression only when some form of conflict of strivings is present (see MacCurdy, 1925): the formulation described merely looks upon the same problem from a different point of view, and in fact implicitly recognizes the "conflict" theory of affect. See Rapaport (1942a).

[48] A summary of the pertinent literature can be found in Rapaport (1942a), Chapters II and IX.

[49] The most thoughtful writing known to the present authors on the nature of affects in relation to schizophrenia is *The Psychology of Emotion* by MacCurdy (1925). This is one of the finest volumes in psychiatric literature, and is too rarely referred to. MacCurdy's views, though having much influenced the writers, are not identical with the above sketchily summarized views.

determinant in connection with the color determinant will add considerably to the clarity of inferences to be drawn from the specific color responses. In our discussion of the form determinant, we stated that a member of our civilization learns to look upon the world in terms of *forms* and *formal relationships* which lend themselves to description and communication in objective, logical terms.[50] As the delay of impulses developed, the possibility arose for the development of thought processes; by means of these, reality was tested and the route to the satisfying object that involved the least danger was searched for. Aspects of thinking—memory organization, concept formation, anticipation—were crystallized into a system usually referred to as logical or purposive thinking, the function of which was not only to make the delay profitable, but also to secure and safeguard the existence of the delay. That is, the course of the thought processes so evolved was dictated not merely by impulses, but also by discernible forms of reality. Thus were built up the ego and a conflict-free sphere in the ego where logical thinking predominated.[51]

Here reference should be made to our discussion of drive cathexes and hypercathexes at the disposal of the ego (see above, pp. 107f.). The hypercathectic energies of the conflict-free sphere of the ego are freely available for whatever purposes conscious logical thinking may require; in contrast, the drive cathexes manifest themselves in affects and action impulses. Having advanced these general considerations, let us now attempt to view the variants of the common color responses in terms of this conception of affects and actions.

The Specific Significance of the Variants of the Color Response. The *FC* response represents a successful integration of the form and color impressions, and requires sufficient delay to allow for the emergence in the course of the associative process of that content possibility which could successfully integrate the two. We interpret these responses as indicators of the capacity for affective rapport, for emotional adaptation. In these responses the strict regard for forms, with an appropriately integrated affective response, means that the course of the subject's associative process in everyday life is guided by a factual assessment of reality, yet includes an appropriate expression of affect. The adaptation to reality is sound, but is not limited to cold reasoning; impulses are not suppressed, but can occur in an appropriate manner—that is, in a degree and form which is in keeping with the reality context. Furthermore, this affective expression occurs to the subjective satisfaction of the subject, carrying both empathy for the

[50] See, e.g., the theory of physics, which since Galileo has been in a constant struggle to get away from the "secondary qualities" of matter by describing these "qualities" in terms of the three dimensions of space, time, and mass.

[51] For a specific elaboration of this point, see Hartmann (1939).

feeling of others and that quality which arouses the empathy of others for oneself. Furthermore, the *FC* response indicates that the subject's actions are smoothly controlled, and a course is taken which allows for a reasonable discharge of tension: here too both sentient environment and subject alike experience the feeling tone accompanying the action. This is the meaning of the terms "affective rapport" and "emotional adaptation." The extent to which such adaptability characterizes a subject can only be inferred from the quantity and quality of *FC* responses he gives, and their relationship to his other kinds of color responses. Thus, qualitatively the *FC* response of a poor form level indicates only misguided and unsuccessful attempts at adaptation. We shall defer discussion of the quantitative interrelationships until later in this section.

The *CF* response indicates a weak perceptual impact of the form of the blot, and carries the connotation that delay or associative and perceptual elaboration have contributed little to the final response. The *CF* response stands for a vivid, unfettered affectivity, for poorly controlled impulses, for spasmodic control of actions, and a general minimization of delay or constraint. Thus, where *CF*'s are massed, impulsive acts and affective outbursts may reasonably be expected. This type of inference must, however, always be modified by the relationship between the number of *CF* and *FC* responses, which we shall come to presently. It must be pointed out here that if control is too rigid in its repressive measures, or takes the form of blocking, the test record may not contain any color responses; yet pent-up impulses may break through this rigid control in the form of tantrums and excitements. These considerations hold true especially for children and psychotics. Thus, the absence of *CF* responses need not indicate the lack of potentialities for outbursts: rigid and brittle control, which restricts the occurrence of all determinants other than form and gives rise to a generally poor form level, particularly on colored cards, must always be suspected of harboring such potentialities. The examiner should also keep in mind that in certain character formations affective outbursts and impulsive acts become transformed into somatic expressions, and will still be represented by *CF* responses.

The pure color response represents either the extreme of impulsive and wild affectivity, or an abandonment of all control. This abandonment of control essentially eliminates affects, as we know them in everyday life, because affects are derivatives of the instinctual impulse brought about by the development of the controlling mechanisms; with the partial or full abandonment of these controls, the conditions are so changed—as in deteriorated schizophrenics—that the clinician usually speaks either of inappropriate affect or of flattening of affect. A great wealth of *C* responses may be given in certain normal constellations, however, in which "affects for affects' sake" are prevalent—an indulgence in one's own affects.

Interrelationships of the FC, CF, *and* C *scores.* The above rationale, together with clinical experience, allows us to present further, more specific hypotheses about the significance of particular varieties and patterns of color responses. In a normal record the absence of all of these color responses indicates more or less shyness, more or less tense alertness to form and to reality, and a more or less rigid suppression of affects, with a leaving of action and thought to cold logic, especially if the form level is high.

A few *FC* responses only—with no other color responses—are given by affable persons who lack zeal and impetus in their actions, and merely fit in with their environment. The presence of these responses in great number (four or more) without other color responses is frequent in overpliant persons, bent upon pleasing everyone, lacking in assertiveness in the pursuit of their own ends, and in extreme cases even lacking cohesive clarity and sincerity of character. In an average-sized record, we expect about two *FC* responses; in smaller records their absence will be understood as inhibition (coarctation), and in larger records as a poverty of affective rapport deriving from sources other than inhibition and most frequently denoting a weakness of object attachments.

About one *CF* response should be present in the average-sized record, where it will stand for impulsive, strong affects, and will indicate that the affective adaptation represented by the *FC* responses is not simple and complacent, but has strong drives behind it. When the *CF* responses are given alone or greatly outweigh the *FC* responses, poor and spasmodic control and inadequate delay become apparent. In children disobedience and in adults irritability are connoted by this state of affairs.

The *C* (pure color) response, if occurring without any other varieties, is indicative of the potentiality for violent emotional storms, or may represent a tepid unconcern in which the function of affects proper has been eliminated. If *FC* and *CF* responses clearly outweigh them, these *C* responses refer more to the general variability of affective display, and indicate only a partial weakness of control which often may not become apparent in everyday situations. When the records are very rich in *FC* and *CF* responses, pure *C* responses may come about sporadically as a result of the tiring of the associative process. The implications of these will be similar to those of the abundant *CF* responses.

The *F/C* and *C/F* responses, with their extremely weak reaction to color and even some vagueness of the perceptual organization of forms, indicate feebleness of emotional responsiveness and adaptation. Responses in which colors are merely "painted on" or "used as marks" can usually be interpreted as indicating something artificial and forced about the subject's affective output; the affect does not blend meaningfully with the action or the situation.

The *FC arb* response indicates an effort at emotional adaptation which has little success, and results rather in a disharmony and even inappropriateness of affective display. Here the subject's emotional comprehension of the situation, or his emotional tie to it, is weak or limited, and in his zeal to be appropriate he becomes inappropriate. These responses occur most frequently in some chronic schizophrenics who are attempting to put up a good front, and sometimes in preschizophrenic conditions, or incipient schizophrenias.

The $F\overline{C}$ (by denial) response is a similar form of the *FC arb* response. In these the affective contact is tenuous but does not become inappropriate, by virtue of the subject's sufficiently critical attitude toward his own affective display and actions. Doubt and lack of spontaneity are connoted by this type of response if it is prominent in a record.

The *C sym* response by itself, in a schizophrenic setting, bespeaks a loss of emotional contact with reality and a pathologically autistic course of the thought processes. More rarely, it is expressive of specific neurotic overvalent ideas, or an overintellectualization of affects.

The *C det* response indicates essentially a blunting or flattening of affect, and is also linked with pathologically autistic thinking.

The color-naming response is usually a sign of a total lack of control over affective reactions, such as is seen in some organic cases.

Color denomination, though not a response, indicates a repression of color reactions especially if mere naming—in the sense of recognition—is all that occurs.

Color description, referring to aesthetic qualities of and subjective reactions to the colors, also indicates a repressive trend. If elaborate and sensitive, and in a setting of good color responses, it frequently connotes a wealth of sublimated achievements and a smoothness and variability of the functioning of the instinct derivatives.

The Sequence of the Color Responses. Subjects who mass their color responses on Cards II and III, and do not give them on the last three cards, are usually inclined to be stimulated to a quick and early affective display in a new situation, but soon tire out; they indicate a degree of artificiality and weakness of emotional responsiveness and adaptability. On the other hand, subjects who avoid color responses in the beginning of the test, and accumulate them slowly on the last three cards, usually act with considerable restraint in new situations, slowly get a feeling of the situation, and then may react with considerable affective variability and empathy.

It is also significant whether the subject gives his responses to the blue-green areas or to the red and orange areas. In the former case, the subjects are usually inclined to control their affects and not make a too vivid display of them; in the latter case, the affective reactivity is usually more vivid and intense. Further research into these and other colors not found on the Rorschach cards is urgently needed to clarify the nature and validity of these relationships.

Finally, it is clinically useful to look for signs of what has been referred to as "color shock." This includes failure or delay in reacting to, or more or less violent exclamation at the sight of, the colored cards—especially the first card which contains colors, Card II. In some instances, color shock becomes apparent when the subject reaches Card VIII after a series of four gray cards. Of all the colored cards, Card IX presents the subject with the most difficult task because of its diffuse coloring and the difficulties it presents for fine articulations and whole responses. Thus, color shock occurs most frequently on this card, but its significance is therefore not as great as on Cards II or VIII. If the subject is generally impulsive and poorly controlled, a turmoil of wild color responses may come about on Card IX; but if he is attempting to cope with his poor control, Card IX may give rise to a considerable setback in productivity and even to failure, or tiny *Dr* responses, or generally poor form responses.

The sequence of color responses on any individual card is also significant. For instance, Card III offers manifold possibilities of interpretation besides the bright red areas, but if the subject goes directly to these areas and clings to them before using the achromatic areas, hysteria must be considered as a possible diagnosis. In such cases the impact of color points to an especially labile and intense affective life, at the expense of the delay and ideational productivity that would be implied in first giving the human movement response. If the subject delays his color responses till the end of any card bearing colored areas, the indication is for caution and reserve preceding affective response in any situation.

Color Responses as Diagnostic Indicators

The Sum C *Score.* Among schizophrenics, we find the greatest amount of color response in unclassified schizophrenics rather than in the paranoid, who clinically show considerable rigidity. Furthermore, with the progressive decrease of control or delay associated with chronicity and deterioration, the average *sum C* of unclassified schizophrenics increases. In a schizophrenic, a *sum C* of 10 or more strongly militates against a paranoid diagnosis. Paranoid conditions tend to show a moderate, average *sum C*. In contrast, simple schizophrenics have the lowest average *sum C* of all psychotics, excepting depressive and involutional cases.

Great intensity and variety of affective experience is characteristic of overideational preschizophrenics, while restriction and poverty of affective output, and even some flattening, characterize the inhibited type; the *sum C* of overideationals is correspondingly much larger. Preschizophrenics of the highly ideational type do display vivid, poorly controlled, and to a formidable degree inappropriate affects and actions.

In depressives, we find a great dearth of color responses, because clinically they manifest the greatest restriction and inhibition of affective output. Thus, an extreme limitation in the number of color responses may serve as a good diagnostic indication for the presence of depression. Differentiation between depressives and paranoid schizophrenics or inhibited preschizophrenics is a diagnostic problem due to the similar effects of depression and rigid inhibition.

Within the neurotic range, the highest average *sum C* occurs in hysterics with their great emotional lability; at the opposite extreme we find neurasthenics, who clinically are characterized by their extreme meagerness of affective expression and action. The incidence of pure *C* in unclassified schizophrenics distinguishes them from hysterics, who accumulate the milder color responses.

It is worth while to summarize these differential diagnostic findings in reference to the rationale we have advanced above. The low *sum C* scores of paranoid as compared to unclassified schizophrenics are consistent with the clinical fact that the paranoids often present a much better systematized psychosis, with less abandonment of control, less disorganization, but considerable rigidity and inhibition. The extreme variability of affective experience clinically characterizing overideational preschizophrenics is demonstrated by their highest average *sum C* of all groups. Low *sum C* scores obtain in inert, apathetic, emotionally retarded or blunted clinical groups, such as depressives, neurasthenics, simple schizophrenics. Hysteria—the neurosis that stands out clinically by virtue of heightened emotional reactivity—shows up with the highest accumulation of color responses of all neurotics.

For a finer differentiation between the clinical groups, we must turn now to a specific consideration of the share which each basic kind of color response contributes to the gross *sum C*.

The FC *Response.* In accordance with our rationale we find the highest *FC* incidence among the neurotics, inasmuch as these responses refer to appropriate affective display and reactivity. In obsessive-compulsives and mixed neurotics *FC* responses are usually well retained. The inhibition associated with depression, and the apathy and inertia associated with neurasthenia and simple schizophrenia, appear to preclude the potentiality for establishing affective rapport and for displaying appropriate affective reactions, as indicated by a very low incidence of *FC* responses.

It is not unusual to find *FC*'s in unclassified schizophrenics of any degree of chronicity. In such cases, however, *CF* usually exceeds *FC,* and the number of pure *C* usually tends to exceed even the number of *CF* responses. This is an important diagnostic lead in connection with the balance struck between *FC* and the other color responses indicative of weak control. With schizophrenic chronicity and to some extent deterioration, the predominance of *CF* or *C* responses increases.

It may happen that *FC* equals or even exceeds the combined number of *CF* and *C* in a psychotic person's Rorschach; but in such a case, this fact points to the retention of a good social façade, as often happens in paranoid conditions. It is diagnostically characteristic of depressives, neurasthenics, and simple schizophrenics to have a dearth of color responses (none or one) rather than any specific balance between the different kinds.

It appears, then, that a predominance of *FC* responses over less form-articulated color responses occurs in those clinical groups which we would expect to manifest more emotional adaptation and appropriate affective expression. Depressive inhibition or flat, blunted conditions appear to preclude giving *FC* responses.

The CF *Response.* On the basis of clinical knowledge, we expect *CF* to run higher in groups characterized by the greatest amount of impulsiveness, vividness of affective display, and general affective dilation: unclassified schizophrenics and hysterics. Unclassified schizophrenics are characterized by a general loosening of control, impulsive affects, and bizarre behavior; incoherence sets in early in them, and brings about a setting which is prohibitive for delay but is a hotbed for color responses. This is in contrast to the paranoid cases whose trend to systematized ideation itself indicates the presence of delay in good keeping with their lower color scores. This does not mean that paranoid schizophrenics will not have violent outbursts, but only that they will show a more coherent front, and less apparent fluctuation of affect and ideation. Thus it is significant to note that, while the *CF* usually exceed the *FC* responses in the unclassified group, they seldom do in the paranoid group. The relatively high *CF* of hysterics is clinically understandable in terms of the impulsiveness of the hysterical personality. It is significant to note that here they exceed obsessive-compulsives, from whom they are not so sharply differentiated by the *FC* averages. Furthermore, the *FC* and *CF* score averages in hysterics are closer together than in obsessive-compulsives. Depressives' *CF* responses have an incidence at least equal to that of their *FC* responses; and this gives the impression— paralleled by the clinical picture—that the affective display in depressive psychoses is likely to be of an explosive, unadaptive nature. The special prevalence of pure C responses in depressive and involutional psychotics is also consistent with this inference.

Thus it appears that the increase of CF responses in clinical cases corresponds to the increase of impulsiveness and poor control of affects in the clinical picture; this is especially the case when the CF prevail over the FC responses.

Pure C responses appear to refer to an abandonment of control over affects and actions, and, under certain conditions, to a generalized inappropriateness or flattening of affect; therefore we should expect to find the highest incidence in schizophrenics and preschizophrenics, and a much lower incidence in depressives, neurotics, and most of all in normals. These theoretical expectations are grossly confirmed by our experience. The number of pure C responses in schizophrenics—especially of the unclassified type—shows a great increase with progressing chronicity and deterioration.

Among schizophrenics, C are often lacking in acute paranoids and simple schizophrenics. In the latter group, the general withdrawal and flattening of affect appears to explain this finding. All color responses run very low in this group; but they are more likely to give pure C responses than the better controlled color responses. In acute paranoid schizophrenics, the general maintenance of rigid control appears to explain the low incidence of pure C responses.

In depressives we find that pure C responses are almost entirely limited to the psychotic groups. Neurotic depressions are characterized by a well-retained inhibition and coarctation, or at least by some control (CF); but psychotic depressions are more open to outbursts and violent display of affect. Still, the inhibitory effects are sufficient to make an important differential diagnostic indication: a neurotic may give occasional pure C responses, but in all categories these are overshadowed by the FC and CF responses. A single C can easily occur in either a schizophrenia or a depression, but the likelihood of schizophrenia increases markedly with each additional C.

Clinically, the content of the pure color responses frequently makes a decided difference in diagnostic evaluation. There are two major kinds of color responses which usually bear less pathological weight than others, especially if occurring alone. These are "blood" in connection with the red areas on Cards II and III, and "palette" or "spilled ink" on the last three cards. Normals, neurotics, and depressives give this type of C as a large share of their pure C responses, in contrast to schizophrenics whose range of content shows considerable variability. (It is particularly common for depressives to see "blood" on Card II.) Thus, inclusion of the more common and less striking pure C responses in the averages should be assumed to lessen the diagnostic differentiations we found. The occurrence of a "blood" or "palette" response by itself need not indicate a schizophrenic process; but if these more innocuous pure *C* responses occur together with more specific *C* responses (such as "meat" or "ocean"), then they make a diagnosis of psychosis more probable. In other words, in clinical practice the weight to be attached to any pure *C* response will depend upon its content *and* that of any other pure *C* responses present.

The Sequence of Color Responses as a Diagnostic Indicator. The average incidence of *FC* responses is greatest on Cards VIII and X. This is understandable, inasmuch as these cards contain a number of different colors, all of which are relatively discrete areas on the inkblot. There are no diffusely colored areas in them as in Card IX, nor is there a dearth of colored areas as in Cards II and III; therefore the two main obstacles to giving *FC* responses are absent. There is no clear-cut trend for *CF* responses to be more or less frequently given to any of the cards, except that they seem to be relatively infrequent on Card III, which appears understandable considering the definitive forms of the three red areas on that card, which facilitate other kinds of color responses and, being distinct from the major portion of the inkblot, need not enter into the responses at all. The pure *C* responses occur most frequently on Cards II, IX, and X.

Schizophrenics, preschizophrenics, and depressives give pure *C* responses on Cards II and III; normal and neurotic subjects tend rather to produce *FC* or *CF* responses here. Thus, the appearance of pure *C* responses early in the test may indicate the possible presence of severe psychopathology. A large share of these pure *C* responses are "blood," however, and the examiner will need to watch the subsequent cards carefully for further clarification of the bearing of this early indication. Very few neurotics or depressives give pure *C* responses on Card VIII, although schizophrenics and preschizophrenics give them frequently. Normals and those neurotics in whom control is better preserved are able to meet this first completely colored card with an emphasis upon *FC,* or at worst *CF.* Schizophrenics, however, to a large extent appear to be unable to cope with this card, and accumulate pure *C* responses.

On Card IX the emphasis in normal and neurotic subjects appears to shift to the *CF* response. Here, then, the first sign of impulsiveness and weakness of control may come to the fore in the neurotic or normal range. To a large extent, this manifestation will be associated with the difficulty Card IX presents to all subjects. Therefore, the weight of these *CF* responses is lessened, and the examiner should be on the lookout for pure *C* responses. It is again the schizophrenics and preschizophrenics who mass these on Card IX. Here the fundamental impairment of control and delay in schizophrenia becomes especially apparent: neurotics still cling mainly to a precarious *CF* level. Finally, on Card X normals and neurotics show a great accumulation of *FC* responses, often overshadowing their many *FC* responses on the other cards. Thus, even after the difficulty on Card IX, normals and neurotics maintain sufficient control to cope with the brightly colored Card X by successfully integrating form and color. Among these groups only hysterics show an inclination to give *CF* responses. Pure *C* responses in neurotics are, relative to their other color responses, exceptionally low on Card X. Schizophrenics—especially chronic and deteriorated—and preschizophrenics stand out with pure *C* responses on Card X.

The examiner then must watch carefully where the different kinds of color responses occur: a pure *C* on Cards II or III bears much less pathological weight than on Card X; an *FC* response to Card IX should indicate a special effectiveness of control of affect and action; a *CF* on Card IX will not have as much impulsive implication as one on Card VIII. The amount of variability within specific clinical groups is great, of course, and no ironclad rule or completely reliable anticipation can be made. Our point is rather that the examiner must always keep in mind the degree to which each inkblot makes it difficult for the subject to work out integrated responses, and the specific kind of task each card poses. If the examiner is aware of the nature of the inkblots, progressive experience with the test will not bring too many surprises nor too many apparent contradictions.

Conclusions. In the average-sized record of 20 to 25 responses, the average normal subject who is neither too inhibited nor too impulsive or outgoing is likely to give about two *FC* and one *CF* responses. In any event, the number of *FC* responses will generally exceed that of all other color responses, thereby indicating a normal control of affect and action, and the capacity for establishing emotional rapport.

In all nosological groups, an extreme limitation of the number of color responses refers to an extreme limitation of affective output, whether as an expression of depressive retardation, prepsychotic inhibition, rigid, coarctated personality formation, generalized flattening of affect, or even of inhibition within the normal range. Conversely, a great number of color responses refers to extensive affective output, whether of a definitely psychotic and inappropriate kind, or referable to the affective lability of hysterics, to the dilation of preschizophrenics, or to normal impulsiveness.

In general, schizophrenia appears to increase the number of *CF* and especially *C* responses, thereby indicating a fundamental abandonment of control, and loss of ability for delay of impulse and for affective rapport. Only those schizophrenics characterized by rigidity—paranoid schizophrenics—are able to maintain to some extent a "normal-looking" balance of color responses. Even in paranoids, however, progressing schizophrenic chronicity and deterioration make the psychotic color pattern more and more clear: pure *C* responses greatly increase, and those blunted and flat color responses to which we attach the label *deterioration* become more and more frequent. Furthermore, schizophrenics show their greatest accumulation of *C* responses on Card X, where the better-controlled neurotics and normals give a preponderance of *FC* responses.

Preschizophrenics appear to follow closely the schizophrenic color pattern, and the greatest weight is placed upon pure *C* responses in their records. In inhibited preschizophrenics, the *sum C* is in general small; in overideational preschizophrenics the *sum C* is frequently quite high.

No real color pattern may be said to characterize simple schizophrenics, inasmuch as their generalized flattening of affect almost entirely eliminates genuine color responses from their records. Paranoid conditions, on the other hand, show a pattern much like that of normality and in general provide no diagnostic leads by the choice and use of colors.

Depressives in general give very few color responses, indicating their extreme limitation of affective output. If the depression is of a psychotic degree, the most usual color response will be "blood" on Card II and possibly Card III.

Among neurotics, the sluggish, inert, and affectively impoverished neurasthenics show, like simple schizophrenics, no genuine color responses. Anxiety and depression shows its continuity with depression proper by a somewhat low number of color responses. Hysterics stand out with the greatest amount, and especially with their emphasis upon *CF* responses, which indicate a weakening but not an abandonment of control. In general, neurotics maintain an *FC* prevalence. Pure *C* responses occur only in isolated instances, and no great accumulation of them is at all likely to occur. Within the normal range, maladjustment appears to allow for the occurrence of occasional pure *C* responses; impulsiveness appears to increase and inhibition to decrease the number of color and especially *CF* responses.

THE EXPERIENCE BALANCE, OR THE RELATIONSHIP BETWEEN MOVEMENT AND COLOR

In laying down principles of interpretation for this test, Rorschach maintained that the quantitative relationship between the number of movement and the number of color responses was of crucial significance. In evaluating this relationship he appears to have been guided to a large extent by the dichotomy of introversive-extratensive personality types. In the previous sections, we stated that such dichotomous thinking does not prove to be clinically fruitful. Instead, we have emphasized that the amounts of movement and color responses are important components of the qualitative wealth of the record, and therefore refer to the qualitative wealth of the subject's psychological experiencing.

More specifically, a protocol which is qualitatively rich in both directions refers, in the normal range, to interesting, rich, freely variable, versatile thought and feeling life and mobile activity; one which is qualitatively poor in both directions—even if quantitatively rich—refers to an inhibited, rationalistic cognitive and feeling life in which there is relatively little variability or enjoyment and the realm of action is narrowed. In the pathological range, the qualitatively rich protocol refers to a variability and luxurious development of symptoms; while a meager protocol refers to inhibitory, inert, and relatively colorless symptoms, which may, nevertheless, occasionally have violent flare-ups.

It is usually the case—especially among clinical subjects—that either the *sum M* or *sum C* is lower. Thus, when *sum C* is lower than the *sum M,* the indication is that affective output and vigorous action are restricted, and the picture is one in which pathological ideational productivity—in the form of fantasying, obsessions, phobias, or delusions—stands in the foreground. If *sum C* exceeds the *sum M,* the emphasis is much rather upon pathologically increased affective output and display which is often inappropriate; usually a poor control of impulse and action, and a general loss of delay for reality testing proceding action is implied. This type of balance refers, therefore, to the presence of some kind of hysterical symptom, or to schizophrenic impulsiveness and inappropriateness of affect.

It is also usual for inhibitory or coarctative tendencies to press unevenly upon the color and movement responses; which of these will be more severely hit will depend partly on the nature of the maladjustment which is exerting the coarctating (ego-limiting) effect, and partly on the premorbid strength of the functions reflected by the color or movement responses. In general, *M* responses are the ones more vulnerable to maladjustment, and especially to longstanding maladjustment.[52] The reason for this is that delay, implicit in the coming about of *M* responses, weakens in maladjustment with the weakening of the control which allows for delay. Maladjustments give rise to conditions which, even in the presence of inhibitory processes, are relatively favorable for the coming about of color responses, especially *CF* and *C.* Thus the relation of *M* to *C,* and the amount of each, provide a crucial indication of the ideational and affective inclinations of the subject, and of the effect upon them of maladjustment. The processes that give rise to movement and to color responses may be devastated by the maladjustment; they may hold up against it, or even extend their influence under conditions created by it; or they may find for the first time a sudden

---

[52] This fact has already been established by Skalweit (1935).

release through it. The "experience balance" *(sum M: sum C)*—the balance between impulses and affects on the one hand, and delay and ideation developing in it on the other—becomes a crucial diagnostic indicator in the Rorschach test.

The Diagnostic Significance of the Experience Balance (EB)

Dilation and Coarctation. Considering coarctation first, we find the lowest incidence of both movements and colors in extremely inhibitory or generally flattened conditions: specifically, the depressions, depressionlike neuroses, inhibited preschizophrenias, dull chronic and simple schizophrenias, and generally inhibited normal persons. Such coarctation is practically absent in overideational preschizophrenics, obsessive-compulsives, and hysterics. Patients with paranoid conditions may or may not be coarctated, because although their ideational productivity takes the form of delusions, they remain exceedingly coherent and great segments of their intellectual functioning are unimpaired by the delusion formation. This limitation of the area of their delusions leaves their previous compulsive, rigid personality make-up still operant, and thus a good share of the cases show clear-cut coarctation.

If we consider a total of *sum M + sum C* equal to or greater than 6 as representing dilation, we find most of the ideationally most productive and affectively most labile overideational preschizophrenics to be dilated. In second place are acute unclassified schizophrenics, who show both great ideational productivity in the form of delusions and considerable affective display and impairment of control. The ideationally productive obsessive-compulsives follow in third place.

Deteriorated unclassified schizophrenics give dilated Rorschach protocols fairly often because the setting in of incoherence and the abandonment of all affective control greatly increase the *sum C* score, especially the number of pure *C* responses. In contrast to unclassified schizophrenics, paranoid schizophrenics do not show an extreme tendency toward dilation even in deterioration. The general rigidity and inhibition that appears to characterize these cases has already been stressed.

The Direction of the EB. In evaluating the diagnostic significance of the direction of the *EB*—the prevalence of movement or of color in it—a basic question must be raised: When maladjustment results in a general coarctation of the qualitative wealth of the record, is its characteristic direction (the movement versus color preference) retained even within the coarctated range? If it is, the direction of the *EB* should gain added weight in our diagnostic evaluations, because it will yield material to breach the diagnostic limitation inherent in coarctated protocols.

In cases with a tendency toward general dilation, the *M* scores, which are dependent upon native endowment, often cannot increase at the same rate as the color responses, which may be given not only on high *(FC)* but on low levels of integration *(C)*. Furthermore, dilation in quantitative as well as qualitative wealth often has a driven, restless quality, which is unfavorable for the delay required in order to give *M* responses but is a hotbed for poorly articulated color responses. *M* prevalences are thus likely to be veiled in these dilated cases; and we should expect characteristic diagnostic directions to come to clearer expression in the relatively coarctated records, where we may see whether the movement or the color tendency is stronger in holding up against the general inhibition.

Clinical experience bears out this expectation. When they are coarctated, acute schizophrenics retain a movement prevalence, as a reflection of their intense delusional or related ideational activity. Coarctated chronic and deteriorated schizophrenics swing much more to color prevalence, as a reflection of their general loss of integrative ability and abandonment of control. Among neuroses, the more hysteriform—hysteria, and anxiety and depression—retain a color prevalence in the face of coarctation; obsessive-compulsives and neurasthenics retain a movement prevalence; and mixed neurotics lie somewhere between these two groups, by virtue of sharing the symptoms of both. Within the normal range, coarctation restricts the number of movement responses much more than that of the color responses, because poor control or inability to delay is characteristic of most maladjustive tendencies.

Regardless of coarctation or dilation, *M* prevalence occurs in acute schizophrenics, overideational preschizophrenics, obsessive-compulsives, and related groups. Paranoid schizophrenics show a somewhat higher incidence of *M* prevalence than unclassified schizophrenics; this is in accord with both the presence of delusions in the paranoid group and the systematic nature of their delusions, which distinguish them clinically in a gross way from unclassified schizophrenics. Coarctation is sometimes extreme enough to make it difficult to distinguish a paranoid schizophrenic from a depressive psychotic; and in such cases a careful analysis of the subject's verbalizations, and recourse to other tests in the battery, are indicated.

Although overideational preschizophrenics fairly often show *M* prevalence, its incidence is not as overwhelming as one might expect: the fact is that, in their extreme dilation, they swing not only into *M* responses but even more extensively into color responses, sometimes to the point where the former vanish while the latter become exceedingly plentiful. The intense ideational activity of the subjects characterized by this last pattern is apparent in the verbalization of their responses, their quantitative productivity, their *DR%*, and the features of their other tests.

In regard to the depressives, it might be argued at this point that we have been overlooking an inconsistency of the test: that in spite of the delusional activity of psychotic depressives—their convictions of having committed the "original sin," of having brought ruin and disaster into the world—M responses or M prevalence are practically absent in their records. This objection overlooks the fact that psychomotor retardation in depressives is extreme enough to prevent the coming about of those sensitive and finely articulated responses which carry movement impressions.

Thus far we may conclude that M prevalence in a psychotic protocol points mainly to the presence of an acute delusional condition; in a preschizophrenic setting it points to the overideational type; in a depressive setting it usually indicates some obsessive or schizoid trends accompanying the depression; in the neurotic range it always points to the presence of obsessive pathology; and in the normal range, it is most regularly associated with a sublimating mode of adjustment.

Color prevalence may occur in many different disorders, such as schizophrenias, depressions, the hysteriform neuroses, or even precariously adjusted normals. Great color prevalence with pure C responses (other than "blood" on Cards II and III) is a strong indication of the presence of schizophrenic psychopathology. In terms of our rationale, if the schizophrenic process is of such a character as greatly to increase the affective and impulsive display at the expense of control and delay, then pure C responses will accumulate in the record; this does not obtain for depressives or normals, and only very occasionally for a hysteriform neurotic.

Finally, we should like to offer some considerations about the effect of general dilation upon the pure C responses. With either coarctation or dilation, potentialities for giving pure C responses are increased. On the one hand, where coarctation has especially hit the M responses, the indication is that the control is rigid and brittle. The rigidity is detrimental to the articulation and integration necessary for the development of M responses and to the rich thought processes they represent, and the brittleness of control allows for a breakthough of uncontrolled affects, by reason of temporary breakdowns of control and delay. On the other hand, extreme dilation appears to favor a luxuriant crop of pure C responses. Experience clarifies this finding: the dilated subjects are too responsive to every aspect of the inkblot, and though they may retain a good capacity for delay, their responsiveness may carry them too far in their productivity, and impulsive pure C responses come about. Also, the dilated subjects tire by reason of their great productivity in the course of the test or of even a single card. The most elaborate and best-integrated products of the interaction of the perceptual and associative processes are exhausted, but the subject's general responsiveness is not, and thus the standards appear to suffer. In such cases the significance of the pure C responses comes very close to that of the *CF* responses, indicating some impulsiveness but no fundamental abandonment of control.

These data teach a practical point to the Rorschach tester. General dilation may unduly increase the number of color and especially pure *C* responses, so that they may overshadow the *M* responses: in such cases the degree of ideational productivity should be assessed by the number of *M* responses alone, and not by the direction of the *EB*. At the opposite extreme, very coarctated cases frequently do not allow for any assessment of ideational activity, either by the number of *M* responses or by the direction of the *EB:* in these cases, often not even the whole Rorschach test can tell the story, and other tests must be consulted for information about the degree of pathological ideational activity in the subject.

THE SHADING AND RELATED RESPONSES

Shading responses are those in which the light-dark (chiaroscuro) shadings of the area initiate, in part or whole, the associative process leading to a response. These responses have been traditionally interpreted to be indicators of the presence of anxiety, and by definition can occur only on the first seven cards. Besides the shading response we shall also deal here with certain responses which appear to be related in their psychological implications to the shading responses proper: (1) responses to areas whose contours are determined by variations in shading, rather than outer contours bordering on the white areas; (2) responses in which the shading or textures of the brightly colored areas are elaborated upon; (3) responses in which black or gray or white are *colors* ("black bat," "white snow").

The scoring of shading has become more refined than that of any other determinant, indicating whether the shading has been used by the subject as a textural quality, a vista effect, a vague diffusion effect, etc. The inferences drawn from each of these varieties, however, have been the least validated of all the Rorschach test indicators. The resulting confusion is in part also ascribable to the great variety of expressions of anxiety which may occur in different clinical syndromes, making it extremely difficult to evaluate the indicators of anxiety in any test.

Scoring and Inquiry

Shading Responses Proper. We adopted Binder's (1932-1933) scores of the shading responses, because these were rather homogeneous with Rorschach's general scoring system and especially with his scoring of the color responses. Specifically, where the shading impression merely accompanies and is well integrated with a definitive form response, the score given in *FCh* (form-chiaroscuro); where the shading impression predominates but some form element is retained, the score is *ChF;* and where the shading is the sole determinant, the score is *Ch.* It is true that all these types of shading responses may be used in such different ways as those mentioned above; but for the sake of simplicity of scoring, as well as because of the relatively infrequent use of shading as a determinant by patients we have seen, we did not employ a different score for each variety. We were content rather to indicate by the score that shading was in some way involved in the response, and that it stood in a subordinate or dominant position to the form impression.

Like the scoring, the inquiry in general is similar for both shading and color responses. Only a few problems more specific to the shading responses must be discussed here. First, inquiry after a shading determinant should not be pursued unless the content of the response given is consistent with the shading of the area chosen. Second, inquiry should be avoided if the subject describes the shading impression spontaneously: here the examiner will be able to score the response from the spontaneous verbalization, as well as from his familiarity with the response itself and the congruence of the response with the area chosen. Third, if no definite statement about shading is made spontaneously—and if shading is relevant to the response—then it is diagnostically most important to determine by inquiry whether the subject is at all responsive to the shading of the inkblot, and whether he did integrate shading impressions into his response. Particularly the "animal skin" and related responses on Cards IV and VI and the "map" and *At* (see below, p. 407) responses on Cards I, IV, and VII should be carefully watched. On the other hand, if the subject plays up the shading impression, the examiner must then try to determine the definitiveness of the form impression; not infrequently the "animal skin" is not sufficiently articulated perceptually to allow for an *FCh* score, and the appropriate score is *ChF.* But the usual *ChF* responses are always strongly suggested by a vagueness and diffuseness of the content—"X rays," "geological drawings," "aerial photography," "microscopic slides." These must therefore be inquired into, unless the spontaneous verbalization makes it clear that shading is being used. As we shall attempt to show below, even if inquiry reveals that only the vague outline of the area chosen and not its shading has determined the response, these vague responses remain indicators of the presence of anxiety—but it is usually that of a subject who has a very poor tolerance for conscious anxiety. Their significance will be especially great if, from other test evidence, we should expect indications of anxiety. The pure *Ch* responses also are usually made conspicuous by their content —"cloud," "smoke," "dust," "dirt"—because only rarely will subjects be able to describe specific cloud or smoke formations, and those who can will usually state spontaneously the presence of some form element in these responses, which are then scored *ChF.*

A general problem of inquiry into the shading impressions is raised when the subject says in inquiry that it was "the darkness of the card." This does not make it clear whether it is the variations of shading or only the undifferentiated impression of blackness that was the determinant. In such a case, the examiner should ask the subject to explain what he means by darkness. In general, inquiry should not be pursued too persistently or far into the presence of shading as a determinant; too many questions evoke speculations and supplementations of the original response, rather than reliable material about the determinant role played by the shading. To press inquiry to the point of asking, "Does it look like a bear skin right side up?" is to start a game of logical manipulation with the subject, in which he will more likely come to see how he *could have* responded than how he actually did. A strong shading impression will either be stated spontaneously or in the first response to inquiry: the further an inquiry is pursued before a shading impression is described by the subject, the weaker its significance becomes.

F(C). This score is used for two somewhat different kinds of responses, the significance of which appears to be grossly the same. If a subject makes out forms within a heavily shaded area without using the shading as shading, or uses the different shadings of some brightly colored area to elaborate his response, the *F(C)* score is given. In regard to the first variety, inquiry should be aimed at establishing whether a sufficient number of details of the response were derived from the variations in shading, or whether merely one contour of the response was delimited by a shading type of variation. Examples of this kind of response are the "faces" in the heavily shaded upper half of Card IV, both "faces" looking away from the mid-line, and the "figure of a man" in the center of the upper projection of Card VI. If, on Card IV turned upside down, the response "two witches" is given to the solid black area of the inkblot, the shading variation has determined only one part of the contour of the response; the score of the determinant is therefore more appropriately *F* or *M*. Similarly, if the subject makes out "an eye" because of some variation in shading of an area he has interpreted as "a head," the *F(C)* is not in place, although a tendency in that direction should be noted. In regard to the second variety, the relevant information is either included in the spontaneous verbalization or is elicited in the inquiry in the pursuit of color determinants. Some responses may warrant specific inquiry, however, for example, the response "flag" to the central blue area of Card VIII may be amplified in inquiry, "It is wrinkled as though it were waving in the wind." Such a response warrants the *F(C)* score.

The C′ Determinant. When the blackness or whiteness of an area used as color is the sole determinant, the score is *C′*. Of course, *FC′* and *C′F* responses also occur. At one extreme we might have a "black bat" or "white porcelain vase"; at the other extreme, "coal" or "snow." If the subject describes something as "dark," he may well be giving a chiaroscuro response; and an interpretation of a white space does not necessarily imply the score C'. Here the problems of scoring and inquiry are similar to those for the shading and color responses. Inquiry aimed at eliciting "whiteness" or "blackness" in a response, (e.g., "bat") is justified only if the spontaneous verbalization is suggestive in this respect. The use of black or white should be explicit, or at least implicit, in the subject's spontaneous verbalization of his response. It is unwise to inquire whether every "butterfly" is a "black" butterfly or not; this is time-consuming and may even impair the significance of the test results.

Rationale of the Shading Responses

We shall forego here a discussion of the perceptual-associative interplay underlying the variants of the shading responses, because we consider it closely parallel to that described in the corresponding variants of the color responses. The reader will, we trust, easily see the relation of the following considerations to those advanced concerning the color responses.

Of all the determinants, shading is the least useful for establishing a definite diagnosis of the patient, and is helpful rather in clarifying the degree of prominence and the type of role which anxiety plays in the clinical picture. Obviously, even thus it can often contribute to a definitive diagnosis. It is of course meaningless to say "anxiety is indicated," because it is present in all of us: the examiner must try to understand how the subject expresses his anxieties, how he attempts to cope with them, and what effects they have on his thought processes. About all this we know little. The clinical symptoms of anxiety show great variability, and there is also considerable disagreement in the field about what should be considered clinical indications of anxiety and what degree and kind of anxiety is normal. Parallel to this variability and lack of systematization in the clinical picture, there is a great variety of anxiety indicators on the Rorschach test, of which the shading response is only one.[53]

[53] Zulliger (1933) lists the following indicators of anxiety: "An increase in the average number of small details; an increase in the number of chiaroscuro responses; a production of many poorly perceived anatomical responses; an increase in original responses of poor quality; coarctation of the Experience Balance; a loosening in the sequence of responses in persons who 'lose their heads,' that is, who lose their previously sharp perception of form as soon as colored cards are introduced, and in consequence experience a color shock which is usually quite strong; an inclination to oligophrenic detail (Do responses); production of a color shock; decrease in the number of whole responses and in the number of movement responses; more human details than complete human figures in the content of the responses; decrease in the number of originals and at the same time in the percentage of popular responses."

Clinically, anxiety may take the form of violent panic attacks, constantly lingering free-floating anxieties, intolerable boredom and restlessness, acute or chronic bodily symptoms; or it may even be impalpable until the subject suddenly gives way to an impulsive or irritable outburst, or unexpected activity. Similarly on the Rorschach test, the subject may not use the shading in his response, but may be restricted to interpreting peripheral details of the inkblot *(De, Dr);* he may be unable to penetrate and structure the diffusely shaded cards, and be left with only *Wv* or at best *Wo* responses. These are presumed here to be different modes of reaction to shading.

In other words, shading responses are not the only mode for reacting to a shading impression. When on the shaded cards the subject for the first time gives no whole responses, the indication is that anxiety impairs his ability to survey and grasp total situations, although not entirely paralyzing his productivity. When on the shaded cards peripheral edge or rare details are resorted to for the first time in a record, the indication is for attempts to avoid or escape anxiety-arousing situations or ideas, or for a quibbling, inappropriate kind of productivity. When the subject falls back upon *Wv* responses, the indication is either of an inability to tolerate conscious anxiety or of a paralyzing effect of anxiety which prevents perceptual articulation of the shaded mass. When the subject who displays an otherwise excellent form level turns to the gross popular responses on the shaded cards, the indication is of a kind of control of anxiety that consists in falling back upon stereotypes and platitudes in anxiety-arousing situations. If the subject avoids the shaded areas and turns to the white spaces on the card, the indication is of an anxiety-determined oppositional or negativistic tendency.

In regard to the use of shading itself as a determinant, the presence of pure *Ch* responses is—in our experience—usually referable to a relatively steady, free-floating anxiety; an accumulation of *ChF* responses usually refers to paralyzing anxieties, more directly related to specific situations and ideas; the *FCh* scores appear to refer mainly to anxieties which are relatively well controlled and/or bound up in bodily symptom formation.

The Relationship Between Shading and Anxiety. Any attempt to develop a rationale of the shading responses must cope with the same problem as that discussed in connection with the color responses: Why is it that a specific determinant appears to relate to a specific psychological manifestation in the subject? The argument here runs grossly parallel to that for the color responses. There are conjectures in the literature that the connection between shading and anxiety is analogous to, or an expression of, the symbolic relation between night and fear. It is likely that this explanation has some core of validity because both in everyday life and in psychological or psychoanalytic investigation of patients this symbolic relationship appears to be quite general. But this explanation would here connect the general darkness of the card with anxiety, rather than the shading of the darkness; as a consequence, the use of shading would appear to be only one of the many possible indicators of anxiety and would no longer constitute the essential link between clinical anxiety and the test indications.

It appears to us, however, that it is not necessary to posit any intrinsic relationship between shading and anxiety. Our assumption is that the diffuse shading impression and the gross articulation of the shaded cards both make articulation of the blots relatively difficult. In anxious persons the articulating and integrating abilities are impaired;[54] thus they fail on these cards more readily than do nonanxious persons. According to this assumption it is not the shading and the anxiety, but the gross articulation of the blots, and the articulation difficulty, which are at work. Obviously, the articulation difficulty can be coped with, and this happens in cases where the impact of the diffuse shading impression does not prevent articulation or initiates strong associative processes resulting in responses primarily based on shadings. Experience and the data to be presented indicate that subjects with relatively little anxiety can bypass this impact or relegate it to a minor role, and can articulate the blot to the point where shading, if used at all, becomes a mere embellishment. Other subjects do not cope with this difficulty so successfully, and will give responses of an adequate form level but with little articulation *(Fo)*: here the shading has merely handicapped articulation, and anxiety is palpable but still relatively mild. In other anxious subjects the shading impact will set off associative processes of greater or lesser intensity which lead to responses based in part *(FCh)* or mainly *(ChF)* on the shading impression. In our experience, these responses are given by subjects who feel conscious anxiety of varying degrees. Other anxious subjects will not use even the disturbing diffuse shading in their responses to indicate their anxiety; they may choose edge details *(De)* or tiny details *(Dr)* and avoid the task of extensive articulation. Here the shading prevents rather than initiates an associative process. Other subjects give responses that account only for the vagueness of the initial impression *(Fv)*, or fail the card entirely. These appear to be mainly the subjects who cannot tolerate conscious anxiety.

Inspection of those cards on which shading responses are most frequent indicates that even objectively they include the most unarticulated blots

---

[54] See in this respect the discussion of attention and anxiety, Chapter 3, pp. 108ff., where good attention was conceived as a free intake of stimulation in which the subject can follow the articulations of the incoming stimulation.

in the series—Cards IV and VI especially.[55] We have maintained above that anxiety is primarily expressed in poor ability for perceptual articulation of the inkblots; hence, blots that do not offer any ready starting points for articulation increase the vagueness of the responses. Here the subject may invoke shading as a justification, and the shading itself will be only weakly a determinant of the final vague response. Let us take, for example, Card IV, where the "animal skin" is a popular whole response. Inquiry almost always elicits the information that something about its general contour as well as its shadings made it look like an animal skin. What the subject is really telling us, perhaps, is that he was unable to work beyond the gross external contour of the inkblot, and that the unarticulated shading—the inherent vagueness—of the inside of the blot restricted him to the gross abstraction, "animal skin." If he had been able perceptually to penetrate and articulate Card IV, he must have been attracted to the solid black areas in the lower side projections, and this might have prompted him to turn the card around and see the two witchlike figures; or he might have been able to begin an articulation of the inkblot from the lower side projections which resemble boots or feet, and work his way up into the card to give a human-movement response. But in the "animal skin" response no such internal articulation comes about, and the subject in a sense pins his own weakness of perceptual organizing ability upon the shading. Thus, shading responses can be understood as merely symptomatic of a more deep-lying difficulty. This view, though not irreconcilable with the darkness-fear connection, would reduce it to merely one of the factors making for difficulty in perceptual organization. Thus, the perceptual impact of shading always makes for some vagueness in the response; this vagueness may be so intense that no predominant form, or only a vague *(Fv)*, arbitrary *(F—)*, or gross response in departure from a better general form level, may come about.

It might be argued here that the shading impression is not always left on a vague level, but is sometimes highly articulated and integrated into a total response. This would be especially true for elaborate and well-seen vista responses. According to our experience, such a free and productive manipulation of the shading does not necessarily refer to anxiety. True, it may be initiated by a shading impact of great vagueness due to anxiety, which then yields to articulation; but it may also be only a final consequence of powerful articulation, which would explain why such shading responses of the highly integrated type may be given by subjects who are

---

[55] [Philip S. Holzman, in a personal communication, comments: "It is also true that variations in shading are most obvious on these blots. If the shading on Cards I and V were also highly differentiated, this issue could be decided."—Ed.]

relatively free from anxiety.[56] It is an obvious consequence of this view that the occurrence of shading responses on cards where they are relatively infrequent suggests more strongly the presence of strong anxieties disrupting the subject's perceptual and associative efficiency and productivity. We find the greatest number of shading responses on Cards IV and VI, which have the most diffuse shading and offer the least possibility for articulation. There is also a high incidence on Card VII, which presents difficulties in the way of a whole response, so that an anxious subject may fall back upon its vague cloudlike or islandlike structure. The lowest incidence of shading responses occurs on Cards III and V. Card III of course is well articulated, lends itself to at least one *W* response and to many *D* responses, and allows for color responses. Card V offers considerable difficulty in the way of internal articulation—because of its almost solid black coloring—but still allows easily for a frequent whole response ("butterfly"), and its well-defined projections permit the subject many responses without need of coping with its impenetrable darkness. Card II appears to run low in the incidence of shading responses because of its better articulation and the presence of colors: nevertheless, the ribbed massive dark portions on this card sometimes do bring about shading responses, and thus it runs somewhat higher than III or V. Card I occupies a middle position: it might be expected that since it lends itself to articulation as well as to a very popular whole response, shading responses should run low on it; nevertheless, "X ray" and to some extent "topographical map" are frequently given, especially by many of our patients who find the first card "tough going." To some extent, the initial anticipation that these are going to be "medical pictures" may account for the "X rays" and "microscopic slides" frequently given on Card I.

It may be concluded from this analysis of the heavily shaded cards that those whose total organization offers the greatest difficulty to articulation and perceptual penetration will attract the greatest number of shading responses. This we believe to be a reflection of the fundamental vagueness of those responses that use shading, and this vagueness we believe to be the anxiety indicator. The impact of shading itself may dictate the course of the associative process, so that shading will be included in the final response; but even such responses must utilize vagueness as one part of the justification for the response. It also follows that the use of shading—as well as the occurrence of vague responses in general—on Cards II, III, and V suggests much more strongly the presence of intense anxiety than on the more difficult Cards IV, VI, and VII.

Rationale of the F(C) *Response.* This was the only shading score

[56] This point, especially in connection with vista responses, has been stressed by Guirdham (1935), Klopfer and Kelley (1942), and others.

Rorschach himself used (Rorschach & Oberholzer, 1923). Rorschach contrasts the *F(C)* and *FC* responses, explaining that the latter reflect free affective adaptation and rapport and the former unfree, anxious, cautious rapport. Clinical experience has shown that watchful affective display, adaptation with little freedom or flexibility and dictated by anxiety, rapport of a calculated and speculative character, are frequent concomitants of an abundance of *F(C)* responses. We have previously pointed out that a great preponderance of *FC* responses corresponds to an overpliant and submissive kind of emotional adaptation, but with the implication that this came naturally or automatically to the subject. In contrast, the subject who gives many *F(C)* responses will assume a role, his spontaneous expression of affect will be greatly restricted, he will watch carefully in order to determine what kind of display is called for and only then attempt to fit in. The significance of the *F(C)* responses that are given in connection with colored areas is essentially the same; but the indication is for a somewhat freer affective display. Good penetration, leading to integration, is usually present in such responses: the subject does not recoil from the colored surface to a pure form abstraction, and although the color does not quite become a determinant in the course of the associative process, the ability to work with and articulate a colored area is a positive sign.[57]

The Black-White-Gray Colors: C'. Very little is known about the significance of responses which use white, black, or gray as colors. Schneider (1937) published a blind analysis by Rorschach interpreting the use of such determinants as representing conscious control of or defense against the subject's own affects. This appears to correspond to some degree with our own clinical impressions. This formulation does not differ essentially from that concerning the two types of *F(C)* responses just discussed: such conscious control of or defense against affects is merely the other side of the coin of anxious and cautious adaptation. The presence of pure C' responses always carries with it some suggestion of severe maladjustment.

The Shading Responses as Diagnostic Indicators

We have already stressed that, inasmuch as shading responses refer to the presence of anxiety, their accumulation in any clinical case can very rarely be construed as a diagnostic sign. We might perhaps reverse the question and ask, "Is the absence of shading responses in any way diag-

---

[57] In the section on color responses we described the *(C)F* response, which is essentially of the *CF* variety but involves also some penetration of the textural quality of the colored area. In that connection we mentioned that the weight given such responses is never as great as that given the typical *CF* response, when the impairment of control is being assessed. When there is an accumulation of *F(C)* and *(C)F* responses to colored areas, it suggests a person given to such mingling of affect and anxiety as is seen in complex emotions like nostalgia (sweet sorrow).

nostic?" Acute paranoid schizophrenics often fail to give shading responses. In contrast, chronic paranoid schizophrenics show a great inclination to give them, especially those of the *ChF* variety, and this is one of their important diagnostic signs. A complete lack of shading responses is common in the Rorschachs of bland and flat simple schizophrenics, and in those of inhibited preschizophrenics whose anxiety may be intense but is often inappropriately expressed. Depressives not infrequently make no use of shading, not because of the absence of anxiety but rather because of the extremely coarctated character of their records; these cases rarely use determinants other than form, and their anxiety comes to expression rather in a limitation of productivity and vague whole responses. Among neurotics, obsessive-compulsives often find other ways of expressing anxiety (*Dr* responses, strained productivity, etc.).

In general, where anxiety is dulled or absent, as well as where it finds ideational expression rather than direct representation, shading responses are likely to be absent. The examiner should neither discount the existence of anxiety when there is an absence of chiaroscuro responses, nor overvalue their presence: he must remain fully aware of the many varieties of anxiety indications on the Rorschach test.

Because of the multifarious ways in which it can find expression, and because of the confusion over its definition, anxiety is one of the most difficult psychological factors to assess. A study is needed that will combine the advantages of a very large control group, which has been carefully explored psychiatrically, with the examination of many individual clinical records; thus we might trace the specific test manifestations of variants of anxiety, and the way in which they correlate with the subject's everyday experiencing of and coping with them.

THE CONTENT OF THE RESPONSE

By "content" in the Rorschach test we mean the appropriate conceptual classification of the particular product of the subject. That is, in the content score we are not interested in whether the subject saw a "bear" or a "wolf," but rather in that he saw an animal; the score of the content refers to the class in which the particular response may be most appropriately subsumed. There are at times specific contents of ideation palpable in the verbalizations of the Rorschach test, as contrasted with the content aspect of the response proper; this is found when the patient sees things as "shriveled," "decaying," "fighting," and when the verbalization of the response has a strong emotional tone. But these descriptive amplifications of responses—which usually lend themselves to some direct interpretation

—do not bear upon the conceptual classification of the content, and we shall defer discussion of them until the next section, in which the analysis of verbalization will be presented.

Scoring and Inquiry

In the *scoring* we distinguish the following main categories of responses: whole animals *(A)*, parts of animals *(Ad)*, whole human forms *(H)*, parts of humans *(Hd)*, objects *(Obj)*, plants *(Pl)*, bony anatomy *(At)*, soft anatomy *(Ats)*, X rays, geography *(Geo)*, geology *(Geol)*, clouds *(Cl)*, blood *(Bl)*, anal responses, sex, architecture *(Arch)*, landscape *(Ldsc)*, or nature scenes *(N)*. Responses which do not fit any of these categories are registered individually. Exceptional responses may occur which carry highly individual characteristics and elaborations, and these should not be forced into the nearest appropriate category. "Dragon" should not be scored simply as an animal, nor should "witch" be scored as a human. The fundamental point of scoring is to summarize the variety of content, in order to gain a picture of the qualitative wealth of the record. Forcing a relatively specific content into a more or less relevant category can result only in understating the wealth of content in the final summary (formal psychogram). But the examiner must also be careful not to overstate this variability by giving special content scores to every response in which the wording differs only slightly from the usual.

The principle of inquiry into content is that it be pursued only—but always—into responses in which the content is not directly and specifically stated in the spontaneous verbalization. A few examples will make this point clear. A subject may respond to the lower side pink areas on Card IX, "A head." Here the examiner must ask, "What do you mean?" because sometimes this area is seen as a man's head, a woman's head, an animal head, etc. Thus, the inquiry should drive the response to a specific clarity. Of course the examiner should not ask, "What kind of head?" because this tends to arouse a critical, reflective attitude in which the subject may revise his impression. A more general question such as "What do you mean?" will be more successful. The vagueness of the spontaneous statement of content is frequently a hiding place of uncertainty or peculiarity of perceptual and/or thought organization. It does not follow that every human figure referred to should evoke inquiry about whether it is male or female: this should be done only where the spontaneous verbalization of the response indicates vagueness or uncertainty in regard to the sex, or where in the record such vagueness has already been impressively encountered. Examples of vagueness are such responses as "two figures" or "two objects" to the black areas on Card III. Here again the subject may be asked,

"What do you mean?" or "How do you mean, object?"[58] Such inquiry usually will elicit either a critical rejection of any definiteness in the figures or a basic doubt about the nature of the objects, and even at times such psychotic reasoning as, "Whatever they are, they are lifeless; they must be objects." Thus, inquiry into the vagueness of the initial statement can elicit much material useful for diagnostic analysis.

Inquiry is also indicated into responses of the "map" or "anatomy" varieties, in which the spontaneous verbalization does not indicate a specific content. It is important to distinguish between "map" responses given because the card is in general vague, and those given because certain parts of the card resemble geographic configurations of specific countries or islands. Anatomical responses may also be merely vague, or may refer to specific organs and bony structures of the body.

Finally, responses such as "animal" or "flower" should be inquired into to establish whether the subject had a more specific idea about the kind of animal or flower. Inquiry may bring forth that the subject had no such specific idea, that he had a specific idea but rejected it, that he considered it too peculiar to be mentioned, or that there were so many specific ideas that no decision could be made. Here the examiner may obtain additional data on the wealth and variability of the subject's productivity, and his self-critical attitude and doubtfulness—none of which is indicated in the gross spontaneous formulation of the response.

The Rationale of Content

The content of the subject's responses refers essentially to his associative processes although, as we shall again attempt to show, the inkblots themselves may exert a considerable regulating influence upon their course. In general, the wealth or stereotypy of the subject's responses corresponds to the wealth or stereotypy of his everyday thinking. In clinical records variability of content may be a reflection of a specific maladjustment rather than of a general wealth of the associative processes.

The question to be asked is, What conceptual realms did the subject's associative processes pass through, and how specific or vague was the available associative material? The greater the limitation of conceptual realms available, and the more general and nonspecific the response, the stronger are the indications for stereotypy of thinking.

What may stereotypy result from? There are several factors here: (a)

---

[58] The question, "What do you mean *by* object?" is purposely avoided; it carries a connotation of asking for a word definition, rather than for a clarification of the response. [The tone of the examiner's voice should remain neutral and matter-of-fact; otherwise such questions may seem too challenging, forcing the subject into a defensive, self-justifying attitude.—Ed.]

Native limitations of endowment and intelligence may seriously limit the range of conceptual realms from which the content of responses may be drawn. (b) A normal adjustment which derives its stability and safety from clinging to convention and the obvious may also restrict the range of associative material. (c) The presence of strong anxiety may impair the fluidity of the subject's passing from one realm of ideas to another. (d) Extreme inhibition, depressive retardation, or psychotic blocking may restrict responses to those which are most patently congruent with well-circumscribed obvious details of blots. (f) An all-pervading preoccupation may result in a relative stereotypy if, in its absence, the wealth and variability of ideas might have been great. The presence of strong preoccupation in a generally unproductive picture may tend rather to increase the apparent variability, however.

There are several avenues of expression for the stereotypy that results from any of these conditions: it may find expression in a great increase of animal, anatomy, or vague responses, in perseveration of a single content, or in an abundance of anatomical-sexual-anal content. In the following we shall discuss each of these modes of expression.

The Animal Responses: A. The most common of all contents in the Rorschach test are the animal responses, whole and detail. Under usual conditions, the average adult around 30 years of age has about 40% of his responses in this conceptual realm. In the literature of the Rorschach test, an increase of the percentage of animal responses above this level has been considered an indication of stereotypy—or of monotony and colorlessness of the associative processes. Explanations of the frequency of animal responses, and of the significance of giving too many, have been mostly conjectural. It appears, however, that the symmetry of the inkblots is one of the crucial factors. That is to say, we experience the greatest variety of nongeometrical forms, which nevertheless show some symmetry, in the world of animal life. Objects usually have definitive contours, or quite rigid geometrical outlines; plant life may be too intensely identified with colors; landscape responses and other complex formations require either unusually sharp perceptual articulation and integration, or else are pathologically vague; and the human form, while symmetrical, lacks the great variety of animal forms. Thus, animal responses are the most easily conceived.

This line of thought helps us to understand why the percentage of animal responses becomes an indicator of stereotypy: when the psychological conditions in the subject prohibit complex articulating or integrating achievements, the most easily seen content becomes the most prevalent. The percentage of animal responses ($A\%$) thus indicates the extent to which the subject is no longer actively digging into the inkblot, but is rather responding only to its grossest articulation. Stereotypy here means that personal, self-expressive[59] material is no longer delivered by the subject; he depends upon the most obvious conventionalities or platitudes in any situation. We frequently see subjects with a strong drive toward quantitative productivity resorting to more and more A responses, in the search for further possibilities, and not infrequently such subjects end up with a very high $A\%$. Even without such quantity ambition, the best and most variable responses are usually given first, with the last responses inclining to the animal variety. But the meaning of the $A\%$ becomes clearest in clinical testing: it is high with primitive, low intelligence, with inhibition, compulsive rigidity, or depression; it is low in a setting of generally flexible and rich intelligence, or of freedom of impulses, elation, or flightiness.[60] To be sure, in the pathological range the $A\%$ does not always follow the degree of coarctation or dilation of the record. In a highly coarctated record we may find a low $A\%$, and the question then is to determine what has replaced the A responses as the expression of the coarctation of ideational content. We shall come to these replacements later. Similarly, a high $A\%$ in a very dilated record will refer to specific conditions of psychopathology; for example, the verbosity and flair for platitudes in an obsessive-compulsive maladjustment. But it appears that, within the normal range, the increase and decrease of the $A\%$ parallel the coarctation and dilation of the record. Specifically, a high $A\%$ usually refers to strong inhibition, and a low $A\%$ to impulsiveness.

The Anatomy Responses: At. There exist other easy ways of finding a response, the first of which is seen in the anatomical responses. The stereotypy indicated by At responses may stem from several sources: (a) feelings of intellectual inadequacy; (b) bodily preoccupations; (c) generalized anxiety; (d) extreme blocking which may even lead to perseveration of At responses.

Intellectual inadequacy is usually indicated in the subject's verbalization of his responses by an inappropriate, though not queer, use of expressions, or by use of terms which seem highfalutin against the subject's background. It appears that the reasoning which leads from feelings of inadequacy to At responses is, "He must expect something fancy of me, and

[59] "Self-expressive" here does not refer to responses that are necessarily based on individual memories; in fact, these are pathological indicators, as we shall see in the section on verbalization. Variability of content is a middle ground between generalities and actual memories; the former are too noncommittal, the latter too specific, to reflect wealth of ideas.

[60] It must be kept in mind that very unusual and sharply seen A responses are also obtained, and may even be original. Therefore, to take an $A\%$ simply at its face value is incorrect: the examiner must know the quality of the responses behind the summary score.

even though I do not know about these things, I will try to meet his level."

Bodily preoccupations do not always find direct expression in the Rorschach test, although this is frequently the case. There are records of severe hypochondriacs without any *At* responses, and others with only a few crucial *At* responses, specifically pertaining to the hypochondriacal ideas. Frequently, however, the overvalent ideational content of bodily preoccupation limits the range of associative material from which responses may be drawn, and finds direct expression in *At* responses.

In regard to generalized anxiety, the *At* are among the most obviously *vague* responses subjects can fall back upon, once anxiety has prevented perceptual articulation and disrupted the associative process. This occurs most frequently where both strong anxiety and strong inhibition are present.

In regard to blocking, *At* responses should be considered as indications of this extremely pathological condition when no other responses occur on any card, or when *At* responses in general predominate in the record without becoming a series of perseverations.

The beginner will often argue that, since the subject came to a doctor's office and was set to encounter "medical stuff," no special significance can be attached to the *At* responses. Experience shows, however, that only persons with anatomical preoccupations, with intense anxiety and inhibition, or with feelings of intellectual inadequacy, get set in this way. Some subjects do start the test with a set for medical pictures, but this set inevitably breaks down as they go through the cards; usually on the first or second card the impact of nonanatomical impressions is strong enough to counteract the general set. If not, then we have one or another of the pathological implications of an abundance of *At* responses.

There is only one exception to this rule: physicians are set to give *At* responses more readily than the average subject, and more justifiably. Furthermore, their *At* responses must be judged differently from those given by laymen: "pelvis" on Card I, sufficiently elaborated, or "gray and white matter of the spine" on Card II, are acceptable and considered of good form level. Yet we have records in our files of doctors who gave few or no *At* responses. Thus, the usual implications of stereotypy must be somewhat modified in the case of medical people, though even to them the *At* responses represent an easy retreat into a professional stereotypy without risk of "giving themselves away." Physicians too are open to feelings of intellectual inadequacy and rigidity of thinking, and those who in everyday life are inclined to replace conversation with shoptalk will be most likely to give a record monopolized by *At* responses. With this latter type, the correct procedure is to repeat the test with instructions to give no more *At* responses.

Experience suggests that a distinction be made between bony or skeletal anatomy, and muscular or visceral anatomy. The skeletal responses appear to refer to blocking and rigidity; the visceral responses frequently carry some disguised sexual or aggressive connotations. The *At%*, however, groups both types together.

One or two *At* responses in the average-sized record of 20-25 *R* carries no significant pathological weight, while greater incidence raises the question of maladjustment even in the normal range.

A final comment about *At* responses is in place: we have indicated that they are almost entirely vague or arbitrary in form, and hence of a poor form level (F $\pm$ or F—). There are a few exceptions: on Card III the upper side red area seen as "stomach and esophagus"; on Card VIII the upper middle white area seen as "ribs"; on Card X the upper middle gray area seen as "trachea and lungs." These three are the only common ones to merit an *F+* score in subjects other than medical men.

The Vague Form Responses: Fv. The stereotypy of a record may be appraised also from the presence of vague form responses. *A* and *At* responses represent easy ways of responding; it is likewise easy for a subject to give only noncommittal, nonspecific *Fv* responses. In these the associative process does not have any intimate and extensive interaction with the perceptual processes; rather, the initial perceptual impressions are quickly generalized into a response which, by virtue of its reference to the vagueness of the inkblot, is safe from being in any palpable contradiction to the area chosen. In other words, the associative process turns to the realm of indefinite forms where anything may be everything. These indefinite realms may be geographical, geological, microscopic, X ray, anatomical, landscapes. In these cases, the absence of any definite content becomes the indicator of stereotypy, and of a parallel lack of specificity in everyday thinking. Rich thinking leans simultaneously upon specificity and upon free handling of abstractions.

It must be kept in mind, however, that some of the contents listed as vague may be sharply articulated and consistently integrated. Such is the landscape given on Card II, "a driveway leading up through a park to a castle, behind which the sun is setting"; similarly, the geographical response "Africa" to Card II turned upside down, and referring to the lower left red area. A well-constructed geological formation on Card VI by someone who knows that field, or a specific microscopic pattern on any of the cards by a medical man or laboratory technician, may also be of a high order of articulation and integration. It is therefore advisable not to include these under a general heading which we have indicated to refer to stereotypy: rather, they should be scored separately under content, to avoid a false picture of stereotypy.

"Preoccupation" Responses. We have already indicated that an ana-

tomical preoccupation may give rise to many *At,* sexual, and anal responses. Here the pressure of associative material foists the content of the preoccupation upon areas of an inkblot, sometimes with more success (good form level) and sometimes with less (poor form level, or even absurd form responses). The preoccupation seems to assume the role of a principle regulating the figure-ground articulations of the inkblot; that is, specific parts of the gross perceptual impression will stand out by virtue of showing a formal resemblance to the images of the preoccupation. Thus, where sexual preoccupation is in the foreground, peninsulalike areas and invaginations in the contour of the inkblot are returned to again and again for responses whose content is genital organs. These responses also represent an easy way out. In contrast to the animal responses, which show much dependence upon the compelling organization of the inkblots, these "preoccupation" responses show too much dependence upon a specific predominant associative content of the subject; but in either case, flexibility of interplay between perceptual organization and associative material—the variability and interdependence of each—suffers greatly, and a picture of stereotypy ensues.

Perseveration represents the extreme form of stereotypy, and must be distinguished from the usually less pathological forms described above. The latter may be distinguished from perseveration by the following criteria: (a) their content is one which *can* be a content of conscious preoccupation; (b) inquiry usually shows that the patient is aware that his preoccupation is shaping his responses ("I have sex organs on my mind all the time"); (c) some effort will be made to base the response on a definite perceptual likeness between inkblot and image; (d) there is usually some variability among responses of similar content. In contrast, a thoroughgoing perseveration may cling to one specific content through all or most of the cards, quite without congruence of form and variability of content; the gross concept perseverates. Sometimes the content of the perseverating idea is such that some of the responses will be on an acceptable form level. For example, if the patient sticks to the idea of "butterfly," he will find good butterflies on some of the cards; but the perseverative nature of his record will be clear by the exclusive occurrence of "butterfly" responses, some of which are apparently totally unrelated to the perceptual mass of the card. The subject may come to the test without a specific content to perseverate with, but may find in the first card some more or lesss acceptable content and stick to it through the test. One patient gave "bone" to practically every card in the test, and almost no other response. In general, perseveration does not reveal the content of a psychosis, but indicates its devastating effect upon the associative processes of the subject. The crowning touch to perseveration is the absence of variation from one response to the next:

neither different kinds of butterflies nor different kinds of bones will be seen. This is crucial in distinguishing anatomical perseverations from a record otherwise dominated by *At* responses: in the latter, the *At* content will vary to some extent with the perceptual characteristics of the inkblot.

These, then, represent a variety of ways in which stereotypy may come to expression. There are other response contents which refer not to stereotypy, but to the degree of variety. These are the human, object, architecture, and plant responses. We shall discuss these in sequence.

The Human Responses: H, Hd. These are generally considered to reflect the presence of interest in other human beings. Interest does not necessarily imply capacity for warm and firm interpersonal relationships: this capacity will be confirmed only by the presence of appropriate color responses, indicating the degree of adaptiveness in the subject's affective life. Yet we can learn something about the nature of the interest from the kind of interest; the inclination to see only parts of human figures indicates an anxiety-ridden, wary, cautious interest.

The question must be asked, Why does this relationship between human responses and interest in human beings obtain? It appears that interest in and/or free contact with other persons results in a wealth of observation and experiences relative to human form, postures, and expressions; the lack of such interest or contact results in a lack of such observations. This fund of associative material will be called into play in the course of the interaction of perceptual organization and associative elaboration leading to a response; and the subject will give human responses in proportion to his wealth of observations. This proposition of course presupposes that no generalized inhibition or depression is limiting the freedom of perceptual organization and associative processes. But it must always be kept in mind that a sharp observation of other persons may come about by reason of preoccupation with and difficulty in human relationships, even though contact with human beings may be extremely limited. This preoccupation in its pathological setting may be the basis for the persistence of human responses even in psychotic conditions which have cut most of the channels of interpersonal communication or contact.

Another hazard in evaluating the human responses must be mentioned. In the section discussing the movement responses, we indicated that only human figures merit the *M* score. We did not maintain that all human figures are *M* responses: the essential criterion was that some imbalance of the perceptual mass be interpreted into a bodily tension corresponding to a movement of a human figure. Many human forms may be seen where no such imbalance is necessarily involved. Thus, the number of human-figure responses often exceeds the number of *M* responses. In certain conditions, however, when the free interest in human beings slackens, the number of responses with human content may be exactly that of the *M* responses. In this case the examiner should beware of a spuriously discrete analysis of the former, and should focus his analysis mainly upon the movements. A similar difficulty arises in connection with the human-detail responses. *Dr* and *De* responses are quite infrequent in the average-sized normal record, but human-detail responses are not; thus human-detail responses will be mostly of the large detail *(D)* variety. However, when an anxious, cautious interest in other persons becomes an extreme preoccupation in a highly obsessive setting, the number of human-detail responses may be identical with the number of *Dr* and *De* responses. Here too the examiner should avoid a twofold analysis drawing inferences both from the *Dr*'s and the human details, which are in fact identical.

Several points about the concrete content of the human responses must be taken up here. As we have already indicated, it is preferable not to obscure variety of content by including such things as witches, ghosts, giants, sorcerers, Teddy Roosevelts, Frankensteins, all under the human response score. These represent a diversity of associative processes and an availability of specific past experiences greatly in excess of that seen in such gross responses as "a head" or "a person." Although they may be justifiably set under the human score, the examiner must indicate—or at least keep in mind—their greater significance for the associative processes.

Facial expressions, expressive movements, and postures of human figures often appear to be expressions of the subject's own conception of himself. The more specific these associative elaborations of the content become, the more self-descriptive they are. Rorschach noted this point especially in connection with the movement responses: he maintained that the bending (flexed) human figures reflect a self-conception as a person weighed down by his problems and shrinking from them; while the upward or outward stretching (extended) figures reflect a self-conception of ambitiousness, of uprising against one's burdens, of active and aggressive coping with life's problems. On the other hand, even such facial expressions as "scared" or "ferocious" may also reflect a generalized feeling tone or affect disposition of the subject, whether or not they are consciously accepted by the subject as characteristic of him. It is erroneous to lean too heavily upon such interpretations, however. First, in only a few maladjustments—overideational and some hysteroid conditions—do these responses persist in any clear and abundant manner. Second, and more important, too much attention to such symbollike content analysis at our present stage of knowledge leads only to speculative and reckless interpretations of the subject's "unconscious," of its content and its "dynamics." The incidence of such wild psychoanalytic interpretations in recent publications appears to have increased, and this is a trend which will be detrimental to the clinical usefulness and status of the Rorschach test.[61]

The Object Responses: Obj. These are relatively infrequent. This may be partly ascribed to the fact that objects of irregular or vague shape are rare. In order to give object responses, the subject must call into play abstractions which are effective enough for the irregularity of the perceptual mass not to prove too disturbing an interference with the associative processes. As a consequence, object responses are almost always either very sharp and well articulated, or absurd and arbitrary. Experience indicates that object responses are most frequent in compulsive adjustments— even after their decompensation—and in psychotic conditions where arbitrariness allows for them.

The Architectural Responses: Arch. These are also relatively rare, and either very sharp or absurd. Their presence refers sometimes to a direct interest in or experience with construction and architecture, sometimes to a general appreciation of abstract, formal spatial relationships (as in connection with painting). Furthermore, the occurrence of these responses in women not infrequently points to the presence of masculine strivings and wishes. But here one should tread very cautiously, and seek confirmation of this indication, especially in the patient's Thematic Apperception Test stories. It has also been claimed (Roemer, 1921) with some justification that such responses may refer to a constructive ambitiousness. It might be mentioned that the most frequent architectural responses are the "castle" in the upper middle *Dd* of Card II, and the "Eiffel Tower" in the upper middle gray of Card X. Although the lower middle *Dr* on Card VII is frequently seen as a house, this response is not on a very high form level and carries less of the implication of the other architectural responses.

The Plant Responses: Pl. These—flowers as well as trees—are less frequent than might be expected from their manifold forms of appearance in everyday experience. They occur more frequently in children than in adults, and in women more than in men. It would not be surprising if an investigation should show that the rarity of "flower" responses is referable to the taboo our times and civilization have put upon sentimentality and sensitivity. In our experience, clearly formed and articulated plant responses always suggest that we may be dealing with a person of sensitivity and delicacy of feeling. Of course, the vague plant responses *(C or CF)* do not carry fineness of integration and specificity of content; thus, they refer not at all to sensitivity, but rather to the uncontrolled use of color as a determinant.

---

[61] [These words, written in 1945, still carry a valid warning, overcautious though they may appear. For a kind of psychoanalytic interpretation of which Rapaport approved, see Schafer (1954).—Ed.]

Thus far we have discussed the content scores referable to stereotypy, and some common varieties of other responses which do not usually carry pathological implications. There are, however, some contents with such implications; these are the cloud, blood, sexual, and anal responses.

The Cloud (Cl) *and Smoke* (Sm) *Responses* refer—at least nine tenths of the time—to a total vagueness and lack of articulation of the percept. Thus they indicate the presence of anxiety in an intense and usually free-floating form.

The Blood Responses: Bl. These indicate a tension of aggression exceeding that to be expected in the average well-adjusted person. Whether this aggression takes a passive form, is expressed in somatic symptoms, or leads to impulsive outbursts can be inferred only from the total test context. It appears that in a context of compulsive adjustment or maladjustment, passive or somatic symptom-producing aggression is expected; in a context of hysteriform maladjustment, outbursts are more likely. Aggressions are most strongly indicated when the blood is seen on some animal or human form (Card II: "Two bloody bears fighting"). The blood responses on Cards II and III, if not combined with any form and if occurring in a record which has other pure color responses, indicate rather a psychotic impairment of control and of capacity for delay.

The Sex Responses are usually pathological indicators, although they may appear in the records of uninhibited, professional, or psychologically sophisticated persons. These subjects will tend to be specific and even technical in the language they use in conveying sex responses, and they will usually give them in a dilated record. In these exceptional cases, the sex responses will be limited to only a few areas. The following are the only sex responses considered of adequate form level and scored plus: the lower middle red of Card II, "vagina"; the upper middle black *Dd* on Card II, "penis"; the upper middle *Dr* on Card IV, "vagina"; the upper projection on Card VI, "penis"; the lower middle *Dr* on Card VII, "vagina." In any other setting sex responses become pathological indicators. Their pathological weight increases if they are given on areas other than those enumerated above; if their verbalization is inadequate or incorrect (e.g., "womb" for the female organ); if they are verbalized with blunt vulgarity; if there is vagueness and hesitation in the reference ("the bottom part of a woman . . . er . . . her privates"); if they refer not to isolated sexual organs, but to sex acts (penis going into the female sex organ); if fabulizing, too much facetiousness, or any incoherence surrounds the response.

But why is it that sex responses are usually absent in normal records, and usually found in a setting of other pathological indications? The explanation appears to lie at least partly in the fact that sexuality is still taboo in our culture, evidences to the contrary notwithstanding. These taboos seem to be especially strong in communicating with a relative stranger, as in the testing situation. The normal subject apparently enters the testing situation with the taboo relatively well established, so that his associations do not stream in the direction of sexual organs or acts.

Sex responses occurring in a neurotic context most often refer to sexual preoccupation, or to a case whose presenting symptom is a sexual disturbance. The neurotic is likely to adhere to the acceptable sex responses enumerated above; he will frequently withhold an already-formed sex response, although later he will possibly report this response as a result of the pangs of conscience. Such withholding of sex responses indicates a better degree of integration than would easy and spontaneous verbalization of them; and still better integration is indicated if, while withholding them, the neurotic is able to give other responses. In contrast, psychotic patients either give many such responses quite easily and confidently, or are likely to block and give no responses at all—and even sometimes to disrupt the entire test situation in the wake of such blocking.

If the examiner carefully watches the shifting of the subject's gaze over the card, he will get the feel of where trouble starts and can intervene to help the psychotic subject verbalize the sex response; thus at times he can keep the remainder of the test running smoothly. If the subject appears to be neurotic, and if the examiner feels relatively sure that some inhibition about sex responses is operative, he may say, "I noticed that you had something in mind which you didn't tell me: what was it?" The examiner may also add, "You are supposed to tell me everything you think of as you look at these cards." Unaggressive, secure, firm inquiry of this type generally yields results. Sex responses elicited only by inquiry have, of course, a more limited pathological weight.

Although *Anal Responses* are even less frequent than sexual responses, the same considerations hold. The usual anal responses are "colon" and "rectum." Less direct expressions of anal preoccupation are seen when the subject centers interest upon the rear of any figure, discussing proportion and altitude and roundedness relative to the rest of it.

The Diagnostic Significance of the Scores of Content: Stereotypy

We shall discuss the $A\%$, the $At\%$, and the $Fv\%$ together, as these may either replace or complement each other as indications of stereotypy.

Stereotypy—and thus the $A\%$—is expected to be high in conditions where rigidity, inhibition, and a general retardation of the associative processes are outstanding in an otherwise coherent picture; it is expected to be low in conditions characterized by flightiness, great ideational mobility, or extensive disorganization and incoherence of thinking. Therefore, in schizophrenics the $A\%$ declines with progressive deterioration.

It might be asked why this decline in stereotypy should be looked at askance. The fact is that stereotypy is not merely a negative characteristic, although it becomes so when excessive. Where stereotypy is too low, it shows a lack of stability in thinking; it indicates that the obvious channels of communication in everyday life have lost their due significance for the subject. In other words, we cannot be receptive or productive of new and unusual ideas only; we often must use the stock of well-worn ideas we have, in order to cope with a situation and to be organized and oriented in receiving or producing new ideas. With increasing flightiness this principle is thrown away; too few of the old systematized ideas are available, or at least the reliance and emphasis on them is gone. It is not true, however, that all chronic and deteriorated schizophrenics show this increasing impairment of cohesive stereotypy; sometimes longstanding schizophrenia results in an extreme degree of stereotypy shading into perseveration, which reflects a general flattening of ideation. This may come to expression in a high $A\%$, though more often in other ways. Thus, a decrease of stereotypy need not mean an increase of variability, but merely a generalized devastation of ideational processes with schizophrenic deterioration.

But what may replace the high $A\%$ of the chronic and deteriorated cases, as the indication of stereotypy or devastation of ideation? Vagueness may be such a factor and anatomy ($A\%$ at least 30) another. For example, in unclassified schizophrenics, the proportion of cases with an $Fv\%$ greater than 20 increases with progressive deterioration. Chronic paranoid schizophrenics very frequently are characterized by flat, vague records. The devastation may also show up in a great increase in the $At\%$.

Simple schizophrenics, by reason of their similarity to chronic schizophrenics, show the kind of stereotypy that reflects a generalized devastation of associative processes.

In contrast, the paranoid conditions most often have an $A\%$ above 50 while $Fv\%$ and $At\%$ do not play a significant role. The picture is therefore one of a tendency to stereotypy as part of a general rigidity.

Overideational preschizophrenics were among the most ideationally wealthy of our groups, and such indications of stereotypy as high are largely lacking. Inhibited preschizophrenics produce a genuine variety of content despite their low $A\%$'s; vague, sexual, and anal responses appear to replace the usual indicators of stereotypy. The fact is that the content of the responses of this group really falls into a few specific categories, and this limited range of content is to be expected from their clinical picture. The most acceptable expression of stereotypy, a high $A\%$, is found among the depressive neuroses; while good animal forms are replaced by anatomical and vague responses in the devastated depressive psychoses. Almost complete stereotypy is to be expected in any depressive.

Among neurotics, the greatest variety of content occurs among the obsessive-compulsives because of their ideational productivity.

The stagnant, impoverished, and blocked conditions are those in which *At* responses appear to predominate. Maladjustive tendencies in an anxious and inhibited normal subject also may give rise to vagueness of perceptual organization sufficient to cause a massing of *At* responses.

THE FIFTH SCORING CATEGORY: FREQUENCY, ORGANIZATION, AND VERBALIZATION

Actually, three different things are scored in this category. First, the extremely frequent *(popular)* and extremely rare *(original)* responses—as established by findings in the general population—indicate how close a subject's response is to the conventional. Second, *complex organization* of a response is scored as "combination" or as "construction." These scores are used when different contents are given to different areas of the inkblot, and yet some meaningful and acceptable connection between them—for example, "two animals climbing a tree"—is established; these reflect the integrative ability of the subject's thinking. Third, the wording or *verbalization* of a response may take many pathological and diagnostically significant forms, to the discussion of which we shall devote a special section. We might mention here only that the disturbances in verbalization are referable to the associative processes of the subject, and usually convey some disturbance in his adjustment to the "reality" of the testing situation and of the inkblot.

Although the fifth scoring category includes three different aspects of responses, it is not as heterogeneous as it might appear at first glance. First of all, the popular and original responses relate to the other two types of scores in this category, by virtue of being the baseline against which complexity of organization and deviant verbalization can be measured. Second, the combination and construction responses are intimately related to the difficulties or deviations in verbalization, because they too are referable mainly to the associative processes and the quality that makes them combinations is intimately bound up with their verbalization.

POPULAR RESPONSES: *P*

Scoring and Inquiry

The criteria for the popular response were set by Rorschach in his *Psychodiagnostics:* they must occur once in at least every four or five records. But there are two other kinds of responses that must be considered together with the *P*. The first is the response we shall refer to as *(P)* or conditional *P*. In this, the formal articulations of the area chosen are identical with those of the *P* response, and only the fact that the content of the response is less common differentiates it from a *P*. Sometimes the main difference will lie in a slight deviation in the perceptual articulation of the response, and in these cases too a *(P)* should be scored. Customarily a *P%* is calculated to indicate what share of *R* these very common responses represent.

Let us consider now the specific *P* responses on each card.

Card I: "Bat" or "butterfly" *(W)*; if seen as a "bug" or "bird" the score is *(P)*.

Card II: "Two men," "two bears," or "two dogs" with the head in the upper red area *(W)*; the black areas seen as the "head and shoulders" of two bears or dogs *(D)*.

Card III: The black areas, with (scored *W*) or without *(D)* the lower middle detail, seen as "two men"; if these areas are seen as "birds" or animals with or without the area that corresponds to the leg of the man, the score is *(P)*.

Card IV: "Animal skin" *(W)*.

Card V: "Bat" or "butterfly" *(W)*; if seen as a "bug" or "bird," the score is *(P)*.

Card VI: "Animal skin," including all *(W)* or only the lower bulk *(D)* of the blot.

Card VII: "Two women talking or dancing" *(W)*; the upper third *(D)* or the upper two thirds *(D)* seen as the "head," or "head and bust," of two women.

Card VIII: The side pink areas seen as "two animals" *(D)*.

Card IX: The upper orange area seen as "two witches" or "Santa Clauses" or "clowns" *(D)*.

Card X: The side blue areas seen as "two octopi" or "crabs" or "spiders" *(D)*; the lower middle green area seen as a "rabbit head" *(D)*.

A few *(P)* responses were included above to show that this score is flexible and allows a certain amount of discrepancy from the usual response. The score is given as long as the perceptual organization of the area is grossly retained and the content is consistent with it: a bird is acceptable on Card III, but a "crocodile" will not do. Another regulating principle in score *(P)* is that the *P* response by definition (frequency) is *F+*; thus no deviation from *P* which is worse than *F+* can be scored *(P)*.

The second kind of response which must be considered together with *P* responses are those frequent responses which are not quite popular. Nevertheless, if massed, these indicate a tendency in the same direction. The outstanding ones among these are:

Card II: The whole card *(W)* or just the lower red areas *(D):* "butterfly."

Card III: The middle red area: "butterfly" or "bow tie" or "hair bow" *(D).*

Card IV: The lower middle projection: "animal head" *(D).*

Card VII: The lower third: "butterfly" *(D).*

Card IX: The lateral half of the lower pink areas: "man's head" *(D).*

Card X: The small brown area in the upper central white space: "wishbone" *(D);* the upper middle gray area: "two bugs" *(D);* the lower middle green area seen as "two caterpillars" or "worms" *(D).*

It must be kept in mind that the popular responses vary to some extent with the population the examiner is working with. We shall return to this point in our discussion of the rationale of the *P* response.

By definition, the *P* responses almost never need any inquiry. Only for the *(P)* score should discrepancies from the usual verbalization be inquired into.

Rationale of the Popular Responses

The *P* responses have been considered to represent compliance with the thinking of the community—in other words, the capacity for thinking in conventional and stereotyped terms. Such a capacity is essential for balanced and realistic thinking, and the lack of it indicates some lack of common sense and of understanding of the simple and common routes of thinking. Of course, this compliance is often carried to extremes, resulting in a lack of individuality and freedom of thinking; flexible common sense then becomes banality.

But why should the popular responses have this implication? The answer appears to lie partly in the nature of the inkblots. The fact that a very considerable share of the general population—regardless of its great variety of adjustments and maladjustments—sees the same responses in a blot indicates that the blot itself is more or less conducive to a specific perceptual organization and consequently specific associative content. In this sense, the areas to which popular responses are given represent a relatively clearcut piece of reality which is so compelling that its meaning is a matter of social agreement. The responsiveness of a subject to these compelling areas on the inkblots thus becomes the measure of his sense of the obvious. Thus the *P* responses have a continuity of meaning with—and the majority of them are—animal responses.

The absence or overabundance of *P* responses have different meanings in different psychopathological settings; their interpretation in terms of common sense is valid only within the normal range. Poor yet not altogether low-grade deficient intelligence, compulsive overcritical pedantry, depressive inertia and self-criticism, a penchant for platitudes of the type frequently found in naïve hysterics, ideational flatness of the type seen in simple schizophrenics—all may make for an unduly high $P\%$. In these conditions, overdependence upon the compelling perceptual qualities of the inkblot reflects impaired freedom of the subject's own productivity. The basis of this impairment must of course be deciphered from the other aspects of the test. Many psychopaths give generally flat Rorschach records with a high $P\%$. This appears understandable if we realize that thinking in terms of common sense *alone* is concretistic thinking, rooted only in the temptations and tribulations of single isolated situations and not guided by such temporally and morally abstract ideas as right and wrong or consequences.

A low $P\%$, provided that R is not too large, generally reflects a weak contact with and responsiveness to reality. Of course, when a record becomes dilated, the $P\%$ will be spuriously low because of the limited number of possible P's; and instead of the percentage, the absolute number of P's will be significant. The larger R is, the more the number of P's should approach the maximum of 12. It must also be kept in mind that an absence of P responses on any card does not necessarily indicate lack of common sense to begin with, but may reflect a disturbance specific to the card. Thus, if P responses stop on a heavily shaded or diffusely colored card, it is justified to conclude that anxiety or affects can play havoc with common sense. The presence of strong anxiety, however, drives one toward vagueness rather than toward platitudes.

In the average-sized record of 20 to 25 responses, there should be four or five P's or a $P\%$ of 20 to 25%. It appears, however, that with increasing age (above 30) a progressive, slow increase of the $P\%$ takes place.

The Diagnostic Significance of the P Responses

The highest $P\%$ occurs in depressives and depressivelike neurotics, in the ideationally flat simple schizophrenics, and generally in persons characterized by marked rigidity and caution.

Considering schizophrenics specifically, there is a progressive decrease in the incidence of P with chronicity and deterioration; this is in accord with the departure from reality found in the progress of the schizophrenic process. For other reasons, preschizophrenics tend to have a low $P\%$.

In terms of the absolute number of P responses, depressives are not outstanding for their great number of popular responses, but rather for the great share their few popular responses have in their meager records. Thus, although depressives usually exceed acute schizophrenics in their $P\%$, they have fewer P's.

Accordingly, the emphasis upon P in impoverished records is reflected by the absolute number of *P*'s. We may conclude that pathologically inhibitory or ideationally flat conditions make for an overemphasis upon popular responses, while dilated overideational conditions and abandonment of reality testing make for a minimal emphasis upon them.

THE ORIGINAL RESPONSES: *Orig*

Scoring and Inquiry

Original responses are those that occur no more than once or twice in a hundred records. This statistical criterion must be modified by further considerations. Responses that are vague in form should never be considered original, nor should fanciful associative elaborations of tiny areas or projections of the inkblot not based upon perceptual articulation and reorganization of the area in question. Thus, original responses may be *F+* or *F—* but never *Fv,* and the examiner should be very conservative in assigning this score to responses referring to tiny areas. Similarly, the examiner should not score as *Orig* such a farfetched response as "elephant" for the "bear" on Card VIII; such responses are not based upon active perceptual work on the area chosen.

The *Orig+* responses are usually immediately convincing. Only when there is some doubt, and the score *Orig—* is in question, should inquiry be made in order to establish whether it is the examiner's blind spot that makes the response appear poor. The score *Orig* does not refer to an unusual choice of area: there are *Orig* responses to areas where *P* responses can be given. What makes the response original is a new perceptual organization of the area.

Like *P* responses, *Orig* responses vary with the character and cultural level of the subjects one works with; hence the examiner must always adapt himself to his population. Only experience with 300 to 500 records obtained from a wide sampling of the cultural group in question should be considered an adequate basis for such adaptation, and data from psychopathological cases should never be taken as indicating popular trends. A much greater flexibility in scoring the originals should be allowed, however. In a psychopathological population which is impoverished in original response, a response that is seen relatively often in the general population may be scored *Orig,* to indicate that in this instance a more vivid ideational functioning has occurred. Such a flexibility of scoring emphasizes that scoring should remain subservient to the analysis of the record, and should help point up significant aspects of it. To be sure, for purposes of any statistical study, a uniform set of criteria for all groups should be established and adhered to.

Rationale of the Original Responses

While the popular responses reflect conventionality and stereotyped thinking, the original responses represent freedom in thinking. The popular responses reflect a great dependence upon the compelling perceptual characteristics of the inkblot; the original responses reflect a marked degree of independence of these configurations, which allows the subject to manipulate them so as to bring forth new articulations and contents. Thus, the elaborate original responses are often carriers of ideas intimately linked with the problems and attitudes of the patient, while the popular responses usually carry no trace of personal flavor. Furthermore, just as the conventionality indicated by the popular responses is double-edged, so is the originality in these responses: originality may be a sign of freedom, but too much may indicate a lack of common sense and an unconcern for the obvious articulations of reality. The *Orig%*, the form level of the original responses, and the general context of the record in which they occur must all be considered in evaluating the significance of the original responses. Any sizable, but not excessive, number of original responses of a good form level usually indicates good native endowment. Such responses may persist even in a pathological context. Poor form level or great abundance of original responses in cases of poor affective adaptation indicates psychopathology.

The incidence of original responses is highest in the ideationally rich clinical group: acute unclassified schizophrenics, overideational preschizophrenics, obsessive-compulsives, mixed neurotics, and paranoid conditions. The lowest incidence of original responses occurs in depression, anxiety and depression, and simple schizophrenia. Furthermore, acute schizophrenics significantly exceed chronic and deteriorated schizophrenics in their incidence of *Orig,* and overideational preschizophrenics significantly exceed inhibited preschizophrenics.

It appears then that the presence of active ideation tends to increase significantly the number of original responses given. As these accumulate in groups where the *M* and *Dr* responses also accumulate, it might be asked, What can original responses specifically contribute to diagnostic evaluation? Under certain conditions *Dr, M,* or *Orig* may be missing, and the indications that persist then become diagnostically crucial. Sometimes the sudden occurrence of a few originals in an otherwise coarctated record will be the only clue to the presence of pathological ideation.

The highest incidence of poor original responses occurs mainly in chronic schizophrenics and in the related simple schizophrenics. It is striking, however, that more than half of the few originals given by acute paranoid schizophrenics are of a very poor quality, and this is sometimes a crucial diagnostic indication of the presence of schizophrenia in the records of such patients: their records usually show coarctation and careful control, but occasionally a fantastic original response will break though. Most depressives give few original responses with great caution and hence only on a good form level.

COMBINATION AND CONSTRUCTION RESPONSES

Scoring and Inquiry

In these responses the subject links together, by means of associative elaboration, responses to two or more parts of the inkblot. If this link is present in the spontaneous verbalization of the entire response, the score "combination" *(comb)* is usually given; if the parts of the response are seen separately and only afterward linked together, the score "construction" *(constr)* is given. For example, the whole of Card I seen as "a winged man" is a combination response, because the wings are conceptually discrete from the figure of the man in the center of the inkblot; this response is in contrast to "bat" on the same card, which is a gross abstractive response in which all the parts are mutually interdependent. Similarly, the response "two bears with blood on their paws" is to be considered a combination; "a colorful butterfly" is not. Combination responses may become even more complex, and correspondingly more easily scored: for example, the response to Card I, "two winged men [side figures] carrying a headless woman" (center figure). It appears from these examples that combinations may consist either in elaborating upon a single response, or in establishing action connections between the relatively autonomous parts of the total response. A construction response differs from these in that, for example, the last response would be derived from seeing first two winged figures, then a middle figure, and then elaborating the action relationship between the two.

These types of responses do not require, nor do they admit of, inquiry. The spontaneous verbalization should make clear whether a combination or construction was involved, and any elaborations elicited in or inferred from inquiry must be considered as secondary indications and of correspondingly minimal significance. In the following we shall not distinguish between the combination and construction responses, because both represent merely different shadings of the same associative process.

Rationale of the Combination Responses

Combination responses appear to emanate from the subject's associative elaboration around two or more spatially contiguous areas of the inkblot. That is to say, the content of the specific combination is not provided in the inkblot: given the condition of contiguity, the rest is up to the subject's associative thought processes. Good endowment and intelligence are prerequisites for giving well-integrated and acceptable combination responses; and the amount and quality of combinations are a reflection of the integrative ability of the subject. Although maladjustment appears to cut down the incidence of combination responses, those combinations which survive are most likely to bear the marks of the specific maladjustments in their arbitrariness or unrealistic establishment of relationships. Here, however, the response passes out of the range of combination, and becomes a pathological indicator of the type we term "fabulized combination" or "confabulation" (see below). In general, the combination responses bear some relationship to the original responses, inasmuch as both represent a new way of looking at the card and of coping with the multifarious perceptual impressions; in both, the subject actively puts something of his own into the response. Maladjustment is much more likely to allow for the persistence and even increase of the number of original responses, while it tends to cut down the combination responses.

The Diagnostic Significance of the Combination Responses

Again, the most actively ideational groups give the greatest number of combination responses: obsessive-compulsives, overideational preschizophrenics, and acute unclassified schizophrenics are all likely to have at least one combination response. We find an almost complete absence of combination responses in depression, anxiety and depression, and simple schizophrenia. Furthermore, there is a progressive decrease of these responses with schizophrenic chronicity and deterioration. It appears then that, like the original responses, combination responses reflect the presence of either pathological ideational activity or normal adjustment; and their absence in the clinical range is referable to extremely inhibitory, retarded, ideationally flat, or disorganized conditions.

THE ANALYSIS OF VERBALIZATION[62]

The subject's verbalization can carry within it crucial indications of the nature of his maladjustment. The subject's verbal communication of his

[62] [This section represents the most distinctive and original of Rapaport's contributions to Rorschach testing. It was in many ways a pioneering effort, and at the time of the first edition it had not been thoroughly worked out—the authors admit as much. The clinical usefulness of the categories described was nevertheless considerable, and is demonstrable in Schafer's books (1948, 1954). They have also been used with some success in research (e.g., Watkins & Stauffacher, 1952; Powers & Hamlin, 1955; Hertz & Paolino, 1960).

Rapaport's students have continued to use and teach his scoring of verbalizations

response *in relationship* to the determinants he used, the area he chose, and the content he attributed to it, is an integral aspect of that response; like the response itself, it is a product of the subject's thought processes and is amenable to scoring, systematization, and diagnostic evaluation. Verbalizations—especially where they seem to admit of symbolic interpretation or interpretation by analogy—have been used by many investigators for interpretation of test results. But what has been lacking thus far was a psychological rationale to systematize the conspicuous verbalizations and to attempt to explain the psychological processes leading to deviant ones.

We began by making a large collection of excerpted deviant verbalizations, from our mixed clinical population. They included all verbal formulations that our experience had indicated and rationale had supported as useful diagnostic indications. Only against the background of material provided by such a comprehensive excerpting could any attempt at systematization or clarification begin. It is not our claim that the following pages present a complete explanation or systematization of final validity of the material we have excerpted, or that the excerpts represent an exhaustive collection of all possible kinds of deviant verbalizations. We do not even maintain that the distinctions we made between different kinds of pathological verbalizations are entirely consistent or correct. Nevertheless, we feel that our material is sufficient to allow for an attempt to make some

---

and have contributed to their clarification and extension. Mayman (in preparation) has concentrated on systematizing and validating the *fab* category. My own work has convinced me that what Rapaport was getting at was in large part manifestations of the primary process. My manual (Holt, 1963b; see also Holt & Havel, 1960) is thus an outgrowth of the scoring presented here. Since it contains a detailed critique of Rapaport's formulations wherever I felt it necessary to modify them, I have left the present text essentially unchanged, even though I do not believe that certain distinctions and conceptualizations attempted here have stood the test of time. For the most part, they are simply noted by a reference to this footnote. In general, further clinical experience has shown that even the more extreme pathological verbalizations are not as specific to schizophrenia as this text implies.

In particular, I have found it difficult to work with the notions of loss and increase of distance from the card. There is undoubtedly a valid insight in this conceptualization, pertaining to the inappropriateness with which schizophrenics approach the task of interpreting inkblots, but in practice the distinction between too-little and too-great distance proves too slippery for reliable use. Concepts such as failure of reality testing, or slippage in set, will probably eventually replace disturbances of distance. The other main respect in which the following text's discussion now seems deficient is that it fails to make use of Kris's concept of regression in the service of the ego. By paying close attention to the effectiveness (or ineffectiveness) with which the subject uses his controls and defenses in coping with the emergence of his own primary processes, I have found it possible and fruitful to distinguish between uncontrolled, pathological breakthroughs of primary-process material (maladaptive regression) and more ego-syntonic, socialized, acceptable expressions (adaptive regression). See Pine and Holt (1960), and Silverman, Lapkin, and Rosenbaum (1962); Holt (1966) contains an up-to-date bibliography of studies using the primary-process scoring system.—Ed.]

tentative order out of the varieties of pathological verbalization. To ignore these altogether would be to discard one of the most crucial segments of the Rorschach material; to present them merely haphazardly without any system would be to confuse the reader. In our own experience, the growth of the rationale which we present below has served in helping us to locate and understand the more subtly deviant and hitherto unencountered verbalizations which are ever-present in clinical Rorschach records.

Our approach to the verbalizations was a gross one. We did not attempt to analyze all verbalizations which, in everyday clinical work, we use as characteristic indicators of the subject's personality organization and maladjustment. Rather, we restricted ourselves to the most strikingly deviant ones, hoping to establish with them some kind of basis that later would permit further development. As a consequence, the bulk of the verbalizations extracted reflect schizophrenic pathology of thinking. Thus we shall surmount the temptation merely to shrug away schizophrenic verbalizations as "nutty as a fruit cake," and attempt to show that there is order and a basis in these verbalizations themselves for understanding them; this basis permits inferences from clear-cut to masked schizophrenic thinking when the course of the thought process is more obscure or entirely hidden.

Scoring and Inquiry

The titles we shall apply to the variants of pathological verbalization are largely our own. Even those which we have borrowed from previous investigators will be somewhat altered in respect to their designation and significance. We could not avoid this arbitrariness, inasmuch as we began our work with whatever scores were already well established in the literature, but in the course of experience they imperceptibly underwent modifications and extensions as we encountered different nuances of verbalization. We shall not attempt here to give the criteria for our scores, because actually our discussions of each score will be in effect a statement of the concepts and criteria necessary to understand and apply it.

It should be stated that these "scores" are qualitative indicators and, unlike those discussed so far, do not need to clutter up the scoring sheets, as long as one is keenly aware of their presence in a record.

In regard to inquiry we can only re-emphasize those principles stated in the general section on inquiry (see pp. 279ff.). Good effective inquiry is not wholesale inquiry, which rather will make the patient aware of those nuances of unwitting verbalization to be described below, and drive him back upon the most conventional and safe expressions. Exactly *when* inquiry is to be made cannot be prescribed, yet the following considerations will give leads.

If the subject sees a "pink elephant" for which there is no perceptual support in a pink area chosen, we have an indication that the subject's associative processes have gone on their merry way without referring back to the inkblot for perceptual regulation and modification of the final response: here there is too much disregard for the inkblot, or too much departure or "distance" from the card. On the other hand, if the subject sees a mountain on the upper part of a card and a flower on the lower part, and therefore concludes that it is a picture of a mountain resting on a flower, we have an indication that the subject is taking the spatial relationships of the inkblot as real and meaningful: here he is attending *too much* to the inkblot, and shows a "loss of distance" from the card. We shall attempt below to show to what extent increase or loss of distance characterizes each, and to what extent—and this is the most usual case—a loss of distance *and* an increase of distance are manifest in the same response.

In his *Psychodiagnostics,* Rorschach pointed out that introspective subjects—those inclined to give movement responses in abundance—will readily recognize that the cards are merely inkblots which they must *interpret;* the more naïve subjects—those inclined to give an abundance of color responses—frequently consider the inkblots as pictures whose meaning they must *discover.* The latter will be inclined to ask, "What is it really?" Though the former is somewhat in the direction of increased distance, and the latter somewhat in the direction of loss of distance, both reactions are within the normal range; in our experience, introspective subjects will never explain a response solely in terms of their own associative process, and naïve ones will never give responses that are so specific, so absurd, or so loaded with conviction as to imply that their response is the inevitable, real content of the blot.

Thus it appears that, from the responses themselves, from the verbalization, or from the verbalized reasoning usually elicited in inquiry, one can infer the presence of thinking which does not adhere to the reality of the testing situation, as defined by attitudes, responses, and verbalizations of the general normal population. Such deviant thinking has been called *autistic* thinking.[63] By "autistic thinking" we mean here cognitive processes that are not ruled by the laws and conventions of logic. Such thinking has been demonstrated to be motivated by wishes. The rules of wish-dominated thinking may be characterized from several different viewpoints. From Freud's exposition of the dream mechanisms, we know that displacement and condensation of ideas may be one set of forms in which such thinking is manifested. Lévy-Bruhl (1921) used the concept of "participation" to

---

[63] In this discussion we are using the concept of autism only in the sense of its pathological extreme as described by Bleuler (1911), and not in the more general sense in which it is applied by G. Murphy (1945, 1947).

describe such thinking in preliterate people. By *participation* is meant a mode of thinking that considers things identical by virtue of their sharing a single common quality.[64] We might also mention here Piaget's concept of "transductive reasoning," that reasoning which makes inferences about whole situations from experience with only a small and relatively discrete part thereof.

The significance of autistic thinking in the Rorschach test is, however, a special one. Here thinking is always related to the perceptual reality of the inkblot, and hence the autistic character of any thinking we observe must and can be judged in terms of the regulative effect of the perceptual reality upon the subject's thought process. This is why the degree and pathological implications of autistic thinking can be conceived of in terms of loss or increase of distance from the inkblot. This is the conceptual yardstick we have found most helpful in systematizing the variety of forms which autistic thinking may take in the Rorschach test situation.

Keeping these considerations in mind we can make one specific point about inquiry here. The questions asked by the examiner should be as vague as possible; they should give the subject no clue to the examiner's intent or to the specific aspect of the response he is concerned with. The examiner should never ask, "What is there about the card or on the card that makes you think so?" Instead, relatively ambiguous questions such as, "What makes it look like this?" or "What makes you think this?" are preferable. In our clinical experience, the former questions drive the subject's attention and thinking to the perceptual characteristics of the inkblot, regardless of his spontaneous inclination. The latter questions permit him to localize the basis of the response in his own thoughts, memories, or reasoning. Experience shows conclusively that all normal and most neurotic subjects will usually not locate this basis in their own thought processes, but that preschizophrenics and schizophrenics frequently will. Thus, the vaguer questions are actually catalyzing questions, helpful in eliciting schizophrenic thought processes. These points will be further elaborated below.

General Rationale of the Analysis of Verbalization

The Reality of the Testing Situation. Fundamental to the understanding of pathological verbalizations is an understanding of the reality of the testing situation. In this connection two questions arise: How shall we conceive of this real situation, that is, what conceptual framework shall we use

---

[64] [Compare the "von Domarus principle" of predicative reasoning (von Domarus, 1944). For further discussion of the theory of the primary process, see Rapaport (1951a, 1959a), Gill (1967), Holt and Havel (1960) and Holt (1967c).—Ed.]

for describing it? and, How can we approximate the "true" situation, in order to detect weaknesses of orientation to reality and reality testing?

In answer to the second question, we may say that the reality can be made palpable only in terms of the records of a large variety of normal subjects. Here we may see how the normal subject, whose orientation toward and testing of reality are reasonably sound, conceives of his role in relation to the inkblot and to the examiner. By and large, normal subjects will understand the testing situation and the test instructions to mean that they are to give responses for which sufficient justification may be found in the perceptual qualities of the inkblot; that their responses must be completely acceptable to everyday conventional logic; and that, just as they should not give responses they cannot confirm by reference to the inkblot, so their responses should not be so dominated by the perceptual configurations of the inkblot that they are no longer subject to critical control, and thus become absurdly combined or absurdly integrated.

The answer to the second question implies the answer to the first. We may profitably conceive of the reality of the testing situation in terms of the distance maintained by the subject between himself and the inkblot. If the subject's responses show too little regard for the inkblot (absurd form responses), or if his responses carry too much associative elaboration of a response which in itself is good, then we have an indication of increase of distance from the card. On the other hand, if the subject's response shows that he is conceptually and/or affectively taking the inkblot as an immutable reality, with its own real affective and logical propensities not admitting of critical control, we have an indication of loss of distance from the card.

Thus, distance here differs from the concept of distance used in the evaluation of the Word Association Test results. The crucial difference is that in the Rorschach test we have a perceptual reality which is to some degree a palpable basis for measuring distance; in the Word Association Test the words called out by the examiner are very elusive realities by reason of their many connotations, and the standard against which to judge distance lies more in the popular reaction.

It must be pointed out also that our indications of the presence of autistic thinking come not only from the patient's verbalizations. We have maintained that a strong prevalence of movement responses—especially if $M-$ is present—with a marked lack of color responses indicate the possible presence of autistic, unrealistic thinking; it was also implied in our discussion of the form level that many of the arbitrary form responses, which are not sufficiently geared to the perceptual reality of the inkblot, are, when abundant, expressions of autistic thinking; and we mentioned that the occurrence of space responses in extreme amounts may refer to negativistic paranoid thinking, which always implies that pathological autism is at work. The fact remains, however, that an analysis of verbalization is the most crucial and most frequently helpful procedure in the search for traces of autistic thinking. Pathological verbalizations are less often scattered in isolated cases; they occur with startling frequency in a very large share of the records of schizophrenics, preschizophrenics, and related conditions.

To make the concept of "distance" clearer, we shall discuss briefly one of the forms each distortion of distance—loss or increase—may take; in a sense, the two examples to follow will represent prototypes of the processes active when the distance relationship is autistically distorted.

The DW Response. As described in the section on the area chosen, the *DW* score is given to responses in which the patient attributes to an entire inkblot a content based on only a portion of it. This procedure is far from the inductive or deductive thinking which we usually accept as logical; it has been called transductive thinking by Piaget, and represents a subtype of autistic, magical thinking. For example, Card VI may be called "a cat" because the fine projections at the top look like "whiskers." The reasoning behind these responses may be formulated thus: "If this looks like whiskers, then it *must* be a cat." It is as though the subject has found a clue to the *reality significance* of the inkblot. In the following analysis we shall return often to the concept of transductive thinking as one expression of loss of distance from the inkblot, because to our understanding it characterizes a number of other pathological responses as well.

The Absurd Response. Responses for which no objective perceptual support is given in the inkblot itself, we have termed *absurd*. Here the course of the associative processes is no longer regulated by the percept, and too many of the patient's subjective processes are involved in the coming about of the response. This too is unrealistic or autistic thinking; but here the reality of the inkblot itself becomes minimal in significance, and the content of the associative processes is overemphasized. Thus, in contrast to transductive reasoning, such "subjective"[65] responses serve as a prototype for *increase* of distance from the inkblot. An example of an absurd response is, to Card VII, "It isn't a shoelace, is it?" (See also below, pp. 457f.)

We must anticipate that some of these specific examples will strike the reader as more or less appropriate introspective comments, or mere flippant remarks. Such expressions as will be analyzed here may appear to be conventional enough even in psychiatric examination, and the fact that they hide autistic schizophrenic thinking may not be noticed. The clinical interview is never a standardized procedure, and in it usually only gross mani-

---

[65] We shall avoid using the term "projective" in connection with responses characterized by too much associative elaboration, because of the possible confusion of meaning. We shall use instead the term "subjective."

festations of queerness will bring the autistic thinking clearly to the fore. Thus, clinical examination has remained a relatively weak tool for demonstrating schizophrenic thought disorder—the primary symptom of schizophrenia (see Bleuler, 1911)—in its early phases, preceding the appearance of the gross secondary symptoms (delusions, hallucinations, inappropriateness, etc.). The testing situation, however, is a *standardized situation*. Furthermore, complete recording of all responses of the subjects gives us a set of reactions which may also be standardized. These two taken together provide a system of coordinates, in relation to which responses may be evaluated to detect any departure from the usual reactions of subjects and any autistic conception of the testing situation. Many of the extracts we shall present will not look peculiar if taken by themselves; but they deserve our attention by reason of their deviation from the standard responses and conceptions of the normal population. This is the basis on which it can be claimed that standardized tests in general, and the Rorschach test in particular, are diagnostic tools which—above and beyond their intrinsic diagnostic potency—are much more sensitive for the evaluation of verbalization than is the clinical interview. It can also be claimed that comprehensive and systematic work with the verbalization on these tests is a highway for investigating disorders of thinking.

Deviant Verbalizations

Fabulized Responses. Examples: On Card II in reference to the black areas and the white space in the middle, "lake . . . dangerous rocks"; on Card II in reference to the lower middle red area, "the inferno." In the first example, the fabulized element is introduced with the subjective, affect-laden adjective "dangerous," indicating that the subject's associative processes have unduly elaborated upon the original percept with little regulation from it. This is a typical reflection of increased distance from the card. In the second example, the "inferno" refers to a red area where the response "fire" would be acceptable. The specificity of the "inferno" response suggests that the associative processes have again departed too far from the card. In these two examples we see that fabulizing denotes too much affective elaboration of the response, or too great specificity. However, neither of these responses seems outrageous to reason nor stands in sharp contradiction to realistic possibilities. As a matter of fact, such responses are frequently given by introspective and sensitive persons who enjoy playing with language of high affective charge and colorfulness of reference. But the normal subject will be *aware* of the fanciful play in the response, will experience pleasure in it, and will be immediately prepared to explain that all he really saw was "rocks" or "something fiery"; whereas our clinical subjects give these responses with an air of reality and an expenditure of affect. Thus, the outstanding thing in these fabulized responses is the increased distance they show from the card; but an implicit loss of distance is expressed by the emotion-laden conviction that "this is what it really is." Nevertheless, we often find such fabulized material even in normal protocols, introduced in descriptions of facial expressions and physiognomic characteristics of animals or objects.[66]

Additional examples: Card IV, *W:* "a bat . . . shadings from gray to black. It gives you the impression of oppression, as if he could envelop you with his wings." Card I, middle figure: "more like a monster than a man; looks as though he would jump at somebody." Card II, usual bear: "creatures in another world [upper red] certainly scared this animal." Card VIII, upper middle *S:* "face, looks very fierce, twitching lips." Card VIII, each half of upper gray: "two old graybeards, very wise, deep in thought, some great problem on their minds." Card VIII, pink *S:* "a dog, German shepherd in the attack, coming in with that slow deliberate grace as though afraid, really good footwork for a fighting dog."

In general, the presence of a few fabulized responses will not be conclusive proof of psychopathology. Only a great massing of them indicates excessive fantasying, which probably includes a pathological amount of autistic thinking.

Fabulized Combinations. Examples: On Card X in reference to the lower middle green areas, "a rabbit . . . worms coming out of his eyes"; on Card VIII in reference to the side pink area and the lower middle pink-orange area, "two prairie dogs, climbing on a butterfly." In both of these examples, the parts of the response that are being combined represent good percepts. The rabbit's head and the worms are frequently given, and so are the animals and the butterfly. But worms do not come out of the eyes of a rabbit—especially not in the size relationship seen on the card—nor do prairie dogs climb on butterflies. The fabulized character of these responses is apparent in the impossibility of the combination effected. Even the acceptable combination responses have a fabulized element, but it is always in full accord with possibilities offered in the real world. Thus, a relation-

---

[66] Such facial expressions and physiognomic characteristics have been considered by some investigators to represent rudiments or vestiges of *M* responses. In terms of our rationale such an assumption is erroneous, inasmuch as they express associative elaborations based on few, if any, minor perceptual aspects of the card. The amazingly balanced relation of perceptual and associative processes achieved in *M* responses is missing here; the associative processes predominate. That they run high in records which also have a high number of *M* responses is understandable in terms of the implications of both for the presence of active ideation; but to maintain that both are on one continuum is to establish a spurious relationship. [It seems debatable that *fab* responses always carry any emotional conviction of reality; see fn. 62.—Ed.]

ship is introduced in these fabulized combinations which represents un-realistic and autistic ideas. If we examine these responses more closely, we see a sharp difference between them and the merely fabulized responses described above. What appears to lie at the core of the fabulized combina-tion is that a spatial relationship in the inkblot is taken as an immutable, real relationship. Here, although the final formulation of the response represents an increase of distance from the card, the response bears mainly the mark of extreme loss of distance. The autistic thinking in these fabulized combinations is usually quite striking, unlike that in some of the merely fabulized responses which the examiner may find himself passing over too quickly. Thus, these responses represent fabulizing associated with a loss of distance from the inkblot, which tends to become entirely unrealistic. It is true that fabulized combinations occur, though rarely, in the records of normal and fairly well-organized neurotic subjects. But these subjects will usually seem startled when such a response possibility comes into their minds; they will give the response with a smile, with some apologetic ex-planation of the fact that "it just struck me this way"; and although the pathological implications of the response are not thereby entirely elimi-nated, their weight is lessened.

Additional examples: Card IX, pink and green: "two hippopotamuses with elephants standing on their backs." Card X, lower middle green: "man with green mustache." Card III, *D*, lower middle: "two men holding kid-neys." Card III: "two African savages cooking something in a pot over a fire . . . only the positions have been transposed so that the fire [middle red] is over the top of the pot instead of underneath it." Card X, blue and green details: "sheep . . . spiders or octopuses, one of them seems to have hold of that sheep." Card II, inverted: "wire-haired terriers with noses on fire."

Confabulations.[67] Examples: In reference to the mid-line of Card VI, "the light streak in here reminds me of the wide and powerfully flowing Mississippi River"; in reference to the three blue areas on Card X, "might be a crab [outer blue]. [What makes it look like that?] Because it has bones here" (inner blue); in reference to Card V, "two people lying down, tired, resting [side figures] . . . somebody helping them [central figure], nature might be helping them . . . might be God." The first of these examples represents an increase of distance from the card so extreme that one can

---

[67] The use of the term "confabulation" here differs from that advanced by Rorschach; it seemed a good concept for subsuming a variety of pathological ver-balizations, and we liberally extended its scope. [Again, the decision to extend the meaning of a term used by many Rorschach workers to designate the *DW* response seems an unfortunate one. I have proposed "autistic elaboration" as an alternative (Holt, 1963b); see fn. 62.—Ed.]

no longer see any justification for the specificity and affect loading of the response; the intermediate steps in the associative-perceptual interplay are no longer apparent. This response stands in sharp contrast to even such a fabulized response as "inferno"; for in the latter the justification for the response is at least palpable, while in the former an extraneous element is introduced without any real warrant.

The second example has somewhat different implications. In this response the middle *blue* area of the card is described as the bones pertaining to the animal of the outer *blue* area. Here we see thinking in terms of "participation" in clear-cut form: inasmuch as both areas are blue, they belong together in a single concept and share each other's qualities and meanings. Such a mediating link as similarity in color reflects the extremely unrealistic nature of the thought process giving rise to this response. In this sense, this example shows some continuity with the fabulized combinations: it is clear from the response that, to begin with, there was a pathological loss of distance from the inkblot, which then led to the farfetched associative elaboration. But unlike the fabulized combinations, in which the combined percepts are of a good quality and maintain their separate identity, here the quality is poor and the separate identity of the parts is lost. In this sense, the response shows a continuity with the *DW* responses, inasmuch as identities are established as well as lost on the basis of only partial impressions. Later, in discussing the contamination responses, we shall see how this type of thinking reaches another pathological extreme.

The third example of confabulation lends itself to a relatively more complete, yet more complex, analysis. The response starts out with relatively clear-cut fabulizing in terms of "tired, resting"; already an increase of distance from the card is indicated. The central figure then enters the picture, and its significance appears to emanate from transductive reasoning based on its spatial relationship to the two side figures, as well as to their "tiredness." That is, as there are two reclining tired figures and one erect figure, the latter must be a "helper." Thus a pathological loss of distance from the inkblot—to the extent that the subject's reasoning is bound by the objective spatial relationships in the blot—has led to the determination of the significance of one part of the response by the significance of the other: this is transductive reasoning at its clearest.

The pathological increase in distance implied in the final elaboration of the response is also clear; it lends the response an extreme fabulatory character by associative elaboration, which leads finally to ascribing the significance of "nature or God" to the central figure. This example is important, because it contains traces of all the steps from pathological loss of distance to pathological increase of distance.

Thus, in general, confabulation responses carry to the extreme those tendencies which are already present in both fabulized responses and fabulized combinations. These three types of pathological verbalization appear to constitute a rough sequence of increasingly pathological indicators. These responses always imply the probable presence of unrealistic, autistic thinking in everyday situations, where fantasies and autism replace adherence to objective orientation to reality. The indications are most clear-cut when confabulations are present, and least when only a few fabulized responses are given.

Additional examples: Card X, *W:* "two boxers [pink], referee in between . . . legs [lower middle green] and eyeglasses [middle orange] . . . pole of the ring [upper middle gray] . . . in the background the crowd yelling them on [the rest of the card]." Card IX, *W:* "oil in the center. Top looks like part of a flame; there seems to be fire at the bottom. Seems to be the evidence for a crime story in this picture. [?] The idea of oil igniting quickly suggested fire to me, and the color red." Card III, *W:* "a fellow's body, just a framework. Nothing here is done right—his back is broken, he is broken in two, here is his kidney . . . part of his body is in the tomb." Card VI, at the bottom of upper proj.: "Bacteriological smear with debris . . . on a vaginal smear of gonorrhea after sulfathiazol." Card X, *Dr* on *S* proj. of *S* blue: "a lady bending down holding onto an erected penis, worshipping it, she looks like she is in love with the phallus." Card V, *W:* "Huge oil storage plant burning down, a lot of action to it. I almost hear the roar of flames and ashes . . . also mixed in the idea of a bomb dropping on one of these tanks contributing to their explosion."

The Diagnostic Significance of Fabulized Responses, Fabulized Combinations, and Confabulations. First of all, schizophrenic chronicity and deterioration make for a greater incidence of all these pathological verbalizations, but especially of confabulation, which is the most autistic and most clearly a part of schizophrenic thinking. The "covering up" that characterizes so many rigid paranoid schizophrenics is likely to limit greatly the pathological implications of their verbalizations. Still, the proportion of paranoid schizophrenics likely to give at least one confabulation ranges from one to two out of five cases.

Paranoid conditions are not likely to have confabulations. These patients are very sparing in their use of any of these pathological verbalizations. This is also true of simple schizophrenics, although for an entirely different reason: the generalized vagueness and stereotypy which characterize their Rorschach records. In this respect inhibited preschizophrenics resemble them very closely; this also is an ideationally flat group, whose great inhibition and anxiety lead to considerable vagueness or to perseverationlike anatomical or sexual responses. If we turn to overideational preschizophrenics, we find them outstanding in the production of fabulized responses and fabulized combinations. Clinically they are rich in fantasies, being possessed by what is psychoanalytically termed "libidinization of thought processes," and abound in obsessions or obsessive ideation, phobias, and even semidelusions. The great accumulation of fabulized responses and fabulized combinations most sharply distinguishes this preschizophrenic group from the schizophrenic group which resembles it most, the acute unclassified. That is, this preschizophrenic condition is replete with the less serious indications of autistic schizophrenic thinking; and although it includes a number of the extremely pathological autistic products, these indicate the presence of a schizophrenic process, rather than its culmination in an acute phase. In acute schizophrenics, the abundant play of fantasy indicated by the fabulized responses appears to decrease considerably, probably because it is replaced by delusions and related symptoms.

Depressives give very few of any of these verbalizations. We see here a diagnostic sign to differentiate depressive psychotics from acute paranoid schizophrenics—two conditions which, by reason of their generalized coarctation, are frequently difficult to distinguish—since the schizophrenic is more likely to give such pathological verbalizations. We shall see later on that the same trend is apparent in other verbalizations.

Among neurotics, we should expect to find no confabulations and few fabulized combinations. In regard to fabulized responses proper, the highest incidence occurs in the ideationally active obsessive-compulsives. Libidinization of thought processes is also characteristic of obsessive-compulsives, but their thought processes never become unrealistic in the extreme (confabulation is very rare). Even fabulized combinations occur relatively rarely in neurotics.

In summary, it appears that a high incidence of, and special emphasis upon, fabulized responses[68] indicate that ideation is quantitatively and qualitatively rich, though not unrealistic to the point of clearly psychotic thinking. When fabulized combinations and confabulations begin to enter the picture, the ideation is taking a pathologically autistic turn, and the suspicion of at least a preschizophrenic condition is raised. When the confabulations begin to predominate, with or without a sizable incidence of the other responses, we are most likely dealing with a full schizophrenia, and more likely with a chronic than an acute one. The absence or near absence of all of these responses is characteristic for those clinical groups

---

[68] Fabulized responses sometimes become marked in the records of delinquent children, in a general setting of poor intelligence and weak ideational development. In such cases, the fabulized responses are likely to have the significance implied in their name—that of tendencies to excessive lying, even to the point where the child no longer can distinguish sharply between what is truth and what he has invented.

in which flattening of ideation, blocking, or generalized retardation is prominent.

Contaminations. Examples: In reference to the upper side red area on Card III, "this bloody little splotch here . . . bloody island where they had so many revolutions"; in reference to Card II, "two people . . . holding up candles . . . like a temple here too . . . might be ringing a church bell" (the side figures are the people and the upper central *Dd* area is simultaneously the candle and the temple); in reference to all of Card III, "a butterfly . . . [What makes it look like that?] Because this looks like a butterfly [the central red area]."

Although each of these examples represents a different kind, the first may serve as the simple prototype for contaminations in general. The area referred to is frequently interpreted as an island, and also as blood; in this response, however, the two ideas fuse. The fusion is not regulated by a sound reality orientation—as in an interpretation of the same area, with the card held upside down, as "a red devil." It appears that the source of this contamination is originally in a loss of distance from the card: apparently two discrete concepts came about in the course of the associative process, but the objective spatial identity of the area referred to was taken as indicating a real relationship between the two concepts; in other words, the formal spatial link between the two was transformed into a conceptual link. This is the contamination: the boundaries of concepts once formed are so fluid that separate abstractions from the same area cannot remain independent side by side, but fuse into a single idea. The final concept that integrates these two impressions represents a pathological increase of distance from the card, as well as from reality.

In the second example, there is some resemblance to a fabulized combination. The subject first clearly perceives the two people, and then clearly perceives the buildinglike *Dd* area and calls it a temple; if this were merely a fabulized combination, the response would be "two people lifting up a temple." But the subject goes further. As the two people are holding their hands up, and where their hands reach there is a temple, the meaning of the card is changed and the farfetched conclusion is drawn that they must be ringing a bell. Here too taking the spatial relationships of the card for reality indicates the loss of distance; in addition, transductive reasoning is apparent in the change of meaning of the response by reason of a single part. Here the change of meaning is the core of the contamination. Of course, the final verbalization of the response, with its establishment of relationships not in accord with the reality of the inkblot, indicates an extreme distance from the card.

In the third example we see a different form of contamination, in which there is not merely a change or fusion of meaning, but a *giving* of meaning. Here a part of the card is given a content, and this content contaminates the percept and meaning of the entire card. The response might seem at first glance merely a *DW*, where a part autistically influences the meaning of the whole; the distinguishing feature of this response, however, is that the original percept loses its identity in the final response, and is no longer a specific part of it. This contamination represents another form of transductive reasoning. In everyday life, a parallel to the reasoning underlying this contamination would be to consider that a man who wore a tie with butterflies printed on it was a butterfly.

If we review these three examples, we see that in all of them some form of objective spatial contiguity in the card is taken too seriously, with too much reality value; and this loss of distance opens the door for schizophrenic autistic thinking and unrealistic conclusions. In these conclusions, discrete concepts may fuse, interact, and change each other's meaning (participation), or even give meaning to a previously uninterpreted area. Spatial relationships are considered to be conceptual relationships, and in such a setting there is no basis for maintaining definite boundaries between any concepts: contaminations result. In the first example, there was little loss of identity of each of the concepts; in the second example, a partial loss and a change in identity occurred; in the final example, the original concept completely lost its isolated identity.

In some schizophrenic records we see such contamination *in statu nascendi,* and the consideration of these might further clarify the nature of the thought processes leading to contamination responses. One acute paranoid schizophrenic gave the following response to the upper middle gray area on Card X: "These look like animals, but in reality they are the lungs of a person." In this response there is still awareness of the distinction between the two percepts and their corresponding concepts, although the subject's own verbalization indicates that the conceptual boundaries are tenuous. If the subject had lost awareness of the discreteness of the two ideas, the contamination might have taken form as, "These are lung animals . . . because they have heads and are shaped like lungs," or "These are animal lungs because taken together they look like the two halves of the lungs, but separately each looks like an animal head." Another example is the response given by a chronic paranoid schizophrenic, in reference to Card I, "It could be a tree and it could be a skeleton: the two thoughts happened simultaneously, although the tree kind of predominated." Here again awareness of the distinctness of the two percepts and their corresponding concepts is still present, but we see the contamination in the making. The verbalization itself, and the concern caused to the patient by the apparent temporal simultaneity of the two ideas, already indicate a weakening of the boundary between these two concepts.

In general, one might say that contaminations are expressions of a schizophrenic's increasing inability to keep percepts and their corresponding concepts distinct from each other; there appears to be a fluidity of conceptual boundaries in schizophrenics which allows for transductive reasoning, or thinking in terms of participation, in which everything may ultimately belong with or be related to everything else. This is autistic thinking at its extreme. To be sure, we have presented merely a schematic description of the process. It is rarely seen in such extremes clinically, partly because the remnants of adherence to verbal conventions—as long as the patient remains coherent—hide the process, and partly because when conventions are eliminated deterioration sets in, and the incoherence of verbal communication now replaces verbal convention in disguising the course of the schizophrenic thought process.

The contamination response stands out among all pathological responses as one of the most reliable indicators of the presence of schizophrenia, and yet in its clear-cut form it occurs with amazing infrequency. We emphasize this to show the diagnostic limitations of this indicator. It must also be emphasized that the mere fact that a subject is schizophrenic, even if chronically so, is no basis for anticipating an abundance of all kinds of schizophrenic responses, verbalizations, and reasoning in the course of the Rorschach test. It is most usual in acute—and even in chronic— schizophrenics that a few very pathological indications will be scattered throughout the entire record; the examiner must weave them together into a diagnosis. Only work with longstanding chronic and deteriorated schizophrenic cases (and with no other type of cases to complicate the diagnostic picture) will lead to complacency about the ease of diagnosing schizophrenia by the Rorschach test.

Additional examples: Card VI, inverted, *W:* "could look like a tree, this [upper wings] a bush in the back . . . on each side like little children. [?] Like someone was holding them up; maybe up in the tree" (children and tree are same area: each half). Card I, *W:* "that looks like a V there [the inner contour of *S* figures] Is it a V? . . . Winged Victory. [?] Here V for Victory and here the wings back of it" (*S*). Example of contamination tendency: Card III, *W:* "a cross between . . . [?] a map and a moth and a butterfly."

Autistic Logic. We coined the phrase *autistic logic* in order to segregate, in our scoring and thinking, one form which pathological autistic thinking may take. These responses are subject to the same principles of analysis as the verbalizations described above, but are distinguished in that the subject reasons out his responses with an air of, or claim to, irrefutable logic. This *logic* bears little if any relationship to reality or to conventional norms of reasoning; autistic logic replaces syllogism in the thinking of the schizophrenic.

Examples: in reference to the very tiny projection in the center of the arc at the top of Card IX, "the north pole . . . because it is at the top"; in reference to all of Card VI, "two people, backs turned to one another, but they are upside down . . . because they are embryonic, I guess"; in reference to all of Card X, "a fashion show, a burlesque, an orchestral score, a fashionable audience. [What makes it look like that?] The tones of the instruments"; in reference to Card VIII, "an animal or a bug . . . an animal would have more color in his system than a bug. [What makes it look like that?] The colors, the way they were in order . . . I associate color with moving around and animals aren't very stationary usually; anything that is colorful is movable . . . like a wall would be of one color and that was a series of colors and therefore movable and animals are usually very active."

The first example, "the North Pole," is one of the responses traditionally scored *Po* (position-determined responses) in the Rorschach literature. Nevertheless, they represent a subtype of that process of reasoning which we have designated autistic logic. This logic is implicit in the verbalization, with its use of the word *because*. This type of response bears clear traces of a pathological loss of distance from the inkblot, in that its spatial relationships are taken too much for reality. The arbitrariness of the reasoning needs no elaboration here, beyond pointing out how original loss of distance leads to farfetched conclusions.

The second example, the embryo, reflects the same process. The subject sees the two figures with the card upright. These figures are usually seen only after the card has been turned upside down. If the subject does notice them with the card upright he will usually turn the card around in order to make sure he has seen the figures correctly. Some preschizophrenics, and occasionally a schizophrenic, show a clear-cut tendency to give responses having this "upside-down" quality without turning the cards; but these subjects will merely point out that these are two figures, and may or may not imply that the correct position would be with the card upside down. But in the example in question the subject accepts the upside-down position as the real one (loss of distance), and so draws the farfetched conclusion (increase of distance) that they must be embryos. This is a relatively simple and transparent form of autistic logic. It is somewhat more florid in the third example, the fashion show. Let us attempt to reconstruct the logical steps in the evolution of this response. At first the colorful blot is responded to in an extremely gross and undifferentiated way, and its colorfulness is understood to represent a fashion show or a burlesque. With the appearance of "an orchestral score" a logical jump is made which is incomprehensible before inquiry, which we shall soon come to. The subject then attempts to link the impression of "an orchestral score" with the impression of "a fashion show," and ends up with a fashionable (musical) audience. The two major segments of this response are not clear until inquiry brings forth the key to the whole response: the colors are the "tone colors of the instruments." It should be apparent from our previous discussions that this entire response is also a contamination, inasmuch as the bright colors simultaneously represent the audience's dress and the tones of the instruments. But the reasoning based upon this contamination falls clearly within the realm of autistic logic. The response itself is characterized by extreme distance from the inkblot. The colors lead the subject to think of bright clothes, of shows, of concerts, of music, of "fashionable" audiences. Of course, the sequence of verbalizations implies that there is a multiple returning to the blot; but this apparently serves only to set the subject off on a new tangent which leads her even farther afield from any realistic considerations or maintenance of conceptual boundaries.[69]

The fourth example does not have the multiplicity of references of the previous example, and is more transparent. The subject was in doubt whether to say "bug" or "animal," and to reach a decision he pursued his way through a maze of autistic logical derivations, none of which was based on a perceptual return to and study of the inkblot, but instead on the laws of "logic." That animals are not usually very stationary can be maintained; but to relate their muscular activity to their external colors, as the patient did, is to set up an if-then relationship for which support exists only in the laws of autistic thinking. The side pink areas are seen by the majority of all subjects as two animals, and it may be presumed that the animallike appearance of these areas had an impact upon the subject's associative processes. In fact the examiner at first understood the subject to be merely referring to these side areas, and only the spontaneous reference to "colorfulness" indicated that a thought disturbance might underlie the response. But it is apparent, from the final conclusion reached by the subject, that

[69] A skeptical reader might argue that diagnosis on the basis of such responses is no longer "Rorschach test interpretation proper," and that subjects giving such responses must be so disorganized that they had to be tested in padded cells. This response occurred in a Rorschach record of a young divorcee whose schizophrenia, though longstanding, was first detected in the examination at this Clinic. Most amazing of all, she came to the Clinic on her own because of clashes with her parents who were disturbed by her promiscuous sexual behavior and adjustment difficulties at home. A few years later, the subject was working and getting along extramurally, although there can be no doubt that her thought processes continued to show a fundamental schizophrenic disorganization.

these parts of the original percept were not discriminated; though most likely of some influence on the content possibilities which were brought to mind, these percepts were not used in a regulative way in the course of the associative processes. Only pathologically autistic thinking could merge a clear-cut impression—that of the side figures—with an amorphous perceptual mass, so that it loses its identity altogether and serves only to set off a chain of ideas held together by autistic logic.

These responses occur only in unclassified and paranoid schizophrenics. This pathological verbalization thus shows its relationship to the contamination response, as an exclusive or almost exclusive indicator of schizophrenia. Furthermore, its incidence appears to be greater in chronic and deteriorated schizophrenias than in acute. Still, as with the contaminations, the averages are not strikingly high, and it is rather their exclusive occurrence in schizophrenias which gives them their full pathological significance: they cannot be relied upon to occur in the record of any individual schizophrenic. Contaminations and autistic logic, more than any other verbalization we shall discuss, with the exception of incoherence, represent the final consummation of schizophrenic disorganization of thinking and extreme impairment of reality testing.

Additional examples: Card X, lower side brown: "Sahara desert. [?] I imagined it; just the oneness of it." Card III, *W:* "another fight that takes place in South Africa . . . [What makes it look like that?] Because Africa is so divided." Card V, *W:* "an abandoned road. [?] Because it is not completed on each end" (upper proj.). Card X, *W:* "various insects seem to be feeding at the time of this portrayal. [?] Because near the mouths of many there was something else; feeding is usually done in large groups."

Peculiar, Queer, and Related Verbalizations

After having administered a few hundred Rorschach tests to normal, neurotic, and psychotic groups, the examiner has a general "feel" for verbalizations which can be considered the norm. In other words, he becomes familiar with the vocabulary and syntax which different kinds of subjects use in the Rorschach test, especially when they deviate from the run of normal groups. In the verbalizations designated as *peculiar* and *queer* we approximate an analysis[70] of verbalization in itself, without specific reference to the percept involved. They differ from those previously discussed also in that there is no explicit pathologically autistic *reasoning* in them, but rather verbal end products thereof.

[70] [What is accomplished is less an analysis than the pinpointing of a problem, which cries out to be solved by the recently developed resources of structural linguistics. Here is a major challenge for psycholinguistics. See fn. 62.—Ed.]

These verbalizations indicate that the subject's relationship to the Rorschach card involves either loss or increase of distance. The boundary between those verbalizations designated "peculiar" and those designated "queer" is quite fluid, and the two shade imperceptibly into each other. The criterion we used for the score "peculiar" was that the verbalization could, outside the standardized test situation, pass as conventional and appropriate; the verbalization scored "queer" could not. In other words, our baseline of evaluation was everyday verbal convention, which we know can obscure milder forms of autistic thought processes but not severe disorganization.

Rationale of Peculiar Verbalizations. Examples of loss of distance: On Card II, in reference to the black areas, "two low-built low dogs"; in reference to the mid-line of Card VI, "part of a lady's vagina"; in reference to the lower middle area of Card VI, "transverse cut of a sore"; in reference to the middle one-third area of Card VII, "belligerent dog . . . might have had its autonomic nervous system aroused and the adrenal glands sent out their stimulation"; in reference to all of Card IX, "I think it's definitely from here down to here" (the subject pointing from his shoulder down to his waist).

At first glance, the first example might appear to be nothing more than a strange manner of expression. But closer scrutiny reveals that this unusual expression is communicating a very subjective and affectively charged attitude toward the card, as though the subject were perceiving a real dog.[71] This affective closeness to the card represents a form of autistic thought. A similar response is that given to the middle yellow areas on Card X, "a fine dog . . . noblest of all dogs." Both examples may strike the reader as being fabulized responses rather than peculiar, and in a wider sense they do involve fabulized elements; but fabulized responses do not carry such powerful reality connotations, and although fabulizing may introduce an affect as part of the content of a response, it will never spend an affect upon a response once conceived. The second example, "a part of a lady's vagina," shows a similar loss of distance. On the one hand, the expression "a part of" makes the response extraordinarily specific, so that it sounds more like *recognition* than *interpretation;* on the other hand, the expression "a lady's" is in sharp contrast to this specificity; it is redundant and sounds like an apology. This extreme specificity, which can be based only upon a conviction that "this is what it is,"[72] is even more striking in the third example, "transverse cut of a sore." The patient in question had probably seen few if any kinds of cuts of sores, even if such a thing as a "transverse cut" existed. The loss of distance is quite pronounced in the fourth example,

71 [See fn. 62.—Ed.]
72 [See fn. 62.—Ed.]

the belligerent dog. The subject in justifying this fabulized impression does not refer to any perceptual quality of the area in question, but explains his response in terms of the physiology of real dogs. To paraphrase this response, "This *is* a belligerent dog: what makes it look belligerent is, of course, the underlying physiological processes of this emotion." In the fifth example, "definitely from here down to here," we see the reality of the card at last fully proclaimed.

These five examples show a pathological loss of distance from the card: the subject views it as though it were replete with reality connotations. Loss of distance is also expressed in such phrases as "medically speaking," "from the artistic point of view," "strictly speaking." The subjects who introduce their responses thus are neither medical men nor artists, nor do they speak in any strict sense. Loss of distance is also expressed when figures are described as obviously Chinese or Oriental, bears *conlusively* Russian, and drawings *definitely* scientific—although the subject cannot adequately explain why he is so sure. The emphasis in the analysis of these verbalizations is not upon their fabulized elements, which to be sure are present, but rather upon the security and definiteness with which the responses are given, indicating the inordinate reality value conceded to the cards.

But let us turn now to the opposite extreme, those peculiar verbalizations which refer to overincrease of distance from the card.

Examples of increased distance: In reference to the whole of Card II, "This might be the part of the back up here [pointing to himself] . . . [What makes it look like that?] I just think so"; in reference to the whole of Card IV, "Could it possibly be a picture of somebody's lungs? . . . [What makes it look like that?] I just thought of it"; in reference to the lower middle *Dr* area of Card VII, "I find myself consciously trying to make this a vagina."

The increased distance is seen in the first two examples, where the subject does not even claim to be able to substantiate his response in the reality of the inkblot. The third example was given by a neurotic who was able to verbalize a usually undiscriminated segment of thought processes. In the third example, before any percept showed definite organization, the subject became aware of his impulse to see a certain thing in the card. Here we see responses representing increased distance *in statu nascendi* under pressure of overvalent ideas. Similar verbalizations are, "The first card you showed me looked like an anus and that made me sure that all the rest would be the same"; "They don't resemble spectacles but it comes to me as I look at it"; "A vagina, I might be thinking that's what you are looking for." In all these, the concern is with the associative rather than perceptual-reality justification of responses: this makes the verbalization peculiar.

Additional examples: Card IX, pink: "some creature without any legs, tongue hanging out. [?] An old man." Card II, *W:* "two individuals; upper reds are probably head formations but not attached to the bodies as yet definitely." Card VI: "the top looks like the cross section of male organ to me . . . the lower part looks like the reverse" (meaning a vagina). Card VII, *W,* each half: "a facing map of the western part of Europe." Card III, meaning the men: "two objects." Card VI, *W:* "I am just sure that it is something that has to be studied microscopically." Card VI, *W:* "looks like some scientific part of hygiene but I don't know what." Card IV, *W:* "it belongs to the bat kingdom." Card II, *W:* "another bone structure. [?] Having the first picture shown, I thought the second would be that." Card V, *W:* "looks like a bat, personally."

Rationale of Queer Verbalizations. Examples of loss of distance: In reference to all of Card VIII, "probably the whole thing is a structure . . . part of some animal . . . because it doesn't make sense that it could be anything else"; in reference to all of Card III, "one of the hipbones . . . the left"; in reference to all of Card IX, "It still reminds me of female sex . . . to me, sort of a laugh . . . would like to have much of it [sex] without being afraid of it; in fact if I go to heaven, it is the first thing I am going to do."

In the first example a pathological loss of distance is seen in the conviction that no other interpretation would make sense. No further explanation is offered. Now, it is true that one may get apparently similar responses from normal subjects; but they will convey, by more or less subtle verbalization, that the content they attribute to the card is the only thing it looks like *to them.* This kind of response is rather an expression of rigidity of percepts and paucity of associations, and is usually accompanied by an awareness of these. But in the example given, the subject assumes his percept to be *the* exclusive real possibility, and there is no further search. Such a conviction of exclusive reality in the test corresponds to queerness in everyday life. Normal persons do not lose sight of the fact that they are the subject in the perceptual-associative process; the schizophrenic who gave this response was no longer aware of this, and the *only* possible meaning of things was that which they had for him.

This example gives merely a skeleton picture of the queer loss of distance; the second example will round out the picture. If someone not well acquainted with anatomy makes a very concrete statement about it, it would be considered peculiar in the sense described above. But when a subject says that the third card is "the left hipbone," not merely the absurd form of the percept but the extravagant specificity, which cannot be supported by rational considerations, gives away the pathological autistic loss of distance.

In the third example, sex in heaven, the process appears to be as follows: there is a small portion in the lower center of Card IX which is rather frequently interpreted as a vagina; this impression apparently had such an impact upon the patient that it resulted in a quick mobilization and verbalization of fantasies very central to her maladjustment and the whole card became involved in the elaboration. It is this forceful impact which indicates the loss of distance from the card.

Examples of increase of distance: In reference to the white space between the two lower central green areas on Card X, "I tell you confidentially I am looking for a twat . . . here it is! A big one though . . . it would be awfully loose . . . if a man needs it badly he tries it"; in reference to Card III, "I don't see the uterus or vagina or anything like that there"; in reference to Card I, "histological plate . . . [What makes it look like that?] The sensation obtaining between light and one's eyes"; in reference to a response on Card VI "[What makes it look like that?] The ink makes it look like that"; in reference to all of Card I, "It is a bat because they have them in Carlsbad Caverns"; in reference to all of Card I, "It looks like a butterfly . . . [What makes it look like that?] Because I have read about these tests."

In the first and second examples, we see the pathological increase of distance in nascent form. In the first, the patient states that he has a predetermined idea in mind and is searching for something on the card with which to connect it. In the second, the patient is no longer aware of, or at least does not verbalize, his preconceptions, and only the resulting disappointment which he expresses indicates their existence. These two examples might seem similar to the one classed as peculiar—"I find myself consciously looking for a vagina"—but there is a crucial difference. The peculiar verbalization is socially acceptable, it is a confession of a tendency which the subject notes in himself and which may be ego alien to him; furthermore, there is a refinement in the formulation which may be considered appropriate. The other is freely expressed, apparently is not felt as ego alien, and its direct and bland vulgarity must be considered queer. The card becomes merely a pretext for dwelling upon overvalent ideational material.

The third example, "histological plate," is also pathologically distant from the card, although in a somewhat different way. Here the subject carries into the testing situation a frame of reference which is appropriate only in a physiological laboratory, no longer considers the card as worthy of inclusion as a segment of reality, and is concerned only with light waves and physiological changes in the eye. The fourth example, "the ink makes it look like that," shows a similar increase of distance, although less "scientifically" worded.

In the fifth and sixth examples, the subjects establish the basis for their responses in their past experience. Again there is a pathological increase of distance from the card, inasmuch as the response is not located in, attributed to, or justified by perceptual qualities of the inkblot. It is easy to miss the difference between these responses and reminiscences of normal or neurotic subjects. The latter may refer to past experiences in explaining their responses, but their reminiscences will not replace the explanation of the response in terms of the percept; rather they will amplify it. The normal or neurotic subject might say, "It looks like a bat, I never saw one in real life but it resembles pictures I have seen with those wings and the body . . ."

One other type of queer verbalization may be mentioned, that in which two symmetrical figures are described as male and female. These responses too represent a degree of distance from the card, seen in the extraneous subjective elaboration of the percept for which no support is offered by the card itself.[73]

Additional examples: Card IX, W: "the whole: psychiatric experiments . . . surrealistic painting . . . soul burning out in hell." Card II, W, referring to upper middle Dd as penis and lower middle Dr as vagina: "intercourse; glorified kiss." Card X, W: "piece of land with many islands . . . you and I know the East Indies." Card VI, W: "X ray of a fly. [?] Looks like there is bones in there." Card X, lower middle green: "a crab, I was hoping for an octopus." Card II, W: "artistic design of fly's foot." Card VII, upper and side proj.: "different genitals, all on exhibition."

Diagnostic Significance of Peculiar, Queer, and Related Verbalizations. Peculiar verbalizations are much more abundant than queer ones. The only real exception to this occurs in deteriorated schizophrenics, where it is not surprising in view of their generalized disorganization, which allows not only for pathological increase or loss of distance from the card, but for the most deviant consequences of this autistic alteration of their relation to reality. That queerness does not predominate even in other schizophrenics is striking testimony to the power of conventional verbalization in obscuring pathological thinking, and shows the extent to which even chronic schizophrenics are able to maintain a good front. Peculiar responses do occur in a few scattered depressive, neurotic, and even normal cases, although nowhere in such quantity as in schizophrenic and preschizophrenic records. This should not be disconcerting: first, we do not claim to have established sufficiently definite boundaries between acceptable and autistic verbalization, and our scores cannot be considered final; second, in those schizophrenic

---

[73] Like any other pathological response, this male-female response carries the implication of a true projection, and in our experience has usually been an indication of strong homoerotic strivings. See also Bergmann (1945).

records where peculiarities occur there is usually additional support for the diagnosis in other scoring categories and other types of autistic verbalization, and this is rarely the case for depressives, neurotics, or normals. Queer verbalizations are absent in all groups other than schizophrenics, preschizophrenics, and paranoid conditions. Thus, carrying autistic loss or increase of distance to its extreme is found only where schizophrenic pathology is involved.

Although the greatest incidence of queer responses occurs in deteriorated cases, their greatest significance is for the diagnosis of acute and some well-preserved chronic schizophrenic cases. The incidence of queer responses in overideational preschizophrenics is also crucial for their differential diagnosis, because in the bulk of the test material these cases—like some chronic schizophrenics—may appear in the guise of a neurotic condition or an eccentric character formation. What distinguishes overideational preschizophrenics from full-blown schizophrenics is that, though they give queer verbalizations, the majority of their autistic verbalizations are peculiar. This finding is parallel to our findings in connection with the fabulized response → fabulized combination → confabulation sequence. The emphasis in overideational preschizophrenics is always upon the earliest signs of the disorganization of thinking, although a few of the more serious indications frequently creep in. Peculiarities are also helpful diagnostic indications for inhibited preschizophrenics, inasmuch as these cases —unlike overideational preschizophrenics—do not abound in queer verbalizations. That peculiar responses are so rare in the nonschizophrenic groups attests to the pathological significance of even these more innocuous deviant verbalizations.

Vagueness. Vagueness, as used here, must be distinguished both from vague form and from confusion and incoherence. *Vagueness* of verbalization refers to the subject's weak hold on a definite form percept; *confusion* refers to a confusion within the response itself or in the subject's experiencing and communication of the response; *incoherence* refers to extraneous materials' being dragged into the response, overshadowing it, disrupting it, or even making it completely incomprehensible. Although these three kinds refer to different levels of verbalization, and vary also in showing increase or loss of distance, they constitute a continuity in terms of the withering of the response itself, whether due to perceptual or verbal difficulty. Vagueness means that the subject himself is unable to keep a percept alive; in the confusion response, the complete percept is never formed nor entirely communicated; and in the incoherent response, little trace of the original percept is left and communication of it is totally ineffectual. These comments are easily recognized, and thus are not in need of diagnostic attention; they conceal rather than reveal the essential nature of the schizo-phrenic thought disorder.

Examples: In reference to Card I, "I can almost get a witch's face but I can't make it"; in reference to all of Card VI, "a skin tacked on a wall . . . I can't quite get it but it is there some place." In these two verbalizations, the subject spontaneously communicates her feeling of vagueness about common percepts which are easily retained by normal and most neurotic subjects. The spontaneous awareness and communi-cation of the difficulty, however, is most likely to occur in severe neuroses. This awareness of the internal process leading to a response contains echoes of the peculiar verbalizations; but here the vagueness is not an integral part of the justification for the response. Still, the vagueness of the response implies some autistic disturbance of the subject's relation-ship to the card and its perceptual possibilities. Such vagueness also occurs in prepsychotic or psychotic conditions, but usually these subjects do not spontaneously communicate their feeling of vagueness: in these cases the first perceptual impression is fleeting and quickly washed away, and despite insistent immediate inquiry the subject is unable to grasp the percept again. The examiner feels in such inquiry as though he were dig-ging in quicksand. Such fleeting impressions are usually embedded in a stream of verbalization where only one or two words, which otherwise might seem simply incoherent, are the clue to the vagueness in a common and well-defined response. Vagueness of this type is quite frequent in toxic or delirious conditions, and obsessivelike, disorganized preschizo-phrenics.

Confusion. Examples: In reference to all of Card IV, "fur skin, a coon . . . [What makes it look like that?] A tail, legs hanging down. Its hot, no! It's cold when you are wearing furs"; in reference to all of Card II and the popular bear response, "If it were a cut on his head, the blood certainly wouldn't be standing up; it would be dripping down"; in reference to all of Card II, "clowns . . . they have three legs [the three bottom pro-jections] . . . they can't have three legs."

In the first example, the subject betrays her confusion in inquiry when, attempting to point out the furry quality of the skin, she says, "It's hot." This verbalization at once points toward the possibility of confusion. The term she used to denote the furry quality is one usually referring to the subjective experience of wearing fur or to weather, and thus points to a weakness of the conceptual boundaries. The subject at this point stands midway between a conceptual level referring to the perceptual appearance of a fur coat and a discussion referring to the subjective experience of fur-wearing or weather. The confusion becomes even more obvious when the patient completely shifts from the furriness into the conceptual level of weather, which results in a logical-verbal contradiction: she now has to deny that it is hot, and to assert that it is cold "when you are wearing furs." Such extreme fluidity of conceptual boundaries is pathognomonic of a psychosis, and suggests what underlies incoherence.[74]

The second example of confusion betrays a pathological loss of distance from the card, of the type seen in the fabulized combination responses. Here the objective spatial position and direction of the upper red splotches on Card II are taken as an immutable reality, and confusion results. The subject does not draw a farfetched schizophrenic conclusion, but recognizes the logical difficulties of the original illogical inference; thus she can only deny what she takes for reality in the inkblot, and says the blood "would be dripping down." We see here two contradictory concepts existing side by side, and clashing with each other.

The third example, "three-legged clowns," is of the same order. Again there is a pathological loss of distance from the card, so that the three projections become three legs; but again the conceptual orientation insists, "They can't have three legs." Normal subjects may sometimes give responses resembling this—as, "a three-legged animal"—but either indicate it is a play of fancy, or suggest that the fourth leg is not showing, or otherwise rationalize the odd number of legs; thus they soon make it clear that they are neither confused nor disturbed about what they have said. In our examples, however, the subject maintains that his response *is* and yet *cannot be,* and reveals in his attitude a definite perplexity about this contradiction.

Such confusional responses in our experience have usually indicated the presence of confusion in everyday life and in clinical examination. Clinically, however, these manifestations of confusion may be subliminal, or perceptible only after thorough examination or protracted observation. Confusion is not very sharply defined clinically, and would require much more study for a definitive statement. Yet it seems to involve either an extreme fluidity and shiftiness of conceptual boundaries and realms, or a simultaneous existence of two contradictory concepts, one logical and the other not.

Incoherence. Examples: In reference to Card I, "desert pictures, shadow pictures . . . you lift your hand up in desert pictures"; in reference to Card IV, "makes me think of the book *Dr. Jekyll and Mr. Hyde,* of moderation because there is good and evil in everyone"; in reference to all of Card IX, "limbs and shoulders of men . . . always inner ambition

[74] In this verbalization we see schizophrenic contamination in thinking alone, and not in reference to a percept as above; such fusion of concepts in verbal communication becomes the clinician's diagnostic sign.

that man could make wings and overcome gravity . . . that the card reminded me, it can be done."

We might best begin this analysis with the third example. The green
areas on Card IX are perceived as shoulders and the upper orange areas
as wings; this is not an unusual percept, and if well elaborated may be
considered to be a good form and even a movement response. But this
patient took the percept as a starting point for farfetched and saltatory
personal associations, so that a mild incoherence is felt. This use of the percept as a starting point for personal associations is contrary to the implications of the test instructions. More generally it is contrary to the
rules of ordered thinking in which the initial link of a thought chain
remains regulative of the whole chain. But we have seen, in connection
with the Word Association Test, that with a disorganized subject any test
stimulus can set off an associative process which will lead him so far
afield that the course of his thinking will no longer be clear, and to the
recipient of his communication it will appear confused. This is the criterion
for incoherence. The usual schizophrenic cannot abide by this first regulative link, just as he cannot eliminate clang or other pathological associations on the Word Association Test.

The first example, "desert pictures," appears more convincingly incoherent because the point where the associative processes intruded into the
perceptual processes is not clear. At first the expression "desert, shadow
pictures" seems to have no relationship to the card; furthermore, the explanation "you lift your hands up in desert pictures" seems irrelevant.
The tests of this patient indicated his inclination to make references to
Bible illustrations, though conveying them with considerable autistic distortion. The middle area on Card I is frequently interpreted as a person
with uplifted hands: this perception—though it remains questionable
whether the figure itself was perceived—may have been coupled with the
association of some Biblical desert scene involving persons with uplifted
hands. It is possible that the associative background of this incoherent
verbalization lay in a picture of Moses and the sons of Israel in the desert
battle against the people of Amalek.[75] This attempted reconstruction of
the thought process may seem arbitrary and farfetched, but it reflects the
true difficulty of making incoherence understandable; not only are the
subject's communications gappy, but the gaps are great and the uncom-
municated cross references almost hopelessly numerous. Such an incoherent verbalization may involve autistic logic, but the extreme encroach-

[75] In this battle Israel was to win as long as Moses held his hands up in the air.
[It is also possible that the patient was referring to the parlor game in which one
makes "shadow pictures" by holding up his hands into a beam of light against a
wall or screen.—Ed.]

ments upon the continuity of thinking go far beyond it; even the attempt at communication or pseudo logic is discarded, and nothing is verbalized but disconnected impressions.

The second example, Dr. Jekyll and Mr. Hyde, is easier to reconstruct. The response refers to the two halves of Card IV which extend in opposite directions. The patient did not state so, but this oppositeness seems to have been taken by him as analogous to the psychological situation of Jekyll and Hyde. Extreme increase of distance from the card is thus apparent. But the associative processes are extended to involve the most abstract moral issues of good and evil, which apparently lead the subject to a statement of the crux of his own ethical system—"moderation," because good and evil are present in everyone. It is also likely that the "moderation" reference is based in some way upon the mid-line of the card, or upon the lower middle area between the two outward extensions. Formal spatial characteristics of the card serve to set off a maze of associations, which are briefly suggested by the verbalizations. Such brevity is the form that incoherence systematically takes.

Incoherence is always a psychotic indication and—provided that no signs of toxicity or organic brain deterioration are present—the diagnosis is likely to be schizophrenia.

Miscellaneous Types of Verbalizations

The Symbolic Response. We shall discuss the symbolic response here because of the continuity with the last example of incoherence, where "good and evil" were symbolized by the inkblot. This example of symbolic interpretation in a schizophrenic's response gives us the clue for evaluating symbolic responses in general. These are given not only by psychotics, but also by many neurotics and highly imaginative normals. To the schizophrenic, the area to which he is responding symbolically *is* the abstract idea or it is *designed* to represent it. Thus, one schizophrenic gave the response to Card VIII, "The one who drew this must have intended to represent the similarity theory of nature." Here the awareness of the play of fantasy is completely lost, and a fundamental conviction—which is experienced by the schizophrenic as "insight" into the card—takes its place. In contrast, very reflective or sophisticated neurotic and normal subjects may integrate symbolic elements into their responses, such as on Card II, "The two people are fighting and the red might be symbolic of the conflict." Thus, outright symbolic responses may be either schizophrenic indicators or imply a quality of highly articulated thinking.

It must be kept in mind that implicitly symbolic responses also occur. If a subject interprets the upper projection on Card VI—where a penis is frequently seen—as "an erect snake ready to strike," the examiner will readily recognize at least the possibility for some latent symbolism. Such responses are not in themselves psychotic indicators, and are frequently obtained in neurotics, particularly hysterics; but some psychotics also give these symbollike responses. One case described the lower middle confluence on Card VII—frequently seen as a vagina, and sometimes as a penis—as a "gun emplacement camouflaged in a strategic position"; by the farfetched elaboration of content to this relatively undifferentiated area, the symbolic implication is established. The occurrence of such overelaborate yet implicit symbolic responses should be considered as a danger signal, and should prompt the examiner to look carefully for other psychotic indications.

The cautious examiner will not attempt to infer unconscious ideas or feelings from any implicit or explicit symbolic responses. The hazards of wild symbolic interpretations are overwhelming, and the examiner will only discredit himself in the eyes of responsible psychiatrists by speculations not based on an intimate knowledge of the patient himself. Nevertheless, symbolic responses can be interpreted in their formal aspects as indications of psychotically autistic thinking, or as reflective normal or obsessive neurotic indications. A farfetched symbollike response in an area of an inkblot where sexual responses are usually given is a suggestive indication of psychosis. With subjects who see too many teeth, too many pincers or scissors or nutcrackers, too many strategic gun emplacements or battleships with cannons raised to shoot, the important thing is to recognize that these are implicit symbolic responses; their occurrence should arouse suspicion of the presence of a psychotic process, but in themselves they should not be used as material for symbolic translation.[76]

The Symmetry Verbalization. These verbalizations are not responses proper, but only verbal expressions thrown in among the responses or in some cases replacing them. Examples: "It is the same on both sides"; "This one also is bilaterally symmetrical"; "What I don't understand about them is their symmetry"; "What bothers me about them is their symmetry; if they were asymmetrical I might be able to make something out of them." Although there is little definite evidence for it, experience suggests that an excessive preoccupation with symmetry contains vestiges or traces of a tendency to give movement responses.[77] It is possible to attempt at least a partial substantiation of this relationship. First of all, the symmetry comments imply an increased distance from the card; the inkblot is no longer a source of stimulation in initiating associative processes, it

[76] [See fn. 7, p. 284 above.—Ed.]

[77] For a discussion of this relationship see the rationale of the movement response, pp. 355ff.

evokes no affective or ideational response in the subject. He is preoccupied only with its formal spatial relationships, and is sensitive to asymmetries; and this, in a sense, is a vestige of that sensitivity to perceptual imbalance which we understand to be the starting point for the development of movement responses. This is largely speculative, but not inconsistent with clinical experience. Among neurotics, those with the lowest incidence of movement responses—hysterics and the anxiety and depression group—show the greatest frequency of symmetry verbalizations; in obsessive-compulsives, where movement responses abound, the number of symmetry verbalizations appears to be lower. This is only a gross trend, and it must be kept in mind that the compulsive, rigid meticulousness in many obsessive-compulsives sharply cuts their number of movement responses and at the same time elevates their number of symmetry verbalizations. Similarly, anxiety-ridden and affectively labile hysterics may react to the inkblot in such a gross undifferentiated fashion that they become almost unaware of the symmetry, and make few if any references to it.

Among psychotics, the incidence appears to be higher in paranoid schizophrenics and paranoid conditions than in unclassified schizophrenics; this too is in inverse relationship to the incidence of movement responses. Although the differences are slight, they are in accord with the consideration advanced by Rorschach—and supported in our experience—that paranoid disorders occur in persons who originally give many movement responses, the number of which sharply declines with the onset of the psychosis. The apparent increase in symmetry verbalizations appears here to represent a replacement of movement tendency. In a few psychotic cases where the Rorschach record is extremely coarctated, an excessive concern with an elaboration of the bilateral symmetry of the cards suggests the presence of paranoid delusions.

The Relationship Verbalization. These verbalizations may be of two different kinds. The first is an integral part of a full response; the other is not related to any actual response, and is more on the order of the symmetry comments. Examples of the former kind: referring first to the whole of Card II and then to its lower middle, "I don't know what these are but they seem to evolve out of this"; referring to the black areas on Card III, "Two human beings coming out of this here [the lower middle dark areas] . . . evolved out of this"; in reference to all of Card IX, "Still part of your back, only dyed"; in reference to Card II, "Might be the butterfly of the previous picture"; in reference to the small green streaks at the bottom of the green area on Card IX, "These are those claws again of the bear" (referring to the response "bear" given to Card VI). Even within the first kind of relationship verbalization, there appears to be a further division. The first two examples refer to relationships between different areas on the same card, and show a pathological loss of distance from the card closely related to that seen in the fabulized combinations; the last three examples refer to a relationship to responses on previous cards and appear related to the perseverative responses which we discussed in the section on content analysis. In a sense they go beyond mere perseveration, as the idea is not that "this too looks like a butterfly," but rather that the present response has some connection with, dependence upon, or even real identity with some previous response. Here too we see a pathological loss of distance from the card, responses being taken at full reality value and their verbalizations intertwined.

The second type of relationship verbalization is of the following order: "It resembles the other pictures . . . they are related, they aren't reproduced just by chance . . . could be a filled-in cousin of one of the others"; "That's the same one you had before"; "Looks like the other one only in a different position . . . the white disappeared, came toward the center, the black spread out"; "Of course I recognize that the picture consists of some of the details of the two former pictures"; "We are going to get down to something . . . I think they all relate down to something"; "Let's see the other one again." These responses, like the symmetry responses, are concerned with formal objective spatial relationships or constructions of the various inkblots and represent an increased distance from the card. In the first few examples, the subject sticks to a level of description, with a tacit assumption of interrelationship between the cards; in the last examples we see a conviction of the interdependence of the cards not only in structure, but even in meaning. In these the patients are no longer responding to objects, they are concerned merely with the formal abstract meaning characteristics of the cards. Normal thought processes—not only as evidenced by the manner in which normal subjects take this test, but in terms of ego psychology also—are concerned with meaningful objects, with all their implications for the self. When a patient indicates that objects are of less significance to him than formal characteristics, we see a pathological increase of distance from the inkblot and an indication for a similar retreat from reality in general.

There is a further aspect of these verbalizations, especially those concerned with what the inkblots all "relate down to." In records where such a search for insight is present, we might even find expression of the fear that "you are going to get me on this one." But even without this comment, a paranoid preoccupation and mode of reasoning are indicated; the patient is looking for systems in the cards, for a hidden meaning, for ultimate relationships, for the catch in it. Experience indicates that these responses occur most frequently in paranoid schizophrenia and paranoid conditions, with isolated instances in other types. When they do occur in other cases, the possible presence of a paranoid trend—though not one constituting the core of the disorder—must be seriously considered.

The examiner must be careful to distinguish these verbalizations from those given by nonparanoid introspective persons, whose introspectiveness is limited in scope by strong inhibition. Such subjects give many symmetry verbalizations, and show an increased interest in abstract spatial relationships; but these subjects do not usually go as far as the examples quoted. Instead, there will be an extensive preoccupation with the aesthetic and general physiognomic characteristics of the blot, which may even lead to acceptable—and from the point of view of content, highly suggestive—verbalization, such as on Card I, "It is as if something were behind a cloudy foreground." This interest in the abstract, to the neglect of the relatively concrete, implications of the inkblot occurs in a setting of overcautiousness, introspection, and inhibition of ideational output.

Verbalization of Reference Ideas. What we score as a reference idea is nothing but a progressive concretization of this flair for relationships, which at its extreme may become queer. Examples: to all of Card III, "Two individuals . . . perhaps the two red blots at the top are keeping these heads together . . . facing each other . . . the red in the center is keeping them from each other"; to all of Card III, "Looks like a body to me . . . these are blood spots . . . I don't know why they should be there . . . might have come out of the body." In reference ideas an arbitrary relationship is established between different areas of the inkblot, where not even an objective spatial relationship exists as a weak justification. These relationships are woven into an extremely concrete setting, as in the "blood" example, or are used as the basis for vague, abstract, symbolic elaborations. The strain in these responses is tremendous; they share characteristics with the fabulized combinations, are suggestive of position responses (where position of the area of the response alone determines its content), and may even have the flavor of autistic logic. Here we see the autistic positing of interrelationships which occurs only with extreme distance from the card.

To make the significance of these examples clearer, let us differentiate them from more acceptable responses. A combination response on Card III coping with the same areas might be, "Two caricatured figures with a backdrop of red decorations behind them," or "Two courtiers bowing with brightly lit chandeliers hanging over them." A simple relationship verbalization to the same card might be, "I don't know what it is but these two [the upper red] balance this central red area and both set off the dark parts . . . but I don't know what it could be." But in the reference example, the relationship idea fuses with the percepts and is concretely interpreted, so that the red areas acquire a dynamic quality and occupy an integral place in the final response. Reference ideas of the type described occur almost exclusively in schizophrenic conditions; if they occur in a setting which does not justify a diagnosis of schizophrenia, they must be considered as indicating extreme schizoid trends.

Self-Reference Verbalizations. These verbalizations convey the subject's feeling that the card or the inquiry has some special reference to him. In the true self-reference, all awareness of the impersonal reality of the card is lost; but there are very mild instances where some problem of the patient immediately fastens upon a specific area of the inkblot, and the affective reaction to that area and its verbalization constitute a self-reference in nascent form. An example of the full-fledged self-reference: a deteriorated schizophrenic woman who appeared somewhat confused gave the response "two dogs' heads" to Card II and when asked to point to the nose, replied, "Now you imply I am too nosy!" An example of a milder form of self-reference: a subject gave the response "menstruation" to the lower red area of Card II, and then in a disgusted tone said, "I revolt against being a woman and not a man!" Self-reference verbalizations are generally rare in Rorschach records; they come mainly where there is schizoid disorganization, and then only in a few cases. These must be carefully differentiated from the reminiscences of some reflective normals who might say, "The two bears I just mentioned to you a few minutes ago brought back to my mind a certain show I once saw . . ." The self-references are distinguished by their abruptness of statement, without the explanatory transition which usually characterizes reminiscences; furthermore, self-references almost always have strong affective concomitants.

Although distinctions can be made between self-references and the reference ideas discussed previously, they show a continuity in that relationships are established for which the only justification lies in pathological autism. Both types, when clearly established, refer almost exclusively to the presence of schizophrenia.

Absurd Responses. Examples: To all of Card III, "This whole thing could be the knee of the human body . . . these little specks carry the water [lower middle] . . . some kind of cartilage [middle red]"; to all of Card IV, "A praying mantis"; to all of Card VII, "Looks something like a grasshopper."

The designation "absurd response" implies that the form of the card has been grossly mishandled. We have deferred its consideration until discussing verbalizations, because the principles of analysis of verbalization appear well suited to shed light on this response. As a matter of fact, we have used this type of response as a kind of prototype of those involving a pathological increase of distance from the card. In the absurd response, the actual form of the blot is so flouted, and the associative chain between the original percept and the final response is so circuitous, that usually the verbalization of the response appears to the examiner quite unrelated to the area referred to. Absurdity is not scored for any response a part of which is adequately seen, even though the rest might be absurd by itself; if a single part is well seen, the score should be confabulation, or *DW,* or some related score. The absurd response is not always utterly incomprehensible; some insight is possible on occasion, but only in terms of a most far-reaching abstraction from the blot, as in the grasshopper. The absurdity of this autistic abstraction is patent. Similarly, if the white space in the middle of Card II—frequently interpreted as a vagina—is called the male organ, this too must be considered absurd, even if the examiner can infer that the association started with the female organ. In general, any response which is so unsupported by the card that the inkblot might as well have been of another form, strongly raises the question of the presence of a schizophrenic process.

Additional examples: Card VIII: "I could call that a baby [*S* pink] and that the umbilical cord" (gray). Card VI, upper middle proj.: "Mountain." Card V, *W:* "Could it be a hippopotamus spread out like that?" Card IV, *W:* "Caterpillar."

Deterioration Color Responses. We have briefly discussed these responses in the section on pure color responses (p. 389), where we stated that their abruptness shows an almost total disintegration of any capacity for delay of impulse or action, and becomes indicative of inappropriate affect and flattening of affect. In terms of our general rationale of verbalizations, the significance of these responses may be formulated in a slightly different way: they are usually given with an air of truth, and thereby indicate a pathological loss of distance from the card; at the same time, some of them, by their goriness and arbitrary symbolic elaboration, indicate a pathological increase of distance from the card.

Examples: To all of Card VIII, "I guess it represents blood . . . blue blood . . . blue blood, red blood, and pink blood"; to all of Card IX, "Looks like sort of virulent disease . . . all the bright colors"; to all of Card X, "Blue water, yellow flowers, red rocks, black concrete, orange earth"; to the red and yellow areas of Card X, "Yellow race trying to get hold of the red race . . . four yellow and only two red"; to the middle yellow of Card X, "Egg spot"; to the inner and outer yellow of Card X, "Urine stains"; to all of Card VIII, "Red and white corpuscles in the blood."

Rapid and arbitrary interpretations of all colors as differently colored blood, or related interpretations, occur most frequently in hebephrenic schizophrenics, but also in any schizophrenic showing deterioration. Such color responses are given almost exclusively by schizophrenics, and increase with chronicity and deterioration. They seem to indicate that affectivity has become detached from objects, is unchecked by intellectual considerations or by ego processes, and is expressed as though it were itself a creator of objects and builder of new autistic worlds which appear weird and incomprehensible to the examiner.

Additional examples: Card VIII, lower middle, *D:* "Brown grass. [?] Withered, disintegrated." Card IX, *W:* "Could be an infection . . . being protected by some serum in the body." "Frame showing different cancer growths, or different functions of the body . . . infection spreading." Card VIII, *W:* "Inside of a cow . . . beef steak . . . roast beef." "Looks like the ground by the colors." Card X, pink: "Orange reminds me of blood . . . very dry, mixed with dirt . . . blood again . . . very much dried . . . mixed with dirt."

Exactness Verbalizations. Examples: In reference to all of Card I, "In consideration of these small vacant spaces it would look more like a bat skeleton than a bat with its body intact"; in reference to all of Card V, "A little bit like the things called bats"; in reference to the upper one third of Card VII, "A person's face but it doesn't look quite right for that." It is apparent that the fundamental weakness in these responses is a weakness of abstracting ability. That is to say, with a minimum of abstraction the irregularities of the inkblot could become rounded, meaningful, and acceptable; but in these responses the subject takes too sharp cognizance of every detail, and either explicitly calls his weak abstractions farfetched or, as in the first example, chooses a content which retains the irregularities as meaningful parts of the response. The overmeticulousness of these responses usually permeates the entire record. They occur most frequently in compulsive personalities who, at the time of testing, have not yet become fully decompensated. Pathological conditions that reflect a decompensation of a compulsive personality—such as paranoid conditions, or anxiety and depression—also foster such exactness. This verbalization in itself can never be diagnostic, but should always be used as a clue for the direction in which the maladjustment lies.

Criticism Verbalizations. Examples: "They all seem like a series of patterns thrown together . . . doesn't look like anything complete"; "Just a silly picture of ink and red paint"; "Crazy face, poor attempt." These criticism verbalizations have several implications. In the first example, traces of exactness are apparent in the reference to incompleteness. There is also a mild flavor of a loss of distance from the card, in that the subject implicitly attributes some real significance or intent to the card. This is clearest in the third example, where the patient states it to be a "poor attempt." In both the second and third examples a direct verbal criticism of the card occurs; in our experience this is usually a thinly disguised expression of aggression against the examiner. This is seen most clearly in depressives, who abound in such criticism verbalizations, and in various other ways—

by their persistent overpoliteness and continual referring to the examiner as "doctor"—express thinly disguised hostility. This mixture of ostentatious politeness and displacement of criticism to the card is indicative of a strong tension of aggressions which the subject cannot directly express; and their most frequent occurrence in depressives seems consistent with this explanation of their significance.

Verbal Aggression. Examples: "What do *you* think it is?"; "Put down that I don't know"; "I won't tell you anything so you won't put down anything"; "I don't think I'm abnormal enough to appreciate this test."

These verbalizations bear little reference to the subject's responses. Nevertheless, they are part of a complete test record and, being given in the standardized test situation, constitute valid material for interpretation. An examiner can hardly fail to notice the aggression in these comments. These verbalizations may refer to the fact that the examiner is taking everything down ("Put that down," or "Don't put that down"), or to the stop watch or other materials or furnishing in the examiner's office, or to the language or behavior or appearance of the examiner, or to the quality of the cards, or to the German name of the test—in short, to anything through which they may strike at the examiner. The greatest accumulation of such comments is found in desperate depressives, subjects with paranoid disorders, and some simple schizophrenics with psychopathic trends. Nondepressive schizophrenics and normals rarely make such comments. In our testing situation great care is taken not to antagonize the patient, and it requires considerable lack of control of aggressions to confront a friendly, polite, interested examiner with such remarks.

Aggression Responses. These verbalizations are not side remarks or expressions of difficulty, but an integral part of the response content. In these responses things are "splashed," "splattered," "split open," "bleeding," "shooting," "fighting"—or other direct or implicit aggressive content is apparent. These differ from the examples discussed above, inasmuch as here the aggression is not directed toward the examiner and does not suggest that the subject cannot control it. Integration of the aggressive idea into the response refers to a great tension of aggressions within the subject, which probably plays an important part in the dynamics of the maladjustment. Every maladjustment has its share of inability to control aggressive impulses, but these responses suggest a degree of prohibition of overt manifestation of these impulses in everyday life and their representation in fantasy life instead. Such an interpretation seems justified in only occasional cases, however, as there has not been a well-defined investigation into the significance of these responses; certainly we cannot infer the form taken by or the objects of the aggression in the subject's everyday life.[78]

[78] [For such an investigation, see Holt (1966).—Ed.]

Self-Depreciation Verbalizations. Examples: "I don't feel so dumb, but I am"; in reference to a response just given, "Disappointing, isn't it?"; "You will have to give me a zero on that"; "I don't like to be dumb"; "I think I must be nuts."

These verbalizations refer to the subject's inefficiency, inability, intellectual incapacity, etc. Such comments are especially striking because implicitly or explicitly the examiner has made it clear that this is not an intelligence test. If, nevertheless, the subject becomes self-critical of his intellectual abilities, it indicates a trend which is strong enough to be interpreted as characteristic of him. As a matter of fact, even if these subjects are reassured after one of these comments ("It is not a question of ability" or "You are doing all right"), they will almost always continue making them. Understandably, these responses occur with the far greatest frequency among the depressives. Such verbalizations occur in neurotic and normal subjects, but rather in the beginning of the test as a passing expression of anxiety about their capacity to give many or definitive responses. The depressed subject will persist in self-depreciation, however, and may sound disgusted with himself or even desperate.

Affective Verbalizations. Examples: "They scare me to look at them"; "Makes me sick to my stomach"; "A hideous picture to me."

In a sense, such verbalizations imply a loss of distance from the card, and contrast with the exactness and symmetry comments. Here the subject does not remain so aloof from the card that it has too little affective significance to give rise to a response; instead the card is taken almost as some horrifying segment of reality, and precipitates a gross affective response. Such ready affects are typical in hysterics and in many labile overideational preschizophrenics. Very anxious neurotic depressives may also give them.

Masturbation and Castration Verbalizations. Examples of *masturbation* verbalizations: To both halves of the lower one third of Card VII, "Book leaves frayed, deteriorated"; to all of Card IV, "Leaf, damaged in some way"; to all of Card I, "Iron support . . . rusted, eroded"; to the upper side projections on Card IV, "Stunted trees, weathered and age-beaten trees." Here the blots are perceived and verbalized as representing mutilated, deteriorated, decayed, shrunken, damaged, dead, wasted, eroded, stunted, ragged things. These verbalizations usually take reference to the irregular outlines of the area chosen or to its shading.

Examples of *castration* verbalizations: To the black areas on Card III, "Two men . . . leg missing . . . many things missing about them"; to all of Card I, "A bat, doesn't have a head"; to all of Card V, "A bat . . . feathers gone"; to all of Card VI, "Penis, torn away from the bottom here"; to the pink areas on Card VIII, which are popularly seen as animals with heads, "An animal, doesn't have a head, it ends at the stump of the neck." These responses are characterized mainly by parts missing, torn, torn off, shot off, blown off.

These verbalizations have been given a place in our general scoring scheme, and will be discussed here in order to indicate the need for segregating them from other qualitative features of Rorschach responses. Whatever they may refer to in the subject's personality, these types of verbalization are sharply differentiated in feeling tone and attitude from the others we have discriminated. We have not succeeded in establishing a clear-cut link between the masturbation responses and masturbatory guilt, and the castration responses and castration anxiety; but these verbalizations have reference at least to conscious attitudes and feelings which, in psychoanalytic thinking, are frequently linked with such guilt and anxiety.

Let us consider first the castration verbalizations. The examiner will be struck that these frequently refer to a part as "missing" at the very spot where most subjects perceive it. In the fifth example, the popular "animal" on Card VIII, we see this in clear form. Another example is the verbalization on Card IV where a giant is described with his head "missing"; most subjects who give this response see the head in the shading in the upper part of the card. The elaborate description of and the search for missing parts in the cards are comparable to the distress certain persons feel at the sight of blood or any kind of bodily mutilation or deformity. Whether the basis for such distress—and for such Rorschach responses—is really referable to "castration anxiety" is open to question. But the responses appear to imply some specific attitude and personal feeling concerning "incompleteness" or "lack of something"; in psychiatric thinking, these feelings of insufficiency or incompleteness are frequently associated with the presence of "castration anxiety."

The examiner will again be struck by the fact that the *masturbation* verbalizations are given without much if any basis in the card. An example is the verbalization which we gave above, "Penis . . . torn away on the bottom here." Here too it appears to require a certain attitude to dwell so upon deteriorated or decayed appearances, whether or not supported in the inkblot by drooping lines, frayed edges, or indistinct shadings; most subjects are not overconcerned with either missing parts or disintegration and related conditions. Preoccupation with these again implies that the subject himself has a special sensitivity, which frequently crops up in persons with masturbatory guilt, where fears of consequent slow decay and insanity are common. This does not constitute proof that such references in the Rorschach responses must be an expression of masturbatory guilt. The feeling tone of these verbalizations strongly suggests, however, a continuity with the feeling tone of ideas clinically encountered in patients with masturbatory guilt.

We must again stress that it is open to question whether these verbalizations can be reliably considered indicative of the presence of "castration anxiety" or "masturbatory guilt." A number of patients we have examined who accumulated "masturbation" verbalizations had conscious severe conflicts over masturbation, according to the clinical history. In other cases, the clinical data were inconclusive. The difficulties are even greater in the "castration" verbalizations. Castration anxiety even in psychiatric examinations is in general an inferred entity, and only psychoanalytic or equivalent treatment can elicit material that may be claimed to substantiate its presence. A few cases giving these verbalizations showed, in subsequent psychoanalytic or hypnotic treatment, that the intensity of conflict and anxiety relating to the "castration complex" was a crucial part of their maladjustment. Also, a few psychotic cases giving these verbalizations had delusions whose conscious content pointed rather clearly to castration fears. But none of these data are conclusive proof. "Castration anxiety" appears to be ubiquitous, although of varying intensity, and its clinical manifestations are in general diffuse.

By including these two types of verbalization in our material we have attempted only to call attention to the need for systematization and further investigation of them. They are well-defined verbalizations, and in the long run an understanding of them may lead to some recognition of the manner in which different types of emotional conflict may penetrate perception, thought, and verbalization. This relationship of experience and verbalization of experience to prominent affective conflicts and attitudes is still an experimentally unattacked problem.

The situation of the Rorschach test is different from that of any of the other tests. Summaries of diagnostic signs—more or less exhaustive, and more or less correct—exist in the literature. The test itself in its multiplicity of aspects exceeds any of the tests thus far discussed. The limitations rather than the scope of this important test should be emphasized, since its scope has often been represented before and amply demonstrated by us in the sections dealing with its various aspects. For all these reasons, a summarizing simplification would have been more dangerous and less necessary than in the other tests. To achieve an appraisal of the interrelationships ("patterns") of its different aspects by a summary would have proved either inconclusive or too cumbersome.[79]

---

[79] [At this point, there followed in the first edition 28 pages of fine print, in which 217 cases were presented in condensed form, with indications of diagnostically relevant data and a differential diagnostic discussion for each.—Ed.]

CHAPTER 10

The Thematic Apperception Test

The Thematic Apperception Test was conceived by H. A. Murray (Morgan & Murray, 1935) as a projective test which, through the medium of the imaginative productions of the subject, made possible inferences about themata of import in the subject's life, and from these in turn about the "needs" and "press" outstanding in the underlying dynamics of his personality. It has become generally known by its initials, and will be so abbreviated here as "the TAT."

THE PLACE OF THE THEMATIC APPERCEPTION TEST IN THIS BATTERY OF TESTS

In the previous chapters we have discussed tests of intelligence, tests of concept formation, the Rorschach test as a diagnostic test of personality and maladjustment, and the Word Association Test. The last was included in this battery to yield information concerning ideational content, but has proved to be of limited significance in this respect and more of diagnostic significance in revealing disturbances of the thought processes. These tests together enable us to draw up a skeletal framework of the structure and dynamics of the personality, of the assets and liabilities (intellectual, conceptual) that result from the development of the personality, and of the equipment with which the personality meets internal and external situations and through which it manifests itself. These tests touch upon what is most characteristic of the human organism—namely, its ability not only to function but to become aware (both unconsciously and consciously) of much of its functioning and to communicate this subjective self-experience. This is readily apparent in self-criticisms, in reflections upon one's own thinking, and in communications of one's own anxiety. What is usually called, in clinical parlance, "the ideational content" of the patient is part of this self-experience. It is difficult to define how much of this ideational content

covers more than the conscious part of the subject's self-experiencing, because certain facets of the conscious ideational content are immediately
revealing of the unconscious ideational content: the patient who does not
tire of reiterating that he does not mean to criticize but would like to ask
why this or that is done the way it is done, reveals not only his curiosity
and interest—a conscious ideational content—but also his aggressive dissatisfaction. It was our purpose to include a test in our battery that would
give us an appraisal of the subject's experiencing of his own world and of
himself as part of it. In a sense, we wanted to obtain thereby a direct picture of the material dealt with by the intellectual conceptual apparatus
and personality dynamics of the subject which were incidentally indicated
by the other tests.[1] Therefore, we have had to find a test which would supply us with more than incidental information about these contents and attitudes.

Two avenues for obtaining it were considered and discarded. The first
was the use of direct questionnaires. These, as used in the conventional
personality inventories, could at best give a true picture of the subject's
conscious attitudes and thought contents. We say at best because the
likelihood of obtaining a correct picture even of these by questionnaires
is small. It is well-known from interviews how difficult it is for the subject
to communicate clearly formulated conscious ideas and attitudes, and how
easy it is for him to avoid communicating even these without becoming
deliberately evasive or deliberately untruthful. ("I thought of it but considered it unimportant.") Furthermore, ideas and attitudes otherwise available to consciousness may simply become temporarily unavailable in the
course of the interview, and later on—when the psychotherapist's skill
brings about a situation in which they are communicated—the patient will
state, "I told myself at home repeatedly that I had to tell you this, but I
never thought of it once I entered your office." Finally, it is known from
the clinical interview that much of a subject's attitudes and needs—material
which has never been clearly put together consciously, but is accessible to

---

[1] To avoid misunderstanding, it should be stated that other tests also give us incidental information concerning specific thought contents and attitudes of the subject.
Sexual and bodily preoccupations will show up in sex responses to the Rorschach
test; fears (as of high places) in specific responses on the Rorschach test (cliffs,
peaks, turrets) and in associative disturbances (for instance on the stimulus *snake*)
in the Word Association Test; feelings of insufficiency and disintegration in torn,
ragged, and dying figures of animals and plants in the Rorschach test and in reactions like *dirt*—"me" in the Word Association Test. Specific attitudes may show up
even in the Wechsler-Bellevue Scale, where for instance the question on why we
should keep away from bad company is answered, "My parents told me so, but I
have found bad company the only sort that is interesting and that I feel well in."
In these tests, however, information about ideational contents and attitudes is only
incidental.

consciousness and can be put together in the course of the interview—can be elicited only by the skillful interviewer. For all these reasons, using direct questionnaires for the purposes of our battery was out of the question. It must be remarked here that all these considerations are valid even if the questionnaire to be used is one developed to obtain reactions freely formulated by the subject, and not the customary ones where the reactions are "No," "I don't know," or "Yes."

The other approach which was discarded was that of play techniques. The wealth of literature on play techniques clearly shows that they are able to elicit ideational content and attitudes, both conscious and unconscious, in children. Yet, the constriction adults experience in relation to play, and the difficulties of developing play techniques that would be as acceptable for adults as the current play techniques are for children, were so great that—though we do not consider them insurmountable, and hope that some investigators will develop them[2]—we discarded the idea. An additional reason for discarding play techniques is worth mentioning. In discussing the virtues of projective tests, we stated that they must set up in the instructions a definite starting point and a definite end point for the behavior segment or thought process to be investigated; otherwise, there can be no hope that an economically feasible, objectively and completely recordable, significant segment of behavior can be isolated, recorded, and made amenable to analysis and interindividual comparison. Play techniques in general involve such a multiplicity of aspects and levels of behavior, and lend themselves so poorly to instructions that set a relatively uniform end point, that this difficulty in itself served as a deterrent to our using them.

Our choice fell on the TAT (Murray, 1943). This test, requiring the subject to make up a story around a picture visually presented to him, clearly delineates the task to the subject, states the beginning and the end of the task unequivocally, and binds the patient to one level of behavior— verbal communication—which is fully recordable. Unlike most play techniques, it gives a springboard to the subject as to the topic about which he is expected to produce, and thereby makes interpersonal comparison easier; furthermore, the presence of a picture supports the subject—especially if he is inhibited and inert—in his efforts at production. The aim in such a test is obviously to confront the subject with a great variety of pictured situations which will elicit from him indications about which of these situations and relationships represented are fraught with danger, difficulty, and personally important implications for him. Obviously there are many ways to set up such a series of pictures. We chose the TAT because its wide use, which makes possible a comparison of results, recommends it over any other

---

[2] See, e.g., Rosenzweig and Shakow (1937).

extant or self-made series. Obviously, the limitations of the picture series become limitations of the material that can be obtained.[3]

TESTING OF IDEATIONAL CONTENT[4]

The problems we face in the testing of ideational content are radically different from those in the diagnostic testing of intelligence and concept formation, or in the Word Association and Rorschach tests. On clearly defining these problems, and adopting the attitude toward ideational content required by them, hinges the efficacious use of such a test. In tests of intelligence and concept formation our questions are couched so as to prompt the subject to draw on his knowledge and ability. Obviously, in these tests also the subject reveals part of his ideation. But in tests of intelligence and concept formation the subject draws on a static or relatively stationary segment of his ideation, namely that which has a claim on interindividual agreement—knowledge verifiable in textbooks or by logic and achievements measured by clearly defined criteria. Single responses contain no indication of how this knowledge is being actually used by the subject in everyday life, and only scatter analysis gives us an idea about the dynamic efficacy of the different aspects of the ideation tested by an intelligence test. Summarily, one could say that only the ideational assets of the subject are assessed by diagnostic tests of intellectual functions, and that the attitudes are only incidentally elicited by them. In these tests the subject knows clearly that his response must conform to an ideal of common agreement, logic, or textbook statement. On the one hand, this makes evasion impossible or hardly possible.[5] On the other hand, the impossibility of evasion also means that if one restricts oneself to this type of testing, one will certainly fail to appreciate the variability in direction, depth, and extent of a person's ideational content. The situation is somewhat similar with the Word Association and Rorschach tests. In these tests our questions certainly are

[3] The construction of an "ideal" set of pictures is dependent first upon gathering extensive material on one standard set of pictures over a wide variety of clinical conditions and over a wide variety of segments of the normal population; and second upon the exploration of a variety of pictured situations with the knowledge so gathered. Sticking to one set of pictures, therefore, is the prerequisite for future development of more comprehensive and revealing tests of this type.

[4] [The conception of the TAT as a test of ideational content was fairly quickly outgrown in the Menninger-Riggs tradition referred to in the Editor's Foreword, in large part because of the approach to the interpretation of the formal aspects of the TAT set forth in this chapter. Rapaport was the first to make fruitful use of the TAT as something *more* than a way of getting at content, and got a number of his students started on an interest in formal aspects that has proved quite productive; see Schafer (1958) and Holt (1951, 1958b).—Ed.]

[5] In the Sorting Test some evasion is possible, since the subject may say of the same object, "I don't know what it is" or "Nothing belongs with it."

couched so as to leave it open to the subject what his response will be, but the subject's subjective experience—as attested to by both his reactions and his recounted introspections—is one of giving the kind of reaction he deems expected of him. Thus we get conceptual definitions in the Word Association Test, statements of what the blot "really is" or "most likely represents" in the Rorschach test. The presence of this inclination in the great majority of the subjects reflects the nature of these tests, which can be summarized thus: in these two tests the subject may suppress or evade to some extent, but *he cannot produce a different type* of material. In the former there are objectively, and in the latter subjectively, no valid alternatives. In other words, as in the intelligence and concept-formation tests, here also the totality of the subject's responses is a set to which there are no alternatives. Therefore, the test material, even though it can be thought of as tapping ideational content, taps only a very restricted segment of it.

The nature of ideational content at large is very different. Perhaps this difference can best be made clear if we keep before ourselves the nature of conversation. One of the participants may make a statement of fact, and draw a conclusion from it. Another may take issue with the fact or the conclusion and initiate a discussion which loses the free-swinging character of conversation and takes on the character of professional dispute or shoptalk; such a turn of discussion may force all participants to adhere to the frame of reference of scientific discussion, and the ideational contents that will come into play will be seriously limited. In a free-swinging discussion, however, someone may join in stating that the fact and the conclusion suggested remind him of the problem faced by modern aeronautics, which if solved would end the war; another participant may then direct the conversation to the war, the world situation, and the death of a national leader; another may continue with what it is that makes a person a great historical figure; the conversation might then pass to a discussion of reactions to great figures and their death. If the tensions for some reason are great in the group, and none of these scientific, political, or psychological issues can be comfortably discussed, the conversation may swing over to the weather or bridge, where everybody can remain noncommittal. This example of a free-swinging conversation versus polarized shoptalk shows that ideational content has a tremendous freedom of movement and therefore a great latitude of evasion, with which the tester of ideational content and attitudes must contend. Furthermore, the capacity for free-swinging fantasy has many variants: it may be completely absent, or temporarily rendered ineffective in a tense situation; it may be sharply limited to a circumscribed field of ideation, yet very mobile and colorful within it; it may be free-swinging, yet without any depth and real content.

It is characteristic of human beings that they are able to think and speak of things not of immediate concern to them, that their ideational content shades from ideas that are direct manifestations of their fundamental interests, needs, and attitudes, to those that have little connection with their essential motives. Yet remarkably enough, the organization of sufficiently large segments of communicated ideational content always bears some traces of the organization of motivating forces—that is, of the personality. But as segments of communicated ideational content range from the commonplace to the idiosyncratic, the testing of ideational content can be efficacious only if it differentiates between conscious and unconscious ideational contents, motivations, and attitudes. These are some of our guiding and orienting principles in using the TAT.

ADMINISTRATION[6]

It is our custom to give the test in two sessions whenever possible, because if it is given in a continuous session to a subject of average productivity, considerable tiring of the subject, with a consequent flattening and emptiness of his stories, is observed. For subjects who give clipped, brief stories, one continuous session may suffice. Extremely productive or circumstantially elaborate subjects may require more than two sessions.

The test is administered with the patient seated upright facing the examiner, as in the other tests. We found it unnecessary to have the patient

---

[6] [Omitted here from the first edition is the description of the test and the reproduction of the pictures. At that time and for some years afterwards, an early and not generally available edition of the TAT was used at the Menninger Clinic—a photographed set of small pictures, nine of which are identical (except for size) with pictures retained in the present, published set (Murray, 1943), while an additional eight are substantially the same though they were redrawn for the 1943 edition. It has been necessary to delete examples of stories told about the 13 omitted pictures. Since the TAT is now so easily obtainable and so widely known, it seemed that a description would be superfluous.

One point from the omitted section bears on administration. Rapaport advocated the giving of all 20 pictures whenever possible, though he noted that "if the earlier stories were conclusive and time was short," certain pictures could be omitted, since they tended not to pull unique material. (The ones he specified are no longer included in the printed set.) He added a warning: "It is inadvisable to use only those cards on which the examiner expects to obtain decisive ideational content: first, the most conclusive material is that given on cards where usually it would not be obtained; and secondly, the way the subject's narratives shape up on cards touching on areas of ideation indifferent to the subject may be used as a baseline for evaluating unusually brief, unusually elaborate, or in other ways disproportionate stories." Since most workers do not have the time to administer a full TAT in routine clinical practice, the following reduced sets may be recommended; they are based on a pooling of experience and practice in several places. For men: 1, 2, 4, 6 BM, 7 BM, 8 BM, (9 BM, 10), 11, 12 M, 13 MF, (15), 16, and 18 GF. For women: 1, 2, 3, (6 GF), 7 GF, 9 GF, 11, (12 M), 12 F, 13 MF, 16, and 18 GF. Parentheses indicate further possible omissions for still briefer sets.—Ed.]

recline on an easy chair or couch for the purpose of obtaining significant ideational contents. It is not impossible that less evasiveness would have been encountered had we used such methods; but the subject would have taken more time, and offered more and mostly unnecessary elaboration of the material. The average subject requires 90-120 minutes for the administration of this test in the upright position and more time-consuming procedures are unjustifiable in clinical work.

The instruction we use is the following: "I am going to show you a series of pictures and I want you to make up a story around each one of them. I want you to tell me what the situation is in the picture, what the events were that led up to it and what the outcome will be, describing the feelings and thoughts of the characters. What I would like you to give is a plot, not an elaborate literary story. I want to write what you say as much as possible verbatim. Therefore, please don't hurry." The instruction is always repeated on request, or in abbreviated form as a warning to the subject who does not comply with it: "What is happening? What led up to it? What will be the outcome? What are the feelings and thoughts of the characters?"

It is our custom to record the time taken by the subject from the presentation of each picture to his starting the narrative, as well as the total time from presentation to conclusion of the narrative. This does not include the time spent in the routine inquiry following each story. Long pauses in the narrative are indicated by a corresponding number of dots.

We found it useful to indicate every mispronunciation, misuse of words, peculiar word construction, and peculiar phrase, by underlining it so as to differentiate it from errors of recording. Among the technical difficulties of administration the following are outstanding:

Handling of the Subject's Speed of Delivery. With subjects who speak too fast, it is our custom to repeat from the instructions our request about speed. In the clinical situation, fast delivery persisting after repeated instructions is either a result of pressure of anxiety or is an outright aggression toward the examiner, and is usually not checked by further repetition of instructions. In these cases it was found expedient for the examiner to read aloud what he is recording whenever the subject outruns him. This procedure may or may not stop the subject's *tendency* to rush ahead, but in practice it prevents his doing so; and it will segregate those subjects for whom the disagreeable experience of being stopped cold is a greater pressure than that of their anxiety or aggressions, and those for whom it is not. The importance of this rule lies in the fact that if the subject runs ahead, the examiner sooner or later must ask him to repeat what he has said; and our experience is that subjects—excepting the compulsive rigid ones—will change their verbalizations and even their stories on second delivery. Slow or hesitant subjects may be prompted by such comments or questions as, "Well?" or "What do you have on your mind?" or "What are you thinking of?"

Handling Refusals to Give Stories. Refusals most commonly take the form of describing the picture: "It's just a man in a window. There is no story in it." The usual way to meet such refusals is to restate and emphasize the instructions: "Remember you are to *make it up* around the picture. It isn't all in the picture." If the subject persists in refusal, the procedure varies according to the type of card. On Cards 8 GF, 12 BG, 13 G, 17 BM, and 20 there is not much object in pressing the subject further; these cards, as compared to the others, offer little support to subjects who find it difficult to mobilize their ideational content, and few compelling features to force a story from those who want to evade giving one. In the case of the other pictures, however, further pressure is usually applied. If this difficulty becomes apparent early in the test, or if it is definitely felt that the subject is evading, he is told squarely: "You came here to obtain help; in order to help you your doctor needs this information. If you don't cooperate, you are defeating your own purpose." The subject's refusal may be an expression of difficulty in mobilizing ideational content, either because of native poverty of ideation, or extreme rigidity and consequent immobility of ideation, or depressive or neurasthenic inertia, or overcaution or suspicious meticulousness. In these cases, help is given in the form of questions: "Won't you just start telling me what the situation is about?"; then, "How could this situation have come about?"; then, "What do you think could be the outcome?"; and finally, "How does he [or she] feel about it?" and/or "What does he [or she] think about it?" After these questions, many rigid or inert subjects will be able to deliver whatever ideational content they can afford to mobilize in relation to the specific picture.

A different procedure is used with very compulsive or paranoid patients, in whom refusal may take the form of meticulously describing every detail of the picture. Once the examiner encounters this manner of refusing to give stories he will discourage it on subsequent cards by reiterating the instruction when presenting the picture: "Remember, please, what we are interested in is the plot and not many elaborate details." If the meticulous enumeration of every detail then continues, the examiner will interrupt the subject: "Please mention only the salient features of the present situation, and proceed to give the story."

In obsessive cases refusal may take the form of obvious rambling and vacillating between possibilities. Here the examiner should state, "Please decide which [or why] and go on giving the plot of the story." Other subjects who remain very vague must be encouraged to be specific—to tell not merely that "a loved one died" but *which* "loved one," or not merely that "he is in trouble" but *what kind* of trouble.

Another form of refusal is what might be termed superficial compliance with the instructions. This is the case when the subject says, "The situation is that a boy is sitting with his violin. What led up to it was that he practiced and the outcome is going to be that he will practice again, and he thinks and feels that he will soon practice again." This is a rather blunt example, and the examiner must be prepared to encounter much more subtle forms of such superficial compliance. There are usually two ways to meet this type of difficulty. With subjects who manifest a paucity of ideational content or inertia, the examiner will proceed to ask detailed questions—though always based on what the subject has already told. For instance, "Why isn't he practicing now? How did it happen that he was practicing before? What makes you think that he is going to practice again? How does he feel about going on with practicing?" Obviously the examiner must be very careful to avoid leading questions and to refrain from asking specific questions until he is quite sure that without them he will get no further material. Subjects who merely evade giving stories by this procedure, especially if intelligent enough and not too badly disorganized, should be faced with the meaning of their procedure, instructed to "try hard," and to stop evading the issues involved in the picture. If the stories still remain completely unrevealing, it is practical to interrupt the examination and ask the subject to come back when he has changed his mind. This need happen very rarely.

Finally, there are subjects who state, "I see not one story but two" or "I see several stories." Our procedure is to let the subject tell all of them, starting with the one that occurred to him first. All alternative stories and their relation to each other will be taken into consideration in interpreting the material; it is characteristic of ideational content that personally significant segments of it may rise to the foreground of consciousness first, but they may be preceded by any number of personally unimportant segments. In any series of alternative stories, the first and the last must be scrutinized with special care; if both the first and the last are commonplace, the one succeeding the first or preceding the last must be considered.

INQUIRY

We have followed four basic principles of inquiry in the TAT. (1) As in the Word Association and Rorschach tests, every lack of clarity must be inquired into. (2) Unlike that in the Word Association and the Rorschach tests, inquiry does not limit itself to the clarification of the subject's responses; it attempts to obtain additional material by forcing the subject's compliance with the instructions and to clarify what parts of the picture were not seen or were seen but not used by the subject. (3) The inquiry in general follows immediately after the patient has finished his story, with the card kept out of sight; but liberal exceptions are made. (4) Suggestive questioning is to be avoided as much as an artificial objectivity which restricts the test to the patient's spontaneous production. Let us now consider each of these points.

Inquiry into Lack of Clarity

Lack of clarity appears on either the perceptual, the verbal, or the story-meaning level.

Inquiry into perceptual unclarity may lead to discovering perceptual distortions which are always indicative of some pathology and, if extreme, may be psychotic indications. For example, in the first picture the boy may be seen as blind or sleeping; the violin may be seen as broken or with a broken string; the bow may be overlooked or misrecognized; the violin may be misrecognized; both violin and bow may be overlooked; or the sheet may be misrecognized for a book. When such perceptual misrecognitions are only hinted at in the stories, unearthing them will be the task of the inquiry; it will succeed only if every ambiguity or unclarity of the narrative is meticulously singled out and inquired into.

Unclarities about the sex of characters may often appear as a borderline instance between perceptual and verbal unclarity. The clarification of such cases is of importance, because it differentiates between slips of the tongue and perceptual misrecognition. The latter is of far greater pathological significance. The word "they" used to refer to one person frequently masks doubt about the sex of that person. Inquiry will establish these differences and unmask doubt.

Verbal Unclarities. The simplest type of verbal unclarity is the slip of the tongue, where the task of inquiry is to establish whether or not the patient means what he has said. The simplest procedure is to repeat the pertinent part of the sentence immediately in the course of administration, as though one is not able to follow: if the slip is repeated by the subject, it usually establishes that he means what he has said; if it is corrected, it is usually to be considered as a neurotic temporary inefficiency. If the slip is repeated with no basis in a perceptual misrecognition present, the suspicion of disorganization in excess of neurosis must be kept in mind. If the slip distorts either the pronunciation or the word itself, the procedure is usually not only to induce a repetition of the word but also to ask the subject, "What do you mean?" The response to such an inquiry will either obviate or make evident the presence of neologistic trends.

Unclarities of Story Meaning. These are the most difficult to discuss in a general way. They are seen most clearly when all coherence of the story is lost. Obviously, this occurs only in very disorganized psychotic adults or children. The attempt of the examiner in these cases is to keep the story in a groove, and to unearth in the inquiry what, if anything, was its core. The degree to which the examiner's efforts in the course of administration and inquiry can unearth a unitary story is inversely proportional to the degree of disorganization present. When the examiner's efforts are used by the subject only as a springboard for new ramblings and new motifs, the examiner must know when to stop. A milder form of this type of disturbance, also mostly psychotic in character, is the introduction into the story of figures not justified by the card. This is not the case when for the mourning man in Card 15 a buried wife is introduced; but it is the case when in Card 14 the man is trying to escape from somebody who cannot be seen in the darkness. This disturbance may shade into perceptual unclarity, when by means of a perceptual distortion a nonexistent figure is discovered in the cards. Use of nonexistent figures must always be inquired into carefully, both as to their perceptual basis and their meaning relationship to the story. Another simple unclarity of meaning is that of contradiction between two parts of a story. For instance (Card 5), the narrative may deal with a ghost, one part of the narrative suggesting that the figure in the picture is the ghost, and another part suggesting that the figure is haunted by the ghost. Such unclarities may easily resolve themselves into mere weaknesses of formulation or, more frequently, omissions of statements which the patient believes he has already made. This type of unclarity may be well within the normal range. Outright denial of having said what was actually said, however, or forceful insistence on having said what was not said, are suspicion-arousing implications; their minor forms are present in long-standing convulsive conditions and even hysterias, their blatant forms only in psychoses.

All these forms constitute only a small part of the unclarities of meaning. The major part is subtle in appearance, and yet of great diagnostic significance. Examples are hard to cite, and the only advice to the examiner must be to familiarize himself zealously with the usual vocabulary and language formation of stories, in order to become sensitive to any departure therefrom. Communications that might pass in everyday conversation and even in the course of a psychiatric examination as acceptable may prove— by reason of being alien to the customary vocabulary and language used in the test—to be pathological indicators. Another suggestion for the examiner is that every shift in the conceptual level of the narrative be watched closely; such shifts also are pathological indicators. A simple example of this type is seen when a subject describes the woman in Card 5 as terrified and, when asked what led up to it, answers "The expression on her face." Here the realm of the story is abandoned by the patient; he shifts to the realm of his own experiencing of the picture and story. One might argue that the subject has simply misunderstood the question. Such an argument may be correct for this example, but is not correct in general, because the majority of such shifts imply serious psychopathology and refer to a weakness of conceptual frames of reference. But if the argument implies that misunderstanding is a category that has its own psychological existence, it must be flatly contradicted. Misunderstanding is a shift in the frame of reference of the subject which, if it occurs in conversation, means a lack of mutual regulation of the frames of reference of the conversing parties. Such a lack may be taken as a normal occurrence in conversation between two or more persons if the conversation is of heavy weight; it may give one pause if it occurs in a light-weight interesting conversation; but if it occurs between examiner and patient in a situation which calls upon the subject to be all there, it must always cause the examiner to consider its implications. If it occurs within the subject's own narrative—where there is no question of "tuning together" with another's frame of reference, but only of the solidity and coherence of one's own—then it always must be considered as a pathological indicator which is at least potentially very serious.

Inquiry Forcing Compliance with Instructions and Exploring Compliance with the Picture

First, wherever the subject has omitted past, present, or future events, or feelings and thoughts of the characters, the examiner repeats the corresponding part of the instructions, thus requesting that he complete his compliance with the instructions. The usual situation faced here is that the subject will say, "I don't know, the picture does not tell it," or "There could be many kinds of events leading up to it, or many kinds of outcomes." This situation is similar to that seen when stories contain statements that "Somebody dear to him died or has gone away, and he is grieved" (Card 6 BM). In all these cases the aim of inquiry is to drive the subject to specificity and decision, even though the subject and even the examiner may experience these as arbitrary. The examiner will ask "Who died?"—and if the answer still offers several alternatives, the first or last must be considered. Sometimes, however, this question elicits a response such as, "It was not his wife, it was his sister"—which in its specificity of negation clearly manifests the direction of aggression.

Second, the examiner should be aware of what the usual story and usual attitudes elicited by the card are, and if the patient's story evades these or implies them in an unclear manner, the examiner's inquiry must try to elicit them.[7] The examiner must keep them in the foreground of his thinking as the context against which he evaluates the patient's narrative as it progresses, when he must make up his mind what openings he can pry into in order to draw information of the type the card usually elicits.

The method of such inquiry deserves a further illustration. When a patient relates about Card 5 that the woman is looking into the room and is "scared," the inquiry will be directed to her fright rather than to the contents of the room: description of the contents of the room may change the subjective experience of the woman's facial expression, while discussion of the "scare" may bring forth a story of what was seen to occasion it. In other words, the inquiry starts directly with the important and stated point. The case is different where the woman in this picture is but once referred to as "he." Now the important point is not clearly stated, and the inquiry will proceed indirectly to obtain other statements about the person. Weighing the advantages of direct and indirect methods of inquiry is one of the most challenging tasks of the examiner.

The inquiry into the perceptual compliance with the picture need not be redescribed here: its main points should be already clear, on the basis of our preceding discussions of perceptual distortions. Not only when the suspicion of perceptual misrecognition is indicated, but also when the story and picture do not seem to conform totally, even though no hint of direct perceptual misrecognition is present, inquiry into the nature of the situation presented by the picture must be made.

The Time and Place of Inquiry

It is advisable to inquire into a story only after it is finished; but it leads only to confusion if one defers inquiry until all the cards or a series of them is finished. This danger is even greater than in the Rorschach test, because of the loosely knit nature of narratives which easily fade into each other in the subject's memory. In our experience, if inquiry is delayed until after a series of 10 cards few normal subjects will avoid mixing the stories. Also, it is often necessary to interrupt the patient's story for inquiry. This is especially the case with verbal unclarities which are afterwards very difficult to recover, judge, or inquire into: they constitute subordinate parts of the narrative, and soon after being uttered lose their identity and submerge in the whole of the narrative. The situation is different with perceptual unclarities; here it is advisable always to delay inquiry until the end of the story or even of the series. As to unclarities of meaning, the examiner must

---

[7] [Summaries of "usual stories and usual attitudes" are available in a number of sources; for example Bellak (1954) and Henry (1956). My experience with the techniques of inquiry advocated here has convinced me that Rapaport's cautions against overinquiry in the Rorschach test are even more applicable to the TAT.—Ed.]

judge for himself whether he can conduct a revealing inquiry afterwards or must interrupt. The general principles are relatively clear. It is better not to make the subject overalert by many inquiries in the course of a story; on the other hand, no point should be left unclarified if it seems that the material will not be amenable to clarification after a few minutes.

The Nonsuggestive Character of the Free Inquiry

Inquiry that merely forces the subject to comply with picture and instructions, to make his statements specific, and to clarify overambiguous points, can be considered nonsuggestive; it is directed at tapping the ideational content of the subject. Any inquiry that makes the subject reflective, so that he realizes there are other possibilities than the one he would spontaneously offer, is a suggestive inquiry. Therefore, it must be kept in mind that the ideational content essential for our understanding of the subject is the content he would think of offhand, whether a commonplace, an evasion, a manifestation of his conscious attitudes and thought contents, or a revelation of his unconscious attitudes and thought contents. All that is thinkable to human beings can be part of the patient's ideation, but it may be of little value for understanding him. The division between the results of suggestive and nonsuggestive inquiry is a division between what is thinkable and what is actually thought offhand by the subject in the given situation.

For instance, a subject may describe the first picture as a boy with a broken violin; the inquiries, "How did it break?" or "How did he break it?" are suggestive to some extent. They suggest that it could have been broken by accident or by the boy. In many cases such suggestive inquiry may appear to be of no consequence because the subject chooses the opposite possibility, yet without the suggestion he might not have thought of the opposite possibility. "What led up to it?" or "How come, broken?" are much safer inquiries. The more noncommittal the inquiry, the more significant the answer. "He didn't break it in anger" is much more revealing if the question was "How come, broken?" than if it was, "How did he break it?"

RATIONALE

To draw up an extensive rationale of the Thematic Apperception Test is for several reasons beyond the scope of this volume. The realm of ideational content comprising imagination and fantasy which is encompassed by the TAT involves almost all the problems modern dynamic psychology and psychopathology deal with. Furthermore, it is very difficult to determine in a general way to what extent the stories obtained on the TAT really are true fantasies and imaginative products, and to what extent they are clichés. For these reasons, a rationale of the TAT lies in the cloudiest and least-explored realm of present-day psychology.[8]

Essential Ideational Content versus Clichés

It might be argued that in the distinction made above between fantasy and imagination on the one hand and clichés on the other, we have abandoned the principle of thoroughgoing psychological determinism— that is, have distinguished between genuine psychological phenomena psychodynamically determined and revealing of the individual person, and stolen goods incidental to and unrevealing of him. We did not intend to make the distinction with any such implication. Clichés are not outside the realm of psychological determinism. They are determined in the sense that *the choice*[9] of what is being used as a cliché is subject to stringent rules. But to uncover these rules, one usually needs broader samples of ideational material than are obtained by one card or often even the whole TAT. To make this point clear a literary example may be in place. Let us take a number of persons who all like Poe's "Ulalume." One who dislikes all that Poe stands for, the clever play of language in the poem, or its *claire-obscure,* may still have a predilection for it because of a close kinship between the psychological constellation pictured in it and his own. But another person who has no such specific affinity to the essential core of the poem may like it for its *claire-obscure,* another for its clever play of language, and another for its reflection of what Poe stands for in poetry. Without knowing what other poems are these persons' "specials," we will not be in a position to judge in what way their predilection for "Ulalume" is characteristic of them. This example should make it clear that clichés given in a TAT story are also characteristic of the subject, but become revealing of him only *in a broader context.* Thus, the first principle of the TAT's rationale is that one must differentiate clichés from essential ideational contents, and attempt to infer—from the interrelationships of clichés—the general rules by which the subject makes his selection of clichés.

The Nature of Ideational Content

The distinction between what the subject spontaneously thinks and what is thinkable is obviously only a different formulation of that made between essential ideational content and clichés. It seems necessary to point out that these distinctions are related to our distinction between drive

---

[8] [For some further suggestions about a general rationale based on Rapaport's conceptions see Holt (1951); on the relation between TAT stories and fantasies, see Holt (1961a).—Ed.]

[9] See in this respect Rapaport (1942b).

cathexes and hypercathexes (see Chapter 3, above). The former refer to the energies of drives, needs, and affects, and it appears to be useful to consider essential ideational contents—spontaneous thoughts—of subjects as ideational representations of these; the hypercathectic energies, which have been described as freely available to the ego, can be considered as those responsible for the emergence of thinkable thoughts as ideational contents. Obviously the relationships suggested here are not intended to be reifications; they are offered merely as a convenient way of describing related phenomena which fell into this formulation in the course of our experience.

But the problem is thus brought clearly into the realm of the theory of memory. In *Emotions and Memory* (Rapaport, 1942a) are summarized experimental and theoretical materials to demonstrate that memory organization is governed by emotional organization, and that emergence, mode of emergence, and failure of memories to emerge into consciousness are determined by the emotional dynamics specific to the person. *Emotions and Memory* was a summary of the pertinent literature, and thus did not undertake to appraise one aspect of memory functioning for the nature of which the literature gives few clues: namely, the segment of memories that is called "knowledge," and which appears to be almost always at our disposal, though extremely variable in different people. For the same reason, the volume in question failed to explore the relationship between emotional organization of memories and the fact—well-known from uncounted learning experiments—that human beings are able to learn things that are remote from their essential drives, needs, and strivings. The volume pointed out a whole hierarchy of emotional factors, ranging from central drives to peripheral attitudes and preferences; and thus it was made plausible to maintain—as we do here and in Chapter 8—that adopting the attitude of cooperativeness in an experimental situation may become a dynamic basis sufficient to organize memory functioning and to accomplish learning in the learning experiment. It should be kept in mind, however, that even the mobilization of an attitude of cooperativeness is ultimately based on more central strivings. Only in the process of studying attention and concentration did we become aware that learning in the course of an experiment appears to be dependent on the degree of availability to the ego of hypercathectic energies.[10]

Strivings and Defenses in the Stories

From a third point of view, the problem here discussed may be stated in different terms. If one wishes to consider the TAT stories as fantasies, one

[10] [On the nature of motives in psychological experiments, see Klein (1956).—Ed.]

may look in them for wish fulfillments, in keeping with psychoanalytic theory. But understanding the TAT stories necessitates some familiarity with the recent development of concepts in psychoanalysis, whose emphasis has shifted in recent decades from the sole exploration of the content and demands of the unconscious id to the defense mechanisms that the ego erects to cope with the danger implicit in these demands.

The distribution of drive cathexes and hypercathexes may take any one of several typical forms: (a) Within the normal range, the drive energies are well controlled, and the hypercathectic energies are freely enough available to the ego to support all voluntary activities. (b) Under conditions characterized as rigid and inhibitory, the drive cathexes are poorly controlled; the dangers to the ego implicit in their encroachments and demands are apparently met by using hypercathexes to enforce a rigid control. (c) Under conditions characterized as overfluid, labile, and impulsive, the neutral ego energies are sparse; drive cathexes easily take over the sluices of motility, and thus manage to direct the subject's behavior. The great majority of conditions in which this third form occurs are psychotic; the minority consists of impulse-ridden hysteroid or psychopathic conditions.

In the first of these conditions—within the normal range—the TAT stories will be a mixture of clichés—stereotypes and fantasylike productions, reflecting both specific defense methods and essential strivings and attitudes. In the second of these conditions—with rigidity prevailing—the TAT stories become extensively stereotyped, and little beyond the subject's *general* defense methods will be readable in them. In the third of these conditions—with fluidity and poor control prevailing—the stories may become fantasylike, representing wishes and strivings directly, and may even take on the contradiction-loaded character of fantasies and become indicators of severe psychopathology. Obviously, this account should be understood as presenting the extremes only; in reality, the TAT stories represent all transitions and combinations of these. No account will be given here of the obsessive, rationalizing form of clichés, which in their wealth differ significantly from the meagerness of the rigid compulsive ones, or of stories that approach artistic poetic creation, with the psychological insight these imply. We believe that the analysis of ideational content will not become a scientifically sound procedure until the whole continuum of production of ideational contents ranging from everyday conversation to poetic creation has been explored.[11]

[11] It is not within the scope of this volume to go into the problems implied in the various phases of this continuum. The interested reader may profitably study Freud (1908), Rank (1907), Sachs (1942), and particularly Bergler (1944) in this respect. He may also derive much information from psychologists', psychoanalysts', psychiatrists', and biographers' analyses of a writer's psychology based on his creations: see, e.g., Rosenzweig (1943), Bonaparte (1933), Freud (1910).

Keeping this change of emphasis in mind, we may formulate the distinction between essential ideational content and clichés as follows: The former allows for inferences concerning strivings of central importance to the subject; clichés allow only for inferences concerning the general character of the patient's defenses. This does not mean that content of central importance can become conscious without first having been molded by defense mechanisms. It means that while the clichés are entirely products of defense mechanisms, prohibiting the coming to consciousness of essential ideational content, stories that permit inferences concerning essential ideational content constitute compromises between defense mechanisms and central strivings. Therefore, stories representing deep-lying strivings will also represent and permit inferring of defense mechanisms from the setting in which these strivings occur and from the consequences they imply.

A few examples may make these issues clearer. A story given to Card 1 may relate that the child sitting in front of the violin does not want to play it, but would rather be out playing baseball with the other boys. This story is a cliché which allows for no inference other than the negative one that a freely active fantasy-life is not characteristic of the subject; only if similar motifs accumulate throughout the stories will we be in a position to make the broader inference that it is characteristic of the patient to be disgruntled with what he is doing, and to consider "the grass greener on the other side of the fence." But another story to the same card may relate that the child's father was a great musician who has died, and the child is holding the violin with the determination to take the place of his father in the musical world and to care for his mother; in this story the patient's oedipal constellation and its consequences are relatively clear. It must be understood, however, that the transition between these two types of stories is entirely fluid; it is possible for a cliché to be transformed by one additional word which indicates real involvement or even by an affective emphasis on one word of the cliché. For this reason, correct recording of the narrative will include notation of such emphases; and correct analysis will take account of every phrase or word that stands out against the cliché. The difficulty of interpreting the test and its apparent subjectivity are rooted in the existence of the fluid transition from near-clichés to material that is similar to genuine fantasy production.

Form-Varieties of Defense

The relationship between essential ideational content and cliché can be profitably looked upon from another point of view. The detailed instructions about what kind of story should be given, and the presentation of a picture as a basis for the story, in themselves are most conducive to eliciting clichés instead of essential ideational content. At first glance this may be considered a deficiency of the test; but it is one of its basic advantages, without which the procedure would not constitute a test. The clichés become norms against which departures from them can be pitted; and only when set against their background does the meaning of the departures become clear. The recognition of this fact is the rationale upon which are based the principles of interpretation, scrutiny of compliance with the instructions and pictures of the test, and analysis of interindividual and intraindividual consistency of the stories.

The defense mechanisms that become obvious in the test utilize the *picture* in deviant ways. The most obvious are constrictions of ideation, corresponding to the defense mechanism, *restriction of the ego* (see A. Freud, 1936, pp. 93ff.). In the TAT this may take several forms. The patient may go through the motions like an empty grinding-machine, when we will obtain such stories as the following to Card 5: the situation is that a woman stands in the door; what led up to it is that she opened the door; the outcome is that she will go into the room, and she thinks that she is going into it. Here the letter but not the essence of the instructions was complied with. The essence of the instructions demands a statement—as evidenced in the general trend of our population—of the situation in the picture, with its implications developed and its past and future elaborated.

Such elaboration may, however, lead to ideas fraught with the danger of intolerable emotions for the subject, who therefore develops rigid formalistic modes of thinking which prevent the emergence of these ideas. There are many form-variants of this mode of thinking. The story given sticks to the picture, and only briefly describes it. In another form of sticking to the picture, the present situation is described with or without its implications, and leading-up events or outcome are omitted: (Card 10) "A man and a woman making love. That's all." (Card 17 BM) "A man climbing a rope. Nothing more to it." Another form of sticking to the picture more clearly defies the instructions. It consists of describing every detail of the picture with painful meticulousness, requiring at times an amazing acuteness of observation and wasting 15 minutes for the examiner: (Card 10) "This looks like the picture of a younger person and this would be her father or some relative; it might be a mother and a child. I see the picture of the hand here, nose and an eye, and an eyebrow and an ear. The pictures are similar; they show the same features, except this one hand, but it doesn't look like it might be the picture of a woman and the boy; looks like the boy . . . she might be having her arms around him, or he might be on her breast. Do you want me to tell more? Well, I just see the features there, the ears, the eyes, and the nose . . ." In another form the subject does make up a story, but insists that every detail of it be derived from some facet of the picture. In such cases every element in the picture becomes laden with implications and far-reaching conclusions are drawn from it. In this type of story the presence of serious paranoid pathology is usually unmistakable. Card 6 BM, after the subject has debated whether it pictures a reunion or a leave-taking: "One factor favoring the leave-taking theory is the presence of the handkerchief in her hand and because, taken by surprise by his unexpected return, she would not be provided with a handkerchief; whereas if it were a case where she was ordering him to leave because of misconduct, knowing in advance that it would be a moving and tearful scene, she would provide herself with a handkerchief and retain it in her hand after a tearful consideration of the action taken or to be taken." All the stories of this subject are merely theories about the picture, and he strives in each to prove his point. In this type of thinking, close tab is being kept on all the minutiae of reality, danger being thus supposedly anticipated.[12] Such thinking develops in persons who externalize (project) all emotional danger, and expect danger to threaten only from the outside world.

While all these types of stories reflect paucity or restriction of ideation, they are of very different origins: intellectual poverty, anxious inhibitions, factualness bordering on the ridiculous, and paranoid overt-alert rigidity are, in sequence, the various likely sources of the restrictions in the stories quoted in the preceding two paragraphs.

Another form of defense is seen in patients who are inclined to make their stories elaborate. Detail-ridden rumination, naïve verbigeration, introduction of many new elements, elaborate exhibitionistic production, are all commonly encountered, but may also take extreme, pathological forms: (Card 5) "The scene is over in France somewheres, and this woman has opened the door and found a man visiting her daughter. She's very surprised and it's in the evening and this man is a former suitor of the girl's, who's been away on a long trip, and she always understood that the daughter did not care for this man and while this man, Henri, was away, the girl has become married and this woman doesn't understand the feelings of her daughter toward Henri. And then the girl's husband walks in and he's enraged at seeing his wife with another man and a hot conversation follows between Henri and the girl asks them if they would like to take a walk in the park. And so the three of them leave and the girl tells her mother that they are going out for a stroll and so they walk a long time and pass some little fishing boats, pass the hanging willow tree until they get to the French quarter on the Left Bank, and there they go to a café and sit down and order some wine . . . and then suddenly Henri looks at his watch and they decide they must return, it's late, and the girl returns home and the old

---

[12] See in this respect our discussion of intellectualizing as a defense in Chapters 2 and 3.

woman, her mother, is wondering what has taken place . . . I never tried this before—it's rather amazing!" Fantasy-ridden or deluded cases will usually produce such stories. In another form of overelaborateness, a series of different possibilities pops into the mind of the subject on every picture; the story vacillates between these possibilities, or describes all of them, or becomes a hairsplitting rumination about which is correct. The doubting character of such productions is easily recognized: (Card 5) "Can't quite get the connection of this room and this door; I guess she is looking into this room. It's a puzzle; this woman who lost her husband looks into the room with some regret that he is missing, thinking of scenes long past; and yet the light isn't lit, might be someone else, can't quite reconcile all those various features; I don't know what this dress represents—servant's dress or lady's of the house; seems probably as though familiar to me; possibly she has heard some strange sounds and commotion in the room, looking in where it happened. What shock: not exactly the expression of a shock, more reminiscent attitude. Thinking of past things rather than present; somewhat conflicting elements in this picture." Another form of such overelaborateness combines rambling and overmeticulous or paranoid analysis of the picture. In this type, extreme departure and extreme sticking to the picture are mixed.[13]

Essential Ideational Content and Memory Organization

Let us turn now to the discoverability of the essential ideational content in the stories. How is it possible that, in a story made up about a picture, the narrator's essential ideational content should be discoverable?

In this test the patient is confronted with pictures of persons in certain postures or interpersonal situations. In order to make up a story around this material, he may either resort to a cliché which he has read or heard about, or draw upon his own past experience.[14] In the latter event, that

---

[13] Neither sticking to nor departing from the picture should be mistaken for loss of and increase of distance from the picture described in the Rorschach test, Chapter 9.

[14] It is important to note that clichés too must be considered as past experiences which are remembered. They differ from actual life experiences in that they are usually movie, fiction, funny-paper, or joke stereotypes—that is, not specific reproductions—which the subject has encountered in a finished form and retained as units in his thought and memory organizations; while what we consider here actual life experiences are those which have occurred step by step in the person's past. This distinction, however, is by no means sharp. On the one hand, we have clichés of a very different origin: happenings and ideas which we once experienced quite vividly may progressively lose their affect and details, and finally boil down to skeletal sketches hardly differing from the clichés just described. On the other hand, there are literary works of fiction which we "lived" while reading them; they are great stories whose temporal development we seem to experience truly, and which become for us far more than adopted clichés.

picture itself is understood by him in terms of these experiences. The fact that an elderly woman on Card 5 is seen by various persons as having an indifferent, scared, worried, surprised, curious, or Peeping-Tom facial expression clearly attests to this point. But this example itself poses a new problem. What kind of past experience is being drawn on, and in what terms? Who are the characters being described in these stories? Are they all representatives of an aspect of the subject himself, or do only some of them represent him while others are figures who have loomed large in his life? This is a difficult question to decide. It might be argued that figures who have played important roles in his life are those whose attitudes and strivings became incorporated into the subject; if this argument is well taken, it would be unjustified to differentiate between story figures that represent the subject and others that represent persons of paramount importance in his world. Yet in everyday clinical work, it is practical to ascertain from the stories what kinds of attributes in the subject's world are given to "the old man," "the old woman," "the man," "the woman," "the young man," "the young woman," "the adolescent boy," "the adolescent girl," "the boy child," "the girl child." Once the subject's view of these types is established, it is easier to recognize which types refer to parental, sibling, child, and self-figures. The ease of recognition is predicated upon the elaborateness and uniformity of the figure by which the subject characterizes himself, and upon the relationships in which this figure stands to others in the stories. The attitudes these other figures display toward each other and the self-figure often reflect actually experienced attitudes of persons who have played decisive roles in the subject's life, and to whom his relationship and attitudes determine his present attitude to his world.

Summing up, we may state that the characteristics, attitudes, and strivings of the figures in the TAT stories are all products of memory; as such, they are subject to the laws of memory organization which order single experiences into patterns conforming with the emotional constellations of the subject's life. This is our theoretical basis for assuming that TAT stories may allow for inferences concerning the make-up of the subject and his world.

If any one affect or mood is overwhelming in a patient's clinical picture, it will spread to many or all the characters in the stories. In such cases, the possibility of inferences concerning the characters of these figures is lessened; most of the figures of the stories become representative only of the subject's own attitudes and feelings. It is as though the patient's problem has grown so overwhelming that all the landmarks of his world—and these landmarks are always the figures of emotional import—vanish, and the patient experiences himself as isolated from all support.

In conditions of extreme disorganization, we find neither clear-cut representations of the subject nor of the figures of import in his world; rather we encounter figures without depth of characterization, unity, or continuity of interrelationships; and much of the happening will appear to be extraneous to the figures, and not explained or understandable from their characterization.

These extreme cases modify but do not abolish the rationale basic to interpreting a TAT: figures described, attitudes attributed, actions related in stories one makes up, are drawn from memory—that is, from past experience; therefore, unless they are clichés accumulated in past experience, they directly represent the real or fantasied figures of personalities, whose attitudes, feelings, and actions loom large in the subject's world.

In the following sections we shall try to describe practical technical procedures, based on this rationale, which are helpful in uncovering and properly appraising essential ideational contents. At the present stage of knowledge—and to our mind, always—the interpretation of the TAT hinges upon the examiner's being sensitized to apperceiving the world of another person in all its variability and perspectives, reflected even in one-dimensional and often very flat story productions.

A Word on the Rationale of Inquiry

A testing situation is one of anxiety for almost any subject, and particularly for the psychiatric patient. The examiner should remember that in anxiety, the most well-prepared and secure knowledge can easily become unavailable, and that in confronting a figure of authority one's wealth of ideas and versatility may vanish. Accordingly, he will not misunderstand relatively stereotyped productions as necessarily signifying ideational poverty, and he will be ready to shape the testing situation so as to reopen the sluices to the personal experiences and essential ideational content of the subject.

ITEM ANALYSIS

The previous discussions have shown how subjects, in making up TAT stories, frequently resort to clichés. The experienced examiner is familiar with these clichés, but the novice may be surprised at their variety. The standard cliché is always approximated but never reached: it is an abstraction from which deviations may be measured. The greater the deviation, the more amenable is the story to diagnostic interpretation. To describe these clichés here would be of little avail; they are more or less clear-cut descriptions of the pictures, with some perfunctory attempts to indicate a course of action of which the picture represents a cross section.

Our item analysis will deal more with the type of information to be expected on different cards if and when the cliché is broken or has gaps through which essential ideational material flows. Equipped with such expectations, the examiner will (1) more easily observe when the cliché gives some clue as to the patient's attitude toward the problem usually hit upon by the picture; (2) easily notice the gaps where he can start his inquiry; (3) be able to assess to which type of information the subject shows the greatest resistance, as indicated by the maximally noncommittal clichés delivered by him; (4) notice in a deviation from the expected information that the story is likely to bear essential ideational content.

Deviations from clichés may be significant in two directions: genuine originality of thinking and great ideational freedom may result in deviations as much as may weighty emotional problems. In both cases, the deviations are characteristic: in the former of the personality, in the latter of the psychopathology. It must be remembered that the more stories show deviations from the cliché, the less any single deviant story can be considered as reflecting the patient's own inside story; and the stories will bear more characterological than psychopathological significance. Records with a great number of deviant stories must also be watched carefully for psychotic material.

The following item analysis presents the type of information which experience indicates is to be expected from each card.[15] We shall refer to these expectancies as the specific significance of the card.

Card 1 usually elicits the subject's attitude toward duty (compliance, coercion, rebellion) and frequently also gives some inkling of his aspirations (difficulty, hope, achievement).

Card 2 usually elicits conceptions of family relationships and attitudes toward the environment generally as giving, supportive, versus barren, depriving.[16]

Card 3 GF usually elicits reasons for despair or guilt.

Card 3 BM usually elicits preoccupation with and causes of depression and suicidal ideas.

Card 4 presents a male-female conflict, fostering expression of attitudes toward feminine demands and masculine wishes not to be tied down or

---

[15] [Because the pictures in the currently available and widely-used set overlap only in part with those discussed in the first edition, I have added my own formulations on the specific significances of the cards that were not used by Rapaport. Where my experience has led me to a somewhat different set of expectations than Rapaport's concerning a picture retained in the present set, I have nevertheless simply reproduced his. Further material of this kind may be found in Stein (1955), Bellak (1954), and Henry (1956).—Ed.]

[16] [Supplied by me; also Cards 4, 6 GF, 7 GF, 8 GF, 8 BM, 9 GF, 9 BM, 16, 19, 20.—Ed.]

problems of controlling impulses. In general, a good picture for learning about conceptions of male and female roles, as well as sexual attitudes. Note handling of picture in background.

Card 5 usually elicits attitudes and expectations toward the mother (seen as oversolicitous, prohibitive, condemning).

Card 6 GF gives the reaction of a woman to a somewhat older and dominant man, only rarely overt attitudes toward the father.

Card 6 BM permits expression of the subject's attitude toward the mother figure (guilt feelings, dependence versus independence, overprotectiveness) and of strong attachment of either toward the other.

Card 7 GF brings out information about the mother-daughter relationship, often the attitudes of mature women toward their own children.

Card 7 BM frequently yields information about the subject's attitudes toward his own father and authority in general (dependence, compliance, rejection, defiance); it also gives him an opportunity to express antisocial trends.

Card 8 GF tends to elicit rather stereotyped themes of daydreaming about the future.

Card 8 BM strongly suggests aggression, but gives the subject a chance to express it in either the socialized, sublimated theme of ambitions to become a doctor, or in the more direct form of a hunting accident. It gives the subject a chance to indicate the target of his repressed hostility.

Card 9 GF is the best in the series for drawing out sibling rivalry; it readily lends itself also to paranoidlike stories about being spied on, which should therefore be interpreted cautiously.

Card 9 BM elicits feelings and attitudes concerning work versus passive ease, male companionship or the homosexual threat of bodily contact; sometimes reveals social attitudes and prejudices.

Card 10 usually reflects the subject's attitude toward separation from love objects, as well as his degree of dependence upon the parent figure of paramount importance.

Card 11 usually reveals the subject's attitude toward danger (aggression threatening from outside) and his manner of experiencing anxiety. Frequently the monster becomes a symbolic representation of instinctual demands threatening from within.

Card 12 F usually affords an opportunity for the subject to express her attitude toward the mother or daughter figure. Attitudes toward aging and marriage also are frequently revealed.

Card 12 M allows the subject to express his feelings and hopes about therapy; at times the attitude toward passive dependence is also strikingly shown by it.

Card 13 MF most usually elicits the subject's attitude toward and conception of sexuality and sex partners.

Card 14 frequently allows for expression of frustrations, worries, hopes, and ambitions. Suicidal preoccupation may also become apparent here.

Card 15 gives the subject an opportunity to single out any person of his environment as the target of aggressions (father, mother, wife, children, siblings) by rendering him dead and buried, and frequently indicates whether guilt feelings accompany these aggressions.

Card 16 tends to elicit material about current life dilemmas, and often stories with an outdoor setting, in which it is important to note whether the scene has vital, generative, optimistic qualities or is one of monotony or desolation. Useful only if given with instructions to imagine a picture and then tell a story about that.

Card 17 GF often elicits strong feelings of unhappiness and the subject's inclination either to sustain hope or to give up (suicide). Attitudes toward a departing or arriving love object also are frequently elicited.

Card 17 BM in general does not elicit any one significant theme with any frequency. If the frequent and usually stereotyped theme of escape is excessively elaborate and intense in feeling tone or outcome, it represents the patient's own expectations or hopes for escape from his difficulties.

Card 18 GF elicits attitudes toward aggression. Relationships to daughter, sister, and mother figures, and to feminine figures in general, are frequently expressed. Jealousy, inferiority feelings, reaction to being dominated are also indicated.

Card 18 BM usually elicits stereotyped stories of robbery or drunkenness; intense aggressions or attitudes toward addiction may also be expressed.

Card 19 by presenting a more ambiguous and unstructured stimulus than most of the others, tests a subject's ability at perceptual integration, and allows the expression of anxiety and insecurity.

Card 20 may elicit attitudes toward loneliness, darkness, and uncertainty.

This enumeration cannot be complete; more experience than one group of investigators can possibly have, and with a greater variety of subjects, will be necessary to establish general trends.

THE TECHNIQUES OF INTERPRETATION

This discussion of the techniques of interpretation in the TAT can only indicate those features in the subject's story production which may guide the interpreter and set him on the trail of the subject's essential ideational content. These techniques are not hard and fast rules like those of scoring on other tests, they are rather viewpoints for looking upon the TAT stories which must become ingrained in the examiner, so that he can use them flexibly and judiciously. These techniques of interpretation are of two kinds: (1) scrutiny of the formal characteristics of the story *structure,* and (2) scrutiny of the formal characteristics of the story *content.*

THE FORMAL CHARACTERISTICS OF THE STORY STRUCTURE

These lend themselves to systematization in terms of compliance with the instructions, consistency within the production of the subject (intraindividual consistency), and consistency of his production with the trend of production of the general population on a given picture (interindividual consistency). There is some evidence[17] in the literature that the structure of language also constitutes a diagnostically significant formal characteristic of the stories, and our experience with the test points up peculiarities and queerness of language which are of diagnostic significance. Yet we are not prepared to give more definite rules about the interpretation of this kind of formal characteristic of the stories.

Compliance with the Instructions

Compliance with the instructions implies that the subject is expected to give a story which will (1) be in the form of a *plot,* and be neither overelaborate, nor merely descriptive of the picture, nor an essay; (2) contain a *situation, leading-up events, and outcome,* as well as *feelings* and *thoughts* of the characters; (3) be made *around* the picture—that is, the subject must comply with the objective picture-context and its implications.

The patient who fails to comply with these implications usually does so because the material that would come to consciousness is such that he cannot tolerate it. To evaluate noncompliance properly, the examiner must assume that it is rarely a result of unwillingness to comply, but mostly of inability to comply. Not even the reluctance or refusal to communicate ideational content once in consciousness should be looked upon as unwillingness, but rather as a specific type of inability to comply. Only this attitude will lead the examiner to an investigation of the bases of noncompliance which may reveal some of the dynamic conditions responsible for it in a given case.[18]

In general, it must be assumed that noncompliance is always an indica-

---

[17] See, for example, Boder (1927); Balken and Masserman (1940); Sanford (1942).

[18] This consideration is in a sense parallel with the modern conceptions of lying and malingering.

tor of an individually significant trend. Whether this trend is generalized, or refers only to a specific idea or areas of ideation, usually cannot be judged from the presence of noncompliance in one story alone; it must be inferred from the degree of inter- and intraindividual consistency of noncompliance. For example, if noncompliance occurs in regard to leading-up events and is generalized in the subject's productions, its presence in any particular story will not indicate that this one is the bearer of a specific essential ideational content; but its presence in only one story is likely to have that significance. Furthermore, if noncompliance is present with respect to Card 19, where it is frequent in the general population, it will have no specific significance; while it will on another, such as Card 8 BM.

The first form of noncompliance consists of deviations from making up a plot, both in the direction of sheer description and in that of overelaborateness with far-reaching inferences from insignificant picture details.

(1) The concept *plot* implies a balanced structure, in the center of which the picture must stand; moreover, since most of the pictures have many facets, it must be clear that the *essential* facets must stand in the center of the plot. Thus, in a story for 7 BM that tells of a father and son who are discussing a crisis in the son's marriage, followed by the latter's successfully carrying out his father's advice, the essential features of the picture stand in the center of the plot. But a story for the same picture of two men watching the consequences of a streetcar accident, to which the drunkenness of a car driver has led, and whose outcome is the litigation of a mother of five children for compensation for her husband's death, has in its center neither the picture nor its essential features.

(2) Considering the cards as "paintings," "models, sitting for an artist," "a theatre scene," "a dream," "a fantasy," "a nightmare," are evasions of different types which constitute noncompliance with the instructions. They are usually followed by the subject's relating the painting's fate, or the overeating at supper that led up to the nightmare, etc. It becomes the task of test administration to interrupt and demand compliance. Similarly, recounting a well-known story with the remark "This reminds me of the story of . . ." is noncompliance.[19]

(3) The noncompliance that consists of omitting either leading-up events, situations, outcome, feelings, or thoughts is common even within the normal range. But if inter- and intraindividual inconsistencies occur in this respect, they become significant. Most common are omissions of statements about the feelings and thoughts of the characters; yet statements to the effect that no feelings are suggested by the face are sometimes pathological indicators amounting to perceptual noncompliance.

[19] In such cases, the distortions of the original story by the subject may be of more significance than his choice of story. See Rapaport (1942a), Chapter VIII.

(4) Two further issues usually involved in noncompliance have already been touched upon in the sections on inquiry and rationale. The first refers to stories that comply only superficially by going through the motions of compliance without revealing any ideational content. If this procedure becomes extreme, it is to be considered noncompliance. The second refers to the effort of the examiner to exert pressure in inquiry to enforce compliance with the instructions in all respects. The examiner may thus obtain important ideational content; but it must never be forgotten that it was not spontaneously thought of, and therefore may be a thinkable content rather than an essential one.

(5) A few more forms of story production must be considered noncompliant, even though some of them are not prohibited by the instructions. Some subjects will attempt to link several pictures into one story, in contradiction to the instructions to build a story around "each one of these pictures"; this procedure is not to be discouraged, but should be noted as an obsessive, intellectualizing connection-seeking or a psychotic disturbance of frame of reference. More subtle deviations are indicated by introducing self-references and descriptions of the subject's own experiences, or making up stories of the "once-upon-a-time" type. The understanding of the instructions by large groups of subjects appears to indicate that such interpretations are not implied by the instructions, even though not expressly prohibited.

Perceptual noncompliance with the picture—rather than noncompliance with the requirement for plot—may take several forms, some of which have been mentioned already:

(1) Perceptual omissions and distortions may be of different degrees, and will correspondingly indicate different degrees of pathology. Thus, omission or misinterpretation of the revolver in Card 3 BM or of the dragon in Card 11 has by no means the weight of the omission or misrecognition of the woman for mussed-up bedding in 13 MF. Misrecognition of the figure in 3 BM for a woman is by no means as serious as misrecognition of the young woman in 12 F, or that of the lower figure in 18 GF for a man. These distortions mean that the position or relationships of the pictured figures or objects touch upon affects, motivations, drives, etc., which then deliver the corresponding ideational content into consciousness; if the pictured figures and objects do not fully fit the ideational content thus mobilized, they must be altered or distorted. The more ambiguous the pictures are, the more easily they will be distorted, even by needs and motivations of little strength; but if an unambiguous figure is distorted—such as an obviously masculine figure seen as feminine—the needs at play must be considered powerful, and such distortions imply the presence of a serious disorder.

(2) Perceptual emphasis may be displaced from the essential to a non-essential part of the picture—for instance, on Card 1, from the boy to the violin in front of him, with an account of its amazing history.

(3) Not the *situation* in the picture, but the picture *itself* may be dwelt upon. This may take very subtle forms. The examiner will be able to spot it if he keeps clearly in mind that while the instructions demand stating the situation *in* the picture, the situation is only *implied* by the picture; and only the degree to which its implications are grasped by the subject and complied with establishes the story as compliant. Thus, what is explicit in Card 6 BM is an elderly woman and a younger man, but the implication of the card is that of a scene between mother and son. If this implication is not grasped, noncompliance is present.

(4) Objects and figures may be introduced into a story even though not pictured and unnecessary to creating a story from the picture. To judge this type of noncompliance, the examiner needs considerable experience; many figures and objects will be introduced as a direct consequence of the expounding of the implications of the picture. Thus, introduction of both a sick child and a doctor into the story to Card 3 GF is not really noncompliance, even though one figure could have made a rounded story. But a patient may state (Card 14), "I see the books and papers scattered around the room" and reply to inquiry, "It isn't there—I just imagined it to be there"; this is noncompliance of considerable significance. Of greater significance is a patient's insistence that there is a third person in the room in Card 6 BM "because of the bearing of the two people seen in the picture."

The extent and forms of the subject's noncompliance and the topics on which he resorts to noncompliance will direct the examiner's attention to cards and instances revealing his essential ideational content.

Consistency of the Stories

The stories may be scrutinized with an eye to their consistency with the general trend of the population on the picture in question, and their consistency with the other stories of the subject. The former is referred to here as interindividual, the latter as intraindividual, consistency.

Interindividual Consistency. To make clear the meaning of interindividual consistency, we must advance some general considerations. To the question "Who wrote Hamlet?" or to problems in arithmetic, there is only one correct answer. The situation is somewhat different when the question is, "Why are laws necessary?" Though there are *correct* answers to this question, there is not "only one"; and it is difficult to judge which correct answer is better than another. The correct answer to "Who wrote Hamlet?"

remains constant all over the world; but "Why are laws necessary?" may be answered on different grounds in different countries. In the latter case, common agreement—the popular trend—must be the scale by which the correctness of the response is measured. This was the procedure followed by Wechsler in establishing scoring norms, and a similar situation obtains for the pictures and stories in the TAT. What the pictures represent and imply can hardly be established by asking the artist who drew them; it must be established by exploration of what the majority of the population sees in them. Such popular trends exist, and some were summarized in our item analysis. Deviations from such popular trends therefore must be considered individually significant. They indicate the presence of strong needs enforcing the deviation, and point to the presence of essential ideational content.

We shall discuss here different forms of interindividual inconsistency:

(a) The perceptual deviations of which we have spoken are distortions only in so far as they deviate from the popular trend. Even if the artist intended the figure in Card 14 to be a man, that would not justify us in considering stories that make it a woman as perceptually not complying; first it must be ascertained that the general trend in the population is to consider the figure a man. Interindividual consistency also extends to the expressive qualities of the figures in the pictures: the mood of the picture and the expressions of the figures elicit responses showing popular trends, and deviations are to be considered significant.

(b) Interindividual consistency also extends to the length and timing of the stories: an average story in the clinical situation is told in about 100 words in about three minutes, and begun about 20 seconds after presentation of the picture. A general trend in a subject to deviate from these averages must be considered significant. Thus extremely long or short stories, extremely slow or fast delivery, long pondering or no pondering before starting the story, are all significant and revealing.

(c) Interindividual consistency extends to the story stereotypes—the clichés—and the essential ideational content that each card is prone to elicit.

The general topic of stories on each card is grossly established in the item analysis, and significant variations or radical flouting of these themes is significant.

(d) Ideally, the language used in the story productions would be clearly formulated, grammatically and syntactically flawless, smoothly flowing, without gaps, inconsistencies, late amendments, or corrections. It is most doubtful that many subjects could live up to this ideal even if these stories were communicated in writing; and in spoken narrative, only an exceptional few approach it. A narrative as a rule is broken, has shifts in tenses and vaguenesses in references; and the logical ideal cannot serve as a measuring rod. Again we must rely upon interindividual consistency. The examiner develops an ear for what is acceptable in narrative looseness, and against this norm evaluates indicators of psychopathology. In the section on Diagnostic Implications we shall give examples of verbalization, to facilitate the development of a frame of reference for such evaluation.

(e) Using the first person singular or plural, names, memories of actual life events and issues, dates, and similar material is a break in interindividual consistency, and should prove helpful in discovering essential ideational content and/or psychopathology.

In short, the examiner must accumulate experience concerning interindividual consistency in perceiving the picture, in appreciating its mood and expressive qualities, in building stories, in responding with certain clichés and essential ideational contents. Where such interindividual consistency is grossly lacking, essential ideational content is usually present.

Intraindividual Consistency. The emphasis we put on intraindividual consistency is based on the assumption that a subject's general approach to story fabrication is a stable one. Ideally, therefore, a subject should take roughly an equal amount of time for considering each picture before his story, proceed with roughly equal speed of narration in each of his stories, and make up stories of roughly equal length. Thus, long delayed or over-quick starting, very long or very short stories, very fast or very slow delivery—all relative to the general run of the individual subject's stories—constitute intraindividual inconsistencies, pointing up which cards or topics implied by them cause the subject to deviate from his general run and, in all likelihood, to reveal essential ideational content.

The demand for intraindividual consistency also extends to other aspects of story production. Thus it is transgressed if on only certain cards a subject omits—or deviates from omitting—leading-up events, description of the situation, outcome, or feelings or thoughts of the characters; and the case is similar for clichés and reflections of the mood and expressive quality of the pictures.

Intraindividual inconsistency plays its subtlest—yet most instructive—role in the patient's language and manner of delivery. Both our everyday and our clinical observations of a person are mainly trained on his intraindividual inconsistencies. Faltering of voice, swallowing, blushing, halting delivery, jumbled sentences, sudden circumstantiality, all call our attention to the special importance of the topic whose discussion they introduce. Consistency of complaint and countenance, as well as of past history related and present status observed, are the fundamentals of our clinical evaluations. We have no means to systematize the different ways in which inconsistencies of verbalization creep into language, because not the grammatical and syntactic ideal but the level of the patient's own narrative is the basis of consistency. The examiner therefore must set his ear to the pitch of the individual patient's narrative, and be sensitive to any dissonance that creeps in. Neologisms, peculiar and queer verbal formulations—such as those excerpted in the Rorschach chapter and in the Diagnostic Implications section of this chapter—are extreme examples, which are recognizable even outside the context of the testing situation and even by an examiner who is not set to the pitch of a particular patient's narrative. In everyday testing work much milder instances will be noticed, and the more extreme forms will set the pattern against which to measure these.

Inter- and intraindividual inconsistencies are not merely dimensions of interpretation of the TAT; they are standards for the evaluation of any interview material. It may be expected that if and when a theory of interview is developed, inter- and intraindividual inconsistency will constitute a chapter of considerable importance in it. Either of these in its extremes may become a pathological indicator, even of psychopathology of psychotic degree. Usually, however, they indicate those stories in which the examiner may justifiably look for essential ideational material.

THE FORMAL CHARACTERISTICS OF THE STORY CONTENT

The formal characteristics of the story *structure,* and their evaluation in terms of compliance and consistency, call attention to those stories in which essential ideational content may be sought. The formal characteristics of the story *content* provide the tools by means of which the essential ideational content may be reconstructed.

If the examiner wishes not merely to paraphrase these apparently significant stories, he must look for abstract categories of content which can be derived from them *as characteristic of the patient's ideation.*

This decision—between the method of paraphrasing and the method of searching for abstract categories of content as the principle of interpretation—is not merely a matter of the interpreter's preference. In the eyes of many scientists it is the distinction between intuition and science, between artistic freedom and scientific rigor. We shall not discuss the place in psychology of "nomothetic" and "idliographic" endeavors, or that of intuition and rigor. As to the former, the scientist will always strive for nomothetic methods; as to the latter, though intuition will long remain an undefined term in psychology, the fact that it is the mother of discovery in all sciences has come to recognition in this century (see Poincaré, 1907).[20]

The search for abstract categories of content in the TAT stories is a

---

[20] [On the nomothetic-idliographic distinction and the role of intuition, see Allport (1961) and Holt (1961b, 1962).—Ed.]

search for the essentials of the stories. The paraphrasing method is necessarily misleading, because in using it the *incidental form* the subject gave his essential trends may easily be taken as a *psychological reality;* whereas in the other method an abstractive step takes place, the incidental form is disregarded, and the category or essential trend inherent to the incidental form is brought to recognition. When a story for Card 6 BM tells of a mother who forces her son to stay at home with her, the inference should not be the concrete one that the subject actually stayed home or that the mother overtly dominated him, but rather that the subject's passive needs are strong and that he views the mother figure as an obstacle to the satisfaction of other strivings.

The main pitfall of "paraphrasing" lies in the fact that the overt content of a TAT story may have a great variety of origins. It may describe how a subject consciously experiences himself or his world, which may be quite different from what the subject and his world actually are; it may represent the fantasy of the subject about himself, with which both his everyday conduct and conscious experience of himself and his world may starkly contrast; it may represent a fantasy which the patient is aware of having about himself, or one of which he is completely unconscious; it may give a reversal of the picture the subject consciously has of himself; it may be merely an expression of the fact that strong unconscious strivings are denied expression by processes that themselves remain unconscious. For instance, a story to Card 14 may describe a person who comes to a strange town and looks out the window down on the town, aware of his unfamiliarity and smallness but with the conviction that one day he will have a place and a name in this town; this story can be that of a self-confident person facing an uphill climb, that of a strong person reflecting upon past experience of his own, or that of a weakling who will be satisfied merely with having dreams. The abstraction *striving* is identical in these three cases, and is safely stated: it is the striving to show one's worth to an indifferent world. On which level this striving is actuated should remain undecided, unless other decisive story material is forthcoming. A story to Card 10 of extreme solicitousness, kindness, or tender love may be that of a person who is merely aware of what he should be and is not, that of a person who tells us what he thinks he is but is actually the opposite of, or that of a person who would want to be thus but cannot. Yet in all these stories—unless they are mere stereotypes—the subject reveals that the pattern he describes is part of his world, one he understands because he has experienced it in relation to one of the figures who have loomed large in his world. The most difficult task in interpreting the TAT is to discern which of the multiple possibilities the manifest content of the story refers to. Such discernment is often not possible on the basis of this test alone, is sometimes not possible even if other tests are available for comparison, and is usually possible only for the examiner with extensive psychological understanding of human beings.

Another warning to the examiner is in place in this connection. The fact that attention is called repeatedly to the possibly incidental character of the manifest contents of the stories may suggest to the reader a comparison with dreams—specifically, with the manifest dream content and latent dream thought. As a matter of fact, the literature on the test contains such comparisons. It must be kept in mind, however, that TAT stories are not dreams, nor daydreams, not even fantasies proper. The methods of dream interpretation—including translation of symbols—cannot and must not play a significant role in interpreting TAT stories. In fact, if and when the stories become symbolically suggestive, the likelihood of the presence of a psychotic process must be considered. What is common to both TAT stories and dreams is merely that they are thought products of a person. The reader will have discovered for himself that certain general principles of interpretation are common to both: but these are predicated merely on the fact that in both cases we are dealing with thought products. In TAT stories we have thought products that come about in a state of full consciousness, unlike dreams, and in an interpersonal testing situation, unlike daydreams; and the system of interpreting TAT stories must be predicated on recognition of this fact. The interpretative principles of inter- and intraindividual consistency and compliance are a reflection of such recognition.

We shall forego here a discussion of the categories suggested by the designer of the test and by others who have worked with it, and proceed to describe the categories that crystallized in the course of our own clinical work.

These categories answer the question "What is the examiner to look for in the TAT stories?" We have distinguished in our clinical work four types of information: (a) prevailing tone of the narrative, i.e., moods, sentiments, and attitudes characteristic of it; (b) the characterization by the subject of himself and of the outstanding figures of his world; (c) the strivings and attitudes of the subject that may be derived from the stories; (d) the obstacles the subject considers himself to be facing.

Before we proceed to discuss each of these, a general point should be made. It has been assumed that the more frequently a theme or motif is reflected in the stories, the more securely we may assume it to have central place in the subject's ideation. It would be misleading, however, to restrict the basis of interpretation to the principle of frequency. The same problem, striving, or need, may emerge in very different forms; only specific knowledge of personality and clinical problems will reveal its identity. Moreover, often different motifs reinforce each other, are dynamically related parts of the subject's "inside story," and mutually clarify each other's place and weight in this inside story. Thus, an adolescent girl, in her story to Card 15, makes a father moan over his daughter's grave: "If I had paid more attention . . . this wouldn't have happened"; in another story (6 GF), a secretary is in love with her boss but learns that "she would never mean anything to him"; for Card 18 GF she relates a story in which an older woman kills a younger one because "she thinks this younger woman is trying to take her husband away from her." These three motifs are not repetitions, yet they reinforce each other's significance by being parts of a unitary fantasy of the girl centering on her relations to her parents.

Thus, the interpretation cannot hinge merely on frequency, but must rely on a knowledge of psychological dynamics—that is, of the general laws governing the relations of motifs. For this reason we shall not enumerate the different strivings, attitudes, and obstacles which may appear in the stories.[21] Nor shall we attempt to give any scheme for which motifs may be considered as meaningfully belonging together in terms of the psychodynamics of a case; that would be impossible. Instead, it must be stated flatly that, although by means of the techniques of interpretation described the examiner will find it possible to identify the patient's essential ideational content, to interpret it efficaciously in its true relationships requires a fundamental knowledge of the psychodynamics of personality.

The Prevailing Tone of the Narrative

The term "tone" here includes moods, sentiments, attitudes, etc. We are concerned not with those that are implicit to the figures, but with those implicit to the narrative itself; it is the flavor of the narrator's personality as it manifests itself in the manner of expression, rather than in the characterization of the figures and their strivings. Obviously, where the figures and strivings are not clichés but richly express the subject's experiencing of his own world, the tone of the narrative will closely shade into their characterization; the story verbalization will capture, encompass, and elaborate in its characterizations what otherwise is indicated *only* in the tone of the narrative. At the other extreme, where one mood—for instance, depression—overshadows a whole record, the prevailing tone will again shade into the characterization of figures and strivings, but for different reasons. In the former case, the verbalization gave form to the tone; in the latter, the tone—the depressive mood—pervades, depletes, and polarizes the verbalization.

In the range between these extremes, the flavor of the individual personality is manifest in the narrative with relative independence of the

21 [Such enumerations can be found in Tomkins (1947).—Ed.]

characters and strivings. Sensitiveness, bluntness, pedantry, childishness, intellectual alacrity, versatility, sloppiness, uncouthness, rudeness, dullness and stereotypy, general affective lability, psychological mindedness, factualness, pleasure in fantasying, pleasure in precision of language—all may be read from the narrative. This medley of terms cannot be subsumed in any commonly used psychological category, and at first glance it may seem incorrect to consider them formal characteristics of the content. Yet experience with the test clearly shows that such characteristics are never incidental to the stories—never forms in which the patient dressed up his essential ideational content—but are always inherent in the experiencing, thinking, and verbalizing of the subject. These characteristics are not reconstructed from the characterizations of the figures and their strivings, but may be found in any part of the story and are implicit to the narrative itself.

It is impossible here to give examples of each of these, so a few must suffice.

(1) An oversensitive preschizophrenic girl gave the following story, 3 GF: "This poor girl, she is suffering mental tortures. She and her husband have been living on a farm and they have been very happy but suddenly her husband becomes ill, she calls the doctor and there seems to be little hope for his recovery . . . she is sick with dread, praying that she won't be left alone [puts down the card as if in fright] . . . Well, he recovers and she finds more happiness with him than ever before." The expressions "this poor girl" and "she is sick with dread, praying that she won't be left alone" are verbal formulations which can be given only by an *oversensitive* person who experiences the full affect of what she is relating.

(2) A woman with anxiety hysteria opened one story as follows: "Oh! Such things! You just don't like to look at such things. It just looks like a picture of two horrid people. When you don't like to look at unpleasant pictures and things, you should just look at them and conquer them. Lately I have just wanted to think pretty thoughts, nothing morbid or blue. I am not crazy; I am just nervous. It's awful to be like that, but it's a good thing we have places like this to go to, don't you think?" These expressions of horror, and the direct discussion of the experience of acute unpleasantness, could have been given only by an *affectively quite labile* person; in others, no such acute experience of strong affect takes place without actual stimulation, and if milder affective experiences are present, they are likely to be suppressed in the narrative.

(3) This example of affective lability is also an illustration of *naïveté*. The examiner need only ask himself what kind of person in the course of a test narrative will talk thus about the clinic she has come to for help— "it's a good thing *we* have places like this to go to, don't you think?"—in order to become immediately aware of the artlessness of the patient.

(4) A domineering alcoholic woman, who managed to terrorize her husband and all her household, gave the following story to Card 17 GF. "Well, it's a girl on the bridge, fixing to jump off and she doesn't because she sees the stevedores down below and knows she will be saved. [What led up to it?] She wanted to jump because of her sorrow or misery, she was starving to death. [Outcome?] She went home to starve some more [laughs callously]. You will have to excuse me for laughing, but I can't help it." The expression "fixing," the contrast between "sorrow or misery" and "went home to starve some more," and the raw laughter and its explanation reflect the cold and even cruel lack of feeling for others which was apparent in the patient's clinical story.

The procedure by which the examiner will most easily notice these generalized sentiments, moods, and attitudes is to read the whole record without special intent to discern the implications of the stories, their figures, and their strivings; those verbalizations which—even in the most obvious clichés—are so specific that they jut out and cease to fit the context of a casual narrative will make the examiner aware that they could be given only by a certain (sensitive, affectively labile, affected, cruel, etc.) sort of person. To be sure, these are not so mechanically observable and scorable as are inconsistencies and noncompliance; they require a trained ear, and oblige the examiner to call upon his own life experience and psychological mindedness; but they are not less objective or obvious than the other formal characteristics.

The Figures of the Story

The figures in the stories are either representatives of the subject himself (identification figures), or of persons who loom large in the present psychological "life space" of the subject. The scrutiny of this formal aspect of the content is relatively easy, because figures of importance are limited to a few varieties: parent, sibling, child, spouse, friend, and occasionally grandparent. The scrutiny is complicated only by the fact that each of these can be of either sex and of considerable variety in age.

In recognizing the identification figures, one must pay strict attention to age; thus we may learn whether the patient thinks of himself as a child, a younger, a mature, or an aged person. Yet it must not be forgotten that most people will tend, in pictures where older and younger persons are together, to identify with the younger; because until and sometimes even after age overtakes people, the parental figures—whether living or dead—loom huge in their psychological world. Therefore, in identifying the parental figures the safest guides are usually the pictures 2, 5, 6 BM, 7 BM, 7 GF, 12 F, and at times 8 BM, 6 GF, and 12 M, where clearly old figures or young and old together are represented. Once the parental figures are identified in stories about these cards, they can easily be identified in other stories, notably to Card 1; their attitudes and strivings will generally show these to be merely different versions of the parental figures already established.

Interference with recognizing parental figures most frequently originates in the paramount importance of problems centering on the patient's child or children where the older figure may become the identification figure while the younger represents the child.

Absence of parental or spouse figures in the stories should not be conceived of as indicating their neutral character in the life of the patient, but rather that the affects directed toward them are of such intensity that the patient prefers to (or must) avoid ventilating them.

When the stories do not permit one to uncover basic interpersonal relationships, there is usually a great poverty of such relationships and object attachments. The converse is not true, because stories replete with interpersonal happenings may be given even by psychotics with extremely impaired object attachments. It must be remembered that memories of and wishes for object attachments may be represented by the stories as well as actual object attachments. Also, in certain psychotic (notably schizophrenic) processes the loss of object attachments is reacted to with frantic efforts to hold on to objects; these come to expression in the stories in the form of profuse references to interpersonal relationships.

Relationship to sexual partner or spouse is most commonly seen in stories told about Cards 4, 10, 13 MF, and at times 5, 15, 17 GF, 3 GF, and 6 GF. Sibling relationships are most clearly represented via 9 GF, but may come to expression in stories about Cards 2, 9 BM, or 18 GF. Attitudes toward children are mostly elicited by 1, 2, 3 BM, 5, 6 BM, 7 BM, 7 GF, 8 BM, and 12 M; for specific exploration of this area, cards 13 B and 13 G may also be used.

Masculine identification of female subjects, and feminine identification of male subjects, may make for some difficulty in determining the identification figures. Minor perceptual misrecognition of the sex of pictured figures, and centering the stories on the figures of the opposite rather than of the subject's own sex, will help reveal it in such cases.

If the examiner keeps clearly in mind the outstanding interpersonal relationships in our civilization that admit of representation in the stories, he will not find it difficult to see which are present and which absent; he will then turn to their attitudes and strivings, as described in the stories, to estimate interpersonal strains and stresses which characterize the patient's world.

Strivings and Attitudes

The strivings and attitudes to be looked for in the stories are those attributed to the identification figures; those of the other figures will mainly support the subject's strivings or hinder them.

The distinction made here between strivings and attitudes is one of quantitative significance only. Where the identification figures are assigned definite strivings, we are usually shown their goals also; where only attitudes are shown, we are told merely of the subject's inclinations without indication of their specific goals. Thus, when the figure on Card 3 GF is described as dependent and grief-stricken, we learn only about an attitude; when it is stated that the only man she ever really loved has left her for good, we are shown the full weight of striving in its frustrated form.

The terms "striving" and "attitude" will here remain grossly undetermined as to their psychological characteristics and place in any system of concepts. We should like to point out only that we conceive of these dynamic trends as derivatives, and thus as indicators, of the basic motivations of the subject. In order to interpret the TAT it is not necessary to clarify the theoretical systemic position of strivings and attitudes; but it is necessary to realize clearly that they are representatives of the underlying dynamic forces and organizers of the subject's actions and thoughts.

The fact that these strivings may be toward dominance or submission, toward success or failure—that is, toward an apparently great yet limited number of directions—would make it appear desirable to enumerate them, and to coordinate each striving with a more static form of it in an attitude. Clinically we have not found such an enumeration or classification necessary. In the clinical stories of each subject only a limited number of such strivings and attitudes is represented; and if the examiner's attempt is to establish the essential relationships between the figures of the stories and corresponding conflicts and tensions, it will be better for him not to be limited by such an enumeration or forced to decide in advance what he is to look for. Obviously, however, the wits and alacrity of any examiner will be sharpened by studying detailed tabulations of the strivings and attitudes of the human being of our civilization, to be found in Murray (1938) [Aron (1949), Stein (1955)], and others.

Obstacles or Barriers

The examiner will most easily discover this formal characteristic of ideational content if he looks for those figures, conditions, relationships, and ideas which appear to hinder the subject's strivings. For example, the story to Card 6 BM may tell of a young man who wants to go away from his small hometown, is sad because he finds it difficult to leave his mother alone, yet goes: Here the responsibility the boy feels for the mother figure (a command of conscience) appears as an obstacle in the way of his strivings for independence and success. Such obstacles may be of various kinds. They may be those of conscience ("I shouldn't leave her alone"), or those of reality ("I cannot leave her alone, she will have no one to support her"). They may be crystallized in a person: when the domineering mother will not let him go, the prohibition—whether he goes or not—remains a live reality in his private world, limiting his freedom in different ways and impeding his movements by pangs of guilt. Finally, these obstacles may themselves be representatives of the subject's strivings, when their crystallization in a person means merely that one of two opposing strivings has been projected outward: Thus, in the example given, the prohibiting mother figure stood for passive, dependent strivings as obstacles in the way of strivings for self-assertion and success.

The Lewinian concept of barriers—both external and internal—may be considered the theoretical construct which corresponds to these obstacles. The emphasis here is twofold: first, that these obstacles and barriers may be external *and* internal; second, that a subject's acting in spite of the obstacles does not mean that their significance in his world can be minimized. Thus, a story to Card 18 GF about a woman who strangles a competitor in a fit of jealous rage, and later goes to the police, to be jailed and executed, is not less indicative of the presence of conscience barriers than would be a version where she collects herself in due time and gets by without murder. Both, however, differ sharply from a story which permits the murder to happen in a premeditated manner, eliminates all incriminating signs, and allows the murderer to live happily ever after.[22]

The relationships of the identification figure and others, which mirror the relationships determining the structure of the subject's world, have not been explored until on the one hand strivings and attitudes, and on the other obstacles or barriers, have been clarified and fitted into the picture. It must be remembered, however, that just as the obstacles can represent strivings, so can they be represented as attitudes. Such attitudes will be, in a sense, in a paradoxical relationship to the subject's strivings.

The use of these formal characteristics of story content will be greatly facilitated if the examiner keeps two considerations clearly in mind:

(1) The four categories of information treated in the foregoing discussion are not pursued for their own sake; they are to be fitted together

---

[22] These considerations obviously apply to strivings also: calming down before murder, self-incrimination after murder, and a premeditated, unpunished "perfect crime" all equally bespeak murderous aggressions, though the narrative indicates that each occurs in a widely different setting.

so as to yield a picture of the world of an individual. Each category is indispensable, but without the first—the tone of the narrative—the examiner will find it most difficult to fit the others into a meaningful picture.

(2) The knowledge of certain basic family data (concerning parents, siblings, spouse, children) will help to simplify the job of the examiner. Yet the examiner who utilizes these four abstract categories of content as the basis for abstractions—such as aggressiveness instead of "the murderer," passive-dependent trends instead of "inability to get away from the mother," maternal figure instead of "*the* mother"—will not slip into describing figures or relationships that have no reality in the subject's world.

DIAGNOSTIC IMPLICATIONS

This test, like the others, requires the patient to think and to verbalize his thoughts. The patient's thinking and verbalization are in their formal aspects shaped by the pathological mode of thinking that is characteristic of the illness itself. In other words, we maintain that every type of maladjustment can be studied through its manifestations in the subject's thought processes, as expressed in the psychological-test performance. An obsessional neurosis may leave its imprint on the general mode of thinking in the form of excessive intellectualizing, excessive doubting, overmeticulousness, and circumstantiality; a hysteria in the form of its labile affects shaping large segments of experience and thinking; a depression in the form of retardation and restriction of thought processes to ideas expressive of and associated with the low mood; and schizophrenia—the most conspicuous—in its pathologically autistic mode of thinking.

The diagnostic implications of the TAT arise from the fact that the patient talks continuously about a wide variety of situations, affects, and motifs, without opportunity of checking back: in this situation he easily reveals his characteristic or pathological mode of thinking. The picture is his only guide, excepting his memory of what he has already said; a relative freeing of his associative processes occurs, and they can interfere with the logical narrative; cautions and cues for correctness frequently become minimal, and verbal material is elicited from which we can infer the patient's general mode of thinking in everyday life.

The study of verbalization of thought processes has been little pursued in the field of psychology, especially in its clinical diagnostic aspects. Perhaps most material has been gathered concerning schizophrenic language, but even here the reports rarely deal with the analysis of *verbalization elicited in a standard situation*. Examples collected from incidentally recorded verbalizations of schizophrenics may teach us much concerning the language and thought in schizophrenia, but systematic understanding can be gained only by studying *complete* samples of *methodically* collected verbalizations of schizophrenics in *standard* situations. In the neuroses and different types of normal personality organizations, the problem of characteristic modes of thinking and verbalization is much more subtle and complex, and has thus far been grossly ignored. For these reasons, we cannot give a systematic treatment of these diagnostic indications.

Here we shall present examples of verbalization of thought processes occurring in TAT stories which we have found to provide diagnostic clues in individual cases. We are not yet ready to offer any rationale of the relationship of these clues to the dynamics of the psychiatric disorders to which they refer, and we think speculation at this point promises little. Therefore, the following examples will be presented merely under general headings, with occasional comments on their significance.

It must be made clear to the reader that not every record obtained from a case will include the diagnostic verbalizations described as appropriate to the patient's nosological group; furthermore, many of these verbalizations overlap from one group to another—especially the ways of talking listed under affective lability and obsessiveness-compulsiveness—and may appear simultaneously in a case. In this event, one of these verbalizations will generally refer to some aspect of the patient's personality organization, and the other to the diagnostically outstanding symptoms; for instance, a depression may occur in either a compulsive or affectively labile personality.

Affective Lability

Affective lability is seen when the patient overreacts affectively to the stimulus picture. This overreacting may take the form of explanations, of criticisms, of affectively charged descriptions, of arbitrary shaping of the story content, of overemphasis on affects in the story, of emotional disturbances even to the point of crying, of blocking on a picture as a result of the interference of affects, or of being able to describe only the mood or affect tone of the picture. In our material, affective lability is outstanding in the records of hysterics, especially females.[23] Affective lability is seen in other clinical groups also, especially in depressives. In otherwise unremarkable records, expressions of affective lability are most likely to refer to the presence of some hysterical disorder. If specific indications of some other disorder are present, the affective lability will represent either one aspect of that disorder—such as the affective lability of depressives—or the character formation of the patient.

Of the 10 to 20 pictures presented, some are likely to be more pleasing

[23] In general, affective lability appears to run higher in female patients, whatever the diagnosis.

to a subject than others; nevertheless the differences warrant at best a passing comment by the subject, and explosive exclamations or other intense reactions will occur only in affectively labile persons.

The following are examples of the different forms in which affective lability may be expressed.

Exclamations. "Oh, goodness, this is a spooky-looking thing!" "Oh how awful looking! Awful looking woman!" "Oh, my, my, my, it just couldn't be that bad!" "That's very pretty!" "Let's forget this one; it looks like a nightmare! It doesn't look very pretty! You give me such weird pictures!"

Interference by Affects with Story Production. Card 15: "It looks like a gloomy picture to me; nothing cheerful; it doesn't even look pretty; I would have to have a very vivid imagination; I like more cheerful things to make a story of." Card 19: "Oh, such things! You just don't like to look at such things!" Card 14: "This looks like a man entering a window, breaking in, entering someplace where he shouldn't, I don't like to make up that kind of stories. I just hope he gets caught, that's all. When I think of things like that I get blue and depressed!" Card 5, stressing the affect of the picture by contrast: "See, there is a quiet peaceful look about the room." Card 10: "This is a boy and a girl dancing with a group of other people put in a small room; the music is slow and sweet; they both feel pleasant and happy in themselves [sigh] and in each other."

Affects Shaping the Content. Card 12 F: "The figure in the background seems to me to be a suspicious old woman, little bit of a leering look on her face, person who knows everything; not terribly sympathetic looking to me; somehow, *from my view* she has no connection with that person in the foreground; I feel the woman in the foreground has a friendly feeling for the world; it seems to be two opposite characters in everything, in what these two people suggest to me."

Depression

Depression may be manifest in the stories in several ways, varying considerably with its depth (psychotic, severe neurotic, neurotic). Almost always it results in a great restriction of ideational activity, so that most of the content is elicited only by persistent inquiry; even then the answers are usually monosyllabic. It may show up in gloomy stories and endings pervading the test, and frequently the patient complains, "Why do you give me such gloomy-looking pictures?" However, it is not rare to find in depressives many wishful fantasies in which love, kindness, and happiness fill the stories to the point of mushiness. In depressive psychoses, typical delusional thinking or perseveration of stereotyped phrases about sin and morality may come to expression; more than in any other group, there is a preoccupation with the characters' being mentally ill, sick, of weak or strong character, etc.

Depressive trends are frequent in clinical groups other than depressions, and these will show similar manifestations. Test behavior such as crying or expressions of despair should be partly discounted by the examiner: these may reflect not an essential depression, but affective lability, anxiety, etc. The examiner is to base his diagnosis primarily on *verbal* behavior.

The following examples are typical of the records of depressive subjects:

Expressions of Depressive Psychotic Delusions. Perseveration of themes: Card 15: "He's terribly worried, probably depressed about having done the wrong things; can't get any rest; he wishes he hadn't lived the way he did; he will be punished in this world and perhaps in the next. [What way did he live?] Violating the laws of God and man." Card 3 GF: "This girl has done something she shouldn't have; she is grieving over it; conscience-stricken. [What did she do?] Committed some sin, conscience-stricken, after which she asked for forgiveness. [From whom?] From God. I don't know whether she improved or not; she is very very sorry."

Psychotic intensity of depression is also seen in distorted perceptions of the affect of the figures, such as seeing Card 18 GF as an essentially melancholic instead of aggressive, conflictful picture. In general, the confounding of aggression, guilt, and depression is often conspicuous, and has interesting theoretical implications.

Paucity of Production. Card 12 F: "Picture of a mother. That's all. [Make up a story.] She has lost her child, buried her, the youngest one in the picture [i.e., *is the mother*]. [Who is the other figure?] Death. [What happened to the girl?] Died. [From what?] Fever. [How does the mother feel?] Sad." Card 15: "Looking at tombstones, the ghost is looking at tombstones. [Why?] I don't know why. [Whose tombstone is he looking at?] A member of his family. [Who?] I don't know. [Make it up.] A child. [What did the child die of?] Fever. [And what is the man doing there?] Wanting to see his child. [How does he feel?] Sad."

Circumstantial Description of the Pictures. Circumstantial description of the pictures will be shown below to be an indication of compulsive rigidity; when it occurs in stories of a blue mood, or accompanies inability to make up a story, the likelihood of depressive retardation of thought processes must also be kept in mind.

Overelaboration or Perseveration of the Theme of Happiness versus Sadness. In one record, this theme was worked into 13 consecutive stories. Card 11 was seen as representing the darker and brighter sides of life, with the idea that one must escape from the darker and move to the brighter; Card 17 BM was seen as a man slipping down a rope to the darker side, when he should have been climbing up to the brighter, etc.

Themes Involving Morality and Sin. These themes, keynoted by such terms as "moral life" or "something one shouldn't do," are also typically depressive.

Obsessiveness-Compulsiveness

The obsessive-compulsive indications are of several varieties and imply differing degrees of decompensation. On the compulsive side, they include circumstantiality in describing the picture, circumstantiality becoming peculiar and even queer, compulsive rigidity seen in dissatisfaction with parts or aspects of the picture that do not fit together; on the obsessive side, they include excessive intellectualizing, too many interpretative possibilities coming to consciousness, doubt, awareness of one's own thought processes, pedantry, essays embedded in the narrative, etc.

Circumstantial Descriptions. Card 15: "This is the picture of a human subject, apparently in declining years, stooping slightly forward, both arms extended forwards from the mid-line of the body pointing towards what I would judge as a tombstone or ground marker of a stone; surrounding the figure are many objects probably representing tombstones, some square, some in the form of crosses, arranged rather irregularly," etc. Card 5: "This is a picture depicting an aged woman opening a door apparently entering a room in which there is a table on which is sitting a vase of flowers, most artistically arranged, behind which there is a piece of furniture, probably a radio or phonograph; the expression on the lady's face is rather drawn, however, her eyes are uplifted," etc. Circumstantial descriptions are also frequent in depressives and decompensated compulsive personalities; they may be accompanied by refusals to make up stories, because "there is no sense to it" or "they are silly" or for any other rigid negativistic reason.[24]

Peculiar Circumstantiality. Circumstantiality may also become somewhat peculiar. Card 6 BM: One subject, having dwelt upon the physical similarity of the two characters even in length and width of head structure, finally concludes that they do not look alike and that the nearer right-hand figure cannot be the son of the left figure; thus "it might be that the man behind him wears the features of his wife."

A preschizophrenic, Card 5: "It's a woman entering a room which contains furniture, victrola or else radio, gate-legged table with a vase full of flowers on it, and also a lamp on it, only part of the shade of the lamp is visible in the picture; the face of the lady contains a lot of surprise; that's

---

[24] [In the above examples, the isolation of affect is also striking; it appears that the subjects have used the self-imposed task of meticulously describing the external, objective features of the pictures as a means of avoiding any recognition of their emotional import.—Ed.]

about all I have to say about it." Here the peculiarity is that the subject feels he has met the requirements, without noting that he has been unable to make up a story. Card 6 BM: "Need to kind of size up the picture first, there is not much study about the background." Card 18 BM: "The same way here, the background doesn't absorb attention, it's all black."

Fragmentation Associated with Rigidity and Doubting. Card 5: "Can't quite get the connection of this room and this door; I guess she is looking into this room; it's a puzzle; this woman who lost her husband looks into the room with some regret that he is missing, thinking it seems of the long past. And yet the light isn't lit, might be someone else, can't quite reconcile all those various features. I don't know what this dress represents—a servant's dress or a lady's of the house. Seems probably as though she possibly has heard some strange sounds and commotions and is looking in where it happened. Not exactly the expression of a shock, more reminiscent attitude. Thinking of past things rather than present. Somewhat conflicting elements in this picture."

Intellectualizing. Records of intellectualizing subjects—most frequently those with obsessive-compulsive symptoms or character make-up—abound in references to controversial, scientific, aesthetic, political, or psychological matters. Particularly often psychological theorizing is encountered. The subject ostentatiously and sometimes incorrectly uses imposing words such as "heretical," "ecclesiastical discipline," "fortitude," "penury," "methodical."

A psychologizing example, Card 4: "This is a story of a conflict between the following of one's instinct—I'd better say passions, it sounds a little better than instincts, because passions is a better term than instincts. There is so much argument in psychology about what you mean by instincts, they are used with so many connotations." In a story about an amnesia case who has committed murder during an amnesic episode, Card 12 M: "He has repressed his desire for revenge in his ordinary life and this had shown up in his loss of memory." Such pseudo insights are frequent in the records of obsessive and intellectualizing subjects. Comments on the intelligence of characters and the "culturedness" of settings are also frequent.

Awareness of Own Thought Process. Card 14: "A woman looking at the moon in a rather pleasant way, not particularly upset; this position looks as though she would be about to commit suicide but you don't . . . I don't . . . the face does not look harassed, as if rather contemplating— appreciating the beautiful scene; *strange to get such an idea when you can see so little of the face;* comfortably relaxed and not tense."

Compulsive Criticism of the Picture. Card 5: "The dish of flowers there is on the end of the table instead of the middle."

Pedantry, Mixed with Free-Associationlike Ideas. Card 1: "I'm not to tell you what the picture reminds me of—that it reminds me of Fritz Kreisler? This young man appears to be studying his violin . . . I cannot tell whether with fondness or disgust. If he is like most other boys it is with —it would be unusual if it is not the latter. He appears to be very thought-ful, perhaps wondering if he can ever master the instrument, or even reach the point where he may like to practice rather than to be outdoors playing. Many musicians, I believe, at an early age found difficulty in choosing between a musical instrument and the attraction of outdoors. Am I to continue? The picture reminds me of Fritz Kreisler, about whom I read an article recently, in which it stated that he not only was a great musician but he had served his country well. Which reminds me also of Paderewski, who was not only a foremost musician, but he obtained world-wide prominence as a statesman. It seems to be rather common that musicians have talents along varied lines. All the members of my family, due to my wife's musical ability and her patience with the children, have all had a musical founda-tion. As is customary in large families some of the children appear to have definite musical talent, while others have not. Do you want more yet?"

Indications of Strong, Unexpressed Aggressions

In a setting of otherwise orderly stories, sudden and not too elaborate aggressive turns which are not required by the card indicate strong aggres-sions that are not being expressed in behavior. Card 18 BM: a man is choked to death; Card 3 BM: the child is grieving because his parents were blown to bits in an explosion; Card 7 BM: two surgeons are watching a patient die on the operating table; Card 17 BM: the man has killed his wife. Aggressive stories become psychotic or prepsychotic indicators when someone in the immediate family is murdered (son kills father, daughter kills mother), when they accumulate, or when they are described intensely, peculiarly, gorily, elaborately, or sadistically. An example of the former, Card 3 BM: the boy has just killed his father "before his father could strike him with a big club for having wrecked the car." Examples of the latter are stories of persons who go insane and kill, or who get in trouble and keep killing others who are trying to kill them and are finally killed, or whose lives are cursed and whose families die in ghastly events.

Paranoid Indications

Paranoid indications may refer to paranoid trends in any kind of pa-tient, in paranoid conditions, or in paranoid schizophrenia. They are seen in themes of suspicion, of spying, of sneaking up and attacks from the rear, in the subject's deducing motives of the examiner from the pictures, in ex-cessive moralizing or moral criticism of pictures and characters, in farfetched inferences from the pictures, in flagrant perceptual distortions,[25] etc.

Paranoid Ideas in the Content. Card 5: In a story which constantly returns to and dwells upon a suspicious woman, "It's more suspicion than anything else; instead of what she sees, all her suspicions are in herself." Card 14: In a story about a man committed to a mental institution by his relatives, "An environment which he felt he should not be in, and which he felt that it would be best for him to get away from; he has been put there by some of his family or relatives who want to get rid of him; his relatives became interested in his welfare and worked towards removing him when they find that his health is in danger; their conscience began to hurt them; though they were sick themselves and felt that his presence might be making them sick; they wanted him to have every advantage as a young man which might be of help to them in later life."

Deducing the Motives of the Examiner or Artist. Card 13 MF: "The ease with which I identify with these pictures makes me wonder if there is a set for dark men and a set for blond men." Card 18 GF: "The artist has been quite skillful in creating an expression that is extremely ambiguous. I suppose that's what the test is for, to see specifically what my interpretation is."

Inferences. There is an unbroken transition between inferences which occur in cautious and rigid normal subjects and those which occur in the most expansive paranoid disorders. The demand of the instructions that the subject make up a story around the picture implies that inferences are to be drawn, and in themselves they cannot be considered pathological indicators. But the examiner should be put on guard as soon as the subject begins to verbalize his inferences as though "proving" his story. At times, proving a story may imply taking the picture as a piece of reality; this amounts to loss of distance (see pp. 428f. above), and becomes an indicator of severe psychopathology. At other times, proving a story shades into inferences concerning the intentions of the examiner or the artist. This still may occur within the normal range in overcautious subjects, as on Card 5: "From the look on her face I would say that there is something displeasing in the room"; or Card 17 BM: "From his appearance he looks more like a murderer than a thief." Paranoid involvement, however, may be seen in the examples that follow.

Card 5, after much speculation about what is implied by the picture: "The table, the vase, the lamp, and the victrola and her clothing and her neck ornament indicate that she is a person of means and the conclusion is that this is a person who has made a comfortable adjustment in life." After debating whether Card 6 BM pictures a reunion or a leave taking:

---

[25] Extreme perceptual distortions can also occur in schizophrenias that show no paranoid symptom formation.

"One factor favoring the leave-taking theory is the presence of the hand-kerchief in her hand because, taken by surprise by his unexpected return, she would not be provided with a handkerchief; whereas if it were a case where she was ordering him to leave because of misconduct, knowing in advance that it would be a moving and tearful scene, she would provide herself with a handkerchief and retain it in her hand after a tearful consideration of the action taken or to be taken." Card 1: "The shadow, the mark: that's the clue to it."

Moralizing. Moralizing is frequent in paranoid schizophrenics, and usually takes bizarre forms.

Card 8 BM: "He may be studying to keep out of trouble. Most boys who don't study and try to do the right thing, if they do what they want to, it leads to penitentiaries." Card 17 GF: "This person has done something which has caused a feeling of shame. [What was it?] You can do a lot of things that you can be ashamed of and want to die for; there are seven sins: pride—that's what keeps you going—stealing, murder, adultery." In a story about a couple getting drunk, Card 13 MF: "They went home and didn't know what they were doing, they had intercourse, shame, and death."

This type of moralizing can be differentiated from that seen in psychotic depressives; in the latter the productivity is meager, the themes are perseverative and, while very specific in content, are vague in their application and imply little criticism of the characters.

Perceptual Distortions. Gross perceptual distortions generally refer to the presence of delusional and often paranoid ideas; apparently the needs or affects elicited by a picture are so strong as to lead to a flouting or distortion of the reality of the picture, analogous to the delusional distortions of reality observed clinically. In many cases where such distortion of reality is not yet clinically apparent, it shows up clearly on the test. Paranoid delusions are most strongly indicated by *extreme* misrecognitions of the sex of figures in the pictures; other misrecognitions of sex need not imply the presence of paranoid schizophrenia or even a paranoid condition. An accumulation of the less extreme perceptual misrecognitions—of sex, objects, or situations—frequently refers merely to a paranoid trend as a symptom in any type of maladjustment. On the ambiguous cards (mainly cards 3 BM and 12 M, the reclining figure), misrecognitions of sex are common and are at best weak evidence of latent homosexuality and feminine identification. A misrecognition of sex on Cards 5, 10, and 12 F, of the female figures on 13 MF or 18 GF, and of the older man in 12 M, are all strong paranoid indications. Misrecognitions of sex on 8 BM (the recumbent figure), 14, 15, and 17 GF are weak indications of paranoid tendencies, and occur at times even in normal subjects.

Other misrecognitions implying paranoid symptoms are the following: Card 1, not noticing the violin; Card 3 GF, the arm of the girl seen as belonging to someone behind her in the shadows; Card 13 MF, seeing the woman on the bed as mussed-up bedding; Card 15 seen as an auditorium, an orchestra section, or the like, or faint figures in the background seen as pursuing the hero; Card 17 GF, the bridge seen as the roof or balcony of a house. There are other frequently encountered perceptual misrecognitions (the object on the floor in Card 3 BM, the pin-up picture in 4, the rifle in 8 BM, etc.), which may be interpreted for their implications of the subject's difficulty in coping with aggressive or sexual drives, but which are too common to mean serious disturbance of contact with reality.

Consistent Denial of Aggression. If a subject consistently denies or evades the aggressive connotations of the pictures, the likelihood of a paranoid disorder is suggested. One subject gave the following series: Card 11, "Just a scene"; Card 3 GF, "A woman dizzy and leaning against the door"; Card 18 GF, "A mother holding her daughter's head to look into her face"; Card 13 MF, "A man worried about his sick wife."[26] The systematic misrecognition of aggressive connotations is akin to perceptual distortions, and if both appear together they are especially indicative of a paranoid disorder.

Miscellaneous. A covered-over paranoid disorder is suggested when in a setting of quite orderly and conventional stories we find a strange one given matter-of-factly.

Cryptic statements, especially when elicited in inquiry, carry paranoid connotations. In a story to Card 10 about a couple that was not happily married, the inquiry, "What do you mean by unhappily married?" elicited the reply, "Some people are and some aren't." Card 18 GF: "Maybe she has something that this woman had and the only way she could get it was by doing this to her. [What was it she wanted?] Well, I don't know, there are only two things she could have, that would be a home and a husband and you couldn't have one without both of them."

Stereotyped phrases perseverating throughout a record also suggest paranoid symptoms. Card 5: One subject told of someone being injured by an "outside force," the man in Card 14 is thrown through a window by the "pulling force of light," and another story involves "the love force." Another kept using the phrase "she soon returns to her normal mind" on every occasion, whether the character is temporarily preoccupied or is in a violent fit of anger.

Such questions as "Do they show all of these to your family?" and re-

---

[26] [In the original, five additional, similar interpretations were given by the same patient for cards not included in the present set.—Ed.]

quests to delete a story, so that it may not be read, are paranoid indications.

Seeing the same person in different pictures is also a paranoid indication.

Indications of a Schizophrenic Process[27]

The indications of schizophrenic psychopathology are of great variety. They lie partly in the content of the story, partly in the subject's reaction to the pictures, partly in the verbalization, and partly in the subject's reaction or attitude to the examiner and the testing situation. We shall discuss first indications seen directly in the content.

Unacceptable Content. Introduction of homosexuality, perversions, or tabooed aggressions (patricide, matricide) into the stories makes careful scrutiny for other signs of schizophrenic psychopathology necessary. The incidence of such content is especially great in preschizophrenics. Example: Card 10 and Card 18 GF, two homosexual lovers; Card 3 GF, a woman grieving because the man who just raped her has also just killed her husband.

Overelaborate Symbolism in the Content. Overelaborate symbolism must also be taken as a lead for schizophrenic or preschizophrenic psychopathology.

Card 17 GF: "The bridge is the dividing line between life and death, the sun being life, the water being death. The girl is undecided what she wants. And the laborers represent drudgery, mean work, because she just has to do tedious work; and the girl knows that if she can't find her place in the sun she will have to become one of the laborers, or else end it all in the river. The outcome: unsettled." Card 11: "We see a number of men, pack animals, apparently they are not aware that the animal is coming out of the cave. There is the possibility that the monster will destroy all of them, one will get across the bridge to safety. There is an undertone of religion in the shape of the bridge, gothic, conveying the idea that perhaps God will protect them from what appears to be impending death."

Withdrawal in the Content. Preschizophrenic subjects will give stories which directly convey their tendency to withdraw.

Card 14: "The man is a keeper of a tower, inside of which it is completely dark except for one window, a French window, to which he goes every morning and looks down at people and civilization living below. He meditates, philosophizing in his mind on all things. Shortly he will return to his duties in the darkness of the secluded tower." Another preschizo-

---

[27] A number of the indications described in the preceding section are also schizophrenic indications, when extreme or accumulated.

phrenic gave several stories about people who were happy and secure only when they could isolate themselves from other people, either in towers or in secluded rooms in their homes.

Delusionlike Content. Schizophrenics sometimes give stories whose content will impress the examiner exactly as typical schizophrenic delusions do.

Bizarre Fantasies in the Content. Bizarre fantasies bespeak excessive and possibly delusional fantasy life. They are most frequent in preschizophrenics, from whose stories the following example is drawn.

Card 12 M: "One business partner is hypnotizing the other one while he is asleep by waving his hands over him and moaning in a low voice to the reclining figure which begins to choke and dies by *drowning*."

Example from records of schizophrenics: Card 18 BM: "He has hallucinations that someone is grabbing him; walking down the street and some unknown power put his skinny fingers around his neck and tried to choke him. Then he sank to the pavement and was later found there dead, by an officer of the law; it was just his imagination that someone he had killed had come back and was on his trail."[28]

Peculiar Turns in the Content. These frequently have the appearance of facetious remarks; but even so, the deviant ideas implied always suggest schizophrenic psychopathology. These are particularly frequent in preschizophrenic conditions, from whose stories the first two examples are drawn.

Card 15: a story about a man visiting his wife in the graveyard, feeling remorse because he had not come on Memorial Day—the subject maintaining there is a Memorial Day for dearly loved ones. Card 11: A story about animals going into the sunlight is transformed into an essay on the benefits of sunlight in keeping animals free of disease and helping them to store vitamins.

Examples from records of schizophrenics, Card 11: "Here we have two angry serpents about to tear at each other. They both have confidence in their own strength since both are lunging towards each other; the confidence of the smallest serpent might help him to win. [Who does win?] You just win by a hairline, the difference between winning and losing. [Who does win?] I have to take sides between the two serpents? I'll follow the story of David among the Philistines and say he found a pebble and shot him in a vulnerable spot. [Who found a pebble?] The small serpent." Card 1: "A little boy, aged 10, introvert, high intelligence, reminding me of my youngest brother, who needs to be adjusted, the boy is considered by parents and others surrounding him to be of unusual ability and intelligence because of the qualities portrayed similar to those of his father . . ." In a story about Card 12 F, a girl has an image of her mother: "Finally

---

[28] This fantasy occurred in an otherwise exceptionally orderly test, and was crucial for the diagnosis of schizophrenia.

the image disappears and she never thinks of her mother again." Card 1: In a story of a boy being mistreated, "His mother was not sexually satisfied the night before and is nervous today." This may sound merely flippant, but flippancy rarely extends to such peculiar rationalizations. Card 1: In a story about a boy not wanting to play the violin, and being forced to take lessons, "The outcome of this lesson, when multiplied many times on following days, has caused the boy to dislike music and very likely to lose confidence in himself. They even cause him to despise his violin teacher, and this may lead to distrust of all teachers and to frustration in his school work." Card 18 GF: "Is this a man or a woman in this picture that's being choked? It is a woman obviously from the dress but I don't think the other one has stopped to think. Her emotions are so involved in a man that she sees in this other woman all her hatred and love combined with the exceptionally abominable treatment which she thinks she is receiving from the man she loves . . ." The subject's own frame of mind usually is palpable only in the tone of the narrative, but here we see the subject carrying her own confusion into the story as an essential part of the theme. An even more direct example occurred when the subject had great difficulty making up the first story and kept repeating, "I don't know what to think, I don't know what to think." Inquiry, to stimulate production: "What is he thinking?" Reply: "He doesn't know what to think."

Vague Generalities in the Content. Vague generalities usually appear as mystifying and redundant formulations.

Card 14: "The fellow of the age of tender years, who is looking to the outside with the window open, trying to see or figure out one of his conclusions; the outcome—the conclusion will probably result as he first figures it out. [What do you mean?] Conclusion is that he may succeed in his purpose. [What is his purpose?] His purpose is to reach his conclusion for a definite decision which he thinks is correct."

The following examples are diagnostic by virtue of their peculiarity of organization and verbalization, rather than content. But just as in the preceding examples of "content" we saw peculiarities of organization and verbalization, so in the following we shall also see peculiarities of content.

Disjointedness of Organization. Disjointedness shades into incoherence, which is patent and requires no examples. Disjointedness may appear in spontaneous productions, or only after persistent inquiry, or only in a passing comment.

Examples of disjointedness elicited by inquiry: Card 13 MF, a story about a man who has shot his girl friend: "[What led up to it?] She had a collection of guns and one was loaded and he shot her; he was just fooling, he was drunk. [Do you mean that it was an accident?] No, he meant to do it; the girl forgot to take the bullet out, he didn't like her and shot her.

[Why?] He didn't like her collection of guns." Card 13 MF: "It is a bad man, he has just attacked the young lady on the bed. He has done it many times. He drinks whiskey. The outcome of this is that she punishes him. Emotion—he feels dull and stupid, she feels angry. [How does she punish him?] Sends the police after him. [And what is the result?] He goes free. [Why?] Because it was partly her fault. [Would you explain that?] She led him on. [What was their relationship?] They were casual acquaintances. [Why did she lead him on?] From curiosity. [Why should she be angry?] With herself. [Why should she want to punish him?] To justify herself." Card 15: "This is a story about a man in his old age who had never forgotten the woman that he had loved when he was young and never married; this must have been, he felt, the woman that God had made for him; environment, such as business, interest, social connections, and religious differences had prevented this marriage; not knowing it really, these two people had walked and worked along the same paths of lines of thought; the woman evidently had saved his life one time which caused enmity politically and she gradually lost her security because she had never married. This man after her death grew to be a very famous statesman and after he had achieved all the things his wife ambitiously sought for him to achieve, he came back to the grave of the woman he loved, and his only thought was to be buried beside her; this is real heavy stuff. [How did she save his life?] She had saved his life because a man when married procreating children by a woman he does not love, grieves inwardly, which causes a gradual failure of health; the woman that he loved must have saved his life by being his mistress." (See also story to Card 5 quoted above, p. 483f.)

An example of disjointedness indicated in a passing comment, Card 1: "The little boy practices the violin and has a nervous stomach and his mother wants him to be the greatest violinist in the world . . ." The nervous stomach was not mentioned again.

Mix-ups. Acute schizophrenics and some preschizophrenics often get mixed up in their stories, which then become contradictory. Contradictions need not be elaborated upon here.

Arbitrariness. Arbitrariness refers to such violations of usual expectations as the subject's flouting—either willfully or through autistic percepts —obvious things in the picture and introducing contents, settings, or ideas not justified by it.

Card 12 F: the old woman behind the young woman is described as attractive looking; one schizophrenic made up a story for this card about a girl imagining "how lovely her mother was"; another schizophrenic described the old woman as "well-preserved and good-looking." Card 18 GF: a schizophrenic described the woman doing the choking as "a lovely young girl, she has every expression of a humanitarian." Card 15: although they recognize it as a man in a graveyard, some schizophrenics make up a different story about it. One schizophrenic began, "It looks like it is a schoolmaster and all these tombstones might represent his pupils"; another says, "Could be an empty music hall although it is a cemetery"; a schizophrenic musician states "This man looks somewhat like Arturo Toscanini and the grave statues seem to resemble orchestra chairs. The man seems to be in thought as to the interpretation of the next piece of music to be conducted; he is creating crescendo markings and the dynamic changes; color and intensity of tone. And the background seems to suggest the unlimited possibilities of the musical interpretation performance"—the last sentence illustrating farfetched symbolism. In blocked schizophrenics who cannot make up stories, arbitrariness takes a different form; "There is nothing happening"; "There is no feeling"; "He doesn't know what to think."

Story Continuations. In inferring schizophrenic psychopathology from run-over stories covering several pictures, the examiner must be cautious: these also occur in neurotic and even normal subjects. Normal and neurotic persons will link two pictures together by choice, however, assuming that they are fully entitled to do so; schizophrenics are essentially disoriented to the situation and the test instructions, and believe the pictures are supposed to be continuations. The schizophrenic subject will ask, "Am I supposed to go on with the same story?" or "Does this have anything to do with the first one?" Yet even such questions may come from naïve subjects; and the examiner must seek other evidence in the record before considering story continuations to indicate schizophrenic pathology.

Disturbances in the Subject's Frame of Reference. Disturbances in the subject's frame of reference are manifested mainly in responses to inquiry.

A common example, which alone is of little pathological weight, Card 15: "The man is in a cemetery and is feeling very sad. [Why does he feel sad?] I see that he is shabby and sad-looking." In other words, the subject misinterprets the examiner's question, "Why?" as "Why do you think so?" Normal subjects immediately understand this question to refer to the frame of reference of the narrative of the stories, not to that of their own thought and perceptual processes. When such misinterpretations do occur in normals and neurotics, they are discarded on restatement of the question by the examiner. If the misunderstanding persists, the presence of a psychotic or prepsychotic condition must be considered. Sometimes such weakness of the frame of reference leads to peculiarities. Card 10: "Sexual intercourse probably. [What is the relationship of these two people?] The man is taller than the woman."

Shock and Embarrassment. Certain schizophrenics experience great difficulty on Card 13 MF. Such reactions should be carefully distinguished from affective lability or mere prudery. Subjects other than schizophrenics will also refuse the card because of its sexual connotation, but not on grounds of its "immorality"; prudish persons will make up stories using such euphemisms or indirect expressions as "revolting" and "indecent."

Peculiar Opening Statements. Peculiar opening statements of a sweeping or intense character should caution the examiner to watch for indications of psychotic thinking. These statements can and should be distinguished from immediate interpretations of the card's emotional implications given by affectively labile people.

A paranoid schizophrenic, Card 11: "This is an imaginary situation suggesting religious conflicts which I am not interested in or worried about." A woman with a paranoid condition, Card 12 F: "Well, I'll say the woman in the foreground is selfish, malicious, suspicious, jealous, cruel . . ." Such statements are likely to be expressive of the subject's attitudes toward himself and/or some outstanding figure of his world.

Peculiar Verbalizations. Since the TAT requires continuous verbal communication in rough narrative sentences, it elicits many peculiarities in phrasing or in sequence of thoughts which may become diagnostic of disorganization of thinking. Many of these have already been described; the remainder must be grouped under the general heading "peculiar." Card 11: the people in the story are "completely slaughtered" by the monster; the monster referred to as "a specimen of antiquity"; Card 7 BM: the figures described as presenting only a "partial view"; Card 15: "There is somebody in a forest of monuments"; Card 13 MF: the woman described as having "a scantily formed body"; Card 11: "The skeleton of some sort of bug"; "A tunnel of water"; Card 3 GF: the girl had "a malicious disease" (not a slip of the tongue); "Somebody might have forced her into rape when she wasn't interested"; the girl had "not been doing her homework and had too much social work" (social activity, not a slip of the tongue); Card 17 GF: the girl jumps into the river because she "has despair of joining the world"; "I can't prophesy anything out of this"; Card 17 BM: two saboteurs upon completing their mission "return to their natural habitat"; Card 3 BM: "There are no signs of livelihood."

Peculiarities of another order are the following: Card 20: the subject speculates that it is probably nighttime because "the shadows seem to be well distributed." Card 17 GF: a story ends with, "seems that there is a light around her, she is not in darkness, she is covered by light." Card 15: an emaciated figure is described as "skin-covered bones although the wrist doesn't look so poor."

The following peculiarities are of still another order:[29] Card 15: "This represents the living and the dead because he is living and the monuments

[29] [The three orders seem to be peculiarity in the choice of words, in the ideas expressed, and in the nature of the reasoning or inference used.—Ed.]

represent the dead." Card 15: a story about a man wondering "what the eternal resting place would be like. [What led up to this?] I knew I'd let myself in deep when I started that one. This picture here represents a graveyard and when you think of a graveyard you think of death and when you think of death you think of life." Card 3 BM: "The extreme broad hemispheres [i.e., *buttocks*] of the man in the picture would suggest doubt if it is a male or a female." Card 18 BM: "This man is stouter than he appears in the picture; his shirt wrinkles indicate that he has a large waist-line, from my experience with third dimension work."

The inclination to use big words ostentatiously, and to spell them out spontaneously for the examiner, also belongs to the category of peculiarities.

CHAPTER 11

Diagnosing with a Battery of Tests

Diagnosing with a battery of tests is not unlike diagnosing with a complex test like the Rorschach test. We shall first take up a few examples of problems in diagnosing with the Rorschach test; these will shed light on the problems of diagnosing with a battery of tests.

It is quite common to find Rorschach test records the first scoring category of which (area chosen) has an extreme distribution of scores which is suggestive of profound maladjustment—such as an all *W* or *Dr* record—while the other scoring categories offer no supporting indications. In such a case, the examiner must pit the evidence from the first scoring category against that of the others, to determine whether the testimony of the first scoring category is sufficient to establish the diagnosis. In diagnosing with a battery of tests, one must often pit very pathological implications of one test—perhaps of minor significance—against indications in the others. Whatever the outcome, indications of psychosis in any test will oblige the examiner to go through the other tests with a fine-tooth comb.

On the Rorschach test, the second scoring category (determinants) and the fifth (verbalization) are those whose diagnostic indications are the weightiest of the test; indications in the first alone will not usually be considered definitive. Similarly, on the Wechsler-Bellevue a severe drop of the essentially verbal subtest scores is of great pathological significance; a drop on Digit Span, Picture Arrangement, and to some extent Object Assembly, usually is not. Similarly, in our battery of tests we have tests of major and minor diagnostic potency.

The verbalization on the Rorschach test is likely to give specific indications of schizophrenic involvement, while high form level indicates preservation of formal reasoning. Similarly, in a battery of tests one kind of specific indication may pertain to the degree of decompensation or of preservation, and another to specific types of disorders. The question is always, on which test are the indications crucial for diagnosis?

On the basis of these considerations, a few general rules for diagnosing with this battery of tests may be safely stated:

Correct diagnosis consists not merely of the diagnostic label; it must account for all symptoms and major trends of the patient. The examiner bent only upon fixing the name of a nosological category proper for the patient is bound not only to miss everything else the tests tell about the patient, but also to misdiagnose the condition: human beings, sick or well, cannot be described only by the name of a nosological category. Though they may suffer, for instance, from a neurosis whose outstanding symptom is anxiety, they may still be alert or inert, sensitive or apathetic, compulsively ordered or flighty and disorderly, intellectualizing or repressive; they may have retained good ego organization, or their defenses may be crumbling; they may be able to put up with their own anxieties or be slipping, slowly or rapidly, into a total decompensation in the direction of a psychosis; their behavior may lie anywhere on the scale from passive dependence to self-assertive independence, from overt homosexuality to normal heterosexuality. The tests indicate many of these complexities of personality and maladjustment; therefore, the examiner who only wants his patients labeled by a category cannot but be confused by the manifold indications of the tests, and impatient in evaluating the place, weight, and significance of each. More likely than not, he will find it difficult to choose from among the manifold indicators those which point to the nosological category proper for the patient.

To evaluate the place of the different indications, one must keep in mind the following rule:

Every indication present in the tests must be evaluated even if the major diagnosis does not encompass it. Such indications may be characteristic either of the personality make-up of the patient, or of his background, or of his status at the time of testing, or of symptoms of minor significance. For instance, if both depressive and obsessive indications appear in a picture and the majority of the tests converge on a depressive diagnosis, the obsessive indications will not be considered artifacts of the test; they will be interpreted either as indications of obsessive symptoms in the depressive setting or, if more generalized, as indications of the patient's original obsessive character structure.

The Differential Diagnosis of Psychosis versus Neurosis

Before the examiner embarks on differentiations between neuroses and psychoses, it must be clear to him that (a) *he is dealing with a set of test records indicating maladjustment;* (b) *any or several of the tests of our battery may be inconclusive for the diagnosis of psychosis;* (c) *all of the tests need not concur, and almost never do, in conclusiveness about the diagnosis of psychosis;* (d) *single psychotic signs other than clearly psychotic verbalizations—particularly on the Rorschach test—should never be made the sole basis of a diagnosis of psychosis.*

The examiner will always be keenly aware of these postulates if he remembers that when diagnosing maladjustment by tests, we diagnose the maladjustment from the thought disorders concomitant with the maladjustment; and that since in any psychosis a part of the intellectual apparatus may be preserved intact, it may conceal in the test performance a clear expression of thought disorder on the basis of which we diagnose; and that specific conditions may bring forth on almost all the tests psychosis-like indications which—excepting clearly psychotic verbalizations—only very extensive experience can distinguish from genuine psychotic indications, if indeed it can be done at all.

One may formulate the conditions under which a psychosis may be diagnosed as follows: (a) If definite psychotic disturbances of verbalization are present. (b) If the Rorschach test record is clearly psychotic, whether the other tests support this diagnosis or remain inconclusive. (c) If suggestive indications in several tests (particularly if these include the Rorschach test and the Wechsler-Bellevue) are present, and if in *any one* test there is a definitive psychotic indication. For example, we may have a few conspicuous but not conclusive distortions of Story Recall, a few distant associations on the Word Association Test, a few unusual stories in the TAT, a few peculiar verbalizations in the Rorschach; then even one definitely established and conspicuously exaggerated loose sorting—*L*—on the first part of the Sorting Test will make the diagnosis of schizophrenia quite likely. (d) If, when the Rorschach test and the Wechsler-Bellevue are inconclusive (but not "clean"), strong psychotic indications are present on several of the other tests. For example, extreme loose sortings in the Sorting Test, poorer delayed than immediate Story Recall and either or both with gross distortions, considerable number or conspicuousness of distant word associations, and a few definitely aberrant stories and perceptual distortions in the TAT will seal the diagnosis of psychosis even if the Rorschach and Wechsler-Bellevue are inconclusive.

Before we proceed further, we must discuss what constitutes an inconclusive Rorschach or TAT. A rich Rorschach test (great *R*, Experience Balance dilated in either or both directions) and an extensive TAT (non-cliché stories, without evasiveness on at least half of the pictures) will either be conclusive in indicating the presence of a psychosis, or will be strong arguments against its presence. The reason for this is that a subject

who is blocked in the Rorschach test, or resorts to clichés in the TAT, may
—even though psychotic—use in his sparse offerings relatively intact parts
of his thought apparatus, as in preserved conventional formulations; thus
he may avoid demonstrating the psychotic nature of his thinking. Tests
showing such "coarctation" are considered inconclusive.[1] For instance, in
a Rorschach test of 10 responses neither the manner of approach nor the
Experience Balance is of necessity conclusive; and even more than these
formal characteristics, the content and verbalization are likely in such cases
to conceal rather than reveal the thought disorder. But if blocking is not
present in the Rorschach test, or if the patient freely creates TAT stories,
it is well-nigh inevitable that if psychotic thinking is present its indications
will become manifest. Therefore, if these are not found in a rich Rorschach
record or an extensive TAT, *only the most conclusive indications in all
other tests* can serve as a basis of a diagnosis of psychosis; and even then
the diagnosis must account for the preservation, evasiveness, or qualitative
coarctation seen in the Rorschach and TAT.

These remarks do not imply that no blocked records can be conclusive.
The emergence of a single definitely queer verbalization or of "deterioration" colors in coarctated records almost always allows a safe diagnosis
to be made. In general, one might formulate that the more meager, coarctated, or flat the test records of a patient are, the greater the significance of
any psychotic indication in them.

THE DIFFERENTIAL DIAGNOSIS OF NEUROSIS VERSUS NORMALITY

We shall assume that we are dealing only with neurotics proper and
normal-neurotic borderline cases. Cases of very deviant score patterns or
verbalizations, and even cases in which the main problem is to exclude
psychosis, will not be considered.

The differential diagnosis of neurosis and normality is relatively easy
in subjects whose test records are neither extremely inhibited nor extremely dilated. In this range, indications of extreme anxiety or utter inability to express anxiety—seen either in the Rorschach test or the Wechsler-Bellevue, or in the clash of their indications—are usually accurate in
pointing to the presence of a maladjustment justifiably labeled neurotic.
Within this same range, it is also relatively easy to distinguish between neuroses and their characterological counterparts, such as between obsessive
character structure and obsessive neuroses, by the fact that the latter often

---

[1] These must be distinguished from test records that are suggestive, having positive but not sufficiently strong indications.

have obsessive indications that go too far;[2] between affective lability in normals and affective lability so excessive as to indicate a hysterical condition.

But in records characterized by meager production, differential diagnosis is difficult. If we exclude from consideration brief records that are expressions of quality ambition—and these are usually easily recognized by their high level—we are left with records in which inhibition and rigidity prevail. Neuroses will frequently find such expression in the tests of any kind of subject, but especially in those of persons with poor educational and cultural background, probably because in these subjects the anxieties link up with feelings of intellectual inadequacy in the test situation, and bring about this test picture. These are the persons who in everyday life are most likely to use ego-limiting mechanisms as a means of adjustment. In records of meager productivity, we usually encounter two types of cases. They can be best distinguished by the Rorschach test: it may be meager and essentially impoverished, or meager but not impoverished. In the latter type—unless the other tests suggest that we are dealing with a maladjustment—an inhibitive, rigid adjustment within the normal range can be expected. In the former case, if the records are really those of a neurotic, we will find abundant evidence in the other tests; because if in spite of inhibition a record is conspicuously poor as an expression of maladjustment, the maladjustment is likely to be so far-reaching as to have a disorganizing effect on the other tests also. When the meager Rorschach record is poor because of the effects of normal anxiety or incidental conditions, the other tests are likely to remain relatively clean. Thus, even in inhibited records differentiation between normal adjustment and neurotic maladjustment is possible.

The situation is even more complex in subjects of great productivity. In these, the absence of inhibition will allow for emergence in the record of much that in a narrow record would be considered indicative of severe pathology. Furthermore, dilated records are usually obtained from persons who in general intellectualize or rationalize; in tests of intelligence and concept formation, their intellectualizing tendency may serve as a screen for disorganization. Thus, when there is great productivity, only the most conclusive signs will allow us to diagnose a neurosis, and only cleanness of almost all the records will allow us to assert that the subject is well adjusted.

---

[2] [I.e., become decompensated.—In my experience, the differentiation of normal and neurotic persons (those who are functioning to their own and others' satisfaction, and those who seek help for their suffering) is much less easy than stated here. Surely the lack of consensus on a definition of neurosis makes it rash to attempt to follow a set of relatively simple rules such as the ones given here, adequate though they may have been for the Topeka setting in the 1940's.—Ed.]

Yet the very fact of dilation, and the types of indications that emerge, point to the type of adjustment or maladjustment present.

In differential diagnosis of normality and neurosis, the examiner should keep in mind the commonplace that neurosis is not a category apart from normal adjustment, but that there is a continuous transition between the two; he should therefore attempt to describe any tendencies toward maladjustment, as well as the functional assets which protect the subject against overt maladjustment. Often he will have to desist from attempting to cubbyhole such subjects into any definite psychiatric category.

Differential Diagnosis within the Major Diagnostic Groups

Here it is much more difficult to give generalized rules; the examiner should have recourse to the discussions presented in dealing with the individual tests. Nevertheless, it will be worthwhile to state a few points.

It is neither necessary nor safe to attempt to diagnose differentially the classical types of schizophrenias (catatonic, hebephrenic, paranoid, simple). It is much more important to diagnose whether a schizophrenic process is in a phase in which it may be labeled a preschizophrenia, or in a phase prodromal to an open schizophrenic break which may be labeled incipient schizophrenia, or in an acute, chronic, or deteriorated phase. These are the diagnostic issues which can be safely tackled by tests, and which are important both from the viewpoint of the psychodynamics of the schizophrenias and from that of their disposition, treatment recommendation, and prognostic evaluation.

We have shown that in many instances one can differentiate the paranoid and simple schizophrenias from the others. Yet these distinctions will help more to segregate paranoids from depressives, and simple schizophrenics from psychopaths, than to differentiate schizophrenics from each other.

In distinguishing preschizophrenics from the others, the examiner will rely on a relatively well-preserved Wechsler-Bellevue, with loose sortings on the Sorting Test and typical Rorschach records, whether coarctated or dilated. In differentiating the acute conditions from the others, the examiner will usually rely on the relative variability of the Rorschach, usually with the presence of movements and colors, together with a probably disorganized Wechsler-Bellevue scatter and a number of revealing word associations. In differentiating the chronic and deteriorated conditions from the others, it will be best to rely on a flattening of the Wechsler-Bellevue scatter with a drop in the Performance scores, a prevalence of concrete, syncretistic, and fabulatory definitions in the Sorting Test, and an increase in the number of conclusive deviant verbalizations in the Rorschach test.

The distinguishing of depression from schizophrenias was extensively treated in the preceding chapters. All that need be added here is that the Wechsler-Bellevue and the TAT will yield the differential indications if the Rorschach does not.

Among depressives, the cruder differentiations—psychotic versus non-psychotic—will most likely be made by the Rorschach test. The finer differentiations will most likely be made by the Performance part of the Wechsler-Bellevue Scale, the Thematic Apperception Test, and the Word Association Test; in the neurotic depressions, both of the latter may lack the essential depressive indications.

Among the neuroses the differentiations will hinge mostly on the Rorschach test. The Wechsler-Bellevue will generally play only an auxiliary role, except where the Comprehension-Information relationship becomes so pronounced as to be helpful in differentiating obsessive-compulsive and hysterical conditions, or where a better Performance than Verbal part will be suggestive of hysteria, etc. The Thematic Apperception Test—especially the tone of the narrative—is also likely to contribute to the differential diagnosis.

Within the normal range, the Word Association, the Story Recall, and even the Sorting Tests become of auxiliary or even less importance; and the diagnosis centers on the Rorschach, the Wechsler-Bellevue, and in certain respects the Thematic Apperception Test.

References

Ainsworth, M. D., & Klopfer, B. (1954), Evaluation of Intellectual Level, Control, Creative Potential, and the Introversive-Extratensive Relationship. In Klopfer, Ainsworth, Klopfer, & Holt (1954), pp. 352-375.

Allport, G. W. (1961), *Pattern and Growth in Personality*. New York: Holt, Rinehart and Winston.

Appelbaum, S. A., & Holzman, P. S. (1962), The Color-Shading Response and Suicide. *J. Proj. Tech.*, 26:155-161.

———— & Siegal, R. S. (1965), Half-Hidden Influences on Psychological Testing and Practice. *J. Proj. Tech. & Pers. Assess.*, 29:128-133.

Aron, B. (1949), *A Manual for Analysis of the Thematic Apperception Test*. Berkeley, Calif.: Willis E. Berg.

Babcock, H. (1930), An Experiment in the Measurement of Mental Deterioration. *Arch. Psychol.*, No. 117.

———— & Levy, L. (1940), *Revision of the Babcock Examination for Measuring Efficiency of Mental Functioning*. Chicago: Stoelting.

Balken, E. R., & Masserman, J. H. (1940), The Language of Phantasy: III. The Language of the Phantasies of Patients with Conversion Hysteria, Anxiety State, and Obsessive-Compulsive Neuroses. *J. Psychol.*, 10:75-86.

Basowitz, H., & Speisman, J. C. (1964), Program Support for Training by the National Institute of Mental Health: 1947-1963. In *Sourcebook for Training in Clinical Psychology*, ed. L. Blank & H. P. David. New York: Springer, pp. 43-60.

Beck, S. J. (1937), *Introduction to the Rorschach Method*. New York: American Orthopsychiatric Association.

Bellak, L. (1950), On the Problems of the Concept of Projection. In *Projective Psychology*, ed. L. E. Abt & L. Bellak. New York: Knopf, pp. 7-32.

———— (1954), *The Thematic Apperception Test and the Children's Apperception Test in Clinical Use*. New York: Grune & Stratton.

Bender, L. (1938), A Visual Motor Gestalt Test and Its Clinical Use. *Res. Monogr. Amer. Orthopsychiat. Assn.*, No. 3.

Bergler, E. (1944), On a Clinical Approach to the Psychoanalysis of Writers. *Psychoanal. Rev.*, 31:40-70.

Bergmann, M. S. (1945), Homosexuality on the Rorschach Test. *Bull. Menninger Clin.*, 9:78-83.

Binder, H. (1932-1933), Die Helldunkeldeutungen im psychodiagnostischen Experiment von Rorschach. *Schweiz. Arch. Neurol. Psychiat.*, 30:1-67, 233-286. Reprinted Bern: Huber, 1959.

Black, H. (1962), *They Shall Not Pass.* New York: Random House.

Blatt, S. J., Allison, J., & Baker, B. L. (1965), The Wechsler Object Assembly Subtest and Bodily Concerns. *J. Consult. Psychol.*, 29:223-230.

Bleuler, E. (1911), *Dementia Praecox or the Group of Schizophrenias.* New York: International Universities Press, 1950.

Boder, D. P. (1927), The Adjective-Verb Quotient. Unpublished Master's Thesis, University of Chicago.

Bolles, M. M., Rosen, G. P., & Landis, C. (1938), Psychological Performance Tests as Prognostic Agents for the Efficacy of Insulin Therapy in Schizophrenia. *Psychiat. Quart.*, 12:733-737.

Bonaparte, M. (1933), *The Life and Works of Edgar Allen Poe, a Psychoanalytic Interpretation.* London: Imago, 1949.

Brenton, M. (1964), *The Privacy Invaders.* New York: Coward-McCann.

Brill, H. (1965), Psychiatric Diagnosis, Nomenclature, and Classification. In *Handbook of Clinical Psychology,* ed. B. Wolman. New York: McGraw-Hill, pp. 639-650.

Bruner, J. S., Goodnow, J. J., & Austin, G. A. (1956), *A Study of Thinking.* New York: Wiley.

———— & Klein, G. S. (1960), The Functions of Perceiving: New Look Retrospect. In *Perspectives in Psychological Theory,* ed. S. Wapner & B. Kaplan. New York: International Universities Press, pp. 61-77.

Buerger-Prinz, H., & Kaila, M. (1930), On the Structure of the Amnesic Syndrome. In Rapaport (1951a), pp. 650-686.

Bühler, K. (1919), *The Mental Development of the Child,* translated from the 5th German edition. New York: Harcourt, Brace, 1930.

Buros, O. K., ed. (1938), *The Nineteen Thirty-Eight Mental Measurements Yearbook.* New Brunswick, N. J.: Rutgers University Press.

———— ed. (1941), *The Nineteen Forty Mental Measurements Yearbook.* Highland Park, N. J.: The Mental Measurements Yearbook.

———— ed. (1949), *The Third Mental Measurements Yearbook.* New Brunswick, N. J.: Rutgers University Press.

———— ed. (1953), *The Fourth Mental Measurements Yearbook.* Highland Park, N. J.: Gryphon Press.

———— ed. (1959), *The Fifth Mental Measurements Yearbook.* Highland Park, N. J.: Gryphon Press.

———— ed. (1965), *The Sixth Mental Measurements Yearbook.* Highland Park, N. J.: Gryphon Press.

Cassirer, E. (1925), *The Philosophy of Symbolic Forms.* New Haven: Yale University Press, 1953-1957.

Cohen, J. (1952), Factors Underlying Wechsler-Bellevue Performance of Three Neuropsychiatric Groups. *J. Abnorm. Soc. Psychol.*, 47: 359-365.

———— (1955), The Efficacy of Diagnostic Pattern Analysis with the Wechsler-Bellevue. *J. Consult. Psychol.*, 19:303-306.

———— (1957a), The Factorial Structure of the WAIS Between Early Adulthood and Old Age. *J. Consult. Psychol.,* 21:283-290.

———— (1957b), A Factor-Analytically Based Rationale for the Wechsler Adult Intelligence Scale. *J. Consult. Psychol.,* 21:451-457.

Cole, D., & Weleba, L. (1956), Comparison Data on the Wechsler-Bellevue and the WAIS. *J. Clin. Psychol.,* 12:198-199.

Cook, R. A., & Hirt, M. L. (1961), Verbal and Performance IQ Discrepancies on the Wechsler Adult Intelligence Scale and Wechsler-Bellevue, Form I. *J. Clin. Psychol.,* 17:382-383.

Eagle, M. (1962), Personality Correlates of Sensitivity to Subliminal Stimulation. *J. Nerv. Ment. Dis.,* 134:1-17.

———— & Wolitzky, D. (1964), Implications of "Action for Mental Health" for Training in Clinical Psychology. In Training in Clinical Psychology, the Matter from Several Perspectives. A Report by the Education and Training Subcommittee, Corresponding Committee of Fifty, Division of Clinical Psychology, American Psychological Association. Mimeographed, pp. 83-107.

Erikson, E. H. (1950), *Childhood and Society,* 2nd ed. New York: Norton, 1963.

Escalona, S. K. (1940), The Effect of Success and Failure upon the Level of Aspiration and Behavior in Manic-Depressive Psychoses. *University of Iowa Studies in Child Welfare,* Vol. 16, No. 3, pp. 199-302.

———— (1948), *An Application of the Level of Aspiration Experiment to the Study of Personality.* New York: Columbia University, Teacher's College, Bureau of Publications.

Estes, S. G. (1946), Deviations of Wechsler-Bellevue Subtest Scores from Vocabulary Level in Superior Adults. *J. Abnorm. Soc. Psychol.,* 41:226-228.

Fairbairn, W. R. D. (1952), *Object-Relations Theory of the Personality.* New York: Basic Books, 1954.

Feifel, H. (1949), Qualitative Differences in the Vocabulary Responses of Normals and Abnormals. *Genet. Psychol. Monogr.,* 39:151-204.

Field, J. G. (1960), Two Types of Tables for Use with Wechsler's Intelligence Scales. *J. Clin. Psychol.,* 16:3-7.

Frank, L. K. (1939a), Time Perspectives. *J. Soc. Phil.,* 4:293-312.

———— (1939b), Projective Methods for the Study of Personality. *J. Psychol.,* 8:389-413.

Freud, A. (1936), *The Ego and the Mechanisms of Defense,* rev. ed. New York: International Universities Press, 1967.

Freud, S. (1900), The Interpretation of Dreams. *Standard Edition,* Vols. 4 & 5. London: Hogarth Press, 1953.

———— (1908), Creative Writers and Day-Dreaming. *Standard Edition,* 9:143-153. London: Hogarth Press, 1959.

———— (1910), Leonardo Da Vinci and a Memory of His Childhood. *Standard Edition,* 11:63-137. London: Hogarth Press, 1957.

———— (1911), Formulations on the Two Principles of Mental Functioning. *Standard Edition,* 12:218-226. London: Hogarth Press, 1958.

———— (1915a), Repression. *Standard Edition,* 14:146-158. London: Hogarth Press, 1957.

———— (1915b), The Unconscious. *Standard Edition,* 14:166-215. London: Hogarth Press, 1957.

Friedman, H. (1953), Perceptual Regression in Schizophrenia: A Hypothesis Suggested by the Use of the Rorschach Test. *J. Proj. Tech.,* 17:171-185.

Gardner, R. W., Holzman, P. S., Klein, G. S., Linton, H. B., & Spence, D. P. (1959), Cognitive Control. A Study of Individual Consistencies in Cognitive Behavior. *Psychol. Issues,* Monogr. 4. New York: International Universities Press.

Garfield, S. L. (1960), An Appraisal of Object Assembly on the Wechsler-Bellevue and WAIS. *J. Clin. Psychol.,* 16:8-9.

Gault, U. (1954), Factorial Patterns on the Wechsler Intelligence Scales. *Australian J. Psychol.,* 6:85-89.

Gibson, J. J. (1941), A Critical Review of the Concept of Set in Contemporary Experimental Psychology. *Psychol. Bull.,* 38:781-817.

Gill, M. M. (1959), The Present State of Psychoanalytic Theory. *J. Abnorm. Soc. Psychol.,* 58:1-8.

———— (1963), Topography and Systems in Psychoanalytic Theory. *Psychol. Issues,* Monogr. 10. New York: International Universities Press.

———— (1967), The Primary Process. In Holt (1967b), pp. 259-298.

Gillespie, R. D. (1937), Amnesia. *Arch. Neurol. Psychiat.,* 37:748-764.

Goldiamond, I. (1965), Training in Behavior Modification. In *Preconference Materials Prepared for the Conference on the Professional Preparation of Clinical Psychologists,* prepared by Conference Committee. Washington, D. C.: American Psychological Association, pp. 56-58.

Goldstein, K., & Scheerer, M. (1941), Abstract and Concrete Behavior; An Experimental Study with Special Tests. *Psychol. Monogr.,* 53: No. 2.

Goolishian, H. A., & Ramsay, R. (1956), The Wechsler-Bellevue Form I and the WAIS: A Comparison. *J. Clin. Psychol.,* 12:147-151.

Griffith, R. M., & Yamahiro, R. S. (1958), Reliability-Stability of Subtest Scatter on the Wechsler-Bellevue Intelligence Scales. *J. Clin. Psychol.,* 14:317-318.

Gross, M. (1962), *The Brain Watchers.* New York: Random House.

Guertin, W. H., Frank, G. H., & Rabin, A. I. (1956), Research with the Wechsler-Bellevue Intelligence Scale: 1950-1955. *Psychol. Bull.,* 53:235-257.

———— Ladd, C. E., Frank, G. H., Rabin, A. I., & Hiester, D. S. (1966), Research with the Wechsler Intelligence Scales for Adults: 1960-1965. *Psychol. Bull.,* 66:385-409.

————Rabin, A. I., Frank, G. H., & Ladd, C. E. (1962), Research with the Wechsler Intelligence Scales for Adults: 1955-1960. *Psychol. Bull.,* 59:1-26.

Guirdham, A. (1935), On the Value of the Rorschach Test. *J. Ment. Sci.,* 81:848-869.

Harris, A. J., & Shakow, D. (1937), The Clinical Significance of Numerical Measures of Scatter on the Stanford-Binet. *Psychol. Bull.,* 34:134-150.

Harrison, R. (1940), Studies in the Use and Validity of the Thematic Apperception Test with Mentally Disordered Patients. II. A Quantitative Validity Study. III. Validation by the Method of "Blind Analysis." *Character & Pers.,* 9:122-138.

Harrower, M. R. (1965), *Psychodiagnostic Testing: An Empirical Approach.* Springfield, Ill.: Charles C Thomas.

———— & Steiner, M. (1943), Modification of the Rorschach Method for Use as a Group Test. *J. Genet. Psychol.,* 62:119-133.

———— ———— (1945a), *Large Scale Rorschach Techniques.* Springfield, Ill.: Charles C Thomas.

———— ———— (1945b), *Psychodiagnostic Inkblots.* New York: Grune & Stratton.

Hartmann, H. (1939), *Ego Psychology and the Problem of Adaptation.* New York: International Universities Press, 1958.

Heider, F. (1957), Trends in Cognitive Theory. In *Contemporary Approaches to Cognition,* J. Bruner et al. Cambridge, Mass.: Harvard University Press, pp. 201-210.

Hein, P., Cohen, S., & Shmavonian, B. M. (1965), Perceptual Mode and Pavlovian Typology. In *Recent Advances in Biological Psychiatry,* Vol. 7, ed. J. Wortis. New York: Plenum Press, pp. 71-78.

Hemmendinger, L. (1960), Developmental Theory and the Rorschach Method. In *Rorschach Psychology,* ed. M. A. Rickers-Ovsiankina. New York: Wiley, pp. 58-79.

Henry, W. E. (1956), *The Analysis of Fantasy.* New York: Wiley.

Hertz, M., & Paolino, A. F. (1960), Rorschach Indices of Perceptual and Conceptual Disorganization. *J. Proj. Tech.,* 24:370-388.

Hilgard, E. R., & Marquis, D. G. (1940), *Hilgard and Marquis' Conditioning and Learning,* 2nd ed., rev. by G. A. Kimble. New York: Appleton-Century-Crofts, 1961.

Hoch, E. L., Ross, A. O., & Winder, C. L. (1966), Conference on the Professional Preparation of Clinical Psychologists. A Summary. *Amer. Psychologist,* 21:42-51. Also in *Professional Preparation of Clinical Psychologists,* ed. E. L. Hoch, A. O. Ross, & C. L. Winder. Washington, D. C.: American Psychological Association, 1966, pp. 79-93.

Hoffman, B. (1962), *The Tyranny of Testing.* New York: Crowell-Collier.

Holt, R. R. (1951), The Thematic Apperception Test. In *An Introduction to Projective Techniques,* ed. H. H. & G. L. Anderson. New York: Prentice-Hall, pp. 181-229.

———— (1954), Implications of Some Contemporary Personality Theories for Rorschach Rationale. In Klopfer, Ainsworth, Klopfer, & Holt (1954), pp. 501-560.

———— (1956), Gauging Primary and Secondary Processes in Rorschach Responses. *J. Proj. Tech.,* 20:14-25.

———— (1958a), Clinical *and* Statistical Prediction: A Reformulation and Some New Data. *J. Abnorm. Soc. Psychol.,* 56:1-12.

———— (1958b), Formal Aspects of the TAT—A Neglected Resource. *J. Proj. Tech.,* 22:163-172.

———— (1960), Recent Developments in Psychoanalytic Ego Psychology and Their Implications for Diagnostic Testing. *J. Proj. Tech.,* 24:254-266.

———— (1961a), The Nature of TAT Stories as Cognitive Products: A Psychoanalytic Approach. In *Contemporary Issues in Thematic Apperceptive Methods,* ed. J. Kagan & G. Lesser. Springfield, Ill.: Charles C Thomas, pp. 3-43.

———— (1961b), Clinical Judgment as a Disciplined Inquiry. *J. Nerv. Ment. Dis.*, 133:369-382.

———— (1962), Individuality and Generalization in the Psychology of Personality. *J. Pers.*, 30:377-404. Also in *Readings in Personality*, ed. R. S. Lazarus & E. M. Opton. London: Penguin Books, in press.

———— (1963a), New Directions in the Training of Psychotherapists. *J. Nerv. Ment. Dis.*, 137:413-416.

———— (1963b), Manual for the Scoring of Primary Process Manifestations in Rorschach Responses. Unpublished Manuscript.

———— (1964a), Imagery: The Return of the Ostracized. *Amer. Psychol.* 12:254-264.

———— (1964b), The Emergence of Cognitive Psychology. *J. Amer. Psychoanal. Assn.*, 12:650-665.

———— (1965a), A Review of Some of Freud's Biological Assumptions and Their Influence on His Theories. In *Psychoanalysis and Current Biological Thought*, ed. N. S. Greenfield & W. C. Lewis. Madison: University of Wisconsin Press, pp. 93-124.

———— (1965b), Ego Autonomy Re-evaluated. *Int. J. Psycho-Anal.*, 46:151-167. Also in *Int. J. Psychiat.*, 3:481-536, 1967 (with commentaries).

———— (1966), Measuring Libidinal and Aggressive Motives and Their Controls by Means of the Rorschach Test. In *Nebraska Symposium on Motivation, 1966*, ed. D. Levine. Lincoln: University of Nebraska Press, pp. 1-47.

———— (1967a), Beyond Vitalism and Mechanism: Freud's Concept of Psychic Energy. In *Science and Psychoanalysis. Vol. XI. Concepts of Ego*, ed. J. H. Masserman. New York: Grune & Stratton, pp. 1-41.

———— ed. (1967b), Motives and Thought: Psychoanalytic Essays in Memory of David Rapaport. *Psychol. Issues*, Monogr. 18/19. New York: International Universities Press.

———— (1967c), The Development of the Primary Process: A Structural View. In Holt (1967b), pp. 344-383.

———— (1967d), Diagnostic Testing: Present Situation and Future Prospects. *J. Nerv. Ment. Dis.*, 144:444-465.

———— ed. (in press), *New Horizons for Psychotherapy* (tentative title). New York: International Universities Press.

———— & Havel, J. (1960), A Method for Assessing Primary and Secondary Process in the Rorschach. In *Rorschach Psychology*, ed. M. A. Rickers-Ovsiankina. New York: Wiley, pp. 263-315.

———— & Luborsky, L. (1958), *Personality Patterns of Psychiatrists*, 2 vols. New York: Basic Books.

Hull, C. L., & Lugoff, L. S. (1921), Complex Signs in Diagnostic Free Association. *J. Exp. Psychol.*, 4:11-136.

Joint Commission on Mental Illness and Health (1961), *Action for Mental Health*. New York: Basic Books.

Jones, A. (1966), Master's Level Training. In *Professional Preparation of Clinical Psychologists*, ed. E. L. Hoch, A. O. Ross, & C. L. Winder. Washington, D. C.: American Psychological Association, pp. 79-93.

Jones, H. G. (1956), The Evaluation of the Significance of Differences Between Scaled Scores on the WAIS: The Perpetuation of a Fallacy. *J. Consult. Psychol.*, 20:319-320.

Jung, C. G. (1906-1915), *Studies in Word Association*. New York: Moffat, Yard, 1919.

Kalinkowitz, B. N. (in press), An Ideal Training Program for Psychotherapists: Contributions from Clinical Psychology. In Holt (in press).

Katona, G. (1940), *Organizing and Memorizing*. New York: Columbia University Press.

Kelly, E. L., & Fiske, D. W. (1951), *The Prediction of Performance in Clinical Psychology*. Ann Arbor: University of Michigan Press.

Kent, G. H., & Rosanoff, A. J. (1910), A Study of Association in Insanity. *Amer. J. Insanity,* 67:37-96, 317-390.

Klein, G. S. (1954), Need and Regulation. In *Nebraska Symposium on Motivation,* ed. M. R. Jones. Lincoln: University of Nebraska Press, pp. 224-274.

———— (1956), Perception, Motives and Personality: A Clinical Perspective. In *Psychology of Personality,* ed. J. L. McCary. New York: Logos Press, pp. 121-199.

Klopfer, W. G. (1962), The Role of Diagnostic Evaluation in Clinical Psychology. *J. Proj. Tech.,* 26:295-298.

Klopfer, B., Ainsworth, M. D., Klopfer, W. G., & Holt, R. R. (1954), *Developments in the Rorschach Technique. Vol. I. Technique and Theory*. Yonkers-on-Hudson: World Book Co.

———— & Kelley, D. M. (1942), *The Rorschach Technique*. Yonkers, N. Y.: World Book Co.

Koffka, K. (1935), *Principles of Gestalt Psychology*. New York: Harcourt, Brace.

Köhler, W. (1929), *Gestalt Psychology,* rev. ed. New York: Liveright, 1947.

Kretschmer, E. (1921), *Physique and Character*. New York: Harcourt, Brace, 1925.

Kris, E. (1952), *Psychoanalytic Explorations in Art*. New York: International Universities Press.

Langer, S. K. (1942), *Philosophy in a New Key*. New York: Penguin Books, 1948.

Lévy-Bruhl, L. (1921), *Primitive Mentality*. Boston: Beacon Paperback, 1966.

Lewin, K. (1935), *Dynamic Theory of Personality*. New York: McGraw-Hill.

———— Dembo, T., Festinger, L., & Sears, P. S., (1944), Level of Aspiration. In *Handbook of Personality and the Behavior Disorders,* ed. J. McV. Hunt. New York: Ronald Press, pp. 333-378.

Light, M. L., & Chambers, W. R. (1958), A Comparison of the Wechsler Adult Intelligence Scale and Wechsler-Bellevue II with Mental Defectives. *Amer. J. Ment. Defic.,* 62: 878-881.

Lindzey, G. (1965), Seer versus Sign. *J. Exp. Res. Pers.,* 1:17-26.

Linton, H. B., & Langs, R. J. (1962), Subjective Reactions to Lysergic Acid Diethylamide (LSD-25). *Arch. Gen. Psychiat.,* 6:352-368.

Lipmann, O. (1911), Die Spuren interessenbetonter Erlebnisse und ihre Symptome. *Beihefte Z. angew. Psychol.,* Vol. 1.

Long, L., & Welch, L. (1942), Factors Affecting Efficiency of Inductive Reasoning. *J. Exp. Educ.,* 10:252-264.

Lorr, M., O'Connor, J. P., & Stafford, J. W. (1957), Confirmation of Nine Psychotic Symptom Patterns. *J. Clin. Psychol.*, 13:252-257.

MacCurdy, J. T. (1925), *The Psychology of Emotion, Morbid and Normal.* New York: Harcourt, Brace.

Masling, J. (1960), The Influence of Situational and Interpersonal Variables in Projective Testing. *Psychol. Bull.*, 57:65-85.

———— (1966), Role-Related Behavior of the Subject and Psychologist and Its Effects upon Psychological Data. In *Nebraska Symposium on Motivation, 1966,* ed. D. Levine. Lincoln: University of Nebraska Press, pp. 67-103.

Matarazzo, J. D. (1965), Postdoctoral Residency Program in Clinical Psychology. In *Preconference Materials Prepared for the Conference on the Professional Preparation of Clinical Psychologists,* prepared by Conference Committee. Washington, D. C.: American Psychological Association, pp. 71-73.

Mayman, M. (1960), Ego Strength and the Potential for Recovery from Mental Illness. In *Festschrift for Gardner Murphy,* ed. J. G. Peatman & E. L. Hartley. New York: Harper, pp. 344-357.

———— (1963), Psychoanalytic Study of the Self Organization with Psychological Tests. *Proceedings of the Academic Assembly on Clinical Psychology.* Montreal: McGill University Press, pp. 97-117.

———— (in preparation), Rorschach Fantasy Scoring Manual.

———— & Rapaport, D. (1947), Diagnostic Testing in Convulsive Disorders. In *Epilepsy,* ed. P. H. Hoch & R. P. Knight. New York: Grune & Stratton, pp. 123-135.

———— Schafer, R., & Rapaport, D. (1951), Interpretation of the Wechsler-Bellevue Intelligence Scale in Personality Appraisal. In *An Introduction to Projective Techniques,* ed. H. H. Anderson & G. L. Anderson. New York: Prentice-Hall.

McNemar, Q. (1957), On WAIS Difference Scores. *J. Consult. Psychol.*, 21:239-240.

Meehl, P. E. (1954), *Clinical versus Statistical Prediction.* Minneapolis: University of Minnesota Press.

Menninger, K. A., Mayman, M., & Pruyser, P. A. (1962), *A Manual for Psychiatric Case Study,* rev. ed. New York: Grune & Stratton.

———— ———— ———— (1963), *The Vital Balance.* New York: Viking Press.

Miller, G. A., Galanter, E., & Pribram, K. H. (1960), *Plans and the Structure of Behavior.* New York: Holt, Rinehart and Winston.

Miller, S. C. (1962), Ego-Autonomy in Sensory Deprivation, Isolation, and Stress. *Int. J. Psycho-Anal.*, 43:1-20.

Morgan, C. D., & Murray, H. A. (1935), A Method for Investigating Fantasies. The Thematic Apperception Test. *Arch. Neurol. Psychiat.*, 34:289-306.

Moriarty, A. E. (1966), *Constancy and IQ Change.* Springfield, Ill.: Charles C Thomas.

Munroe, R. (1942), An Experiment in Large-Scale Testing by a Modification of the Rorschach Method. *J. Psychol.*, 13:229-263.

Murphy, G. (1945), The Freeing of Intelligence. *Psychol. Bull.* 42:1-19.

———— (1947), *Personality. A Biosocial Approach to Origins and Structure.* New York: Harper.

Murray, H. A. (1938), *Explorations in Personality*. New York: Oxford University Press.
———— (1943), *Thematic Apperception Test*. Cambridge: Harvard University Press.

Neuringer, C. (1956), A Statistical Comparison of the Wechsler-Bellevue Intelligence Scale, Form I, and the WAIS for a College Population. Unpublished Master's Thesis, University of Kansas.

Packard, V. (1957), *The Hidden Persuaders*. New York: McKay.
———— (1964), *The Naked Society*. New York: McKay.
Paul, I. H. (1959), Studies in Remembering: The Reproduction of Connected and Extended Verbal Material. *Psychol. Issues,* Monogr. 2. New York: International Universities Press.
———— (1967), The Concept of Schema in Memory Theory. In Holt (1967b), pp. 218-258.
Piaget, J. (1927), *The Child's Conception of the World*. New York: Harcourt, Brace, 1929.
Pine, F., & Holt, R. R. (1960), Creativity and Primary Process: A Study of Adaptive Regression. *J. Abnorm. Soc. Psychol.,* 61:370-379.
Poincaré, H. (1907), *The Value of Science*. New York: Science Press.
Polanyi, M. (1958), *Personal Knowledge: Towards a Post-Critical Philosophy,* rev. ed. New York: Harper Torchbooks, 1964.
———— (1962), Tacit Knowing: Its Bearing on Some Problems of Philosophy. *Rev. Mod. Phys.,* 34:601-616.
Pottharst, D. E., & Kovacs, A. (1964), The Crisis in Training Viewed by Clinical Alumni. In *Sourcebook for Training in Clinical Psychology,* ed. L. Blank & H. P. David. New York: Springer, pp. 278-300.
Powers, W. T., & Hamlin, R. M. (1955), Relationship Between Diagnostic Category and Deviant Verbalization on the Rorschach. *J. Consult. Psychol.,* 19:120-124.
Prado, W. M., & Schnadt, F. (1965), Differences in WAIS-WB Functioning of Three Psychiatric Groups. *J. Clin. Psychol.,* 21:184-186.

Rabin, A. I. (1945), The Use of the Wechsler-Bellevue Scales with Normal and Abnormal Persons. *Psychol. Bull.,* 42:410-422.
———— & Guertin, W. H. (1951), Research with the Wechsler-Bellevue Test: 1945-1950. *Psychol. Bull.,* 48:211-248.
Rank, O. (1907), *Der Künstler*. Leipzig: Internat. Psychoanal. Verlag, 1925.
Rapaport, D. (1939), Should the Rorschach Method Be Standardized? In Rapaport (1967), pp. 52-54.
———— (1942a), *Emotions and Memory*. New York: International Universities Press, 1950.
———— (1942b), Principles Underlying Projective Techniques. In Rapaport (1967), pp. 91-97.
———— (1946), Principles Underlying Nonprojective Tests of Personality. In Rapaport (1967), pp. 221-229.
———— (1950a), On the Psychoanalytic Theory of Thinking. In Rapaport (1967), pp. 313-328.

———— (1950b), The Theoretical Implications of Diagnostic Testing Procedures. In Rapaport (1967), pp. 334-356.

———— ed. (1951a), *Organization and Pathology of Thought*. New York: Columbia University Press.

———— (1951b), The Autonomy of the Ego. In Rapaport (1967), pp. 357-367.

———— (1952), Projective Techniques and the Theory of Thinking. In Rapaport (1967), pp. 461-469.

———— (1953a), On the Psychoanalytic Theory of Affects. In Rapaport (1967), pp. 476-512.

———— (1953b), Some Metapsychological Considerations Concerning Activity and Passivity. In Rapaport (1967), pp. 530-568.

———— (1957a), Cognitive Structures. In Rapaport (1967), pp. 631-664.

———— (1957b), Book Review: *A Study of Thinking*, by J. S. Bruner, J. J. Goodnow, & G. A. Austin. In Rapaport (1967), pp. 674-681.

———— (1957c), The Theory of Ego Autonomy: A Generalization. In Rapaport (1967), pp. 722-744.

———— (1959a), The Structure of Psychoanalytic Theory: A Systematizing Attempt. In *Psychology: A Study of a Science*, Vol. 3, ed. S. Koch. New York: McGraw-Hill, pp. 55-183. Also in *Psychol. Issues*, Monogr. 6. New York: International Universities Press, 1960.

———— (1959b), The Theory of Attention Cathexis. In Rapaport (1967), pp. 778-794.

———— (1960a), On the Psychoanalytic Theory of Motivation. In Rapaport (1967), pp. 853-915.

———— (1960b), Psychoanalysis as a Developmental Psychology. In Rapaport (1967), pp. 820-852.

———— (1967), *Collected Papers*, ed. M. M. Gill. New York: Basic Books.

———— Gill, M. M., & Schafer, R. (1945-1946), *Diagnostic Psychological Testing*, 2 Vols. Chicago: Year Book Publishers.

———— Schafer, R., & Gill, M. M. (1944-1946), *Manual of Diagnostic Psychological Testing*, 2 vols. New York: Josiah Macy, Jr. Foundation.

Reichard, S., Schneider, M., & Rapaport, D. (1944), The Development of Concept Formation in Children. *Amer. J. Orthopsychiat.*, 14:156-161.

Roe, A., & Shakow, D. (1942), Intelligence in Mental Disorder. *Ann. N. Y. Acad. Sci.*, 42:361-490.

Roemer, G. A. (1921), Über die Anwendung des psychodiagnostischen Verfahrens nach Rorschach auf Fragen der Berufsberatung. *Kong. Exper. Psychol.*, Marburg, 7:165-167.

Rogers, C. R. (1951), *Client-Centered Therapy*. Boston: Houghton Mifflin.

———— & Dymond, R. F. (1954), *Psychotherapy and Personality Change*. Chicago: University of Chicago Press.

Rorschach, H. (1921), *Psychodiagnostics*. New York: Grune & Stratton, 1949.

———— & Oberholzer, E. (1923), The Application of the Interpretation of Form to Psychoanalysis. *J. Nerv. Ment. Dis.*, 60:225-248, 359-379, 1924. Also in Rorschach (1921), pp. 185-216.

Rosenwald, G. C. (1963), Psychodiagnostics and Its Discontents. *Psychiatry*, 26:222-240.

Rosenzweig, S. (1943), The Ghost of Henry James: A Study in Thematic Apperception. *Character & Pers.*, 12:79-100.

————— & Shakow, D. (1937), Play Technique in Schizophrenia and Other Psychoses. I & II. *Amer. J. Orthopsychiat.,* 7:32-35, 36-47.

Rotter, J. B. (1940), Studies in the Use and Validity of the Thematic Apperception Test with Mentally Disordered Patients. I. Method of Analysis and Clinical Problems. *Character & Pers.,* 9:18-34.

Sachs, H. (1942), *The Creative Unconscious.* Cambridge, Mass: Sci-Art Publishers.

Sanford, R. N. (1942), Thematic Apperception Test. Directions for Administration and Scoring. Cambridge: Harvard Psychological Clinic. Mimeographed.

Sarbin, T. R., Taft, R., & Bailey, D. E. (1960), *Clinical Inference and Cognitive Theory.* New York: Holt, Rinehart and Winston.

Sargent, H. D. (1953), *The Insight Test.* New York: Grune & Stratton.

Saunders, D. R. (1959), On the Dimensionality of the WAIS Battery for Two Groups of Normal Males. *Psychol. Rep.,* 5:529-541.

————— (1960a), A Factor Analysis of the Information and Arithmetic Items of the WAIS. *Psychol. Rep.,* 6:367-383.

————— (1960b), A Factor Analysis of the Picture Completion Items of the WAIS. *J. Clin. Psychol.,* 16:146-149.

Schafer, R. (1948), *The Clinical Application of Psychological Tests.* New York: International Universities Press.

————— (1949), Psychological Tests in Clinical Research. *J. Consult. Psychol.,* 13:328-334. Also in *Psychoanalytic Psychiatry and Psychology; Clinical and Theoretical Papers,* Austen Riggs Center, Vol. I, ed. R. P. Knight & C. R. Friedman. New York: International Universities Press, 1954, pp. 204-212.

————— (1954), *Psychoanalytic Interpretation in Rorschach Testing.* New York: Grune & Stratton.

————— (1956), Test Review: Wechsler, David. Wechsler Adult Intelligence Scale (WAIS). *J. Consult. Psychol.,* 20:157-159.

————— (1958), How Was This Story Told? *J. Proj. Tech.,* 22:181-210. Also in Schafer (1967).

————— (1967), *Projective Testing and Psychoanalysis.* New York: International Universities Press.

Schilder, P. (1920), On the Development of Thoughts. In Rapaport (1951a), pp. 497-518.

————— (1935), *The Image and Appearance of the Human Body.* New York: International Universities Press, 1950.

Schneider, E. (1937), Eine diagnostische Untersuchung Rorschachs auf Grund der Helldunkeldeutungen ergaenzt. *Z. Ges. Neurol. Psychiat.,* 159:1-10.

Schwartz, F., & Rouse, R. O. (1961), The Activation and Recovery of Associations. *Psychol. Issues,* Monogr. 9. New York: International Universities Press.

————— & Schiller, P. H. (1967), Rapaport's Theory of Attention Cathexis. *Bull. Menninger Clinic,* 31:3-17.

Selz, O. (1913), *Über die Gesetze des geordneten Denkverlaufs.* Stuttgart: W. Spemann.

Shakow, D. (1965), Seventeen Years Later: Clinical Psychology in the Light of the 1947 Committee on Training in Clinical Psychology Report. *Amer. Psychologist,* 20:353-362.

Shapiro, D. (1956), Color-Response and Perceptual Passivity. *J. Proj. Tech.,* 20:52-69.

———— (1960), A Perceptual Understanding of Color Response. In *Rorschach Psychology,* ed. M. A. Rickers-Ovsiankina. New York: Wiley, pp. 154-201.

———— (1965), *Neurotic Styles.* New York: Basic Books.

Silverman, L. H. (1959), A Q-Sort Study of the Validity of Evaluations Made from Projective Techniques. *Psychol. Monogr.,* 73, No. 7.

———— Lapkin, B., & Rosenbaum, I. S. (1962), Manifestations of Primary Process Thinking in Schizophrenia. *J. Proj. Tech.,* 26:117-127.

Simpson, G. G. (1965), Current Issues in Taxonomic Theory. *Science,* 148: 1078.

Sinnett, K., & Mayman, M. (1960), The Wechsler Adult Intelligence Scale as a Clinical Diagnostic Tool: A Review. *Bull. Menninger Clin.,* 24:80-84.

Skalweit, W. (1935), Der Rorschach-Versuch als Unterscheidungsmittel von Konstitution and Prozess. *Z. Ges. Neurol. Psychiat.,* 152:605-610.

Sohler, D. T., Holzberg, J. D., Fleck, S., Cornelison, A. R., Kay, E., & Lidz, T. (1957), The Prediction of Family Interaction from a Battery of Projective Techniques. *J. Proj. Tech.,* 21:199-208.

Solley, C. M., & Murphy, G. (1960), *Development of the Perceptual World.* New York: Basic Books.

Sontag, L. W., Baker, C. T., & Nelson, V. L. (1958), Mental Growth and Personality Development: A Longitudinal Study. *Monogr. Soc. Res. Child Developm.,* 23, No. 2.

Stein, M. I. (1955), *The Thematic Apperception Test, an Introductory Manual for Its Clinical Use with Adults,* rev. ed. Cambridge: Addison-Wesley.

———— (1963), Explorations in Typology. In *The Study of Lives,* ed. R. W. White. New York: Atherton Press, pp. 280-303.

Stekel, W. (1924), The Polyphony of Thought. In Rapaport (1951a), pp. 312-314.

Stoddard, G. D. (1943), *The Meaning of Intelligence.* New York: Macmillan.

Symonds, P. M. (1955), A Contribution to Our Knowledge of the Validity of the Rorschach. *J. Proj. Tech.,* 19:152-162.

Szasz, T. S. (1961), *The Myth of Mental Illness.* New York: Hoeber-Harper.

Thorne, F. C. (1948), Theoretical Foundations of Directive Psychotherapy. *Ann. N.Y. Acad. Sci.,* 49:869-877.

Tomkins, S. S. (1947), *The Thematic Apperception Test.* New York: Grune & Stratton.

Varendonck, J. (1921), *The Psychology of Daydreams.* New York: Macmillan. Also (abridged) in Rapaport (1951a), pp. 451-473.

von Domarus, E. (1944), The Specific Laws of Logic in Schizophrenia. In *Language and Thought in Schizophrenia: Collected Papers,* ed. J. S. Kasanin. Berkeley: University of California Press, pp. 104-114.

Watkins, J. G., & Stauffacher, J. C. (1952), An Index of Pathological Thinking in the Rorschach. *J. Proj. Tech.,* 16:276-286.

Watson, R. I. (1946), The Use of the Wechsler-Bellevue Scales: A Supplement. *Psychol. Bull.,* 43:61-68.

Weber, M. (1904-1917), *The Methodology of the Social Sciences,* trans. & ed. E. A. Shils & H. A. Finch. Glencoe, Ill.: Free Press, 1949.

Wechsler, D. (1939a), *Measurement of Adult Intelligence,* 3rd ed. Baltimore: Williams and Wilkins, 1944.

———— (1939b), *Wechsler-Bellevue Intelligence Scale, Forms I and II.* New York: Psychological Corp., 1947.

———— (1955), *Wechsler Adult Intelligence Scale.* New York: Psychological Corp.

———— (1958), *The Measurement and Appraisal of Adult Intelligence,* 4th ed. Baltimore: Williams & Wilkins.

Wellman, B. (1940), Iowa Studies on the Effects of Schooling. In *Intelligence: Its Nature and Nurture, The Thirty-Ninth Yearbook of the National Society for the Study of Education,* Part 2. Bloomington, Ill.: Public School Publ. Co., pp. 377-399.

Werner, H. (1940), *Comparative Psychology of Mental Development.* New York: International Universities Press, 1957.

Wertheimer, M. (1912), Experimentelle Studien über das Sehen von Bewegung. *Z. Psychol.,* 61:161-265.

White, R. W. (1963), Ego and Reality in Psychoanalytic Theory. *Psychol. Issues,* Monogr. 11. New York: International Universities Press.

Whyte, W. H., Jr. (1956), *The Organization Man.* New York: Simon and Schuster.

Wiggins, J. S. (1965), Review of Kent-Rosanoff Free Association Test. In Buros (1965), pp. 455-460.

Wittenborn, J. R. (1949), An Evaluation of the Use of Bellevue-Wechsler Subtest Scores as an Aid in Psychiatric Diagnosis. *J. Consult. Psychol.,* 13: 433-439.

———— & Holzberg, J. D. (1951), The Generality of Psychiatric Syndromes. *J. Consult. Psychol.,* 15:372-380.

Yacorzynski, G. (1941), An Evaluation of the Postulates Underlying the Babcock Deterioration Test. *Psychol. Rev.,* 48:261-267.

Zener, K., & Gaffron, M. (1962), Perceptual Experience: An Analysis of Its Relations to the External World through Internal Processings. In *Psychology: A Study of a Science,* Vol. 4, ed. S. Koch. New York: McGraw-Hill, pp. 515-618.

Zulliger, H. (1933), Die Angst im Formdeutversuch nach Dr. Rorschach. *Z. Psychoanal. Päd.,* 7:418-420.

———— (1941), *Einführung in den Behn-Rorschach Test.* Bern: Hans Huber.

Publications on Diagnostic Testing by David Rapaport

(1939), Should the Rorschach Method Be Standardized? *Rorschach Res. Exch.,* 3:107-110. Also in *Collected Papers* (1967), pp. 52-54.

(1941), The Szondi Test. *Bull. Menninger Clin.,* 5:33-39.

(1941), Detecting the Feeble-Minded Registrant. *Bull. Menninger Clin.*, 5:146-149.

Brown, J. F., & Rapaport, D. (1941), The Role of the Psychologist in the Psychiatric Clinic. *Bull. Menninger Clin.*, 5:75-84.

(1942), Principles Underlying Projective Techniques. *Character & Pers.*, 10:213-219. Also in *Collected Papers* (1967), pp. 91-97.

(1942), Recent Developments in Clinical Psychology. *Trans. Kans. Acad. Sci.*, 45:290-293.

(1943), The Clinical Application of the Thematic Apperception Test. *Bull. Menninger Clin.*, 7:106-113.

Reichard, S., & Rapaport, D. (1943), The Role of Testing Concept Formation in Clinical Psychological Work. *Bull. Menninger Clin.*, 7:99-105.

Knight, R. P., Gill, M. M., Lozoff, M., & Rapaport, D. (1943), Comparison of Clinical Findings and Psychological Tests in Three Cases Bearing upon Military Personnel Selection. *Bull. Menninger Clin.*, 7:114-128.

Reichard, S., Schneider, M., & Rapaport, D. (1943), The Development of Concept Formation in Children. *Trans. Kans. Acad. Sci.*, 46:220-223.

(1944), The Psychologist in the Private Mental Hospital. *J. Consult. Psychol.*, 8:298-301. Also in *Collected Papers* (1967), pp. 160-164.

Reichard, S., Schneider, M., & Rapaport, D. (1944), The Development of Concept Formation in Children. *Amer. J. Orthopsychiat.*, 14:156-161.

Escalona, S. K., & Rapaport, D. (1944), The Psychological Testing of Children: Intelligence and Emotional Adjustment. *Bull. Menninger Clin.*, 8:205-210.

Schafer, R., & Rapaport, D. (1944), The Scatter in Diagnostic Intelligence Testing. *Character & Pers.*, 12:275-284.

Rapaport, D., Schafer, R., & Gill, M. M. (1944-1946), *Manual of Diagnostic Psychological Testing,* 2 vols. New York: Josiah Macy, Jr. Foundation.

(1945), The New Army Individual Test of General Mental Ability. *Bull. Menninger Clin.*, 9:107-110.

Rapaport, D., & Schafer, R. (1945), The Rorschach Test: A Clinical Evaluation. *Bull. Menninger Clin.*, 9:73-77.

Rapaport, D., Gill, M. M., & Schafer, R. (1945-1946), *Diagnostic Psychological Testing,* 2 vols. Chicago: Year Book Publishers. Revised edition by R. R. Holt. New York: International Universities Press, 1967.

(1946), Principles Underlying Nonprojective Tests of Personality. *Ann. N. Y. Acad. Sci.*, 46:643-652. Also in *Collected Papers* (1967), pp. 221-229.

(1947), On Personality Testing. In *Redirecting the Delinquent.* New York: Yearbook of the National Probation and Parole Association, pp. 160-172.

(1947), Psychological Testing: Its Practical and Its Heuristic Significance. *Samiksa,* 1:245-262. Also in *Collected Papers* (1967), pp. 261-275.

Mayman, M., & Rapaport, D. (1947), Diagnostic Testing in Convulsive Disorders. In *Epilepsy,* ed. P. H. Hoch & R. P. Knight. New York: Grune & Stratton, pp. 123-135.

Menninger, K. A., Rapaport, D., & Schafer, R. (1947), The New Role of Psychological Testing in Psychiatry. *Amer. J. Psychiat.*, 103:473-476. Also in *Collected Papers* (1967), pp. 245-250.

(1948), The Status of Diagnostic Psychological Testing. *J. Consult. Psychol.*, 12:1-3.

(1948), Discussion in "The Psychologist in the Clinic Setting" Roundtable. *Amer. J. Orthopsychiat.,* 18:493-497, 521. Also in *Collected Papers* (1967), pp. 299-303.

(1950), Diagnostic Testing in Psychiatric Practice. *Bull. N. Y. Acad. Med.,* 26: 115-125.

(1950), Theoretical Implications of Diagnostic Testing Procedures. *Congrès International de Psychiatrie,* 2:241-271. Also in *Psychoanalytic Psychiatry and Psychology; Clinical and Theoretical Papers,* Austen Riggs Center, Vol. 1, ed. R. P. Knight & C. R. Friedman. New York: International Universities Press, 1954, pp. 173-195. Also in *Collected Papers* (1967), pp. 334-356.

Mayman, M., Schafer, R., & Rapaport, D. (1951), Interpretation of the Wechsler-Bellevue Intelligence Scale in Personality Appraisal. In *An Introduction to Projective Techniques,* ed. H. H. Anderson & G. L. Anderson. New York: Prentice-Hall, pp. 541-580.

(1952), Projective Techniques and the Theory of Thinking. *J. Proj. Tech.,* 16: 269-275. Also in *Psychoanalytic Psychiatry and Psychology; Clinical and Theoretical Papers,* Austen Riggs Center, Vol. 1, ed. R. P. Knight & C. R. Friedman. New York: International Universities Press, 1954, pp. 196-203. Also in *Collected Papers* (1967), pp. 461-469.

Index

545